I0418965

Electric Dreams

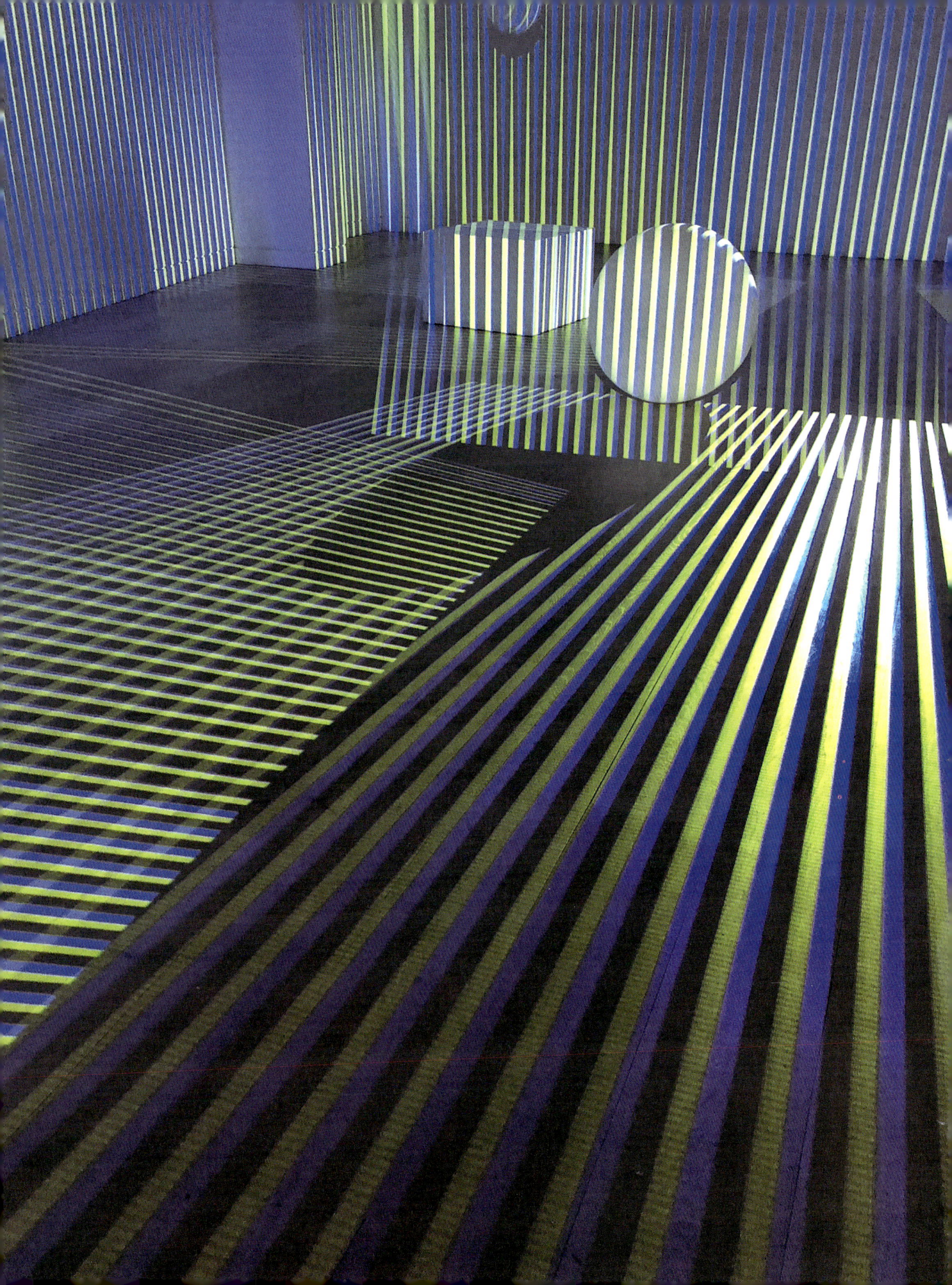

Electric Dreams

Art and Technology Before the Internet

Edited by Val Ravaglia

With contributions by
Sarah Cook, Carlos Cruz Delgado, Bronac Ferran,
Darko Fritz, Nina Horisaki-Christens, Bilyana Palankasova,
Val Ravaglia, Tina Rivers Ryan, Ming Tiampo, Suzanne Treister,
Kira Wainstein, Odessa Warren

Contents

Materialising Invisible Forces

A Programmed Openness: Art as Visual Research

Dialogues with the Machines
104

Electronic DIY:
Tinkering with Tech
152

Supporter's Foreword

At Gucci we remain steadfast in championing initiatives that foster community, inclusivity and artistic diversity. We are delighted to support the *Electric Dreams: Art and Technology Before the Internet* exhibition, a significant milestone in our four-year partnership with Tate, which began in May 2024, alongside the Gucci Cruise 2025 fashion show.

Our partnership with Tate underscores Gucci's dedication to cultural expression and innovation. This commitment is exemplified by this exhibition. By celebrating early innovators of optical, kinetic, programmed and digital art, the show reflects Gucci's pioneering spirit and dedication to exploring creative frontiers.

Through this partnership, we reaffirm our commitment to promoting exceptional cultural landmarks and institutions worldwide that inspire our creative journey.

Jean-François Palus
President and CEO, Gucci

GUCCI

Foreword

For most people living in 2024, digital technologies seem inescapable. Electronic devices are so entrenched in everyday experience that it is rather difficult to even *think* of life without them. Meanwhile, the recent leaps in the development of artificial intelligence and machine learning have become the subject of heated debates, including of course on their repercussions on the arts. It is shockingly easy to forget that only a few decades ago the idea of having a computer in every home – or indeed artist's studio – seemed completely outlandish, and when it became a reality it generated the same level of anxiety about the future of labour and creativity that AI and automation do today.

At a time when such innovations raise fundamental questions on the role of art and of artists, *Electric Dreams: Art and Technology Before the Internet* offers a historical perspective on the subject, focusing on the influence of science and engineering on artistic practices in the period between the end of the Second World War – when discourses around information theory and machine interaction first emerged – and the rise of personal computers. This exhibition and accompanying publication point at the widespread impact of conversations about 'art and cybernetics', showing how they shaped movements ranging from Jikken Kōbō and Gutai in Japan to the wave of optical and kinetic art that took over Europe and the Americas in the 1960s, and shine a light on ideas and approaches from the 'pre-internet age' that are still relevant and thought-provoking today.

Electric Dreams brings together more than seventy artists working across four continents, often connected in complex transnational networks, whose interest in scientific methods and experimentation with technological tools translated into expanded formal possibilities for their works, and suggested new ways to engage the viewers' senses. Their works often emphasised the audience's role in the activation of art, whether by enhancing their acts of perception, by making them become part of walk-through environments or by including interactive and responsive elements. Otto Piene's mesmerising *Light Rooms* of the early 1960s, Wen-Ying Tsai's cybernetic sculptures of the late 1960s, Carlos Cruz-Diez's dazzling *Chromointerferent Environment* from 1974 and Fleischmann & Strauss' early 'augmented reality' work *Liquid Views - Narcissus' Digital Reflections* of 1992 all achieve this effect in uniquely inventive ways, paving the way for the technology-aided immersive installations that have seen an explosion in popularity in recent years.

The narrative here follows a particular and often overlooked evolutionary branch of mechanical and algorithmically generated art, connecting conversations around concrete, kinetic and 'programmed' art with the early adopters of computers as tools for art-making. In particular it follows the evolution of the international *New Tendencies* movement, which brought together artists from the Americas, Eastern Europe, Western Europe and Japan: recurring references to the New Tendencies exhibitions organised between 1961 and 1973 in Zagreb position this city, situated in the non-aligned country of Yugoslavia, as the epicentre of a nuanced art historical phenomenon that deserves far more credit for its role in shaping early digital visual culture.

With their emphasis on sensual experience and formal experimentation with shiny new materials, many of the works in *Electric Dreams* can appear at first glance to offer a naively optimistic view of technology as a bountiful source of visual tricks and modern conveniences. Yet artists often took a far more critical and socially engaged stance than their work seems to suggest. They often wrote about the necessity to reclaim technology from its destructive uses, aware of its environmental impact and of the military interests that had historically driven its evolution.

Overall, the range of artists and works showcased in *Electric Dreams* brings together established names and narratives in the history of art and tech with a number of lesser-known stories, emphasising the overtly international reach of those conversations but also pointing at some more isolated but equally interesting cases and overlooked narratives – from the first examples of electronic music produced in India at National Institute of Design in Ahmedabad in 1969, to the computer-aided video choreographies of Brazilian visionary Analivia Cordeiro. *Electric Dreams* thus weaves a tapestry of episodes from art histories that are worth revisiting at a controversial time for the relationship between human creativity and technology, as the digital 'arms race' continues to accelerate and its consequences become ever harder to predict.

The show has been assembled by Val Ravaglia, Curator, International Art, Tate Modern, who has also edited this volume. Val has been capably assisted by Odessa Warren, Assistant Curator, International Art (Hyundai Tate Research Centre: Transnational), Tate Modern, with further support from Kira Weinstein, former Curatorial Research Assistant, Curatorial, Tate Modern, and Intern Bilyana Palankasova. Many thanks to the exhibition's Curatorial team at large for expertly delivering a project of such complexity, and to all the colleagues across the organisation without whom this exhibition would not have been possible. We would also like to thank the authors who contributed their brilliant essays to this publication: Sarah Cook, Darko Fritz, Tina Rivers-Ryan and Ming Tiampo, along with Suzanne Treister for the interview with Val which rounds up the volume, and Carlos Cruz Delgado, Bronac Ferran and Nina Horisaki-Christens who provided fascinating short texts.

We express our deepest gratitude to Gucci for their support of this project, only the first in a series of extraordinary partnerships. We are also very thankful for the additional support provided by Anthropic, and for the generosity of The Electric Dreams Exhibition Supporters Circle: The David Bermant Foundation and Marcin and Izabela Wiszniewski, Tate Americas Foundation, Tate International Council and Tate Patrons.

Hyundai Tate Research Centre: Transnational provided support for key research on the exhibition in partnership with Hyundai Motor. Bold group exhibitions such as *Electric Dreams*, with their focus on transnational artists' networks and new perspectives on global art histories, exemplify the crucial contribution of the Hyundai Tate Research Centre: Transnational to Tate's programmes, enabling our Curators to develop innovative projects that encourage the idea that art, artists and art histories are connected beyond their countries of origin.

The exhibition in London has also been made possible by the provision of insurance through the UK Government Indemnity Scheme, and we thank HM Government, and the Department for Digital, Culture, Media and Sport, and Arts Council England for arranging the indemnity.

Our most heartfelt thanks of course go to the artists, estates and lenders, private and institutional, who have so kindly supported the exhibition, and without whom this ambitious show and publication would simply not have been possible.

Karin Hindsbo
Director, Tate Modern

Catherine Wood
Director of Programme, Tate Modern

Acknowledgements

The *Electric Dreams* project was originally conceived as an expansion of the dazzling touring exhibition *The Dynamic Eye* (Shanghai, Porto and Istanbul, 2022–4), originally assembled by former Tate Senior Curator Clara Kim with Tate's International Partnerships team as a showcase of Tate's strong holdings of op and kinetic art. *The Dynamic Eye* emphasised transnational encounters between artists and the convergence of certain ideas across cultures and geographies, using localised groups of artists or landmark exhibitions as anchor points for the curatorial narrative. After serving as the project's Curator for the second and third incarnations, I took its structure as a model for *Electric Dreams* – a debt that is especially evident in the first half of the exhibition (and of this publication). Clara Kim therefore deserves a special acknowledgement, along with Matthew Watts, former Curatorial Assistant; Neil McConnon, Director of International Partnerships; Senior Project Curator Katie Chester; Exhibitions Assistants Hannah Cassens Marshall, and the many colleagues from Tate and the hosting venues who contributed to the success of *The Dynamic Eye* tour.

I would like to join Karin and Catherine in thanking the sponsors, participating artists, estates and lenders to *Electric Dreams* for making this ambitious project possible; too numerous to mention here, they are listed in the back matter. I also owe my utmost gratitude to the rest of the Curatorial team, starting with Assistant Curator Odessa Warren for her key contributions and remarkable endurance, and to Kira Weinstein, former Curatorial Research Assistant, for her crucial additional support. Intern Bilyana Palankasova has also provided much needed assistance and research skills, with kind support from the Scottish Graduate School for Arts and Humanities. An exhibition this complex would be inconceivable without the contribution of Exhibitions Registrars Stephanie Busson and Sevinc Duvarci, expertly advised by Travis Miles, Senior Exhibitions Registrar, and the vital help of Exhibition Assistants Jarelle Francis and Sandrine Bergeron. Manuela Buttiglione, Exhibitions Project Manager, enabled us to deliver the exhibition with diligence and enthusiasm. I also thank Senior Design and Production Manager Phil Monk, Senior Art Installation Manager Adam Wozniak, Technical Manager Tom Matthews and the rest of the Production and Installation team for their creative contributions to the design and assembly of the exhibition. My heartfelt thanks also go to Catherine Wood for her trust and stewardship of the project.

I am deeply grateful to the contributors to this publication, Sarah Cook, Darko Fritz, Tina Rivers-Ryan and Ming Tiampo, for delivering such expertly crafted essays despite the compressed timeline, and to Suzanne Treister for being such a keen and involved interviewee. Many thanks also to Carlos Cruz Delgado, Bronac Ferran and Nina Horisaki-Christens, who provided insightful short texts as well as curatorial advice, and to Odessa Warren and Kira Weinstein who also contributed short texts for the catalogue and compiled the illustrations' captions, along with Bilyana Palankasova. Special thanks go to Johanne Lian Olsen for her delightful book design, and to the Tate Publishing team: senior editor Nicola Bion, picture researcher Emma O'Neill, and production manager Bill Jones.

I would also like to thank the following colleagues: Kirsteen McSwein, Senior Learning Curator for Interpretation, along with Giulia Calvi and Elliott Higgs, Assistant Curators for Interpretation; Scott Morris, Antonio Martinez, Ben Wells and Lilly Daniell of Tate Digital; Marketing Manager Isabella Szukilojc and Lead Designer Sam Jones; Tate's Conservation teams, and especially George Morris, Jake van Dugteren, Patricia Falcao, Chris King (and the Time-Based Media Conservation Team at large), Luz Vanasco, Deborah Cane, Elizabeth McDonald, Carla Flack, Alice Watkins, Jacquie Moon and Charity Fox; AV Technician Gareth Fox and Sara Smith of Adi; Sandra McLean and Khaled Sofian of Visitor Experience; Sarah Monteath, Head of Programmes for Major Gifts and Public Sector, as well as Catherine Dunn, Executive Director of the Tate Americas Foundation; and the many other colleagues at Tate in Curatorial, Collection Care, Communications, Development, Digital, Enterprises, Learning, Legal, Library and Archive, Press, Special Events and Visitor Experience who have played a key role in the making of this exhibition.

Finally, I am indebted to a number of scholars and critical friends who, in addition to the many credited artists and lenders who went above and beyond their already generous contributions, have left a significant imprint on the project by providing advice, contacts and research materials: Jonathan Arnold, Mila Askarova, Valentino Catricalà, Christophe Charles, Sean Clark, Dunja and Maja Donassy, Becky Cohen, Paul Cohen, Robert Devcic, Rudolf Frieling, Michael Goldberg, Ben Houston, Mizuho Kato, Melanie Lenz, Laura Leuzzi, Sarah Macaulay, Thomas Machnik, Kathleen Maguire, Julie Martin, Sadanand Menon, Peter Oleksik, Anna Olszewska, Pedro Cid Proença, Paul Purgas, Jasia Reichardt, Kiran and Ravin Sachdev, Marinko Sudac, Victor Wang and Alex Zivanovic. Thank you all for your help in completing this electric circuit and making its energy flow.

Val Ravaglia
Curator, Displays and international Art, Tate Modern

General Editor's Note
Titles of artworks are in given in English; original titles,
where different, of works exhibited at Tate Modern,
are provided in the list on pp.222–7.

Authorship of the extended captions is indicated by initials:
EH – Elliott Higgs
BP – Bilyana Palankasova
VR – Val Ravaglia
KW – Kira Wainstein
OW – Odessa Warren

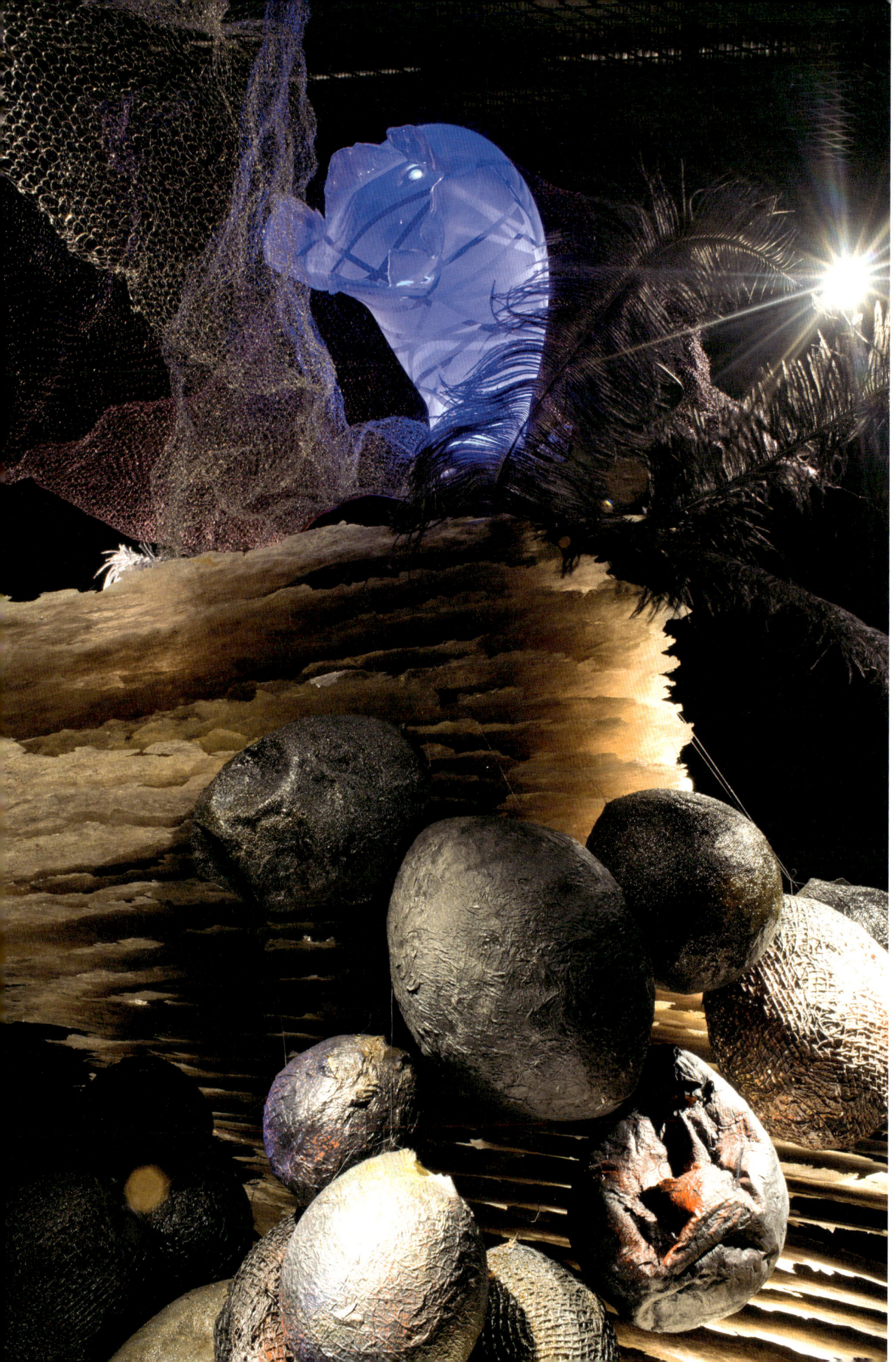

Together in Electric Dreams: Circuits of Art and Technology

Val Ravaglia

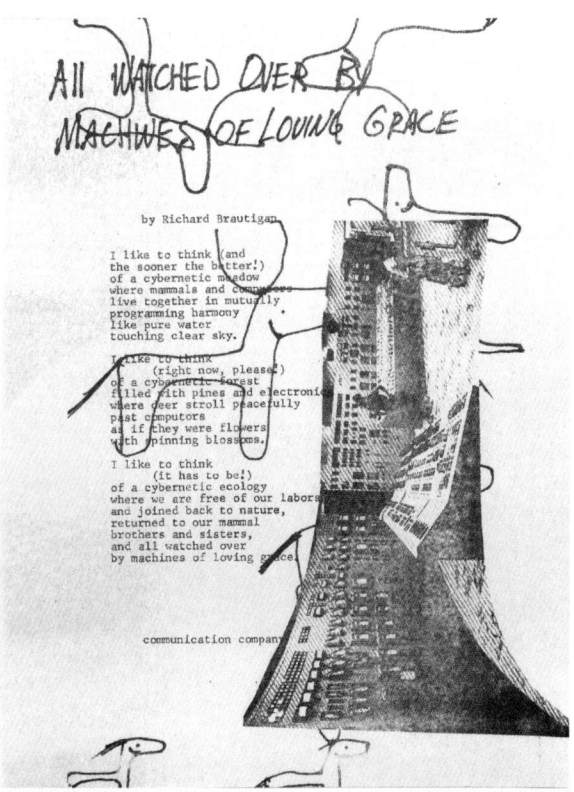

Electric Dreams presents a network of stories about artists who, between the 1950s and the early 1990s, made works inspired by the methods and tools of science and technology, still considered new or emerging at that time, and expressed through them their visions for art's relationship with these fields, their increasing presence in everyday life and their relevance for the future.

Over these decades, consumer electronics spread among ever-increasing sections of the world's populations, becoming ubiquitous (at least in affluent urban centres) and so ingrained in everyday experience as to become commonplace, second nature: 'extensions' not just of people, as the subtitle of Marshall McLuhan's 1964 book *Understanding Media* suggested, but of the environments they inhabit.[1] These appliances included the machines spreading mass media imagery and, alongside, popular ideas about science and technology themselves, profoundly changing worldviews and creating new science-fiction scenarios as others fast became obsolete. Computers went from the size of a room to discreet boxes fitting on a desk, and began to transform the way people – including artists – worked. The idea of information went from a niche mathematical theory to the single most fundamental element defining our age. It was inevitable that a growing number of artists would feel the need to channel these societal transformations in their work. *Electric Dreams* focuses on a number of artists and practices that put that drive at their very core, manifesting scientific and technological thinking as a transformative force on the role of art as well as on its forms.

The period covered by *Electric Dreams* concludes just before the next watershed moment in the social history of technology: the widespread adoption of the internet in its 'domestic' form, enabled by Tim Berners-Lee's model of the World Wide Web. Berners-Lee invented the model in 1989 and made it available to the wider public in 1991, but it would take a few years for the internet to penetrate into public consciousness to the point of becoming the paradigm-shifting technology that currently dominates our daily life. The later examples included in *Electric Dreams* cover the arrival of personal computers, early forms of networked communications through private terminals, and the first appearances of immersive virtual reality environments in the early 1990s. This was also a time when discourses around visual culture and technology began to change: the category of 'new media' emerged in this decade, under the growing influence of the academic field of cultural studies (along with the very notion of 'visual culture' as an expanded field that includes but is not limited to art in the age of mass media), and in turn deeply affected artistic production. The later cases offer a glimpse into some of the themes that would become central to the digital culture of the 1990s, but stop short of the birth of net art: to address this paradigm shift would require far more space than this volume allows.

While this book is structured over four thematic sections that also provide a chronological sequence, *Electric Dreams* does not seek to present a unified narrative in the style of a historical survey; rather, it is a knowingly partial

↖ Richard Brautigan, *All Watched Over by Machines of Loving Grace* 1967, original broadsheet
← Liliane Lijn, *The Bride* 1988 (detail, see p.199)

and selective account of a subject too vast and complex to define and contain. It links well known artists and moments with others that have historically received less attention, as a way of pointing at countless artists and moments that remain yet underexposed.

Many of the stories presented in *Electric Dreams* are directly connected, with artists establishing conversations and collaborations, exhibiting and publishing together, moving across geographical locations and making increasingly effective use of communication technologies to expand their networks – the very communication technologies that also often constitute the mediatic channel and subject matter of their work.

The first section of *Electric Dreams*, 'Materialising Invisible Forces', looks at artistic practices from the 1950s and 1960s, a period still reckoning with the traumas of the Second World War but also witnessing the whirlwind of technological acceleration that went hand in hand with the driving forces behind post-war economic recovery in the countries affected by the conflict and the new economic dynamics of the postcolonial age. Although these effects were felt in different areas and demographics at different speeds, their repercussions on the arts were capillary, the ease and speed with which products and peoples circulated across borders also applying to ideas about art – and of course, to artworks and artists themselves, migrating or travelling by necessity or choice.

Many developments in post-war art were fuelled by a renewed curiosity about the creative potential of science and technology, after a period of diffidence caused by the traumatic revelation of their destructive and dehumanising power during the war – a diffidence that, for many, never completely dissipated, but rather transformed into critical engagement. From the theories of relativity and quantum physics to the mathematical bases of indeterminacy and information theory, to think scientifically no longer meant to strictly *measure* the world, and the speculative aspects that were always a part of scientific processes now appeared more prominent even to non-specialists: new science seemed ever more abstract, at times hardly distinguishable from sci-fi. The huge expanses of space and the microscopic forces disclosed by new scientific approaches challenged these artists to visualise what was barely thinkable; their increasingly immersive and often electrified works, 'programmed' with simple motorised mechanisms, suggested cosmic landscapes and explored the properties of light and refraction, organic growth and chaotic change, as well as human behaviours.

The field of cybernetics, originally defined as the science of 'control and communication in the animal and the machine' (as per the subtitle of Norbert Wiener's foundational text on the subject, published in 1948), was a source of inspiration for many artists interested in ideas of interaction, as it offered a new language – intentionally cross-disciplinary in scope – that allowed them to think of their works as 'systems' to transmit information, with

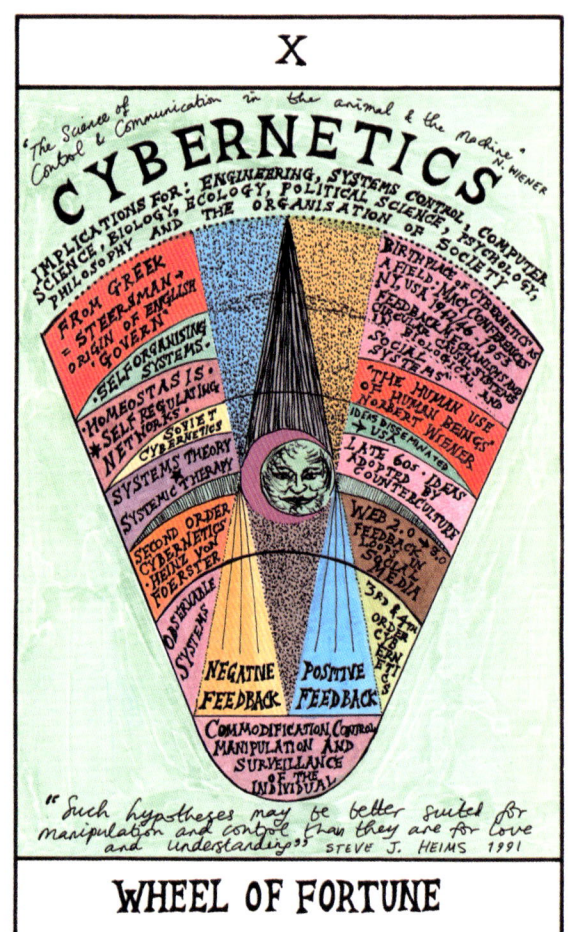

↑ Suzanne Treister, *HEXEN 2.0 / Tarot / × Wheel of Fortune – Cybernetics* 2009–11
→ The opening of *Nul 1965*, Stedelijk Museum Amsterdam 1965 Photograph by André Morain

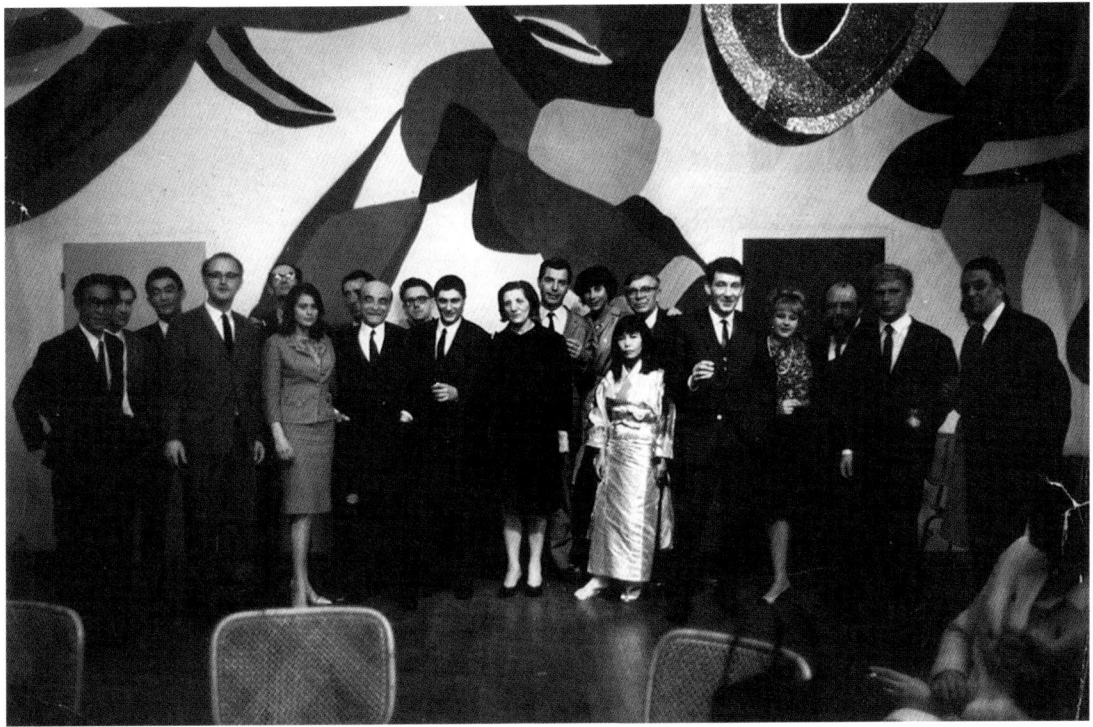

self-regulating and responsive behaviours (feedback loops) in which the viewer or their environment becomes an active component.[2]

'Materialising Invisible Forces' spotlights two examples of post-war artistic milieus that were deeply inspired by ideas from twentieth-century scientific developments, but which also overtly promoted transnational conversations and aided the movement and exposure of artists from distant locales: the expanded ZERO movement (as distinct from Zero, its German core group founded in 1957) and aspects of the London art scene in the 1960s, particularly the network gathering around Signals Gallery (1964–6). These two spheres of influence shared several formal and thematic concerns, from a recovery of geometric abstraction after a period in which expressive abstraction dominated, to their interest in recent scientific developments. Both groups championed the adoption of movement and light as integral components of their works, along with the language and material of industrial design.

ZERO and Signals exhibitions offered a number of likeminded artists from Latin America and East Asia their first opportunities to exhibit in Europe. The exhibition *Nul, negentienhonderd vijf en zestig* (dubbed *Nul 1965* to distinguish it from the earlier *Nul 62* exhibition), held at the Stedelijk Museum, Amsterdam in 1965, was especially notable for its inclusion of artists from the Japanese Gutai group, including a small participation by Atsuko Tanaka, key member of Gutai's first wave and one of very few to use electricity in her practice – indeed, to put the concept of electrical connections at its very core, from her groundbreaking wearable sculpture *Electric Dress* 1956 to her circuit-like drawings and paintings.

In her essay for this volume, 'Electric Worlds', Ming Tiampo focuses on Tanaka alongside founder of the original Zero group Otto Piene and David Medalla, the Philippines-born artist who was a key figure in Signals. The three artists' distinctive individual practices are put in a dialogue alongside their roles in intersecting networks 'that saw the potential of imagining international connectivities as radical acts of hope after two world wars'.[3] This is followed by a short text on Brion Gysin, the British-Canadian artist and writer who invented the cut-up technique adopted by many of the Beat authors, including his friend and collaborator William S. Burroughs. Gysin sometimes resorted to computers to create playful word permutations, and his psychedelic light sculpture *Dreamachine* (from 1960) anticipated the fascination of 1960s countercultures for mind-bending, immersive lightshows.

Also featured in this section is Katsuhiro Yamaguchi, an important figure in Japanese art who continued to push boundaries between media and disciplines over a six-decade career, from his role in Tokyo's Jikken Kōbō (Experimental Workshop) circle to his inventive contributions to the video installation format, yet is still little known outside Japan.

The second section, 'A Programmed Openness: Art as Visual Research', takes the earlier phase of the international New Tendencies movement as its anchor point to revisit the narrative around the 'op and kinetic art' umbrella by drawing attention to more than its formal concerns. In 1960, inspired by recent developments in geometric abstraction and a surge of works focusing on perception and colour theory, including those by ZERO artists, the Brazilian artist Almir Mavignier and Croatian art critic Matko Meštrović devised a proposal for Zagreb's Gallery of Contemporary Art to gather artworks based on mathematical principles, optical effects, motion and direct sensual engagement. The result was the *Nove Tendencije* (New Tendencies) exhibition of 1961, the first in a series of events which made Zagreb the de facto hub of an international movement dedicated to redefining the social role of art at the intersection with scientific ways of thinking about cognition and experience.

Though definitions and internal allegiances shifted dramatically over time, many New Tendencies artists thought of their practice as systematic forms of 'visual research' and of themselves as more than, in the words of François Morellet of the French Groupe de Recherche d'Art Visuel (GRAV), 'deluxe artisans'.[4] For most of these artists, the appeal of art based on geometric and optical principles was its accessibility and immediacy, which allowed it to convey its ideas through direct experience and thus, in their view, more democratically. The emphasis on perception was for these artists a way to activate the audience, to make them participants in the activation of the work rather than passive spectators: again, cybernetics often offered a model to think about feedback and interaction in art.

Several New Tendencies artists identified with the ideas of the Italian *arte programmata* (programmed art) movement, named after a 1962 exhibition titled and organised by Bruno Munari in Milan.[5] As the exhibition's full title – *Programmed Art. Kinetic Art. Multiplied Works. Open Work* – spells out, these artists promoted methodically planned practices based on rigorous scientific principles and mathematical formulae. The notion of the 'open work', coined by philosopher Umberto Eco (who wrote the catalogue for this foundational show), theorised a type of artwork with indeterminate or variable form, whether because of chance processes or public interaction.[6]

Darko Fritz's essay for this section, 'No to Op Art: Visual Research and Programmed Arts of the 1960s and 1970s', revisits the history of the New Tendencies constellation through the phases of its development in Zagreb, including its later years (from 1968) when ideas around 'programmed works' and systems led artists towards the use of computers in art and even provided a link to the nascent conceptual trends.

Also included is a brief overview of GRAV, a paradigmatic New Tendencies group based in Paris with a strong complement of émigré Latin American artists. The section concludes with an in-focus text on *Chromointerferent Environment*, a dazzling immersive installation by Venezuelan artist Carlos Cruz-Diez, which since its first conception in 1965 has taken different forms as new technologies provided the artist with fresh ways to realise his vision.

'Dialogues with the Machines', the third section, focuses on the rise of computers and digital code as tools for art-making, along with the possibilities electronics offered to create increasingly sophisticated forms of interaction. This development was a continuation of ideas around 'programming' as a means of generating or automating processes to produce artworks according to certain rules. The adoption of computers and electronic devices by artists exponentially increased the complexity of the systems and processes at their disposal to generate their works, and at the same time facilitated the inclusion of responsive components with faster and far more nuanced capabilities.

Programming languages allowed artists not just access to unprecedented computational power, but also to *communicate* with their mechanical tools in completely new ways. At the same time, electronic sensors provided their artworks with more sensitive interfaces for responding to environmental conditions and communicating with their audiences; consider, for instance, the sound-activated sculptures of artists Edward Ihnatowicz and Wen-Ying Tsai. Tina Rivers Ryan's essay 'Dialogues with the Machines: Early Computer and Cybernetic Art' shines

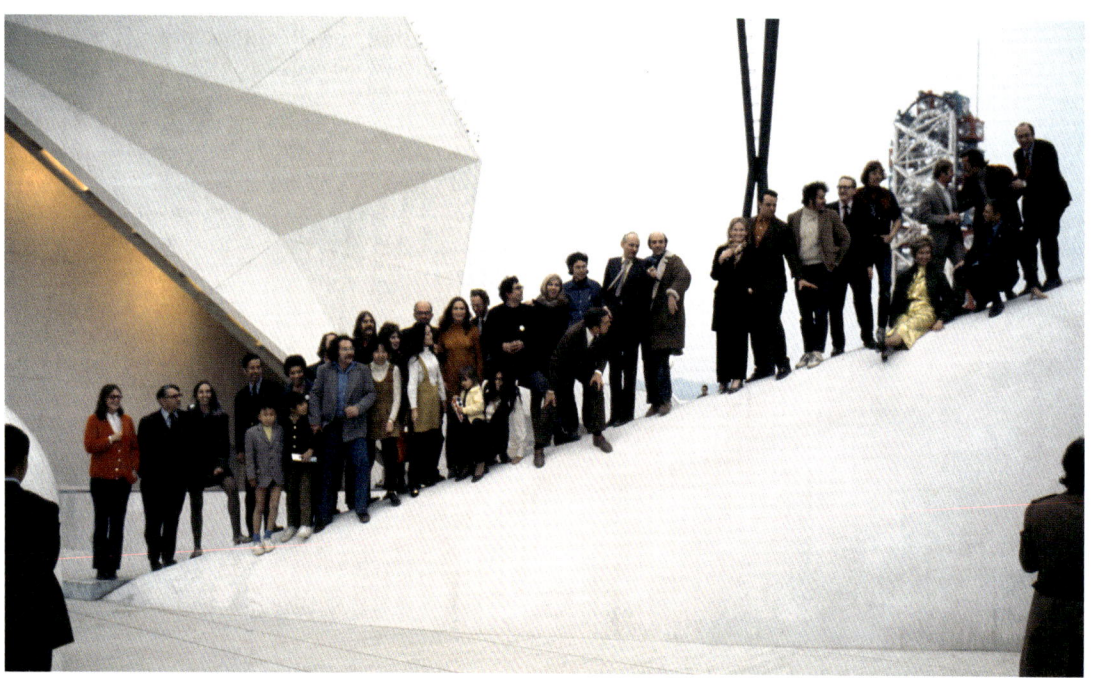

↑ Shunk Kender, group photo of E.A.T. and collaborators outside the Pepsi Pavilion, Osaka, 1970

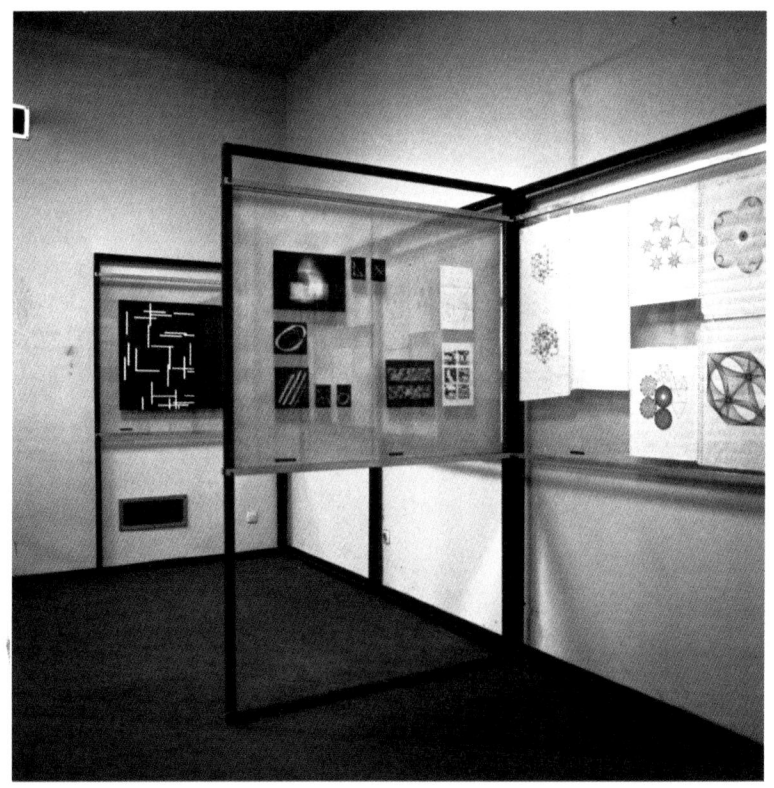

from Japan's Computer Technique Group to the Grupo de Arte y Cibernética, connected to Buenos Aires's Centro de Arte y Comunicación, another hub of experimentation influenced by the intersection of art, systems thinking and communication theory; and from the UK's Computer Arts Society, founded in 1968 in the wake of *Cybernetic Serendipity*, to *Arteônica,* a 1971 exhibition organised by concrete art veteran Waldemar Cordeiro in São Paulo and Campinas, Brazil.

Although the first wave of 'computer-aided art' was somewhat short-lived – partly due to the limitations of computer graphics at that time – some artists persevered in exploring the creative possibilities of digital media. This section spotlights the practices of Analivia Cordeiro, a Brazilian visionary whose works triangulated between choreography, programming and the new language of video art, and Harold Cohen, an established British artist who gave up traditional painting to develop AARON, the first piece of software to use narrow artificial intelligence to generate pictures with a degree of autonomy, though always in a process of 'collaboration' with its creator.

The fourth section, 'Electronic DIY: Tinkering with Tech', presents a diverse range of practices, from the late 1960s to the early 1990s, which exemplify a certain attitude often demonstrated by artists towards emerging technologies: a drive to appropriate and bend their purposes in order to push their boundaries in creative and critical directions. For many years the only way creative practitioners could access expensive hi-tech tools was to work with institutions and corporations, to gain entry to their restricted facilities and collaborate with knowledgeable staff. As consumer electronics became more portable and affordable, artists wasted no time in adopting them – and immediately taking them apart and inside out to experiment with them with full autonomy.

For many, this attitude was a way to reclaim technology from the military and corporate interests that historically drove its evolution, and to inject it with ethical and humanistic values. Artists recognised the potential of video, for instance, to construct grassroots alternatives to mainstream media, and often shared their handheld cameras and video-editing equipment pools with community groups, inviting them to document their interests and social conditions.

Many of those who chose to collaborate with established structures also found ways to hijack the 'master's tools', often navigating negotiations and compromises in order to achieve their creative visions. The period covered by *Electric Dreams* saw a proliferation of the model of the 'artist-in-residence' and other forms of collaboration with private companies and think-tanks, framed as mutually beneficial. This model was the very foundation of Experiments in Art and Technology (E.A.T.), an organisation initiated in the USA in 1967 whose mission was to connect artists and practitioners from various scientific fields.[7] This section includes various examples of E.A.T.'s activities outside the United States, including their collaborations with Ahmedabad's National Institute of Design and their *Utopia Q&A 1981* project of 1971, which

a light on Tsai's years building 'cybernetic sculptures' at MIT's Center for Advanced Visual Studies, along with the groundbreaking work of A. Michael Noll, one of the very first artists to produce computer-generated images as artworks – and to ponder the repercussions of this leap.

This development can also be seen in art reflecting the shift towards the principles of 'second-order cybernetics', which around the same time expanded the study of feedback systems by emphasising the role of the observer as an active participant: electronically-enhanced artworks as increasingly complex 'organisms', capable of operating with a higher degree of autonomy and therefore making their responsive behaviours much more obvious as they 'talk back' to their audience. The observed system becomes an *observing* system, and the observer becomes aware of their role as an interlocutor in a responsive environment as the artwork visualises the effects of their presence and actions on their surroundings: a brief object lesson in interconnectedness.

The late 1960s and early 1970s saw a concentration of exhibitions looking at these themes, with *Cybernetic Serendipity* opening at London's Institute of Contemporary Arts in August 1968, succeeded immediately by *Computers and Visual Research* – the first in a series of events connected to the fourth New Tendencies exhibition (*Tendencies 4*, 1968–9) in Zagreb – which presented an international lineup of computer-aided artistic experiments; *Tendencies 5* then followed in 1973 with an even larger roster. Tracing their participants' other activities in those years reveals even more activities and overlooked connections:

↖ *Tendencies 4 – Computers and Visual Research* (*Tendencije 4 – Kompjuteri i vizuelna istrazivanja*) exhibition at Centar za kulturu i informacije, Zagreb, 2–8 August 1968

connected chapters in Ahmedabad, New York, Stockholm and Tokyo in a long transcontinental chat via telex. Also included is a short text on Expo '70, the world exposition held in Osaka in 1970 where E.A.T. presented their legendary Pepsi Pavilion, featuring an enormous mirror dome and Fujiko Nakaya's first fog sculpture.

Also featured is Sonia Landy Sheridan, who as artist-in-residence at Xerox PARC showed new possibilities to lab technicians and engineers by pushing the boundaries of what photocopiers could do. In 1969, she started the Generative Systems programme at the School of the Art Institute of Chicago, and a student of hers went on to develop one of the very first applications for digital image manipulation, EASEL, which used an intuitive graphics interface, a camera, a tablet and a stylus. Landy Sheridan then adopted it to make some of the earliest artworks of this kind.

The main essay for this section, Sarah Cook's 'The Patchy History of Artists and Electronics: Typewriter, Telephone, Television, Telecommunications', reflects on many of these themes, as well as video synthesisers, performances using live telecommunications such as satellite links, and pre-internet forms of networking. This section also covers the spread of personal computers and the new wave of digital experimentation this sparked from the mid-1980s. Also included is a short text on Palestinian-American painter Samia Halaby, who at that time taught herself how to code and turned her Amiga 1000 computer into a unique instrument to create dazzling 'kinetic paintings'.

The last two short texts examine Tatsuo Miyajima's installations of LED displays as meditations on the flow of time and data, and return to Liliane Lijn, whose kinetic installations were first featured in the programmes of Signals Gallery. Her practice continued (and continues) to evolve through reflections on technology as a way to harness cosmic forces and as an interface between humans and their environment. Her works of the 1980s took the form of totemic light sculptures that embodied the continuum of nature and culture as female mythological figures, and were often accompanied by poems cautioning against the misuse of technology for the domination and destruction of the planet. As the volume draws to a close, Lijn reminds us that scientific knowledges are a double-edged sword, and humanity has a choice: whether to continue to use them to hurtle towards extinction, or to put them towards better ways of interfacing with the cosmos.

An interview with British artist Suzanne Treister serves as an epilogue of sorts. Her *Fictional Videogame Stills* series (1991–2), also created on an Amiga 1000, reflects a new set of questions emerging at the end of the 1980s with the rise of discourses around virtual reality and their effect on perceptions of identity and authenticity. Treister also reminisces about the early days of the internet, and how her disillusionment with its later developments led to her interest in the history of cybernetics, making new links with ideas that inspired many of the practices addressed in the previous pages.

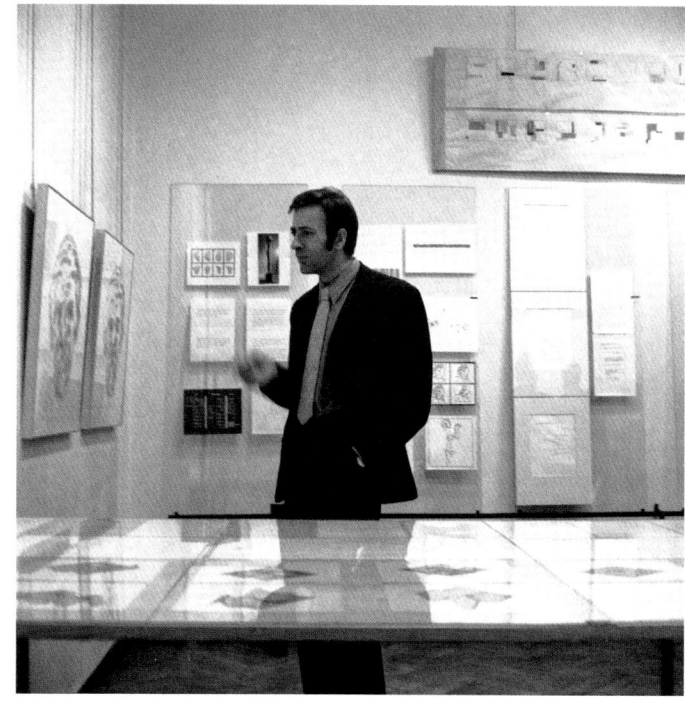

The research behind the *Electric Dreams* exhibition revealed many more stories of artists, movements, moments that we were not able to address in this instance but demonstrate further fascinating parallels. Two standout examples, hailing from geographical areas that tend to be excluded from narratives on art and technology in the twentieth century, are the acrylic light sculptures by Lebanese Nadia Saikali from Lebanon, which were exhibited in Beirut in 1971, and the case of the Crystalists from 1970s Sudan, whose works inspired by physics and natural geometries showed a sophisticated engagement with scientific ideas and process-based practices. Considering the intersecting histories of art, science and technology as a thick tangled web, with *Electric Dreams* we can barely claim to have provided a glimpse into a small section of its fragmented surface. It might, however, offer a starting point for those curious to follow some of the threads presented here and see what else can be found hidden underneath.

↗ *Tendencies 4 – Computers and Visual Research* (*Tendencije 4 – Kompjuteri i vizuelna istrazivanja*) exhibition, 5 May – 30 August 1969

TO CURE TECHNOPHOBIA YOU NEED ILLUSIONS THAT WORK.

A lot of people aren't fooled by the new technology. They know it means new levels of tedium wherever work is required for survival.

At AT&T, we're worried by their hostility.

That's why we're watching reactions to automation so closely. To find out what people will accept. And where they draw the line.

Our calculations can help them view their domestication as inevitable, almost nice.

You see, at AT&T we know even the most advanced technology can be dismantled by people who want to live for themselves and not us.

AT&T. We help keep domination up to date.

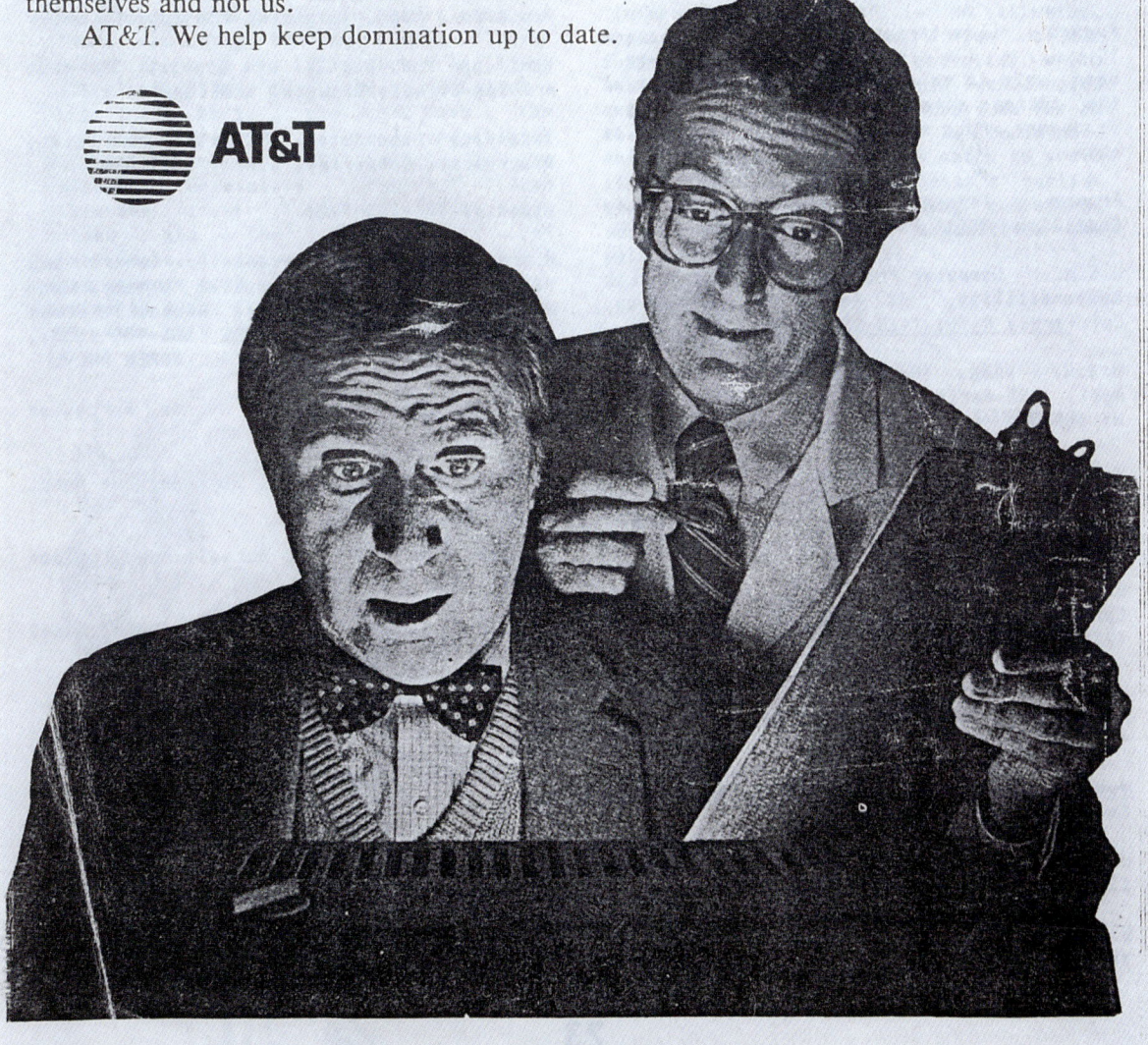

↖ Back cover of *Black Chip* no.86:1, Spring 1986

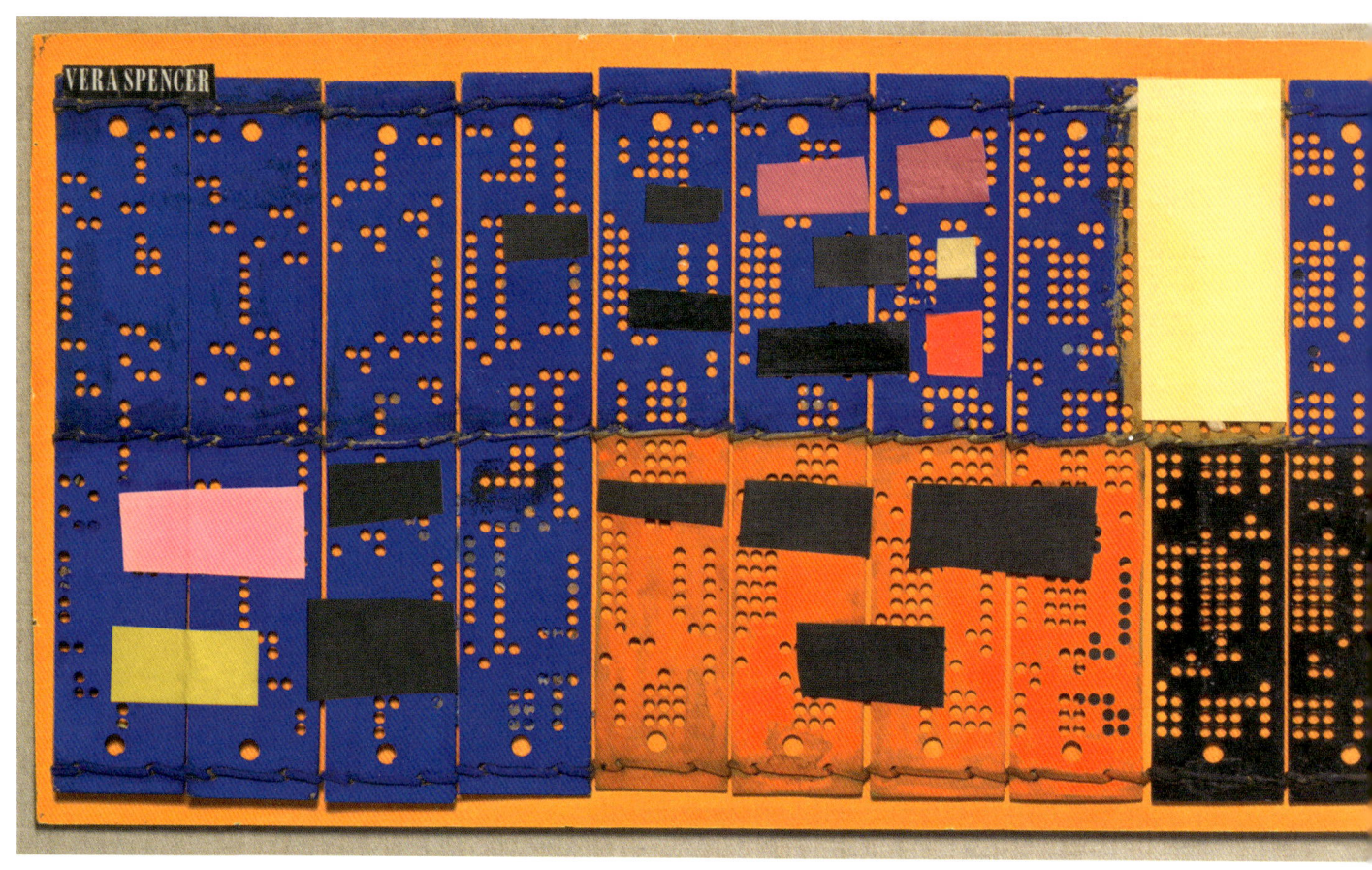

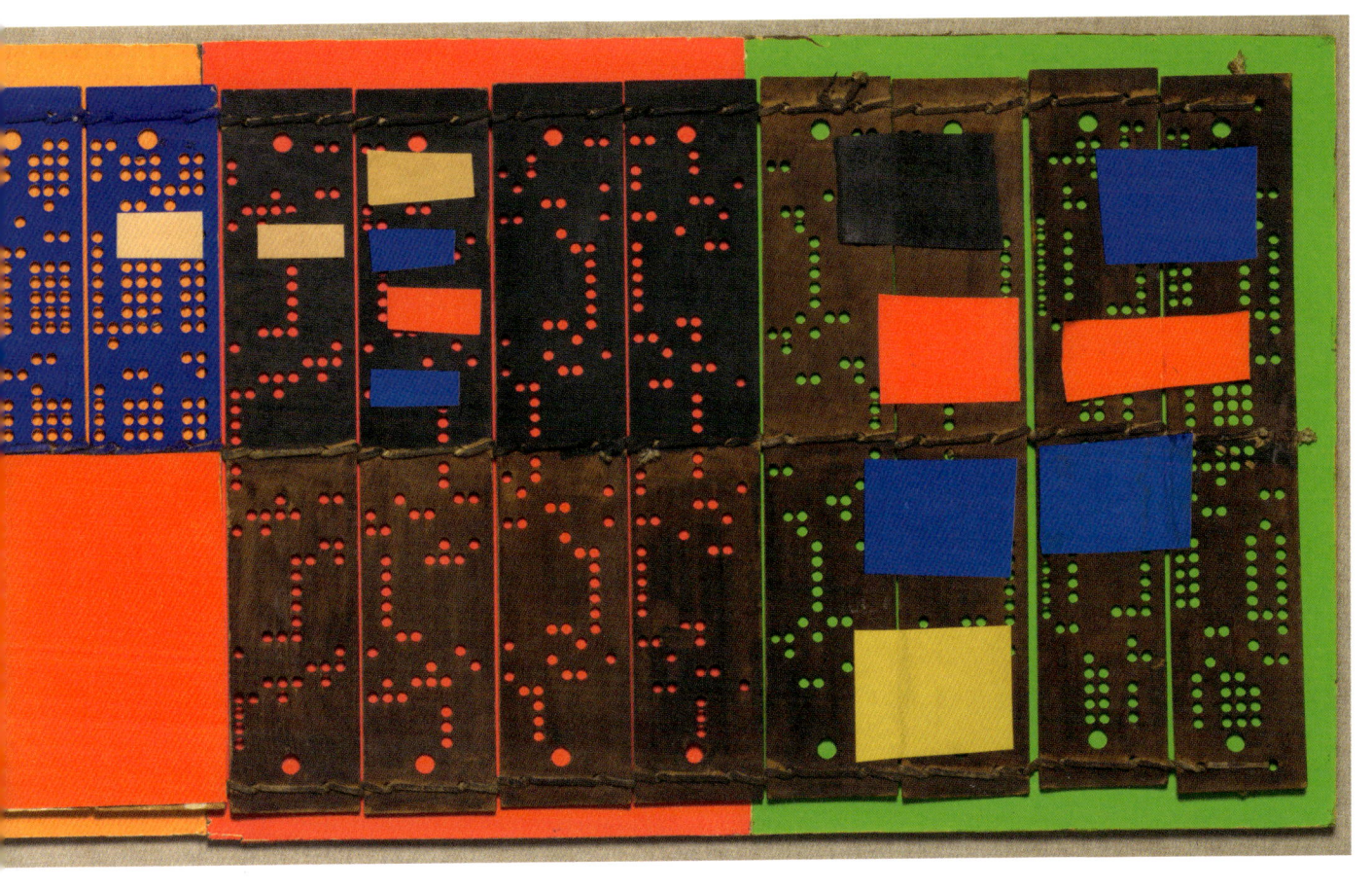

Vera Spencer
Artist Versus Machine c.1954

In 1954, artists Victor Pasmore, Kenneth Martin and Robert Adams, together with the architect John Weeks, organised an exhibition titled *Artist Versus Machine* in London. The majority of the included works are geometric reliefs where 'machine aesthetics' translates into highly regular and polished forms, dissimulating the hand of the artist to the point of appearing mass-produced. Standing out among these is a gently dissenting work by Vera Spencer, also titled *Artist Versus Machine* c.1954. Her colourful collage played with the formal language of geometric abstraction while having an unmistakeable handmade quality, as if to interfere with the approach that would see the artist imitate the machine to the point of disappearing. She applied two rows of twenty punched cards, painted with gouache in violet, red, black and browns, and applied pieces of brightly hued paper roughly cut into irregular rectangles over some of the hole patterns.

The punched cards used in this work are those used to operate Jacquard mechanical looms, patented in France in 1804 to automate the production of woven textiles featuring complex patterns. These punch cards essentially made the loom 'programmable' using a binary language, communicating to the machine through the presence

or absence of a hole. In the 1830s, Charles Babbage took inspiration from Jacquard's punched cards when designing his Analytical Engine, which is considered the first general-purpose computer. Mathematician Ada Lovelace used the analogy of the Jacquard loom to explain Babbage's machine: 'The Analytical Engine weaves algebraic patterns, just as the Jacquard-loom weaves flowers and leaves.'[1]

Just as Lovelace is often credited as the first computer programmer, it may be possible to describe Spencer as one of the first 'glitch artists': in *Artist Versus Machine* she interferes with a programmed motif with her own semi-random insertions, which could generate errors if run through the machine.[2] It is a challenge between approaches to abstraction, appearing at a time when the notion of computational abstraction was only beginning to form in the popular imaginary. By the 1950s punch cards were commonly associated with the nascent field of computer science, so the programmes Spencer imagined herself disrupting with her artistic gestures were not just of the woven kind. And by displaying the source of the information rather than the finished product, she may even qualify as the first artist to display the code itself as a kind of data abstraction. VR

AUTO-DESTRUCTIVE ART

Demonstration by G. Metzger

SOUTH BANK LONDON 3 JULY 1961 11.45 a.m.—12.15 p.m.

Acid action painting. Height 7 ft. Length 12½ ft. Depth 6 ft. Materials: nylon, hydrochloric acid, metal. Technique. 3 nylon canvases coloured white black red are arranged behind each other, in this order. Acid is painted, flung and sprayed on to the nylon which corrodes at point of contact within 15 seconds.

Construction with glass. Height 13 ft. Width 9½ ft. Materials. Glass, metal, adhesive tape. Technique. The glass sheets suspended by adhesive tape fall on to the concrete ground in a pre-arranged sequence.

AUTO-DESTRUCTIVE ART

Auto-destructive art is primarily a form of public art for industrial societies.

Self-destructive painting, sculpture and construction is a total unity of idea, site, form, colour, method and timing of the disintegrative process.

Auto-destructive art can be created with natural forces, traditional art techniques and technological techniques.

The amplified sound of the auto-destructive process can be an element of the total conception.

The artist may collaborate with scientists, engineers.

Self-destructive art can be machine produced and factory assembled.

Auto-destructive paintings, sculptures and constructions have a life time varying from a few moments to twenty years. When the disintegrative process is complete the work is to be removed from the site and scrapped.

London, 4th November, 1959   *G. METZGER*

MANIFESTO AUTO-DESTRUCTIVE ART

Man in Regent Street is auto-destructive.
Rockets, nuclear weapons, are auto-destructive.
Auto-destructive art.
The drop drop dropping of HH bombs.
Not interested in ruins, (the picturesque)
Auto-destructive art re-enacts the obsession with destruction, the pummelling to which individuals and masses are subjected.
Auto-destructive art demonstrates man's power to accelerate disintegrative processes of nature and to order them.
Auto-destructive art mirrors the compulsive perfectionism of arms manufacture—polishing to destruction point.
Auto-destructive art is the transformation of technology into public art. The immense productive capacity, the chaos of capitalism and of Soviet communism, the co-existence of surplus and starvation; the increasing stock-piling of nuclear weapons—more than enough to destroy technological societies; the disintegrative effect of machinery and of life in vast built-up areas on the person,...

Auto-destructive art is art which contains within itself an agent which automatically leads to its destruction within a period of time not to exceed twenty years. Other forms of auto-destructive art involve manual manipulation. There are forms of auto-destructive art where the artist has a tight control over the nature and timing of the disintegrative process, and there are other forms where the artist's control is slight. Materials and techniques used in creating auto-destructive art include: Acid, Adhesives, Ballistics, Canvas, Clay, Combustion, Compression, Concrete, Corrosion, Cybernetics, Drop, Elasticity, Electricity, Electrolysis, Electronics, Explosives, Feed-back, Glass, Heat, Human Energy, Ice, Jet, Light, Load, Mass-production, Metal, Motion Picture, Natural Forces, Nuclear energy, Paint, Paper, Photography, Plaster, Plastics, Pressure, Radiation, Sand, Solar energy, Sound, Steam, Stress, Terra-cotta, Vibration, Water, Welding, Wire, Wood.

London, 10 March, 1960   *G. METZGER*

AUTO-DESTRUCTIVE ART   MACHINE ART
AUTO CREATIVE ART

Each visible fact absolutely expresses its reality.

Certain machine produced forms are the most perfect forms of our period.

In the evenings some of the finest works of art produced now are dumped on the streets of Soho.

Auto creative art is art of change, growth movement.

Auto-destructive art and auto creative art aim at the integration of art with the advances of science and technology. The immidiate objective is the creation, with the aid of computers, of works of art whose movements are programmed and include "self-regulation". The spectator, by means of electronic devices can have a direct bearing on the action of these works.

Auto-destructive art is an attack on capitalist values and the drive to nuclear annihilation.

23 *June* 1961   *G. METZGER*

B.C.M. ZZZO London W.C.1.

Printed by St. Martins' Printers (TU) 86d, Lillie Road, London, S.W.6.

Gustav Metzger, *Recreation of First Public Demonstration of Auto-Destructive Art* 1960, remade 2004, 2015

After starting out as a traditional painter and sculptor, in the 1950s Metzger began to use industrial materials such as steel and corrugated cardboard, and to take an interest in scientific methods. In 1959 he published his first 'Auto-destructive Art' manifesto, theorising about artworks made to decay and disintegrate over time as 'a public art for industrial societies'. To demonstrate these ideas, he started painting with acid on nylon. His first public demonstration was at the Temple Gallery, London, on 22 June 1960. At first, Metzger was hidden behind a pane of glass covered with a white nylon sheet. He then applied a hydrochloric acid solution to the fabric with a brush; as the nylon dissolved, he slowly became visible through the holes. The presentation also included waste in plastic bags and models for auto-destructive sculptures, which would later evolve into his proposal for *Five Screens with Computer* 1963–70 (p.135). Metzger distributed the leaflet illustrated here at a later acid painting demonstration, carried out on the Thames river front in 1961. In 1969, after joining the Computer Arts Society, he co-authored the *Zagreb Manifesto*; this was first presented at the symposium 'Computers and Visual Research' in Zagreb, organised by the New Tendencies movement. VR

Gustav Metzger, Gordon Hyde and Jonathan Benthall, from the *Zagreb Manifesto*, May 1969

'It is now evident that, where art meets science and technology, the computer and related disciplines provide a nexus ... Some artists ... are alive to the possibilities which are opening up in the application of advanced techniques for organising and transforming information. These evolving techniques ... include the use of computers not only for processing inputs into new forms, but also for optimising the creative potential at the man-machine interface. This interface is perhaps the least satisfactory aspect of present-day computers, because of the rigid mathematical constraints imposed, the design of the internal logic of the machines, and the inadequacy of existing programming languages for handling information in open systems. A great deal of computer art embodies the limitations of existing techniques. The aesthetic demands of artists necessarily lead them to seek an alliance with the most advanced research in natural and artificial intelligence.

'Artists are increasingly striving to relate their work and that of the technologists to the current unprecedented crisis in society. Some artists are responding by utilising their experience of science and technology to try and resolve urgent social problems. Others, researching in cybernetics and the neuro-sciences, are exploring new ideas about the interaction of the human being with the environment. Others again are identifying their work with a concept of ecology which includes the entire technological environment that man has imposed on nature. There are creative people in science who feel that the man/machine problem lies at the heart of making the computer the servant of man and nature. Such people welcome the insight of the artist in this context, lest we lose sight of humanity and beauty.'

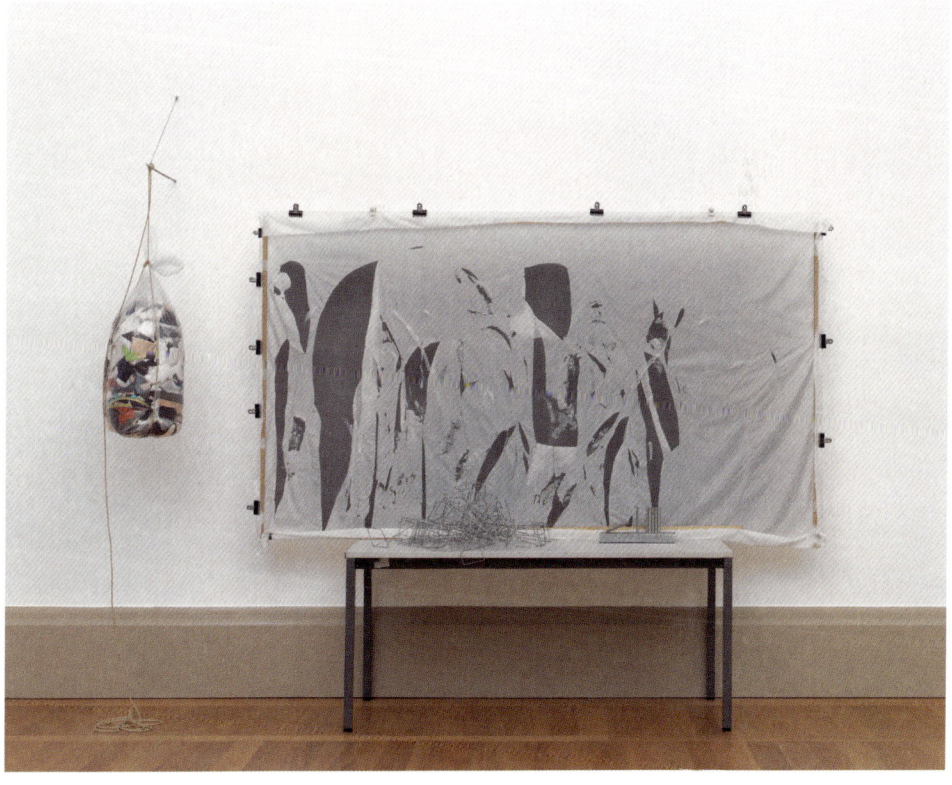

← Gustav Metzger, *Auto-Destructive Art Demonstration*, 1961
↑ Gustav Metzger, *Recreation of First Public Demonstration of Auto-Destructive Art*, 1960, remade 2004, 2015

Materialising
Invisible
Forces

Materialising
Invisible
Forces

22

Materialising

Electric Worlds

Ming Tiampo

For artists working in the fragile peace of the Cold War and the ambivalent optimism of post-war reconstruction, a sense of connectivity to larger worlds expanded hand in hand with technological and economic development. Changes in media, communications and transportation technologies – from the increasing accessibility of rapid, long-distance train travel and air travel to the speed of airmail, as well as the range and ubiquity of radio and television – contributed to an increasing sense of what Canadian media theorist Marshall McLuhan described as the 'global village'.[1]

This short essay considers the work of three artists included in *Electric Dreams*, examining their artworks through a relational comparison that engages their artistic networks and imagined connectivities as both technological and social. Self-consciously making worlds, these three artists, Atsuko Tanaka (Gutai), Otto Piene (Zero) and David Medalla (Signals), were members of artistic movements and larger artistic networks that saw the potential of imagining international connectivities as radical acts of hope after two world wars and the ongoing Cold War. Working respectively from post-war Japan, post-Marshall Plan Europe, and as a Filipino migrant situated between London, Paris and beyond, these three artists with very different sensibilities and histories saw the risks and possibilities of technology differently, yet all three understood it as a fundamental and world-opening part of their artistic practices.

Less than ten years after the end of the Second World War, in a newly electrified landscape that promised prosperity and new horizons – but also the anxieties of rapid economic, social and technological change – the young Atsuko Tanaka created the paradigm-shifting *Electric Dress* 1956 (p.24), one of the canonical touchstones of post-war global art. The idea for the work came to her as she sat waiting for her train at Osaka Station, surrounded by trains rumbling and screeching, dispersing passengers to all corners of the country. Daydreaming, she allowed her eyes to be drawn in by the mesmerising glow and dancing forms of the neon advertising signs that populated the surrounding cityscape. One, in particular, stood out to her: a pharmaceutical advertisement, brightly illuminated by neon lights, that provoked a 'eureka' moment in the young artist. 'This was it! I would make a neon dress!'[2]

A costume, a sculpture, a painting, an installation and a time-based work, *Electric Dress* is a garment composed of hand-painted Edison and tubular incandescent bulbs, wired through a switching device of Tanaka's own invention to flash, blink and dazzle at irregular intervals. When electrified, the work comes to life in an explosion of colour, light and motion that evokes the bustle, energy and connectivity of the post-war city – an energy whose boundaries expanded beyond Japan to a larger conception of an international art world as envisioned by both Tanaka and the Gutai Art Association (1954–72).[3] Extremely heavy and composed of handmade circuits, however, the dress is also potentially hazardous, its dangerous beauty capturing the ambivalence and disquietude provoked by rapid change

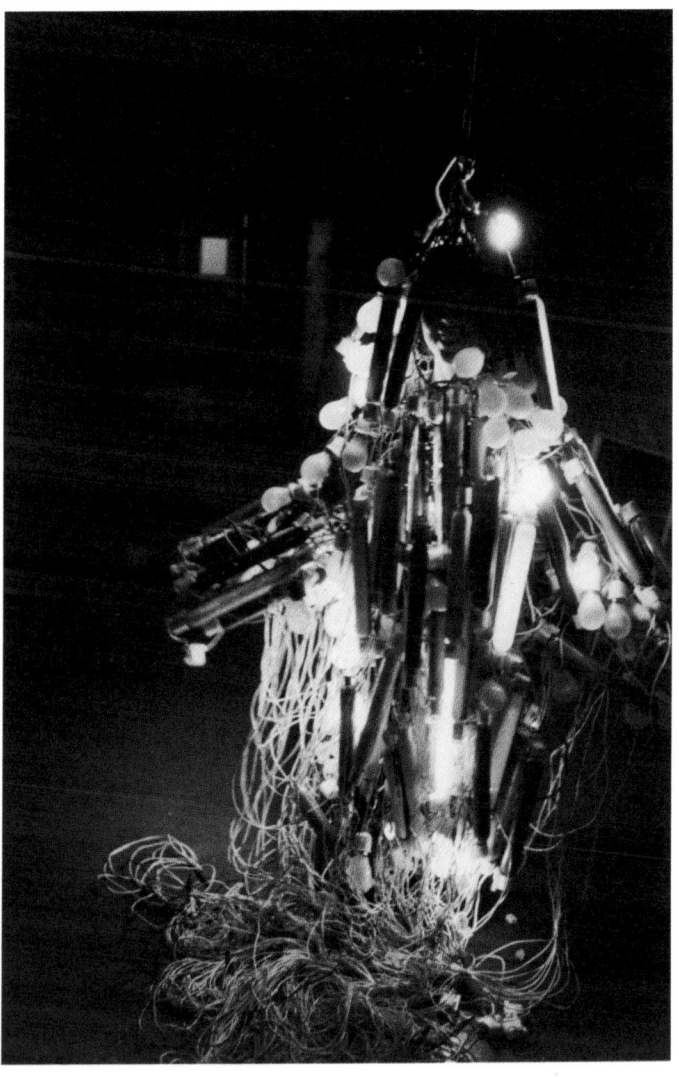

↖ Kiyoji Otsuji, *Atsuko Tanaka's Electric Dress, 2nd Gutai Exhibition* 1956

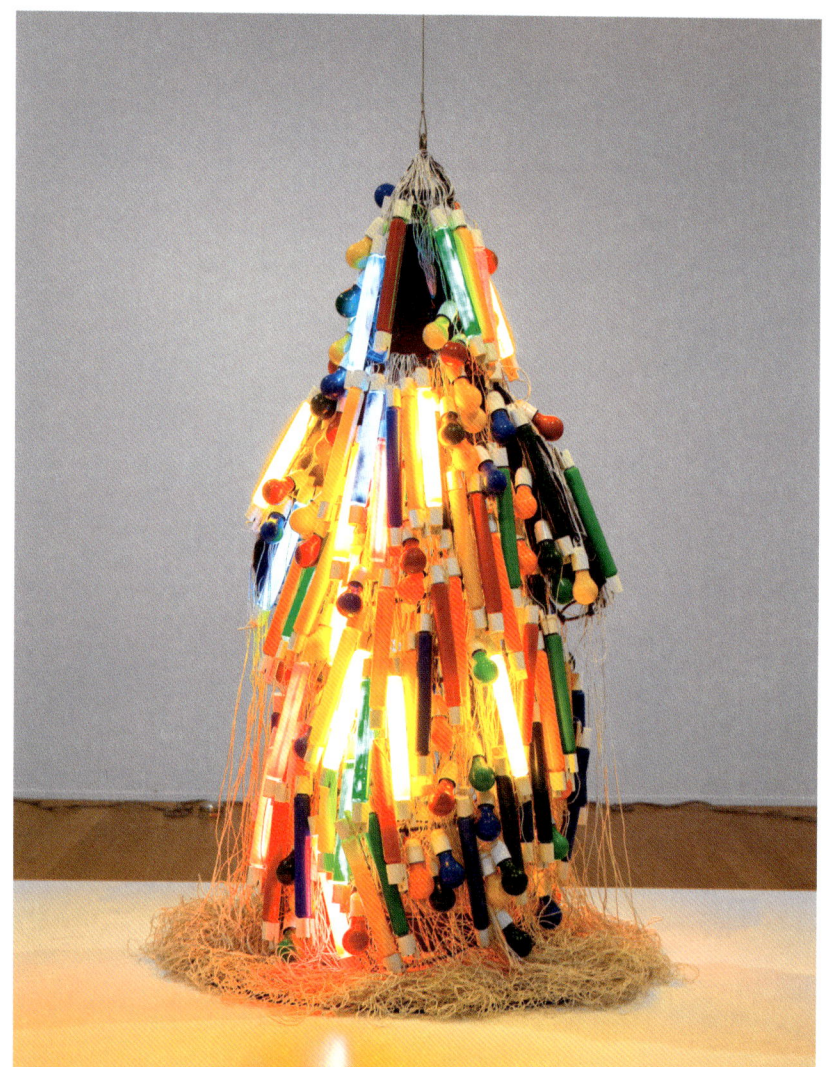

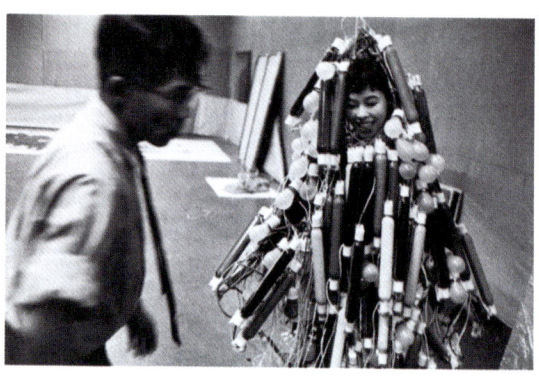

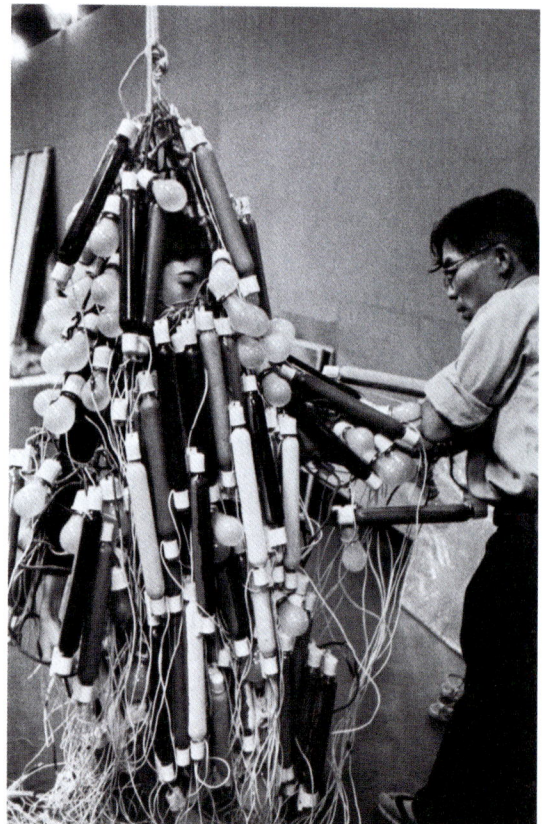

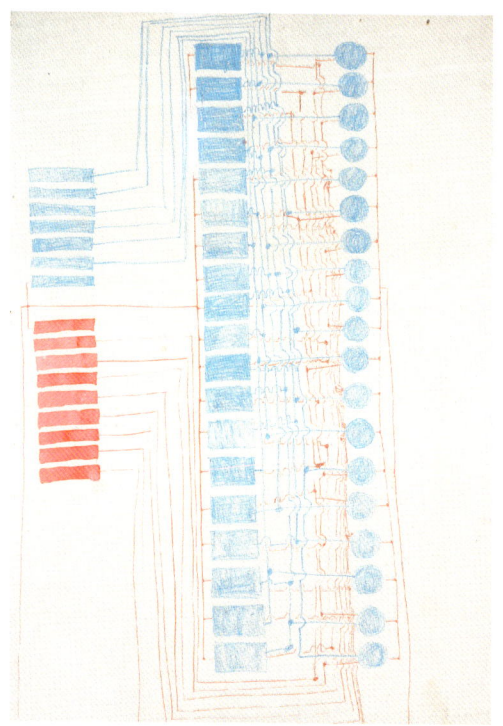

↖ Atsuko Tanaka, *Electric Dress* 1956, reconstructed 1999
← Atsuko Tanaka, *Drawing after Electric Dress* 1956
↗ Kiyoji Otsuji, *Atsuko Tanaka's Electric Dress, 2nd Gutai Exhibition* 1956

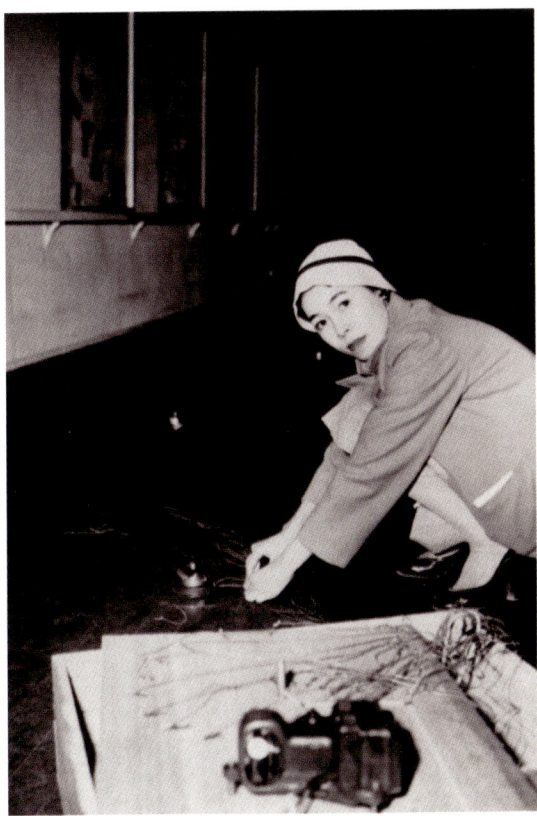
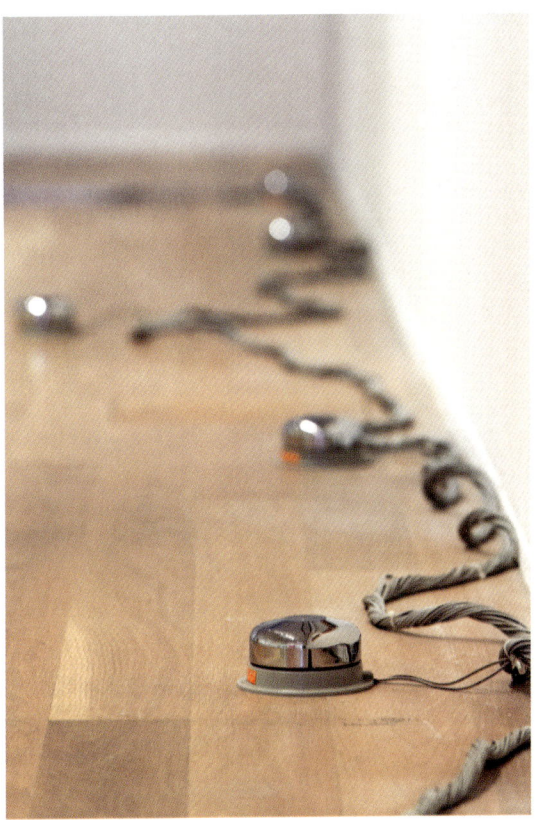

wired through the body in a Japan haunted by the spectre of war.[4] Indeed, when Tanaka tried the dress on for the very first time, testing her skills as an amateur electrician, she commented, 'I had a fleeting thought: Is this how a death-row inmate would feel?', not sure if her experiment in galvanism would result in certain death or new life.[5]

Tanaka created *Electric Dress* in the context of her work in Gutai; it was one of two significant works she made using electricity, the other being *Work (Bell)* 1955. In both cases, the works comprised both electrified objects and a suite of two-dimensional works (drawings and paintings) associated with them. An interactive sound installation, *Work (Bell)* is made up of twenty electric bells controlled by a small, nondescript button, in front of which a modest sign reads, 'Please feel free to push the button, Atsuko Tanaka'.[6] When pressed, the button sets off a series of loud, alarm-like bell sounds that ring sequentially for as long as the activator keeps their finger on the button. The result, as Gutai artist Sadamasa Motonaga wrote, is that the work creates 'a unique [experience] in which a line is drawn clearly within one's inner vision'.[7] In this spatio-temporal sound installation, the sonic experience materialises into form, defining not just a two-dimensional line, but also a three-dimensional space delimited by the string of bells' physical emplacement. Like electronic, radio and television networks that make spatial relationships tangible, *Work (Bell)* conjures space through electric signals and sound. Along with her partner Akira Kanayama, who made

paintings with an automatic toy car, Tanaka represented a conceptual strand of Gutai. This tendency questioned the expressivity of gesture, and imagined the possibilities of an art conceptualised to circulate at great distances, as well as the relationships between art and technology. This development gained further traction in the group's second phase (1965–72), through artists such as Norio Imai and Minoru Yoshida.

In 1965 both Tanaka and Kanayama were invited as part of Gutai by Dutch artist-curator Henk Peeters to participate in *Nul 1965*, an exhibition at the Stedelijk Museum in Amsterdam (p.29). As with Gutai, Nul was a movement that operated in critical relation with gestural painting, and Peeters's exhibition was envisaged as a presentation of post-painterly practices conceived as an international tendency. As Peeters commented, 'I couldn't make a revolution by myself', so he invited others from around the world to help realise 'a new global culture', in which 'art is not nationalist' but opens up global networks of artistic exchange.[8] With a similarly internationalist mindset, Gutai leader Jiro Yoshihara and his son Michio travelled to Amsterdam to install works, armed with preparatory drawings provided by the participating artists; Tanaka's contribution was a series of technical drawings intended to help the curators reconstruct *Stage Clothes* 1956, an outdoor installation related to *Electric Dress*.[9] Although her presence in the exhibition was, in the end, scaled back to a fabric work animated by an electric fan, electrical

↑ Atsuko Tanaka with *Work (Bell)* at the 3rd Genbi Exhibition in Kyoto Municipal Museum of Art, November 1955

↑ Atsuko Tanaka, *Work (Bell)* 1955

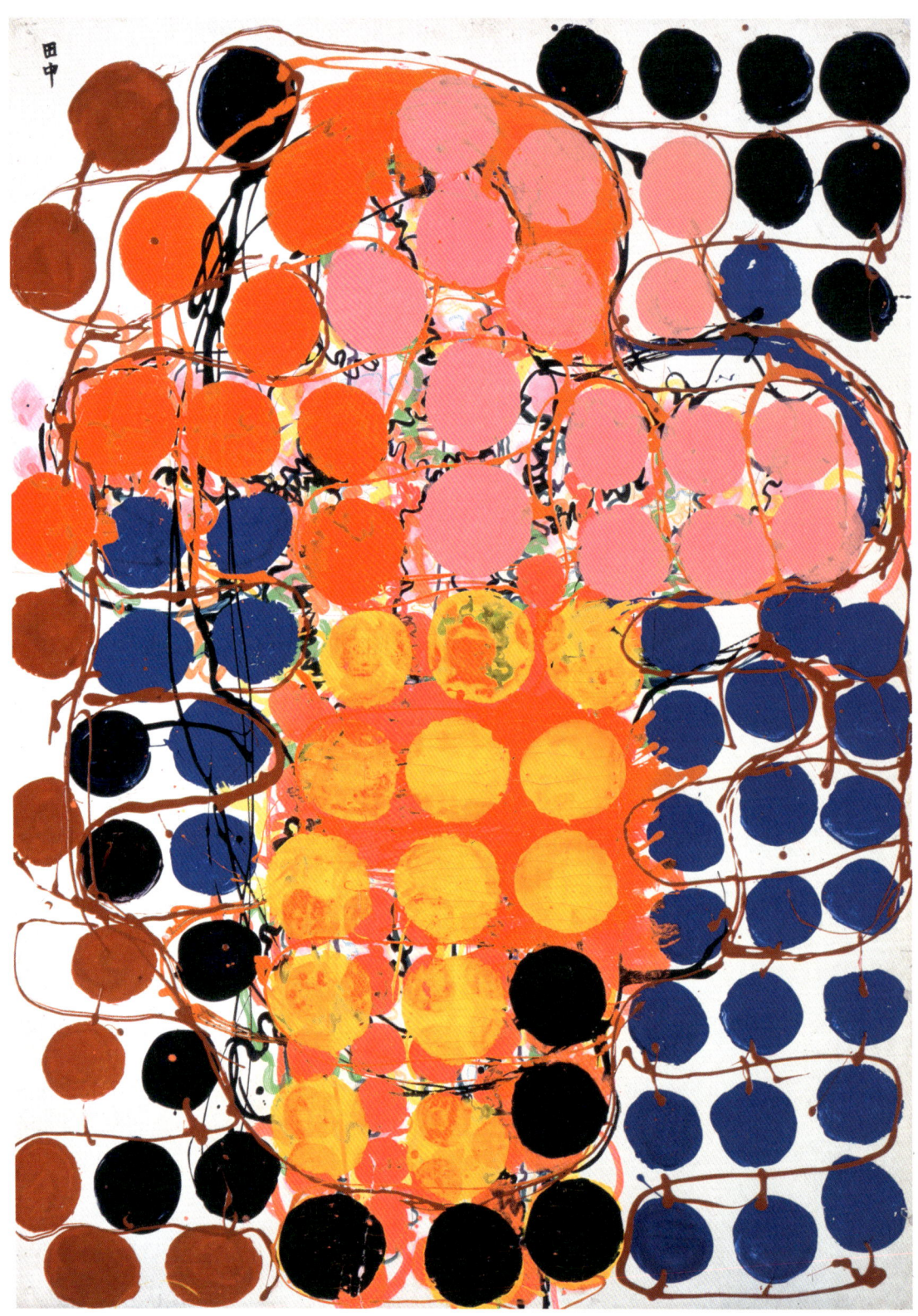

↑ Tanaka, Atsuko, *Work* 1957
→ Tanaka, Atsuko, *Drawing after Electric Dress* 1956

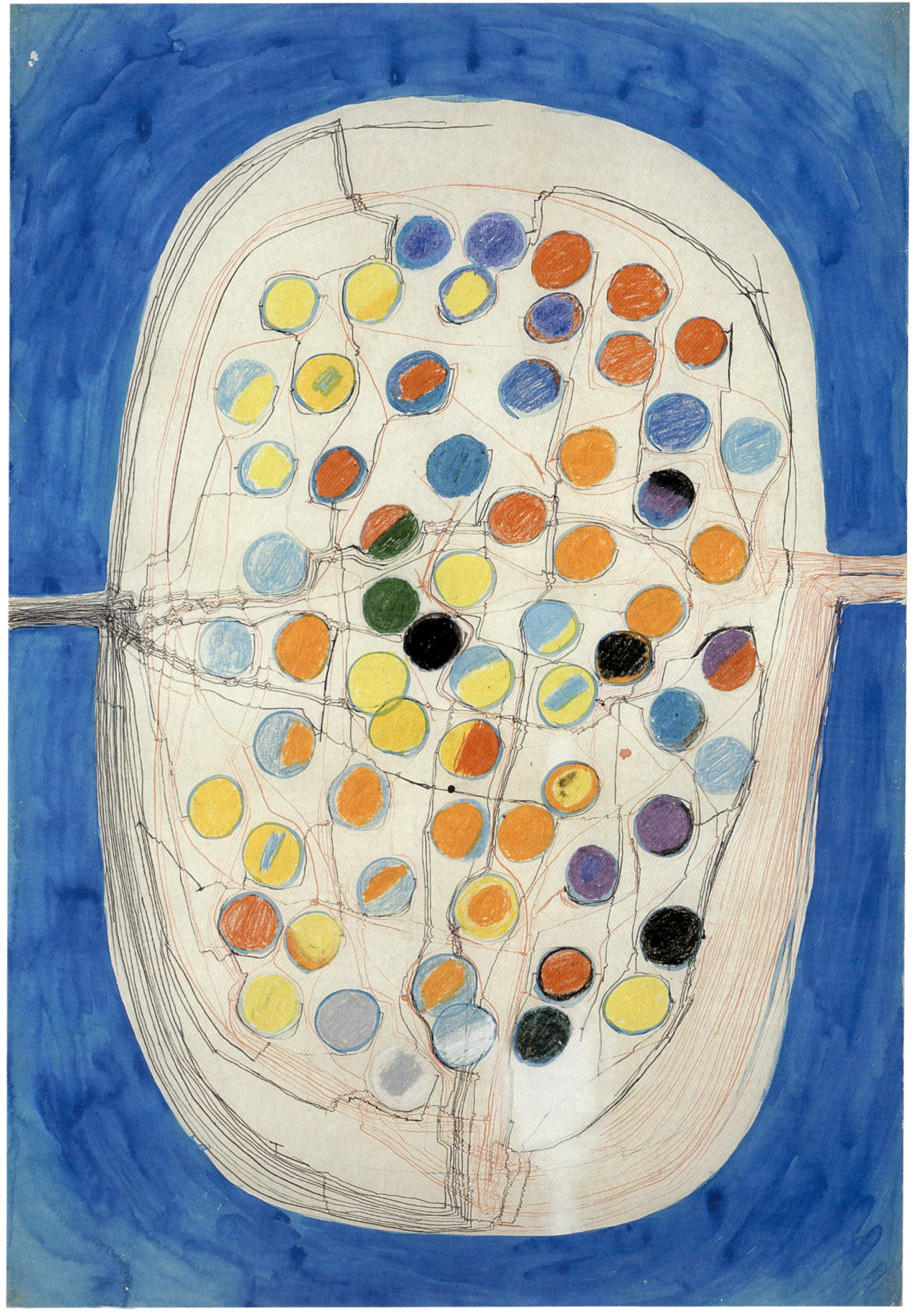

light entered into the Gutai installation through Michio Yoshihara's work *Light in Sand* 1965, a sand box filled with glowing incandescent light bulbs that referred back to his *Hill of Sand* 1962 and *Discovery* 1956.

The exhibition *Nul 1965* activated the ZERO network, bringing together artists from Zero (Germany), Nul (Netherlands), Gruppo T (Italy) and Gutai (Japan), as well as Yayoi Kusama (Japan).[10] Not just isolated inclusions, these groups represented a larger international cartography of practice that ZERO imagined as contemporaneous through circuit diagrams such as those by Heinz Mack from 1971 (p.30) and Henk Peeters from 2011. The ZERO network confidently redrew the geographies of contemporary art beyond Paris and New York, centring themselves as an expanded and expanding network, and including many of the artists featured in *Electric Dreams*, such as Pol Bury (Belgium), Dadamaino (Italy), Heinz Mack (Germany), Almir Mavignier (Brazil), François Morellet (France), Otto Piene (Germany), Jesús Rafael Soto (Venezuela), Takis (Greece), Jean Tinguely (Switzerland) and Nanda Vigo (Italy). Several of these artists participated in the many single-evening exhibitions that took place in Mack and Piene's studios in Düsseldorf.

Otto Piene's mesmerising light ballets, first presented at the Galerie Schmela in Düsseldorf in 1959, took on new life in the context of the ZERO network, expanding the boundaries of art beyond materiality and nation, creating galaxies of form that resonated with the experiments being done by Gutai, Nul, Gruppo T and others. Piene wrote that during the Second World War, into which he was conscripted as a gunner at the age of sixteen for the German Labour Corps Infantry Division, 'fear came before beauty; seeing was aiming.'[11] *The Light Ballets*, such as *Light Room (Jena)* (pp.31–3) were rooms animated by dancing patterns of light cast by perforated forms lit from within, acts expressing hope in the ability of humanity to poetically usurp technologies developed for war beyond the 'technology-happy behaviour of the obedient consumer'.[12] Experimenting with searchlights, Piene longed to present the light ballets as projections into the night sky, writing that 'Up to now we have left it to war to dream up a naive light ballet for the night skies … When will our freedom be so great that we conquer the sky for the fun of it … without being driven by fear and mistrust?'[13] Seeing the light ballets as scalar experiments, Piene wished to expand artistic practice beyond painting and also to critically interrogate the uses of technology, to reimagine human capacities and to envision human worlds within ever-expanding spheres.[14]

Beginning in 1964, the Nul group started to advertise their activities in *Signals*, a small art bulletin issued by the Centre for Advanced Creative Study (CACS), which comprised critics Paul Keeler and Guy Brett, and artists David Medalla, Gustav Metzger and Marcello Salvadori. Whereas Nul and the ZERO network imagined worlds that expanded across Europe to Japan, CACS, which became known as Signals, embraced worlds that were even more expansive,

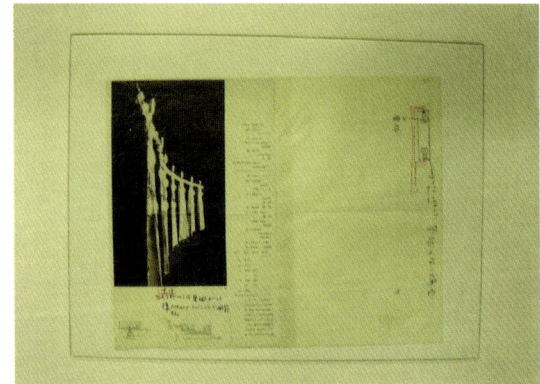

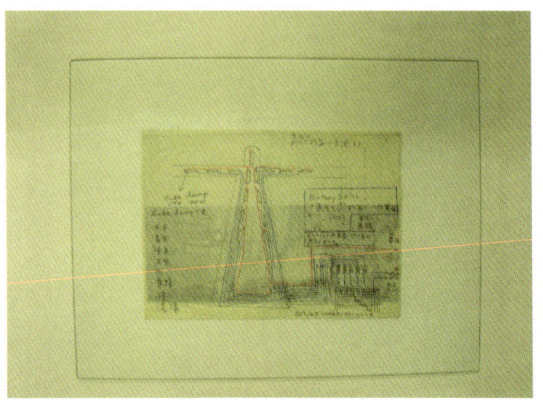

↑ Atsuko Tanaka, *Stage Clothes*, preparatory drawings for *Nul 1965* exhibition

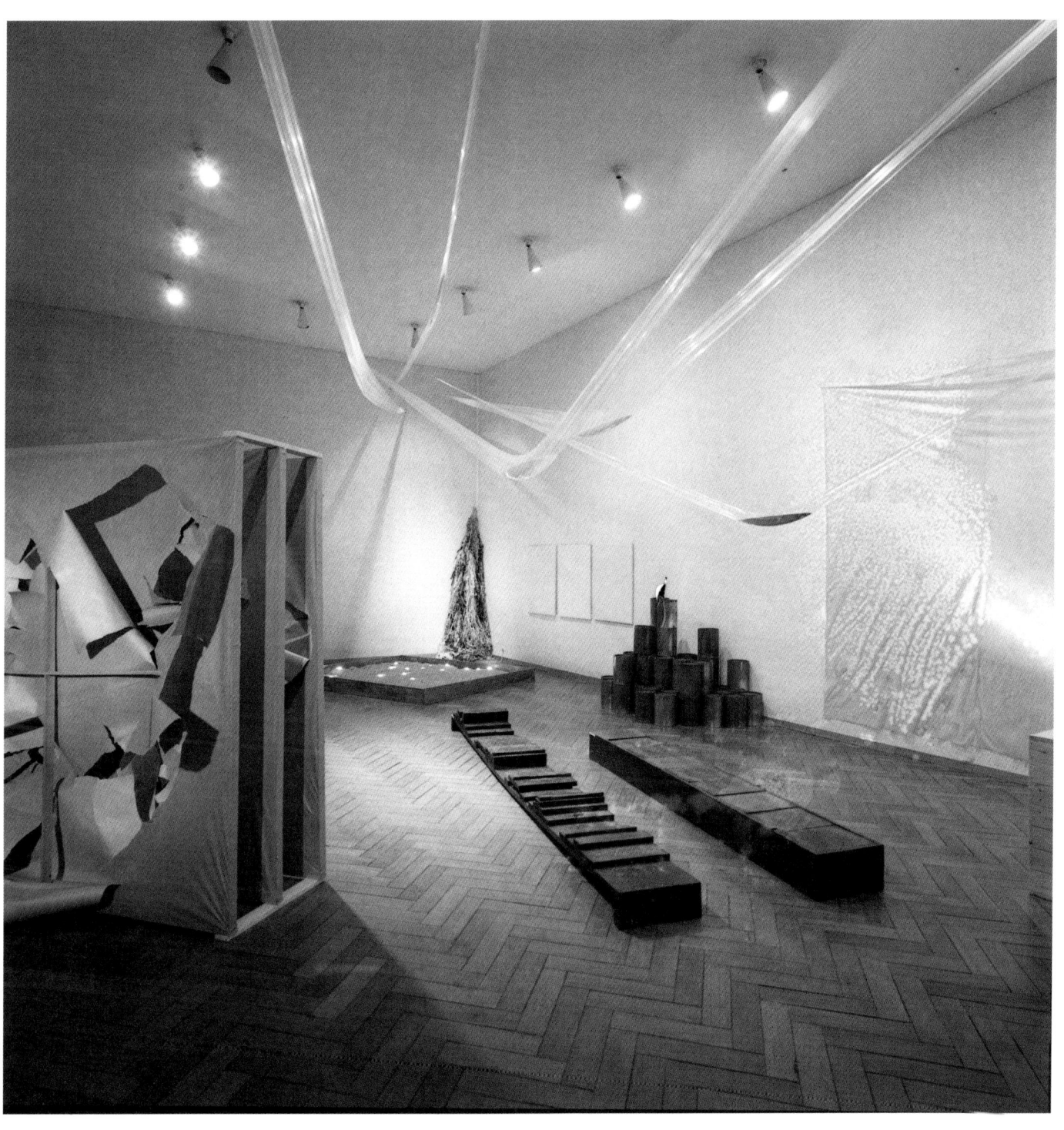

↑ Gutai Room, with works by (clockwise from left) Saburo
Murakami, Michio Yoshihara, Jiro Yoshihara, Tsuruko Yamazaki,
Sadamasa Motonaga, Atsuko Tanaka and Shozo Shimamoto,
Nul 1965 exhibition, Stedelijk Museum, Amsterdam, 1965

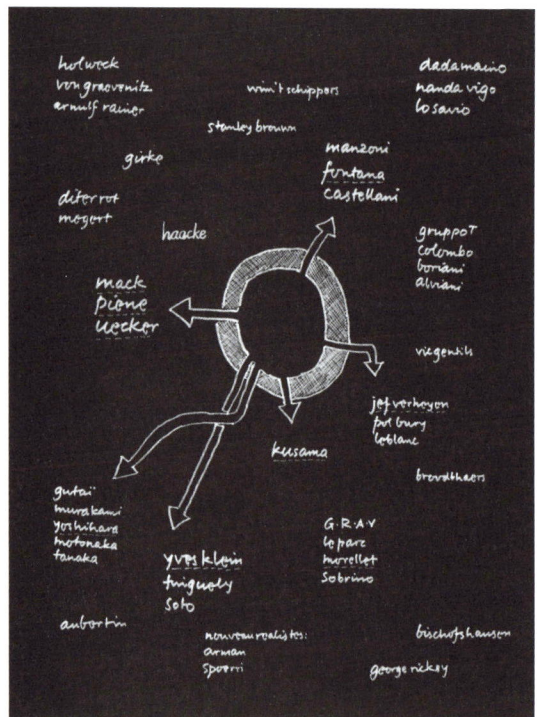

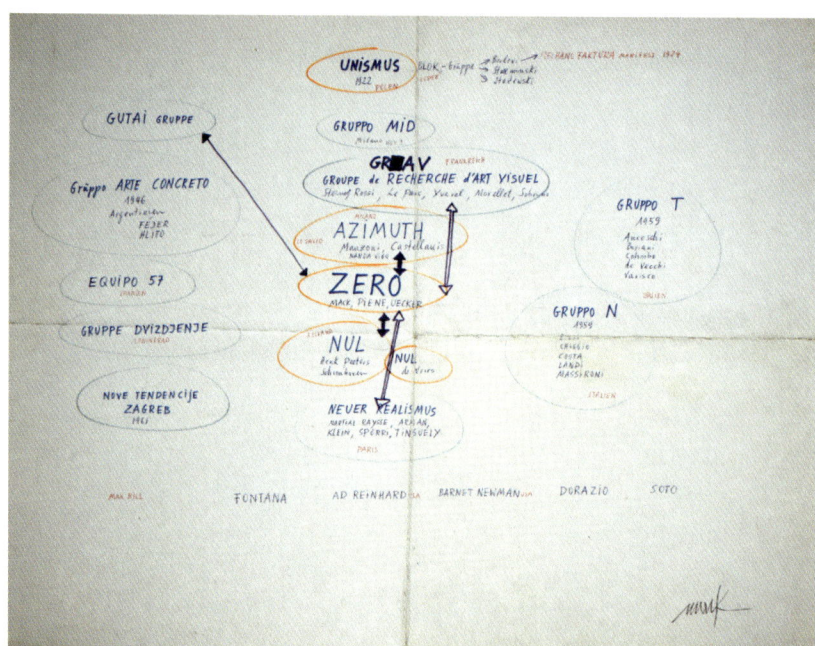

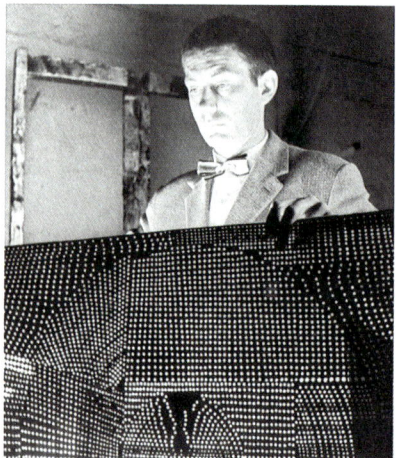

animated in part by the charismatic editor David Medalla, whose geographies included Manila, New York City, Paris, London and Berlin, as well as travels across Africa, South and East Asia, Europe, and Latin America.[15] This apparent cosmopolitanism was hard-won; Medalla was constantly on the move in part so he did not overstay the three-month British and French visas he was entitled to on a Filipino passport.[16] The news bulletin, which featured articles in Portuguese, Spanish and French as well as translations from many different languages, gives the impression of making its own expansive worlds; transcultural friendships and entanglements are traced carefully in its pages through braids of human relationships.[17] The group name, Signals, was inspired by a series of sculptures by the Greek artist Takis, such as *Télélumière No.4* 1963–4 (p.55), which explored light as a medium of communication and technology of transportation, switching mechanisms in the regulation of global flows that, in Takis's hands, became themselves personified.

In the very first issue of *Signals*, Medalla published a photograph of himself with *Sand Machine* 1964 (p.35). The text reads: 'David describes himself as … "one of Those-who-think-Matter-is-Alive"', a tendency in kinetic art that used machines to make visible the invisible enchantment of materials, which Medalla would later call biokinetics.[18] *Sand Machine Bahag - Hari Trance #1* 1963–2015 (p.35), shown in *Electric Dreams*, does just that.[19] It consists of an organic, handmade structure composed of a rotating platform mounted on a wooden trunk, from which a beaded form dangles and erratically combs through the sandbox below, like an inebriated monk at Ryōanji temple in Kyoto.

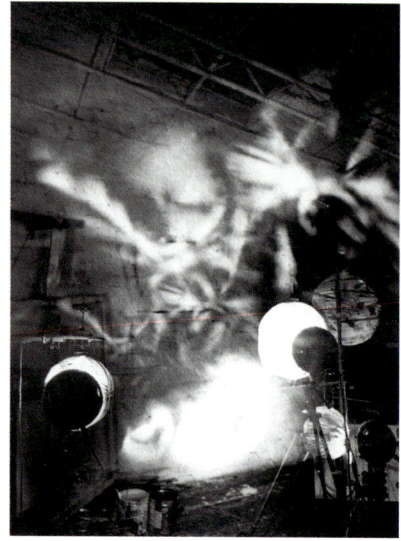

↑ Heinz Mack, *Diagram* 1971
↗ Otto Piene performing his Ancient *Light Ballet, Dynamo 1*, Galerie Boukes, Wiesbaden, 1959
→ Otto Piene, *Archaic Light Ballet* 1960

↑ Henk Peeters, *ZERO Network* published in 2011

30

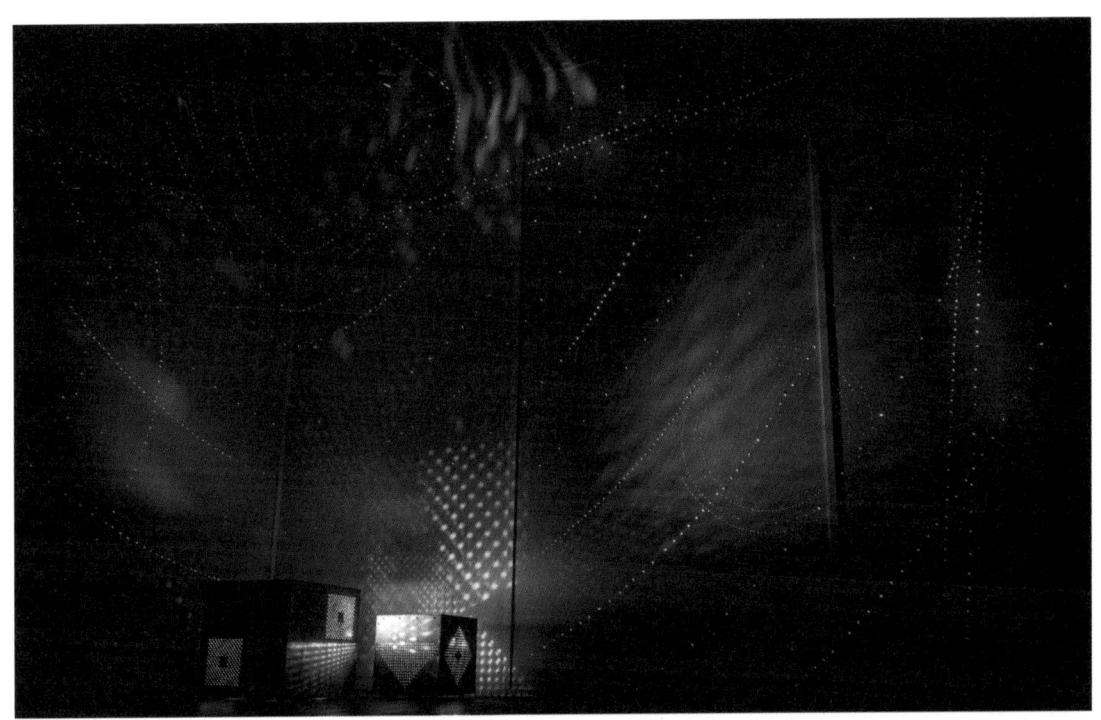

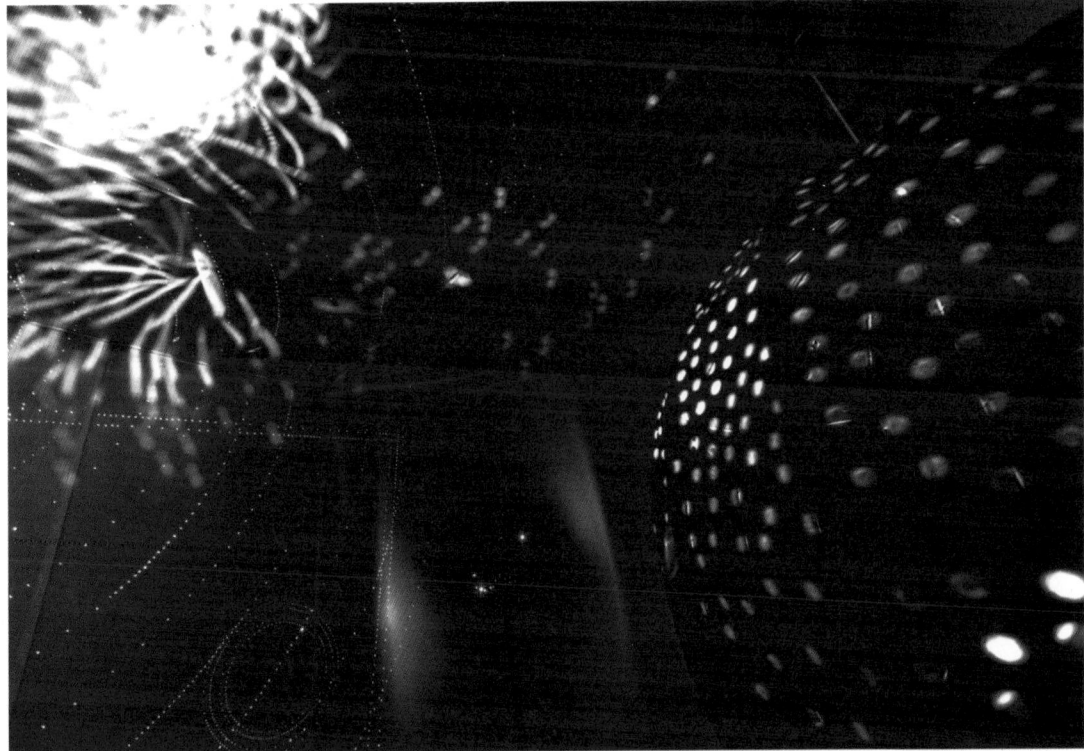

⬆, ↦ Otto Piene, *Light Room (Jena)* exhibited 2007

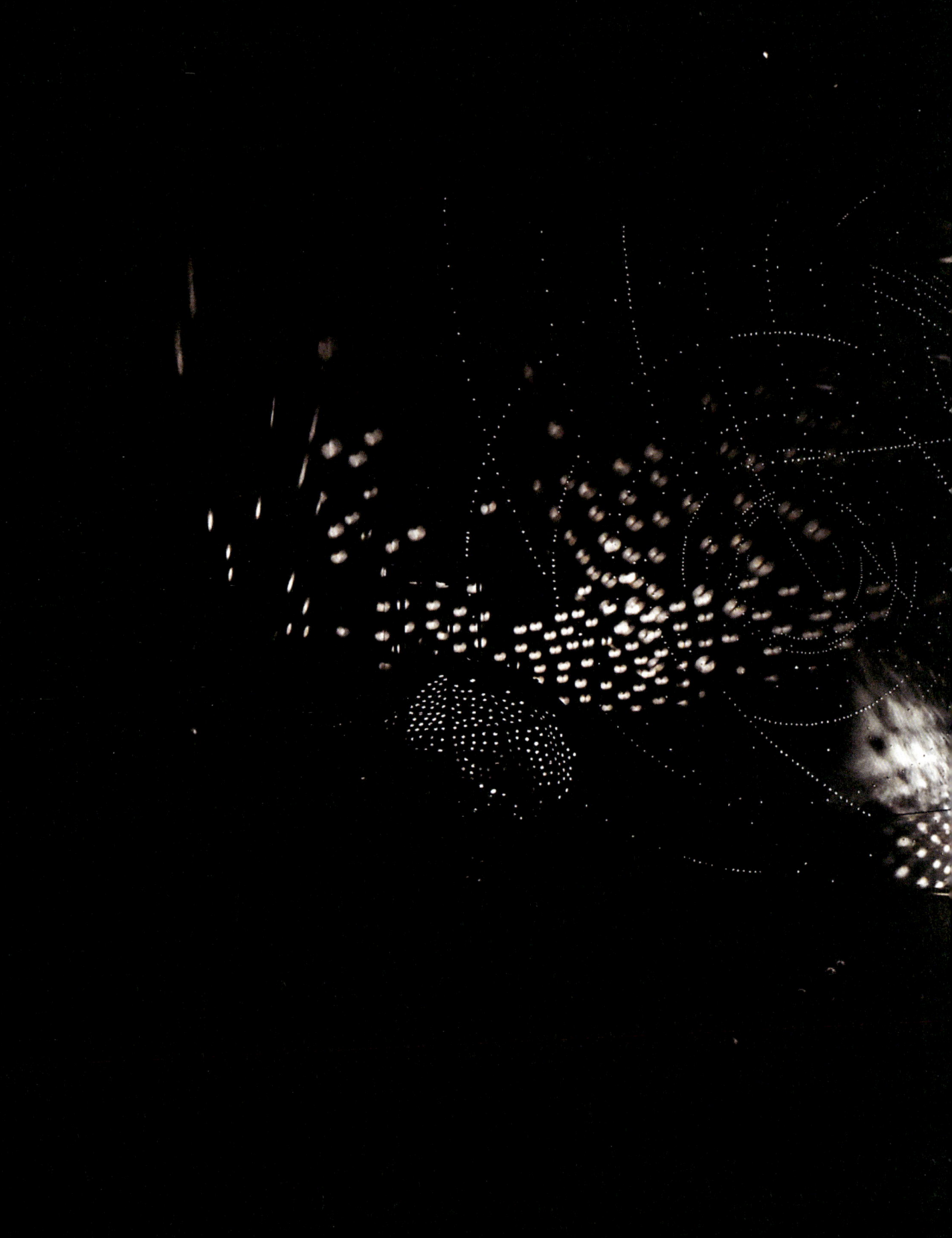

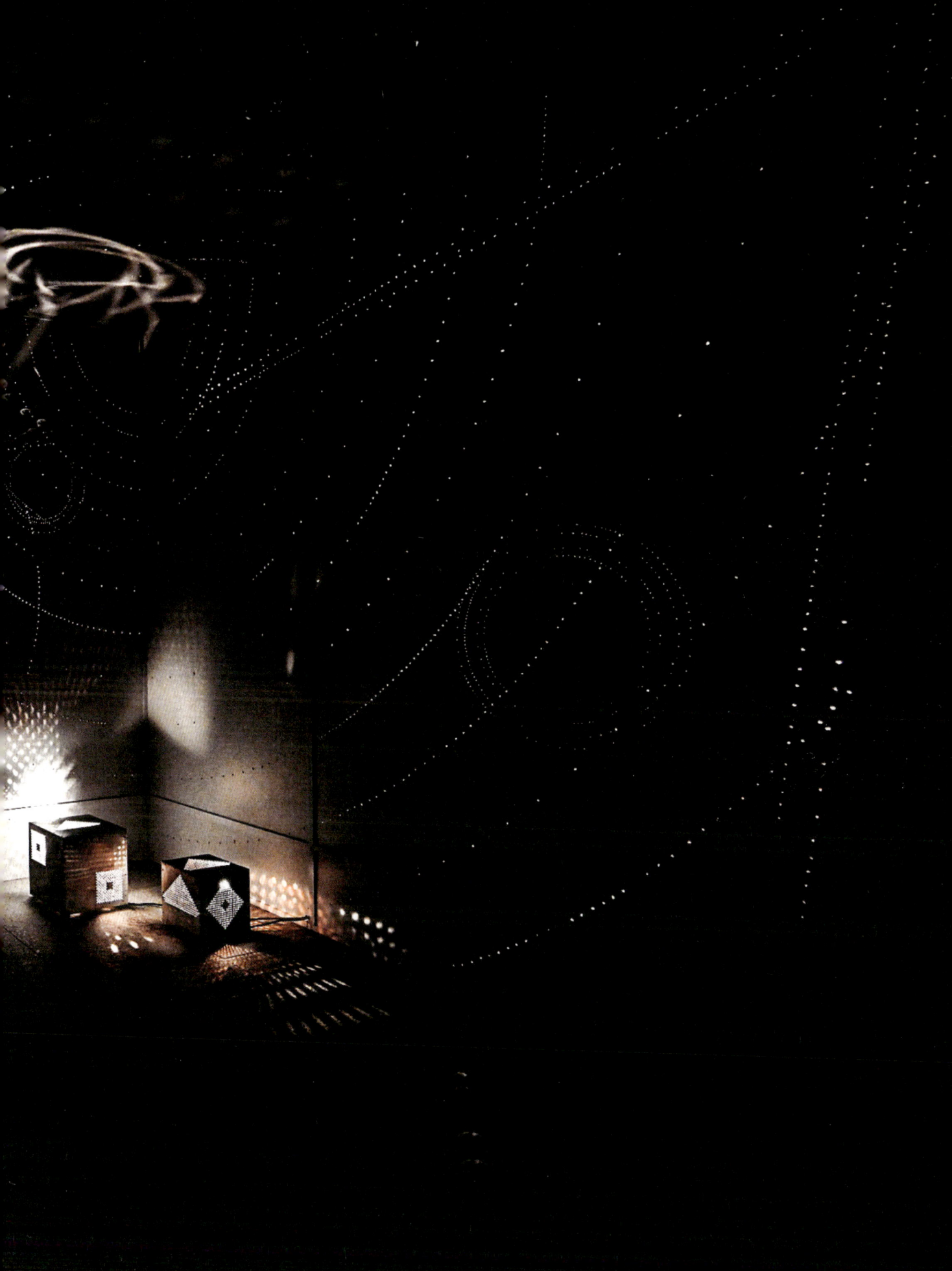

Medalla's close friend, critic Guy Brett, described this form as a snake, 'quivering at the end of an old world and the beginning of a new'.[20] This work, and his renowned *Cloud Canyons* series of the 1960s, a series of bubble machines that created endlessly morphing organic forms which changed shape in response to the breeze generated by passing viewers – liberated the artwork from the mastery of artist, technologist and *homo faber*. Opening kinetic art up to an ethics of relationality and an erotics of form, these works were also notably portable, resonating with 'Medalla's awareness of his status and the status of many Signals colleagues as migrants'.[21] In Medalla's oeuvre, these two concerns – the relational and the political – would ultimately become a more explicitly radical agenda in the Artists For Democracy movement (1974–77, co-founded with Brett, John Dugger and Cecilia Vicuña), which conceptualised love through solidarity, and freedom through economic, political and anti-colonial liberation.[22]

The advancement of transportation, media and communications technologies in the decades after the Second World War contributed significantly to a shift in artistic practice and global perspectives. As McLuhan wrote in 1964: 'during the mechanical ages we had extended our bodies in space. Today, after more than a century of electric technology, we have extended our central nervous system itself in a global embrace, abolishing both space and time as far as our planet is concerned.'[23] For the artists and networks explored in this essay and in *Electric Dreams* more broadly, technology expanded art practice beyond the restrictive confines of traditional media. Taking a humanistic approach to technology as medium, these artists sought to reclaim technology from the military-industrial complex and to critically employ its capacities to free creative practice from the narrow and rarefied pursuits of painting and sculpture. The liberties and worlds that they imagined out of this transformation were in many respects conditioned by their geopolitical circumstances, but what they had in common was the production of new, broader electric worlds visualised and traversed to overcome isolationism, injustice and uncritical techno-utopianism.

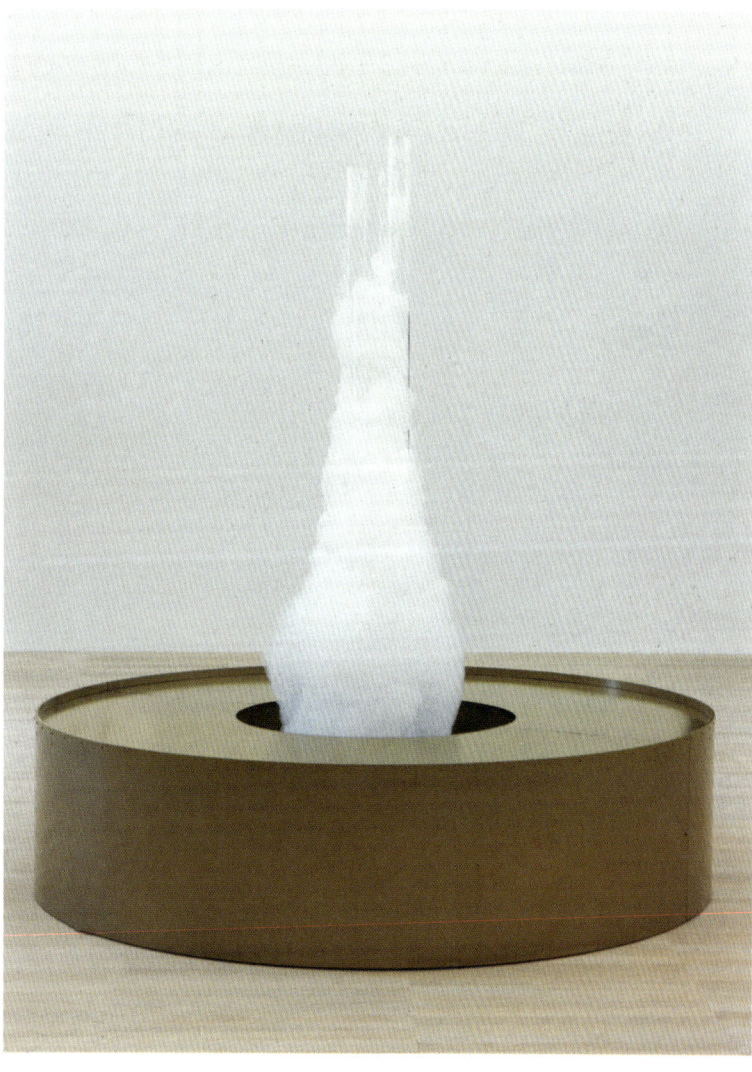

↑ David Medalla, *Cloud Canyons No.3: An Ensemble of Bubble Machines (Auto Creative Sculptures)* 1961, remade 2004

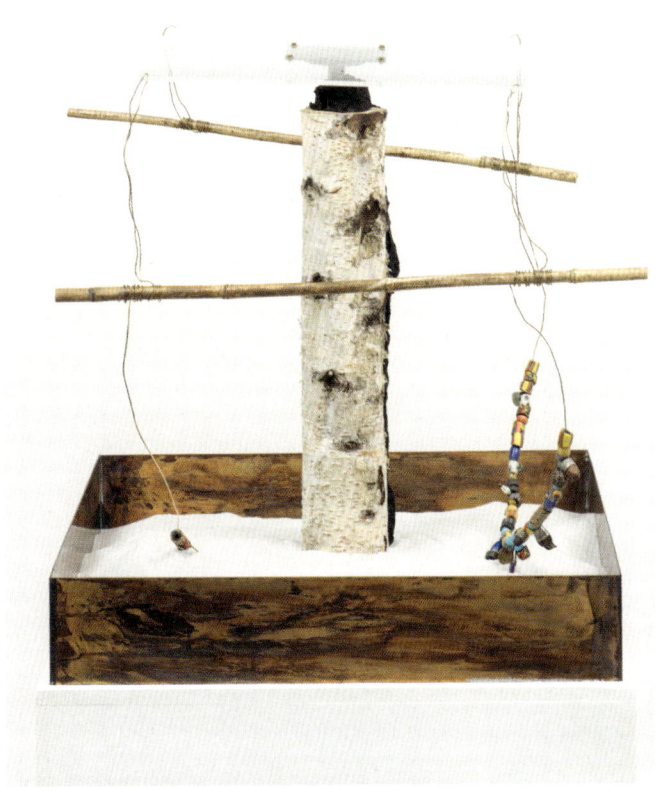

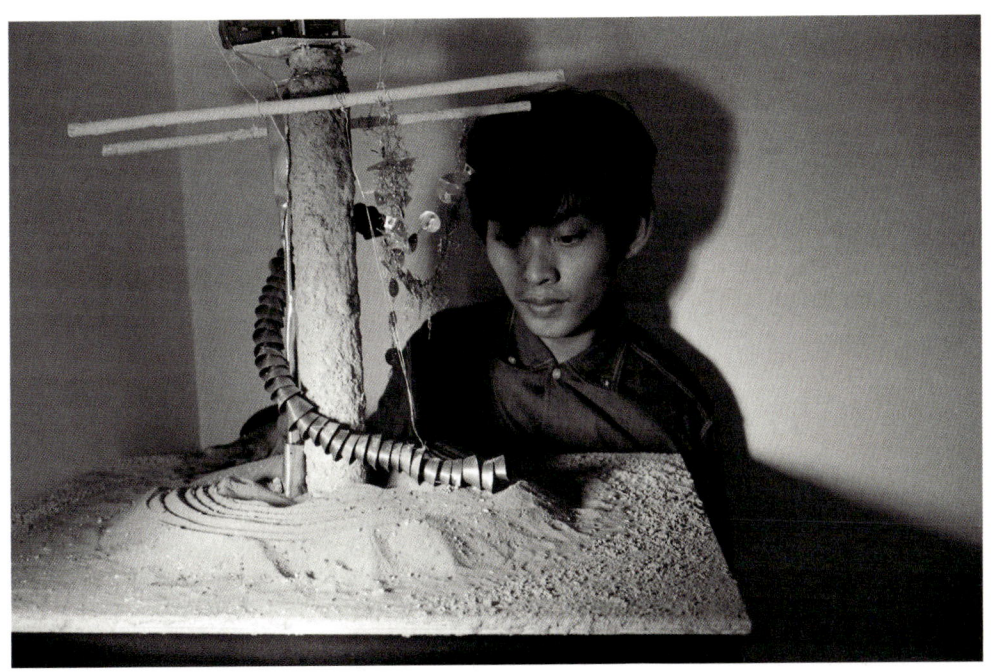

↑ Clay Perry, David Medalla with *Sand Machine*, 1964
↗ David Medalla, *Sand Machine (Behag – Hari Trance #1*
1963–2015

↪ *SIGNALS: Newsbulletin of the Centre for Advanced Creative
Study*, London, vol.1 no.2, 1964, with photographs of Medalla's
Cloud Canyon sculptures by Clay Perry

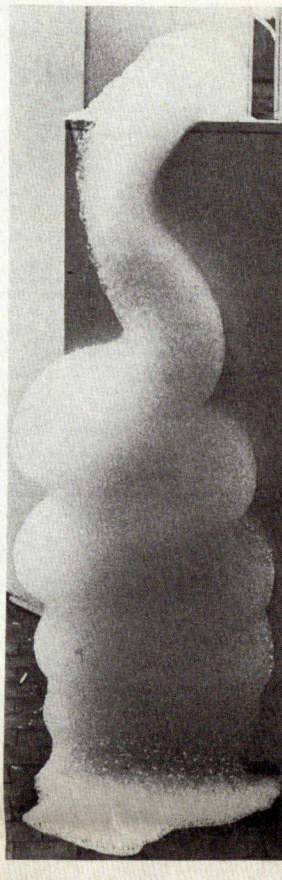

**DAVID MEDALLA: CLOUD CANYONS:
BUBBLE MOBILES 1964.**

PHOTOGRAPHS BY CLAY PERRY.

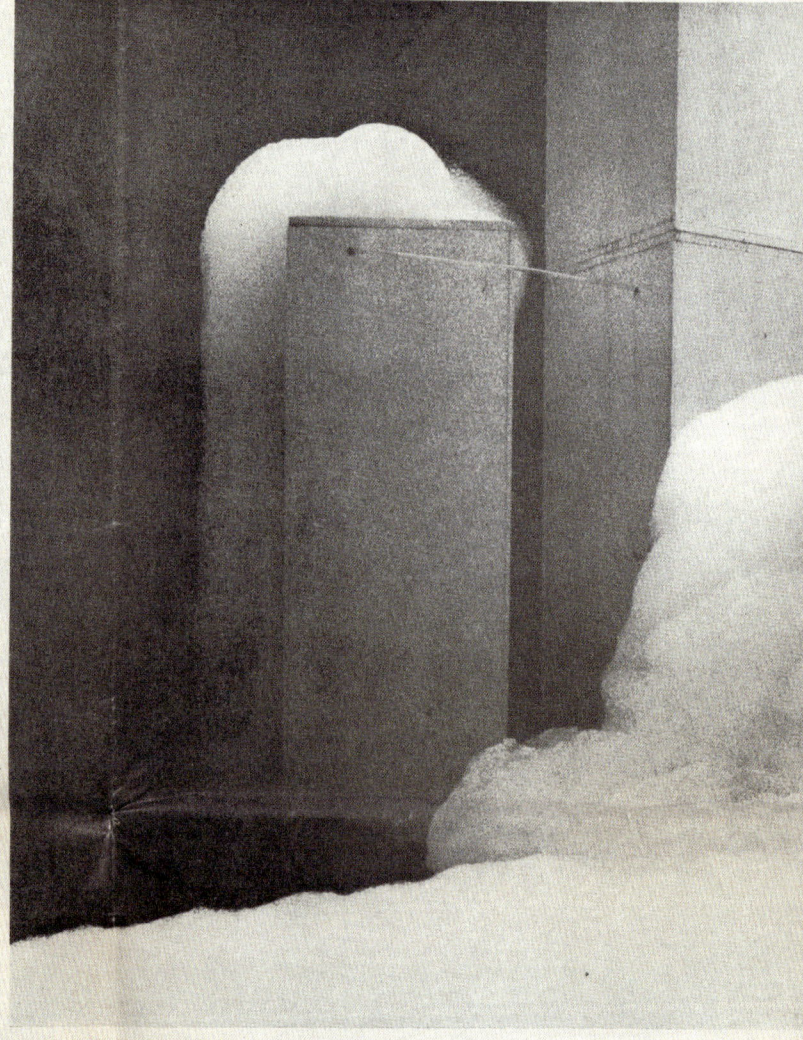

". . . the universe begins to look more like a great
thought than like a great machine . . The old
dualism of mind and matter . . . seems likely to
disappear, not through matter becoming in any way
more shadowy or insubstantial than heretofore, or
through mind becoming resolved into a function of
the working of matter, but through substantial
matter resolving itself into a creation and manifestation of mind . . .
A soap bubble with irregularities and corrugations
on its surface is perhaps the best representation,
in terms of simple and familiar materials, of the
new universe revealed to us by the theory of
relativity."

—Sir James Jeans.

"IF YOU LIKE I SHALL GROW

IRREPROACHABLY GENTLE,

NOT A MAN, BUT A CLOUD

IN TROUSERS. . ."

Vladimir Mayakovsky.

With the five bubble machines exhibited this
year in London **David Medalla** has achieved a
leading position in art.
A quarter million forms continuously changing
reflecting, growing, disintegrating.
Random activity is at present among the most
crucial questions in art.
Apart from other contributions his works have
made, **Medalla** has shown conclusively that
random activity in material/transforming art is
capable of achieving not only the most complex
forms and motions but also an aesthetic content
of the highest order.

—Gustav Metzger.

Bubbles in flight over Cornwall Gardens

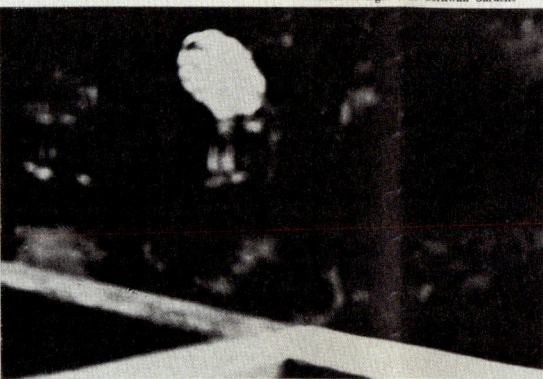

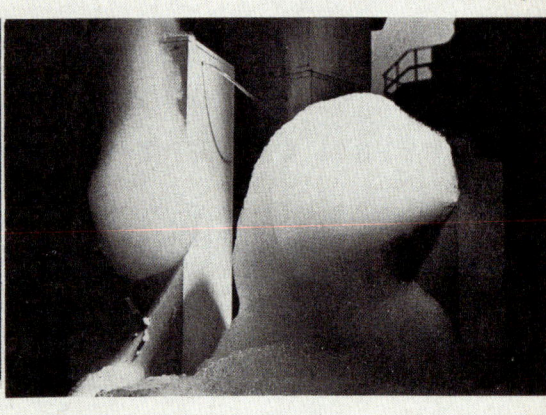

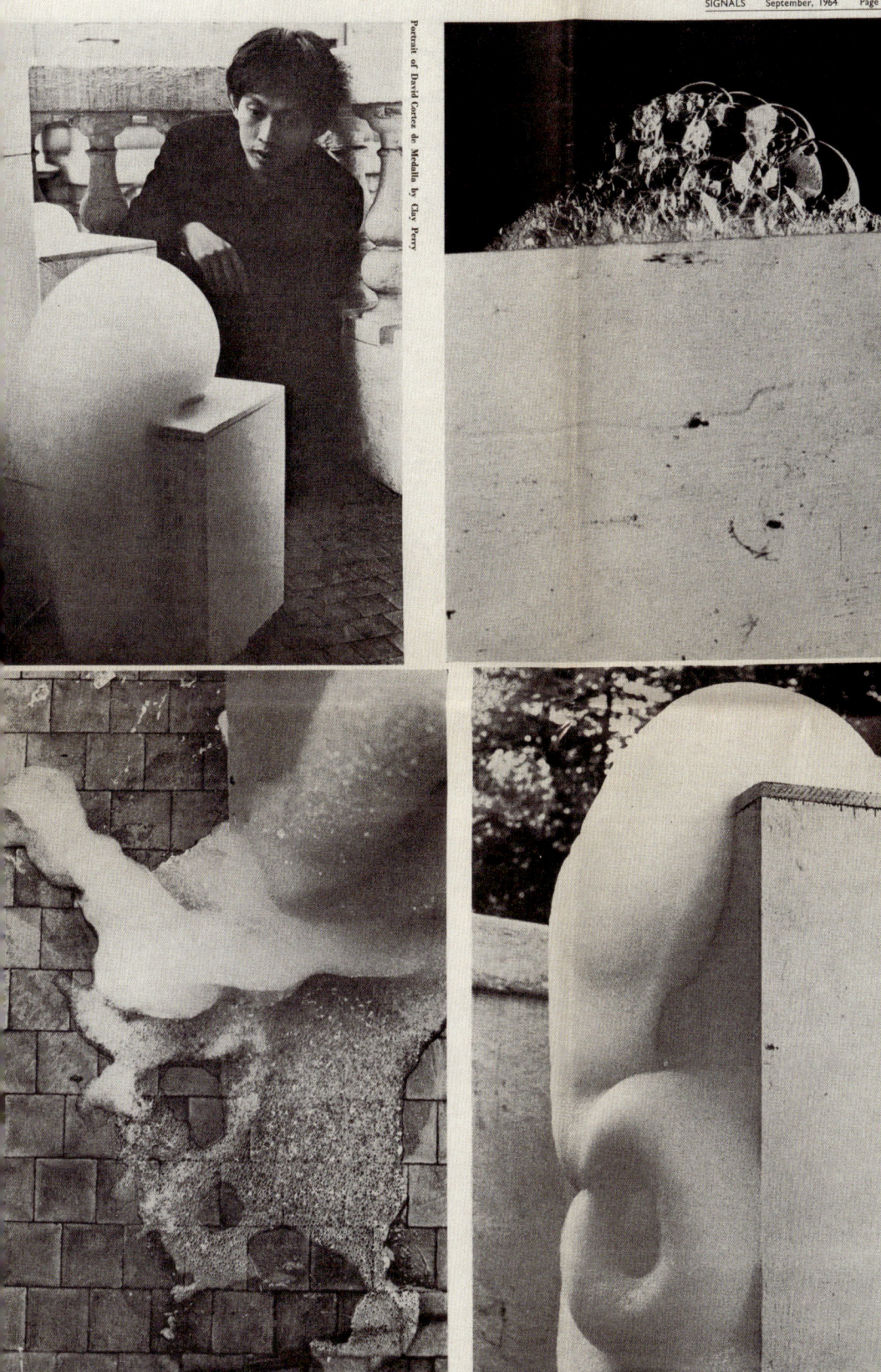

Portrait of David Cortez de Medalla by Clay Perry

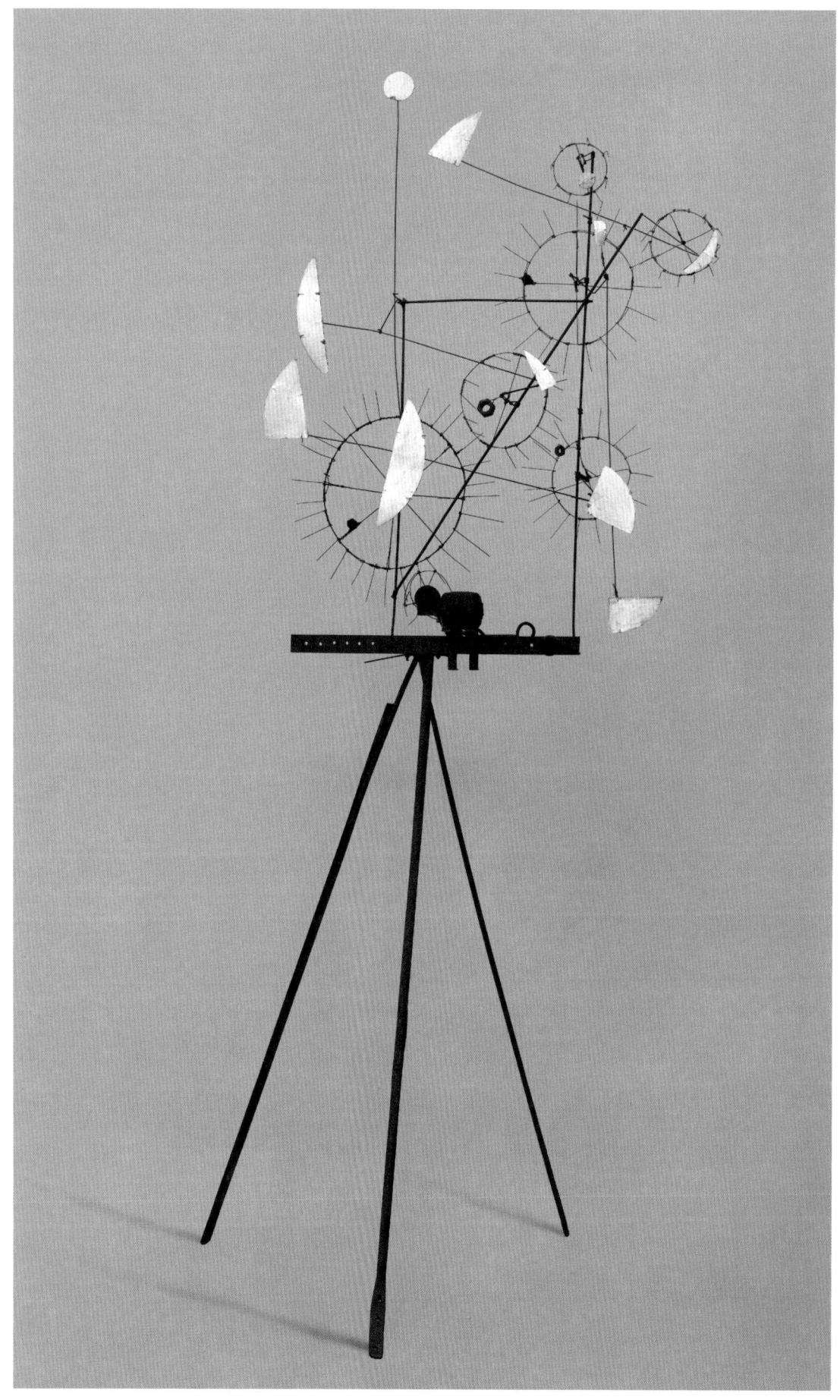

Jean Tinguely

Tinguely's Metamechanical Sculpture with Tripod comprises eleven cardboard shapes attached to straight wires, which are, in turn, attached to seven wire wheels. Driven by a motor, the wheels spin, acting as cogs, while the straight wires are driven back and forth, acting as pistons. Due to the imperfect construction of the machine, the movement of the cogs and pistons is irregular and unpredictable. Occasionally a cog will not properly engage, breaking the pattern of motion as the element of chance generates change within the work. Tinguely, one of the foremost kinetic artists, is known for these 'méta-méchaniques' and his 'painting machines', which he began to make a few years later. In the early 1960s Tinguely became interested in the concept of destruction, creating self-destroying machines such as *Homage to New York* 1960, made up of found objects including bicycle wheels, a self-playing piano, a go-cart and a bathtub, and *Study for an End of the World No.2* 1962, which self-destructed using explosives. KW

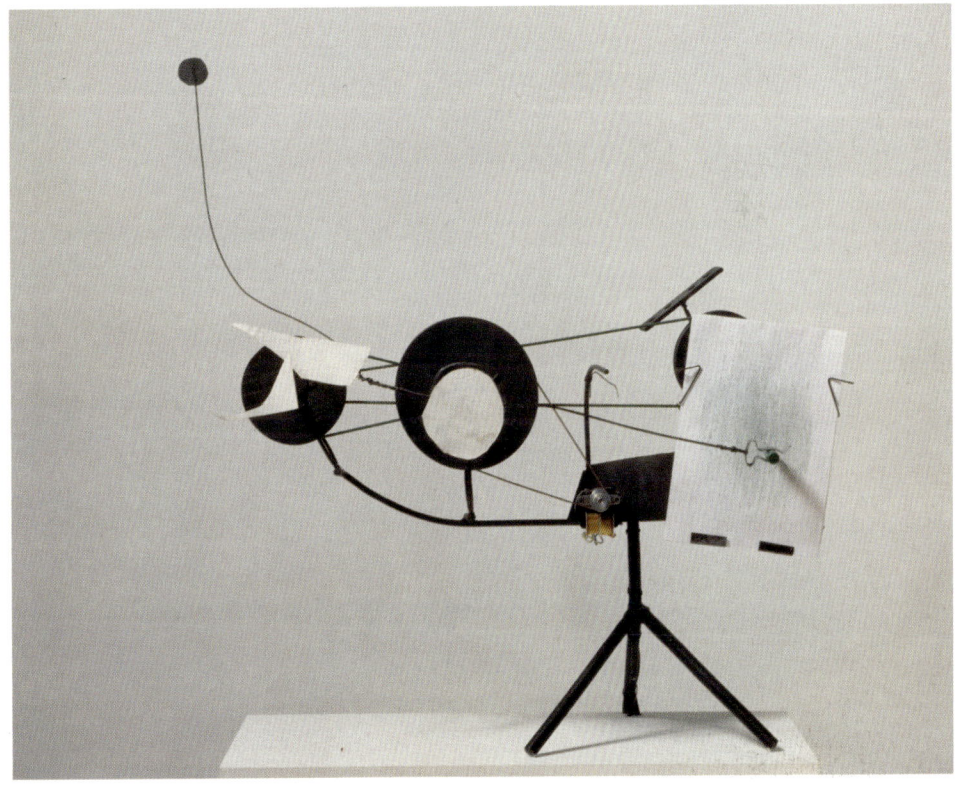

← Jean Tinguely, *Metamechanical Sculpture with Tripod* 1954
↑ Jean Tinguely, *Meta-matic n°1* 1959

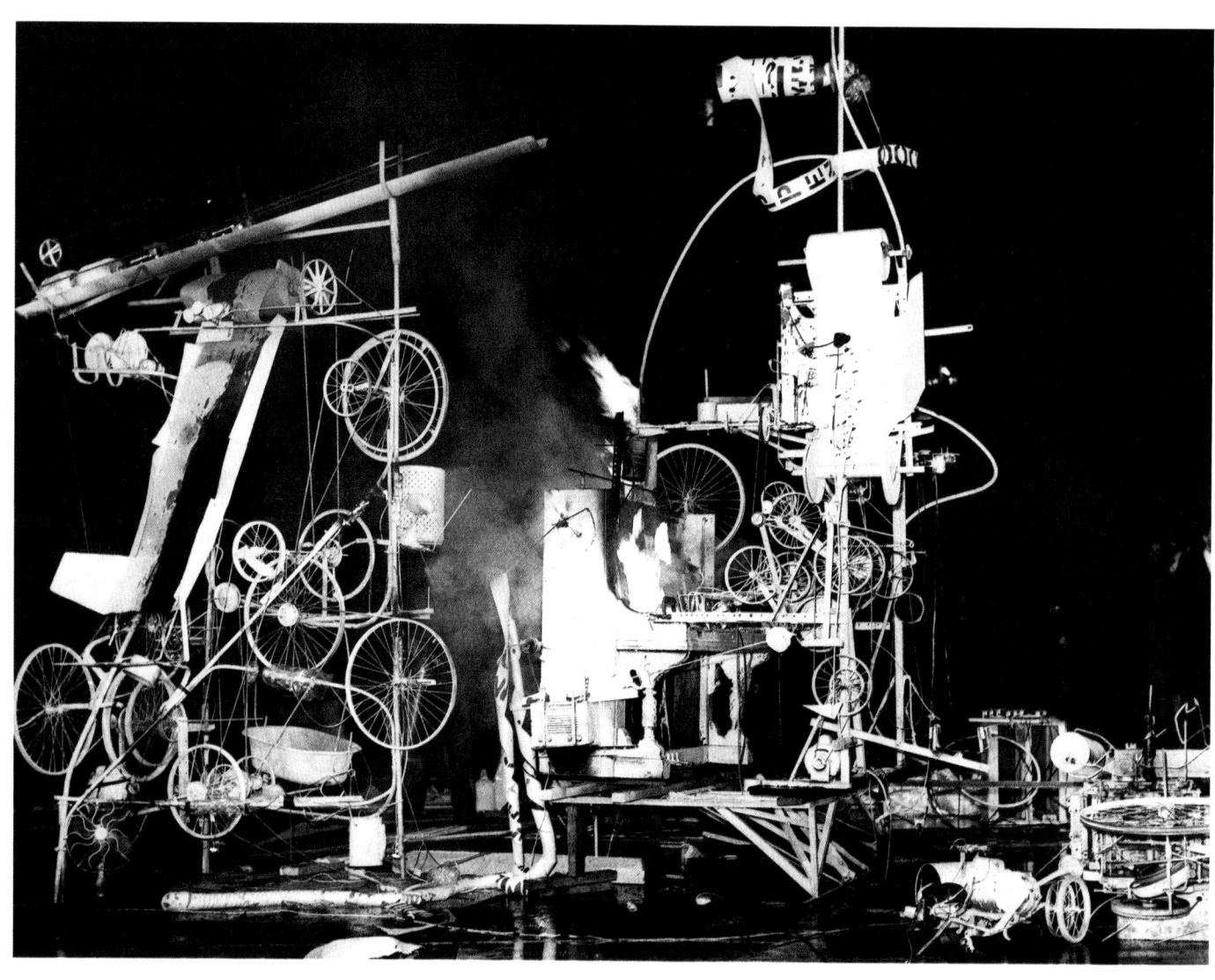

↑ Jean Tinguely, *Homage to New York* 1960
→ Heinz Mack, collage for *ZERO*, no.3, 1961

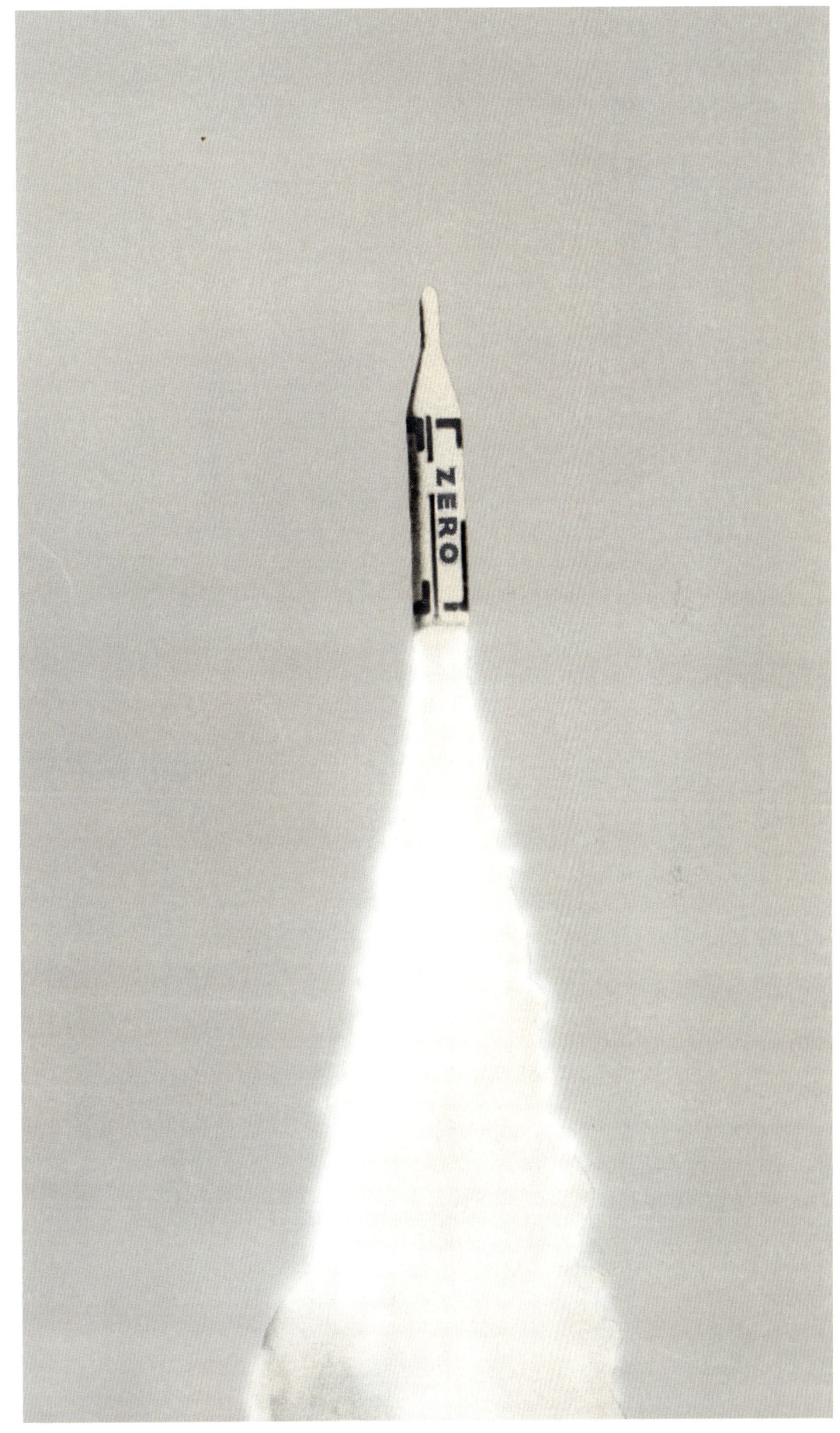

Heinz Mack

One of the founders of the Zero group, Mack sought to make works characterised by 'structural movement' and a 'vibration' effect, achieved with or without the help of motorised parts. In *Light Dynamo* 1963, the shape and surface texture of an aluminium disc appear to constantly transform thanks to the rippling light effects created by overlapping patterns. Mack often used light as a key element on his 'dynamic structures', with reflective surfaces deployed to amplify its effects. Mack was also attracted to vast expanses like 'the sky, the sea, Antarctica, the deserts' as spaces of possibility, where light effects can stand out even in the daytime. In 1959 Mack began to create temporary works in the desert; these were captured in photographs and films for what would become his long-running *Sahara Project*. The 1968 film *Tele-Mack*, produced for a German TV station, features scenes of Mack exposing his sculptures to sunlight in the Tunisian sand dunes while clad in an all-silver suit. VR

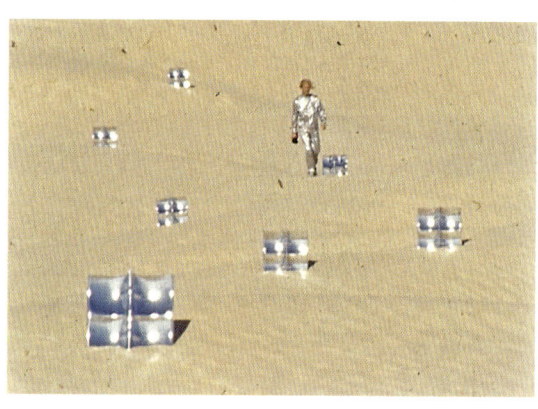

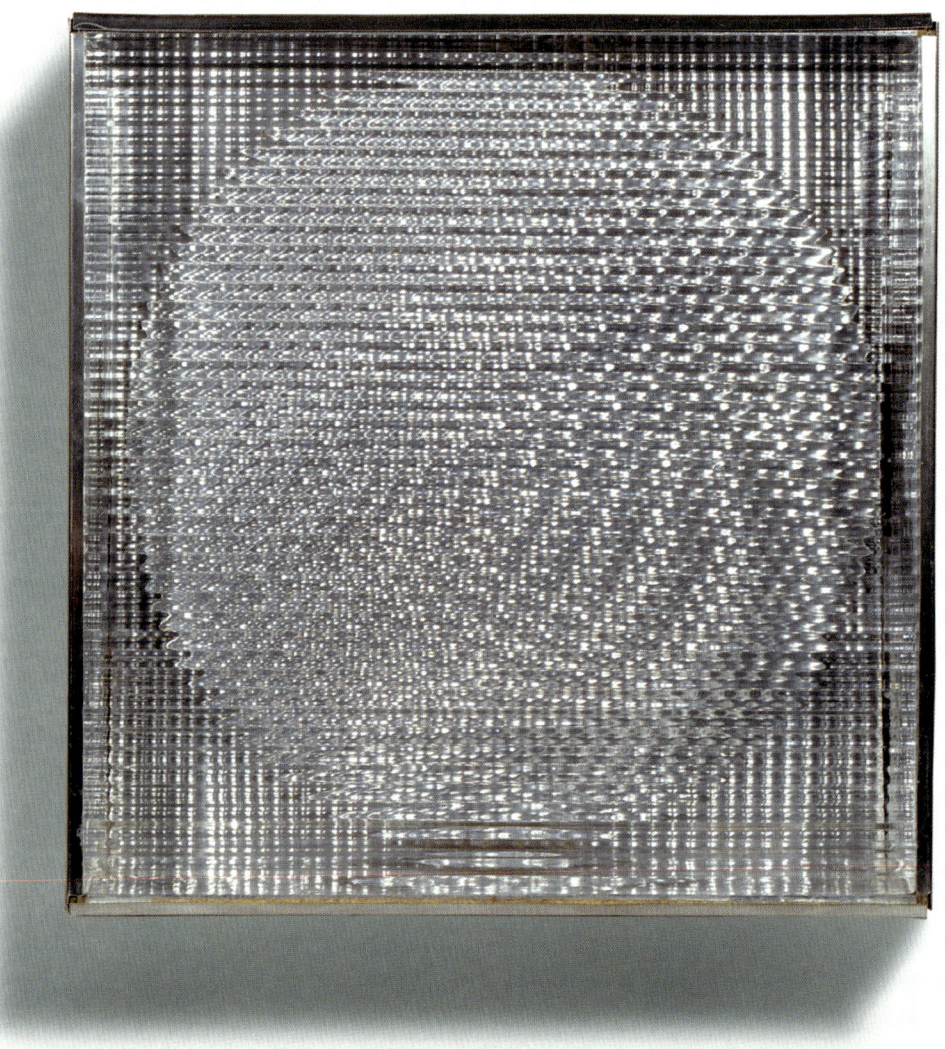

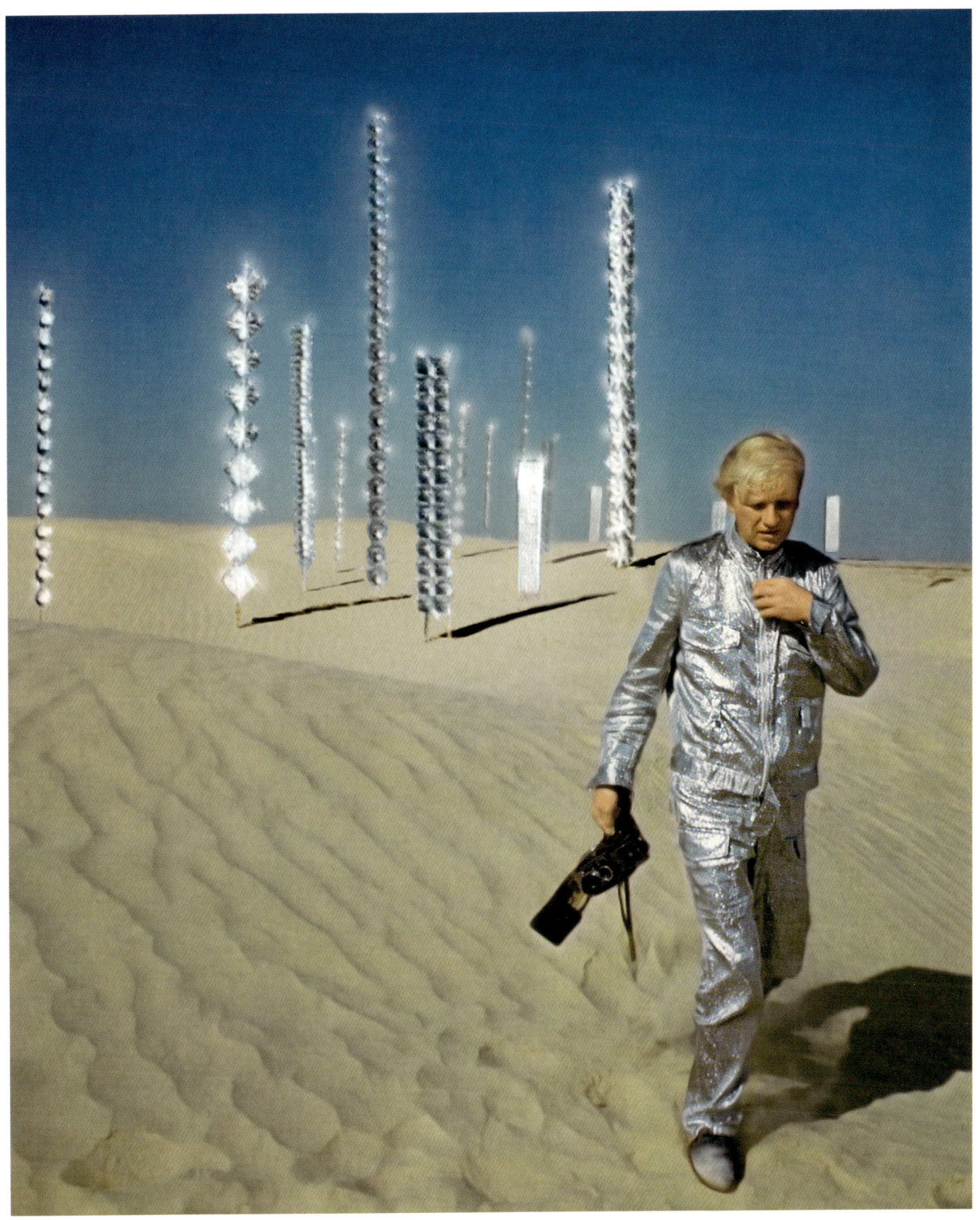

↖ Heinz Mack, *Tele-Mack* 1968
← Heinz Mack, *Light Dynamo* 1963
↑ Edwin Braun, Heinz Mack during the filming of *Tele-Mack* 1968

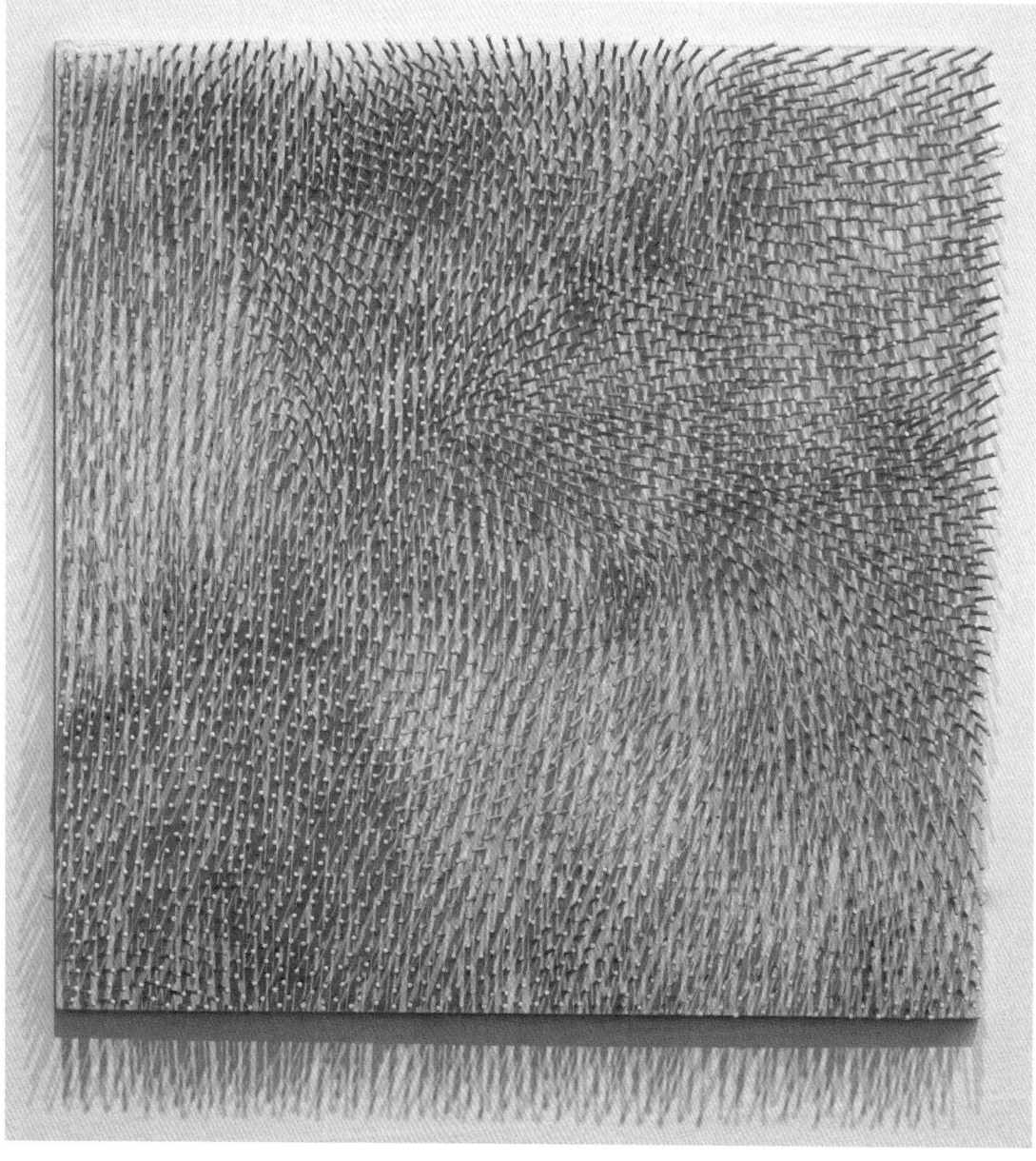

Günther Uecker

Uecker began to make reliefs using nails in the late 1950s. The white composition allows the nails to create patterns of shadow across the surface, responding to the light in the room but also seeming to change in relation to the viewer's own position. This work is part of a series of works entitled *Fields in Movement*.
In a 1964 poem Uecker compared 'the vibration of light' that he achieved in these works to 'the white of the beach | where the visible, crowned by light, is lost in the invisible'. Some of Uecker's works use light and motors, but even those consisting primarily of painted surfaces and nails speak of technology, understood in its purest form: the use of a tool, here the humble hammer. The repetitive puncturing gesture of hammering the nails into the boards also brings the artist close to a certain idea of automation. Uecker compared the process of making these works to a form of meditation, during which he could achieve a state of deep spiritual awareness through monotonous physical actions. Yet Uecker saw this combination of technology and monotony as a way 'to overcome the personal gesture, to objectify, to create the conditions for freedom.' VR

↑ Günther Uecker, *White Field* 1964

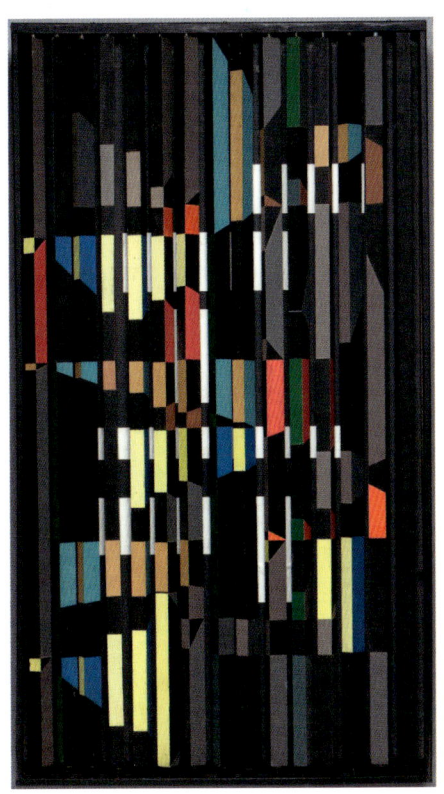

Pol Bury

Bury was interested in what he called an 'aesthetic of slowness', creating mechanical constructions that were characterised by almost imperceptible movement. In *3069 White Dots on an Oval Background,* white dots at the end of thin nylon stalks move intermittently in front of a plain surface. Sudden twitches of movement are often caught on the periphery of the spectator's vision, creating a sense of disorientation. In a poetic text for the publication *Zero 3* (1961), he wrote: 'There is that imperceptible moment between the motion and immobility ... set between waiting for what will come and the present that is already moving away ... and yet it moves ...' VR

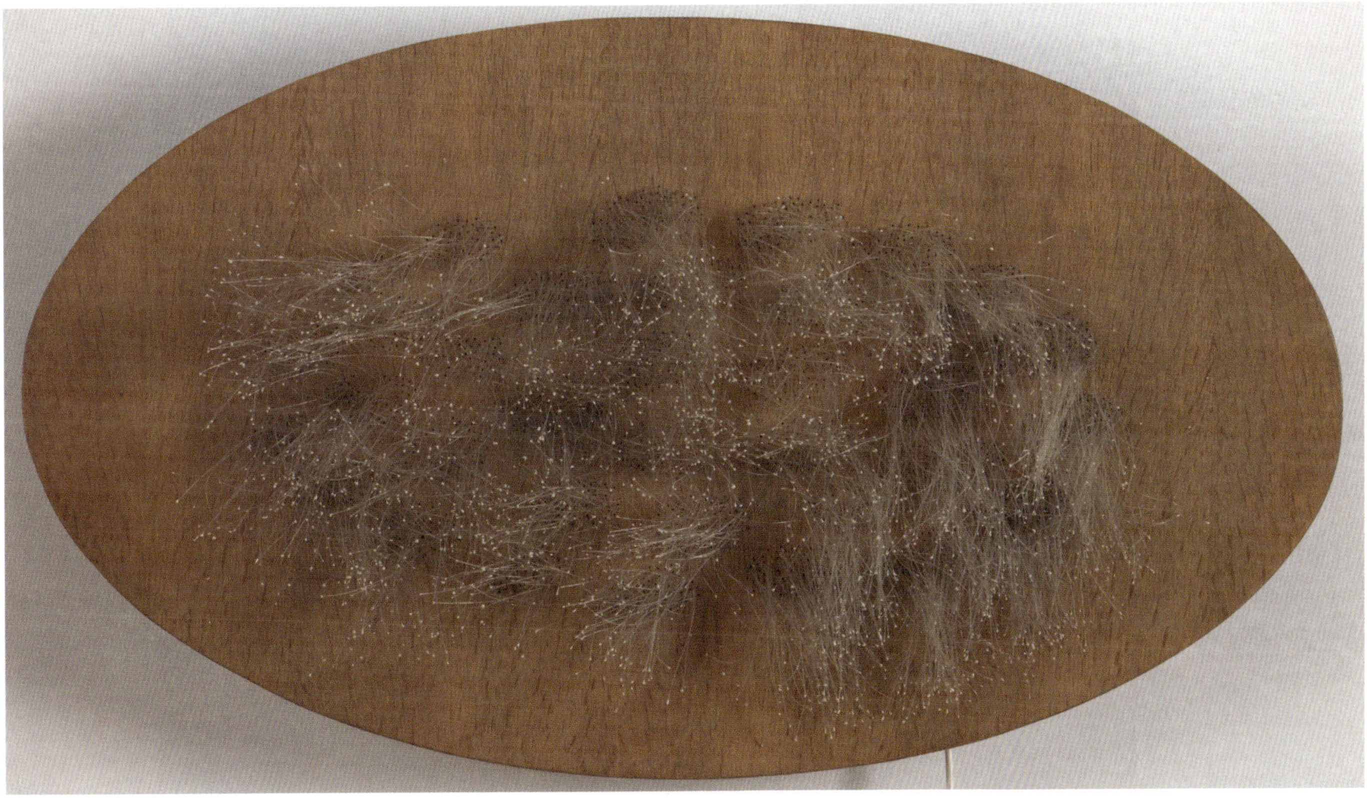

⬆ Pol Bury, *CLICHÉ* 1957
↑ Pol Bury, *3069 White Dots on an Oval Background* 1966

Zero

Founded in Düsseldorf in 1957 by Heinz Mack and Otto Piene, who were joined by Günther Uecker in 1960, the Zero group was a loose-knit group of artists who came together through their shared interest in exploring light, motion and material transformations. Taking their name from the rocket launch countdown, Zero artists took positive inspiration from the technological innovations of the time and adopted aspects of their visual languages to create 'a zone of silence and of pure possibilities for a new beginning'. Reacting to the then dominant languages of gestural painterly abstraction, they sought different ways to achieve a freedom of expression, working with mechanical means, rather than against them. Often working collaboratively, they mounted ambitious exhibitions with invited artists, beginning with a series of *Abendausstellungen* (one-night shows) in their shared studio space. These gradually expanded into festival-like open air events featuring live performances. Zero crossed paths with several other international movements at the time and developed a wide network of international artists hailing from Europe, Japan, and North and South America, often referred to as ZERO in all capital letters. VR

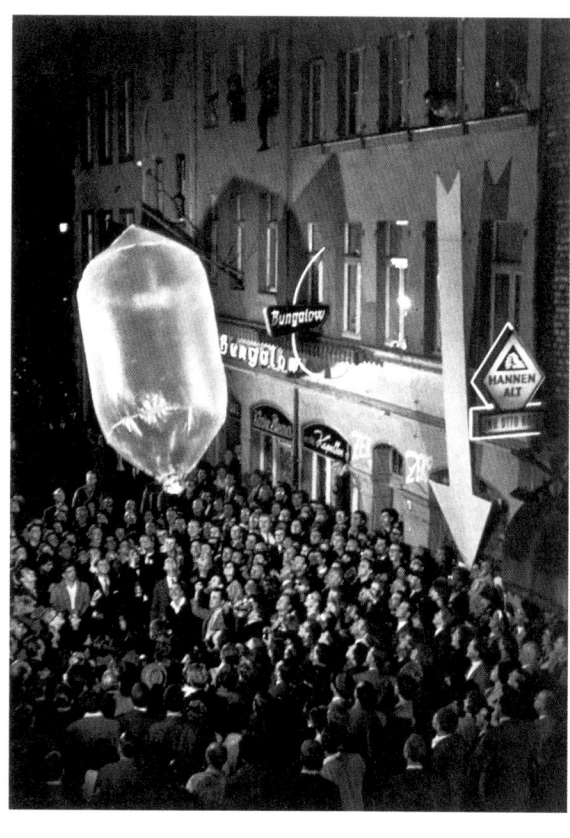

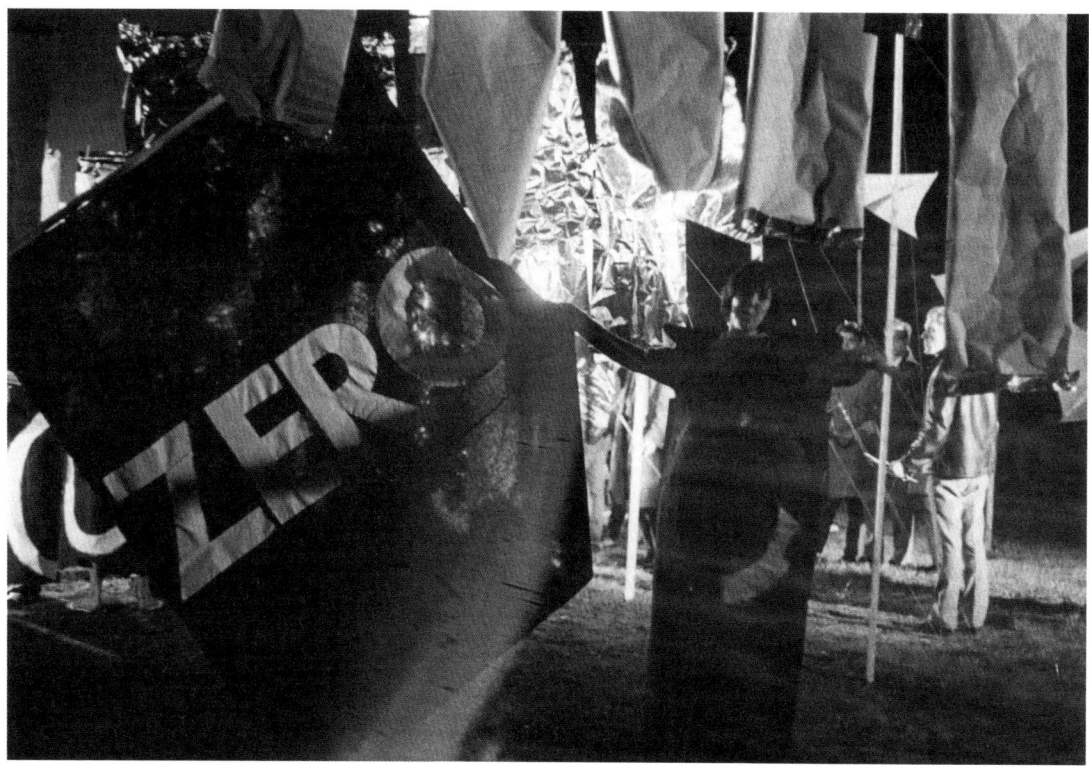

↗ *Zero: Edition, Exposition, Demonstration*,
Galerie Schmela, Düsseldorf, 5 July 1961
↑ *Zero-Fest*, 17 May 1962, Rheinwiesen, Düsseldorf

→ Poster for the exhibition *Nul 62*, Stedelijk Museum, Amsterdam

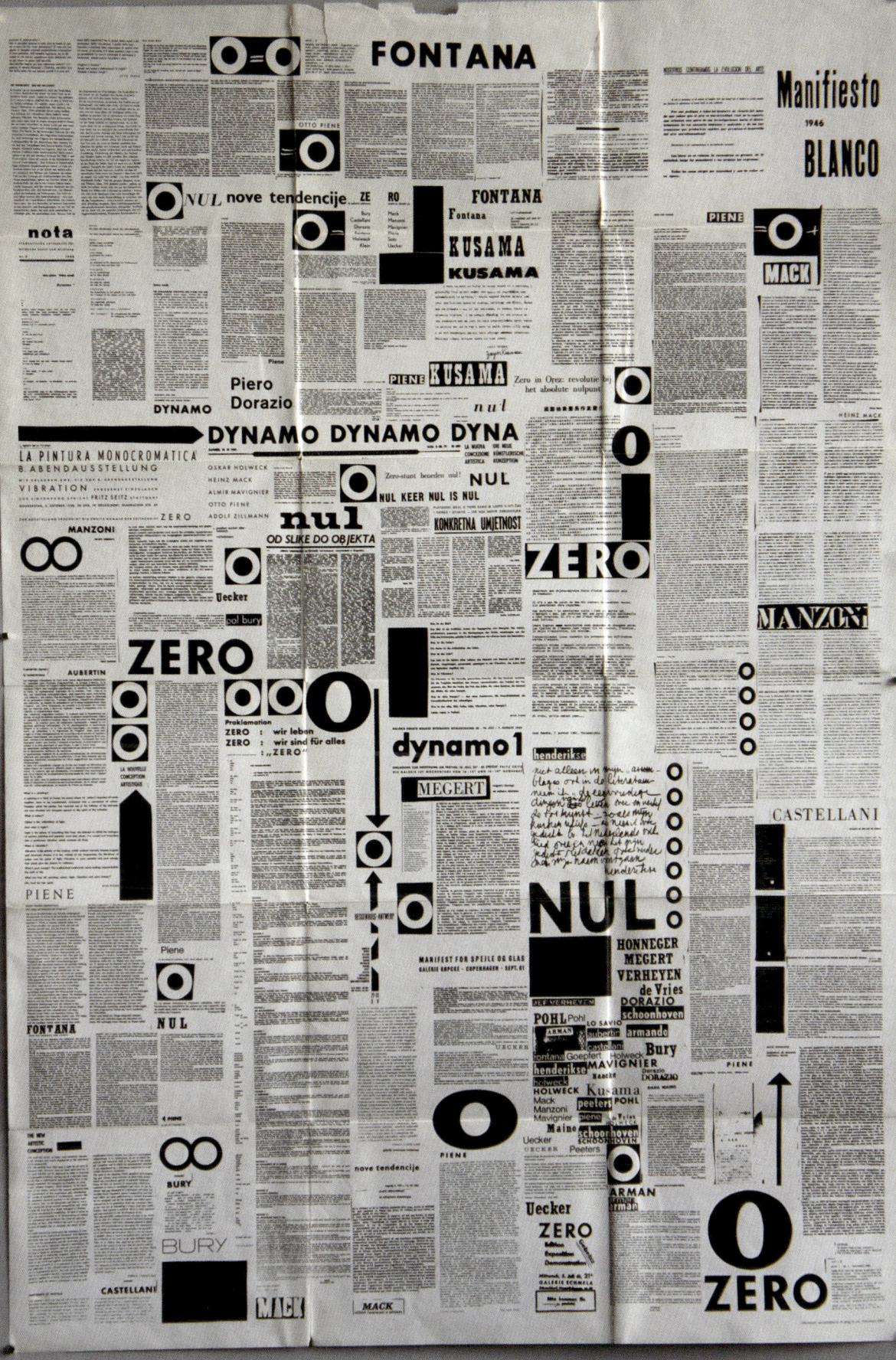

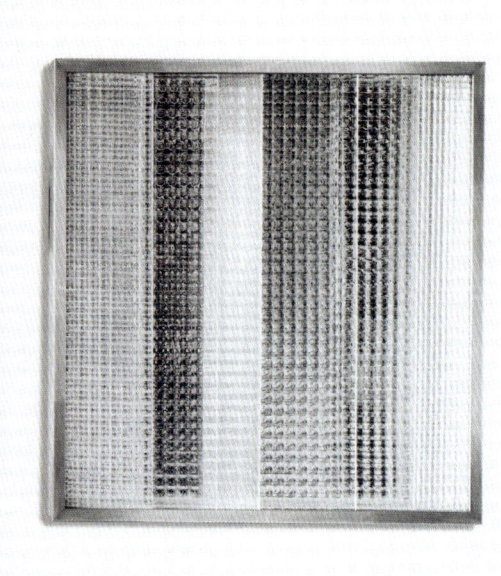

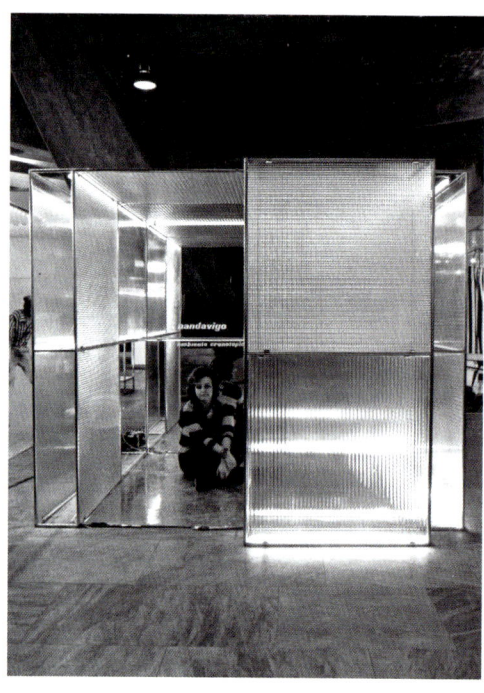

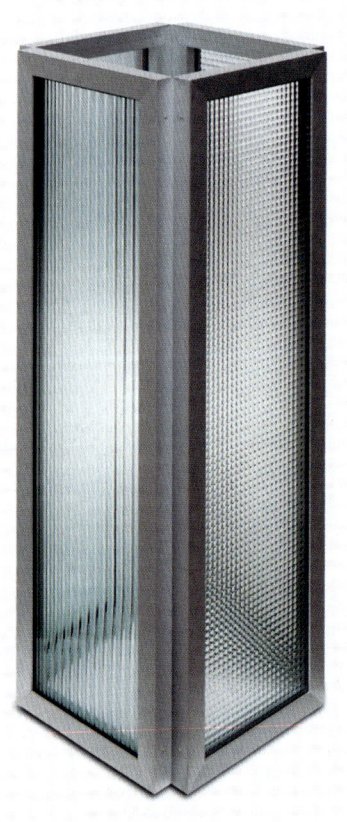

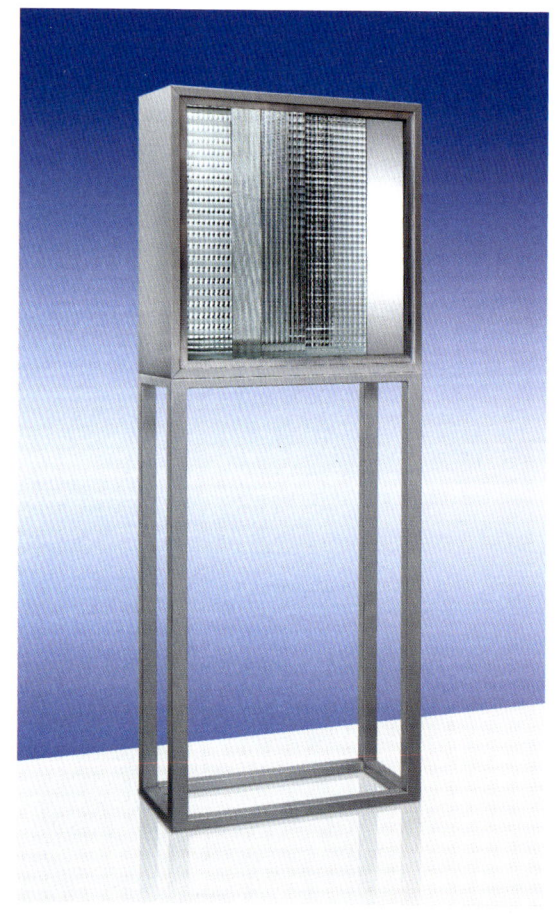

⚑ Nanda Vigo, *Chronotope* 1963
↑ Nanda Vigo, *Chronotope* 1960

⚑ Nanda Vigo, *Chronotopic Environment* 1968,
Eurodomus, Turin, 1968
↑ Nanda Vigo, *Chronotope* 1960–5

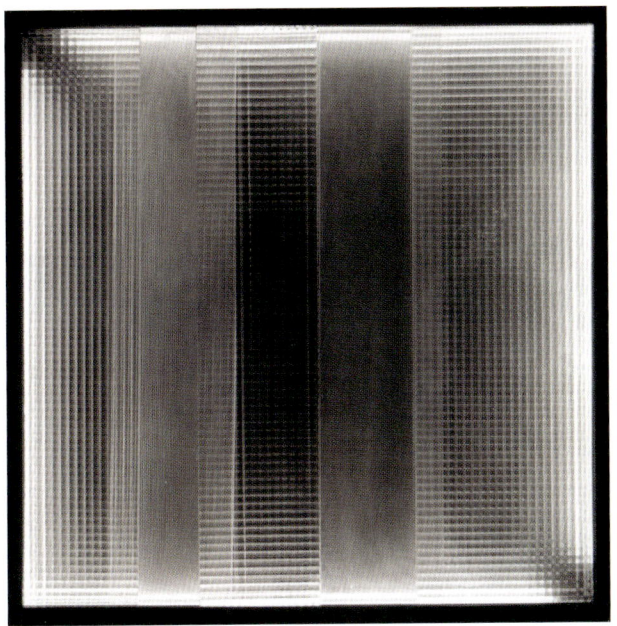

Nanda Vigo

Nanda Vigo, an Italian artist, designer, and architect, was active in the Milanese art circle gathered around Piero Manzoni and mentored by Lucio Fontana. Alongside them she participated in the activities of the ZERO group. In the late 1950s she began experimenting with light and motion in her work. She believed that light had no dimension and could adapt itself to any form. Her *Chronotopes* 1962–8 – the name derived from the Greek for time (*chronos*) and space (*topos*) – are aluminium and industrial glass structures that reflect and transmit light, which spills out of its sculptural frame to immerse the viewer and create otherwordly environments. Vigo's aim was to create emotional reactions in the viewer through the iridescent and heightened sensory effect of her works. Using a range of materials associated with industry and hi-tech architecture, such as textured glass, mirrors, neon, acrylic and aluminium, Vigo created dynamic visual experiences, sometimes taking the form of chambers and labyrinths – among the earliest examples of walk-through immersive installations. OW

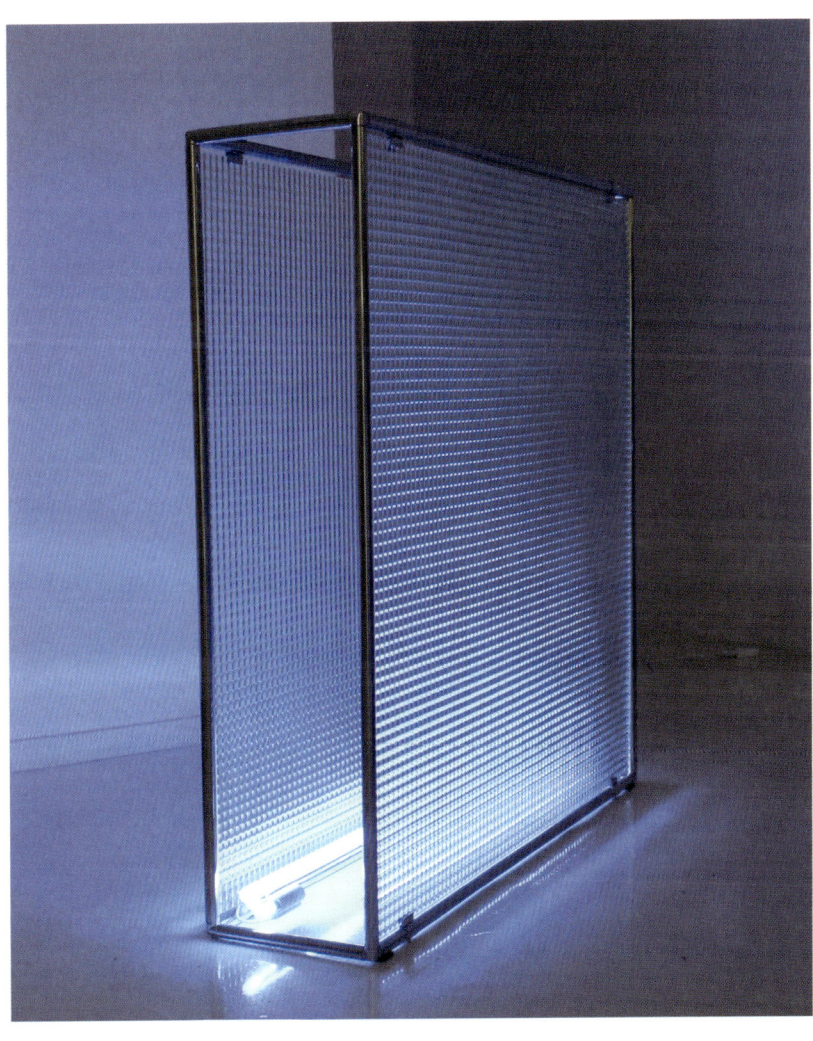

↖ Nanda Vigo, *Chronotope* 1960–5
↑ Nanda Vigo, *Diaphragm* 1960–5

Otto Piene and Aldo Tambellini

Black Gate Cologne is widely considered one of the earliest television programmes by artists. The broadcast was based on a multimedia art event that included films, light objects and audience participation. In this expanded cinema event, Tambellini's films were projected on light objects and inflatables by Piene; the audience could move these objects around the space. Images from five television cameras were superimposed and mixed in a collaboration between artists and TV directors to create a condensed visual aesthetic. A 23-minute version was broadcast on German public broadcasting service WDR on 26 January 1969. The 47-minute video illustrated here includes footage from two, original, consecutive 45-minute recordings with different audiences, filmed at the WDR 'Electronic Studio' in Cologne. BP

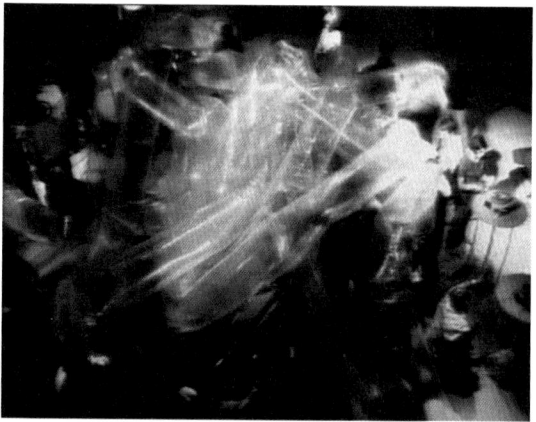

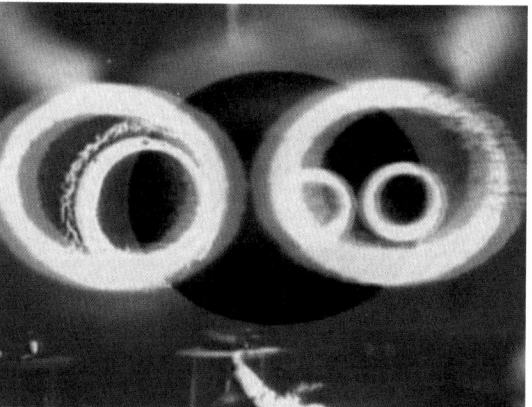

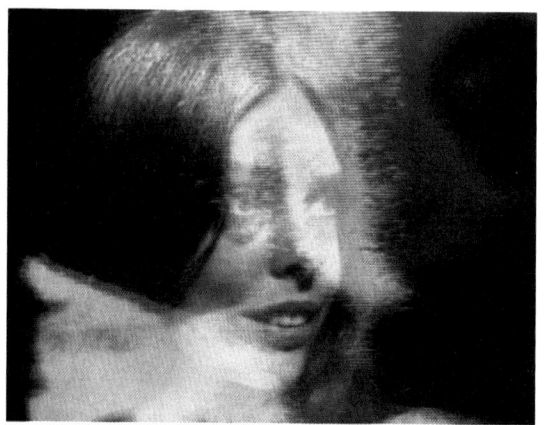

↗ Otto Piene and Aldo Tambellini, stills from
Black Gate Cologne 1968

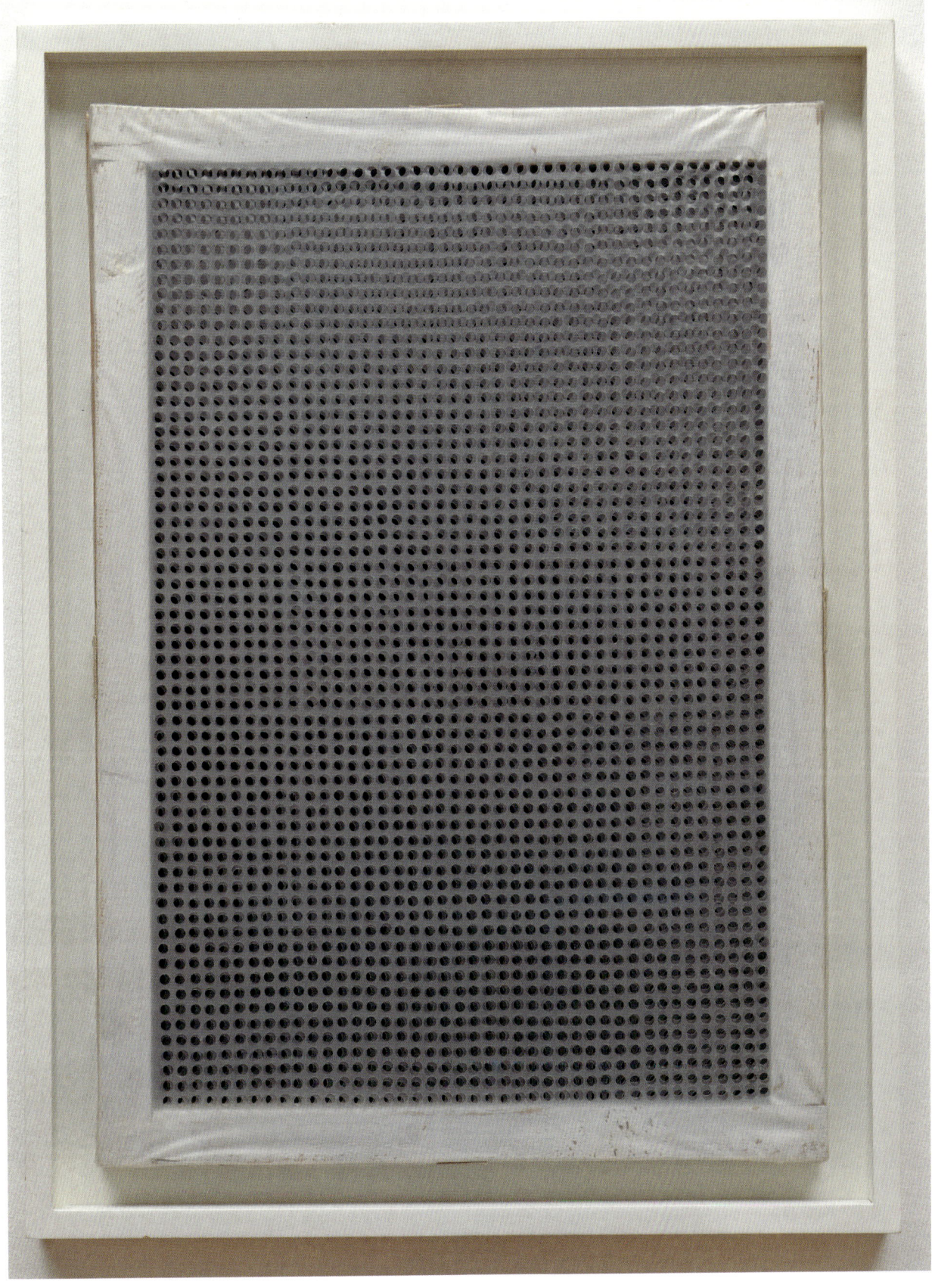

↑ Dadamaino, *Volume of Displaced Modules* 1960

Mary Martin

Mary Martin was a key figure in the British constructivist movement, which emerged in the early 1950s. Inspired by earlier twentieth-century Russian constructivism, this group of artists shared a commitment to geometric abstract art, creating mostly three-dimensional works using a reduced visual vocabulary and colour palette. Using systematic processes and new approaches to materials, these artists aimed to make works that presented themselves as self-contained realities rather than illusionistic representations. Martin had a modular approach to composition, whereby she began with an individual unit and subjected it to a logical process, allowing the work to develop freely within given parameters. In *Permutation of Six* 1966, made of thirty-six parts collaged to form a larger square grid organised in six-by-six, Martin used the half-cube as her unit, and applied a permutative logic to transform six forms drawn in ink. The work exemplifies her artistic process, particularly her experimentation with generative number patterns, geometrical units and reciprocal movement. OW

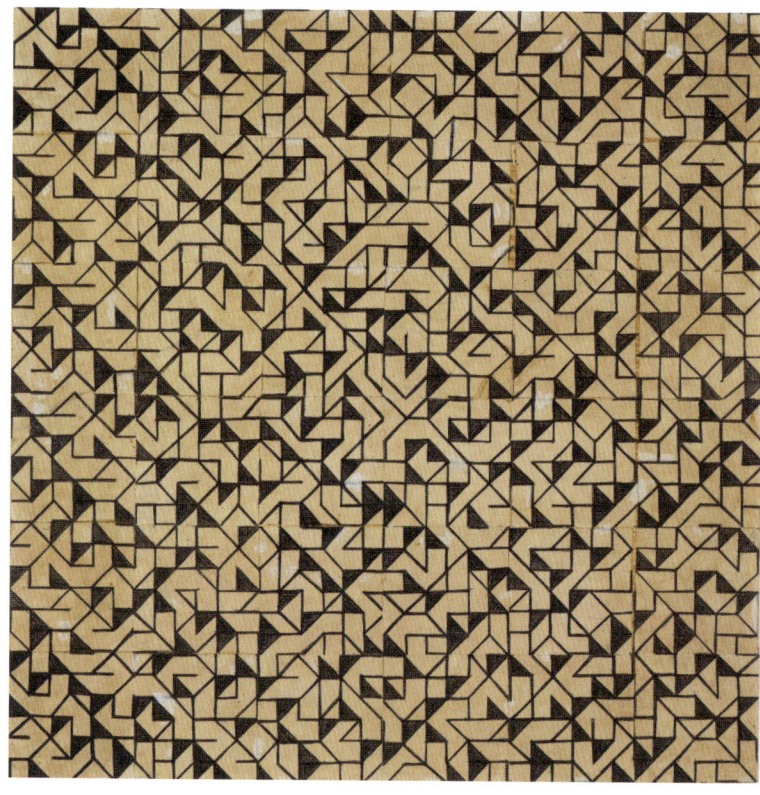

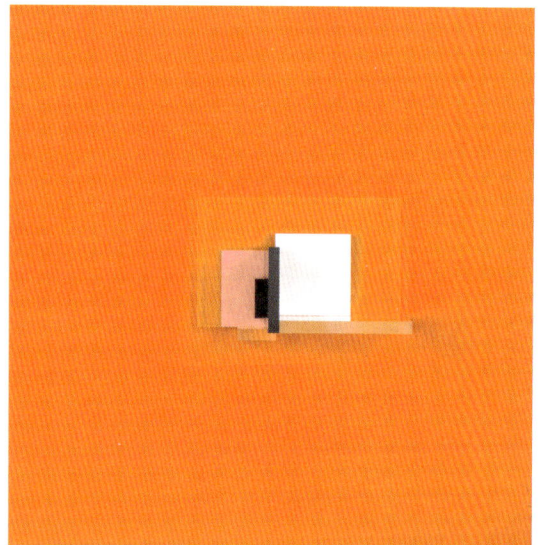

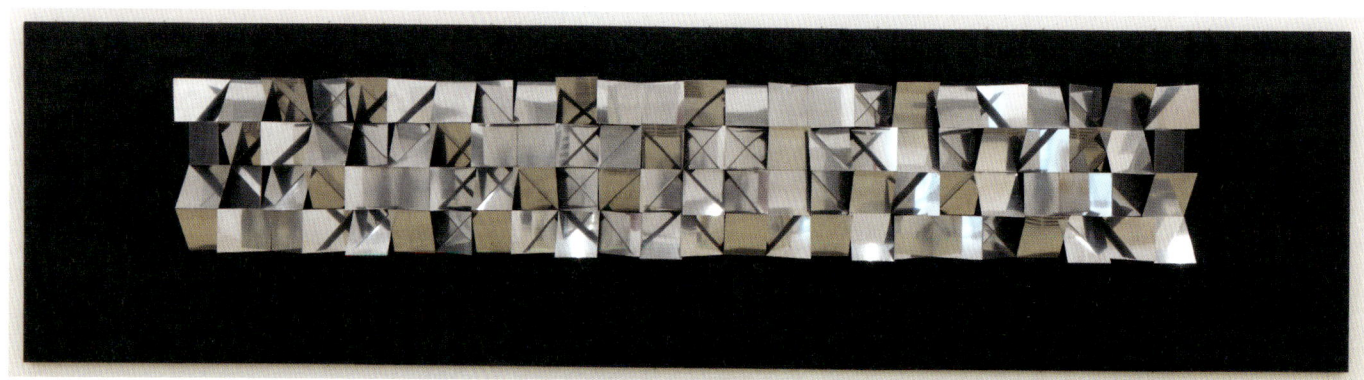

✻ Mary Martin, *Perspex Group on Orange (B)* 1969
↑ Mary Martin, *Inversions* 1966
↗ Mary Martin, *Permutation of Six* 1966

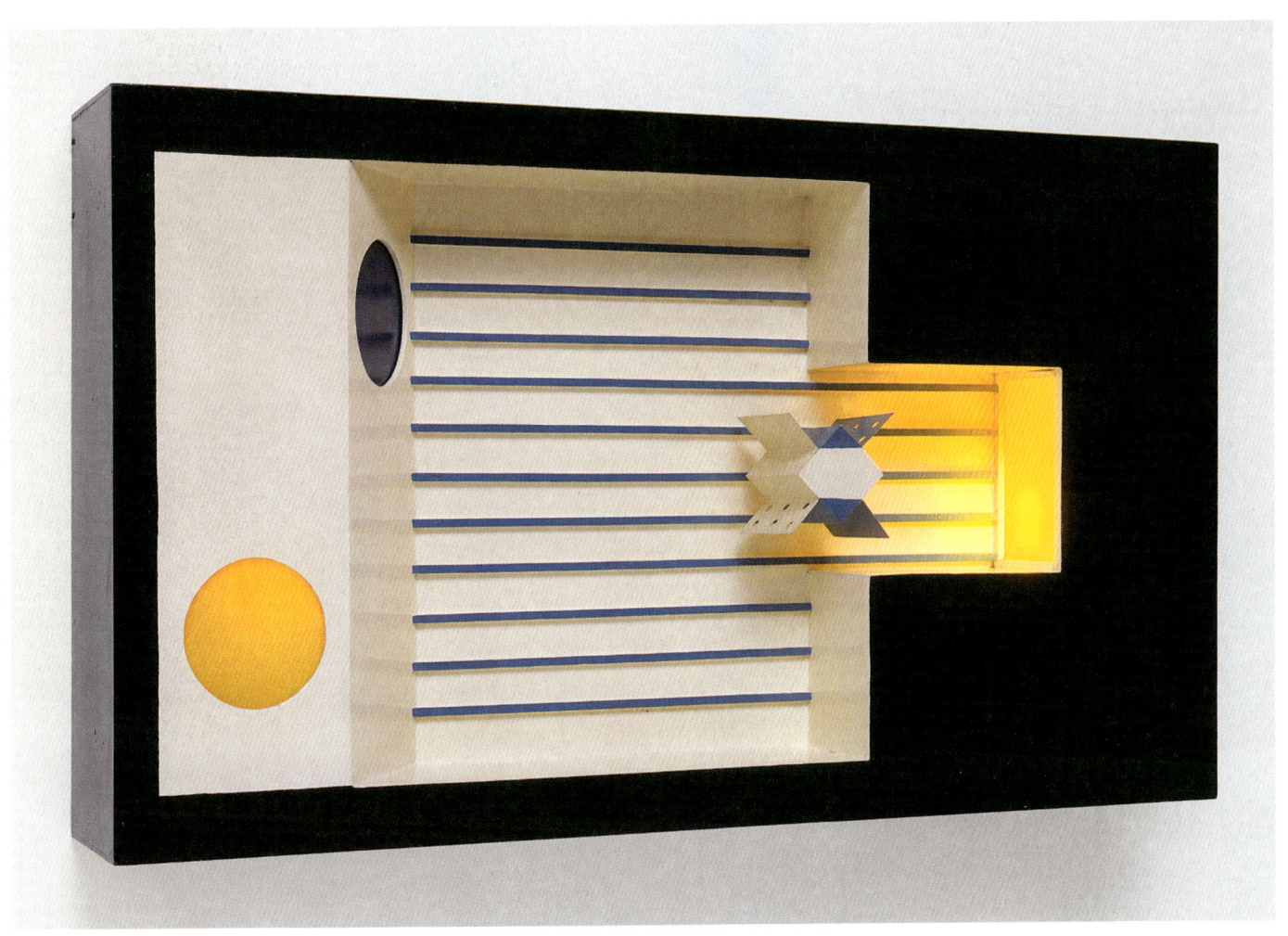

Stephen Willats

In the 1960s, Willats created a series of objects he called *Visual Automatic*, through which he aimed to investigate the relationship between art and social behaviour. He was especially interested in the mechanisms of pattern recognition as a way in which the mind finds order and meaning in an otherwise chaotic situation ('noise'). In this work he included coloured circles lighting up in a random sequence, controlled by hidden environmental sensors. At the same time, a rotating object in the centre of the structure creates a flickering light effect, blinking approximately ten times per second. This speed reflects the frequency of the brain's alpha waves, which occur when an individual is awake but mentally at rest. The viewer's brain thus innately tries to make sense of the flickering lights, while the light pattern created by the metal oscillator encourages relaxation. In the years just before producing his *Visual Automatic* works, Willats had attended and taught at the experimental Groundcourse at Ealing Art School in London (1961–4), led by British artist and theorist Roy Ascott, which encouraged a multidisciplinary approach to art practice through the understanding of semiotics, learning theory, the behavioural sciences and cybernetics. VR

↖ Stephen Willats, *Visual Automatic No.5* 1965

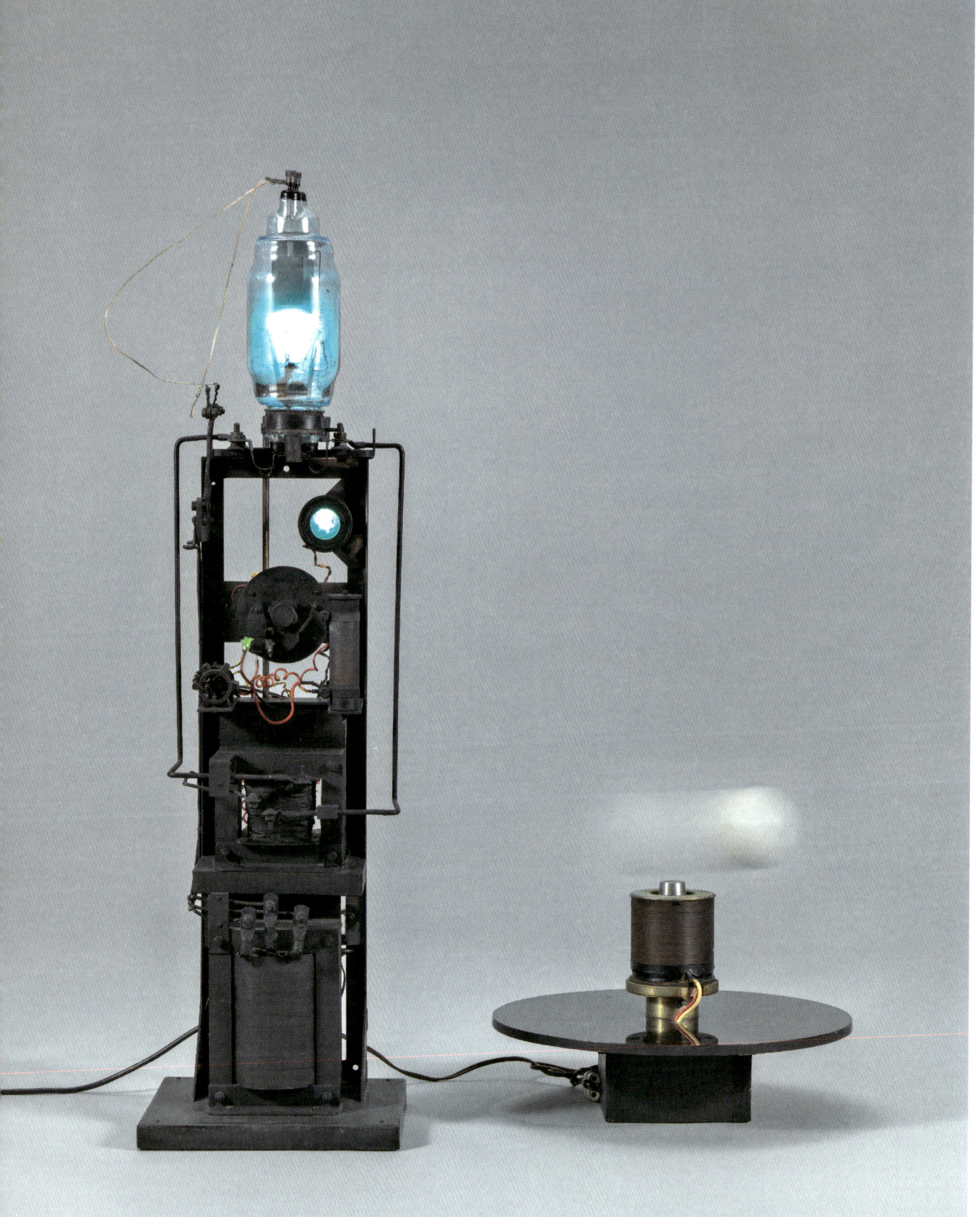

Takis

Télélumière No.4 is part of a series of works utilising mercury rectifiers, devices that convert AC to DC electricity and were once used to power electric railways, industrial motors and radio transmitters. They operate by passing a current through mercury vapour, causing the mercury to ionise and emit a distinctive blue-tinged light. Beside the rectifier – which stands upright, almost like a figure – is a structure Takis refers to as a 'Magnetic Ballet', a sphere suspended from above that is kinetically activated by an electromagnet. *Electro-Magnetic Music* 1966, one of Takis's first musical works, also uses electromagnetism: it comprises a taut metal wire and a needle that moves as an electromagnet switches on and off. As the needle strikes the wire, sound is created (and is amplified through speakers). Takis harnessed fundamental forces in his work, aiming to make visible the energy fields that surround us. KW

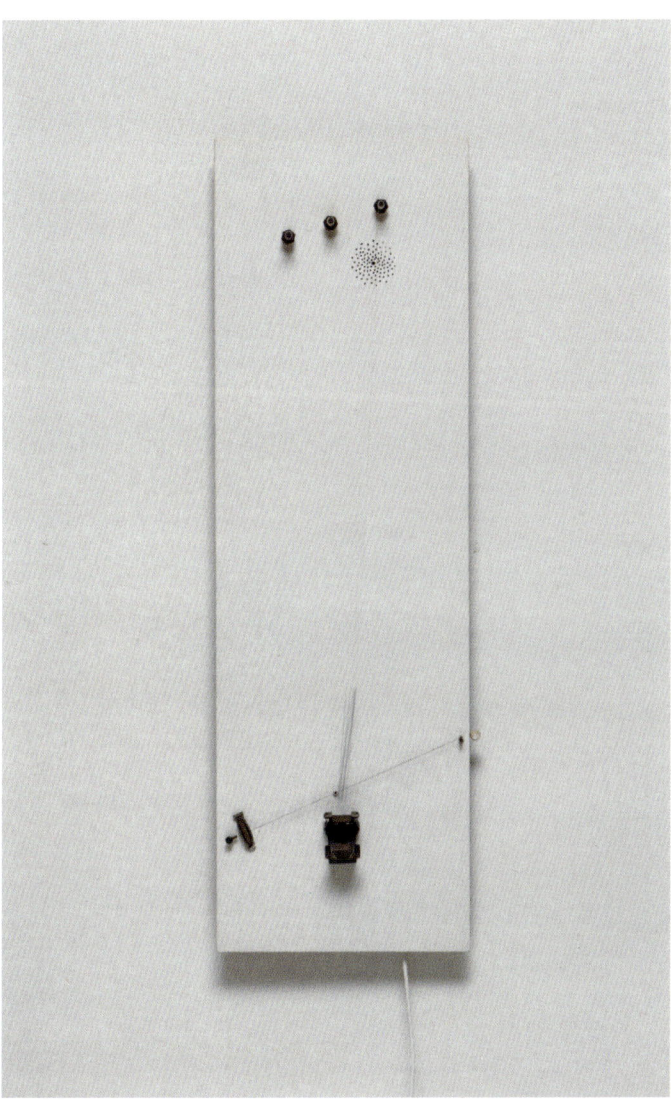

← Takis, *Télélumière No.4* 1963–4
↑ Takis, *Signal* 1965
↖ Takis, *Electro-Magnetic Music* 1966

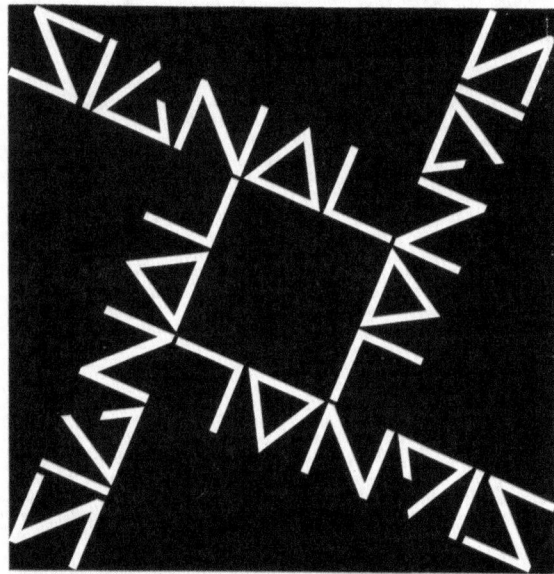

TATE GALLERY LIBRARY

Signalz

Newsbulletin of the Centre for Advanced Creative Study

Director : Paul Keeler
Flat 4, 92 Cornwall Gardens
London, S.W.7   Kni. 0138

Vol. I   No. I   August 1964

STOP PRESS
NOVEMBER: INAUGURATION OF CENTRE SHOWROOMS (FOUR FLOORS, 39, WIGMORE STREET, LONDON W.I): **TAKIS** RETROSPECTIVE AND **LILIANE LIJN.**

Signalz, the name of our newsbulletin, was inspired by a series of tensile sculptures by the Greek artist **Takis.** Our symbol and the layout of this paper were designed by **Keith Potts.**

Price per copy of **Signalz** is one shilling and six pence.

Subscription rates :
One year (12 issues monthly), fifteen shillings for U.K. and Northern Ireland; £1 10s. 0d. sterling for any address abroad, payable in advance by cheque or postal order to **Signalz,** 92 Cornwall Gardens, London S.W.7. *Telephone :* Knightsbridge 0138.

Advertisement rates on request.

Photographs and manuscripts should be submitted with a self-addressed stamped envelope.

" The actual origin of civilization depended on the simultaneous mastery or possession of a number of techniques, some new, some old, which, taken together, sufficed to turn man from being mainly a food-gatherer into being mainly a producer of food. A permanent surplus of food is the necessary basis for the emergence of civil society. Then greater concentrations of population became possible, urban life began, and the neolithic village was overshadowed by the mighty town. The fundamental techniques were the domestication of animals, agriculture, horticulture, pottery, brickmaking, spinning, weaving and metallurgy. These ways of imitating and co-operating with nature constitute a revolution in man's science and a revolution in his way of life. The first area where civilizations based on the combination of these techniques came into existence was in the Near East, in the river valleys of the Nile, the Euphrates, and the Indus. The vital period in which the new techniques were developed is roughly the two millenia from 6000 to 4000 B.C.

" When history is really taught as it ought to be taught, so that everybody is made to understand, as the foundation of his intellectual life, the true story of human society, one of the most fundamental lessons will be the concrete and detailed exposition of the nature of this great revolution in man's control over his environment. The film, the museum, the workshop, the lecture, the library will combine to make the significance of these vital two thousand years sink into the historical consciousness of mankind. This technical revolution constitutes the material basis of ancient civilization. No comparable change in human destinies took place between it and the industrial revolution of the eighteenth century. The cultures of the ancient empires of the Near East, of Greece and Rome, and of Medieval Europe, all rest on the technical achievements of the Neolithic Age. Their resemblances to one another result from this fact. Their differences from us today can only be understood when we realize that we are separated from them all by the second great technical revolution, the coming of the Machine Age."

Professor Benjamin Farrington
Greek Science, Pelican Books, 1963

" Not the occupation, not the object to be manufactured, should be put in the foreground, but rather the recognition of man's organic functions. With this functional preparation, he can then pass on to action, to a life evolved from within. Thus we lay the organic basis for a system of production whose focal point is man, and not profit interests."

Lazlo Moholy-Nagy

" It is the social function of great poets and artists continually to renew the appearance nature has for the eyes of man. Without poets, without artists, Man would soon weary of nature's monotony."

Guillaume Apollinaire

" Let us first of all kill our egocentricity. From now on only teams, groups, whole disciplines can create : co-operation between scholars, engineers and technicians, industrialists architects and sculptors will be the first condition of work."

Victor Vasarely.

" I feel there is a need to affirm that, in terms of the building of objects which embody principles of construction not possible through painting and sculpture, we can extend the framework of creative vision; and in the exploration, transformation and use of raw materials, we have an unlimited field upon which to develop new analogies between what exists in form, space, time, surfaces, dimensions and what grows in perception."

Marcello Salvadori

" Each material has its specific characteristics which we must understand if we want to use it. We must remember that everything depends on how we use a material, not on the material itself , . . And just as we acquaint ourselves with materials, just as we must understand functions, so we must become familiar with the psychological and spiritual factors of our day. No cultural activity is possible otherwise : for we are dependent on the spirit of our time."

Mies van der Rohe

" As for me, I don't subscribe to any theory. I have no theories, only a certain way of life. I like these lines by Walt Whitmen : *Do I contradict myself? Very well then, I contradict myself. I am large, I contain multitudes."*

David Medalla

" I shall give up the use of colour, I think. I shall work with the perspiration of the models, mixed with dust, and even, perhaps, with their own blood; with the sap of plants, the colour of the earth and so on."

Yves Klein.

" This consequence brings us, in a future perhaps remote, towards the end of art as a thing separate from our surrounding environment which is the actual plastic reality. But this end is at the same time a new beginning. Art will not only continue but will realise itself more and more. By the unification of architecture, sculpture and painting in their highest development, a new plastic reality will be created. Painting and sculpture will not manifest themselves as separate objects, nor as ' mural art ' which destroys architecture itself, nor as ' applied art,' but, being purely constructive, will aid the creation of a surrounding environment not merely utilitarian and rational, but also pure and complete in its beauty."

Piet Mondrian.

" The image of man is like the spectrum of a sunbeam, hiding its presence with its rays, yet ever ready to unfold its full radiance the moment we open the prism of ourselves for him to pass through our gates."

Naum Gabo.

Stele to Takis

(Creator of modern aeolian harps/Apollo to the Magneto-Muses/Donor of Votive Figures to the Lares & Penates of nuclear hearths)

Full follow-through
On-site erection
Erecting three antennas
Simultaneously
In three wide-spread
Locations
Maintains a high Degree
Of coordination
(In all reflector altitudes)
With other coordinators
Operational readiness
Accurate performance
Full-field operation
Anywhere in the world

David Medalla,
Paris 1961.

This is the first number of **Signalz,** the monthly news bulletin of the *Centre for Advanced Creative Study.* **Signalz** will contain news items on the activities of the Centre, documentation and critical studies on the Centre's artists, as well as original writings by the artists themselves. From time to time **Signalz** shall also publish pamphlets and books of experimental prose and poetry.

We hope to expand and increase our pages in the future : to include essays by architects, art historians, scientists, technologists, economists, sociologists and town planners. **Signalz** shall print book reviews, notices of important exhibitions in London and the provinces, as well as accounts of pioneering work in the dance, cinema, theatre and music. **Signalz** shall bring to the attention of the artist new developments in technology and science which might be of assistance in the formation of the artist's discipline, in the choice of his materials and the improvement of his technique. We hope to provide a forum for all those who believe *passionately* in the co-relation of the arts and Art's *imaginative* integration with technology, science, architecture and our entire environment.

We believe that such an integration can only be accomplished by most rigorous means: by the exercise of the highest aesthetic standards, and when society gives to the artist its available materials, its support, —*and complete freedom in the pursuit of his* (the artist's) *art.*

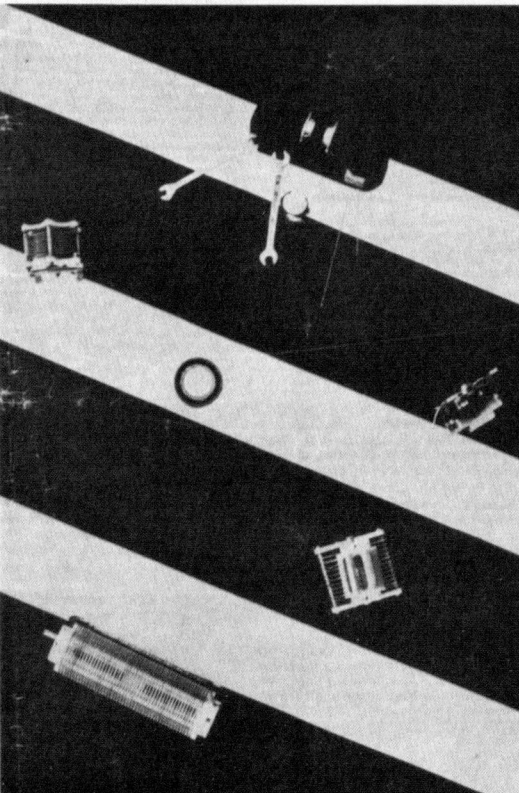

Takis Magnetic Sculpture. 1964

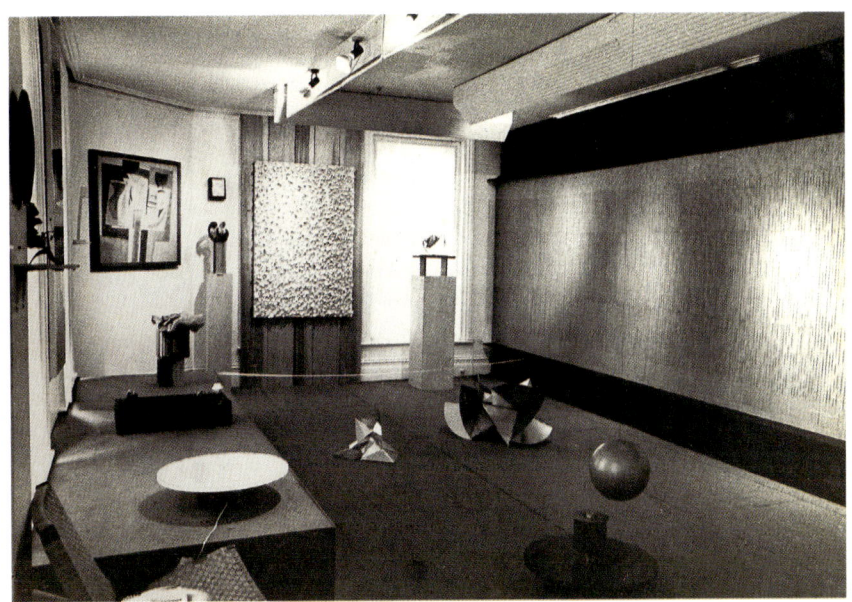

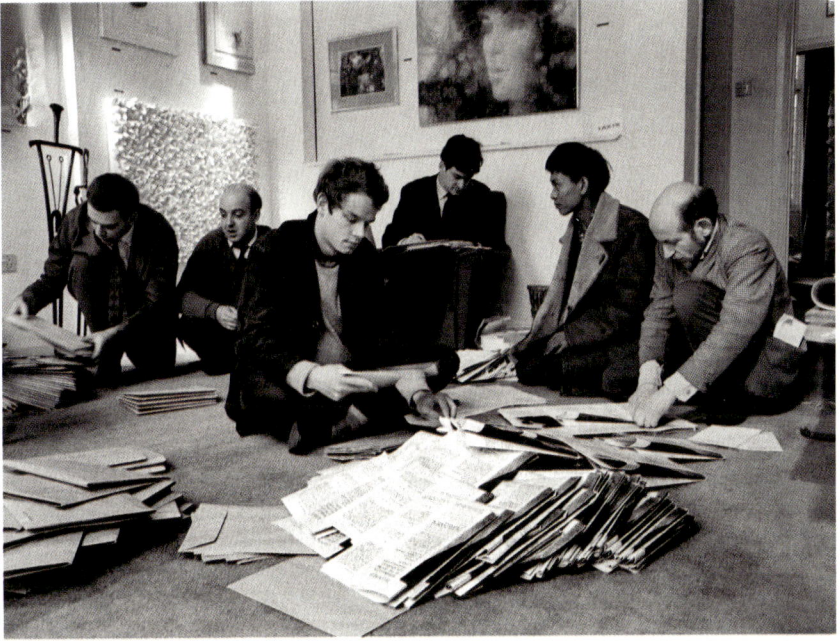

↟ *Soundings Two*, Signals Gallery, 1965, installation view with works by Liliane Lijn, Takis, Lygia Clark, Sergio de Camargo and Jesús Rafael Soto
↑ *Signalz: Newsbulletin* mailing, 1964. From left to right: Paul Keeler, Sergio de Camargo, Guy Brett, Christopher Walker, David Medalla and Gustav Metzger
← Cover of *Signalz: Newsbulletin of the Centre for Advanced Creative Study*, vol.1, no.1, August 1964

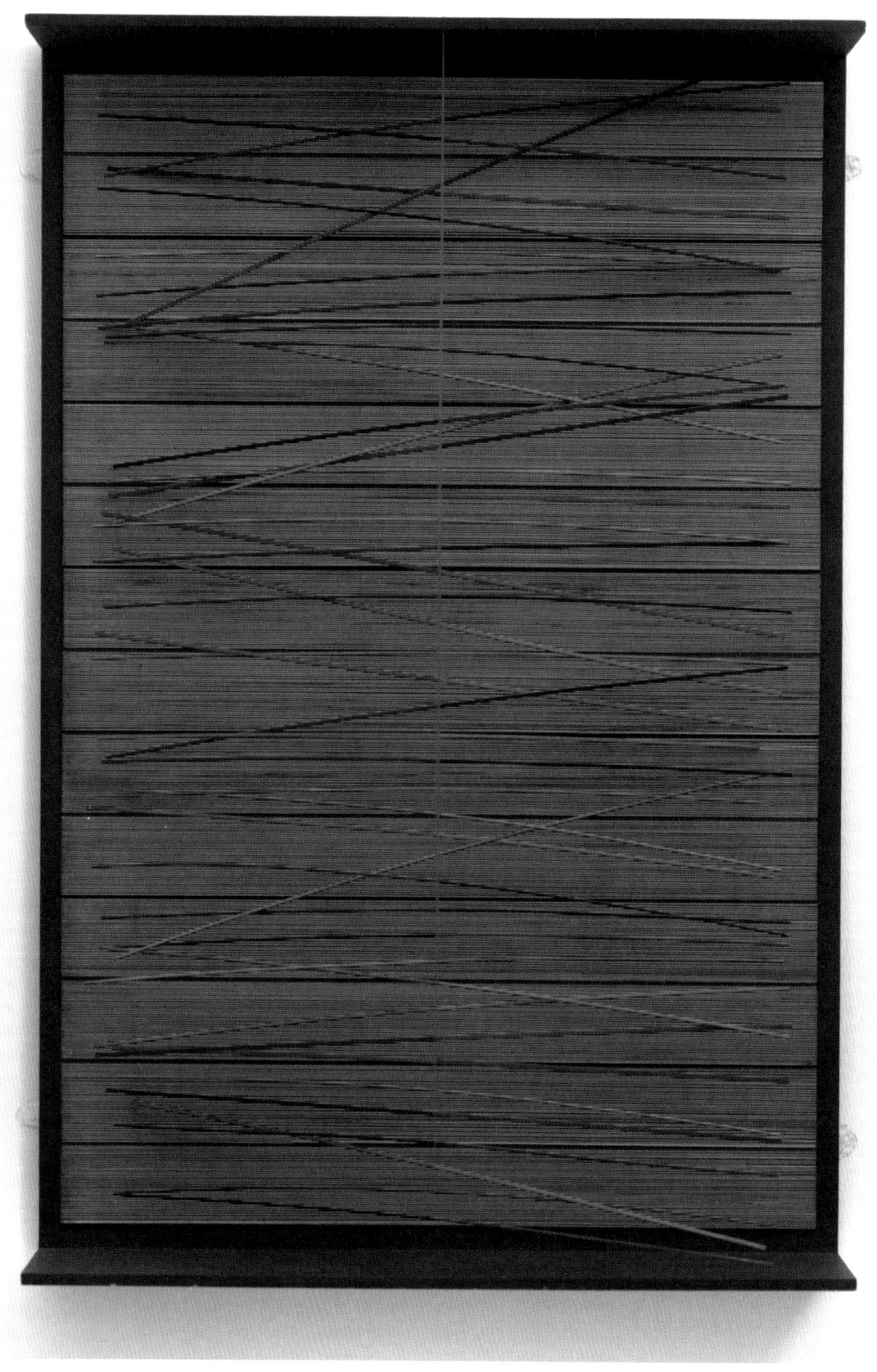

↑ Jesús Rafael Soto, *Cardinal* 1965

Jesús Rafael Soto

Soto left Venezuela for Paris in 1950 where, influenced by Piet Mondrian's late works, he developed a vocabulary based on repeating and superimposing straight lines, squares and circles, usually over a black and white lined background. His interest in the transformation of matter into energy led him to create a series of reliefs he called vibrations. In these works, layers of lines produce an optical disturbance by interfering with perception of the edges of elements – either static or mobile – hovering in front of them. In *Cardinal* 1965 a cascade of painted sticks hangs in front of a striped background, gently swinging with the air around it. This work heavily relies on the viewer's physical presence: the rods' oscillations are partly caused by the viewer's own movements creating small air currents, which in turn enable optical effects that are best appreciated when standing in front of the work, experiencing its subtle shifts in three dimensions. VR

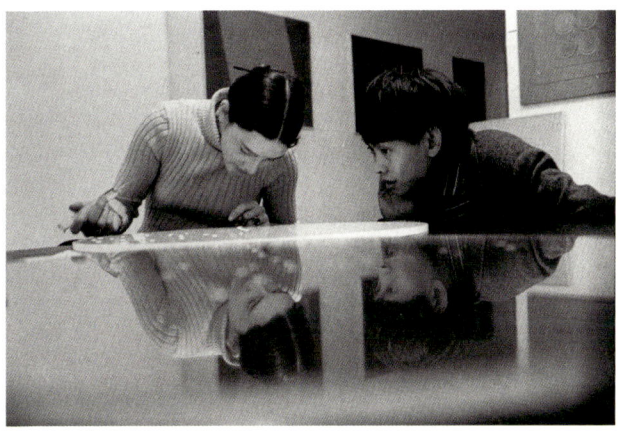

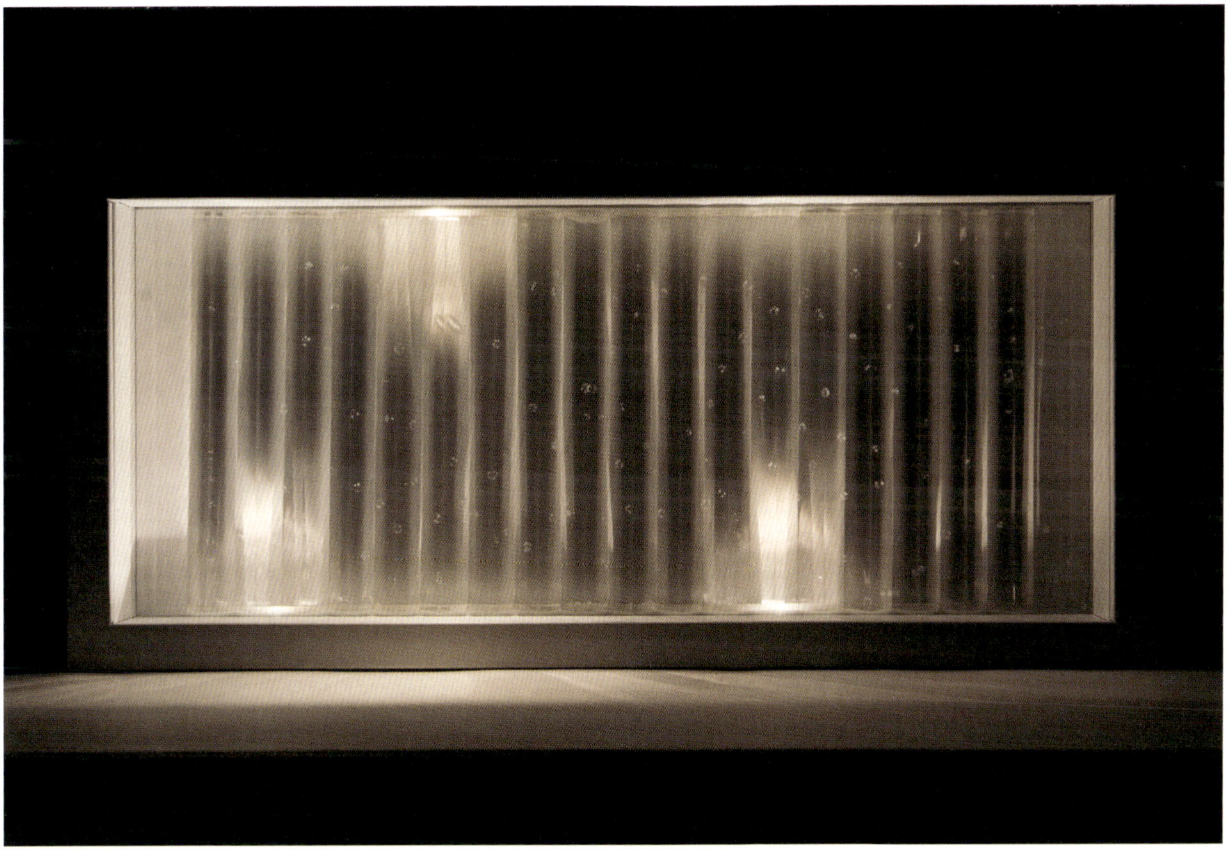

✿ Clay Perry, photo of Liliane Lijn and David Medalla with *Liquid Reflections* c.1966
↑ Liliane Lijn, *Prism Flares* 1967

Brion Gysin is best known for the *Dreamachine* (p.62) a meditative yet dynamic turning flow of light that has had various incarnations since it was first made at the beginning of the 1960s.[1] It was developed within a context of highly creative collaboration that evolved between Gysin, the novelist William Burroughs and the creative technologist Ian Sommerville.[2]

Both famously peripatetic and countercultural figures, Burroughs and Gysin first met in Tangiers in 1954.[3] They were living at the 'Beat Hotel' in Paris in 1959 when Gysin first devised 'cut-up' methods: 'Cut through the word lines to hear a new voice off the page.'[4] Burroughs became a leading advocate of this technique, extending it in his works of the 1960s. Sommerville suggested they could do something similar with the relatively new medium of tape recording. They were co-evolving dadaist processes of chance and randomness into a post-war information age, in which various artists and writers sought to produce depersonalised, radical juxtapositions in language. Such tendencies anticipated the cut-and-paste, hyper-textual and open-source potentialities of the World Wide Web.

The first book that resulted was *Minutes to Go* (1960). It contains cut-ups of text from magazines, from Rimbaud and Shakespeare, with three extraordinary permuted poems by Gysin (p.63). Burroughs cut up a text about language as a virus, a theme that recurred in his later writings. As Barry Miles has described it, Gysin and Burroughs took the view that 'anyone who owned a pair of scissors could write poetry', and the new game was 'fighting subjectivity'.[5]

Gysin became known for his sound poetry – in particular, for his multiple permutations of the phrase *IAMTHATIAM*, inspired by reading Aldous Huxley's 1954 novel *The Doors of Perception*, with its reference to *IAMTHATAMI* (or 'The Divine Tautology') from the Biblical Book of Job. Gysin described having had, 'like Newton', a 'sense of a wild pealing inside my head like an ether experience', realising immediately that he was hearing at least 120 variations of the phrase.[6]

In 1960, Gysin, with Sommerville, developed the world's first 'Dream Machine', patented by Gysin in 1961 under the title *Dreamachine*. Writing in 1962, Gysin linked its conceptual origins to his experience, in 1958, of travelling on a bus along a tree-lined road near Marseille with his eyes closed: 'an overwhelming flood of intensely bright patterns in supernatural colours exploded behind my eyelids: a multidimensional kaleidoscope whirling out through space'. Burroughs gave him a copy of W. Grey Walter's *The Living Brain* (1953) which revealed to him that what had occurred, through the conjunction of the moving bus and the sunlight passing through the even

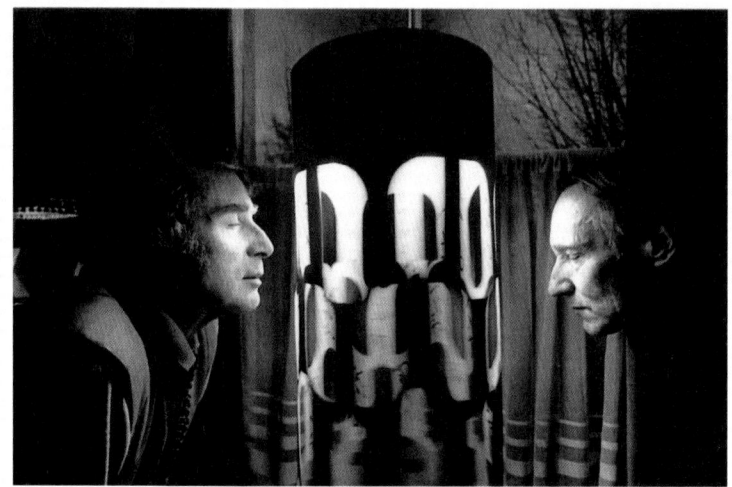

trees, 'at the precise rate of seconds', was a natural flicker effect with 'a many million to one' chance of happening.[7]

Sommerville wrote to Gysin from England in February 1960 saying he had designed a basic apparatus to trigger images in the viewer's brain by means of stroboscopic flickers. Openings are cut into an inner cylinder that rotates around a light source (at least 100-watt) at 78 rpm, so as to stimulate neural alpha-waves. This was the basic *Dreamachine* recipe, to which Gysin added an inner layer of images within the cylinder, seeking to reflect in turn the bright, light-filled patterns he recalled from his bus journey, the viewing of which could also be enhanced by staring at the images with open eyes. Included in *Olympia* magazine in 1962 were instructions for how 'To Construct Your Own Dream Machine'; in his accompanying, highly informative text, Sommerville noted 'The intensity of the effect varies with the individual. Melancholics tend to be irritated; others see nothing.'[8]

Gysin's calligraphic paintings and drawings also draw the eye. He would frequently run Arabic script from right to left across a page and place Japanese characters vertically, creating a grid that has been linked both to kabbalistic writings and to computer programs.[9] In 1960, Sommerville used a Honeywell computer to rework Gysin's *IAMTHATIAM* sound poem into every possible combination. In the same year the BBC gave Gysin three days of access to producers and some new eight-track machines to turn his poems into highly experimental radio. His poems also found their way onto vinyl in Henri Chopin's *OU* magazine in 1964.[10]

In his book *The Third Mind* (1978), created in collaboration with Burroughs, Gysin recalled further of *IAMTHATIAM*, 'I merely undid the word combination, like

Brion Gysin:
Before and After the Dreamachine

Bronac Ferran

the letter lock on a piece of good luggage and the poem made itself.'[11] French critic Gérard-Georges Lemaire meanwhile has observed: 'The Third Mind is perpetually re-beginning, in perpetual contestation. It is never ending – not that it remains forever unfinished but that it is open to all optics. To all possibilities.'[12]

Burroughs's hauntingly prescient solo publication *The Electronic Revolution* (1970) tells us that 'you can construct fake news broadcasts on video camera' and 'scramble your fabricated news in with actual news broadcasts'. He attributes to cut-ups the source of such interventions while noting that 'Playback is the essential ingredient.' He refers to Sommerville's 'tape-recorder experiments' of the mid-1960s; 'He had discovered that playback on location can produce definite effects. Playing back recording of an accident can produce another accident.'[13]

Today's normality seems ever closer to the stuff of 1960s hallucinations and projections. But do we still need to dream with our eyes shut or is it now time to throw them open?

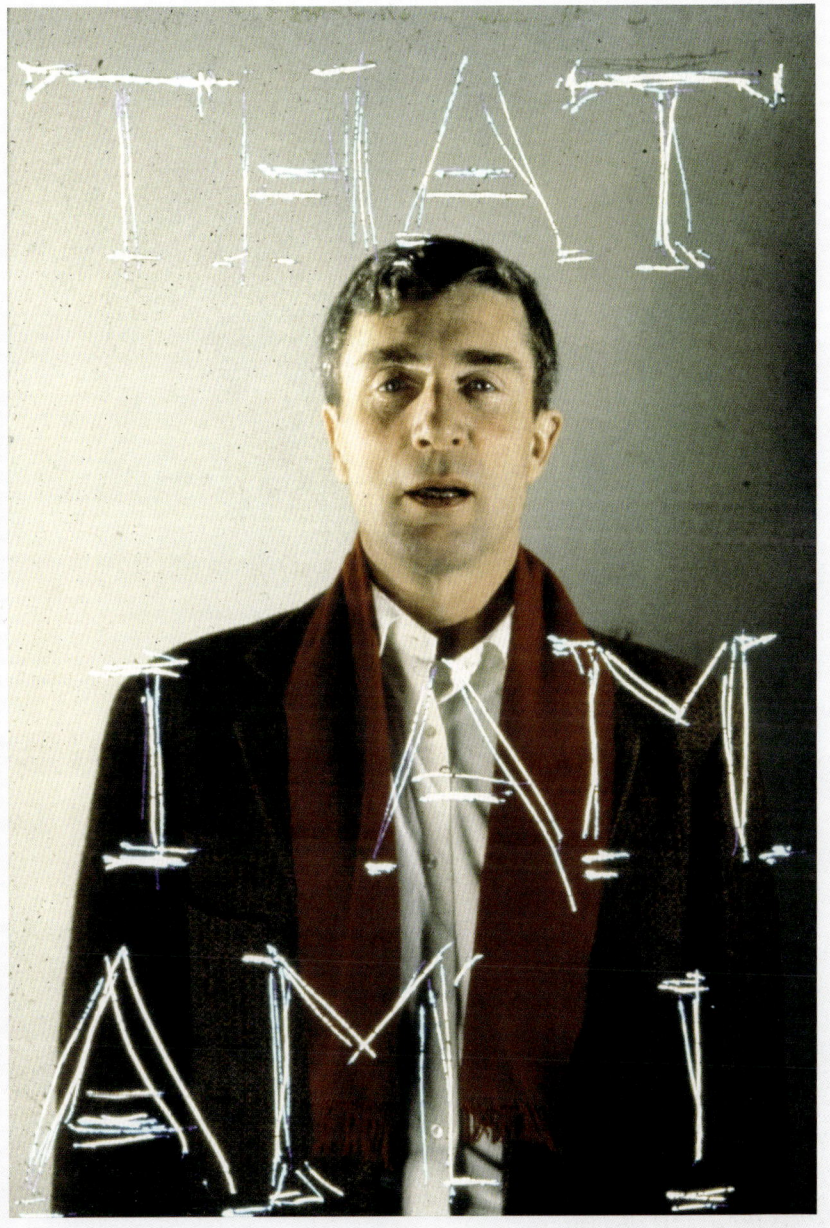

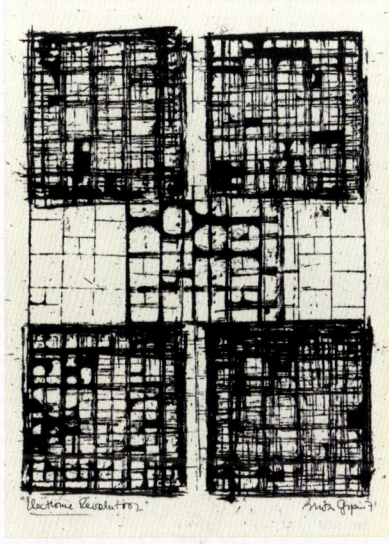

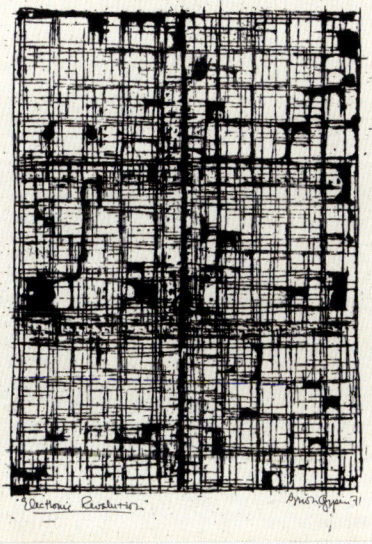

↖ Brion Gysin and William Burroughs with Gysin's *Dreamachine* 1973

↑ Brion Gysin, *That I Am Am I* c.1961

↑ Brion Gysin, *Electronic Revolution* 1971

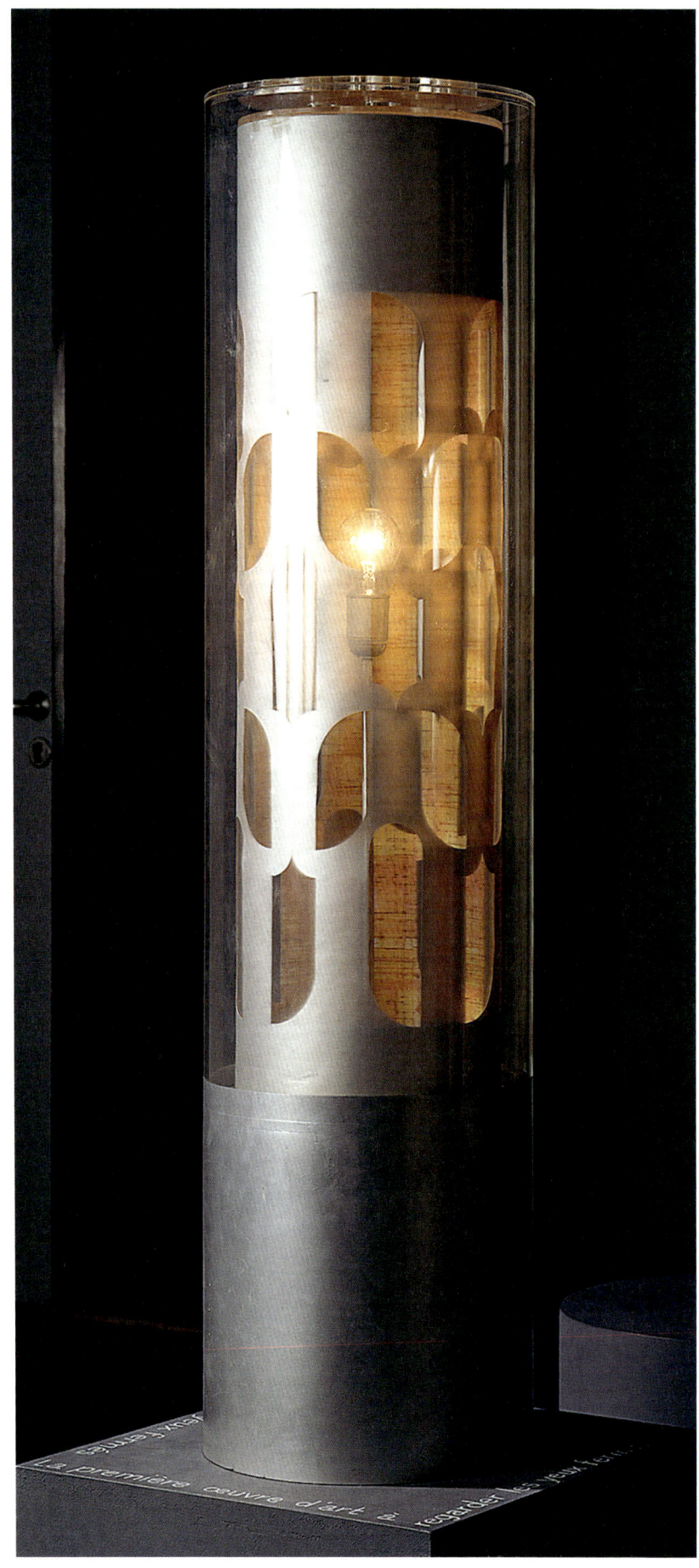

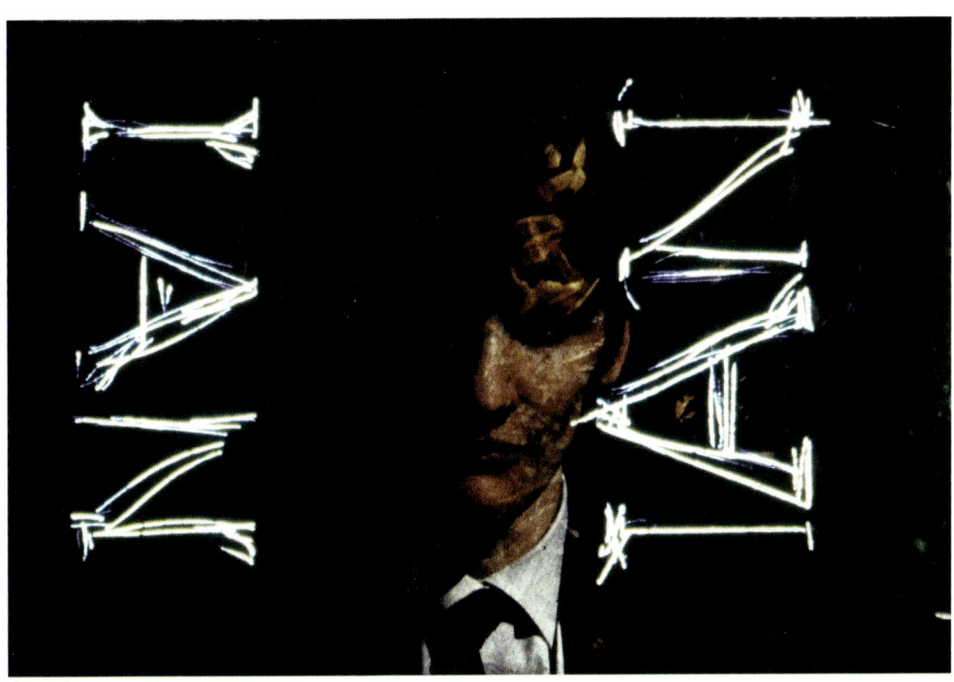

```
I THINK THEREFORE I AM .          1 §  ** 1 % .
I THINK THEREFORE I AM            1 §  ** 1 . %
I THINK THEREFORE I AM            1 §  ** . 1 %
I THINK . THEREFORE I AM          1 §  . ** 1 %
I   THEREFORE THINK I AM          1 . § ** 1 %
  I THINK THEREFORE I AM            1 § ** 1 %

I THINK THEREFORE I AM .          1 §  ** 1 %
I THINK THEREFORE I .             1 §  ** 1 % .
AM I THINK THEREFORE .              %  1 § **
I AM I THINK .                    1 %  1 § .
THEREFORE I AM I .                ** 1 % 1 .
THEREFORE THINK I AM .            ** §  1 %

I THINK THEREFORE I AM            1 §  ** 1 %
I THINK I AM THEREFORE            1 §  1 % **
I THINK AM THEREFORE I            1 §  % 1 **
I THINK THEREFORE AM I            1 §  ** % 1
I THINK I THEREFORE AM            1 §  1 ** %
I THINK I AM THEREFORE            1 §  1 % **

I THEREFORE THINK I AM            1 ** §  1 %
I THEREFORE I THINK AM            1 ** 1 % §
I THEREFORE AM I THINK            1 ** % 1 §
I THEREFORE THINK AM I            1 ** §  % 1
I THEREFORE I AM THINK            1 ** 1 % §
I THEREFORE AM THINK I            1 ** % § 1

THINK THEREFORE I AM I            §  ** 1 % 1
THINK THEREFORE AM I I            §  ** 1 1 1
THINK THEREFORE I I AM            §  ** 1 1 %

I AM I THINK THEREFORE            1 %  1 § **
I AM THINK I THEREFORE            1 %  § 1 **
I AM THEREFORE THINK I            1 %  ** § 1
I AM I THEREFORE THINK            1 %  1 ** §
I AM THINK THEREFORE I            1 %  § ** 1
I AM THEREFORE I THINK            1 %  ** 1 §
```

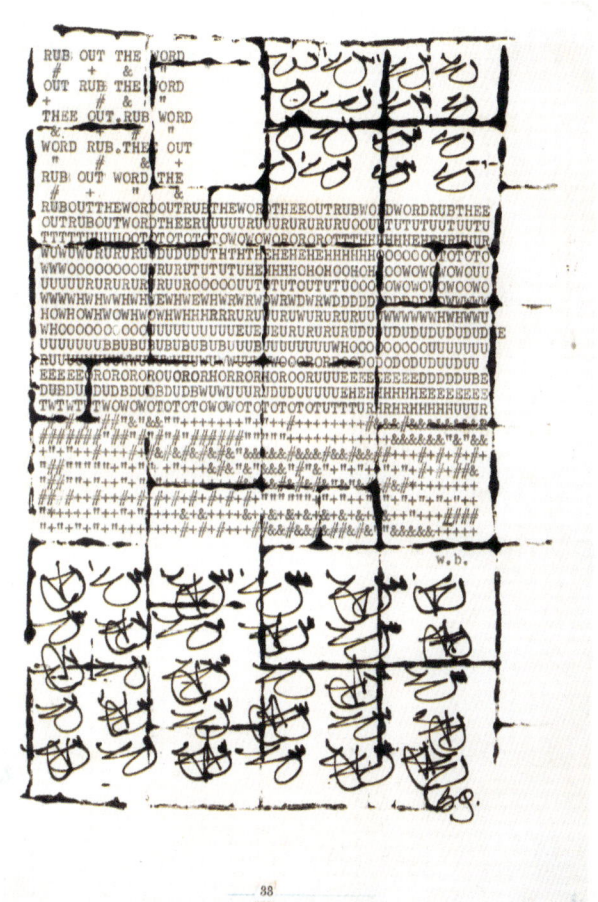

THE THIRD MIND   1978   38

← Brion Gysin, *Dreamachine no.9* 1960
↑ Brion Gysin, *I Think Therefore I Am*, from *Minutes to Go*
(with Sinclair Beiles, William S. Burroughs and Gregory Corso) 1960

♠ Brion Gysin, *Ian Sommerville* c.1961
↑ Brion Gysin and William S. Burroughs, *Rub Out the Word*,
from *The Third Mind* series, c.1965

63

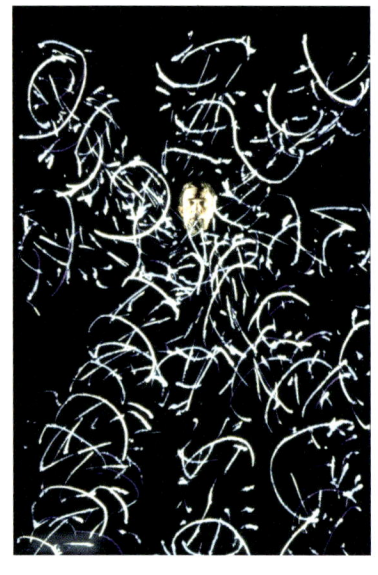

1

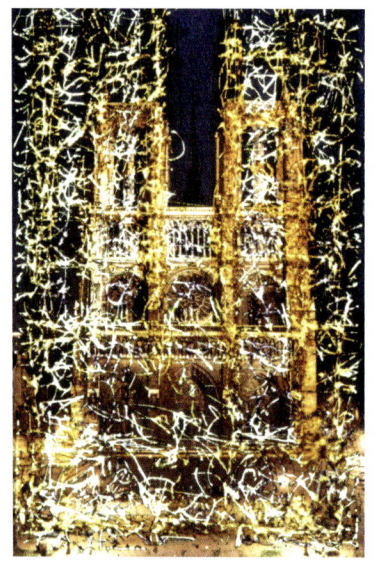

2

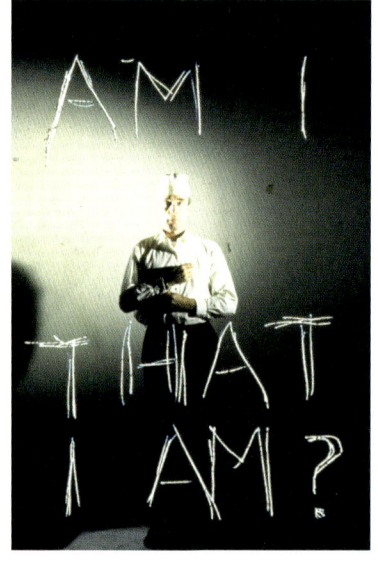

3

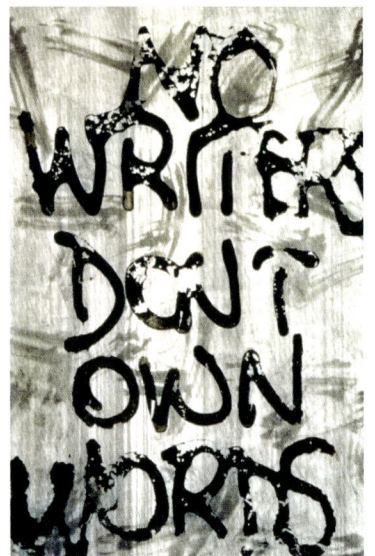

4

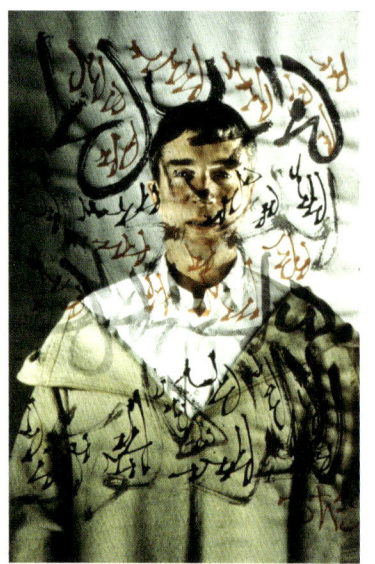

5

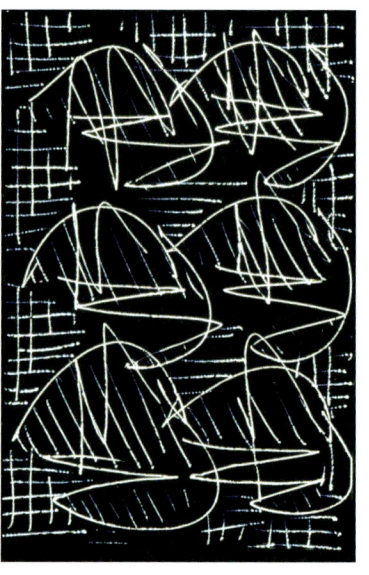

6

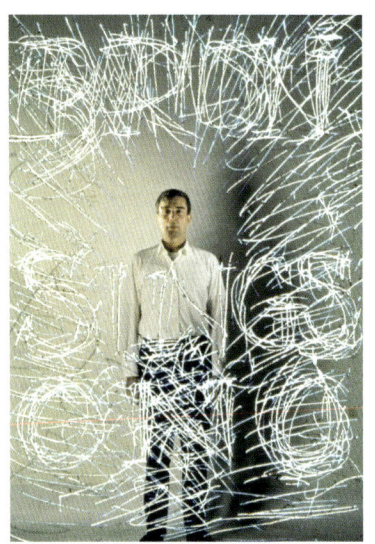

7

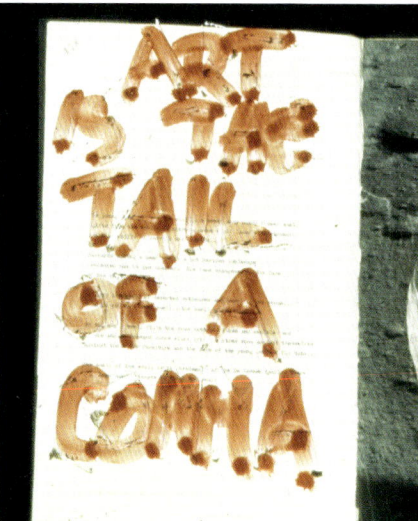

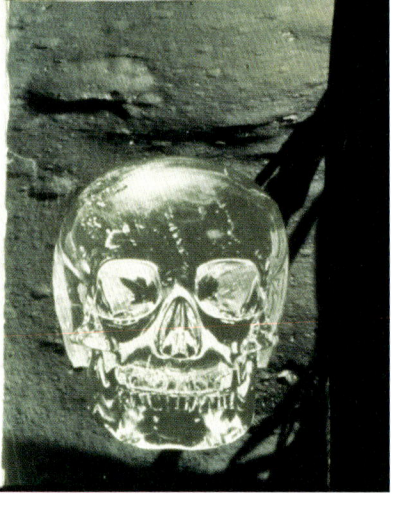

8

9

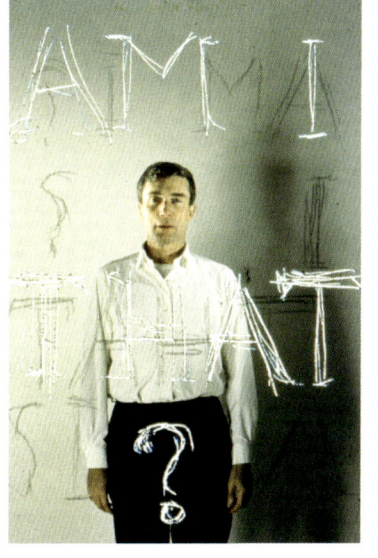

10

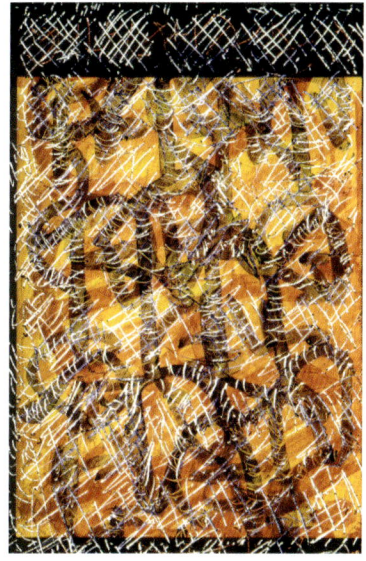

11

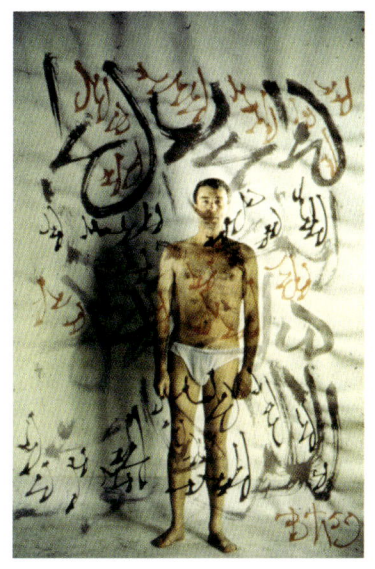

12

13

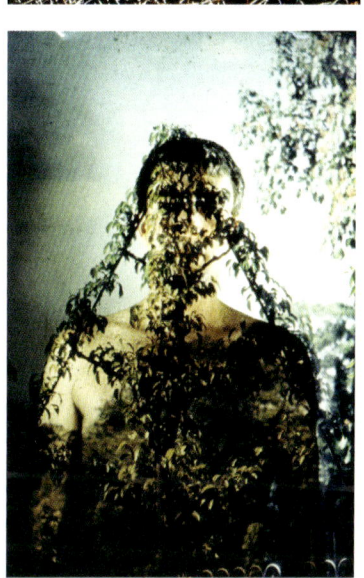

14

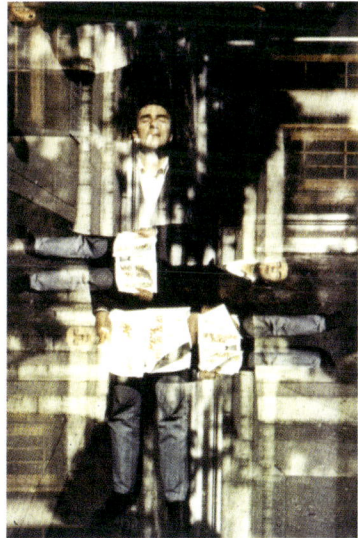

15

Brion Gysin
1. *Self-portrait* c.1961
2. *Untitled* c.1973
3. *Am I that I Am?* c.1961
4. *No Writers Don't Own Words* c.1961
5. *Self-portrait* c.1961
6. *Untitled* c.1976
7. *Brion Sings Ono* c.1961–80
8. *Art is the Tail of a Comma* c.1977
9. *Weapon Tear Alarm* c.1978
10. *Am I That?* c.1961
11. *Untitled* 1973–9
12. *Self-portrait* c.1961
13. *The color of a tree* 1976–9
14. *Self-portrait* c.1961
15. *Self-portrait* c.1980

Katsuhiro Yamaguchi was arguably Japanese art's most prolific media theorist. Over his lifetime, Yamaguchi published at least ten books and hundreds of articles on the material and conceptual developments of reproductive media, industrial materials and electronic technologies, which worked in tandem with the aesthetic effects and experiences produced by his numerous artworks.[1] Through his participation in collectives including *Jikken Kōbō* ('Experimental Workshop', 1951–7), *Environment Society* (1966), *Video Hiroba* (1972–5), and *ArtsUnis* (1982–8), he pushed against media boundaries and artistic categories, collaborating with creatives including architects, graphic designers, industrial designers, sculptors, painters, filmmakers and musicians.

Yamaguchi did not attend art school, but even before graduating from the Department of Law at Nihon University in 1951, he took part in a series of early postwar avant-garde collectives. Eventually Yamaguchi co-founded Jikken Kōbō, which served as a space to explore modernist aesthetics, progressive themes and cross-genre collaborations inspired by mentor and surrealist poet Shūzō Takiguchi and his advocacy of Bauhaus, constructivism and other European avant-gardes. In the 1960s, Yamaguchi found inspiration in the groundbreaking work of László Moholy-Nagy and György Kepes, as well as Frederick Kiesler's genre-bending experiments that treated space and architecture as forms of communications media.

As a member of Jikken Kōbō, Yamaguchi stretched the boundaries of art and the venues for visual exploration in pursuit of new audiences and aesthetic experiences. Collaborating with photographer Kiyoji Otsuji, he produced miniature sculptural assemblages out of reflective and translucent materials that interacted with studio lighting, resulting in a series of photographic inserts in the popular weekly magazine *Asahi Graph* that featured the publication's abbreviated English title *APN* (Asahi Picture News). He designed dynamic, sculptural set pieces for musical concerts that bridged audience and stage (*Space Construction*, 1956) and created shadowbox paintings to be inserted into domestic furniture and commercial architecture (*Vitrine* series, 1952–8). This desire to reach beyond the conventional gallery or museum space to insert art into the everyday spaces of the street, the home and the media continued throughout his life, in his writings, public commissions and conceptual proposals. From 1977 onwards, he repeatedly revised his (ultimately unrealised) proposal for *Imaginarium*, an interactive, video-based network connected by satellite to sculptural multimedia terminals that would allow audiences to collaboratively experience and contribute to creative visual experiments.[2]

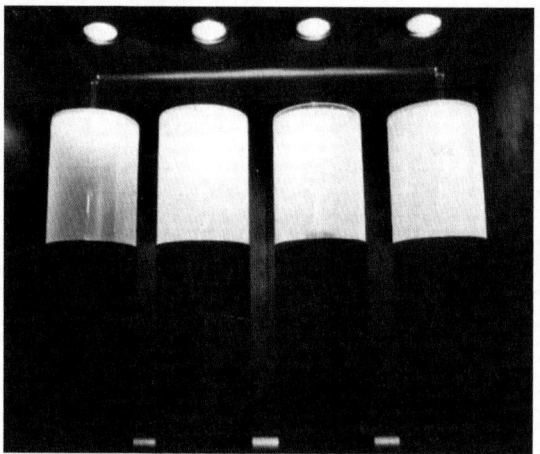

This was envisaged as an alternative to institutional art museums. The proposal served as the inspiration for video sculptures he placed in department stores and public spaces in the 1980s and 1990s.

In his search for art that reached beyond the conventional gallery space, Yamaguchi turned to the new materials and futuristic technologies that linked Tokyo's post-Second World War urban fabric to that of other world capitals, most notably New York. Started in the 1950s, Yamaguchi's *Vitrine* series consisted of shadowboxes with sheets of painted glass layered behind panes of corrugated glass. Inspired by department store window displays, the painted compositions, mediated (and distorted) by corrugated glass, disturbed fine-art perspectival conventions, instead gesturing towards the shifting reflections and refractions experienced while strolling down shopping streets. Along with other members of Jikken Kōbō, Yamaguchi turned to the cutting-edge auto-slide projector – developed by Tokyo Tsushin Kogyo (later Sony) as an audio-synchronised presentation device for schools and other educational settings – and used it to convey the tragic story of a test pilot in *Adventures of the Eyes of Mr. W. S., a Test Pilot* (1953). An allegory for the dangers of technology in the nuclear age, the slideshow followed Mr. W. S. as he explored the scientific wonders of a metropolis on a new planet, only to go blind from the clear brightness of the advanced materials used there.[3]

In the mid-1960s, Yamaguchi made large, translucent acrylic quasi-letter forms containing fluorescent and coloured lights that cast coloured shadows on the surrounding environment. These works materialised Marshall McLuhan's concept of the lightbulb as a technology of communication and transmission, transforming spaces of economic consumption and artistic display

The City Refracted: Katsuhiro Yamaguchi's Applied Media Theory

Nina Horisaki-Christens

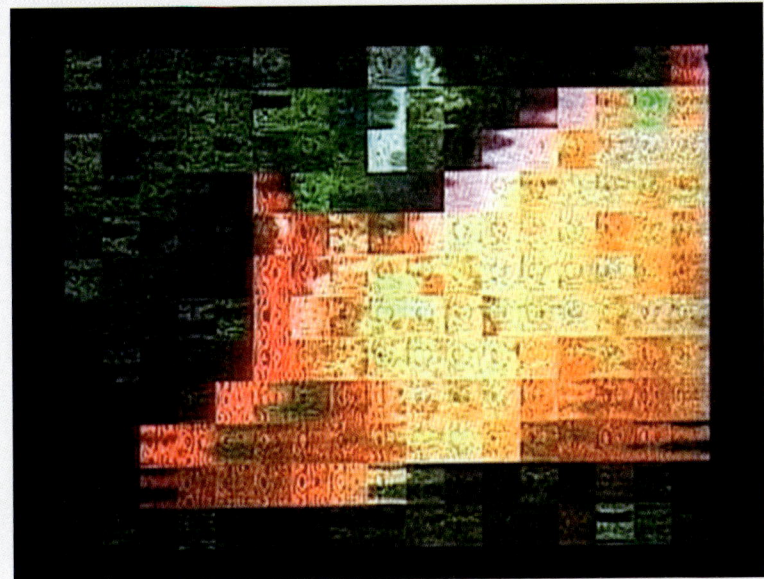

equally, gesturing toward the all-pervasive effects of new media on our everyday urban environments. Even his earliest forays into moving images, such as *Image Modulator* 1969, placed colour television screens behind corrugated glass to abstract mass media images, focusing on the effects of light in urban space. Exhibited in *Electromagica '69* – a show curated by Yamaguchi for the Sony Building in Ginza, Tokyo, that applied cybernetic ideas to urban space to create a non-printed media space – the work presents light as a transmitter of information.

From the 1970s, in the wake of designing the Mitsui Pavilion for Osaka's Expo '70, Yamaguchi launched himself fully into the emerging medium of video, but now specifically as a counter to the centralisation of authority in broadcast media. Establishing the collective Video Hiroba with artists including Fujiko Nakaya, Hakudō Kobayashi and Toshio Matsumoto, he worked on video-mediated urban planning collaborations with communities in Yokohama and Niigata, at the same time as developing his own video performances (*EAT* 1972) and immersive video sculptures (*Las Meninas*, 1974). While his video sculptures focused on deconstructing viewer-object relationships within fine art settings, the video-mediated planning processes Video Hiroba employed used video to deconstruct social hierarchies between citizens and government or corporate authorities. Up until his death in 2018, by repurposing media technologies and linking creativity to media, Yamaguchi pursued a more open, more democratic and collaborative vision of our urban surrounds – one that relies on media processes of reflection, duplication and transmission to refract, distort and generate new ideas, democratic cultures and dynamic social forms.

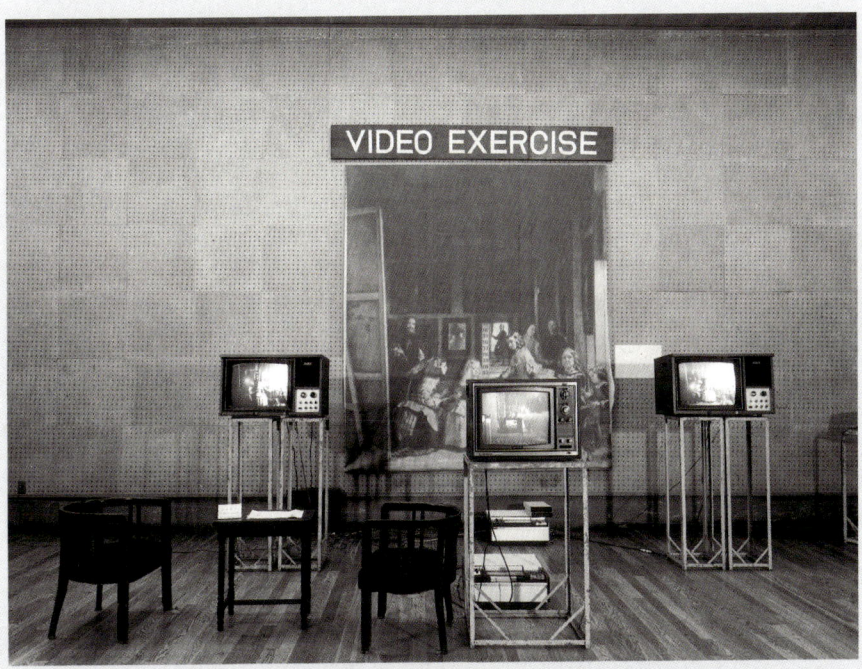

↖ Katsuhiro Yamaguchi, *Water Modulator* 1969, installation view at *Electromagica '69: International Psychech Art Exhibition*, Sony Building, Tokyo, 1969

↟ Katsuhiro Yamaguchi, *Image Modulator* 1969
↑ Katsuhiro Yamaguchi, *Las Meninas* 1974, installation view at the Tokyo Metropolitan Art Museum, 1974

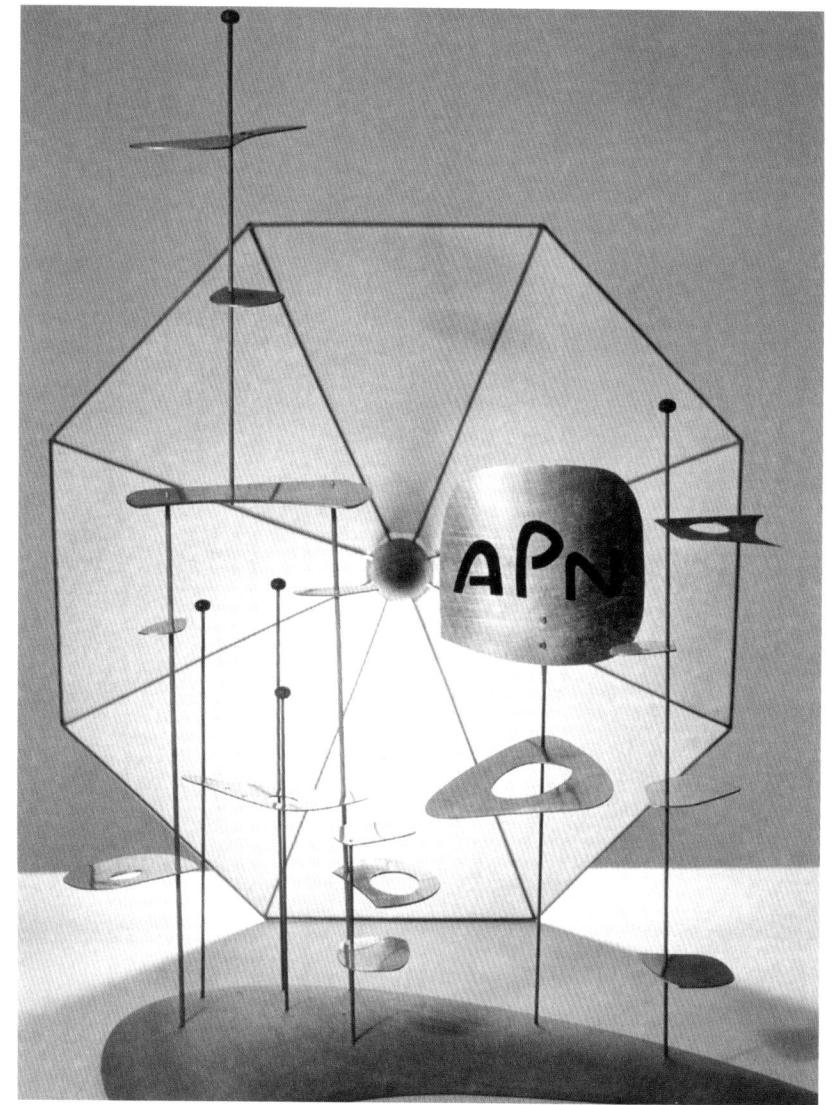
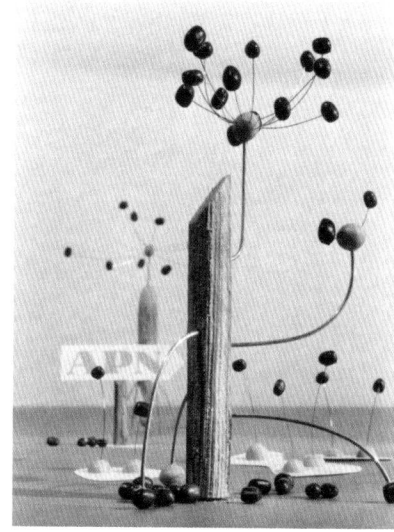
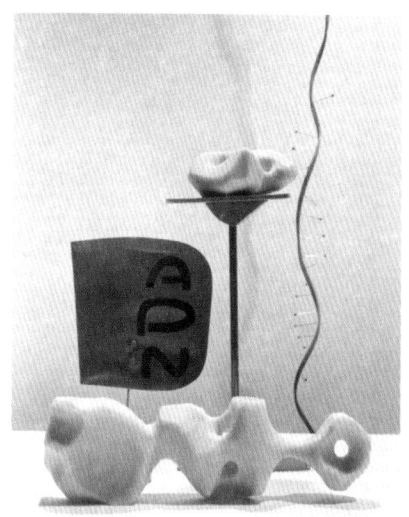
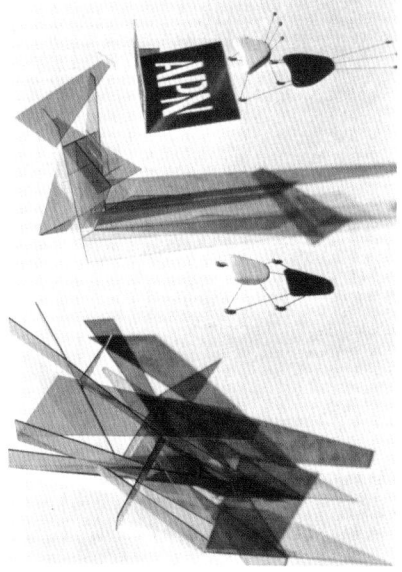
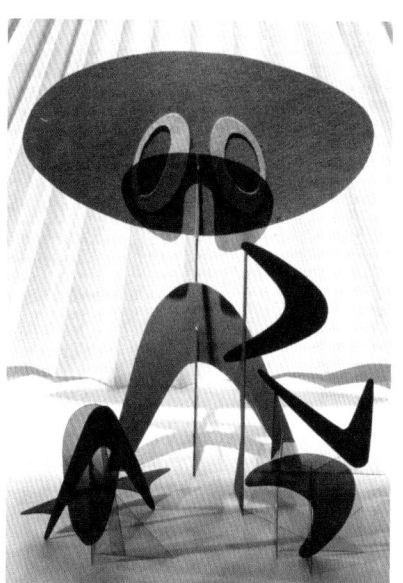

↑ Katsuhiro Yamaguchi, *Composition for APN* 1953–4

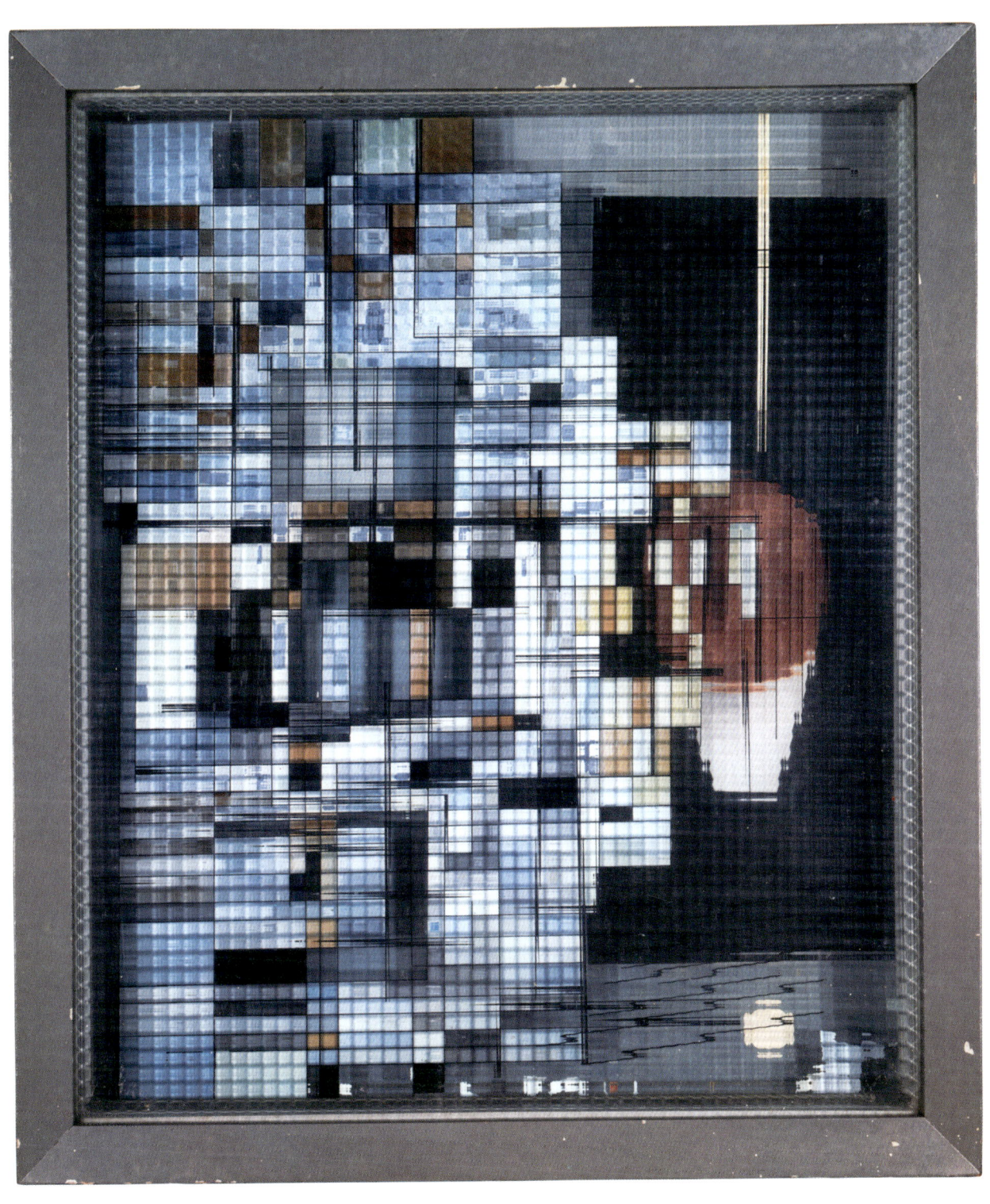

69   ↑ Katsuhiro Yamaguchi, *Vitrine: Deep Into the Night* 1954

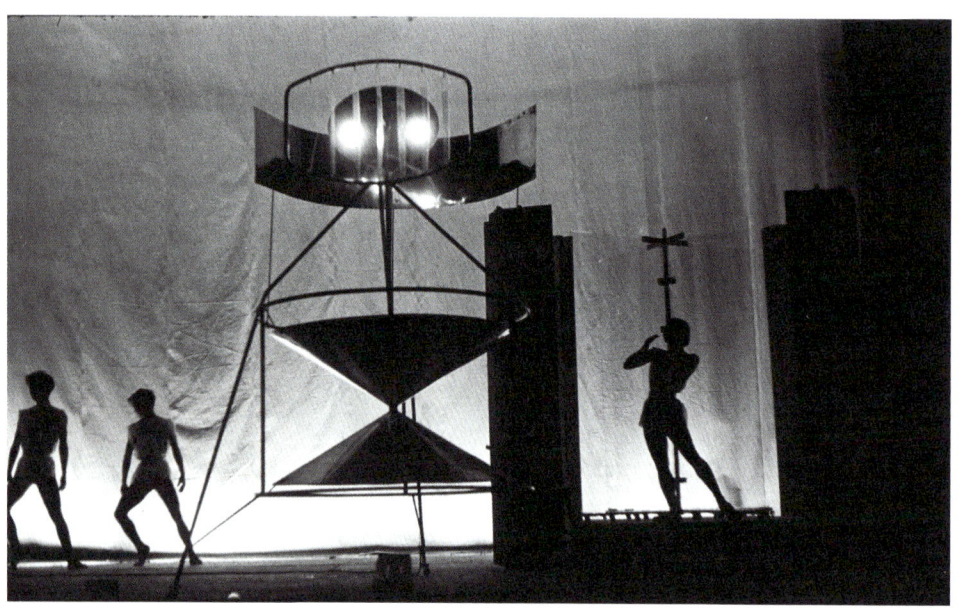

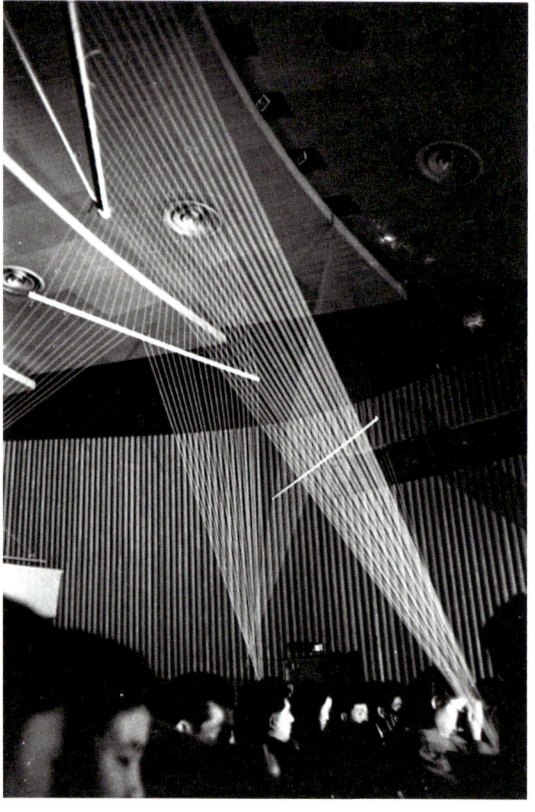

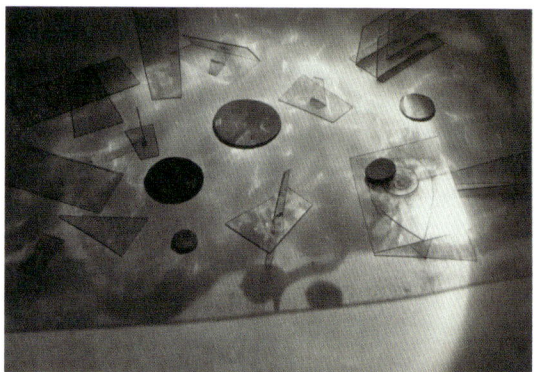

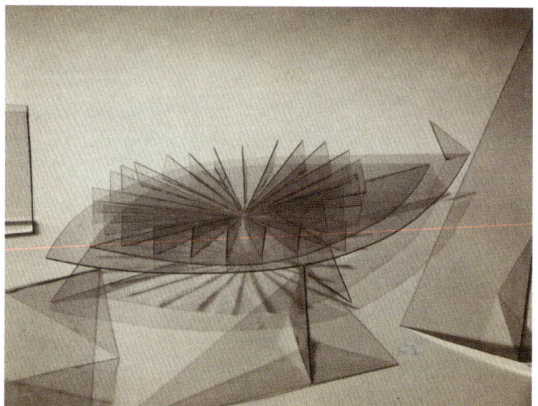

⊼ Jikken Kōbō, *Ballet Mirai no Eve* (Eve Future Ballet), 1955, performance documentation, Haiyuza Theater, Tokyo, March 1955. Photographed by Kiyoji Otsuji
↑ Katsuhiro Yamaguchi's environmental installation for Jikken Kōbō's concert 'Musique Concrète / Electronic Music Audition' at Yamaha Hall, Ginza, Tokyo, 4 February 1956
↗ Katsuhiro Yamaguchi, two photographs from the slideshow *Adventure of the Eyes of Mr W.S., a Test-Pilot*, 1953 (with soundtrack by Hiroyoshi Suzuki)

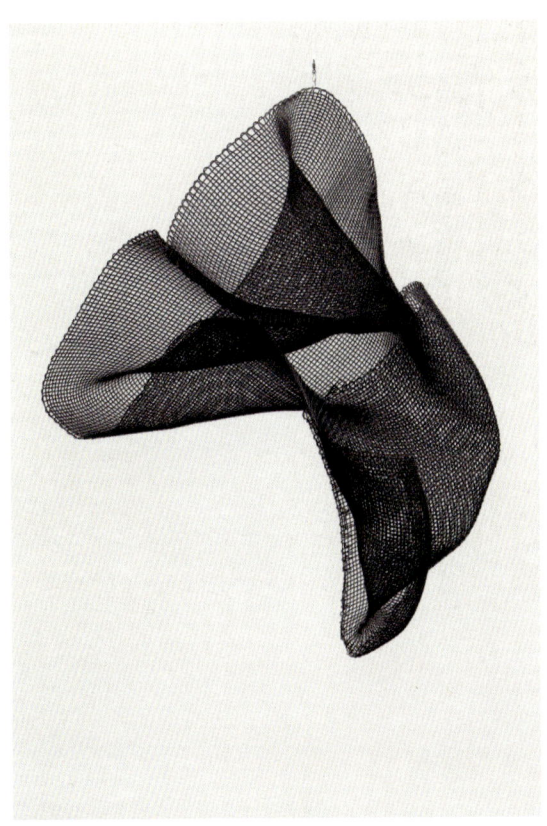

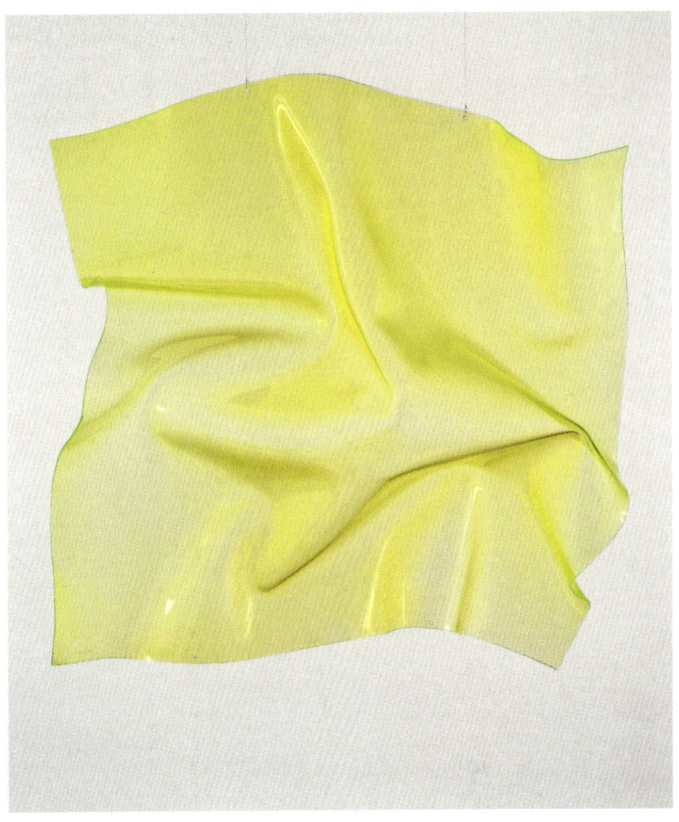

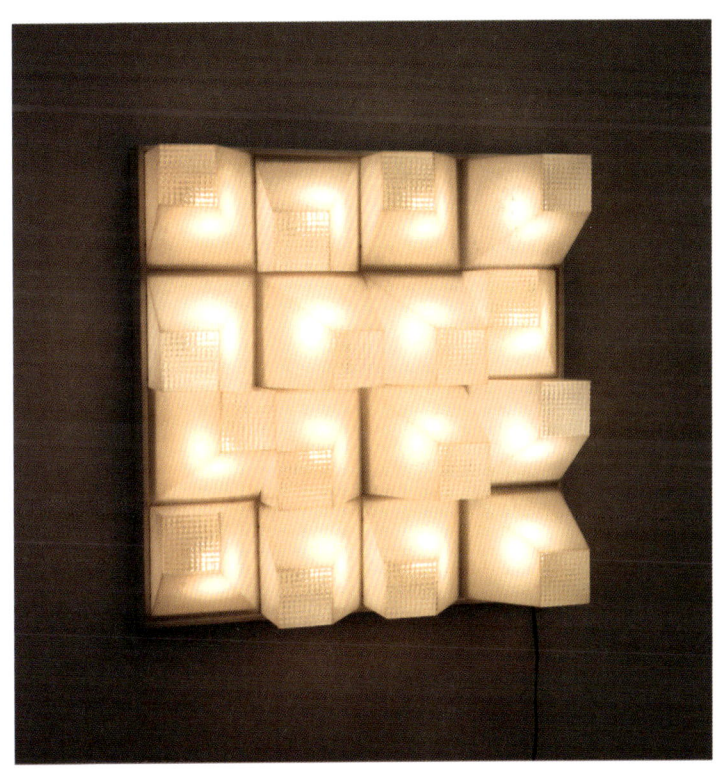

↖ Katsuhiro Yamaguchi, *Mesh sculpture* 1961
⬆ Katsuhiro Yamaguchi, *Trial Object in Acrylic Plastic* 1960s
↑ Katsuhiro Yamaguchi, *Barnacle* 1966

Openness:
Art as Visual
Research

A Programmed
Openness:
Art as Visual
Research

72

A Programmed

No to Op Art: Visual Research and Programmed Arts of the 1960s and 1970s

Darko Fritz

Several segments of twentieth-century contemporary art practice use information as their primary material: concrete art, conceptual art and digital art.[1] Concrete art is composed of basic visual features such as planes, colours and forms that may be programmed through the algorithm – a set of rules applied to selected visual elements; information is therefore used as the building block of newly designed, programmed art. Conceptual art uses the idea as information, while digital art embodies the information in a digital software. We may distinguish between different kinds of programmed art that circulated in the 1960s and 1970s, which bounced between techno-utopian and techno-dystopian and marked the twentieth-century arts during the transition from the industrial age to the information society. It is possible to understand programmed art through the development of international exhibitions, movements and art networks established in the framework referred to as 'New Tendencies' (or 'New Tendency', or 'Tendencies'), which I will refer to as 'NT'.

Zagreb's Gallery (today Museum) of Contemporary Art organised five NT exhibitions between 1961 and 1973, and some key exhibitions were also held in Paris, Venice and Leverkusen, while the last event officially associated with the movement was held as a symposium in Zagreb in 1978. A plurality of artistic trends with a rational approach was presented through exhibitions and symposiums, publications, the journal *Bit International* and a dynamic international network of various progressive artistic theories and practices of the 1960s and 1970s. I intend to look at three distinct phases of NT, articulated through the formation of three different networks of people and institutions: the formation of the international NT movement and its dispersal, 1961–5; the introduction of the computers and visual research section, 1968; and the introduction of the conceptual art section, 1973.[2]

The international movement for visual research

NT brought together artists, gallerists and theorists, first from East and West Europe (and South American dissidents) and, from 1965, also from the United States, USSR and South America; subsequently also from Africa and Asia. The NT stamp, made in 1964 in Paris, read 'New Tendency' in seven languages, reinforcing its international context. Such a unique situation was made possible by the cultural and geopolitical position of Zagreb, in what was then a socialist but non-aligned Yugoslavia, which at a practical level enabled cultural exchange and unrestricted travel to Zagreb for those on both sides of the Iron Curtain.[3]

The first NT exhibition of 1961 represented the plurality of the avant-garde tendencies of the time. It was possible to observe shifts away from painting to object, particularly in the works produced by Otto Piene and Heinz Mack from the Zero group, Almir Mavignier, Enrico Castellani, Piero Manzoni, Julije Knifer and Ivan Picelj. Most of the works were oriented towards visual research through algorithmic practices, which marked the further development of NT

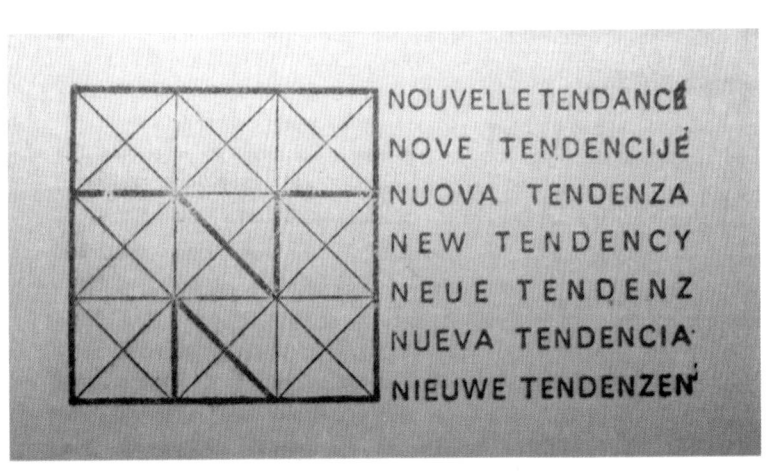

↖ The Stamp of the New Tendencies group, 1964

(as seen in the works of Piero Dorazio, François Morellet from the Groupe de Recherche d'Art Visuel, or GRAV, and Karl Gerstner), and a shift towards research into optical and perceptual structures (Marc Adrian, Julio Le Parc from GRAV, Günther Uecker from Zero, Gruppo N).[4] The catalogue included a positioning statement by François Morellet: 'We are faced with a revolution in art which will be just as great as that in the sciences. Hence reason and the spirit of systematic research have to replace intuition and the individual expression.'[5]

A large group of artists met again in November 1962 in the Paris studio of GRAV, and in 1963 the exhibition *New Tendencies 2* was held. Intuitive art processes shifted towards rational structured experiments following determined programmes, and individual artistic creation shifted towards the strategy of group work. Many NT protagonists abandoned the word 'art' altogether and replaced it with the notion of 'visual research', therefore presenting themselves as 'researchers' instead of 'artists'. Movement and light were brought in as themes and materials, along with the promotion of unstable media and (inter)active participation of the public in the works of art. Those 'open' works were only 'completed' by the specific standpoint or the manipulation of the viewer. NT was framed theoretically by, among others, Matko Meštrović, Giulio Carlo Argan, Frank Popper and Umberto Eco.

Umberto Eco also wrote a text on 'arte programmata' for the catalogue of an exhibition with the same title in Milan in 1962, featuring works by members of GRAV, Gruppo T and Gruppo N. The exhibition was sponsored by Olivetti, the company known for its product design, ranging from typewriters to Italy's first electronic computer, released in 1959. With reference to the works – 'constructions of unmovable structures', which changed with the perspective of the viewer, and 'kinetic movable structures' – Eco defined a specific class of the 'open work', which he had described in his book *Opera aperta* in the same year. This specific class of works consisted of programmed 'event fields'. He wrote: 'It is possible to program with the linear purity of a mathematical program event fields, in which random processes can happen … We therefore can talk about programmed art.'[6] Eco focuses on the possibility of the rational construction of a specific situation for the observer.

François Morellet's 'programming' referred to the self-discipline of an artist, which guarantees a rational and traceable procedure and structure, allowing 'the public to take part in the "creation" of the works'. In his view, this would help with 'demystifying' and democratising art.[7] Morellet wrote: 'Departing from controllable elements the artist has to follow a program. The development of an experiment should realise itself, almost outside of the programmer.'[8] From the moment he sets up the rules, the artist does not intervene or correct the process. It seems that Morellet's definition establishes the link between 'arte programmata' and 'computer art', and can also be widely

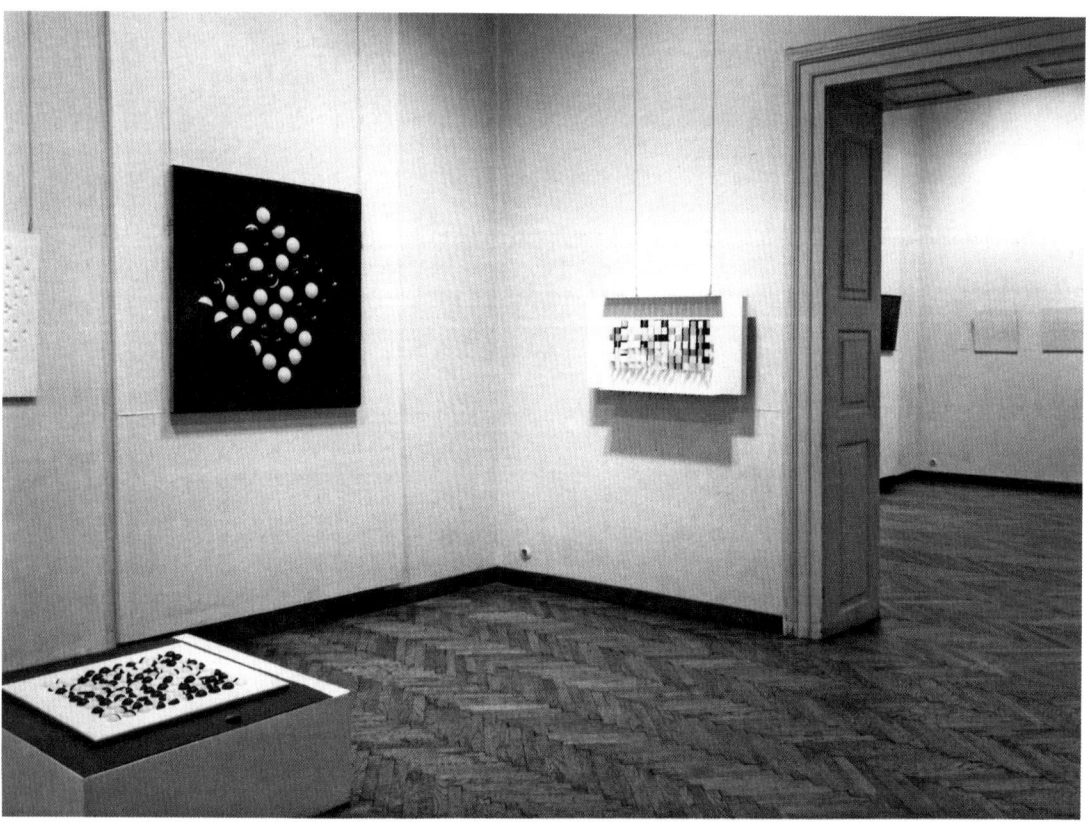

↑ *New Tendencies*, exhibition view at the Gallery of Contemporary Art, Zagreb, with two artworks by Paul Talman and one by Julio Le Parc, 1961

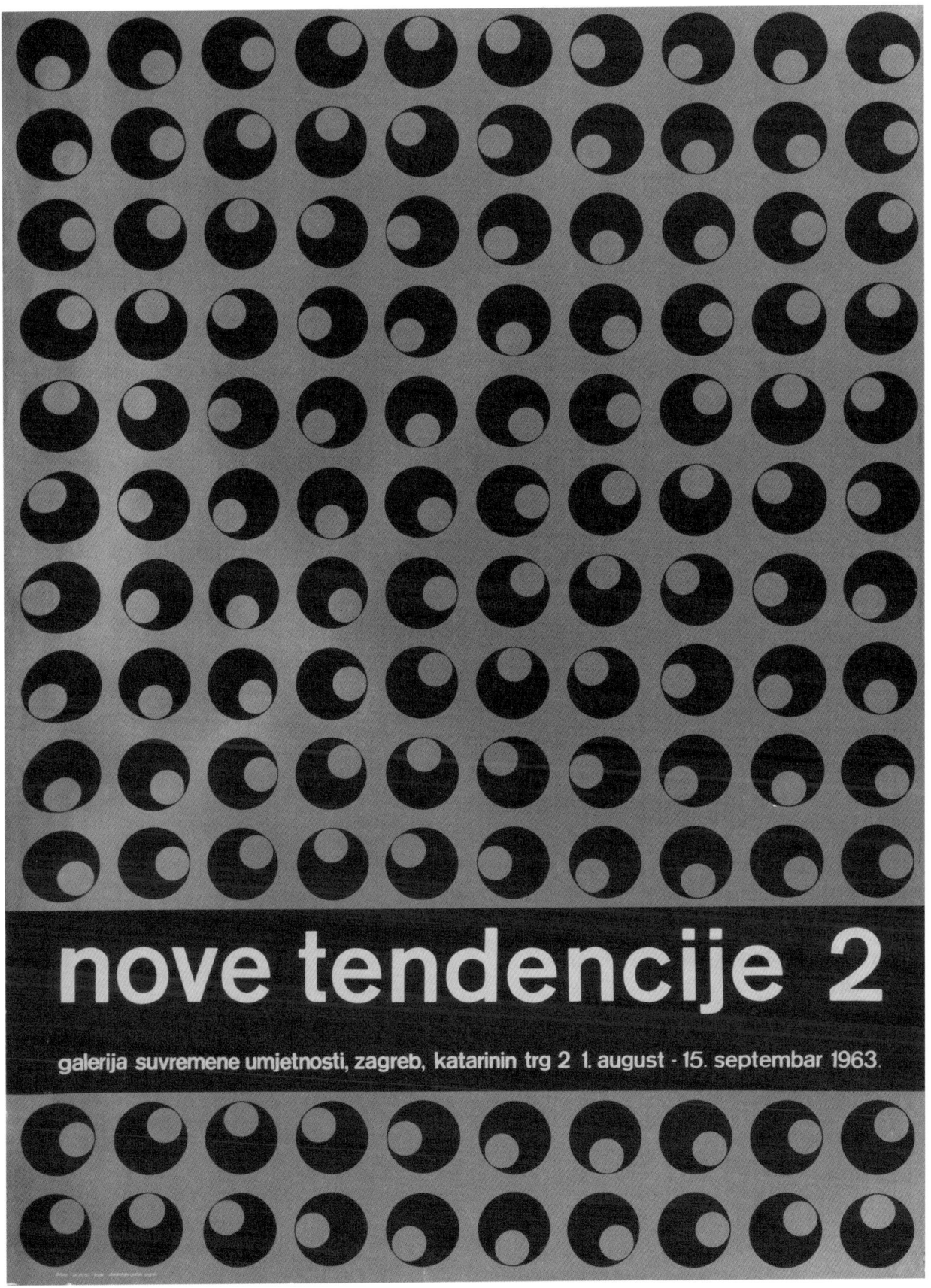

↑ Ivan Picelj, poster for *New Tendencies* 2 1963

applied to contemporary digital art, in particular generative and software art. The same approach is applied to part of the spectrum of conceptual art practice from the 1960s until today, and was incorporated into NT in 1973.

In a 1963 text by thirty-year-old Croatian Marxist, art historian and theoretician Matko Meštrović, who co-curated the first NT exhibition with Almir Mavigner, the demythologising of art and the demystification of the creative process were announced by the positive approach to the industrial production of artworks. Meštrović called for an acceleration of human evolution through the (utopian) process of 'scientification' of all human activities. He thought it was possible to begin this process actively, at once, and to present the global model that was his ultimate objective on smaller scales, through the synthesis of science and art. There was the problem of distributing all material and spiritual goods in equal measure and returning the results of scientific research to the public domain. Meštrović saw the works of NT not as one-of-a-kind commodities for the art market but as 'plastic-visual research with the endeavour to establish the objective psychophysical bases of the plastic phenomenon and visual perception, thus excluding in advance any possibility of the interference of subjectivism, individualism and romanticism.'[9] Then came the development of his thesis: the ultimate transcendence of art by raising awareness of the world through the transformation of the social act into the artistic act, with the aim of actively changing the whole world.

The international impact was such that NT began to be labelled a kind of artistic trend and style, though in its first phase (up to 1965) it brought together more than 150 artists, artistic groups, critics, theorists and gallerists, representing a variety of positions and formal concerns, often developed independently of one another. The travelling 1963–64 NT2 exhibition in Venice changed its name to *New Tendency* (singular), 'because of the striving for the conceptual concentration of purposes and shared ideas', as was explained two years later in the NT3 catalogue. According to increasingly rigorous formal criteria, NT's committee assembled a list of previous NT artists labelled as suitable or unsuitable for further participation. This situation caused conflicts among factions of the NT network.

At this point, despite its radical positions, NT quickly started to enter the art mainstream. NT artists became established and exhibited at prestigious galleries and exhibitions such as Kassel's *Documenta*. The NT2 exhibition travelled, after Zagreb, to Venice and Leverkusen. The new exhibition in Paris in 1964 included fifty-two artists – Lili Greenham and Bridget Riley among them. Julio Le Parc won the grand prize at the 1966 Venice Biennale, then Bridget Riley and Gianni Colombo in 1968. In 1965, thirty-three NT artists participated in *The Responsive Eye* exhibition at MoMA, New York, but their work was immersed in a commercial context that focused more on the retinal effects propelling the op art boom. NT ideas were reshaped and simplified, while the social engagement that had once been a very prominent component was ignored. Through open and interactive art, NT artists rehearsed a democratic process. The op art boom, however, turned their efforts into decorative patterns in popular culture, fashion fabrics and interior design. As fashion comes in, fashion quickly goes out.

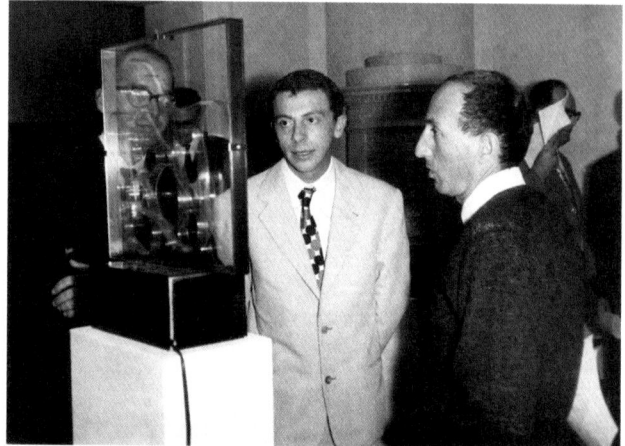

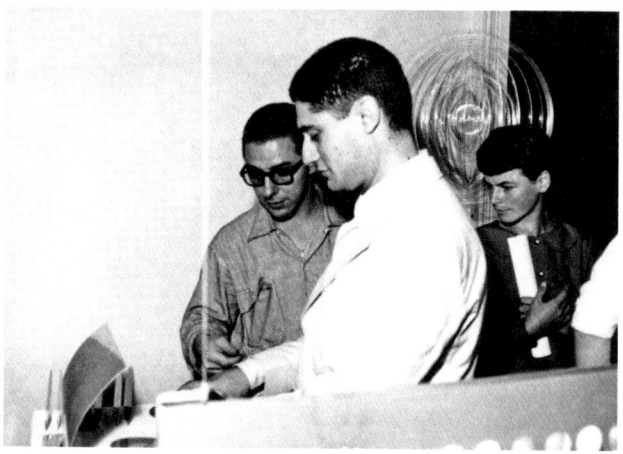

⬆ *New Tendencies 2*, exhibition view with Giovanni Anceschi and Davide Boriani with an artwork by Gianni Colombo, Gallery of Contemporary Art, Zagreb, 1963
↑ *New Tendencies 2*, exhibition view with Getulio Alviani and Eugenio Carmi with an artwork by Joël Stein, Gallery of Contemporary Art, Zagreb, 1963

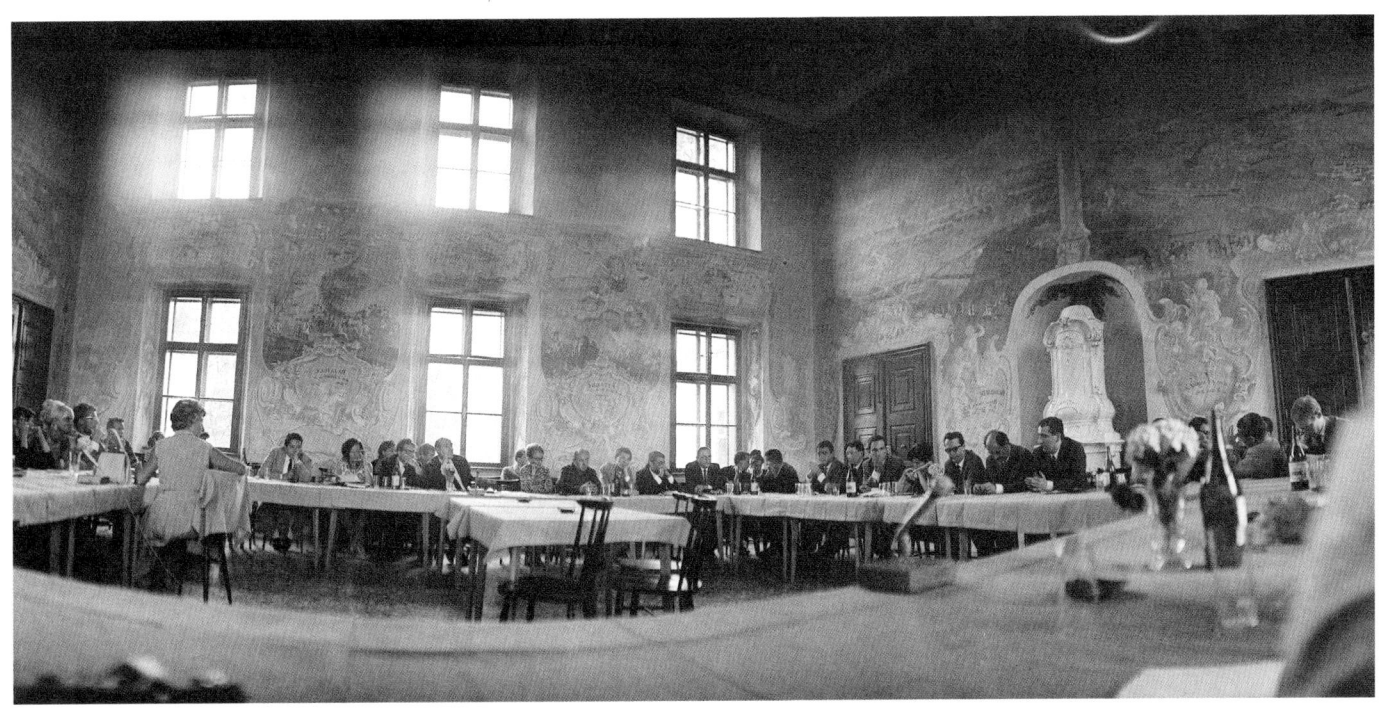

It was the time of the Cold War, which included a US cultural positioning not only toward global socialism but also toward European culture. In a 1973 *Artforum* article, the art critic Max Kozloff argued that abstract expressionism was 'a form of benevolent propaganda', in sync with the post-war political ideology of the American government via the Congress for Cultural Freedom (CCF), which the CIA helped to establish and fund.[10] In 1999, the British historian Frances Stonor Saunders published a book about the CIA and the 'cultural Cold War', in which she asserted: 'Abstract Expressionism was being deployed as a Cold War weapon ... In the manner of a Renaissance prince – except that it acted secretly – the CIA fostered and promoted American Abstract Expressionist painting around the world for more than 20 years.'[11] It was the myth of the genius individual artist that NT dared to deconstruct, preferring group work and machine-made art instead. There were no more genius artists touched by some higher intelligence and producing artworks by their hands that required worship by a passive audience. In 1964, the American artist Robert Rauschenberg was awarded the grand prize at the Venice Biennale and so began American domination of the global art scene. In the American cultural agenda, the success of pop art was to be followed by any further form of art that would exclude the social unrest and critical reflections of the arts of the 1960s. We might ask, was op art, in the shape of appropriated NT aesthetics tailored to new needs, an attempt to fill the need for a new art movement by US mainstream culture of the mid-1960s?

NT organisers reacted to this situation by making their methodologies and criteria even more rigorous. An example of the (over)rationalisation of the artistic process is found

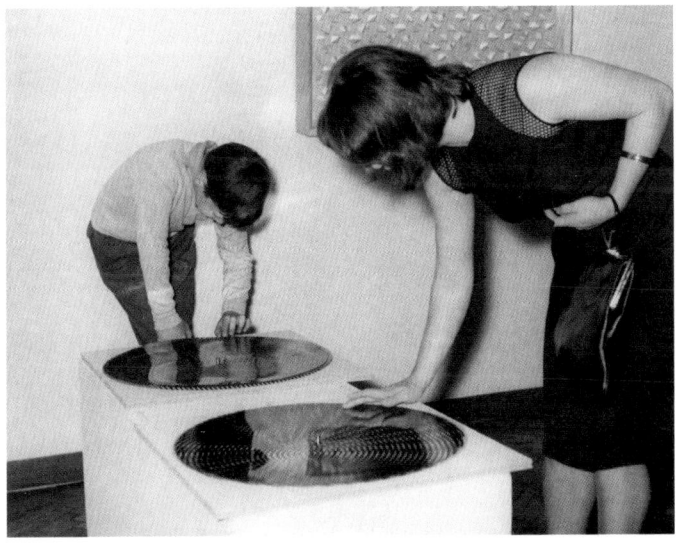

↑ Meeting at *New Tendency 3*, Brezovica, near Zagreb, 1965
↖ *New Tendency 3*, exhibition view, showing visitors interacting with works by Rudolf Kämmer, Gallery of Contemporary Art, Zagreb, 1963

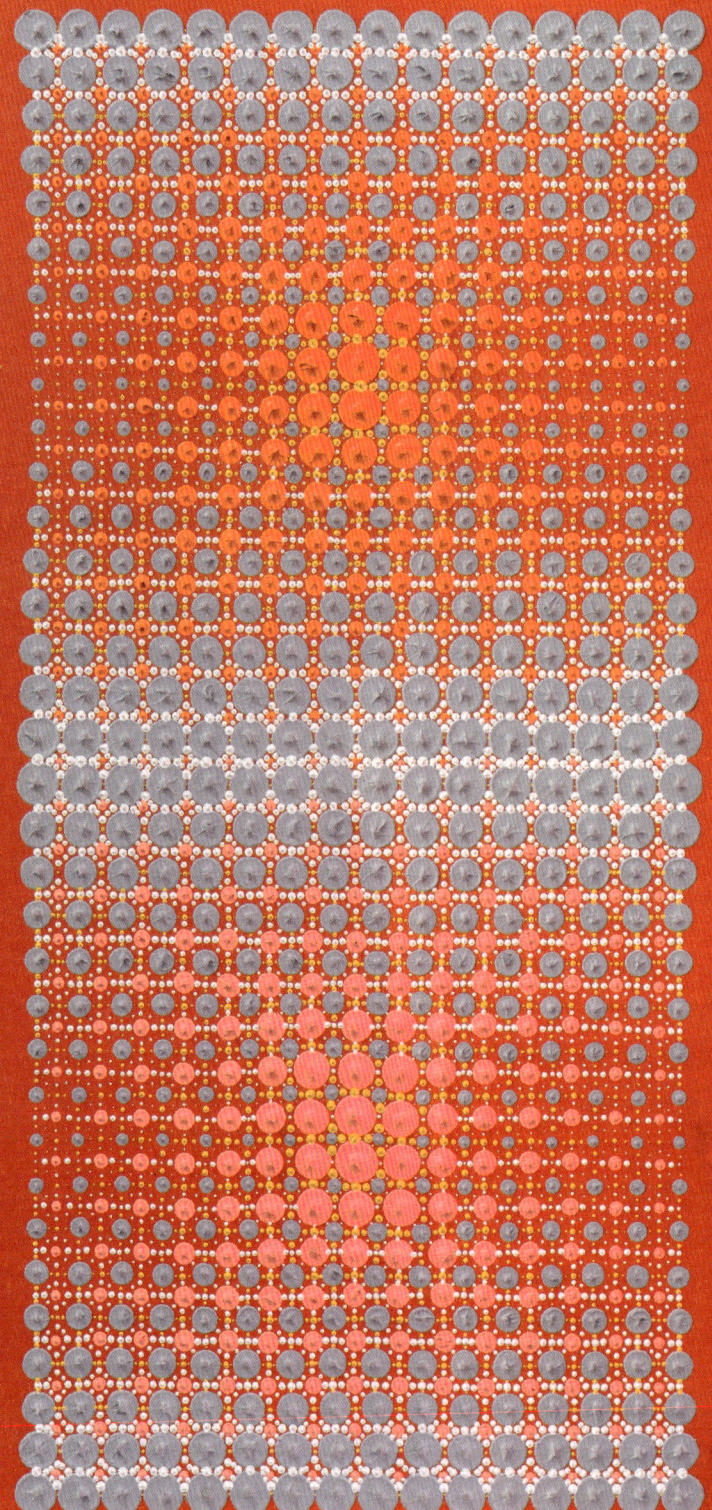

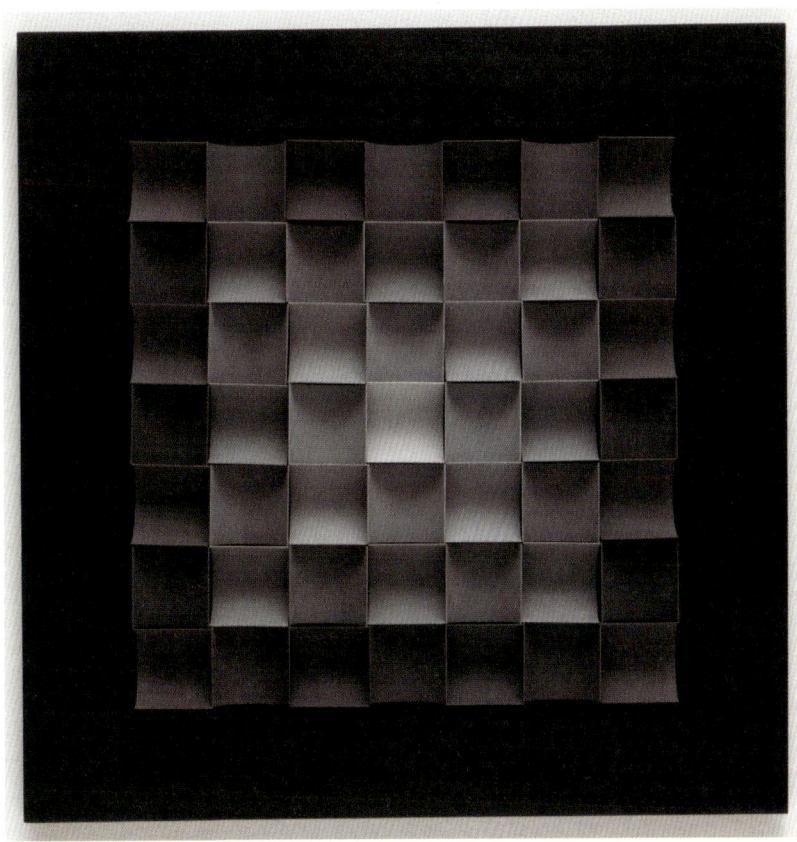

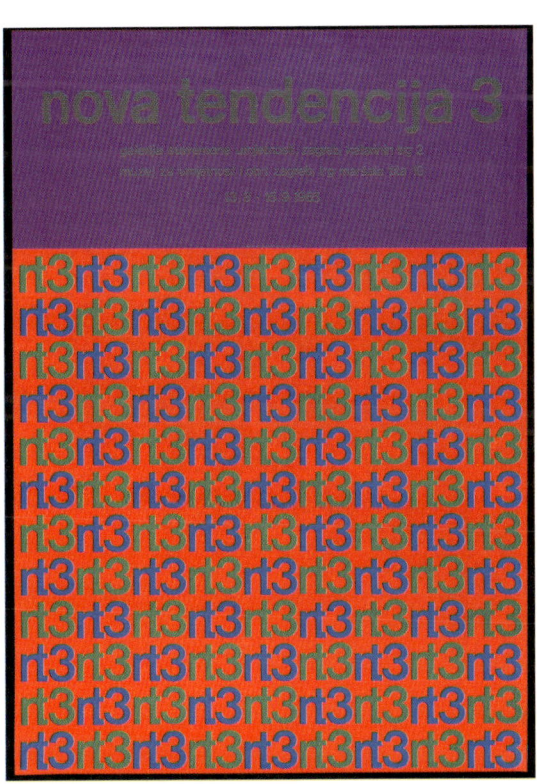

Ivan Picelj

One of the founders of New Tendencies (NT), Picelj was interested in how the perception of a work changes in relation to the movement of the viewer, and explored this idea in his geometric reliefs and graphic works. His posters for New Tendencies events gave visual expression to the experimental character of this new international movement. In the catalogue for *New Tendencies 2,* Picelj spoke of an 'active' art which should imperceptibly permeate society: 'Active art will be realised when elements it consists of become identical. Identical does not mean the same, but subjected to higher structural order ... It should direct creative forces to positive social action. It should be present everywhere. It is imperceptible. It is international and universal. It will transform our visual habits in the direction of perceiving structure, order, and wholeness in relations.' VR

← Almir Mavignier, *Grey/Pink/Orange/White/Yellow on Red Structure* 1964
↖ Ivan Picelj, poster for *New Tendency 3* 1965
↑ Ivan Picelj, *Suasum* 1965

in the *Elements of Criteria for a Systematic Categorisation of Works of the NT*, the document used to select artworks for the *New Tendency 3* exhibition of 1965. The criteria considered: the spatial, material, technical, constructive, formal and functional dispositions of a work. Every disposition was divided into several sub-groups: for example, the constructive dispositions were static, variable, kinetic, mechanised, motorised and repeatable; the formal were composed, structured, fortuitous, monophase-structured, progressively structured and continually programmed. At a meeting of NT members and participants, French theorist Abraham Moles initiated a debate on the relationship between cybernetics, information theory and art that would profoundly change the course of the NT movement.

Computers and visual research

In August 1968, two exhibitions opened just one day apart: *Cybernetic Serendipity* in London, and *Computers and Visual Research* in Zagreb. The latter was the beginning of the series of events organised under the title of *Tendencies 4* and spanning a year, up to August 1969.[12] By 1968 the political situation in the world had been changing radically for several years, as was reflected in art, particularly the kind that considered its role to be emphatically societal. At the 1968 colloquy, Matko Meštrović commented on the current state of affairs in NT:

> During the years after the first, second and third tendencies in Zagreb it became clear that the consistency of the movement would not be kept up, but it was not clear where the real reasons for the impossibility of

its internal coherence lay. These reasons lay in social resistance to ideational radicalisation, and as for science, which was itself alienated and manipulated, there were no real connections with it. It was also not clear that engagement at the level of the idea also had to be political engagement.'[13]

At the same colloquy, artist of the first NT grouping Alberto Biasi got into a fierce discussion with digital artist Frieder Nake about the political situation in 1968, the student protests and the artist's social commitment. Regarding digital art, the leading discourse was the information aesthetic theory of Max Bense and Abraham Moles. Using the same methodology, the new visual research with computers could now be analysed according to the same principles as that from the previous NT phase, and it seemed that the aesthetic value of these works could now even be scientifically measured, using the methodologies of information aesthetics. At the exhibitions and symposiums, the works and ideas of leading figures in digital art from around the world were gathered together, including the authors of the earliest digital graphics: Frieder Nake, Georg Nees, A. Michael Noll and Hiroshi Kawano. Digital images by Ken Knowlton, Leon Harmon and Manfred Schroeder investigated visual perception in photo-image resolution, using pictograms rather than the ASCII standard coding signs used in teleprinters (this was the beginning of prints of digitalised photo images). Computer films showed morphing animation in Charles Csuri's *Hummingbird* and a computer-generated ballet by Noll. Vladimir Bonačić put up a 36-metre-long, computer-generated light installation

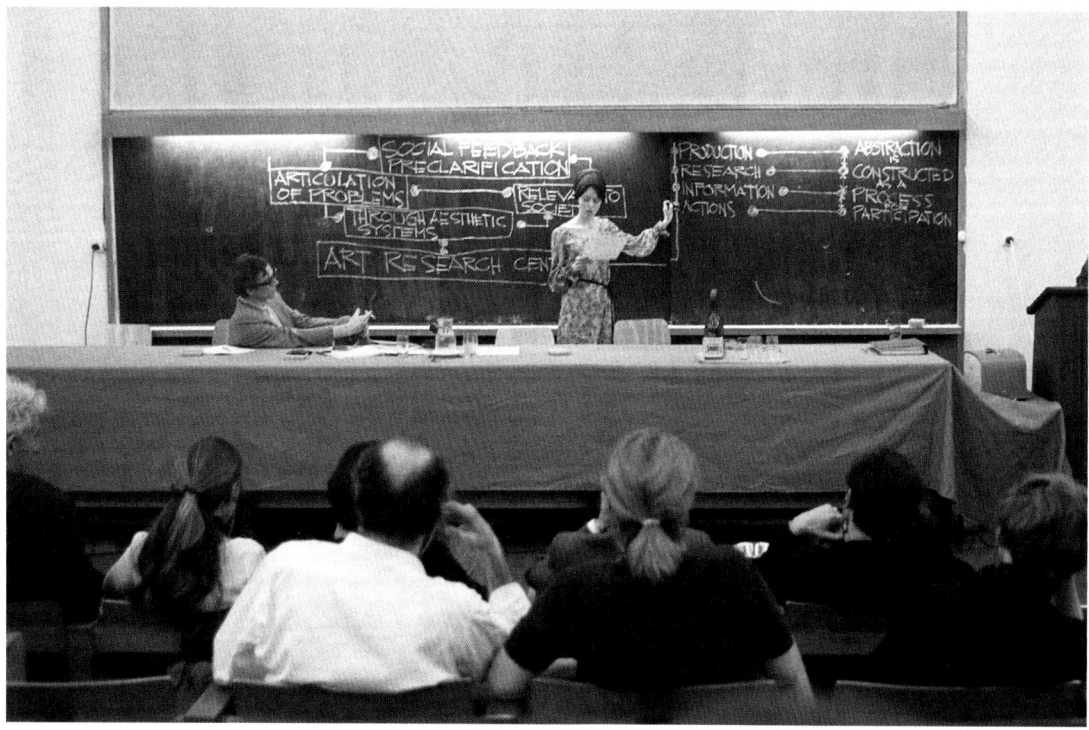

↑ Nancy A. Stephens of ARC (Art Research Center) speaking at the *Computers and Visual Research symposium, Tendencies 4*, Moša Pijade Workers' University, Zagreb, 1969

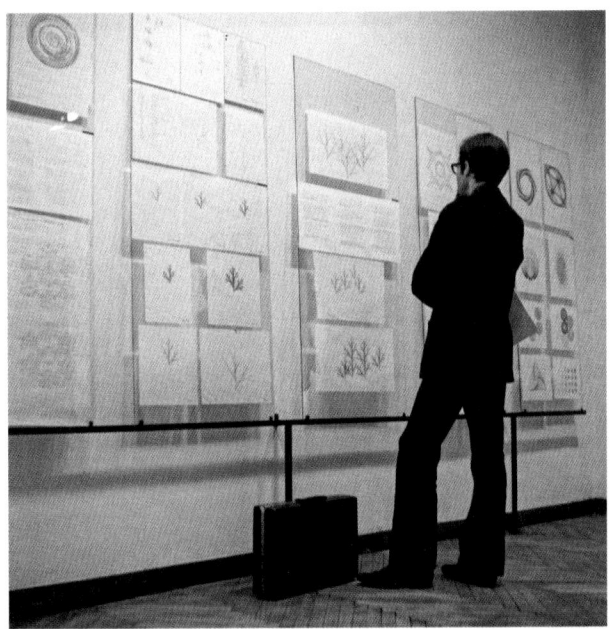

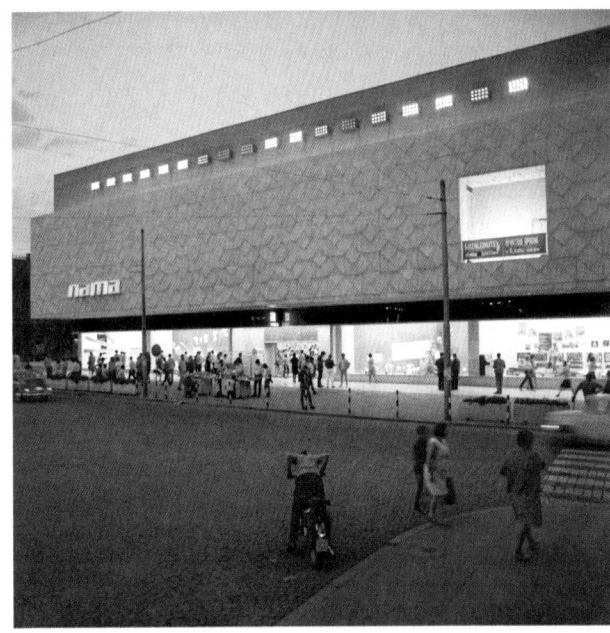

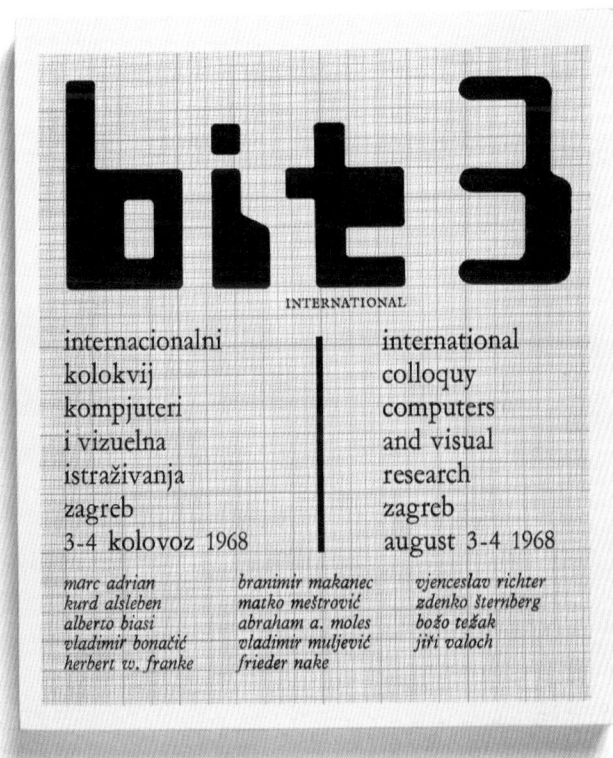

in a public space in Zagreb. The curators established a direct link between concrete and digital art; one of the curators, Radoslav Putar, described it as follows:

> *Even before the 1960s, Karl Gerstner had spoken about the programming of procedures; he mentioned the routine procedures of encoding the elements of the image. Uli Pohl while NT2 was on spoke of the anonymity and exclusion of subjectivity; all spoke about the ending of the importance of one-off or unrepeatable creative acts of an individual genius; they spoke of collective work of a team that would make examples of the visualisation of plastic ideas; many members of NT endeavoured in this work to give the habitus of the machine, or else founded their procedures on the application of mechanical or electrical devices; they all dreamed machines and now the machines were here. And machines had arrived from directions that were a bit unexpected, they were accompanied by people who were neither sculptors nor painters.*[14]

Artist Enzo Mari underlined that, even before the advent of the computer, the application of 'programs' was already characteristic of the work of a number of NT researchers.[15] At a symposium, art critic Jonathan Benthall read out the *Zagreb Manifesto*, which he had written with cyberneticist Gordon Hyde and artist Gustav Metzger from the

✽ *Computers and Visual Research, Tendencies 4*, Gallery of Contemporary Art, Zagreb, 1969: Jonathan Benthall in front of the works of Petar Milojević
↑ Cover of *Bit International* no.3 (1968) published by the Gallery of Contemporary Art Zagreb

↑ Vladimir Bonačić, *DIN. PR 18 – 15* (NaMa I), 1969, computer-controlled dynamic object / light installation in the storefront of NaMa in Kvaternikov Square, Zagreb, part of the *Tendencies 4* exhibition

Computer Arts Society (CAS) in London. The conclusion of the *Zagreb Manifesto* was richly imbued with ideas that are arguably still current:

> Artists are increasingly striving to relate their work and that of the technologists to the current unprecedented crisis in society. Some artists are responding by utilising their experience of science and technology to try and resolve urgent social problems. Others, researching in cybernetics and the neuro-sciences, are exploring new ideas about the interaction of the human being with the environment. Others again are identifying their work with a concept of ecology which includes the entire technological environment that man has imposed on nature. There are creative people in science who feel that the man/machine problem lies at the heart of making the computer the servant of man and nature. Such people welcome the insight of the artist in this context, lest we lose sight of humanity and beauty.[16]

Metzger presented a mock-up of his own artwork – a self-destructing computer-generated sculpture titled *Five Screens with Computer*, imagined for public space and relying on interaction with the public.[17] This was one of the rare moments in the 1960s when one socially engaged international network of digital art was in fertile communication with another.[18]

The use of computers in the context of visual and artistic research expanded the understanding of the idea of 'the program' in art, as something that, from now on, could be found in the software itself: the computer program. Flow chart diagrams and computer code became integral components of artists' applications for the 1969 exhibition *Computers and Visual Research*. Documents concerning the working process were published in exhibition catalogues and in the periodical *Bit International* (which published nine issues between 1968 and 1972). For example, Robert Mallary's paper 'TRAN 2 - a Computer Graphics Program to Generate Sculpture', presented at the 1969 symposium, was later published bilingually in the magazine.[19] New participants, scientists from universities, private corporations and public organisations unintentionally radicalised certain notions in 1960s arts, such as the central position of 'idea', 'structure' and 'concept'. The viewpoint of Brazilian artist Waldemar Cordeiro, an active participant in NT events – that computer art had taken the place of constructivism – can thus be observed in action throughout the history of NT.[20]

Programs and Conceptual Art

The 1973 exhibition *Tendencies 5* consisted of three parts: 'constructive visual research', 'computers and visual research' and 'conceptual art'. The accompanying symposium *Rational and Irrational in Visual Research Today* was also an Association Internationale des Critiques d'Art (AICA) congress. In the conceptual art section, Sol LeWitt exhibited a *Wall Picture*, created by the hanging

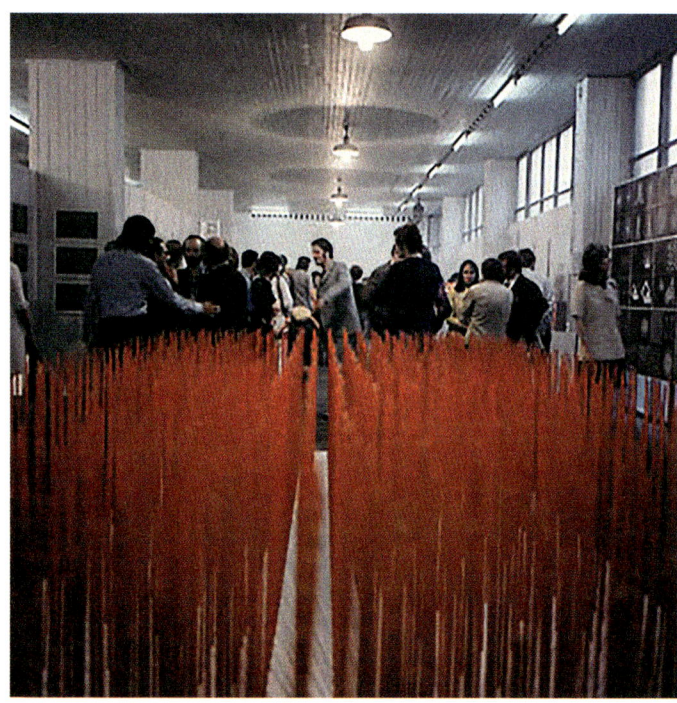

team according to textual instructions summed up in one sentence; we can look at this as another kind of programming, an algorithm of descriptive geometry expressed in writing.[21] In the section 'computers and visual research', a new generation of digital artists presented their works. They included the Groupe art et informatique de Vincennes from France, the Computation Centre of Madrid University, Spain, and the Centro de Arte y Comunicación from Argentina.

NT organisers attempted to link up various artistic practices via the understanding of the concept of programme in the context of artistic work.[22] Radoslav Putar used the phrase 'data processing' to describe the methods of conceptual art.[23] Frieder Nake remarked on the similarity between digital and conceptual art at the level of 'separation of head and hand', while being critical of this production structure as following the logic of capitalism.[24] Boris Kelemen emphasised the importance of constructive and computer visual research, while the papers of Nena Dimitrijević and Marijan Susovski put forward positively inclined theses about conceptual art through the promotion of non-object-based, non-material art and the non-visual.[25] The notion of programs in art binds all three kinds of art as well as the point that the artwork is not necessarily executed by the hand of the artist, but rather by a machine or another person.

↗ *Tendencies 5*, exhibition opening, 1973, Museum of Technologies, Zagreb, with a work by Jesús Rafael Soto in the foreground

The event *Tendencies 6* was planned for years, but ultimately never held in its entirety; only the symposium *art and society* was eventually held, in 1978, with four themes: 'Culture and the changes in contemporary societies', 'The human environment', 'Creativity and the personality' and 'Media and action'. Taking part in the symposium were representatives of all three phases of NT artists. We can pick out Hans Haacke, who had himself in his early work used system theories, and only afterwards the methods of conceptual art. The organisers' idea of re-examining social problems was still very much in evidence. Artistic practices and the cultural and political trends of the time erred heavily on the side of conceptual art, asserting what are still the dominant canons of contemporary art – canons in need of reconsideration, especially in light of recent and inextricably connected developments in technology and society.[26]

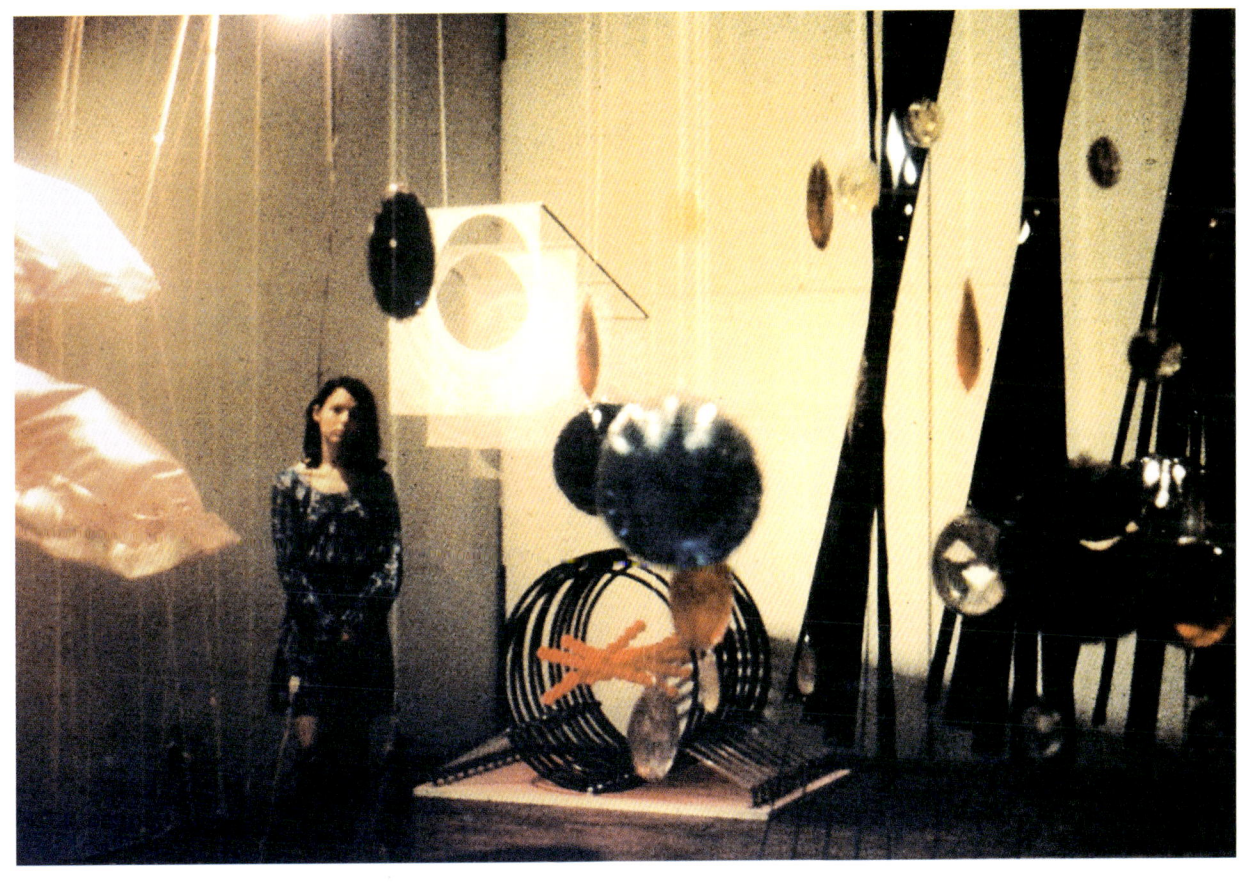

↑ *Tendencies 4*, Museum of Arts and Crafts, Zagreb, 1969, including works by the Art Research Center (T.M. Stephens, N.A. Stephens, P.J. van Voorst, John Abbick, J.B. Thogmartin)

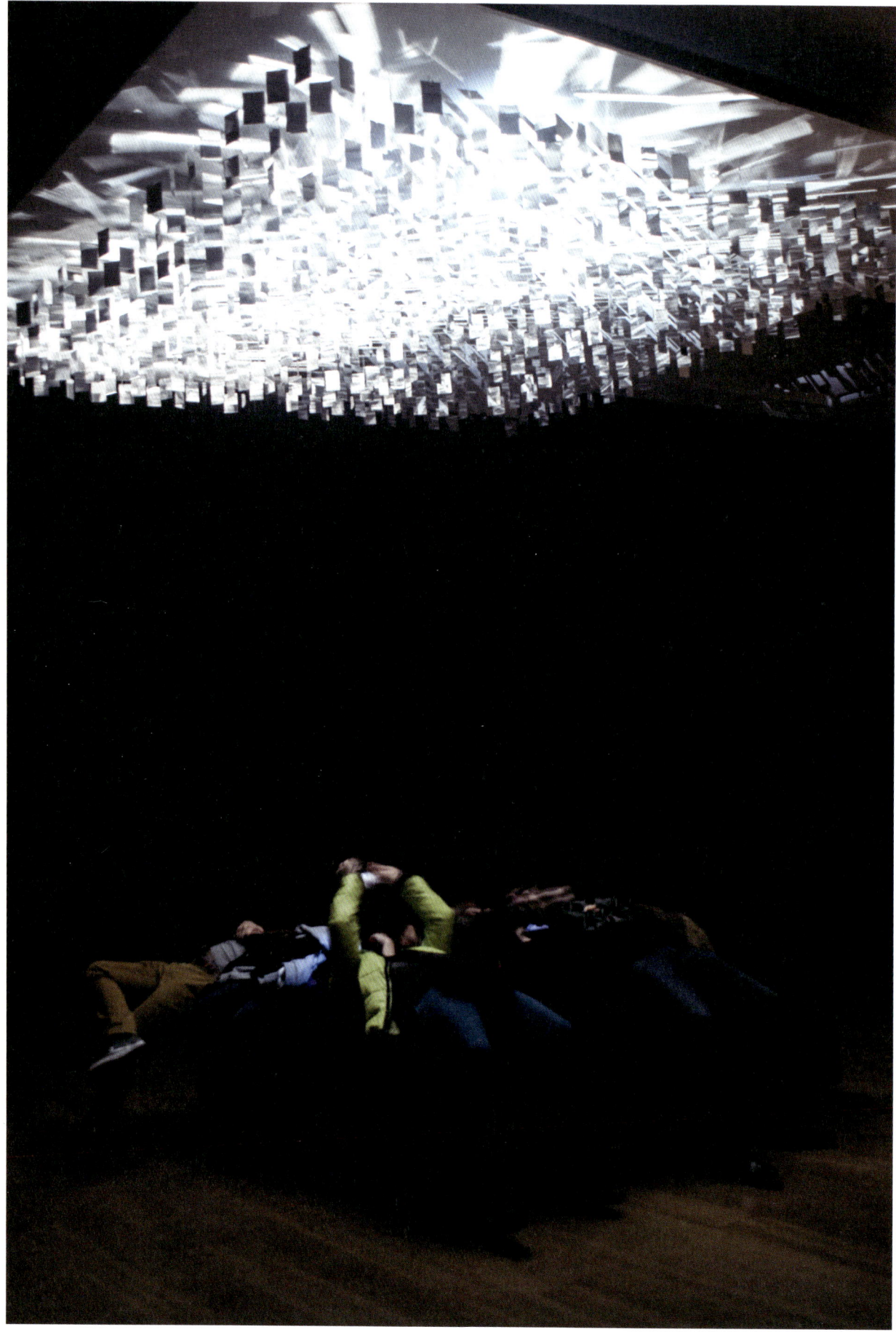

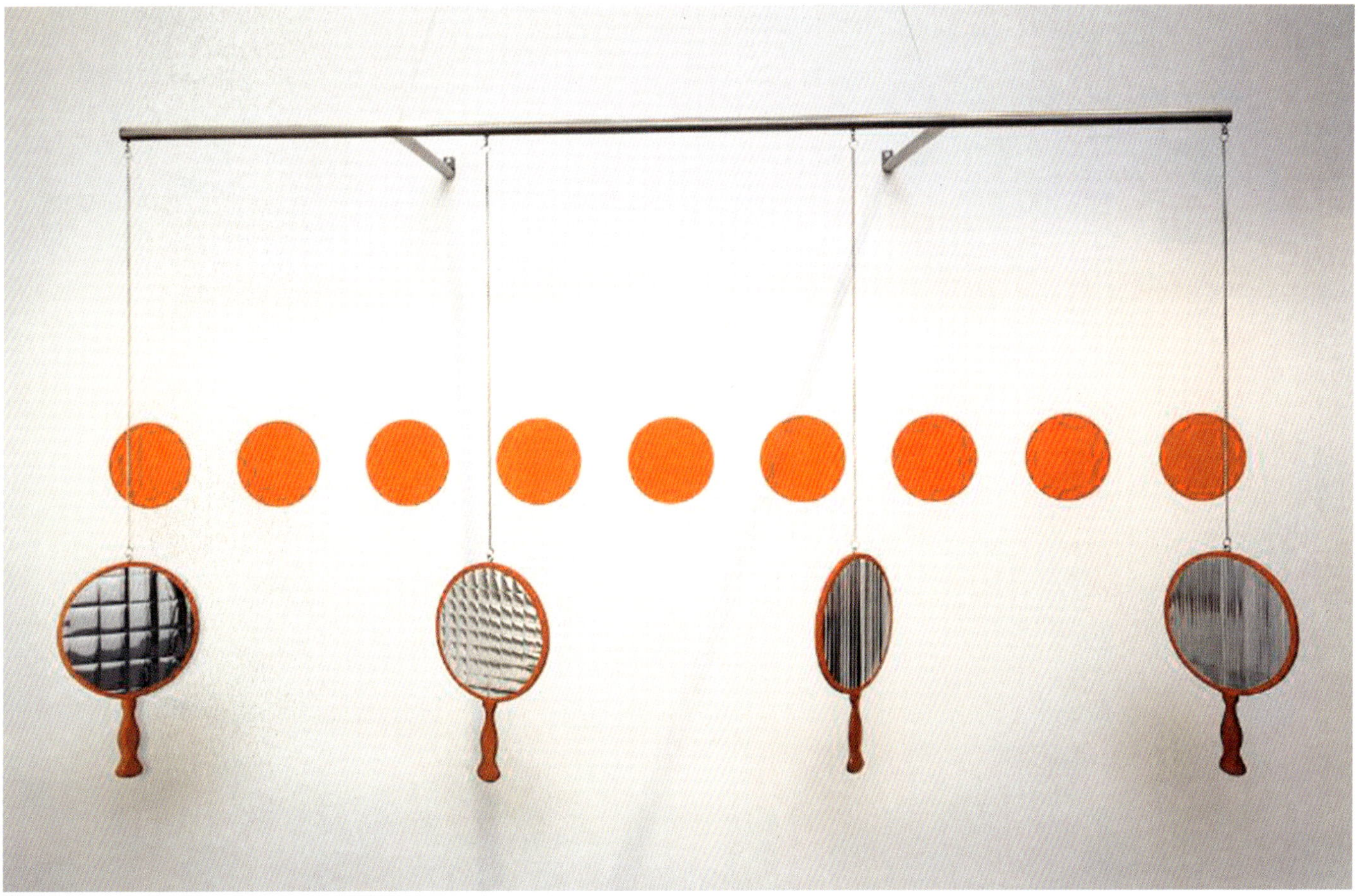

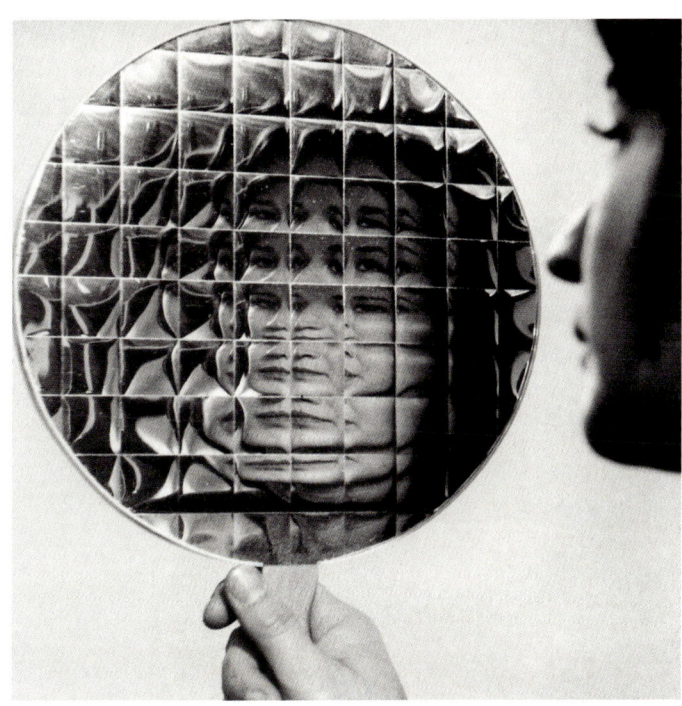

Julio Le Parc

Argentinian artist Julio Le Parc moved to Paris in 1958, and in 1960 he became a founding member of the Groupe de Recherche d'Art Visuel (GRAV). In the same year, he made his first reliefs and *Continual Mobiles*. In writings and interviews from the period, Le Parc expressed his desire to move away from the 'absolute' or 'definitive' artwork and to engage more fully with ideas of 'movement', 'indeterminacy' and 'unpredictability'. Le Parc was determined to expand the role of the spectator in the works and consider how external contingencies such as the space of the gallery and the ability of the viewer to interact with the artwork impact its meaning. He often used reflecting surfaces in his works, both to create dynamic light effects and to make viewers aware of their presence in the same environment as the works. Le Parc paricipated in four editions of the New Tendencies exhibitions in Zagreb, both as a member of GRAV and as an individual artist. VR

← Julio Le Parc, *Continuous Light on Ceiling* 1963/1996
↑ Julio Le Parc, *Four Double Mirrors* 1966
↖ Julio Le Parc, *Double Mirrors* 1966

Martha Boto

Martha Boto, a pioneer of kinetic art, was one of the first artists in Argentina to incorporate movement into her work. In 1956 she joined the concrete art group Arte Nuevo, co-founding Artistas No Figurativos Argentinos (the Non-Figurative Artists of Argentina) the following year. In 1959 she moved to Paris and cemented her position as a kinetic artist, taking part in the Biennale de Paris. Initially working in geometric abstraction, Boto began to investigate space and movement in her work, experimenting with materials which could absorb and reflect light, such as acrylic plastic, aluminium and stainless steel. In Paris she also began to work with electric motors in her sculptures, as in *Helicoidal Chromokinetics* 1968. Through their repetitive movements and their simple yet striking play with light, Boto's works seek to elicit emotional and psychological reactions such as joy or tension in the viewer. OW

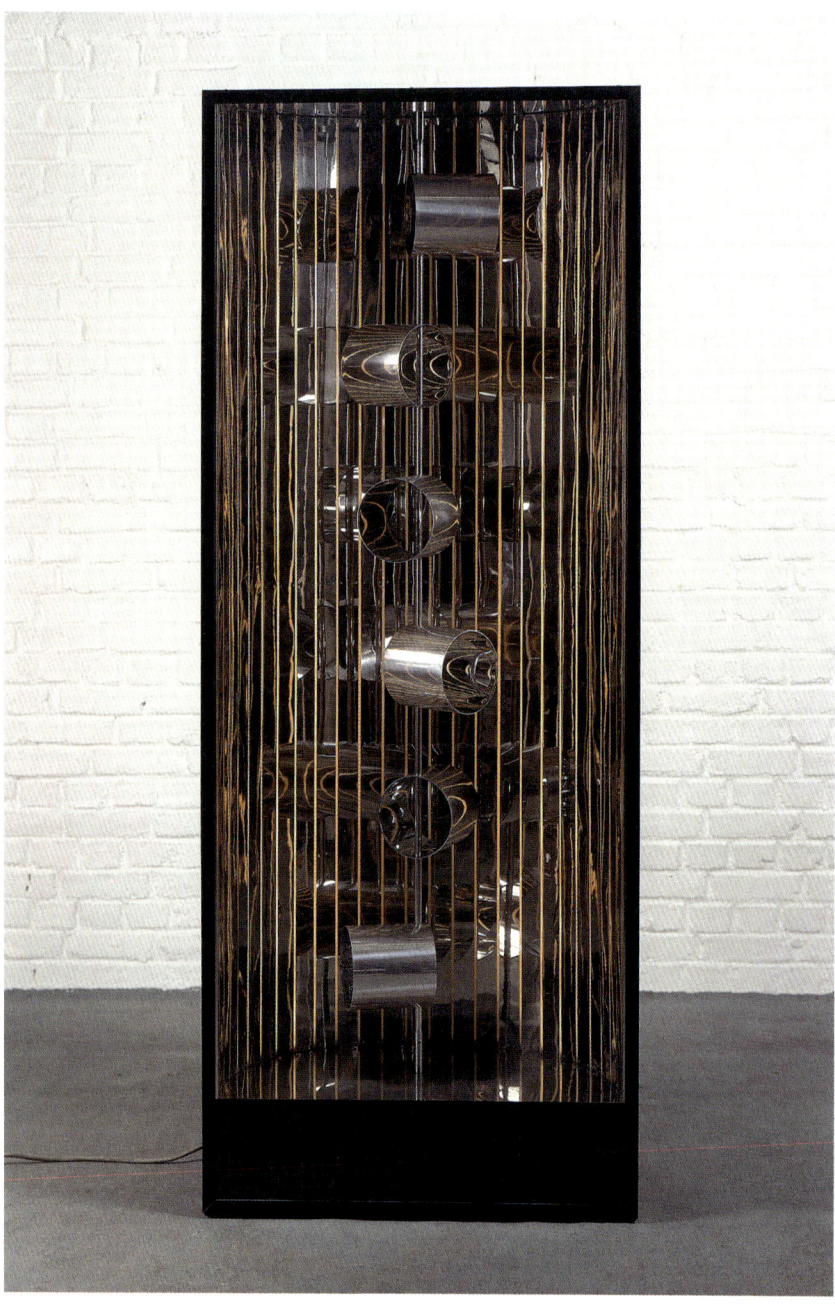

♠ Martha Boto, *Helicoidal Chromokinetics* 1968

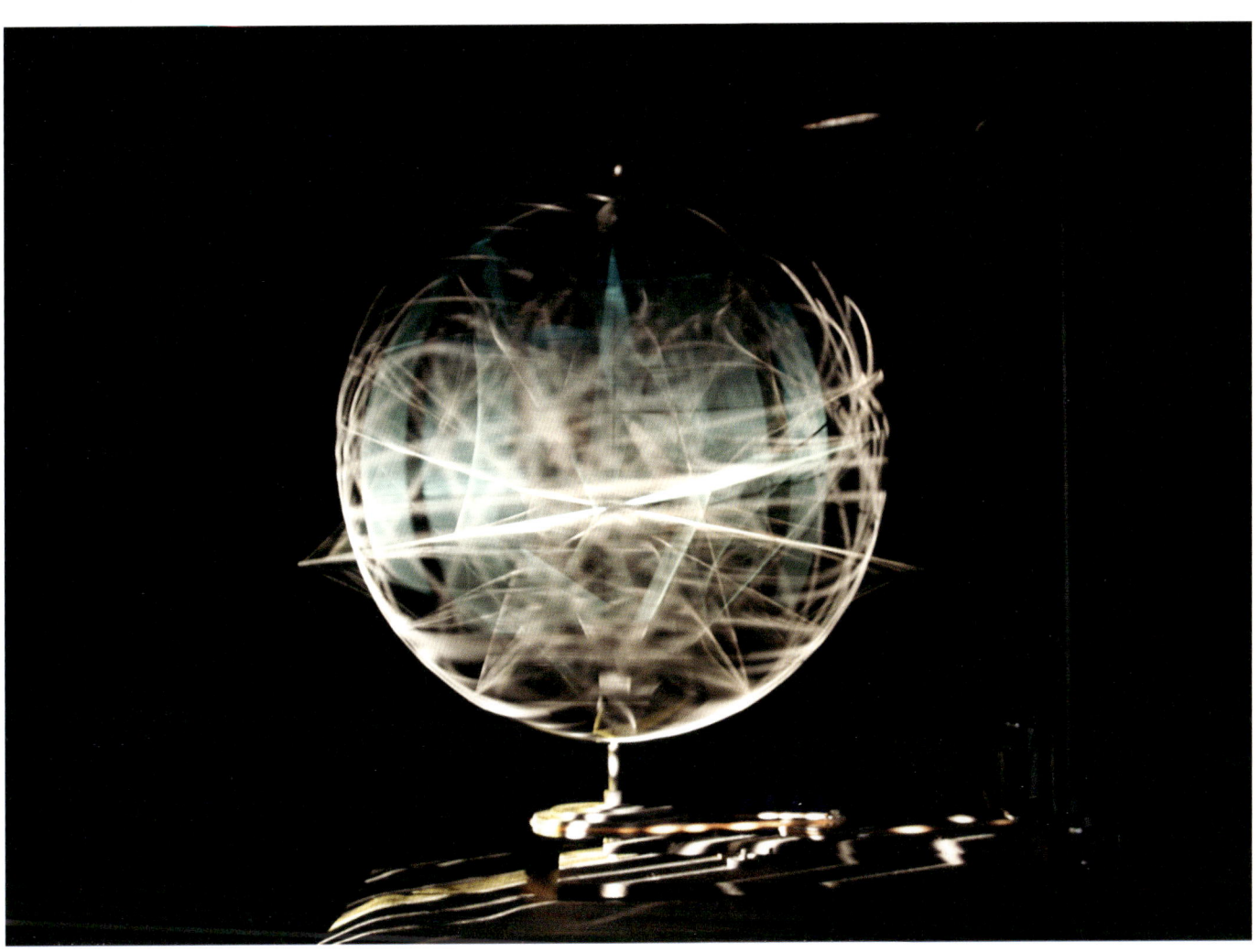

Aleksandar Srnec

Srnec, a prominent Zagreb-based member of the New Tendencies (NT) movement, created *Luminoplastic 1* in 1965–7; it was the first in a series of kinetic artworks featuring light, and probably the first such in Croatian art. The work uses electric motors from sewing machines and, originally, 35mm slides projecting colourful abstract shapes on rotating forms made of thin metal wire. Displayed inside a black box that conceals the projector, the effect is ghostly: lines hover and mutate as they catch the light in unpredictable and ever-shifting patterns. Srnec had been a member of the EXAT 51 group, active in Zagreb in the early 1950s, which proposed experimental approaches to art, inspired by historical precedents of geometric abstraction such as Russian constructivism, De Stijl and Bauhaus. Many of EXAT 51's members would later participate in the activities of New Tendencies and shape the debates of its earlier years. VR

↑ Aleksandar Srnec, *Luminoplastic 1* 1965–7

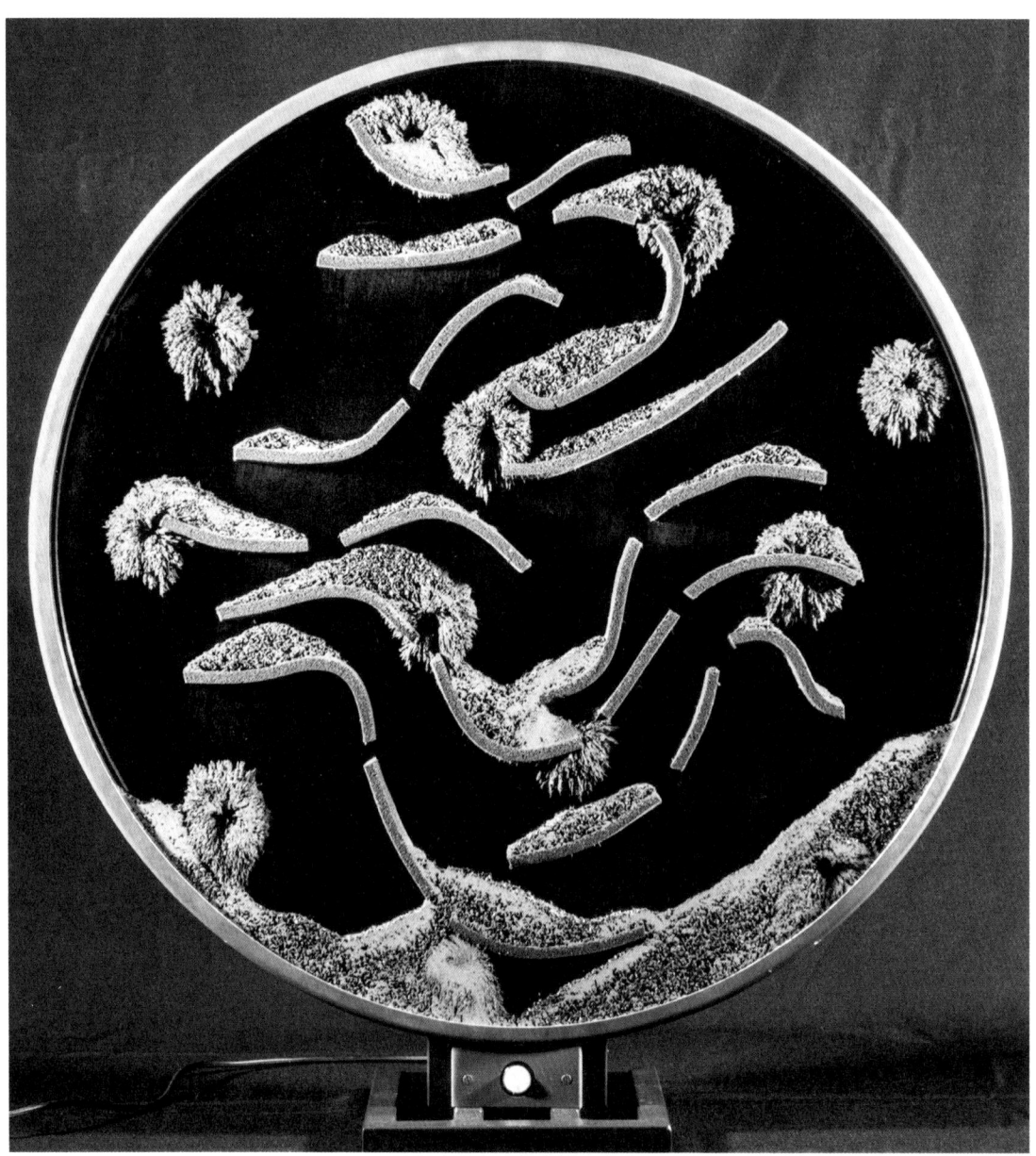

Davide Boriani

In 1959, Boriani became one of the founding members of Gruppo T – an avant-garde collective formed in Milan, working with the effects of spatial and temporal variation on material, surface and colour. Their work emphasised research, novel methods and interventions by the audience, and in 1962 Gruppo T became active members of the New Tendencies movement. For *Magnetic Surface*, Boriani enclosed iron shavings within a circular acrylic plastic and aluminium container. Driven by a motor, magnets move in circles behind the container and pull the metal shavings into shifting and unpredictable configurations. Boriani was particularly interested in the sensorial and temporal experience of an artwork and contributed to discourses on the role of variations (such as repetitions, patterns and frequencies) in aesthetic perception. BP

↑ Davide Boriani, *Magnetic Surface* 1965

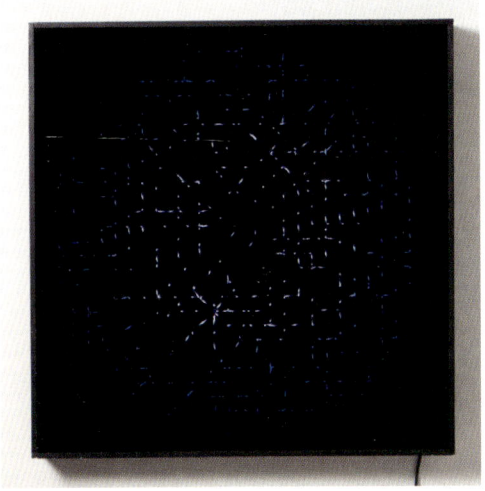

Grazia Varisco

Grazia Varisco joined Gruppo T in Milan in 1960 and participated in shows such as the *Miriorama* series in Italy (1960–3), *Arte Programmata* (Milan, 1962) and *Nove Tendencije* (Zagreb, 1963). Varisco's works explored the concepts of time, interactivity and perception. Through simple geometric lines and overlapping forms, often using materials with dynamic physical properties, such as magnets, mercury and patterned glass, she experimented with the illusion of movement, depth and space. In the series of works titled *Schema Luminoso Variabile* 1961–8 she showcases her interest in combining light and movement to generate constantly changing visual phenomena. Powered by motors, these works create illusory and kaleidoscopic shapes by alternating light and dark in rhythmic patterns that appear to contract and change the speed of their movement. OW

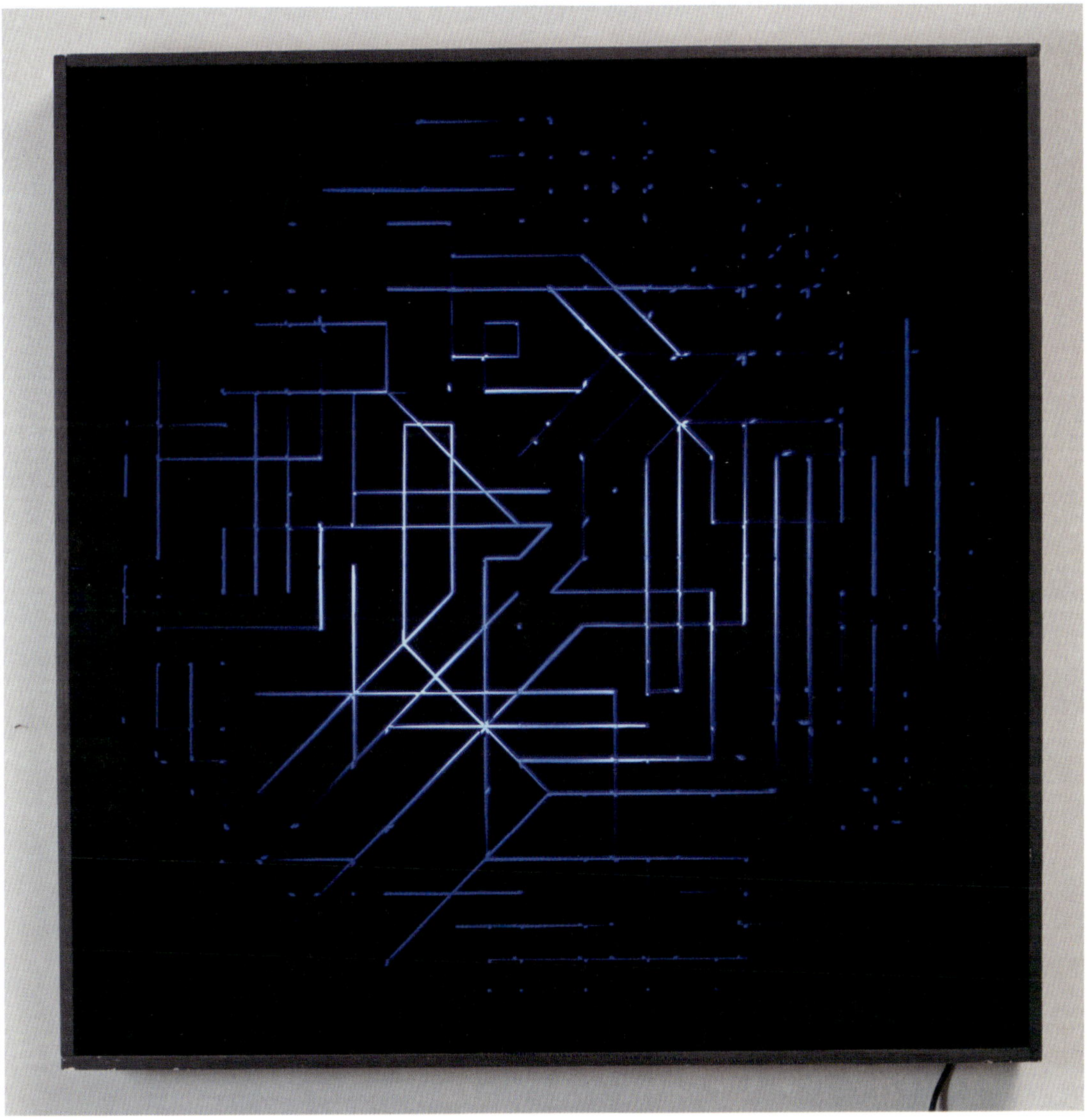

↖↑ Grazia Varisco, *Variable Light Scheme R. VOD LAB* 1964

Alberto Biasi

In *Light Prisms. Spectral Kinetic Mesh*, dancing beams of coloured light are created with prisms and mirrors, making use of reflection and refraction, two of the basic laws of optics. White light, originating from two bulbs, travels through four motorised transparent prisms, where it is dispersed into coloured beams through refraction. The prisms rotate, causing the beams to constantly shift, while mirrors multiply the beams through reflection. Centring light and movement within his practice, Biasi was one of Italy's leading kinetic artists. He was a co-founder of Gruppo N, associated with the New Tendencies movement, and was an instigator of Arte Programmata. He participated in every edition of the New Tendencies Zagreb exhibitions up until *Tendencies 4* in 1968–9.KW

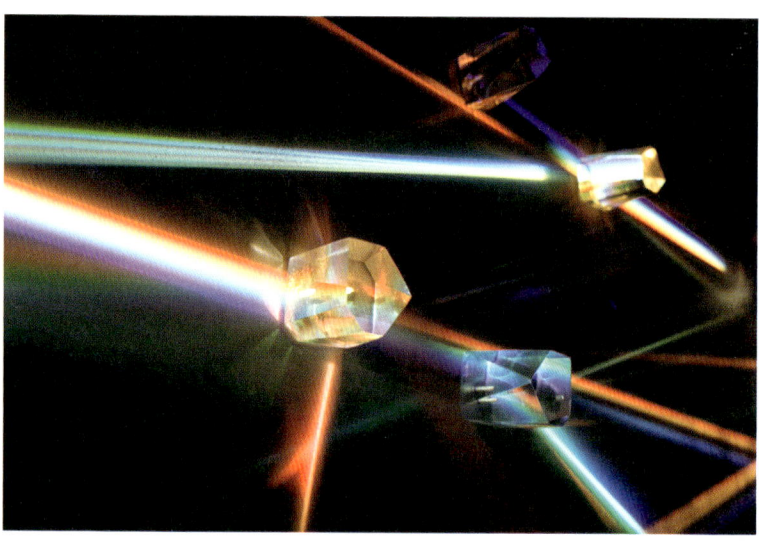

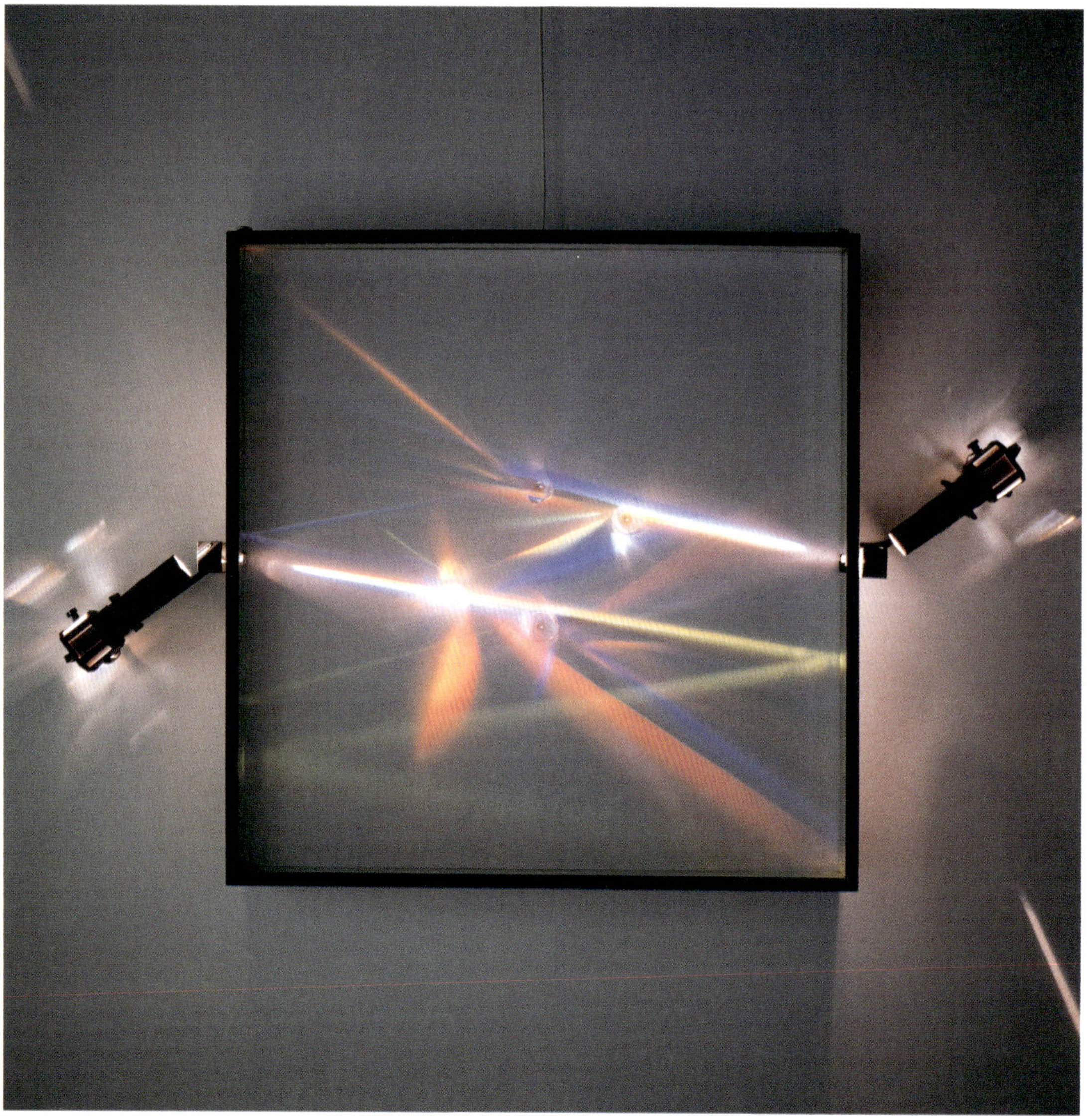

↑ Alberto Biasi, *Light Prisms. Spectral Kinetic Mesh* 1966
(↗ detail)

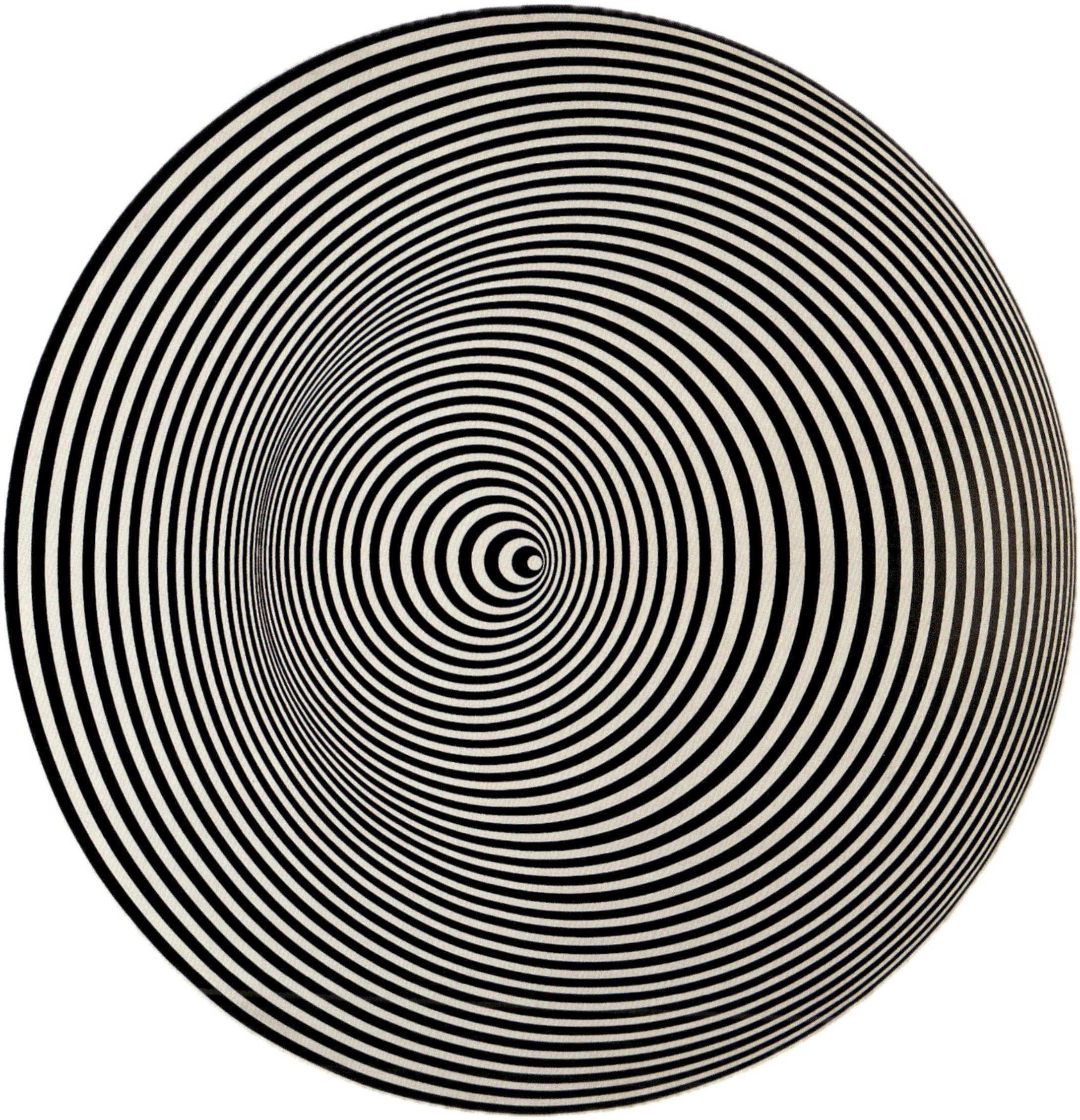

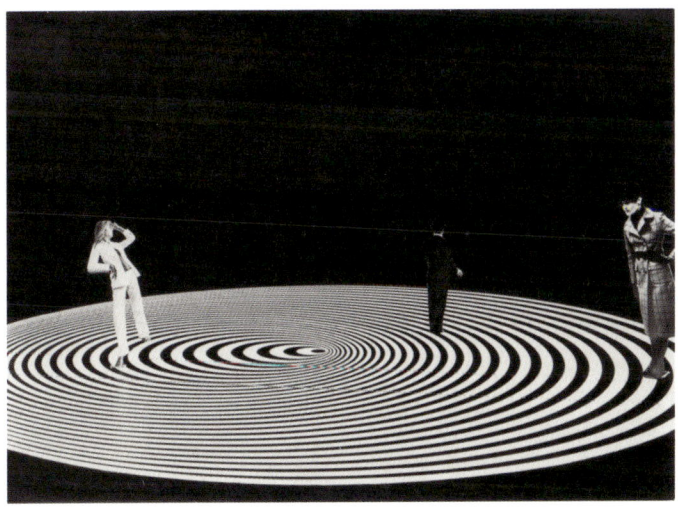

Marina Apollonio

Apollonio began her investigations into geometric abstraction and the nature of human vision in the early 1960s. Her works often derive from mathematical sequences of concentric circles and other simple shapes, inspired by the Gestalt theories of visual perception that form a common reference point for artists associated with the Italian Arte Programmata movement, among others. In her *Circular Dynamics* series, spinning patterned disks create the illusion of depth and elliptical oscillation. Apollonio was close to Italian Arte Programmata collectives like Gruppo N from Padua and Gruppo T from Milan, and artists such as Piero Manzoni and Dadamaino; she also participated in the activities of the international New Tendencies movement, showing work at *New Tendency 3* (1965) and *Tendencies 4* (1968) in Zagreb. VR

↑ Marina Apollonio, *Circular Dynamics 6S+S II* 1968–70
↖ Marina Apollonio, collaged design for *Kinetic Activation Space* 1967–71

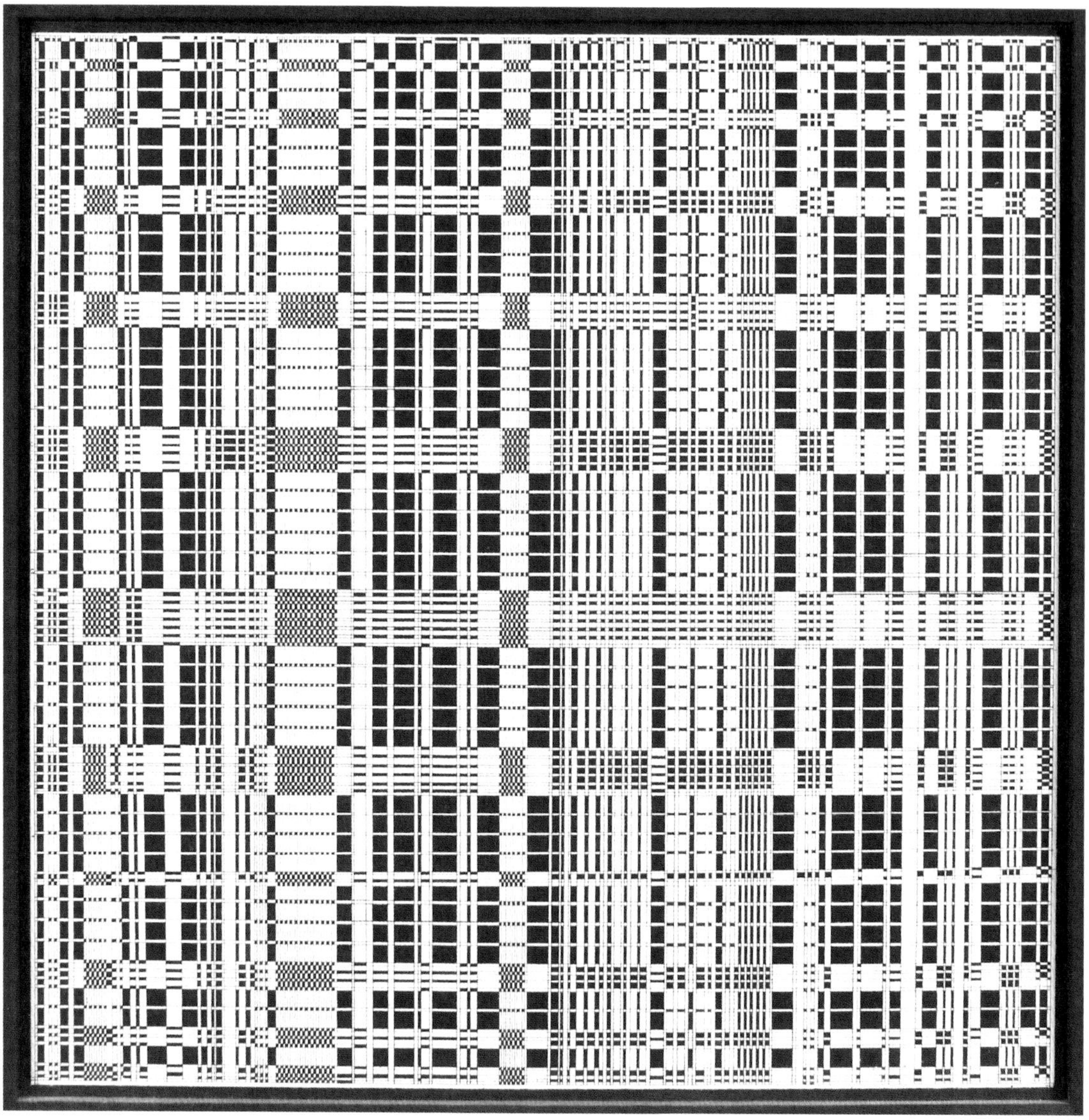

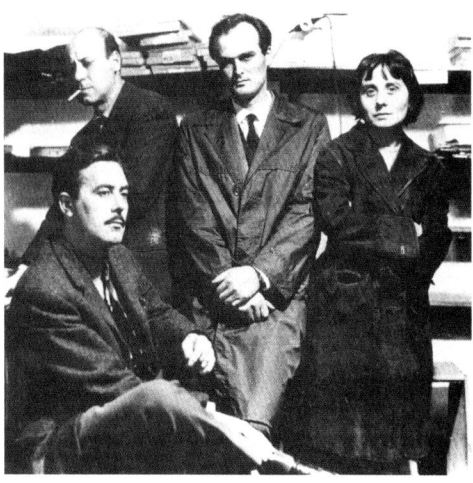

Lucia Di Luciano

Di Luciano considers her work a continuous process of 'visual research', begun in the early 1960s when she started drawing and painting patterns derived from mathematical principles. She played an active role in the Italian Arte Programmata movement, co-founding the artist groups Gruppo 63 in 1963 and Operativo R in 1964. The black and white paintings she produced during this period, such as *Discontinuous Structural Articulation* 1964, feature sequences of thin lines and thicker rectangles, which form banded motifs as horizontal rows and vertical columns intersect. While the mathematical rules governing the work are always predetermined by the artist, some follow a strict computational logic while others introduce random 'discontinuous' numerical shifts. Gradually, Di Luciano also added lone colours and symbols to her compositions, and in the 1970s expanded her palette to the full colour spectrum. VR

↟ Lucia Di Luciano, *Discontinuous Structural Articulation* 1964
↑ Left to right: Carlo Carchietti, Franco Di Vito, Giovanni Pizzo and Lucia Di Luciano, of Gruppo Operativo R, 1964

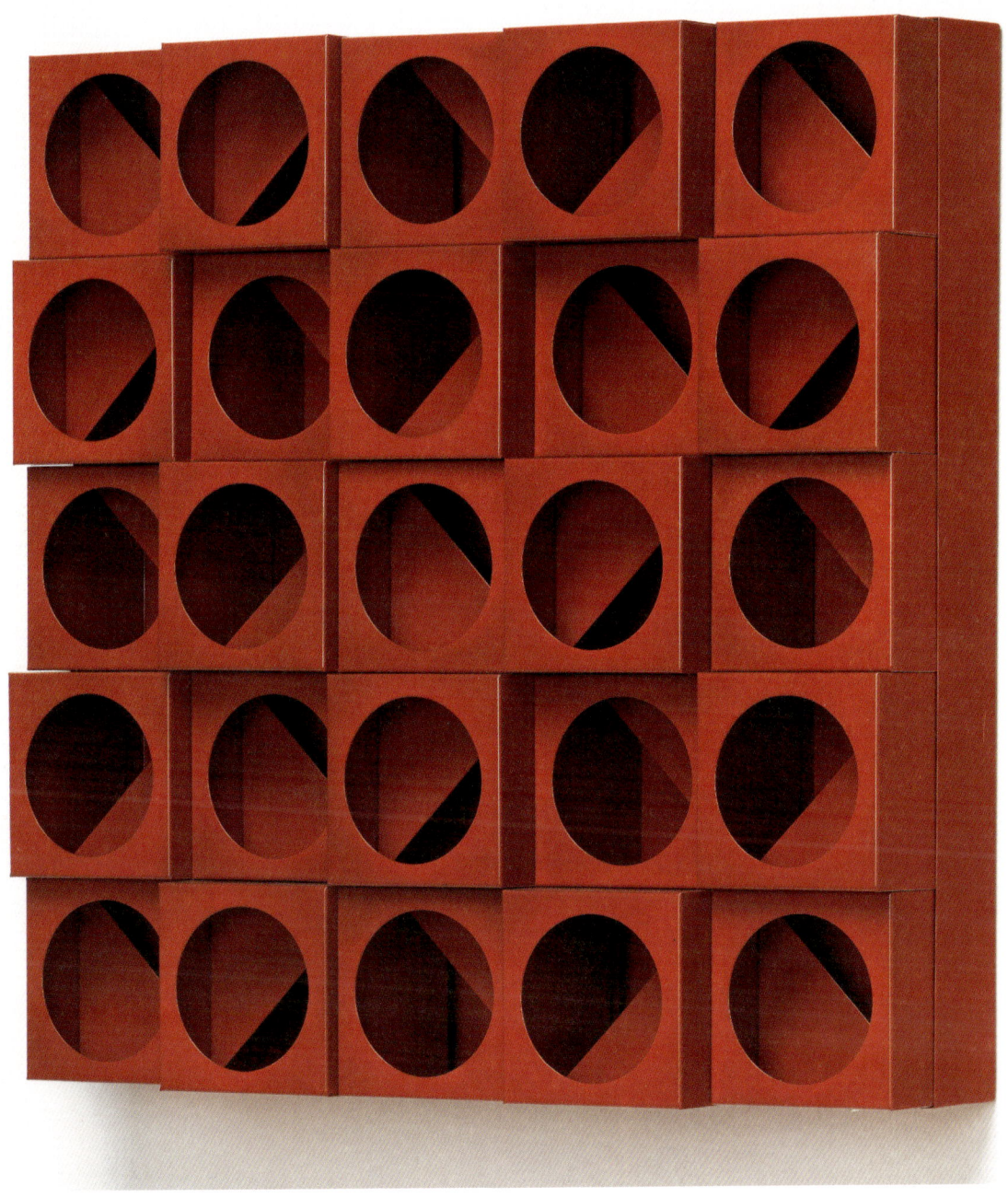

↑ Paolo Scheggi, *Inter-ena-cubo* 1970

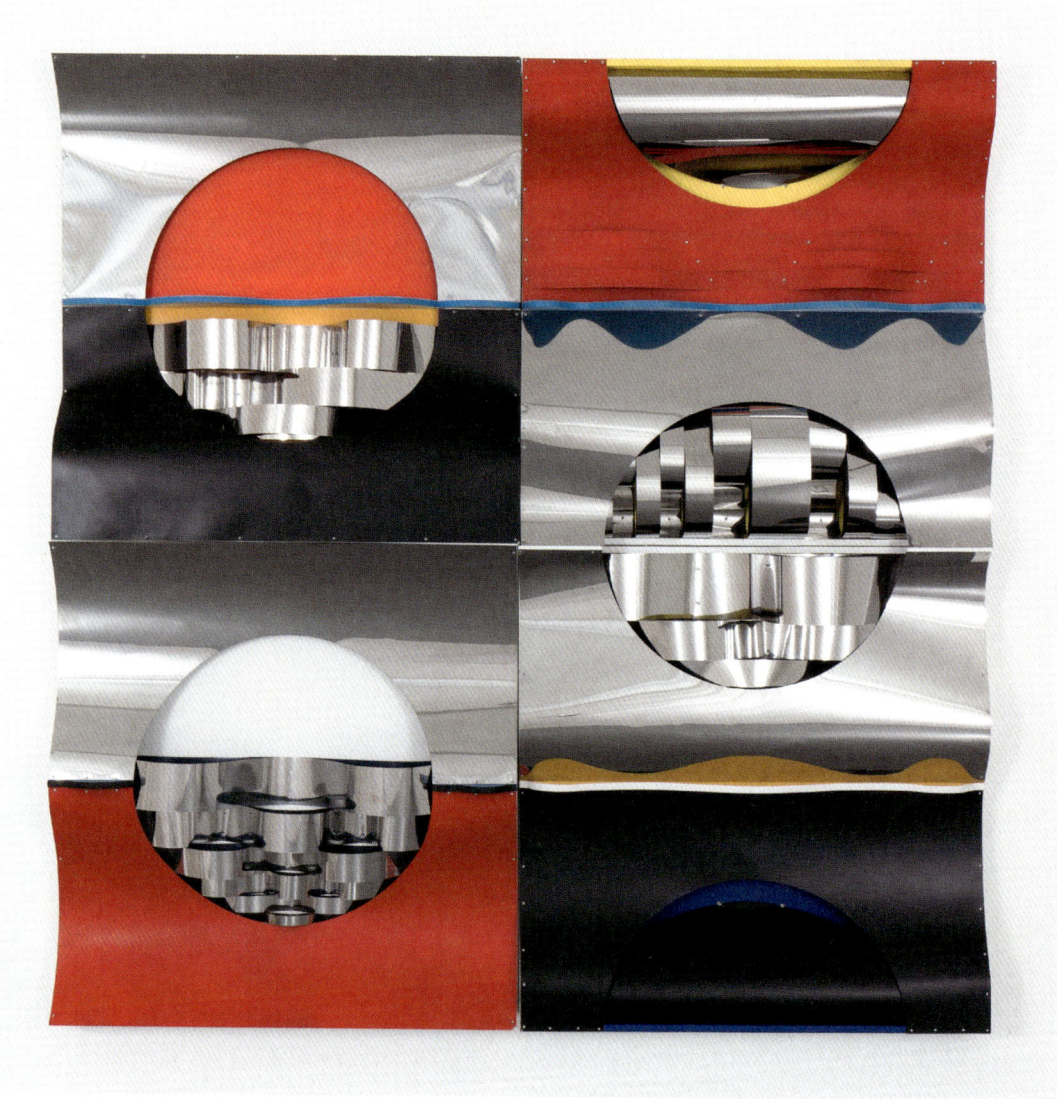

Mohsen Vaziri Moghaddam

In 1955, Iranian artist Mohsen Vaziri Moghaddam moved to Rome
to study at the Accademia di Belle Arti. His years spent in Italy
were a turning point, during which he pointedly moved away
from figurative painting towards abstraction and, later, geometric
reliefs. At this time, he also started to experiment with aluminium.
Untitled 1968 features four modules made of wood and aluminium sheets partially painted in blocks of primary colours which
optically vibrate against one another. Undulating waves cut out
of the aluminium amplify the dynamism by echoing the forms of
the base. It is one of the earliest works in which the artist further
dismantles the closed form of his sculptures by exploring the
interactions between the modules and the space around them:
the four modules can be hung in any orientation or configuration.
He would later produce a series of large hinged sculptures, which
the public was invited to reconfigure at will. OW

↑ Mohsen Vaziri Moghaddam, *Untitled* (*Geometric Reliefs Series*)
1968, remade 2015

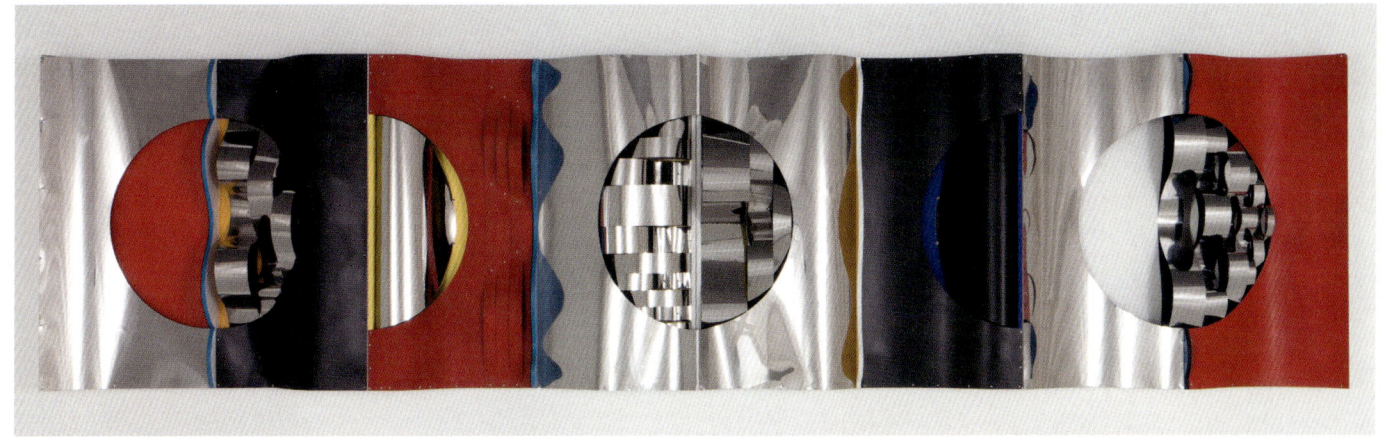

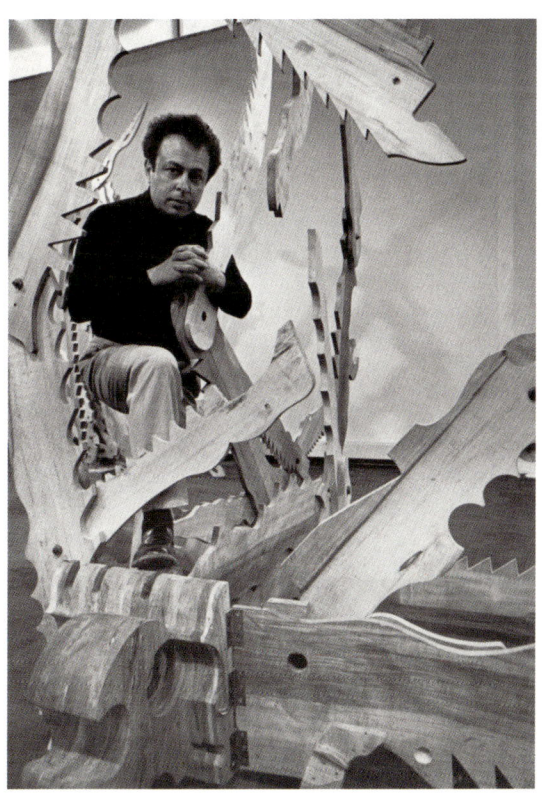

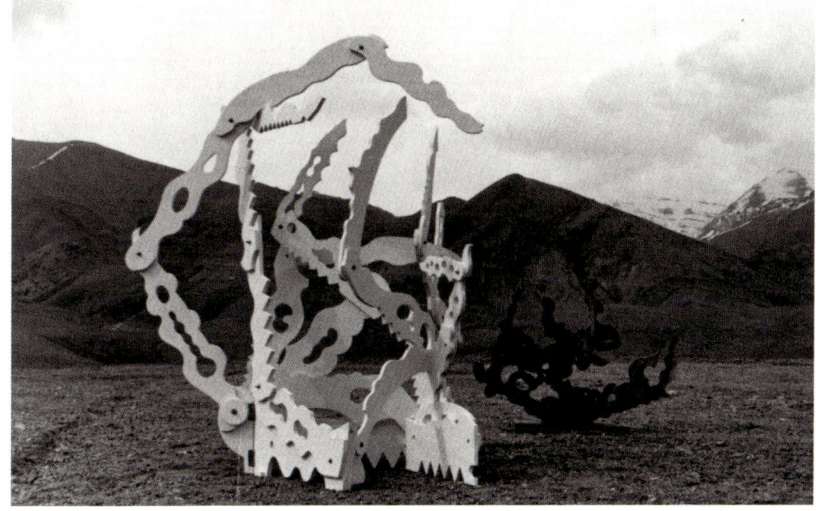

↟ Mohsen Vaziri Moghaddam, *Untitled* 1968, remade 2015
↖ Mohsen Vaziri Moghaddam with his *Transitional Forms* 1971,
at the Iran-America Society exhibition of his wood sculptures
↑ Vaziri's articulated sculptures from 1970 pictured in the out-
skirts of Tehran, 1971

François Morellet

One of the founding members of the Groupe de Recherche d'Art Visuel (GRAV), Morellet used regular grids and repetition in an attempt to reduce the role of the artist's individual choices to a minimum, and to inject his practice with aspects of scientific methodology. Morellet usually based his works on strict mathematical rules, but he also occasionally adopted chance operations as compositional strategies. The pattern for this wallpaper was originally created for a series of square paintings he started in 1960. 'With *Random Distribution*,' he wrote, 'the purpose of my system was to cause a reaction between two colours of equal intensity. I drew horizontal and vertical lines to make 40,000 squares. Then my wife or my sons would read out the numbers from the phone book ... and I would mark each square for an even number while leaving the odd ones blank. The crossed squares were painted blue and the blank ones red.' For the 1963 Paris Biennale, Morellet made a walk-through version of this work, covering the walls, floor and ceiling with this random pattern. 'I wanted the visitors to have a disturbing experience when they walked into this room – to almost hurt their eyes with the pulsating, flickering balance of two colours.'[1] VR

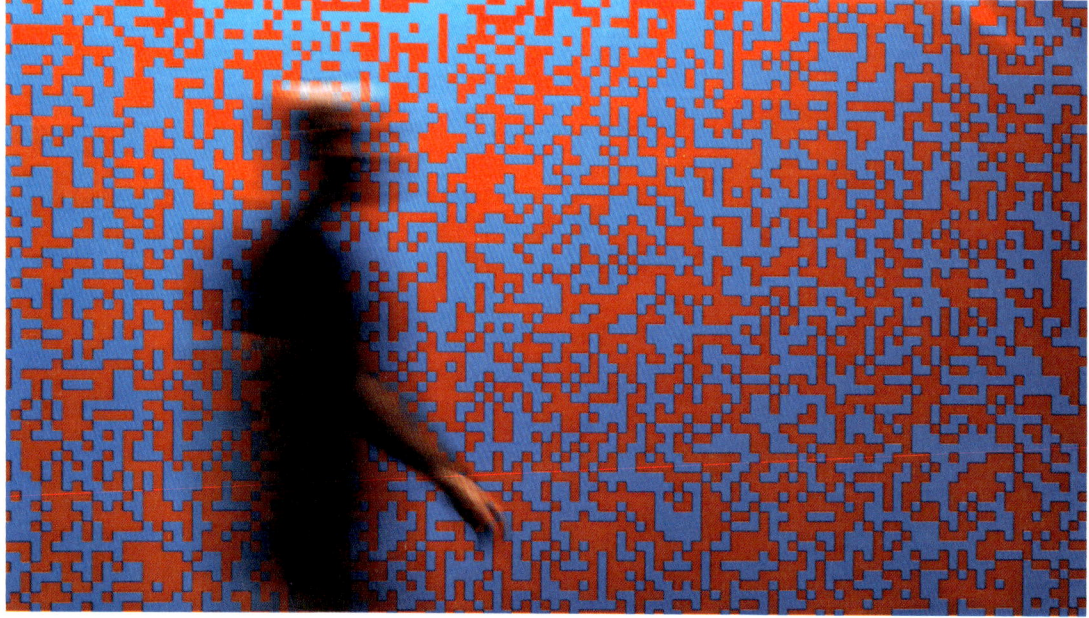

⬥ François Morellet, *Two Warps and Wefts of Short Lines 0° 90°* 1955–6

↑ François Morellet, *Random distribution of squares using the π number decimals, 50% odd digit blue, 50% even digit red* 1963

➔ François Morellet, *Random distribution of squares using the π number decimals, 50% odd digit blue, 50% even digit red* 1963

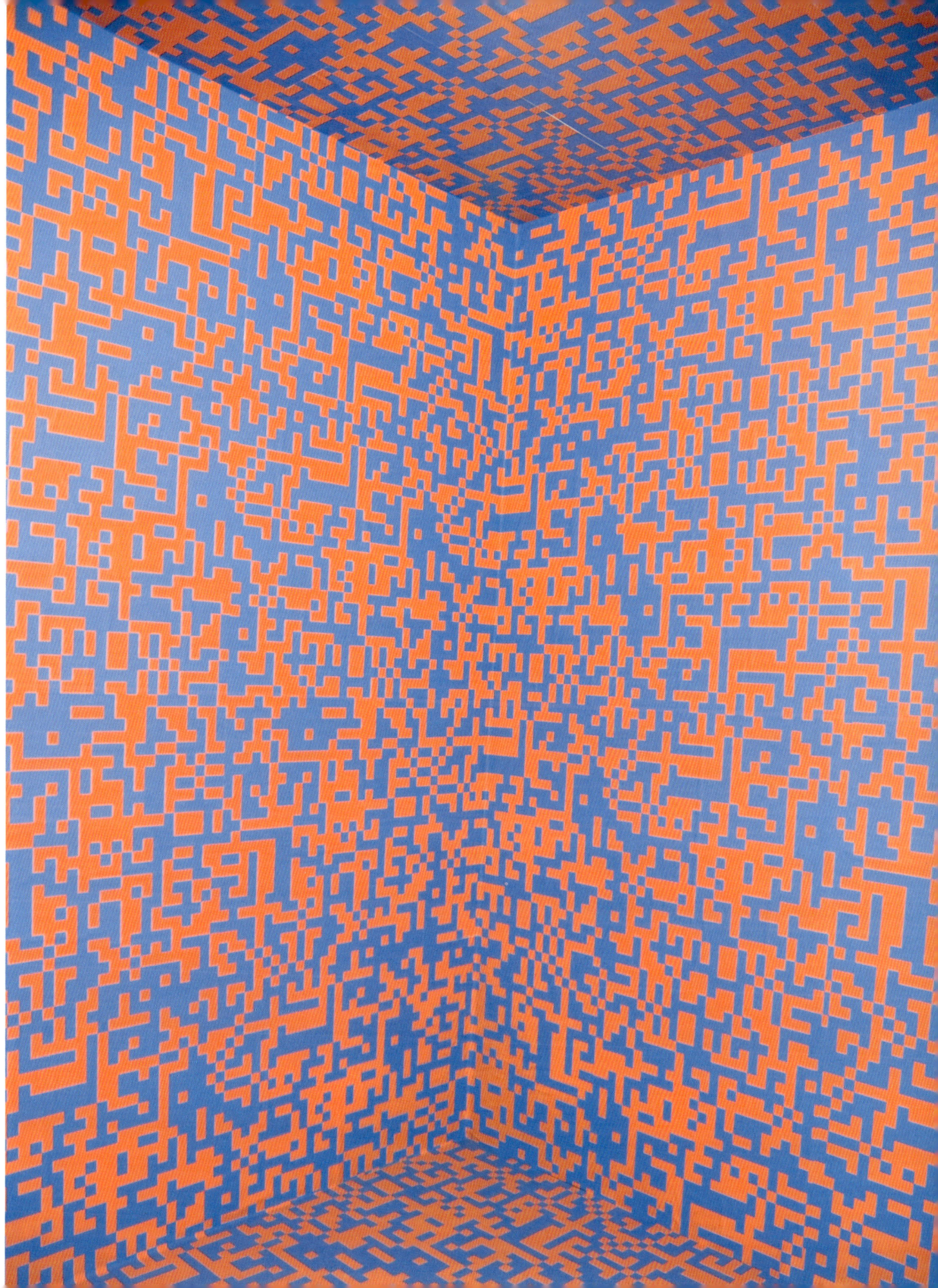

In 1960, a group of artists from Argentina, France, Hungary and Spain rented a garage in the district of Le Marais, Paris, and founded the Centre de Recherche d'Art Visuel (CRAV). Among them were Héctor García Miranda, Horacio García Rossi, Hugo Demarco, Julio Le Parc, Vera and François Molnar, François Morellet, Sergio Moyano, Servanes (Simone Revoil), Joël Stein, Francisco Sobrino and Yvaral (Jean-Pierre Vasarely). CRAV later evolved into the smaller Groupe de Recherche d'Art Visuel (GRAV), with García Rossi, Le Parc, Morellet, Sobrino, Stein and Yvaral. This split occured as some CRAV members advocated for pure research and a break away from museums and galleries, while those who formed GRAV believed that maintaining these links was necessary to stay connected with the public.[1]

Nevertheless, these artists converged in Paris at a time when there was a heightened awareness of societal problems and when avant-garde artists were increasingly marginalised.[2] In addition, movements based on gestural abstraction, such as tachisme and art informel, which the group considered to be stiflingly conservative, dominated this post-war period. Indeed, GRAV marked a generational shift among younger artists interested in redefining art and experimenting with new formats and materials. Among other things, GRAV artists experimented with Plexiglas, nylon, vinyl, light and neon, vowing to abandon the two-dimensional image and its 'complicity with the pictorial aesthetic'.[3]

They rejected the idea of the sole artistic genius, inspired by Victor Vasarely, who proclaimed in 1960 that groups of experimental workers engaged in scientific disciplines would be 'the only true creators of the future'.[4] Seeking to upend and demystify the traditional role of the artist as a producer of masterpieces, GRAV rejected individual labels and instead produced work as an anonymised collective. They reacted against the cult of personality that they felt dominated the art world, underpinned by what they saw as a 'subjective lyricism' that assigned value to artworks.[5] They were dedicated to the process of 'visual research', a term they used instead of 'art', and which implied a scientific attitude as well as freedom from a predetermined outcome.[6] They were interested in the concept of the 'open work of art', which was nevertheless always 'precise, relevant and intentional'.[7] This concept was initially formulated by Umberto Eco in 1961, and had a focus on research and establishing a set of rules, while also expanding the interactive use of visual elements.[8] In rejecting the importance of questions around form, GRAV emphasised the relationship between the artwork and the viewer.

GRAV's work is characterised by its experimentation with participation – namely that of the spectator-actor

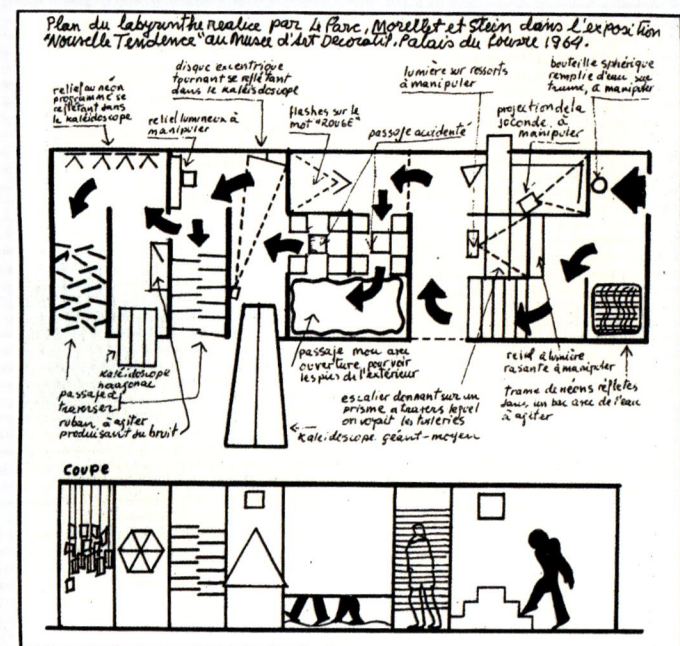

– through which the group sought to unravel the established frameworks of the art world. In doing so, they intended to trigger people into exercising their political agency and galvanise greater participation in society more widely.[9] GRAV believed that liberating both artist and viewer from questions of formalism would, inherently, lead to the liberation of society.[10] Their reflection on the passivity of art viewing was influenced by Guy Debord's 1957 critique of the spectacle, which identified a contemporary consumer society plagued by non-intervention of the social actor.[11] Following this, Le Parc coined the description of GRAV's participatory works as 'situations' rather than spectacles.

Inspired by mathematical principles and predetermined systems, their works dealt with patterns and repetition. In addition, the short-lived nature of some of their interventions was intended to further 'demystify' art and avoid what they viewed as the danger of the art object being treated as a luxury good or fetish.[12] Another important feature of their work was the instability of representation and perception, heightened by the artwork's movements as well as by the viewer's movements in relation to it.[13] These works were meant to test the limits of perception, as epitomised by Le Parc's early mobile works, which offered the potential for an infinite array of visual experiences, with viewers witnessing a constantly changing composition characterised by material instability.[14]

GRAV: Visual Research and the Politics of Participation

Odessa Warren

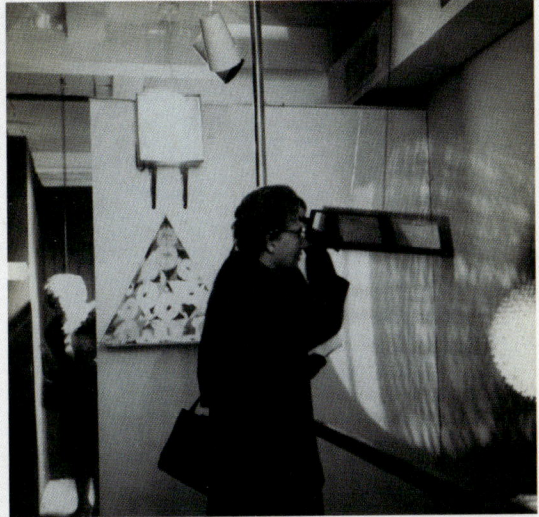

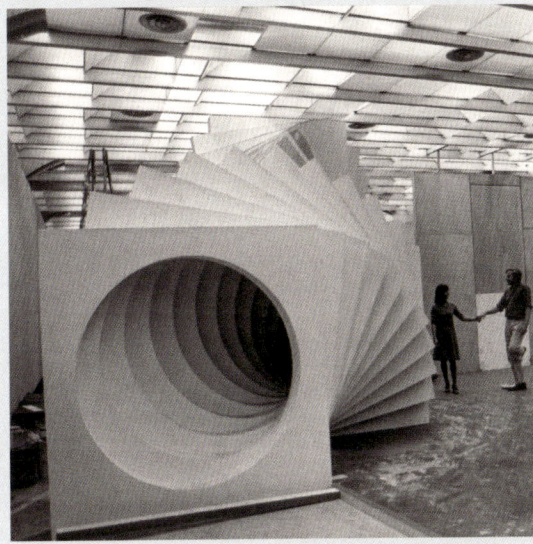

GRAV published their manifesto *Assez des Mystifications!* ('Enough of the Mystifications!') in 1963 for the third Paris Biennale, where they presented their first labyrinth. A collective work, it comprised twenty immersive spaces populated by reliefs, installations of strobing lights, wall-to-wall patterns and mobile bridges. The entrance instructed the audience to 'Entrez – Cassez/Enter – Break', directly in line with their manifesto, which proclaimed 'IT IS FORBIDDEN NOT TO PARTICIPATE'. In April 1966, GRAV decided to take their work into the streets to engage with a public that had not been 'forewarned'.[15] They organised 'Day in the Street', a day-long tour of Paris, during which interactive encounters engaged passers-by in 'situations' such as walking on uneven blocks of wood or looking through a kaleidoscope. Through these playful, kinetic works, GRAV pioneered an early approach to participatory art in which traditional roles of the spectacle-spectator were subverted.[16]

The events of May 1968 saw widespread social and political mobilisation as students took to the streets in protest and workers went on strike across France. Along with international differences within the group, these events precipitated the end of GRAV and they dissolved later that year.[17] In many ways, the vast social change that took hold in 1968 realised what GRAV had always set out to do in their own work.

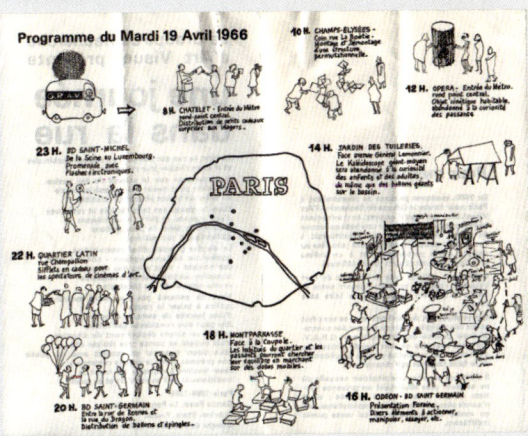

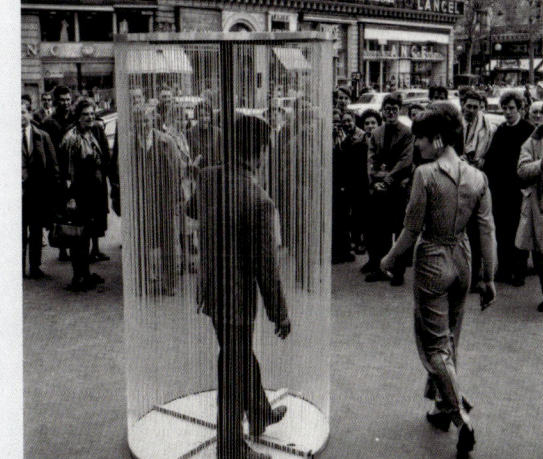

← GRAV, *Plan for a labyrinth for the exhibition Nouvelle Tendence*, Musée d'Art Decoratif, Palais du Louvre, Paris, 1964
↟ GRAV, *Labyrinth – Technological Environment*, third Paris Biennale, 1963
↟ GRAV, *Labyrinth II, Propositions visuelles du mouvement international/Nouvelle Tendance*, Musée des Arts Décoratifs, Paris, 1964
↑ François Morellet, Yvaral, Francisco Sobrino, Vera Molnar, Joël Stein, Julio Le Parc, Horacio García Rossi, *A Day in the Street* 1966

↑ François Morellet, Yvaral, Francisco Sobrino, Vera Molnar, Joël Stein, Julio Le Parc, Horacio García Rossi, *A Day in the Street*, 1966

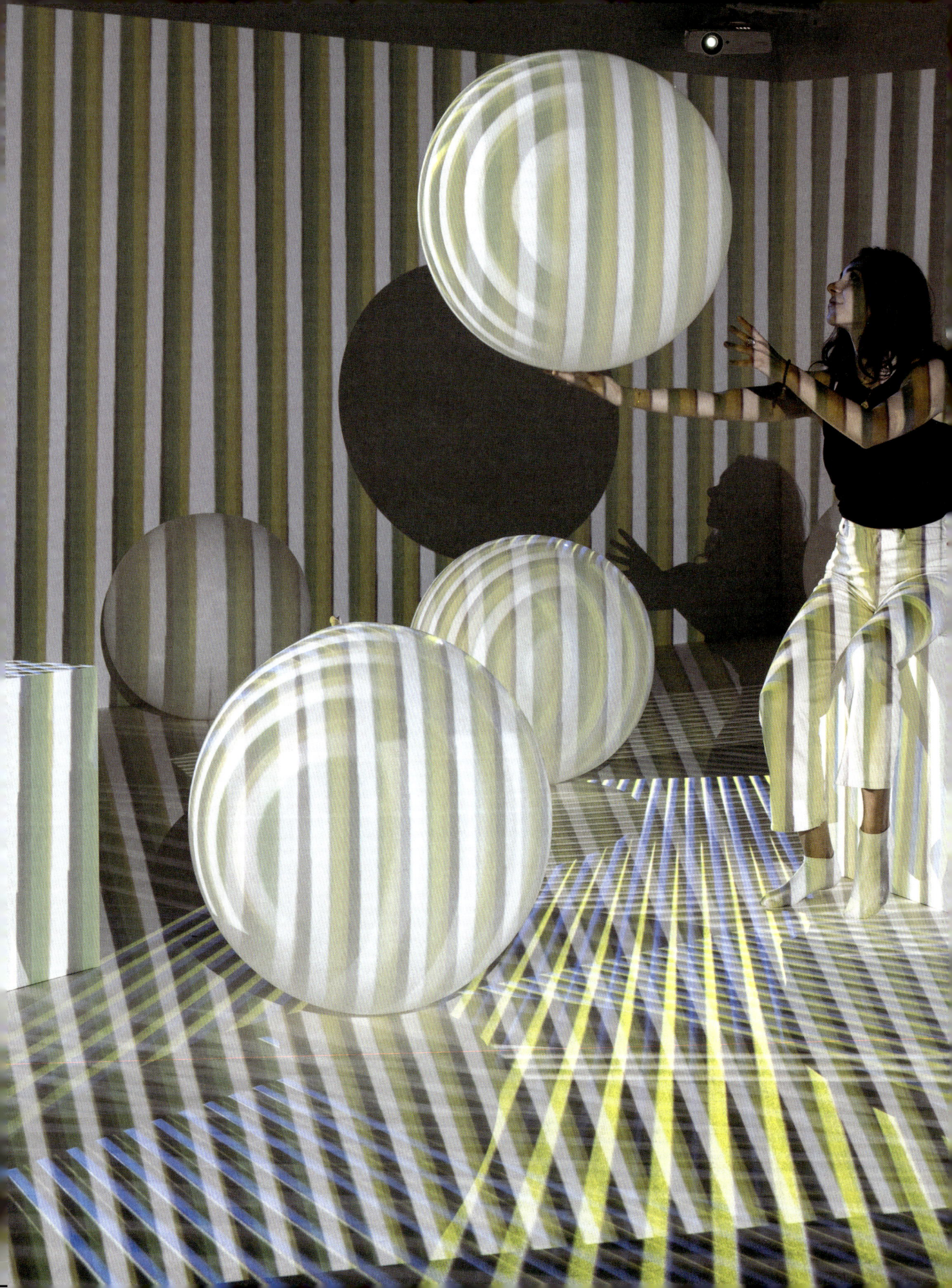

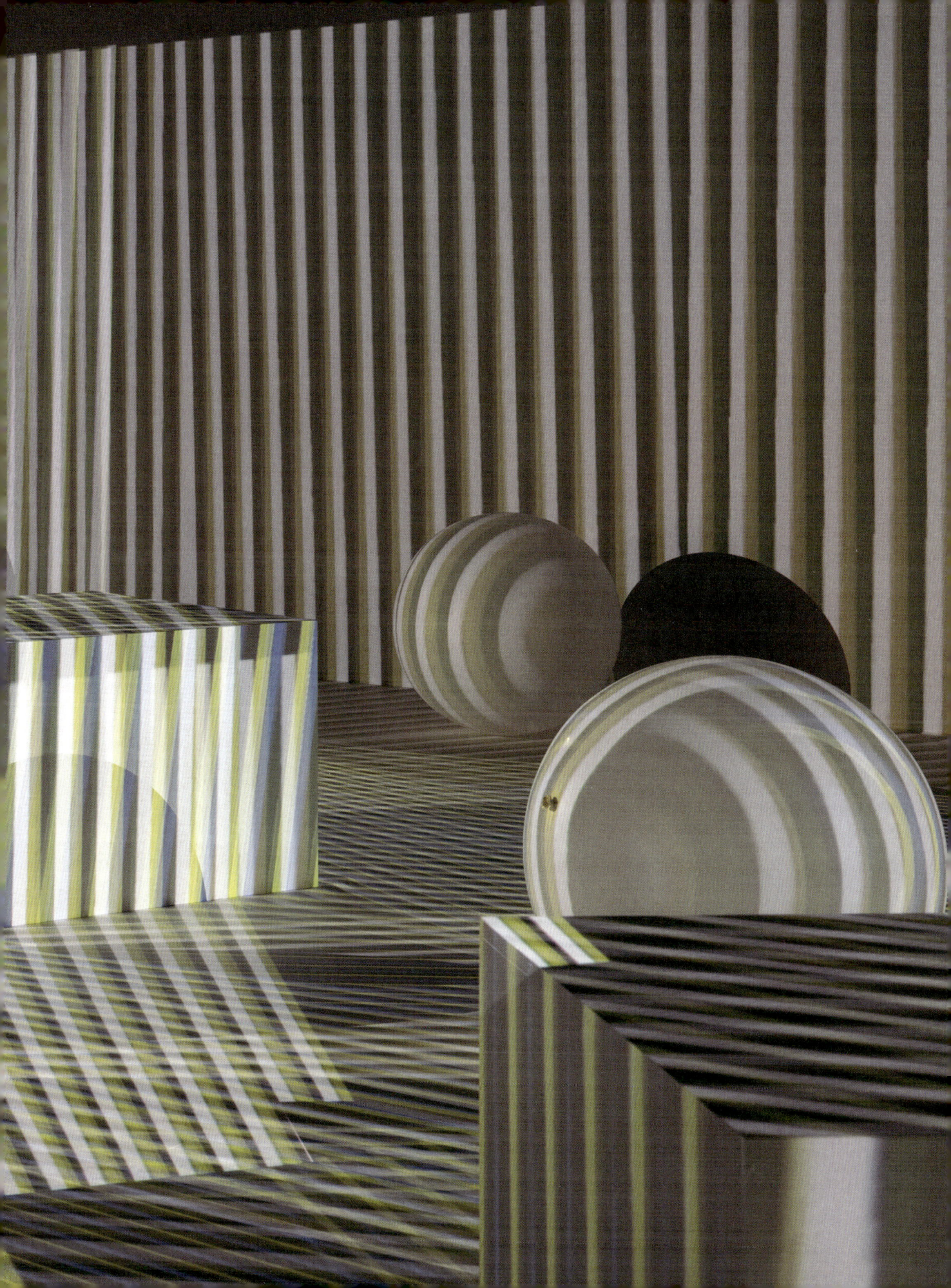

Carlos Cruz-Diez's *Chromointerferent Environment* (*Environnement Chromointerférent*) originated in the concept developed as *Deconditioning Labyrinth* 1965, which Cruz-Diez defined as 'a complex of perceptual and sensory discharge that brought primary sensations into play'.[1] Its purpose was 'to reactivate or awaken, through elementary manifestations, the dormant perceptions of a hyper-baroque society, which unloads onto people an immense, heterogeneous, and continuous bombardment' of information.[2]

This labyrinth, which was never fully realised, was to be composed of a set of environments, such as a 'Temperature Corridor' (annotated 1); a 'Touch Compartment' (2); a 'Pneumatic-walled Cubicle' that progressively compresses the body (3); a 'Sound Chamber', 'where there would be shouting but no echo' (4), followed by an 'Echo Chamber' (5); a 'Chamber for Sound Multiplication' (6); a 'Percussion Room' with rhythmic activations (7); a 'High and Low Electronic Sonic Frequencies and Textures Chamber' (8); a 'Smell Tunnel' (9); a 'Vision Chamber' (10), featuring a 'Square Interference Projection Room'; a 'Chromosaturation Labyrinth' (11–16) and an 'Intense and Progressive Light Chamber' (17).

Cruz-Diez was eventually interested in developing only the aspects of this project related to colour: the *Chromosaturation* section and the *Chromointerferent Environment*. However, their production depended on the possibilities offered by the materials at that time. It was a question of finding the most effective and coherent solution that technically corresponded to the discourse he aimed to achieve. I had the role and privilege of assisting my father in the advent of every development.

Chromointerferent Environment creates a situation of immateriality, transfiguration and ambiguity of colour in space through movement and thanks to the phenomenon of subtractive colour, whereby we perceive colour as a result of white light having been filtered through colour-absorbing media.

The constantly moving projection onto people and objects makes them appear transparent, virtually changing their form and condition. Simultaneously, the spectators take on a dual role as 'actors' and 'authors' of a chromatic event that evolves in real time and space. Fixing our gaze on the shadows on the walls, we have the sensation of moving in the opposite direction to the coloured lines. A dialogue then takes place between the 'variable' of the chromatic interferences and the 'constant' of the shadows on the wall.

In 1974 the work was installed for the first time at the Museum of Contemporary Art in Caracas, in a different configuration from that laid out in the original 1965

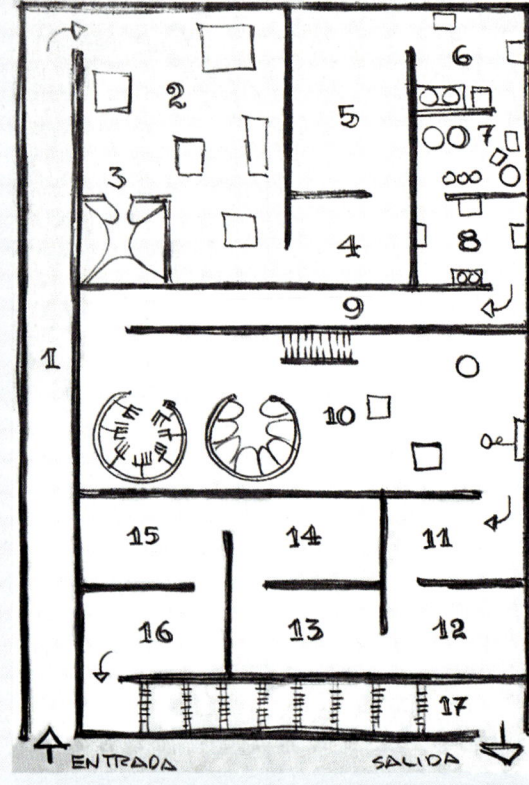

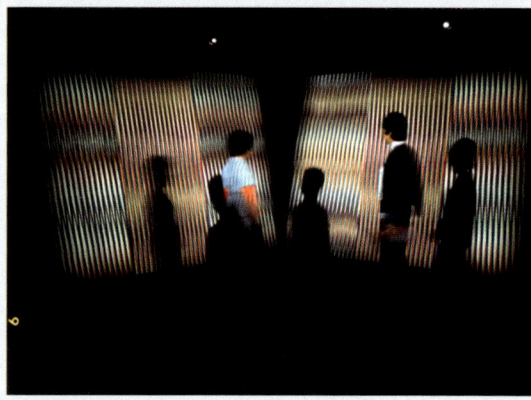

⬥ Carlos Cruz-Diez, drawing for *Deconditioning Labyrinth*, Paris 1965
↑ Carlos Cruz-Diez, *Chromointerferent Environment*, Caracas Museum of Contemporary Art (MACCAR), Venezuela 1974
Previous pages, 100–1: Carlos Cruz-Diez, *Chromointerferent Environment* 1974/2016, installation view, *Unlimited Sector*, Art Basel, 2018

Chromointerferent Environment: A Work in the Making

Carlos Cruz Delgado

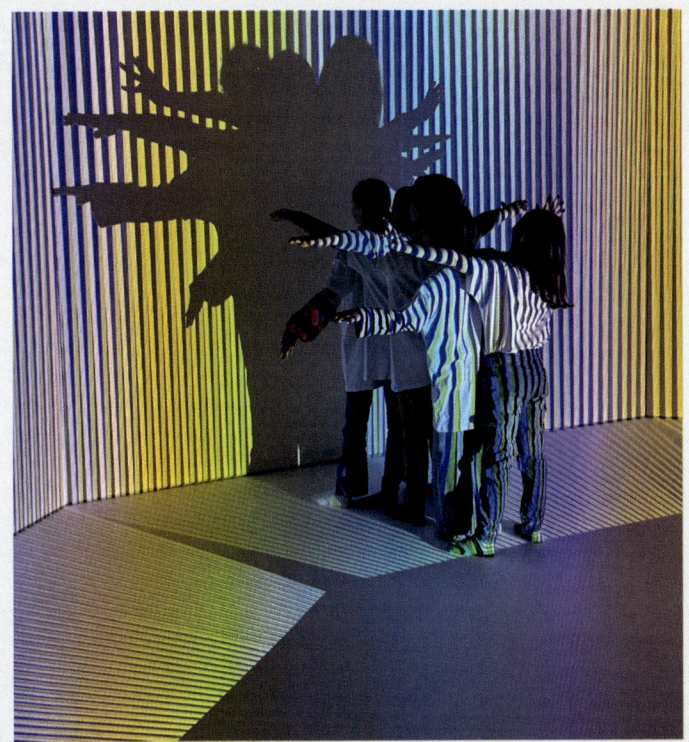

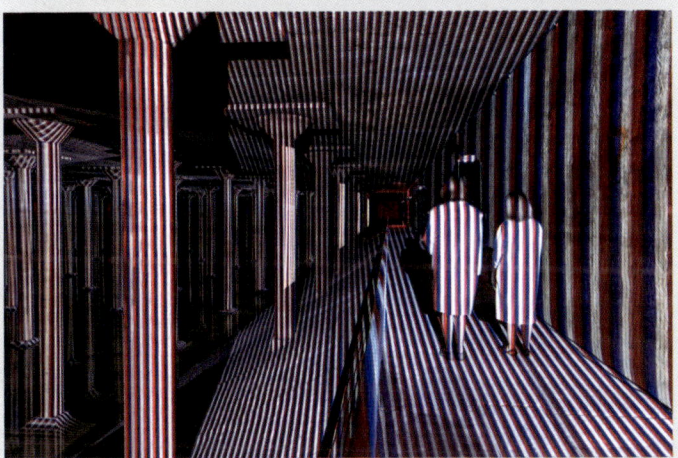

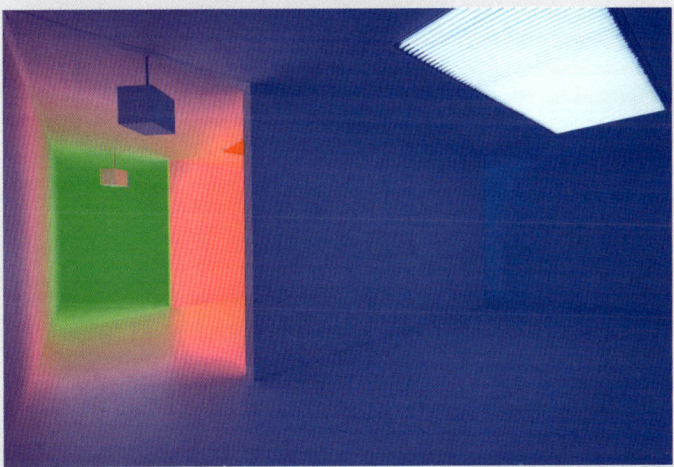

concept. It was made using slide projectors that projected a roll of 35mm frameless images. A small electric motor was added to the projectors to spin a transparent disc at a low rpm. On that disc was a pattern of black lines that I made on high-contrast Kodalith film. The black pattern was projected onto red, blue and green lines painted on white panels. The thickness of the lines of the black patterns had to match the thickness of those painted on the panels.

When the motor was set in motion, the disc rotated slowly, projecting the black fixed pattern, which produced an interference effect on the coloured lines and on the visitors.

This solution defines the essential elements of the artwork, its spatiality and its ability to welcome the viewer into a genuine chromatic experience, a participatory work. However, Cruz-Diez would wait more than twenty years to revisit its execution.

During the 1990s, my father studied and progressively adopted the tools offered by digital technology, which allowed him to perfect and develop various aspects of his works with the use of programming and the language of computers.

The exhibition *Cruz-Diez: From the Participatory to the Interactive*, held in Caracas in 2001, from a series of exclusive exhibitions in digital format, allowed my father and me to install *Chromointerferent Environment* using high-definition video projectors with a vector-based program, which I programmed following his prompts. I set the sequence, width and frequency of the lines, and specified his personal colour palette. The chromatic possibilities of the work increased, something that had been impossible in the 1974 artwork when the coloured lines were painted with gouache on a surface. These initial mechanics were replaced by the movement prompted by the program, allowing different speeds of displacement and direction of the frame. The interference was unexpected and generated infinite possibilities, with which my father was very satisfied.

The results we obtained allowed my father to resolve the configuration of the 1969 artwork and thus produce the definitive technical solution of his original proposal.

Since then, the discourse and experience of the work has gained in technical relevance, and the richness of its chromatic spectrum has contributed in turn to the pace of technological advance. *Chromointerferent Environment* is engraved in the rhetoric of computer-assisted creation, and of the dematerialised and immersive work.

↟ Carlos Cruz-Diez, *Translucent Chromointerferent Environment C* 1974/2009, installation view, *Headlong into Art*, Museum Ostwall, Dortmund, 2009
↑ Carlos Cruz-Diez, *Spatial Chromointerference* 1974/2018, installation view, Buffalo Bayou Park Cistern, Houston, 2018
↖ Carlos Cruz-Diez, *Chromosaturation* 1965/2013, installation view, *Light Show*, Hayward Gallery, London, 2013

Dialogues
with
the Machines

Dialogues
with
the Machines

104

Dialogues

Dialogues with the Machines: Early Computer and Cybernetic Art

Tina Rivers Ryan

Any survey of the first decades of 'computer art' comprises a bewildering array of materials, mediums and aesthetic approaches. How can we possibly make sense of a field that includes plotter drawings of biomorphic lines in ink on paper; prints of geometric patterns photographed off a screen; figurative images rendered in typewriter symbols; machine-milled wooden sculptures; frenetic flicker films; blinking kinetic-light sculptures; and interactive audiovisual 'cybernetic' environments?

The field of 'digital art' that emerged from this heterogenous mix has proven difficult to define, let alone articulate into stable taxonomies. (Is an algorithmically programmed image printed on paper more or less 'digital' than an image rendered in freehand using a light pen on a screen?) But what if this slipperiness of digital art is in fact 'a feature, and not a bug', in so far as it evidences the *mutability* of medium-specificity that lies at the core of the digital medium? At the risk of being reductive, this essay attempts to elucidate this point by describing early computer art according to two general tendencies. On the one hand, we have those 'computer artists' who turned to the computer as a kind of tool, akin to a paintbrush, albeit with its own advantages and limitations; on the other, we have those 'cybernetic artists' who understood the computer as a kind of system, ultimately leading them to investigations of broader concepts such as ecology or intelligence. These two positions are here represented by a close reading of the artists A. Michael Noll and Wen-Ying Tsai, respectively, who stand in for a larger number of artists: the former might include Lillian F. Schwartz and Vera Molnar, while the latter might include Analivia Cordeiro and Harold Cohen. Needless to say, these nominations are debatable, and may shift depending on the project – and yet they allow us to cut across a wide swath of early computer art and to understand how these two different ways of dialoguing with digital machines led to similar conclusions about the nature of the digital as an artistic medium.

'Portrait of the Machine as a Young Artist'

The first persons to recognise the artistic possibilities of the computer were not usually mainstream contemporary

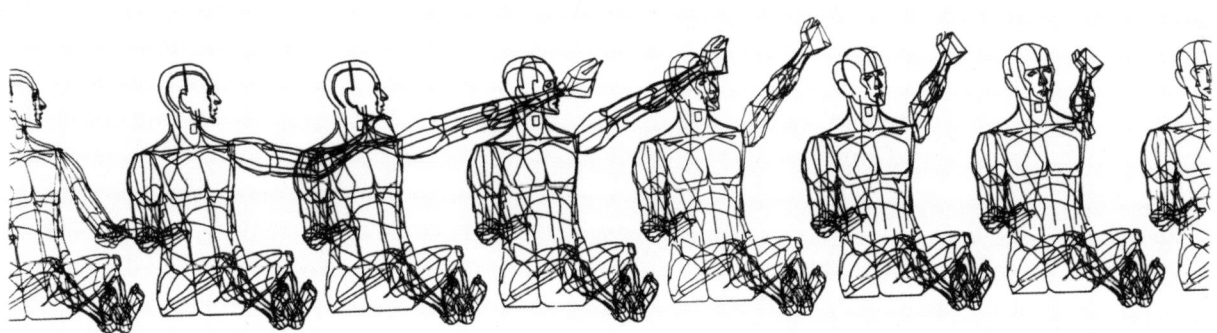

↑ William Fetter, *Human Figure*, model for Boeing Computer Graphics, 1966–8

artists but rather members of the military-industrial complex; in fact, the term 'computer graphics' was coined at Boeing in 1960. By the mid-1960s, however, the idea of using the computer as an artistic tool was beginning to catch the attention of those outside the industrial sphere. Notably, in 1965, *Playboy* published J.R. Pierce's article on recent attempts to use machines, including computers, in art. 'Portrait of the Machine as a Young Artist' included references to the drawing machines of Jean Tinguely, the intermedia work of John Cage, and the digital designs of Bell Labs researcher A. Michael Noll, among other examples, and concluded that artists, not engineers, 'must school the computer' for computer art to achieve any aesthetic success.[1]

The oft-repeated criticisms of the quality of computer art belie the fact that in the late 1960s, the fledging medium had achieved a modicum of institutional success. In 1970 alone, computer theory and computer technology were included in the New York shows *Software* at the Jewish Museum and *Information* at the Museum of Modern Art (MoMA), and the work of computer graphics pioneer Georg Nees was exhibited at the Venice Biennale.[2] But the flurry of excitement regarding the computer as a new medium proved short-lived. By the mid-1970s, computer art had lost its traction thanks to a confluence of forces, including the apathy or enmity of the mainstream art world, the inaccessibility of computer technologies, the limitations of early output devices, and public fears of computer-driven automation and centralised bureaucracies. More profoundly, the use of the computer in art threatened some of the major tenets of modernism, including originality and autonomy, pitting these against the variability and anonymity of the machine. As a genre, 'computer art' consequently became 'possibly the most maligned art form of the twentieth century', as art historian Grant Taylor has explained.[3] And yet these same works – which are now starting to find their audiences – are nevertheless reflective of significant aesthetic theories.

'Computer-Generated Pictures'

In April 1965, the first public exhibition of computer-generated images in America was presented by the Howard Wise Gallery in New York.[4] In February, Wise had seen the cover of that month's issue of *Scientific American*, featuring a colourful example of the computer-generated random-dot stereograms with which Béla Julesz, a scientist at Bell Labs, was investigating depth perception and pattern recognition.[5] Wise invited Julesz to have a show at his gallery in April, and Julesz in turn invited A. Michael Noll, another scientist at Bell Labs, to exhibit his own *computer-generated images* as well.[6] The show featured about eight works by Julesz and twice as many by Noll.[7]

Both the gallery and the artists were conscious of the stakes of presenting computer-generated images as objects of aesthetic contemplation. As Noll later recounted, 'Béla was always very careful not to call his images "art," since the images were stimuli for psychological investigations of

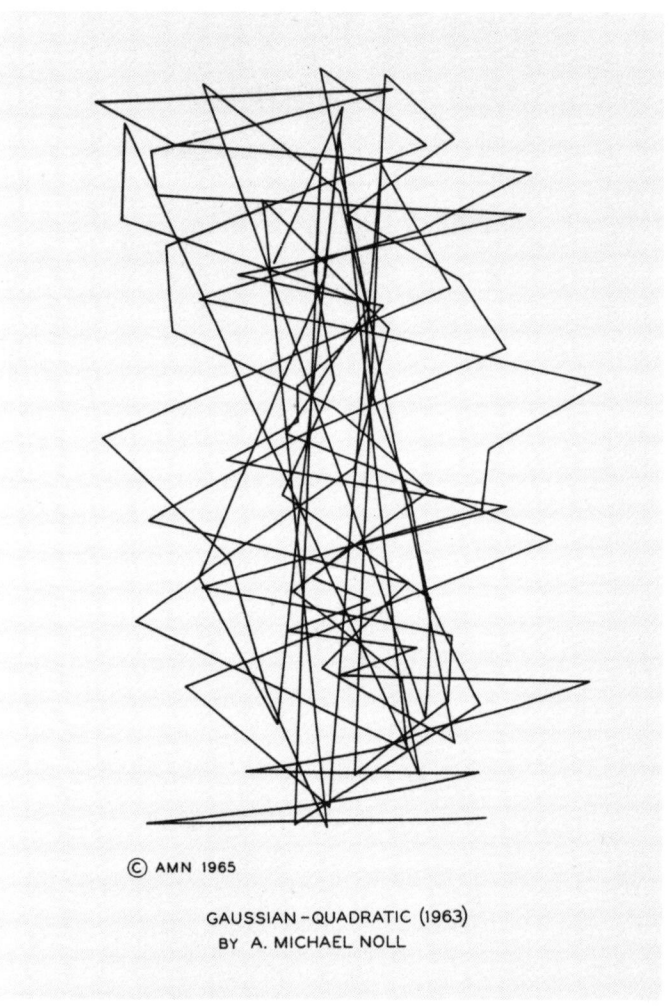

© AMN 1965

GAUSSIAN – QUADRATIC (1963)
BY A. MICHAEL NOLL

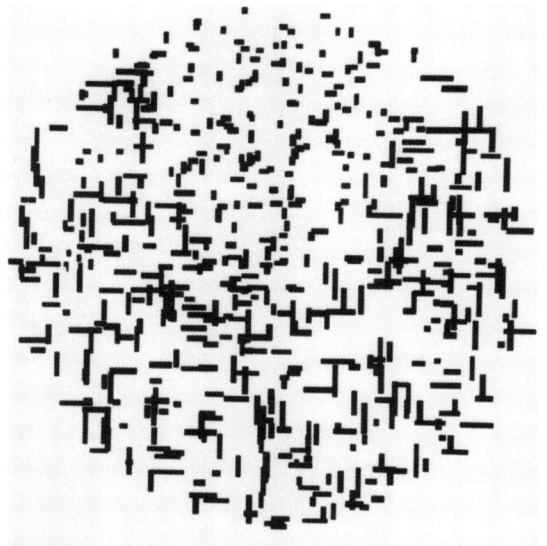
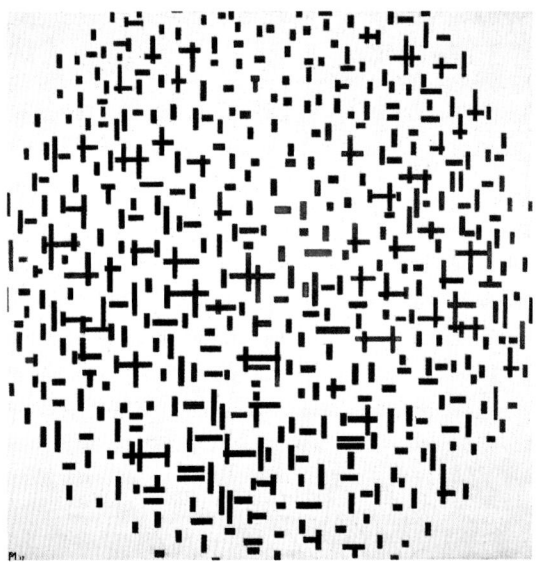

visual perception. I, however, had generated many of my images solely for their aesthetic or artistic effects and was much more willing to call them art.'[8] They compromised by titling the show *Computer-Generated Pictures*. The press release similarly emphasised that, while the computer had been conscripted as a new 'tool' for the artist, it was not itself the artist of the work:

> *This exhibition demonstrates, to some small degree, the potentialities of the computer as a tool in the service of the artist ... Noll and Julesz see the day when a computer can draw – or paint – almost any kind of picture in any one or combination of colors. Both scientists stress, however, that the artist need not fear being automated out of existence; rather, as they see it, the computer will free the artist for creation, unburdened by the tedium of the mechanics.*[9]

The emphasis on the importance of human agency was motivated by the fact that the works demonstrably and not incidentally relied on the use of a computer to produce random numbers and to create variations on a visual theme at speeds far surpassing what could be achieved without a computer. That said, the use of randomness to generate the works was moderated by the artists, who set out parameters for the program and then selected from among the results, or modified the program according to some idiosyncratic personal aesthetic. The computer simply expedited the creative process by making it more an act of selection than execution (foreshadowing the subsequent comparisons of digital art to conceptualism). Noll's work *Gaussian-Quadratic*, the creation of which he discussed in his text for the show, is exemplary of this 'feedback' process between man and machine:

> *Gaussian-Quadratic (1963) is an example of randomness in the horizontal positions but complete order in the vertical positions of the end points of the lines. The exact range for the randomness and the particular equation for the order were determined in a feedback trial-and-error process with the computer. The advantage of this method was that once deciding upon a particular combination of types of randomness and order, the computer very quickly generated pictures, and ... the person was ... therefore able to devote himself to the more creative aspects of actually designing the desired picture in cooperation with the computer.*[10]

While most studies of early computer art, both in the 1960s and since then, contend with how randomness relates to our understanding of artistic creativity, the impact of Noll's work on the notion of the artistic medium is equally profound. Importantly, all of the work in *Computer-Generated Pictures* existed as binary data before it existed in visual (let alone object) form. In other words, Noll's art implies that art can result from – and exist as – the pure abstractions of code, before it is realised in any particular physical medium. Of course, in order to be exhibited, the designs produced with the computer had to be made material; this was achieved through a multi-step process of translating digital data through various technologies and across medium formats, in a manner necessarily limited by the output capacities of computers at the time. First, the plotter would 'draw' the design on a device for making televisual images called an image orthicon tube; the resulting image would then be photographed on 35mm film, with the negative becoming the permanent and unique 'original' work of art. For the show, these negatives were used to

↑ A. Michael Noll, *Computer Composition with Lines* 1964

↑ Piet Mondrian, *Composition with Lines* (*Composition in Black and White*) 1917

make enlarged prints, which were in turn mounted on Masonite (or, in the case of the stereographic works by Julesz, between sheets of acrylic plastic). This process of translating data into art across formats seemingly discards the notion of medium-specificity. In sum, even in very early computer art, we see the computer situated as not simply a new medium for art, but more profoundly, as a medium that makes the very notion of materials, and by extension medium-specificity, obsolete.

'Tsaibernetics'

In 1968, the Howard Wise Gallery presented another show that foregrounded a different conception of having a 'dialogue with the machine'. Trained as a mechanical engineer, Wen-Ying Tsai decided to quit engineering and devote himself to painting full-time in 1963. He travelled to Europe for three months, where he encountered kinetic and op art for the first time at the Galerie Denise René in Paris. In February 1965, his painting *Random Field* 1964 was included in the MoMA survey *The Responsive Eye*. A quintessentially op artwork, the painting comprises an enormous plane of fluorescent green that is mounted approximately 12 mm in front of another plane of fluorescent red, which we see on the sides and through circular cutouts. When viewed under ultraviolet light, the red circles appear to float in *front* of the green panel.[11]

By that fall, Tsai's art was itself moving, rather than simply dealing in optical effects and the illusion of motion. While in residence at the MacDowell Colony, New Hampshire in 1965, he had an epiphany: he wanted to create work as awesome as light shimmering through the leaves of the forest. The result was his *Multi-Kinetic Wall* of 1965. While repeating the same circular motifs and bright colours of *Random Field*, the work deployed motors to animate its thirty-two self-contained units. Within each unit, the concentric rings were programmed to revolve eccentrically, giving them the appearance of a mechanical device run amok. Importantly, the work's kinetic action produced sound, which the artist included in the list of materials of the work. The correlation of image and sound – albeit here mechanical – foreshadowed his subsequent *Cybernetic Sculptures*, which he began making in 1966. Primarily taking the form of either stainless steel rods or polished metallic plates, these vibrating works were shown in Tsai's first solo show at the Howard Wise Gallery in May of 1968.

The first key to the development of Tsai's *Cybernetic Sculptures* was his rediscovery of stroboscopic lights.[12] As Tsai himself explained, he had been familiar with the strobe as a student: 'In engineering school, it was used in laboratory tests of material – modular elasticities, waveform amplitudes. I never thought the strobe could be part of artistic expression.'[13] It was an encounter with the intermedia environments of media art collective USCO that alerted him to the strobe's potential application in art.[14] Without the strobe, Tsai's sculptures moved so quickly that the space across which they moved appeared to be filled

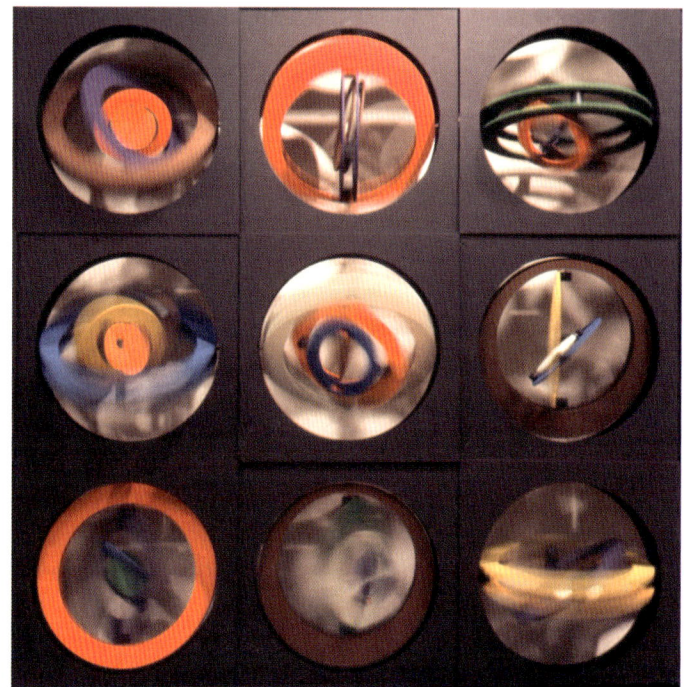

⌐ Wen-Ying Tsai, *Multi-Kinetic Wall* 1965

with a solid mass – an illusion of 'virtual volume' that was first pioneered by kinetic forefather Naum Gabo's *Kinetic Construction (Standing Wave)* of 1919–20. But the addition of the strobe allowed Tsai to modulate the appearance of his virtual volumes, adding another layer of illusionism and, in some cases, making the sculptures appear to change over time, giving them a durational aspect.[15]

Beyond the strobe, the second key to the development of the *Cybernetic Sculptures* was their responsiveness to the viewer. Tsai's initial idea was to rig the stroboscopes with burglar alarms and timers. However, this method could not produce proportional effects, because it was binary (on or off), allowing for no spectrum of action or control. Tsai then turned to the group Experiments in Art and Technology (E.A.T.), which paired him with Frank T. Turner, a senior engineer with Western Union. According to documents supplied to E.A.T. as part of Tsai's entry into their 1968 juried show at the Brooklyn Museum, *Some More Beginnings*, Turner's solution was to modulate the strobes using a voltage-controlled variable-frequency

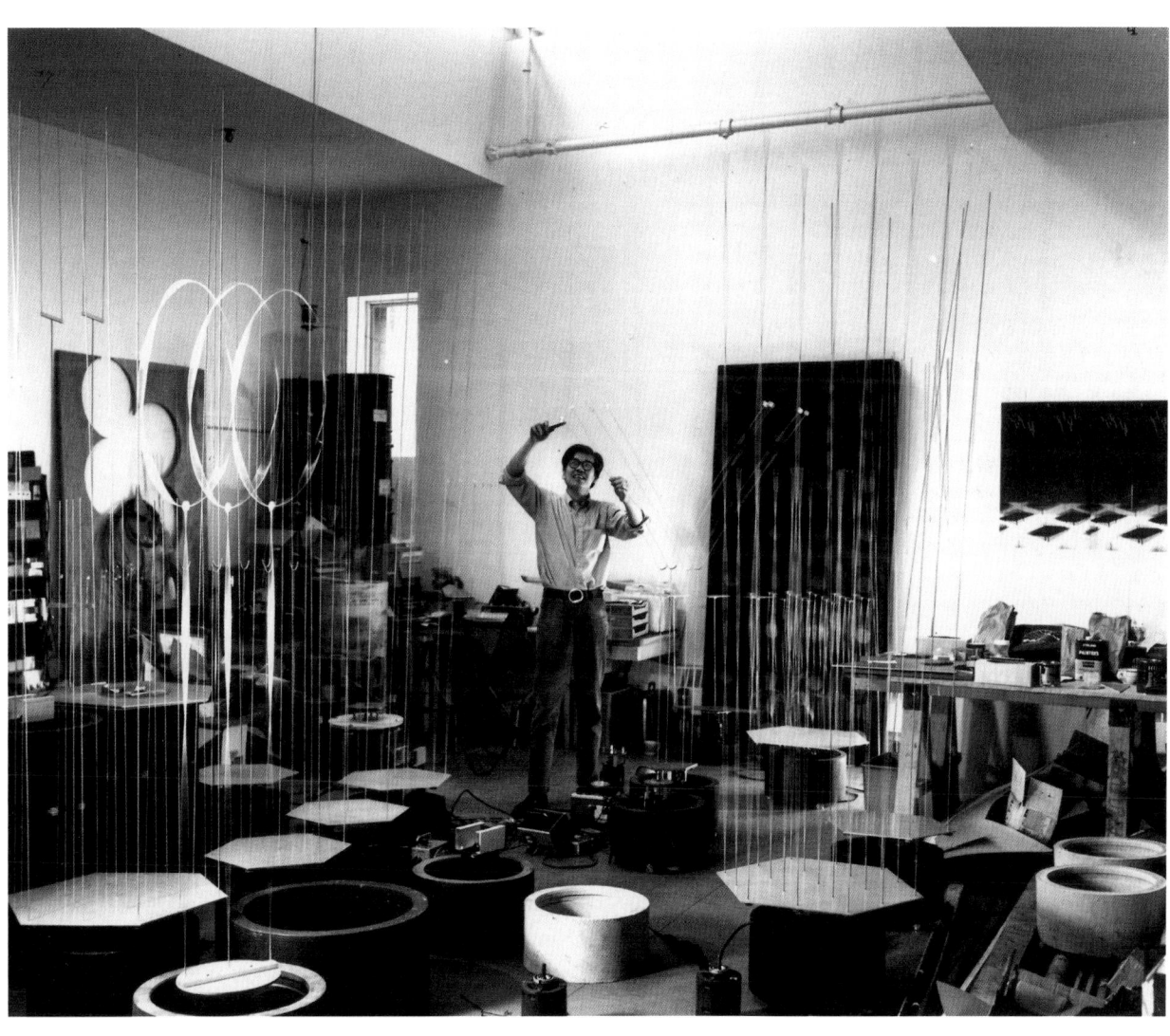

↑ Wen-Ying Tsai's studio at the Center for Advanced Visual Studies, MIT, Cambridge, MA, 1969

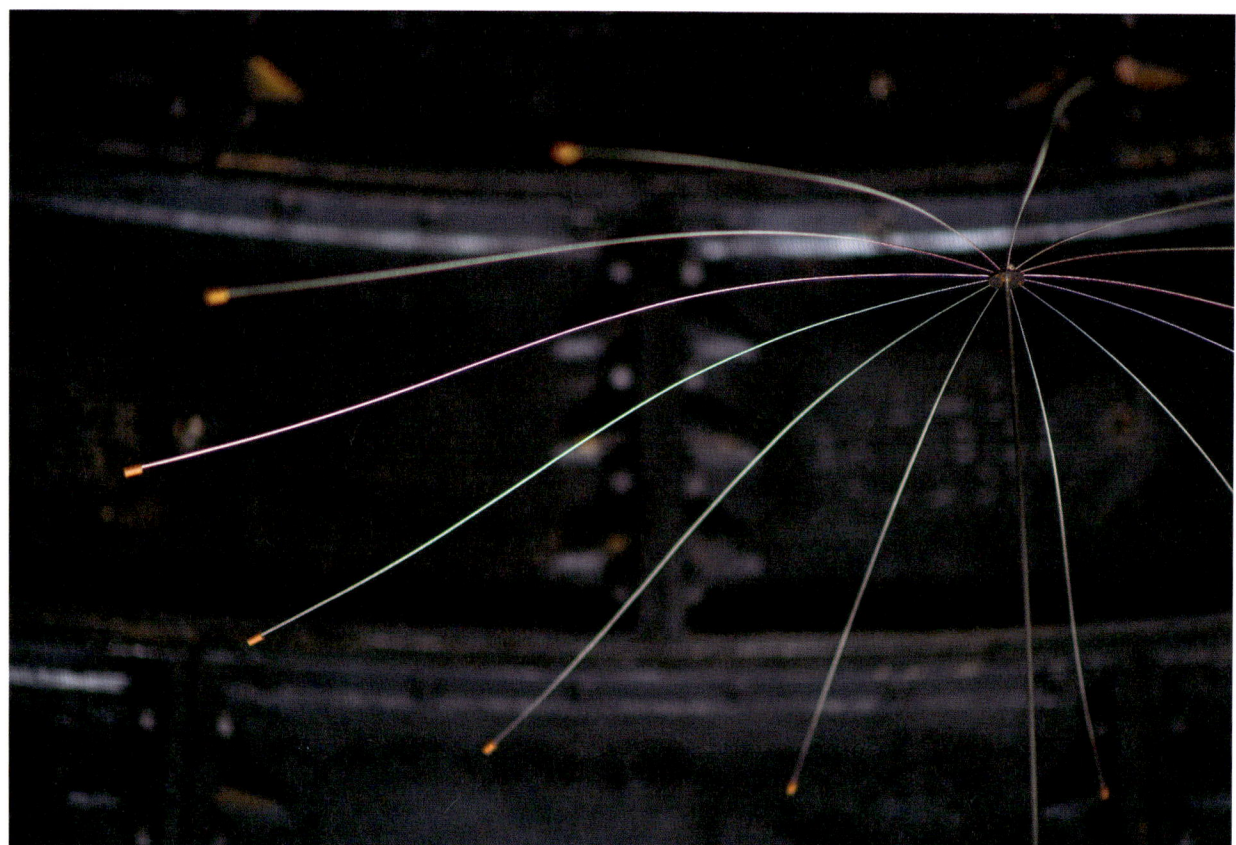

Wen-Ying Tsai

Square Tops 1969 and *Umbrella* 1971 are two of Tsai's *Cybernetic Sculptures,* each made up of thin vibrating metal rods lit by flashing strobe lights. Although the rods vibrate at a constant, rapid rate, the stroboscopic effect of the flashing lights makes the rods appear to slowly undulate, as the viewer is able to see them only at certain moments in their oscillation. The works contain microphones, which allow them to respond to sounds made by viewers, increasing the frequency of the strobe flashes; this makes it appear as if the frequency of the rods' vibrations have also changed. Awoken by viewers, the works seem to shift between slow undulation and rapid pulsation. Prior to his artistic career, Tsai studied engineering and worked as an architectural engineer; this scientific background allowed him to create these complex works. KW

↑ Wen-Ying Tsai, *Umbrella* 1971
→ Wen-Ying Tsai, *Cybernetic Sculpture: Square Tops* 1969

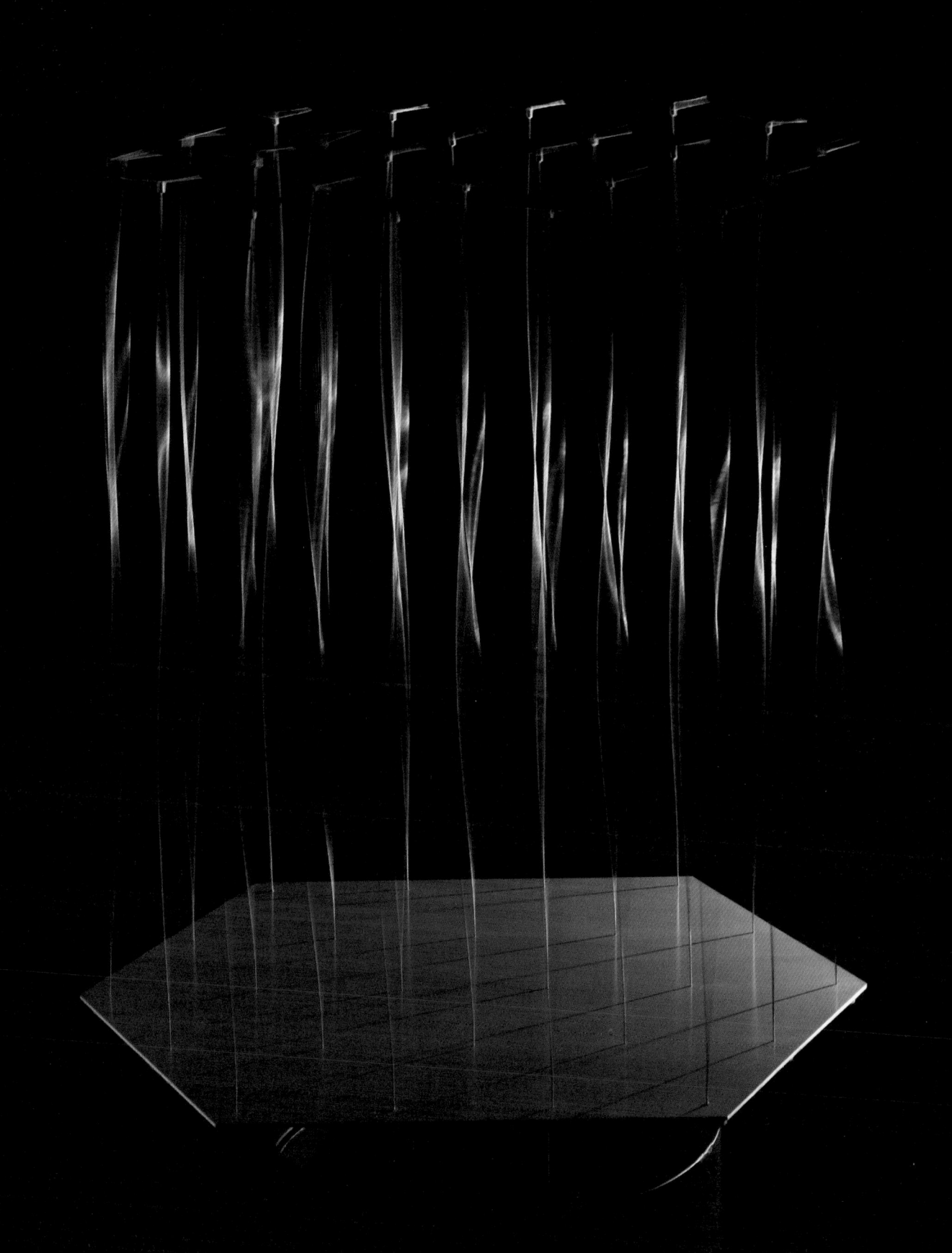

oscillator, built from scrap parts and a low-cost PA amplifier.[16] For the Howard Wise show, this cybernetic technology was applied in three bodies of work. These included a line of eight tall columns that responded to sound ('Speak loudly or just clap your hands to speed them up or slow them down', the gallery encouraged); a piece in the corner that responded to the viewer's proximity; and two pieces near the entrance that responded to the turning of knobs on their respective strobe lights.[17] Thus, in Tsai's work, the light of kinetic light art came to be technologically coordinated with external information, including sound, via electronic signals.

It is in this regard that these works are 'cybernetic'. Although the extent of his reading on the subject is unknown, Tsai was clearly interested in cybernetics: in addition to calling his works *Cybernetic Sculptures*, he also produced a work punning on his name, *Tsaibernetics 1968*. More importantly, his works mobilise a cybernetic sensibility, in so far as they create a closed-loop feedback system in which the viewer responds to the sculpture's appearance by coming closer or making an audible noise, which modulates the appearance of the work, prompting the viewer to respond again, *ad infinitum*. While the viewer can choose how much or how long to engage with the work, Tsai's sculptures are not so much 'participatory' as fully 'cybernetic', in the sense that a viewer cannot wholly opt out of interacting with the work: even the sound of your footsteps walking away can trigger changes in some of the sculptures.

The influence of cybernetics on the intellectual history of the twentieth century is wide-ranging, but of particular relevance here is its correspondence with the development of digital computing. In fact, the two discourses were so closely aligned that cybernetic environments became a kind of ersatz computer art. To wit, the pioneering 1968 museum exhibition of computers and art at the Institute of Contemporary Arts (ICA), London, was called *Cybernetic Serendipity*.[18] In addition to including computer graphics by the likes of Noll and Julesz, the show also included four of Tsai's sound-responsive sculptures. In a book published after the exhibition, the curator Jasia Reichardt explained that cybernetic environments, which are the 'direct development of kinetic and light art', are also genealogically related to computing:

> there are many works based on the ethos of computer technology but which have not been made with the aid of the computer or its peripherals. Many interactive devices, sound and visual systems and ingenious cybernetic environments which operate on a feedback system owe their existence directly to those principles on which computer hardware and software are based.[19]

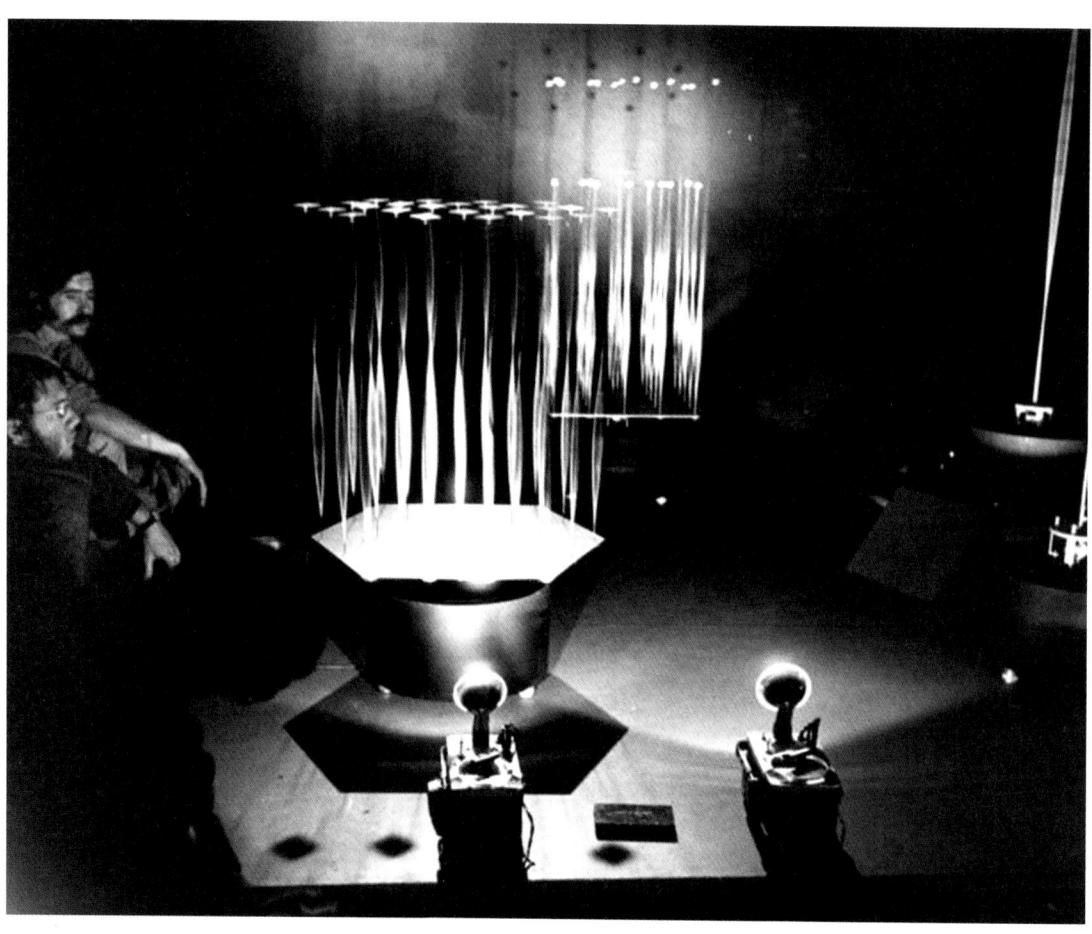

↑ Wen-Ying Tsai, *Cybernetic Sculpture System*, at Center for Advanced Visual Studies exhibition, *Explorations*, Hayden Gallery, MIT, 1970

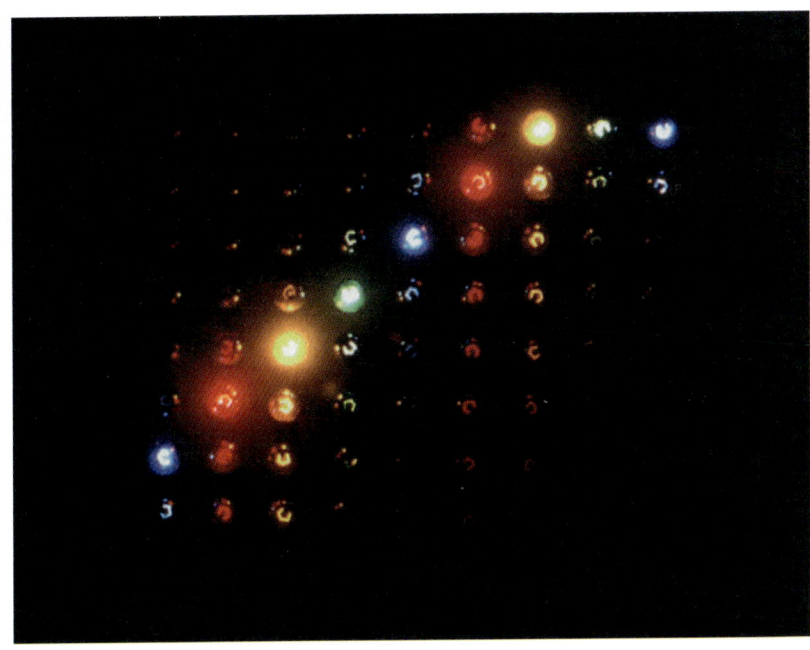

Thus, while Tsai's 'cybernetic' sculptures are not digital works, one may claim, following Reichardt's precedent, that they represent the 'principles' of computer technology, to which they also 'owe their existence'.[20] And perhaps not coincidentally, the feedback system governing the interaction between Tsai's sculptures and their viewers is directly analogous to the feedback system between artist and computer described by Noll in regards to his own works in 1965.

Beyond invoking the general association of cybernetics and computing, Tsai's sculptures engage a very specific attribute of electronic media: namely, the ability of electronic information to be translated across sensory modalities, leading ultimately to the 'metamedium' of digital data. Reichardt herself had noted the importance of translation across media to early computer art, arguing in 1971 that 'it is no longer possible to talk about computer-generated graphics as an art medium without mentioning environmental art, cybernetic systems and spectator participation – events which have grown out of and around the idea of converting images into their equivalents either in sound or movement.'[21] Writing that same year on Tsai's 'cybernetic sculptures', György Kepes similarly highlighted the role of electronic 'transducers' in recent contemporary art:

> Sophisticated instrumentation opened up traffic between all ranges of signals, thus making it possible to convert sight to sound, space to time, and interchange phases and events. [They] convert, amplify, transform, and translate patterns into patterns, introduce new relations into any set of signals – distorting, magnifying, reducing.[22]

In the late 1970s and early 1980s, Tsai began working with computers directly. This new work was enabled by the evolution of the computer into a consumer commodity, in the form of smaller and more powerful 'microcomputers' sold to individuals at greatly reduced costs. Somewhat typical of this period of his art, Tsai's *Computer Light* 1980 is a vertical grid of coloured bulbs programmed to light up in a sequence of geometric shapes. In the 1990s, Tsai embraced the latest iteration of electronic technology: the World Wide Web. In 1995, he completed an online project for Time Warner Electronic Publishing's 'Artslink' initiative that was originally viewable on Netscape (an internet browser that had just been introduced the previous year).[23] In pursuing a path that led him from kinetic sculptures to cybernetic light environments, digitally-programmed light sculptures and finally to the internet, Tsai traced the development of what would later be known as 'digital art' – a field that to this day paradoxically encompasses works as disparate as prints on paper and interactive sculptures, remaking our concept of the artistic medium in the process.

Note: This essay is drawn from Tina Rivers Ryan, 'McLuhan's Bulbs: Light Art and the Dawn of New Media', PhD thesis, Columbia University, New York 2016.

↑ Wen-Ying Tsai, *Computer Light* 1980

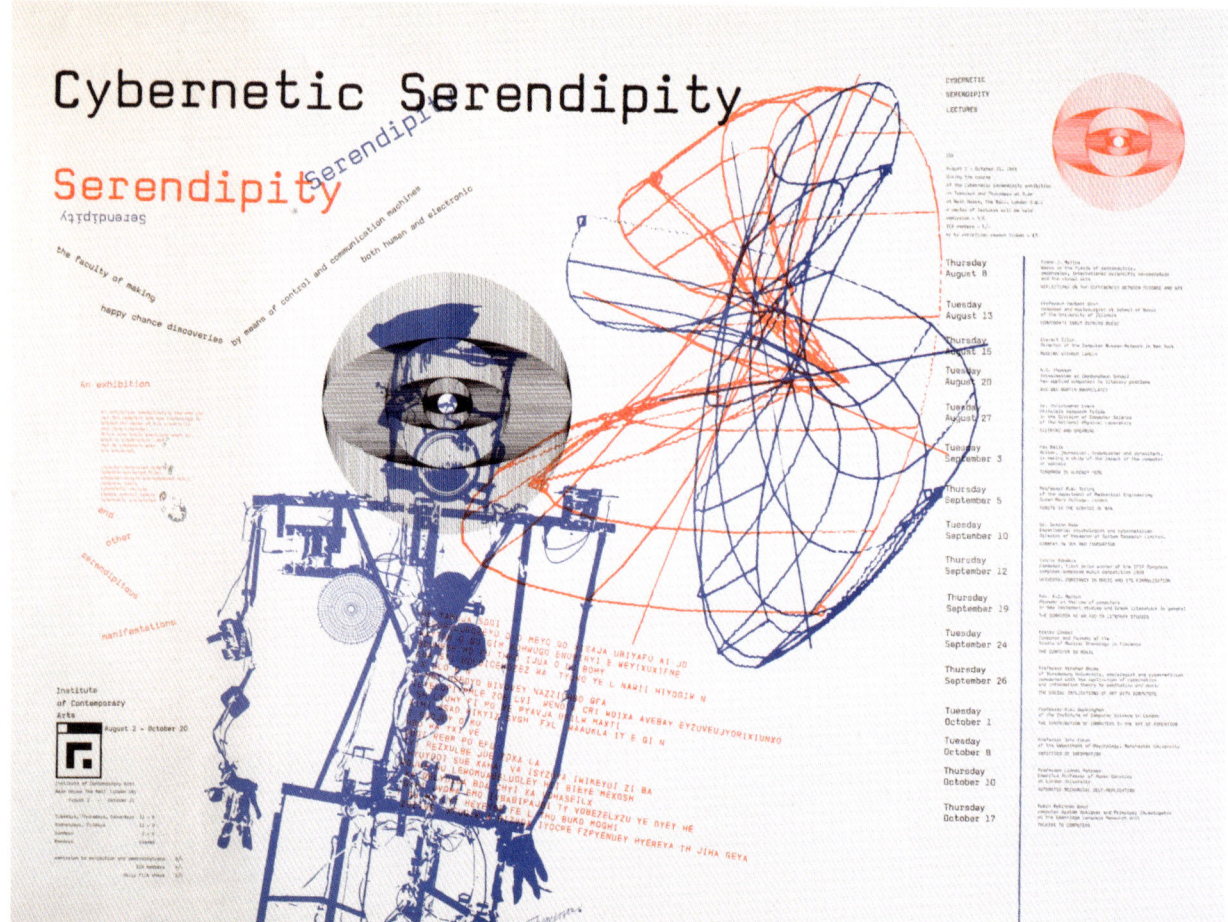

Cybernetic Serendipity

The exhibition *Cybernetic Serendipity*, held at London's Institute of Contemporary Arts (ICA) between August and October 1968, was the first large-scale exhibition dedicated to the use of the computer as a medium or a source of inspiration in the arts, showcasing visual art as well as music, choreography and poetry, alongside experimental projects by people working primarily as engineers and scientists, such as psychologist and cybernetician Gordon Pask. The exhibition, designed by artist Franciszka Themerson (who also designed the poster), included a section illustrating the history and principles of cybernetics and an area dedicated to electronic music, with spherical listening booths. It featured functioning robots by Bruce Lacey and Nam June Paik, several early interactive sculptures (by Nicolas Schöffer, Wen-Ying Tsai, Edward Ihnatowicz) and a vast international survey of computer-generated drawings, poetic texts and music scores. Despite its stated intent, not all featured works used computers in a strict sense – not least due to the fact that very few artists had access to those machines – but demonstrated the potential for thinking and making art with and through programmable machines. The exhibition also reflected the principles of 'second-order cybernetics', which expanded the study of systems based on information feedback loops and self-regulation by including the observer as an active participant: in this case, the exhibition's visitors interacting with responsive machines. VR

↑ Franciszka Themerson, *Cybernetic Serendipity* poster, 1968

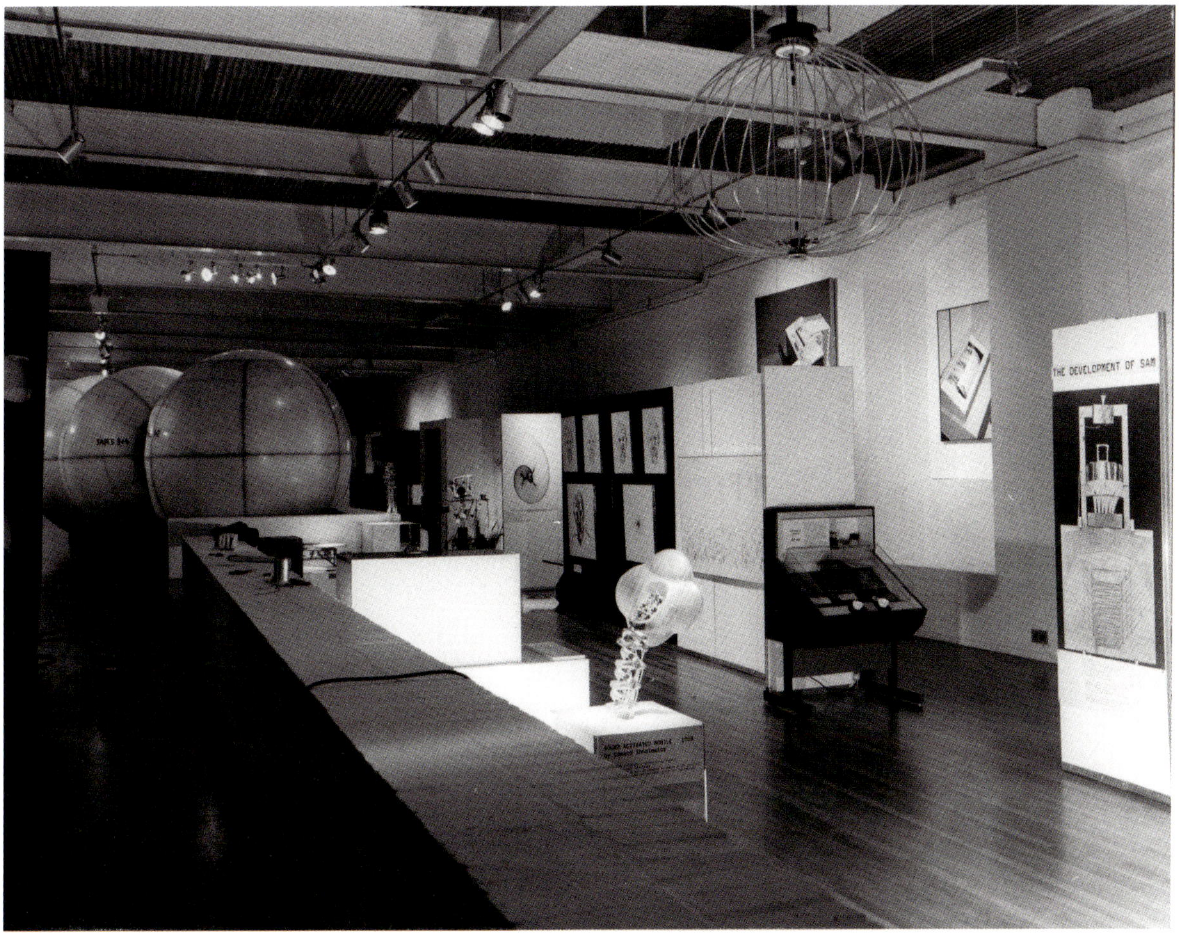

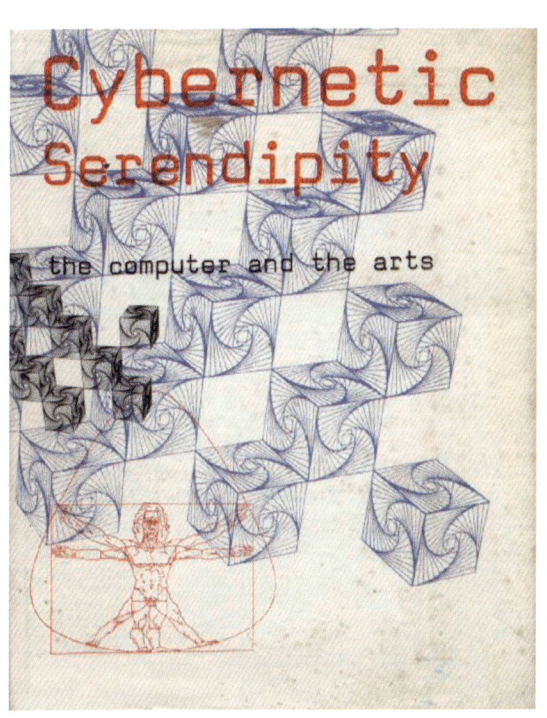

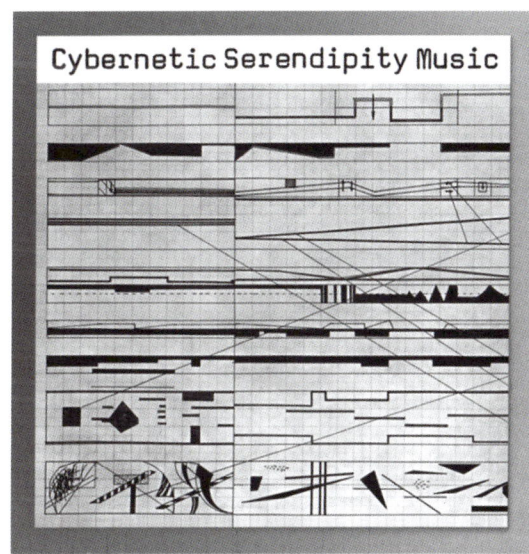

↑ Cover of *Cybernetic Serendipidity: The Computer and the Arts, Studio International Special Issue*, London, 1968, cover design by Franciszka Themerson incorporating designs by Donald K. Robbins and Charles Csuri

⤒ *Cybernetic Serendipity*, Institute of Contemporary Art, London, 1968, installation view including Edward Ihnatowicz, *SAM* (*Sound Activated Mobile*) 1968, and James Seawright, *Scanner* 1966 (on the ceiling)

↑ *Cybernetic Serendipity Music*, vinyl compillation released alongside exhibition, Institute of Contemporary Art, London, 1968. The design on the cover is a graphic score by composer Peter Zinovieff.

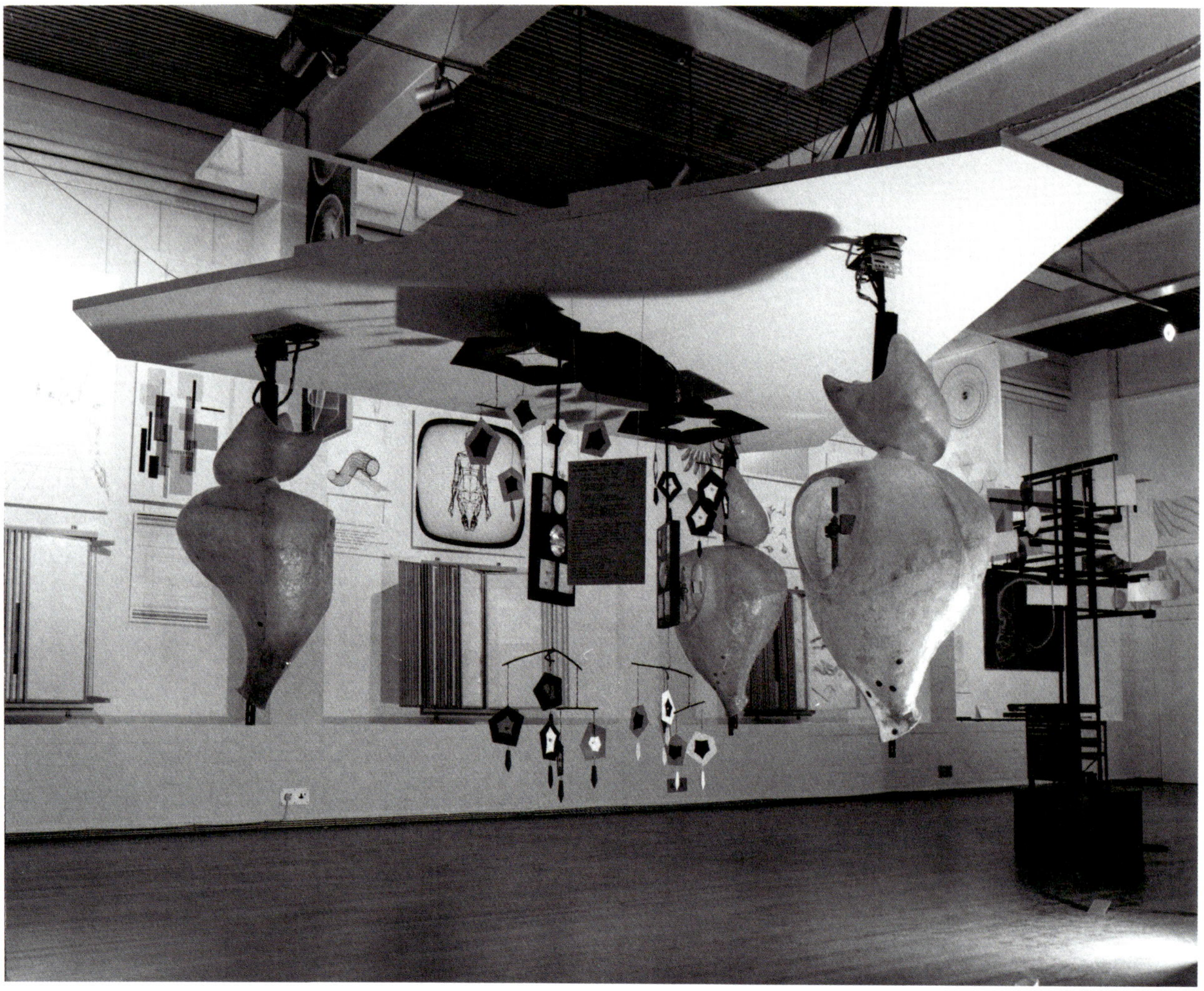

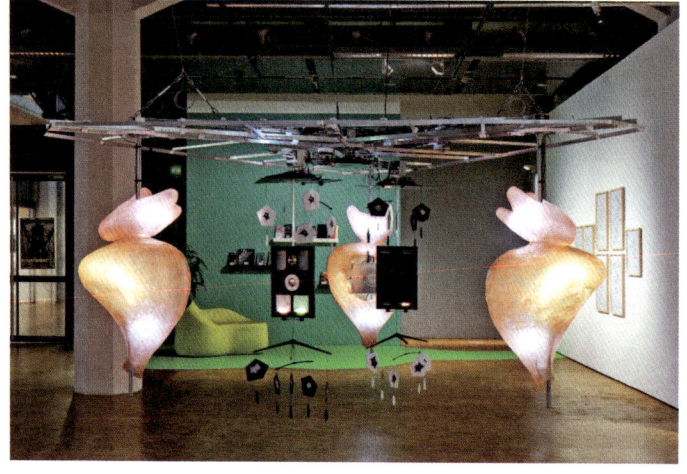

Gordon Pask

Colloquy of Mobiles 1968 is an installation of sculptural figures which move and interact, with each other and the public, through light and sound. Large rotating mobiles are hung from the ceiling – blinking, squawking, and sometimes synchronising with each other, while visitors can interact with them using flashlights and mirrors. The work explores the nature of machine-to-machine and person-to-machine conversations in an interactive and immersive environment.

Pask was a cybernetician and a prolific artist, writer and theorist. *Colloquy of Mobiles* is an installation representation of his 'conversation theory', which suggests that learning occurs through conversations leading to shared understanding. The work was part of *Cybernetic Serendipity* (1968); a 2018 replica including some of the original components was created on the occasion of its fiftieth anniversary and is held in the collection of ZKM Center for Art and Media, Karlsruhe. BP

↑, ↗ Gordon Pask, *Colloquy of Mobiles* 1968

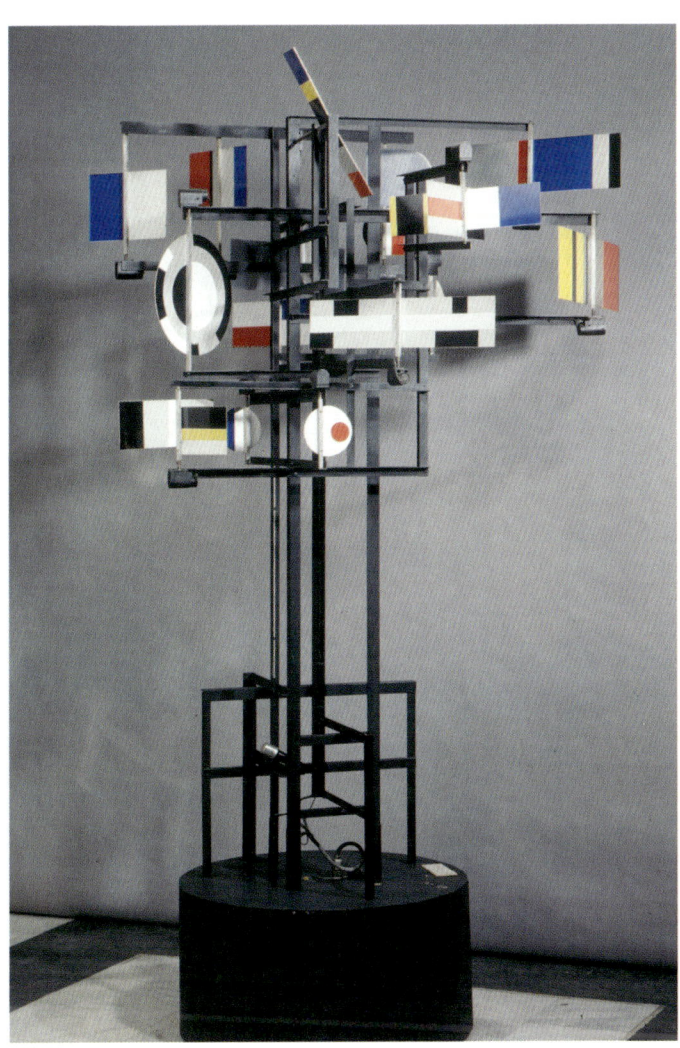

Nicolas Schöffer

Schöffer is one of the earliest artists to combine kinetic art with cybernetics, creating reactive sculptures using computation based on feedback loops. In the 1950s, Schöffer begins to investigate ideas of spatiodynamics and luminodynamics with semi-mobile works. *CYSP 1* 1956 emerged out of these experiments. The work is set on a base monument on four rollers, which contain the mechanisms, while the plates are operated by small motors located under each axis. Photo-electric cells and a microphone built into the sculpture catch all the variations in the fields of colour, light intensity and sound intensity. The title represents the first letters of 'cybernetics' and 'spatiodynamics' and was the first spatiodynamic sculpture with some autonomy of movement. *CYSP 1* was prominently featured in *Cybernetic Serendipity* in 1968, along with a scale model of Schöffer's *Cybernetic Light Tower*, an unrealised project for La Defence in Paris. BP

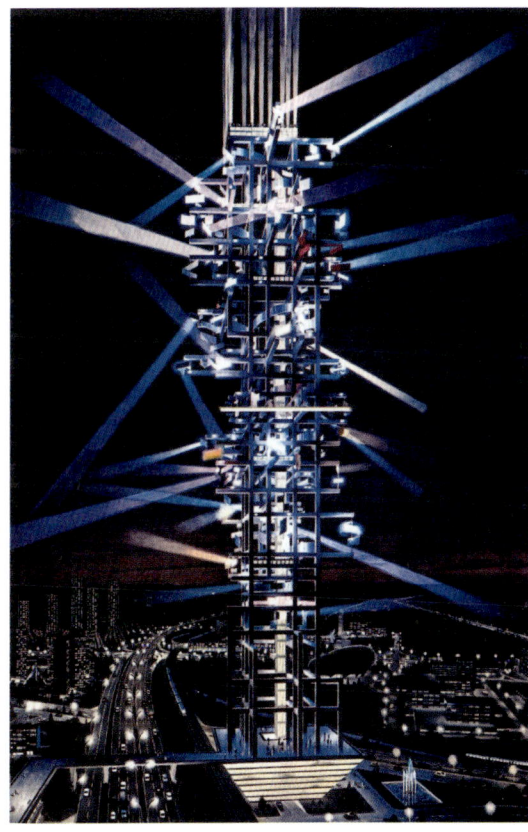

↖ Nicolas Schöffer, *CYSP 1* 1956
↑ Nicolas Schöffer, *La Tour Lumière Cybernétique*, concept 1963, unrealised

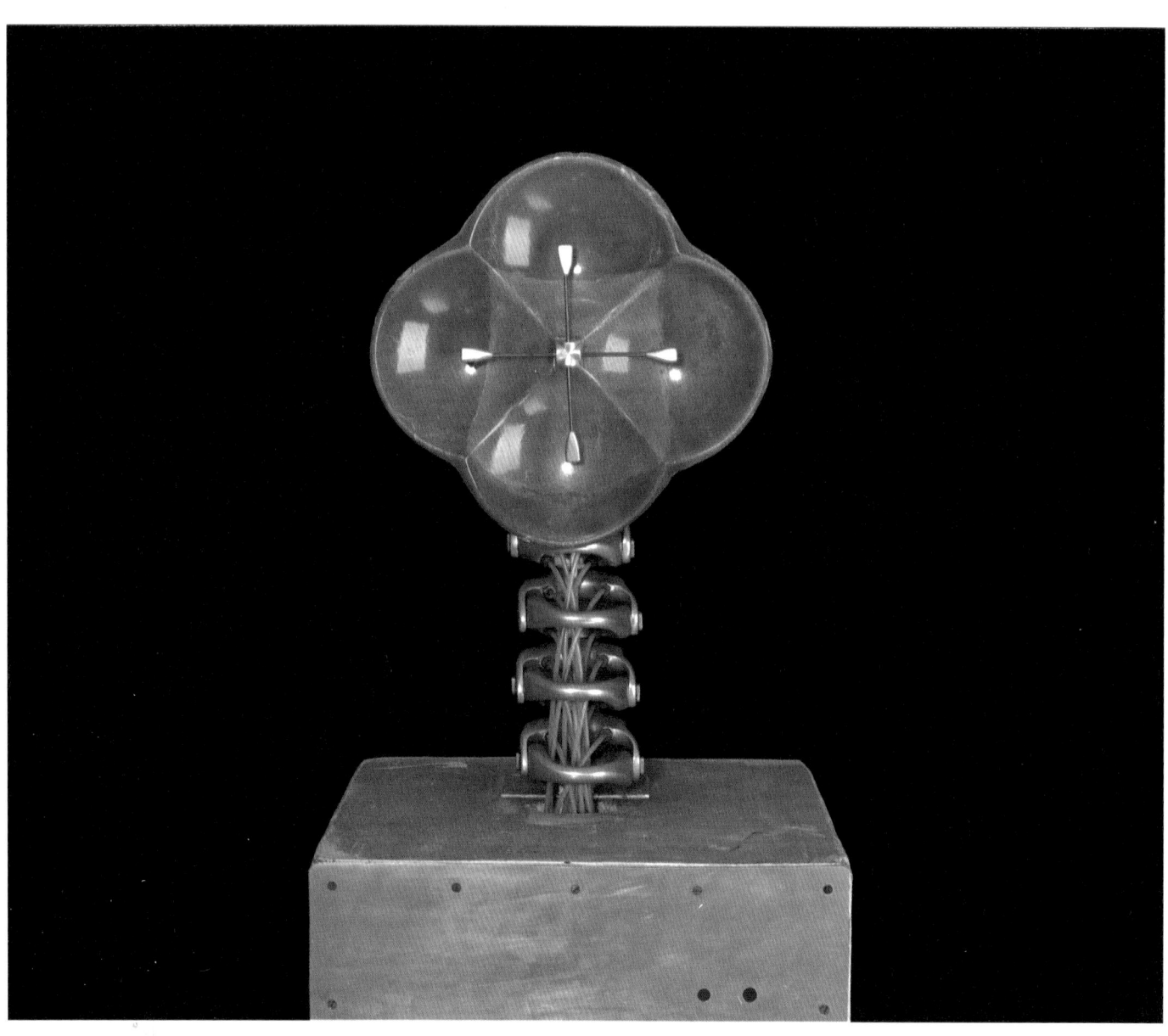

↑ Edward Ihnatowicz, *SAM – Sound Activated Mobile* 1968

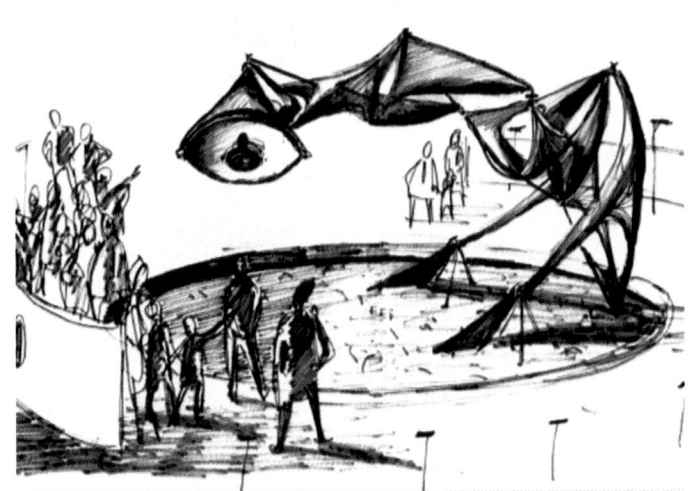

Edward Ihnatowicz

Having moved to the UK from Poland after the Second World War, Ihnatowicz mixed his classical art training with a self-taught passion for engineering to create unique biomorphic sculptures that responded to their environments using custom-built electronic systems connecting a sophisticated array of sensors with hydraulic actuators. These interactive artworks, the very first of their kind, embodied key cybernetic ideas on the communication between people, machines and the environment. Ihnatowicz developed his own hardware and software for his work. His *SAM (Sound Activated Mobile)* 1968, which debuted at the *Cybernetic Serendipity* exhibition at the Institute of Contemporary Arts in 1968, featured an aluminium, spine-like structure surmounted by a four-lobed fibreglass dish holding microphones. As these picked up noises from the environment, the sculpture turned its 'face' towards the source of the sound. In 1970 he went on to create *The Senster*, a 4.5-metre-long robotic sculpture that responded to both sound and movement with startling speed and precision. VR

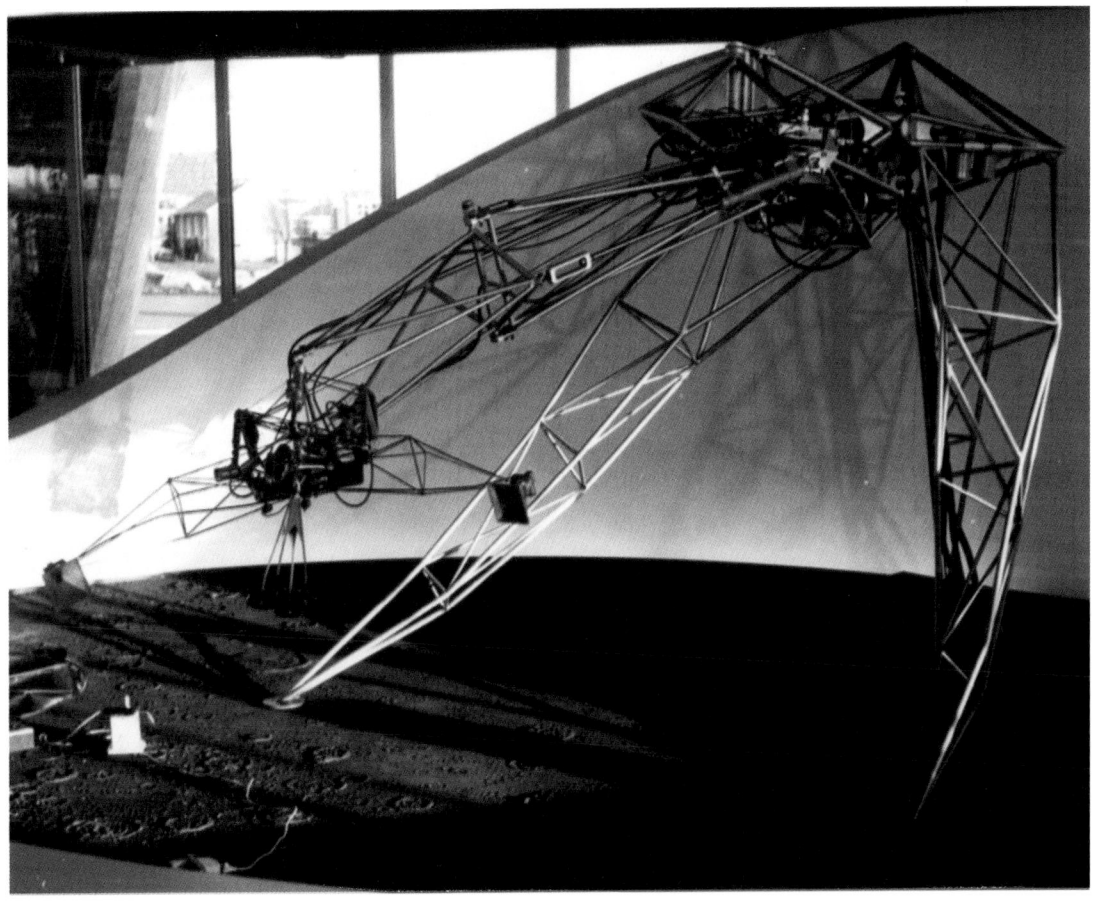

↖ Edward Ihnatowicz, concept sketch for *The Senster* 1970
↑ Edward Ihnatowicz, *The Senster* 1970, installation view at the Evoluon, Philips exhibition space, Eindhoven, c.1970–4

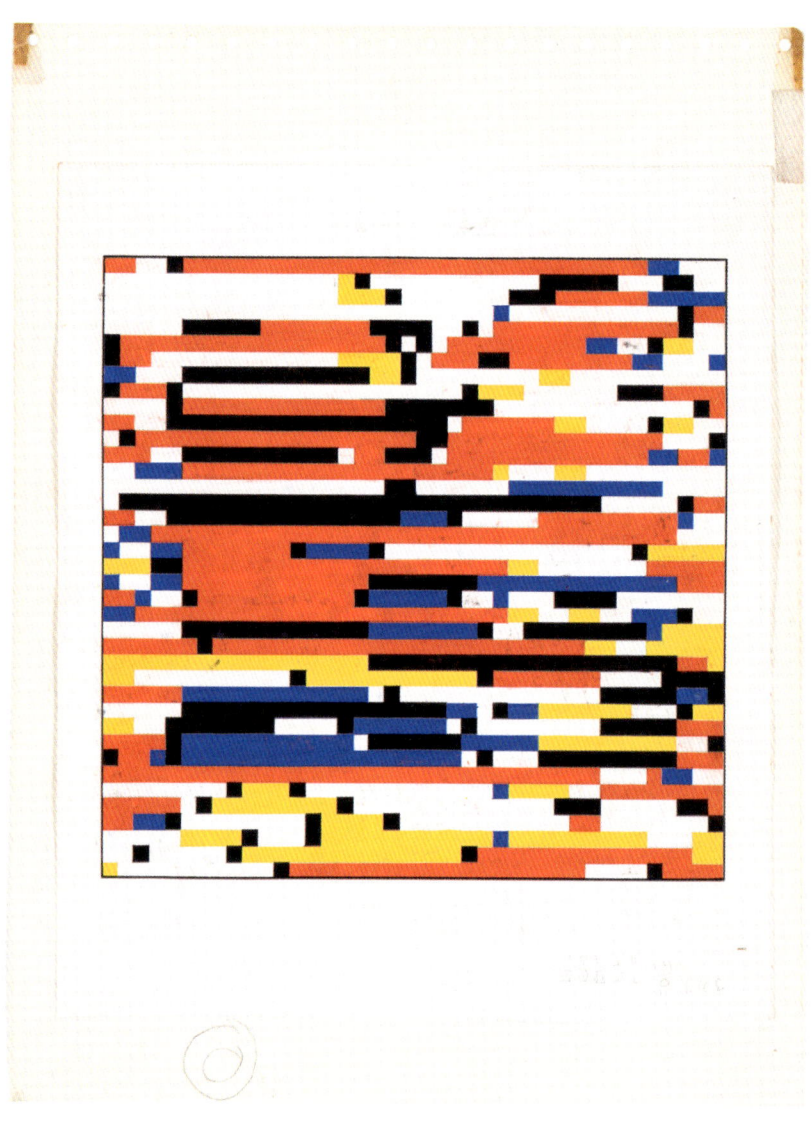

Hiroshi Kawano

Kawano was a Japanese philosopher and artist, one of the first to experiment with computer art in Japan. He was deeply inspired by the writing of German philosopher Max Bense, which led him to learn to program as a way of practising the theories of aesthetic information. His first computer-generated designs were published as early as September 1964 in the Japanese *IBM Review* No.6. Kawano worked with 'pseudo-random' number generators that allowed for the automatic variation of defined forms. At the same time, he could control certain parameters – dimensions, direction and number, for example – to visualise objects such as circles, squares or lines. This method allowed for many different drawings to be realised from the same inputs. BP

← Hiroshi Kawano, *Design 6 Data A* 1965
↑ Hiroshi Kawano, *3 of 7 d2 // Design 1-4* 1964
→ Hiroshi Kawano, *KD 29 – Artificial Mondrian* 1969

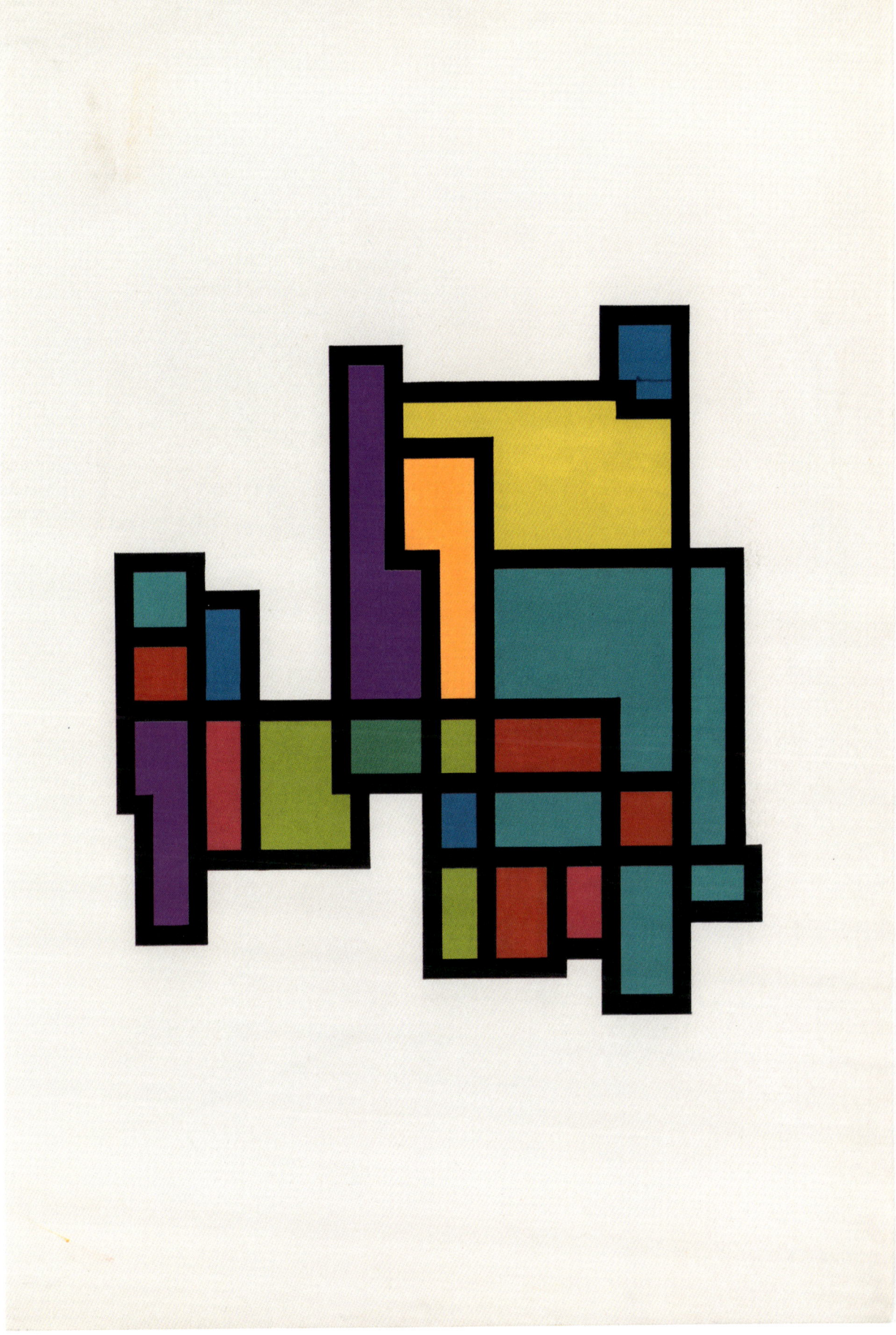

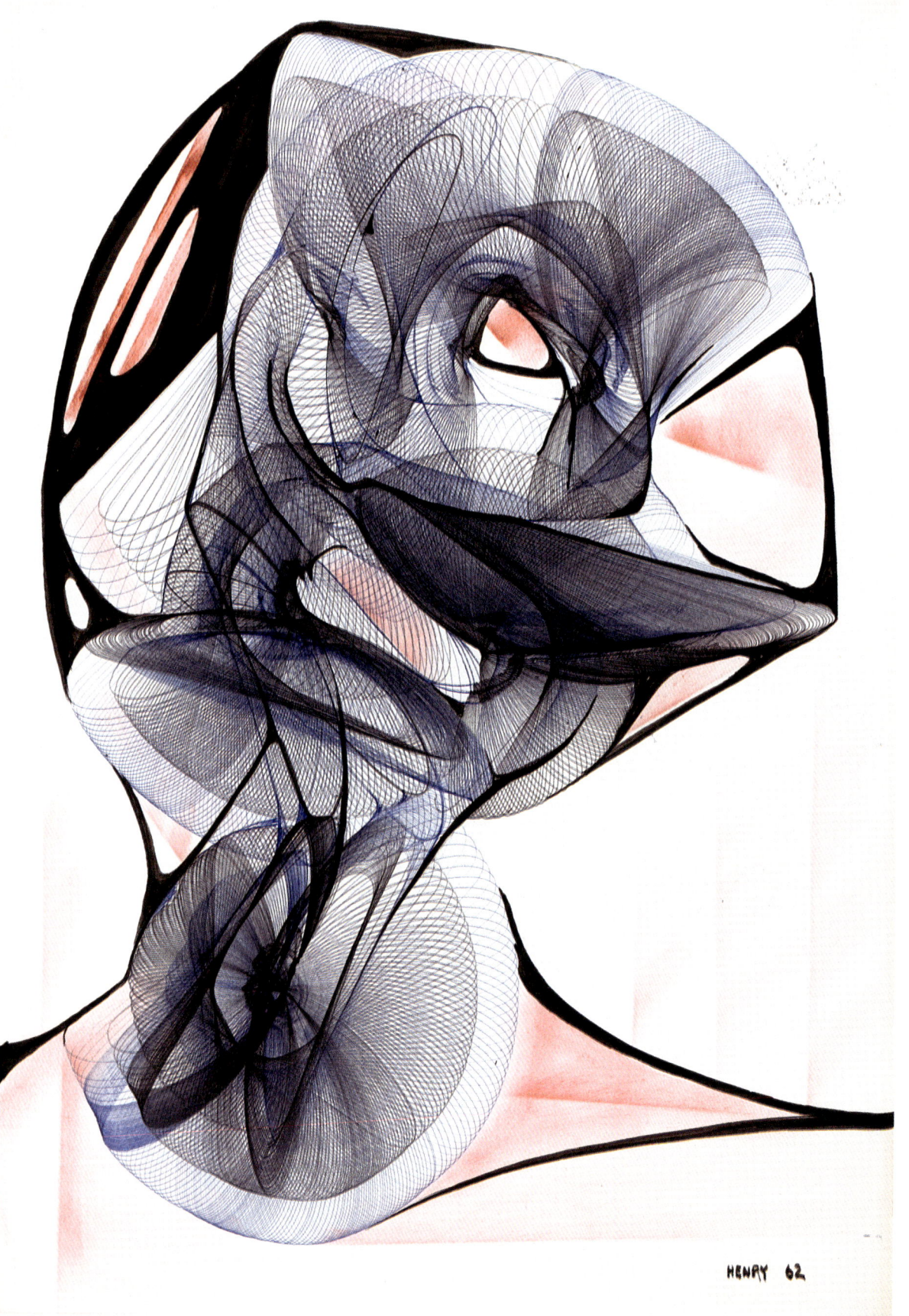

HENRY 62

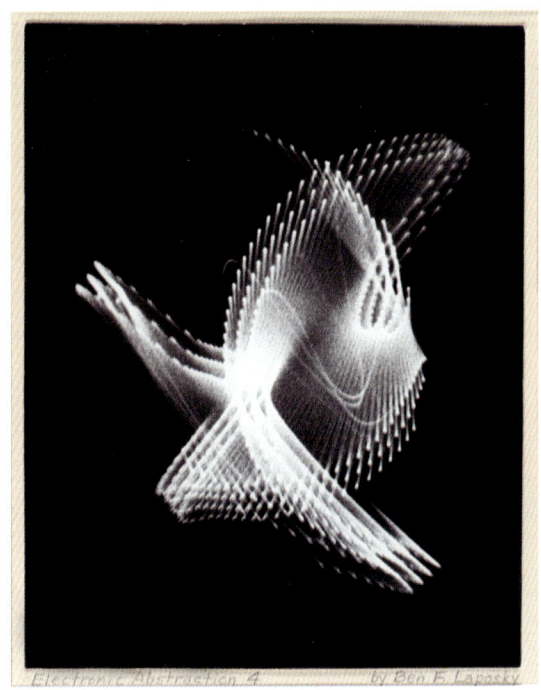

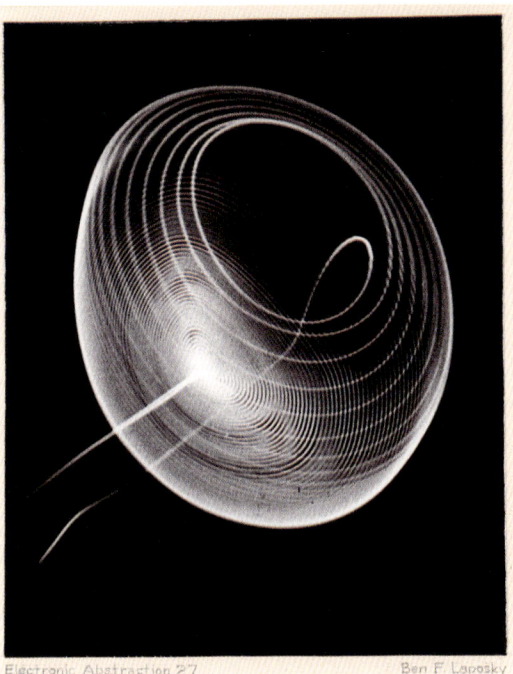

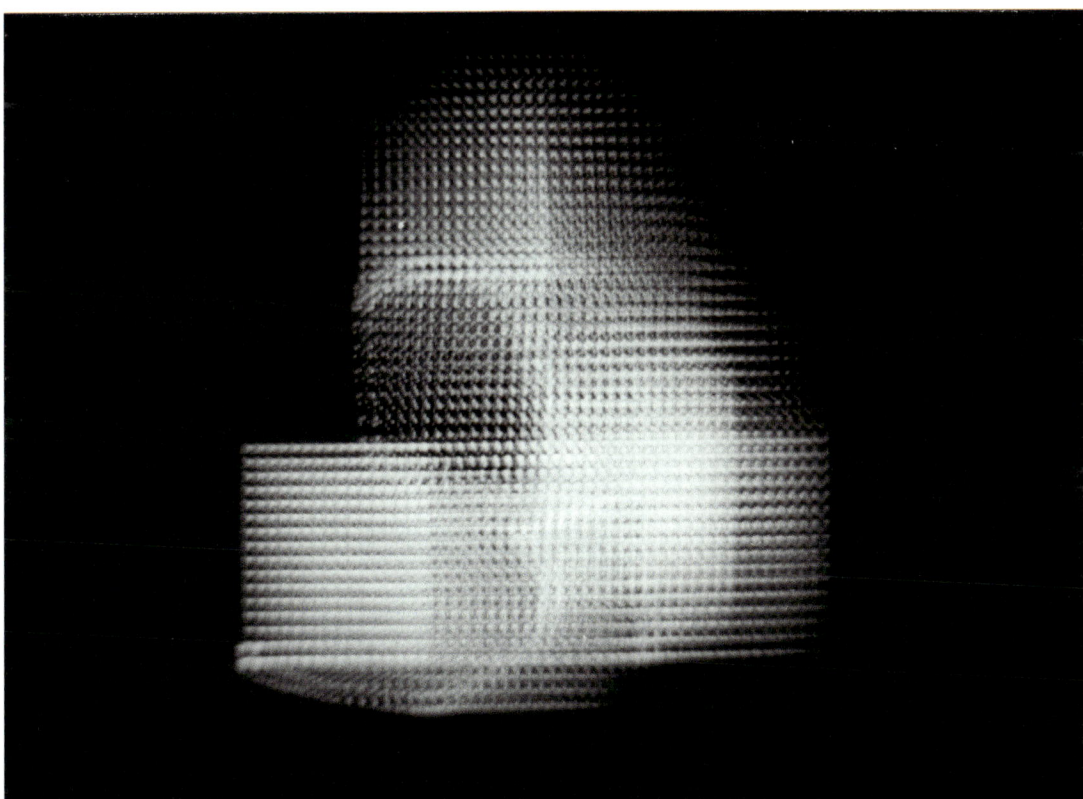

123

← Desmond Paul Henry, *Untitled* 1962
♣ Ben Laposky, *Electronic Abstraction 4* 1952

♣ Ben Laposky, *Electronic Abstraction 27* 1952
↑ Vladimir Bonačić, *IRB 8-9 (I'RB')* 1968

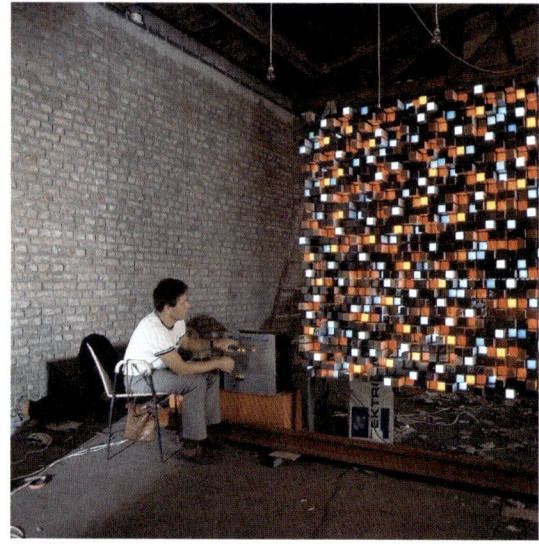

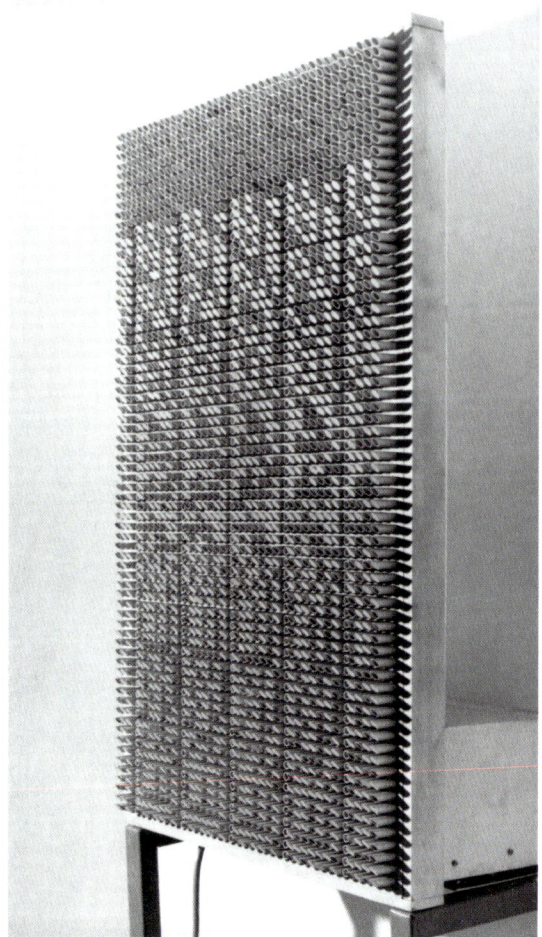

↑ Ivan Picelj, *Tendencies 4* 1969

♠ Vladimir Bonačić with his work *GF.E 16,4 CNSM* 1969, c.1971
↑ Vladimir Bonačić and Ivan Picelj, *T4* 1968

124

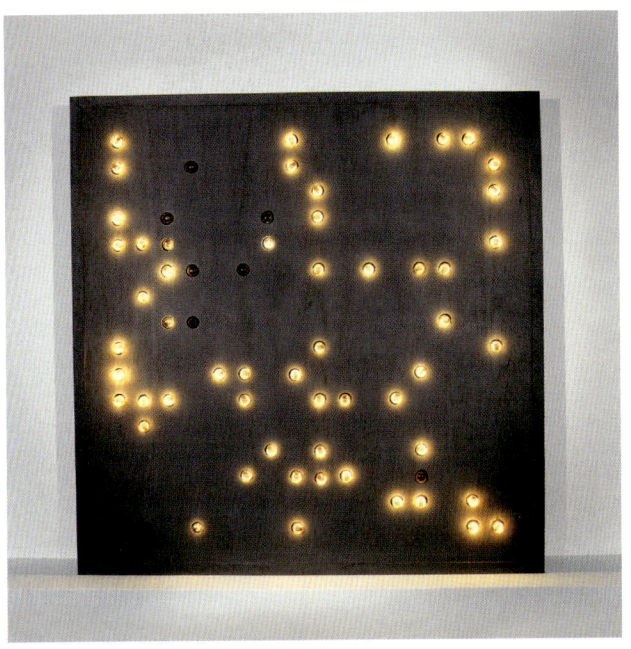

Vladimir Bonačić

While working as a cybernetics researcher in Zagreb, Bonačić started making art to give visual form to Galois fields – mathematical structures that produce symmetries and patterns. Bonačić turned these fields into light arrays on a computer screen and photographed the results. After exhibiting some of these photographs at *Tendencies 4* in 1968–9, he became an active contributor to the later phase of the New Tendencies movement. Bonačić collaborated with Ivan Picelj to create the light relief *t4*, based on Picelj's poster for *Tendencies 4*. This was the first of a series of 'dynamic objects', kinetic artworks using custom hardware and software to visualise Galois fields as light patterns, and sometimes as sounds. Bonačić used software to generate 'pseudo-random' structures that embodied mathematical principles of order and complexity, but thought that relying on computers to generate truly random patterns could only create meaningless results. To demonstrate this, he created *Random 63* 1969 as a kind of paradoxical object, where the bulbs are placed according to a Galois pattern but the sequence in which each turns on or off is truly random, resulting in a friction between signifying pattern and senseless noise. VR

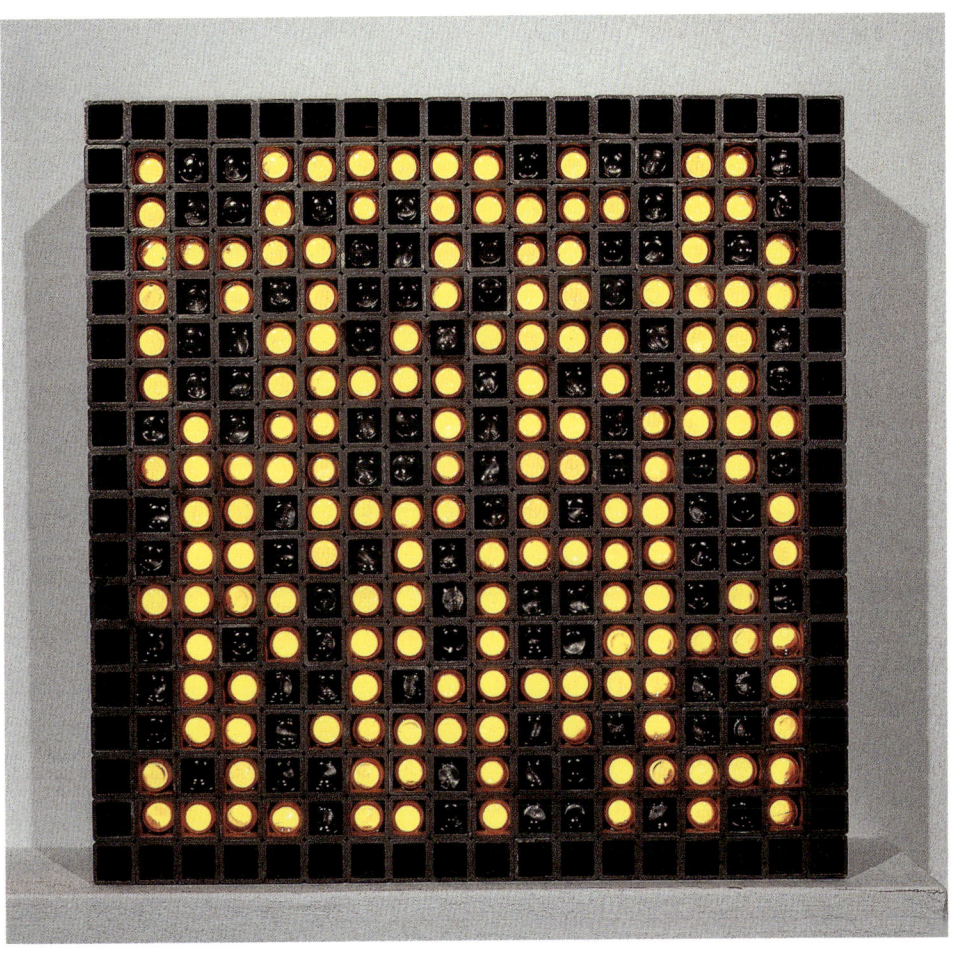

↑ Vladimir Bonačić, *GF.E 16 - NS* 1969

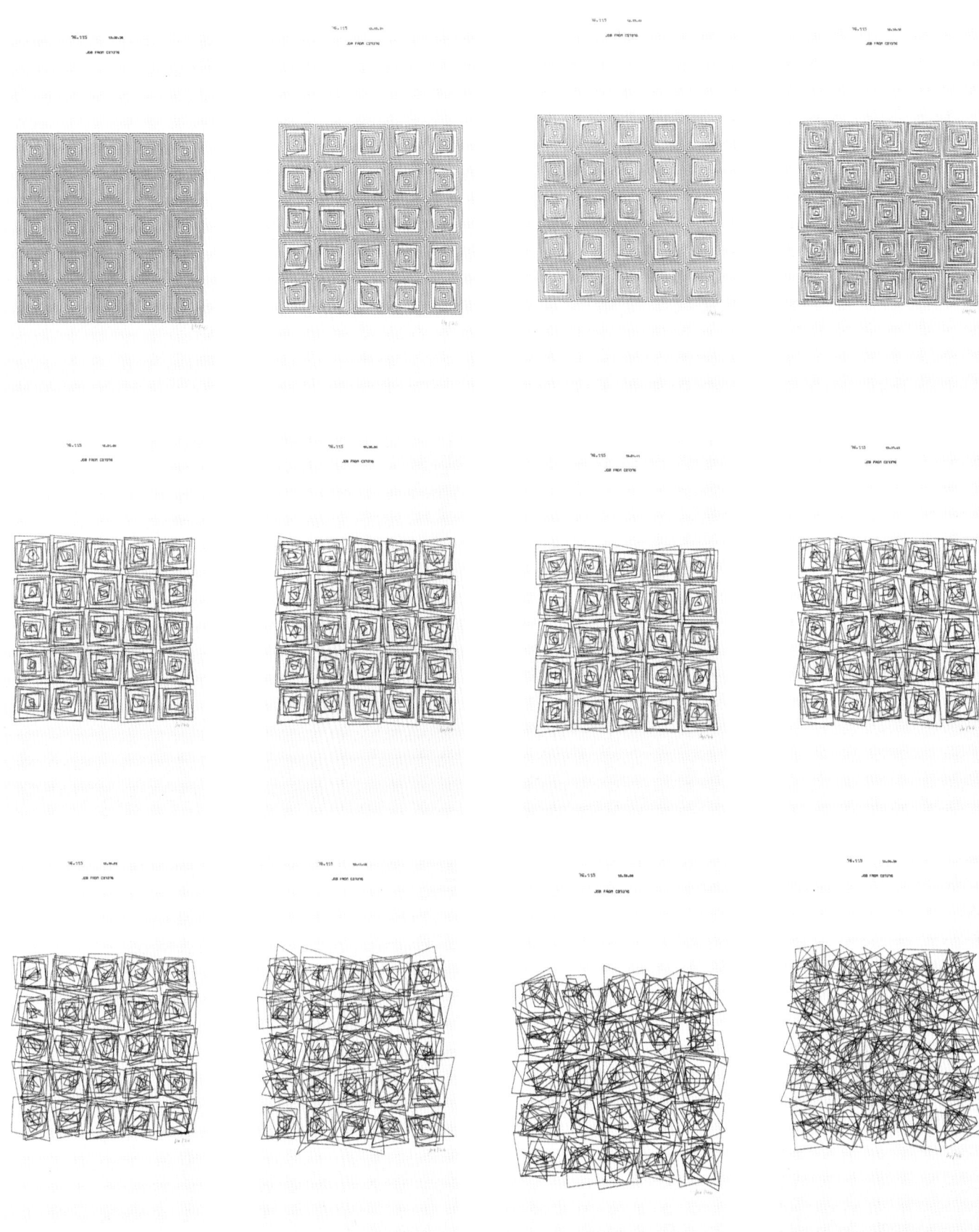

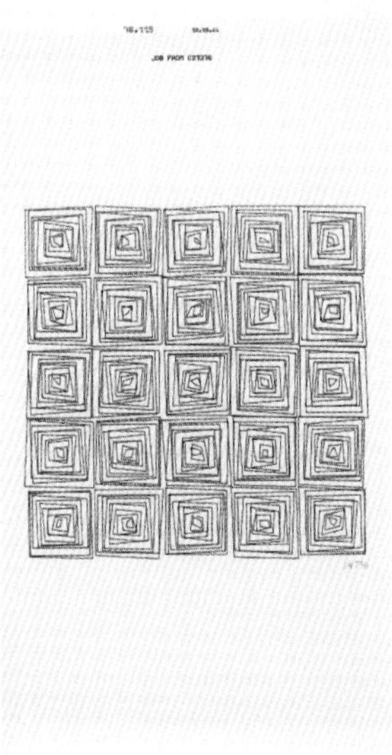

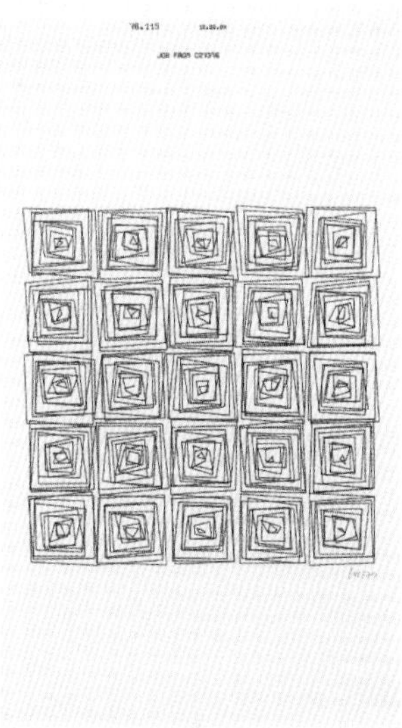

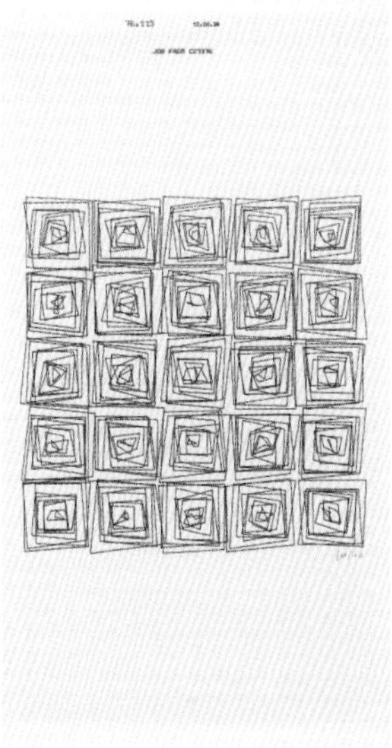

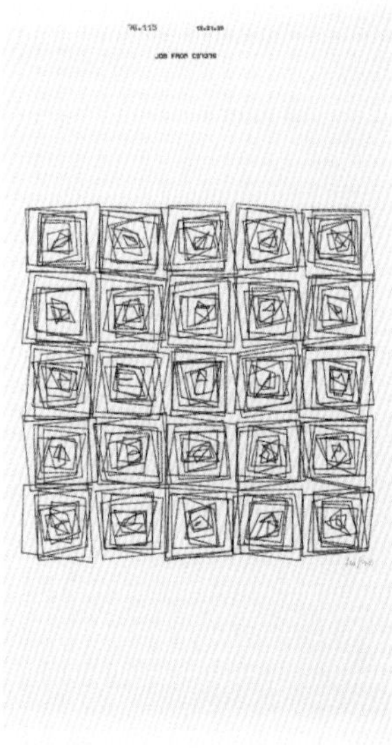

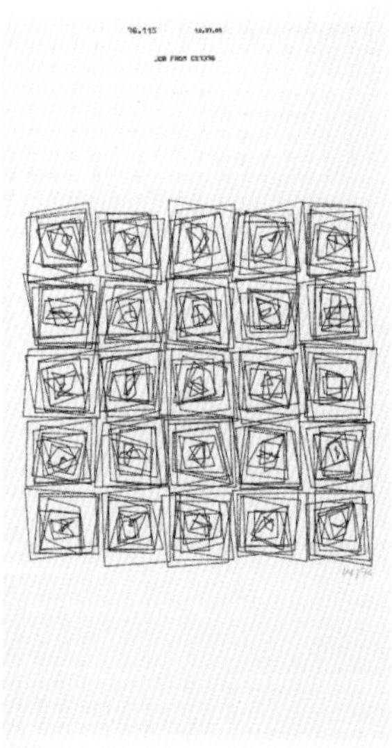

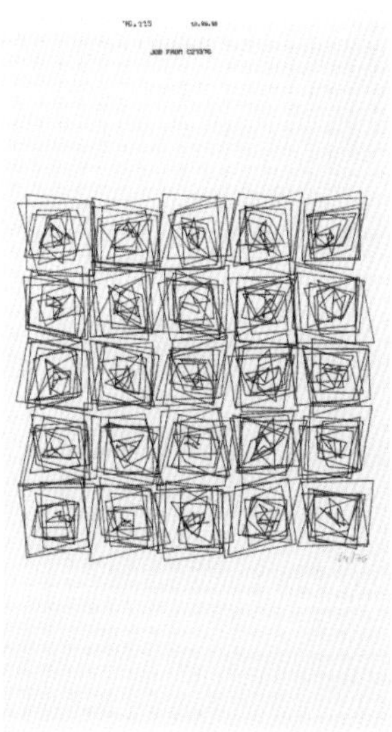

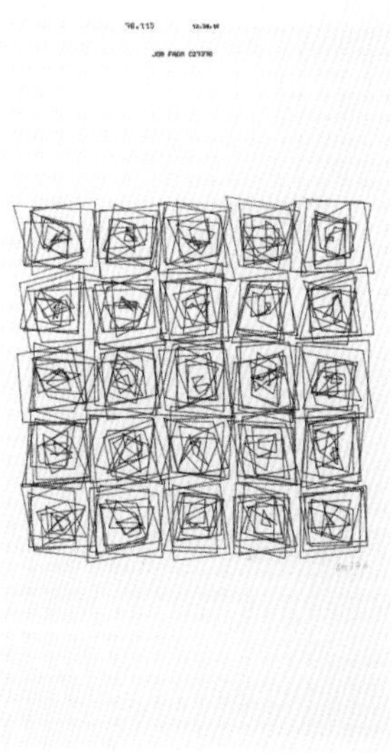

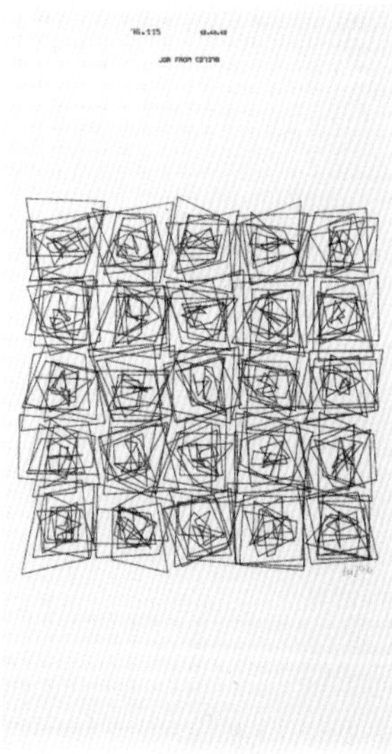

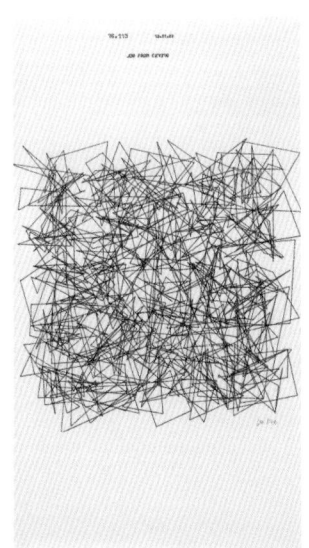

Vera Molnar

A key figure in the first wave of computer artists, Vera Molnar studied painting, art history and aesthetics in Hungary before moving to Paris in 1947. She co-founded both the Groupe de Recherche d'Art Visuel (GRAV) in 1960 and the Group Art et Informatique in Paris in 1967. She created her first computer graphics in 1968, developing the 'Molnart' software with her husband François Molnar in 1976. *Transformations 1–21* 1976 is a series of twenty-one computer plotter drawings on white Benson paper, each showing a stage in the progression of a five-by-five grid made up of concentric-square graphics. The work shows the transformation of the squares from a state of order to disorder, creating a sense of movement and vibration across the series. Molnar experimented with algorithms and systematic approaches to evidence – what she called her visual research. OW

← Vera Molnar, *Transformations 1–21*,1976

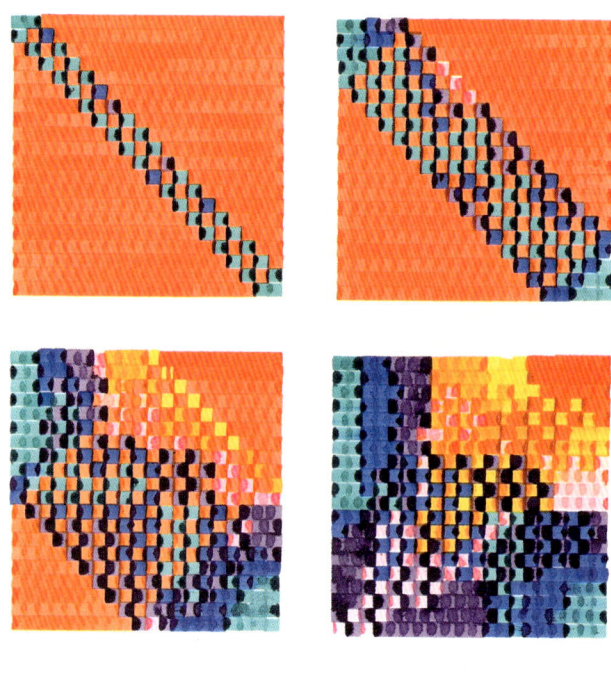

NAKE/TH4/264   1967   MATRIZENMULTIPLIKATION   SERIE 29

↑ Frieder Nake, *Matrix Multiplication Series 29* 1967

Frieder Nake

Nake is a computer scientist and a key figure in early computer art. In 1963, at the Technische Hochschule Stuttgart, he programmed a SEL ER65 computer to connect to the university's newly acquired automatic plotter – the drawing machine ZUSE Graphomat Z64. Nake started with technical test patterns and was soon creating artistic graphics, presented for the first time in 1965 in Stuttgart. He created *Matrix Multiplication Series 29* 1967 by filling a square matrix with numbers on a TR4 computer. The matrix was multiplied successively, and the results were translated into images using the Z64 plotter printer, with each number assigned a visual sign with a particular form and colour. This method speaks to Nake's frequent use of random number generation as a way to add complexity and chance to elements of an artist's decision-making process. Nake also actively participated in animated discussions taking place in publications on the use of computers in art, in which artists, scientists and theorists passionately argued about the potential and limitations of the machines and their capabilities at that time. BP

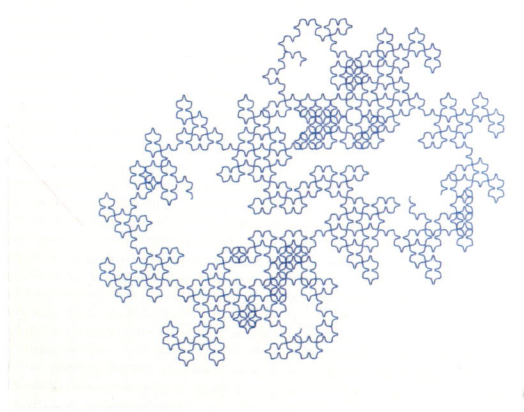

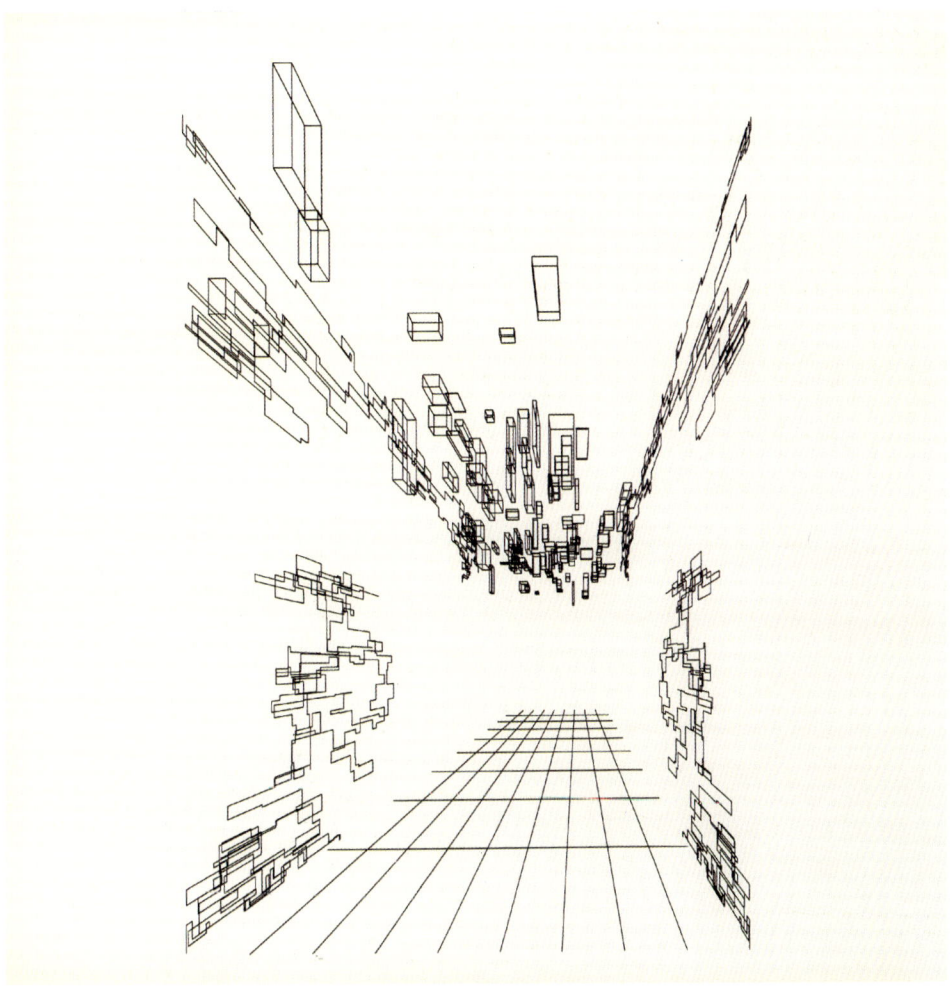

✷ Herbert W. Franke, *Untitled from the DRAKULA Series* 1971
↑ Georg Nees, *Hall (Corridor)* 1966, printed 1970

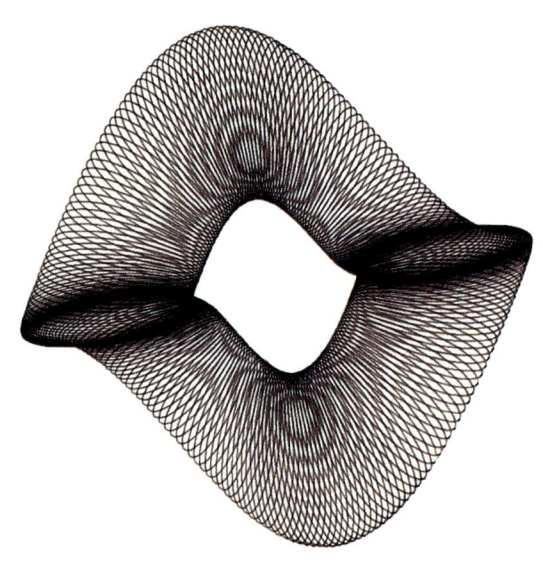

ROTA -45

INC. ANAHEIM CALIFORNIA CHART NO 00   CALIFORNIA COMPUTER PRODUCTS INC. ANAHEIM CALIFORNIA CHART NO 00

↗ Manfred Mohr, *P-026 Logical Inversion* 1970
↑ Tomislav Mikulić, *Rota – 45* 1972

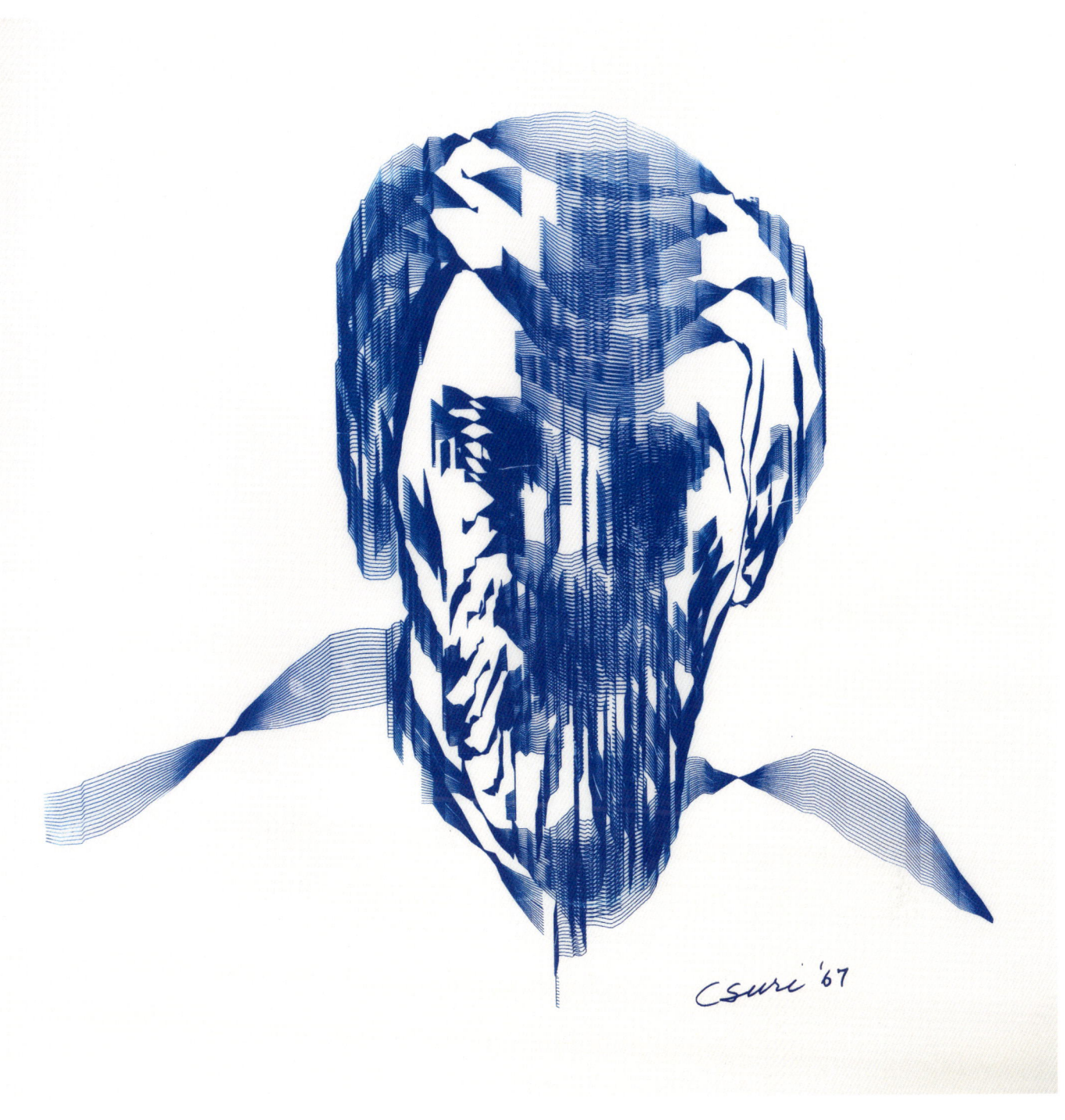

↑ Charles Csuri, *Sine Curve Man* 1967

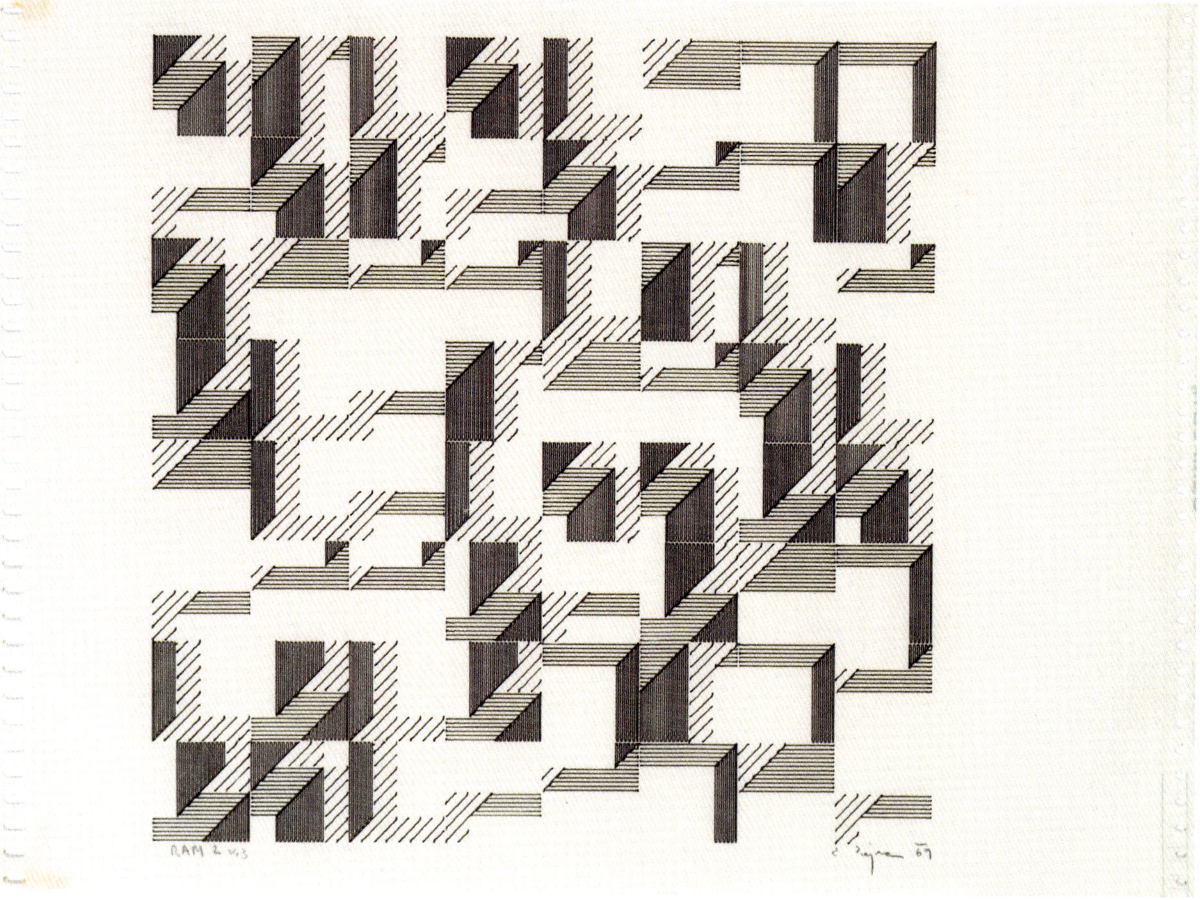

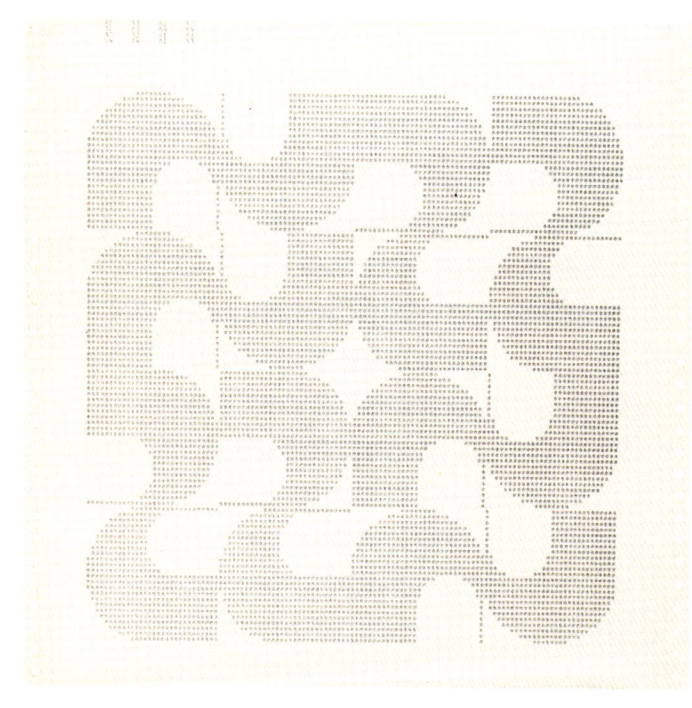

↑ Edward Zajec, *RAM 2 V.3* 1969
↗ Manuel Barbadillo, *Untitled (Cuadro Numero)* c.1968–72

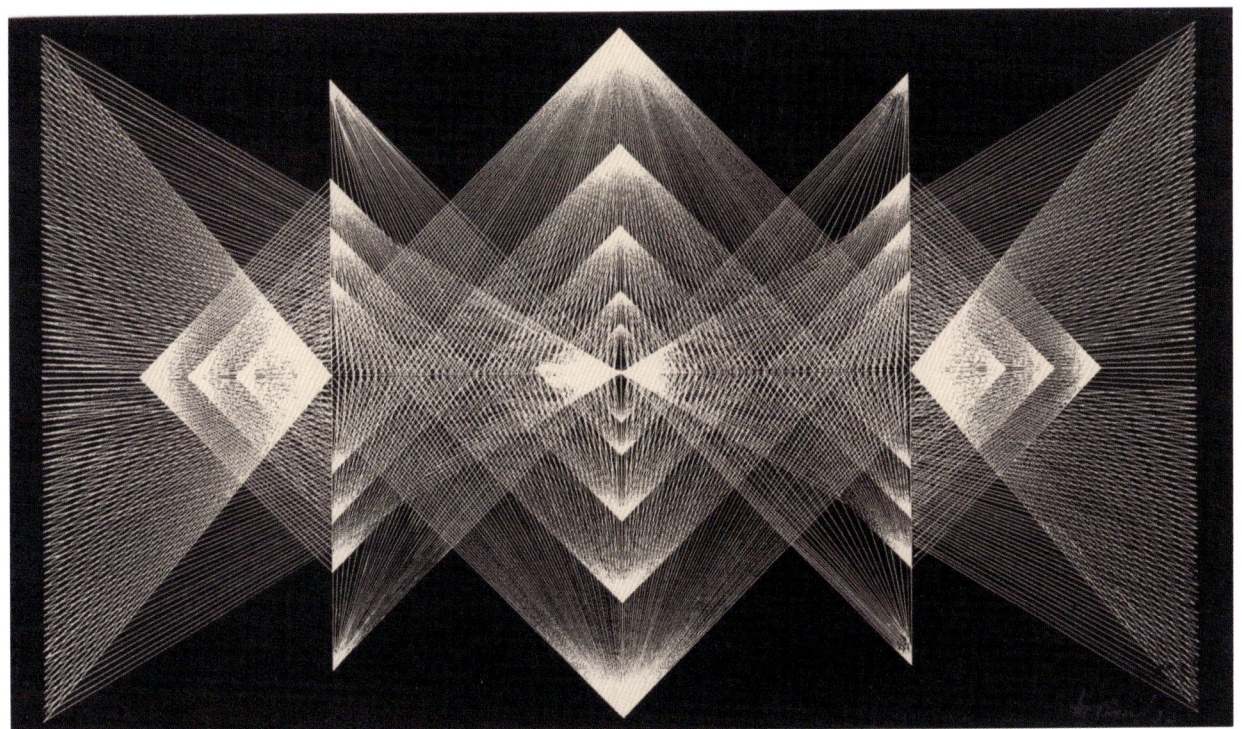

Miguel Ángel Vidal

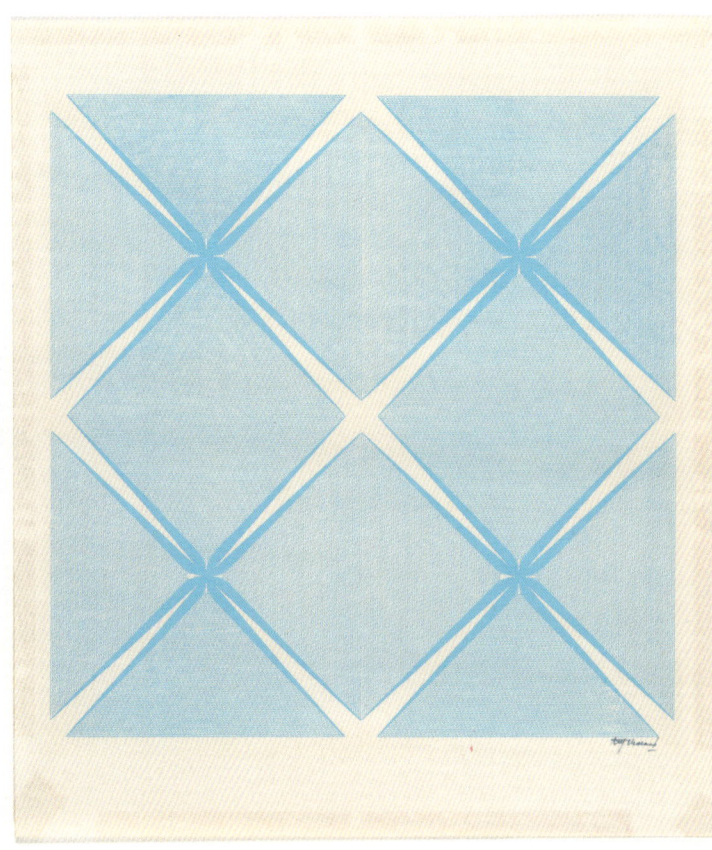

Miguel Ángel Vidal, a painter, printmaker and graphic designer, was one of the founding members of the Grupo de Arte y Cibernética Buenos Aires in 1969, along with other artists associated with the Centro de Arte y Comunicación recently founded by artist and curator Jorge Glusberg. The Grupo de Arte y Cibernética brought together a group of programmers, engineers, system analysts and artists to produce art using computer technologies, collaborating with local universities and the technology manufacturer IBM to access its cutting-edge equipment. It was also well connected to a far-reaching international network of artists working with computers and complex feedback systems. In 1959 Vidal had also co-founded, with Eduardo Mac Entyre, Argentina's Arte Generativo movement, a form of geometric abstraction that emphasised the line as the basic and most versatile element for producing new forms of non-representational art. In his screenprints from computer-generated drawings, Vidal explored depth and pattern through arrays of lines, creating effects like the illusion of three-dimensionality and varying transparency in diagonal compositions. OW

↑ Miguel Ángel Vidal, *Untitled* 1970
↖ Miguel Ángel Vidal, *Untitled* 1969

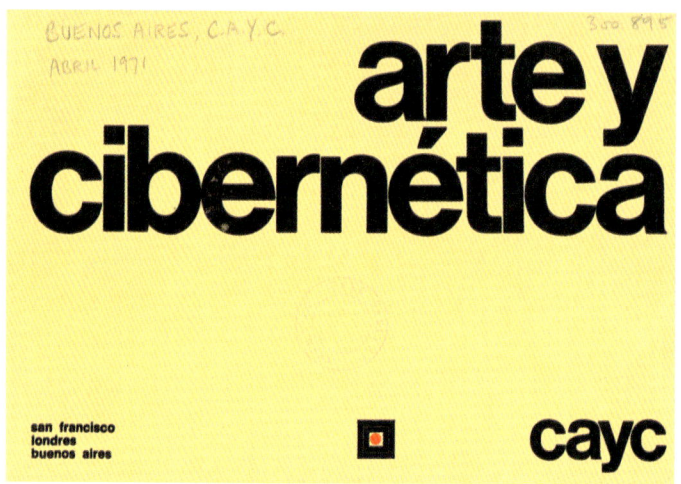

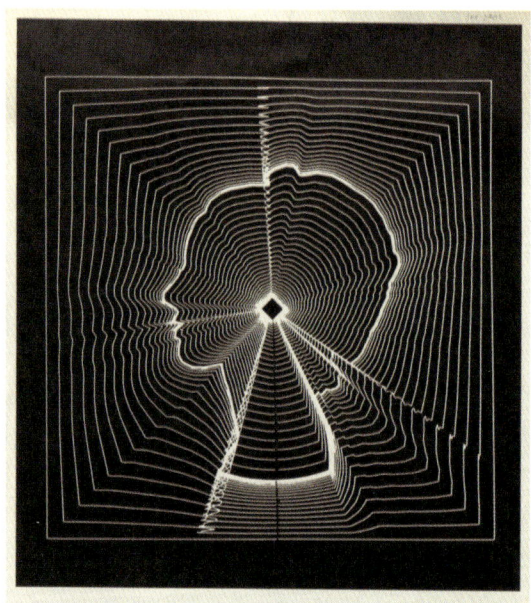

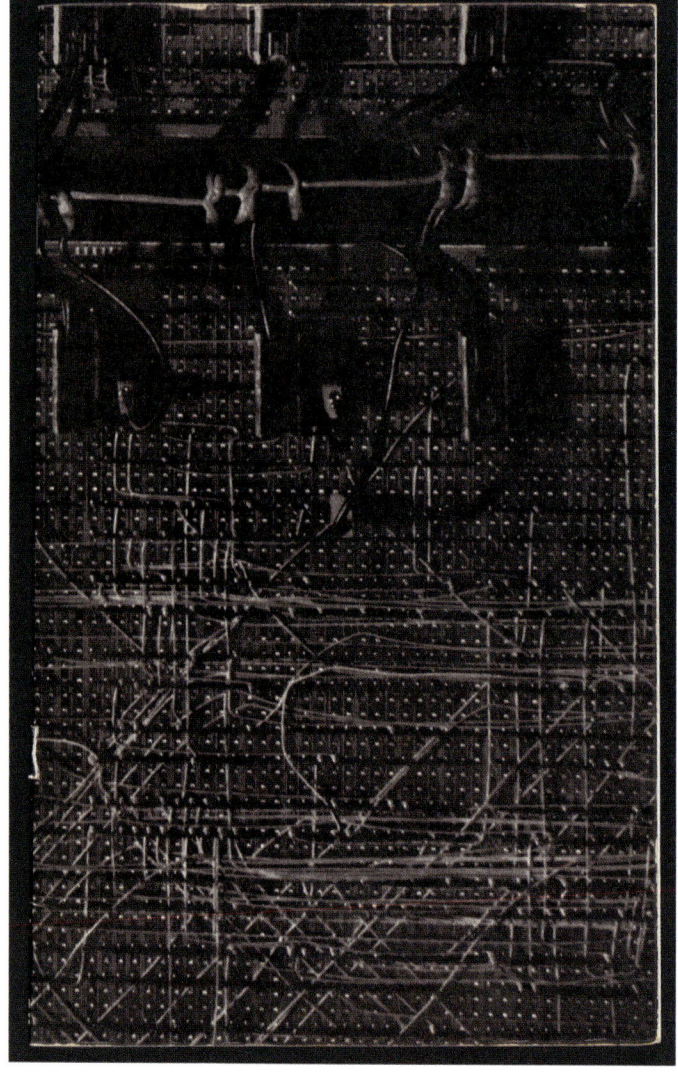

↑ *Arte y Cibernética* exhibition poster, Centro de Estudios de Arte y Comunicación, Buenos Aires, 1969, featuring an image of *Return to Square (b)* by the Computer Technique Group (CTG), 1968

↟ *Arte y Cibernética: San Francisco, London, Buenos Aires* exhibition catalogue, Centro de Arte y Comunicación, Buenos Aires, 1971
↑ *Arte e Cibernética* exhibition catalogue,
Centro de Arte y Comunicación, Buenos Aires, 1970

134

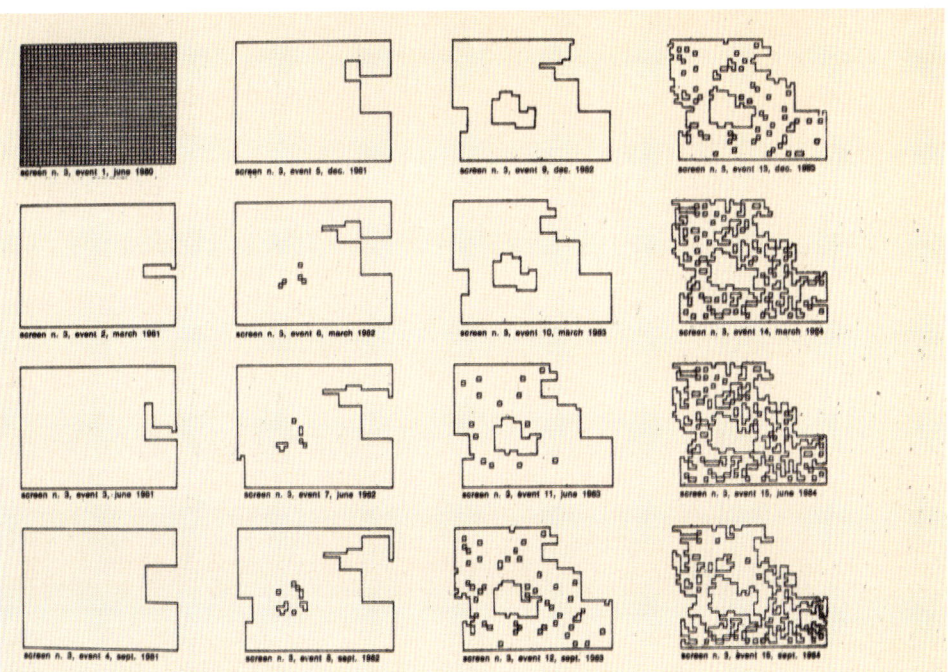

Gustav Metzger

From the 1950s, Metzger's artworks reflected on the destructive power of technology, from its deadly use in modern warfare to its negative effects on the environment; yet he strongly believed that it was only by engaging with technology that artists could hope to counter its harmful and oppressive uses. In 1959 he published his first manifesto on 'Auto-destructive Art', introducing the idea of artworks that were made to change, decay and disintegrate over time (see p.20). *Five Screens with Computer* 1963–70 was his ambitious (and ultimately unrealised) project for an auto-destructive installation controlled by a computer programme, which he described as 'five screens made of stainless steel each made up of over 1000 identical elements. Over a ten-year period the elements are ejected, and the sculpture disappears.' Metzger was a member of the Computer Arts Society (CAS) and the first editor of PAGE, its newsletter, through which he often expressed his critical views on the ongoing role of computers in warfare. VR

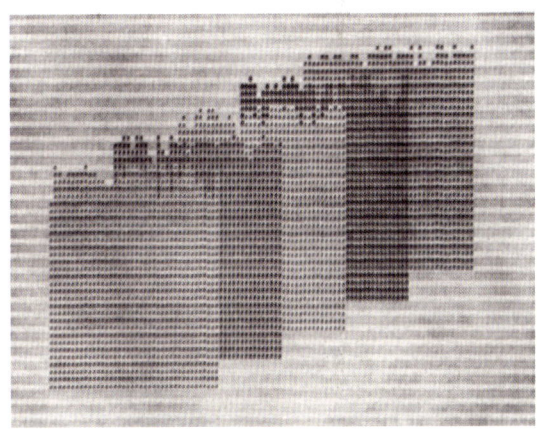

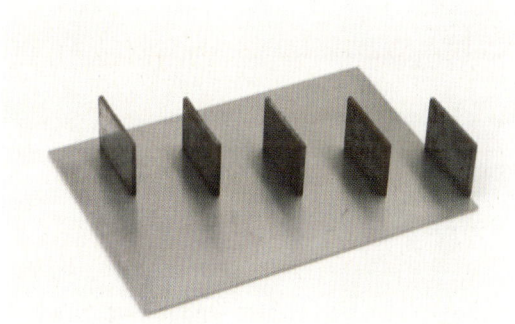

↑ A page from the *Arte y Cibernética* exhibition catalogue, with Gustav Metzger's studies for the gradual disintegration of *Five Screens with Computer* 1969

♣ Gustav Metzger and Beverly Rowe, computer-generated study for *Five Screens with Computer*, March 1969
↑ Gustav Metzger, steel model for *Five Screens with Computer* 1969

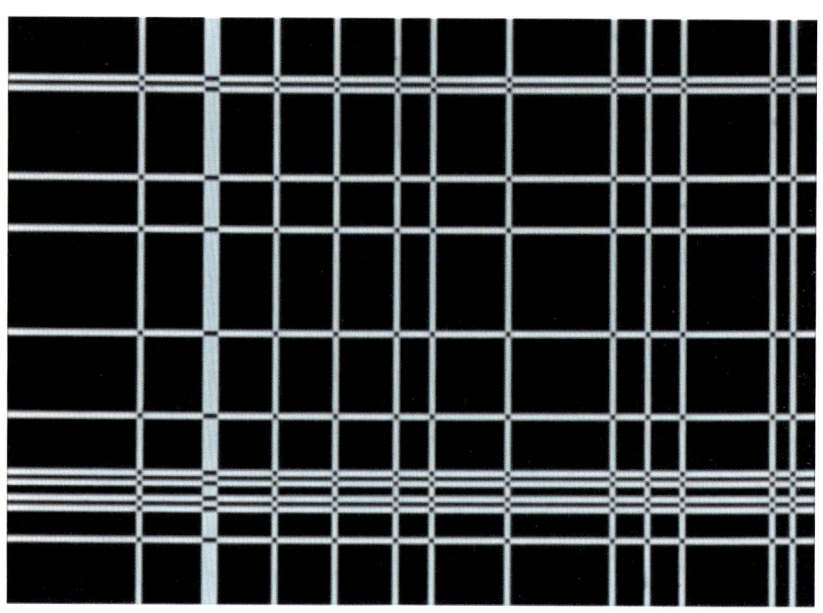

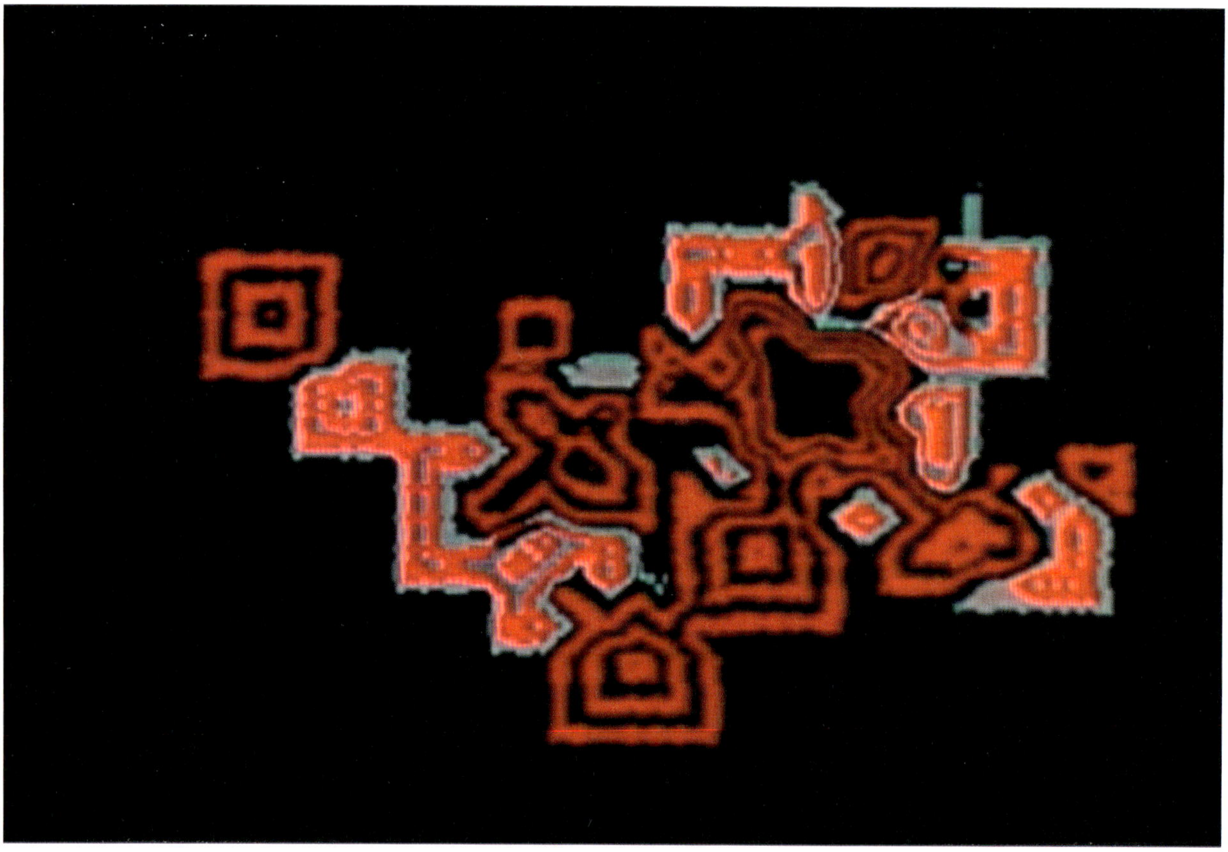

Lillian F. Schwartz

Enigma 1972 was made during Schwartz's decade-long residency at Bell Labs, to which she was the first female artist to be invited. With access to new technology, Schwartz created abstract computer-generated visuals that she edited using traditional filmmaking techniques on an optical printer, a device used to add effects such as fades and superimposition. *Enigma* begins with flashing black-and-white orthogonal patterns which become progressively more colourful and complex, accompanied by an electronic soundtrack by Richard F. Moore. Questioning mechanisms of perception, Schwartz made use of effects such as chromatic variation, where colours appear altered in complex images, and stroboscopic effect, which produces after-images on viewers' retinas. KW

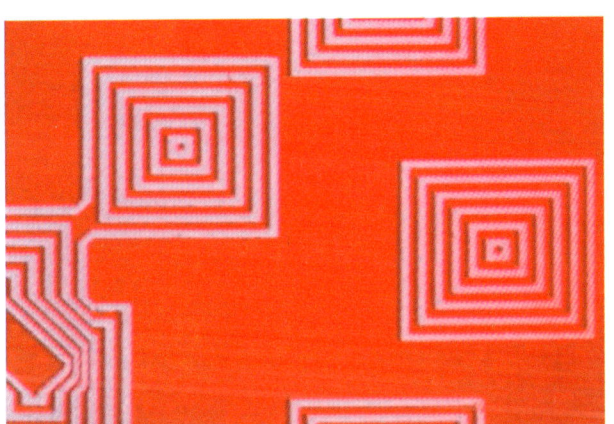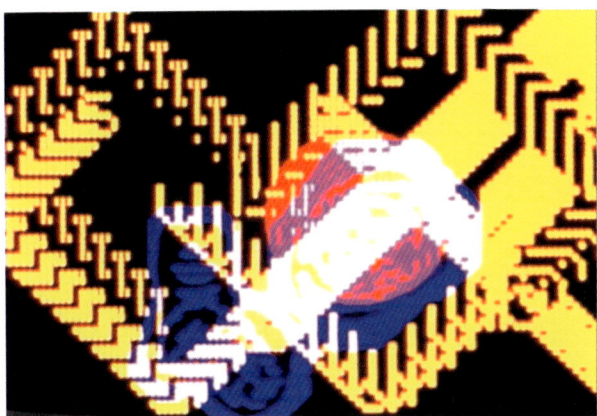

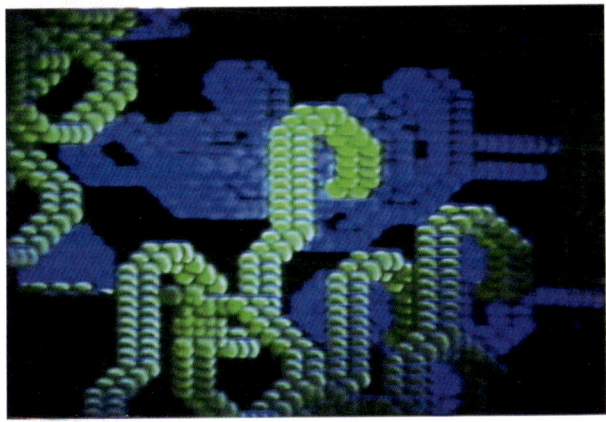

Lillian F. Schwartz, stills from: (top left) *Pixillation* 1970; (top right) *Kinesis* 1975; (bottom left) *UFOs* 1971; (bottom right) *Affinities* 1972

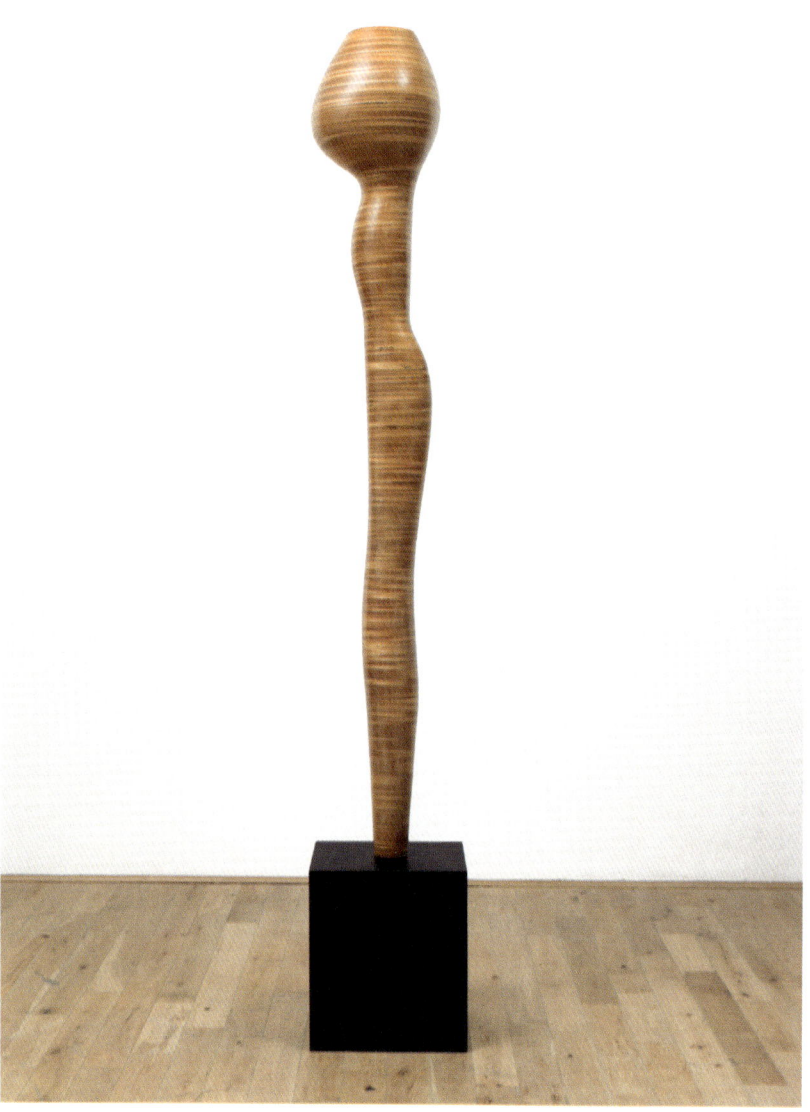

Robert Mallary

Quad III 1969 is one of Mallary's most significant early comput-er-generated works. The tall, elongated sculpture is composed of over 100 sections of plywood, drawn with the computer design program TRAN2. The program generated a vertical sequence of 48 forms, which were printed and used as patterns to cut the individual plywood 'slices' using a band saw. The sections are layered upon each other over a metal rod, glued together, sanded to a smooth surface and laminated. The sculpture was first shown at the *Tendencies 4* exhibition in 1969. *Quad I*, a prototype for *Quad III*, is considered one of the first computer-generated sculptures and had been exhibited in *Cybernetic Serendipity* the previous year. BP

↑ Robert Mallary, *Quad III* 1969
↗ Robert Mallary, computer-generated drawings for *Quad III* 1969

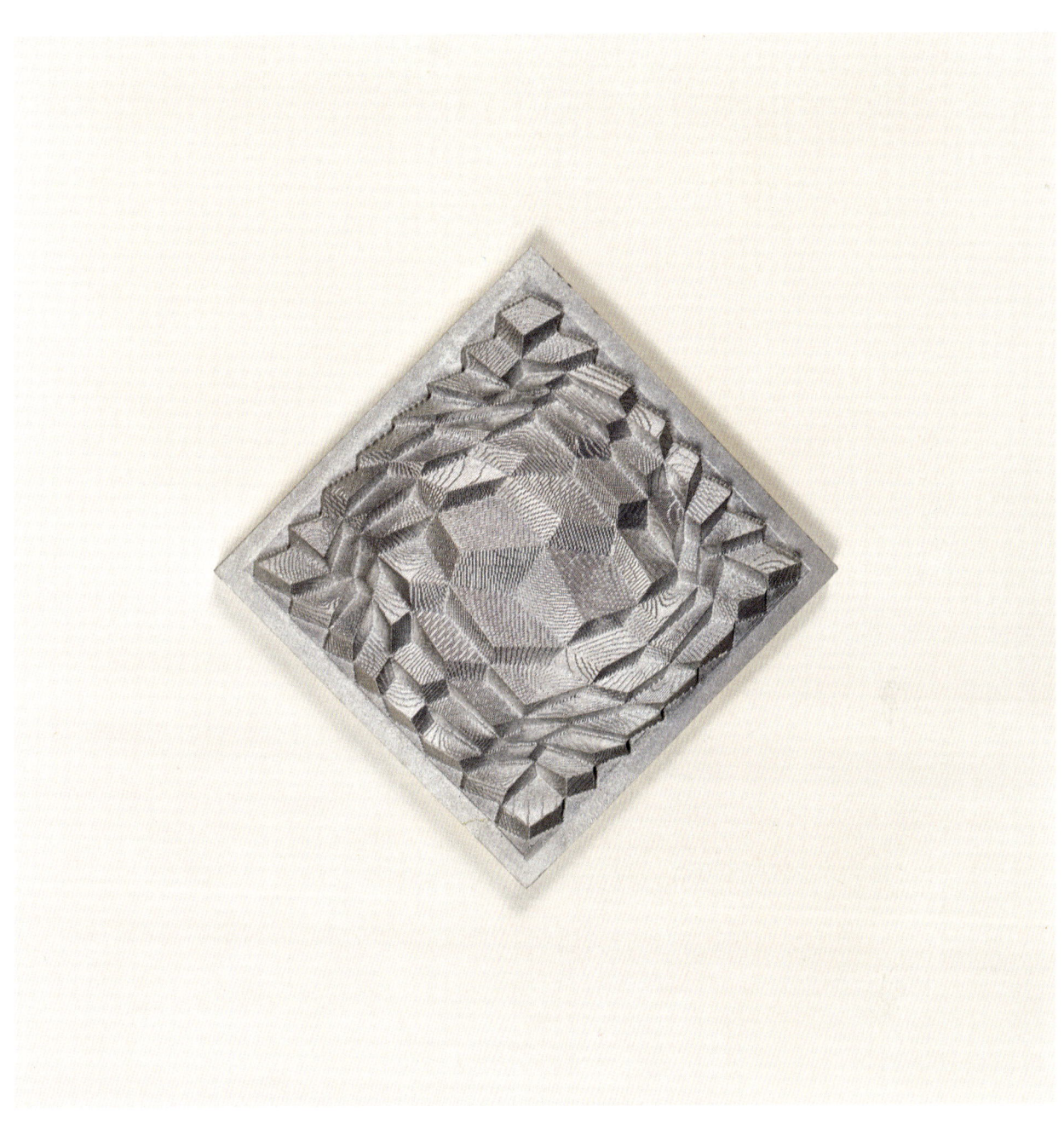

↑ Ruth Leavitt, *Computer Milled Sculpture* 1971

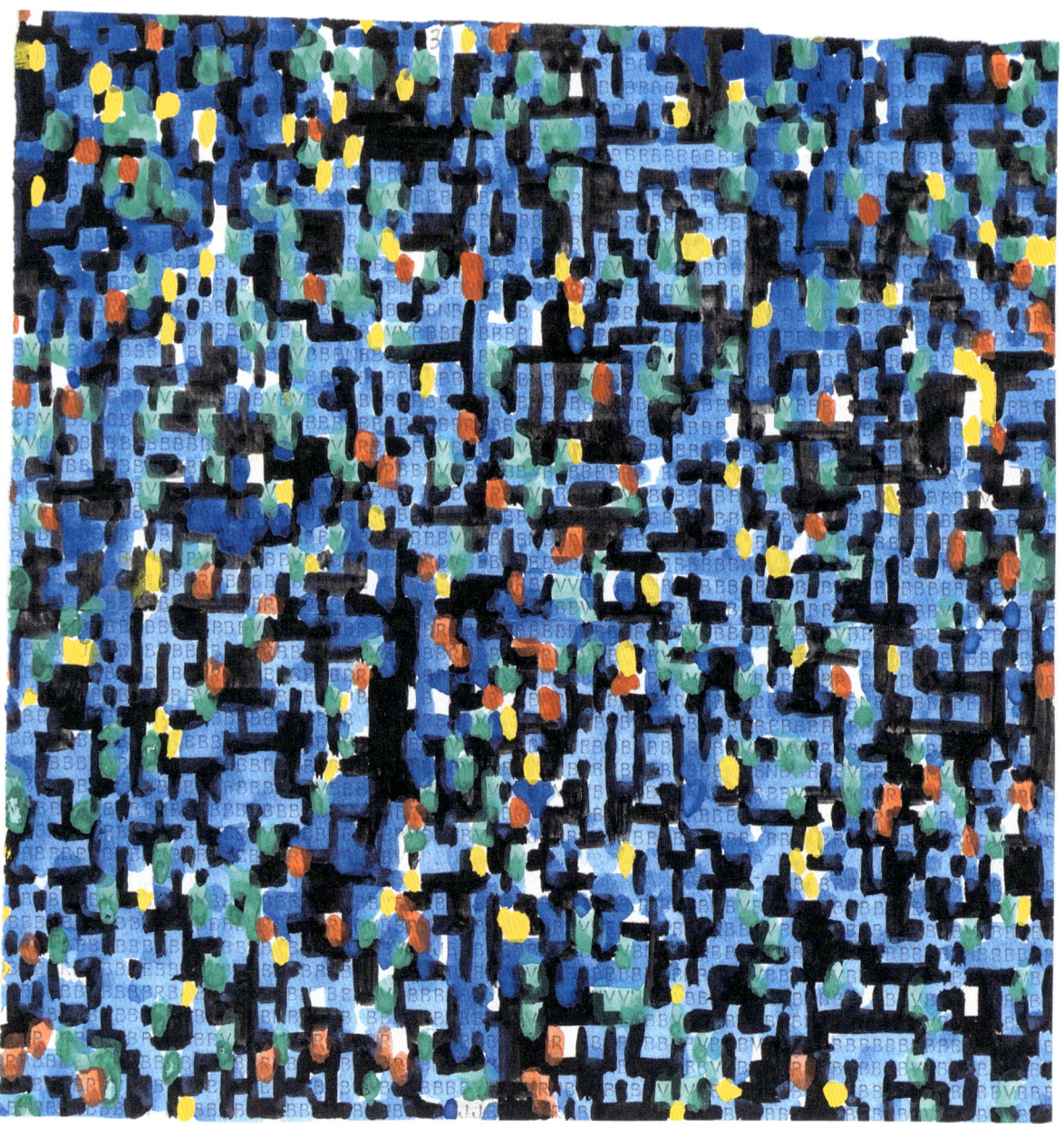

↑ Hervé Huitric and Monique Nahas, *No.3* (from the *Handmade Pixel Series*) 1971

Waldemar Cordeiro

*People Ampli*2* 1972 is a manually digitised photograph of a protest that took place in São Paulo during Brazil's military dictatorship, processed and printed on an IBM S360 computer. Cordeiro divided the image into a grid, replacing each square of the image with a series of alphanumerical symbols, overlaid one on top of another. The density of the symbols depended on the tone of the image within that square: the lightest squares were left blank, and the darkest squares were filled with the most symbols. The identities of the photograph's subjects are obscured, emphasising the collectivity of their political action. Cordeiro was part of the concrete art movement in Brazil before he took a keen interest in computers and their potential to democratise art and culture. In 1971 he organised the first exhibition of computer art in Brazil, *Arteônica* (a compound of the words for 'art' and 'electronics'), which he intended to turn into a series – a plan cut short by his untimely passing in 1973. KW

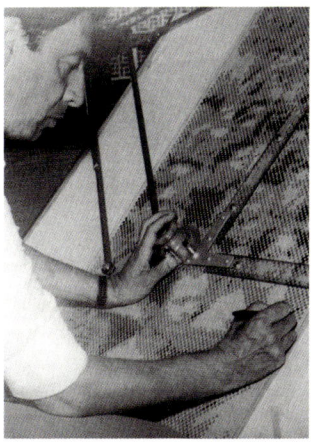

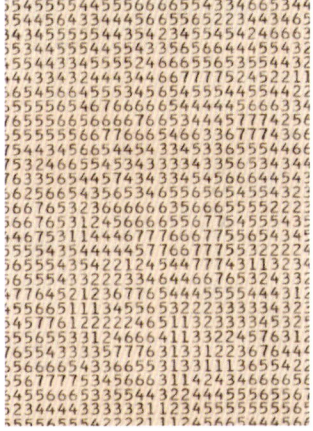

↑ Waldemar Cordeiro, *People Ampli*2*, 1972
↗ Cordeiro manually adds numbers in a grid laid over the enlarged image, each number corresponding to a 'pixel'
↗ The numerical grid as a computer printout: each number indicates the darkness of that point on the image
→ A computer algorithm translates the numerical values into alphanumeric characters to generate various greyscale tones that recreate the image

Analivia Cordeiro created one of the earliest works of video art in Latin America. *M3x3*, filmed in a television studio in São Paulo in 1973, depicts nine female dancers in high-contrast black and white, performing on a three-by-three grid – one on each square. Three cameras were positioned – front-on, side-on, and from above – and the video cuts between the three viewpoints. The dancers appear almost abstracted, carrying out mechanised movements to the minimalistic soundtrack of a metronome. Made at the height of Brazil's military dictatorship, during a period known as *anos de chumbo* ('years of lead'), *M3x3* has been interpreted as a reflection on the repressive regime.[1] Cordeiro created *M3x3* after being invited by the Computer Arts Society to contribute a work to their exhibition and conference *INTERACT. Machine: Man: Society*, held in Edinburgh, alongside international artists working at the intersection of art and technology, including Vladimir Bonačić and Vera Molnar.[2] The work is groundbreaking, not only for Cordeiro's use of video to record the dancers, but also her use of a computer to choreograph their movements.

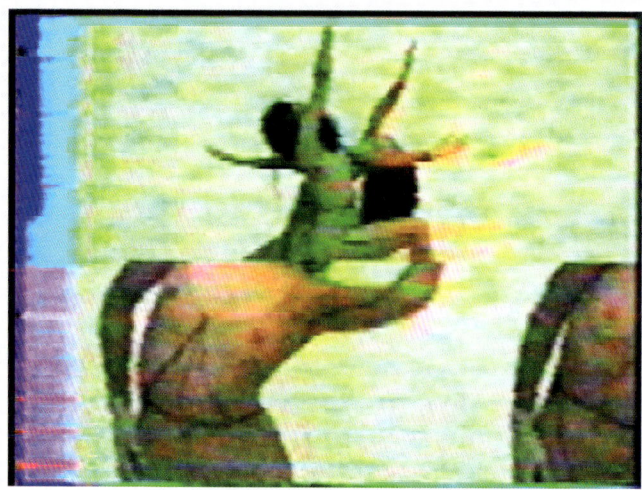

Born in São Paulo in 1954, Analivia is the daughter of Waldemar Cordeiro, a member of the concrete art movement in Brazil and later one of the pioneers of computer art. She was trained as a dancer from age seven by Maria Duschenes, a student of Rudolf von Laban, who developed Labanotation to record human movement. By the age of twelve, Cordeiro was already dancing with professionals.[3] Two aspects of Cordeiro's dance practice contributed to her developing her computer-based video dance methodology. The first was her role assisting Duschenes by noting down choreographies so that they could be more easily remembered, with Duschenes eventually teaching Cordeiro Labanotation after sensing her interest in the subject. The second was her frustration when dancing in front of TV cameras, in works such as *Structured Improvisation* with the Clyde Morgan group, as she felt 'there was no dialogue between the camera shooting and what I was dancing'.[4] For Cordeiro, the computer seemed poised to provide solutions to both choreographic notation and the recording of performance, and the two came together in *M3x3*.

To create this work, Cordeiro utilised the FORTRAN IV programming language to input information into a computer. She then interpreted the output, using it to define the position of the dancers' bodies, the length of time each position was held, where in space they would move next, and the camera angle. The dancers' bodies were separated into six parts (right leg, left leg, right arm, left arm, trunk and head), and a six-digit output defined the position of each body part. Cordeiro translated these outputs into stick-figure drawings, which were shown to the dancers. While much of the performance and its recording were predetermined, some subjectivity remained in the process, with the dancers interpreting how they would transition between the positions.[5] In the making of *M3x3*, Cordeiro developed a methodology that simultaneously created and notated choreography, while also defining the way in which its performance is recorded. As such, the choreography, its notation and the recording of the performance are considered holistically, creating an interdependent and non-hierarchical relationship between all three elements.

In 1974 Cordeiro embarked on a series of videos titled *0°—›45°*. Using the same computer output for the choreography of each version, Cordeiro varied the stage and costume design, and the recording and editing style, creating different interpretations of the code.[6] In all versions a single dancer, Cordeiro, performs to the soundtrack of *Fox Trot* by William Russell, conducted by John Cage. In *0°—›45° Version I* 1974 (p.144), the dancer and stage seem to merge, the horizontal lines of the set intersected by the curved and diagonal lines created by the dancer's body. *0°—›45° Version II* 1974/1975, similarly, utilises this blending between dancer and stage, but here the staging is made up of polygonal shapes chosen randomly by the computer. *0°—›45° Version III* 1974/1989 (p.144) is the most distinct, in which 'computer static notation', demonstrating the dancer's positions through computer-generated stick figures, is interspliced with close-ups of the dancer performing each movement. Cordeiro states this work 'is a study of the degrees of visual intelligibility of movement and a portrait of our fragmented corporal image, consequence of the hectic lifestyle and stress of modern society'.[7]

Analivia Cordeiro:
The Computer as Choreographer

Kira Wainstein

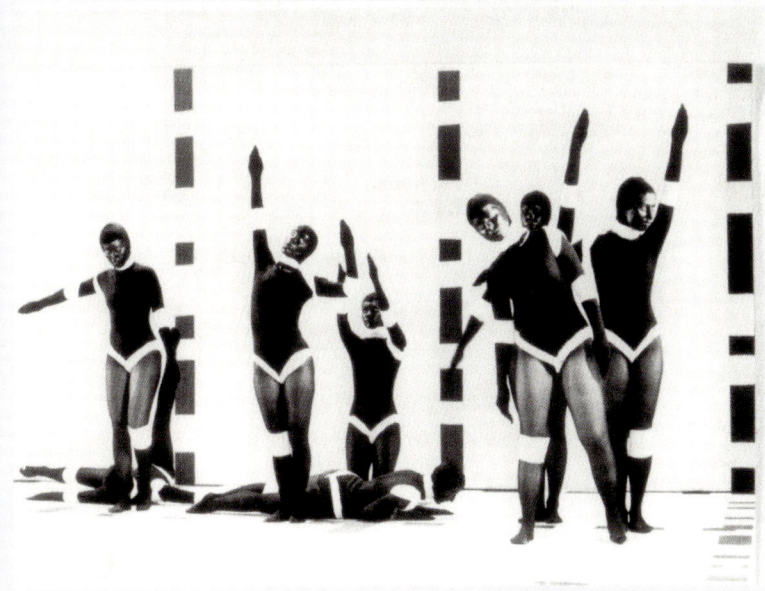

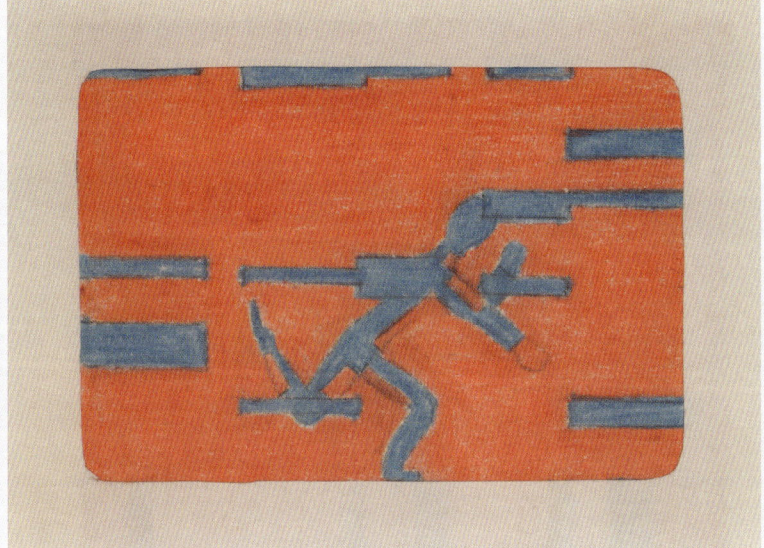

Cordeiro continued exploring the intersection of video and dance throughout the 1970s and 1980s. Works include *Cambiantes* 1976, in which the dancers' makeup and movements are inspired by Cordeiro's time living with the Kamaiurá in their indigenous Xingu lands in the Amazonian Basin.[8] *Slow Billie Scan* 1987 demonstrates Cordeiro's experimentation with telematics, in which a performance by Cordeiro and Lali Krotoszynski at the Museu da Imagem e do Som, São Paulo was broadcast by slow scan television to Carnegie Mellon University, Pittsburg. The slow scan process causes distortions in the tone, and requires twelve seconds per image, creating abstracted compositions of bodies and limbs as the frames overlay.[9]

Alongside video and dance, Cordeiro has made a wealth of work in performance, photography, film, software, installation and sculpture. In 1982 she began research to develop Nota-Anna, a computer movement notation system, which she programmed with Nilton Lobo from 1983 to 1994. Cordeiro describes it as 'the result of a union of theoretical and practical experience in two areas of knowledge: computer graphics and non-verbal communication'.[10] In 2015 Cordeiro created the first of her *Chutes Inesquecíveis* (*Unforgettable Kicks*), sculptures 3-D-printed from Nota-Anna models produced decades earlier. This perfectly demonstrates Cordeiro's practice: she utilises contemporary technology in radical and interdisciplinary ways, waits years for technology to catch up with her ideas, and then starts the process all over again.

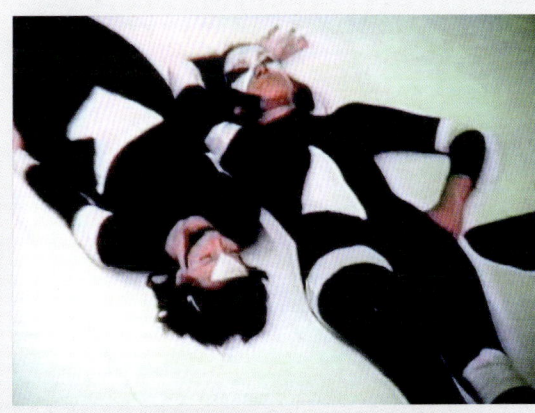

← Analivia Cordeiro, still from *Slow Billie Scan* 1987
↟ Analivia Cordeiro, still from *M3x3* 1973
↑ Analivia Cordeiro, chromatic possibilities drawings for
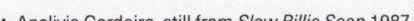
0°←→45° Version I 1974

↑ Analivia Cordeiro, still from *Cambiantes* 1976

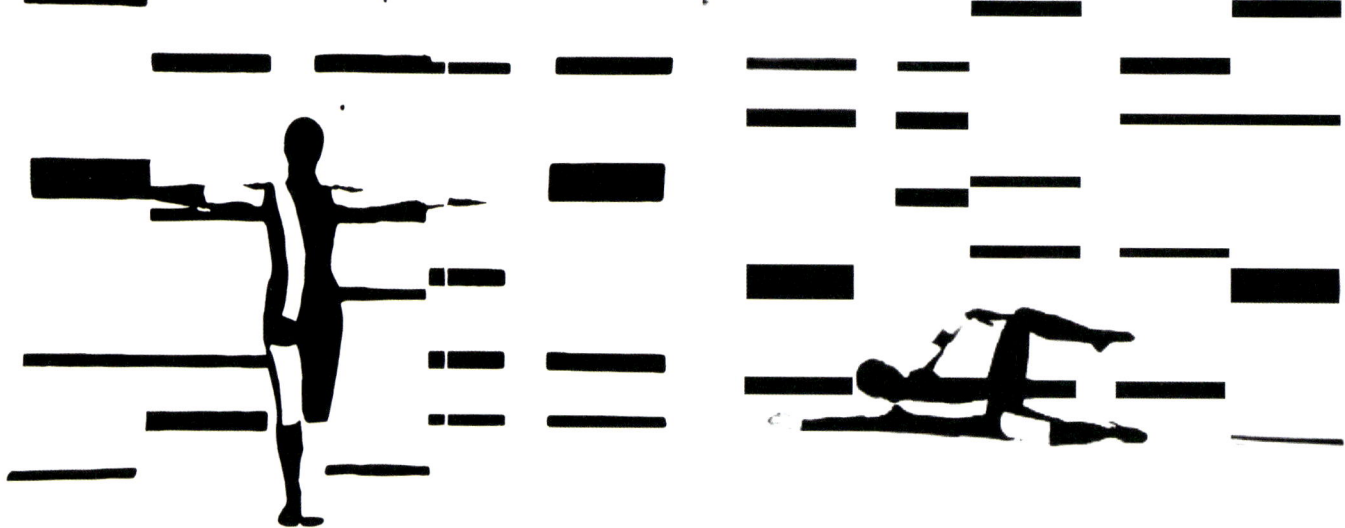

Analivia Cordeiro, still from *0°‹—›45° Version I* 1974

Analivia Cordeiro, still from *0°‹—›45° Version I* 1974

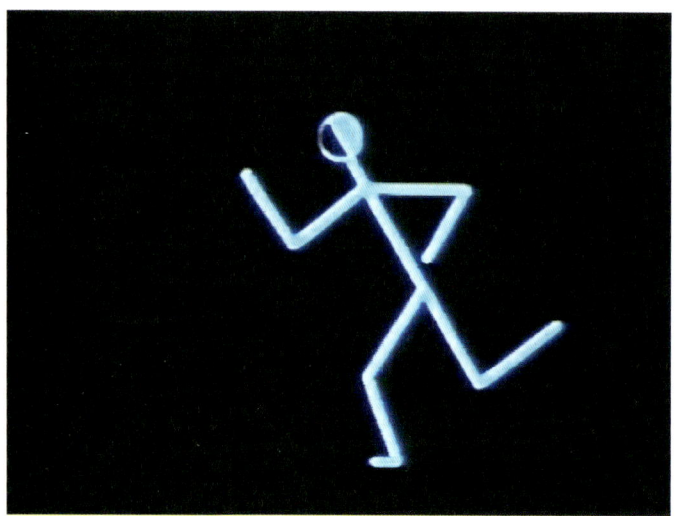

Analivia Cordeiro, still from *0°‹—›45° Version III* 1974/1989

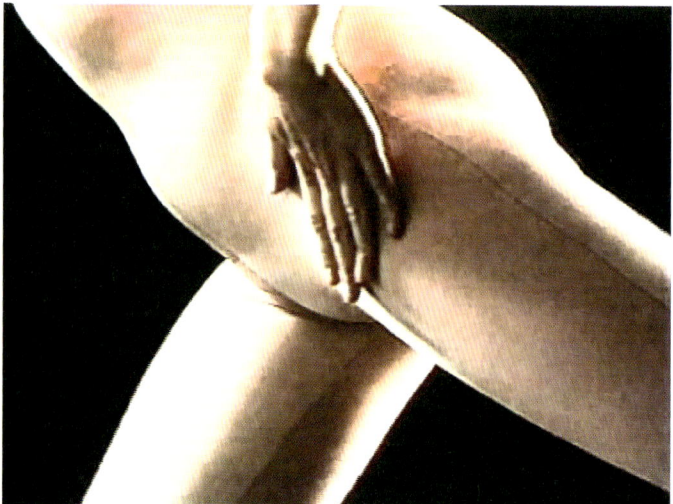

Analivia Cordeiro, still from *0°‹—›45° Version III* 1974/1989

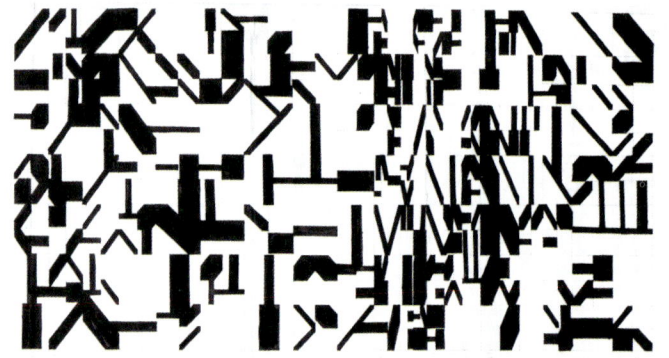

Analivia Cordeiro, still from *0°‹—›45° Version V* 1974/2024

THE PROGRAMMING
CHOREOGRAPHER

by Analivia Cordeiro
905 West End Avenue, #123
New York City, N. Y. 10025

The author, formerly from Sao Paulo, Brazil, is now living in New York City for a year. She describes her experiments in choreography and television at the University of Campinas, Brazil.

Until a short time ago, few people could have imagined that the computer would play any role in the field of the arts. However, its use in the current art scene is an undisputed fact, characterized by a dynamism, manifested through many experiments in the fields of the visual arts, music and dance. For the public, the principal difference in the use of the computer in each of these areas is in the output, which could be an actual work of art or a series of instructions, the interpretations which will permit the production of the work of art.

The use of the computer in the field of dancing is of the second category. The output consists of information for the performance of the dancer, as well as for the technical team producing the show.

The objective of this article is to show how the computer can be used in choreographical programming for television, a field to which the author has been dedicating herself, in a pioneering fashion, in Brazil for the last few years.

This process, instead of using the dancers as choreographic instruments, allows the choreographer to utilize the computer in the creative act, giving greater potential for new aesthetic results.

THE FAILINGS OF TRADITIONAL CHOREOGRAPHY

As I observed, the choreographer's function, when working in television, is to direct the movements of the dancers and establish an understanding with the television producer and director. They determine how the pre-arranged movements of the dancers will be registered by the television cameras, which transmit the dance. The message received by the spectator is a function of the movements of the dancers, captured by the cameras.

It could be be said that the camera is the eye of a dynamic spectator.

The relationship between the dance-TV-spectator can be represented as follows:

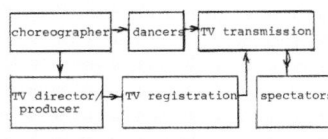

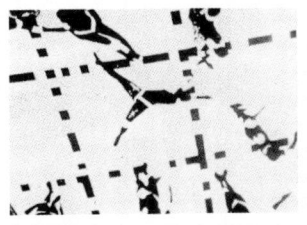

ABOVE: "M3X3" - Camera in overview, from dance experiments by Analivia Cordeiro, from the film, "Computer Dance/TV Dance," 1974.

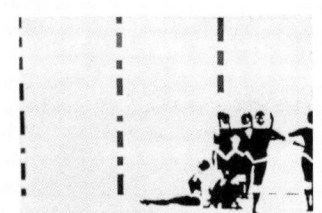

ABOVE: "M3X3" - Camera in lateral view, from experiments in dance at the Computer Center, State University of Campinas, Campinas, Brazil.

09 → 45°
Computer Dance
Analivia Cordeiro
1974

↖ Analivia Cordeiro, first page of 'The Programming Choreographer', *Computer Graphics and Art 2*, no.1, 1977, pp.27–31
↑ Analivia Cordeiro, dance notation for *0°⟨—⟩45°* 1974–84

Before moving to California in the late 1960s and devoting his career to developing AARON – the first computer program capable of autonomously generating drawings using the principles of symbolic artificial intelligence – British-born Harold Cohen was already a well-established abstract painter. Though his shift towards computer-aided art, at a time when the machines could only produce simple geometric line drawings, initially appeared as a radical departure from the lush colours and organic forms of his canvases, in many ways this leap was simply a further step in Cohen's investigation into the processes behind the making and interpreting of images – a quest that was to inform his development of the AARON software right up until his death in 2016.

In 1963, while teaching at the Ealing College of Art, Cohen had attended a lecture given by cybernetician Gordon Pask as part of Groundcourse, an experimental design course led by artist Roy Ascott. Pask's 1963 lecture, which addressed ideas of information feedback and cognition as a process emerging through interaction, left a lasting impression on Cohen.[1] In 1968 Cohen had his first opportunity to work with computers at the University of California in San Diego, and started learning how to code using the FORTRAN programming language. Applied to image-making, the process of coding appeared to him as an interesting model for thinking about drawing as the construction of forms through the application of certain rules and choices. As he put it, he wished 'to answer a very fundamental question … what are the minimum conditions under which a set of marks on a flat surface functions as an image'?[2]

Cohen devised a program that would be able to make a series of marks and base its decisions on how to draw the next marks on a set or parameters defined by the artist. A separate algorithm then fed the instructions to a specially made drawing machine, which could be either a plotter printer or a small device on wheels capable of moving freely on large sheets of paper; the latter was known among computer engineers as a 'turtle'. Initially, Cohen's predetermined rules defined basic relationships between lines, so that the program would be able to determine, through a feedback process, whether a form it had drawn was 'open' or 'closed'; an early version of the program was thus able to generate simple designs which Cohen described as 'mazes'. Gradually, Cohen added more rule sets, so that the machine could distinguish between 'inside' and 'outside' or determine 'figure' from 'ground'. It could then fill in, superimpose or shade forms to suggest a sense of depth and three-dimensionality.

Another characteristic Cohen built into his program, which he called 'AARON' beginning in 1973, was the

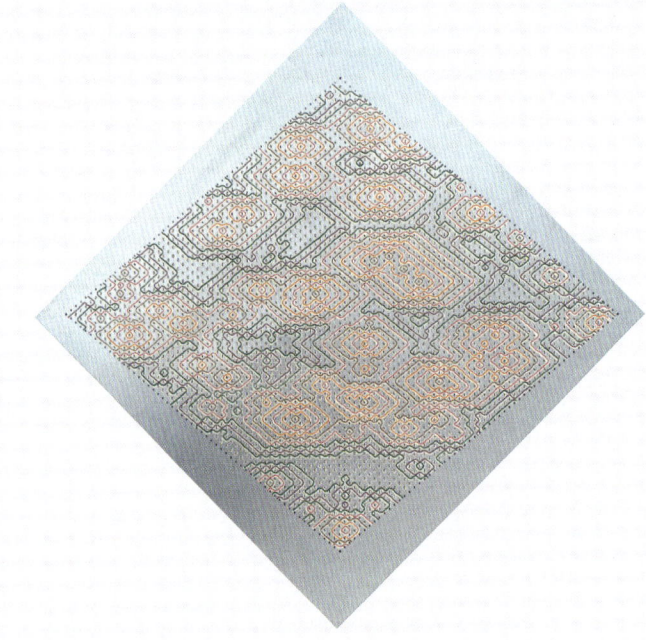

'Freehand Line Algorithm': a set of randomising parameters which complicate the path of the lines enough to dissimulate their mechanical origin. While continuously developing AARON to improve its ability to draw with increasing degrees of autonomy, Cohen also continued to see his practice as a dialogue with his creation and his involvement as absolutely necessary for AARON's outputs to be considered artworks. He also personally coloured in many of AARON's line drawings, or invited members of the public to do so.

For his major exhibitions between 1979 and 1982, Cohen realised murals or large canvases based on enlarged AARON drawings, where the colours are entirely his own. He painted the canvas *AARON #1 Drawing* 1979 (pp.148–9) for an exhibition in Reno, Nevada, where he ran the program on a minicomputer in the gallery and generated 'turtle' drawings in front of amazed visitors. From 1983, having noticed that the turtle's scurrying proved too much of a distraction from the drawings themselves, Cohen retired the device and continued to exhibit AARON at work in the gallery using plotter printers.

From the mid-1980s, Cohen gave the AARON software the ability to generate figurative drawings, with a focus on human figures, interiors and plants. By the early 1990s AARON could finally also colour in the drawings on its own using a custom 'fingerpainting' machine, although Cohen would later reprise his role as principal colourist in the duo, limiting AARON to the task of

Meaning Generators:
Harold Cohen and AARON

Val Ravaglia

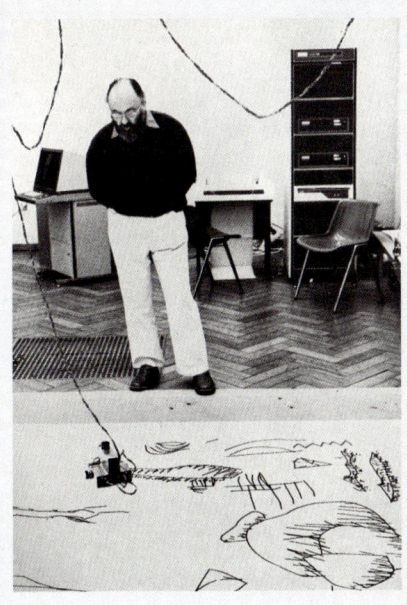

drawing lines only. In his later years, Cohen also returned AARON to the production of primarily abstract works, bringing its progress full circle. The second time around, however, AARON's image-making was freed from the task of simulating human decision-making processes altogether. By 1996, Cohen had come to a realisation: 'I want the work to look as if it has been made by an intelligence, but it doesn't have to be a human intelligence. I am much happier now when I see the program produce an image that looks as if it had been made by somebody who is seeing the world for the first time: seeing the world from a different point of view than someone who grew up human.'[3]

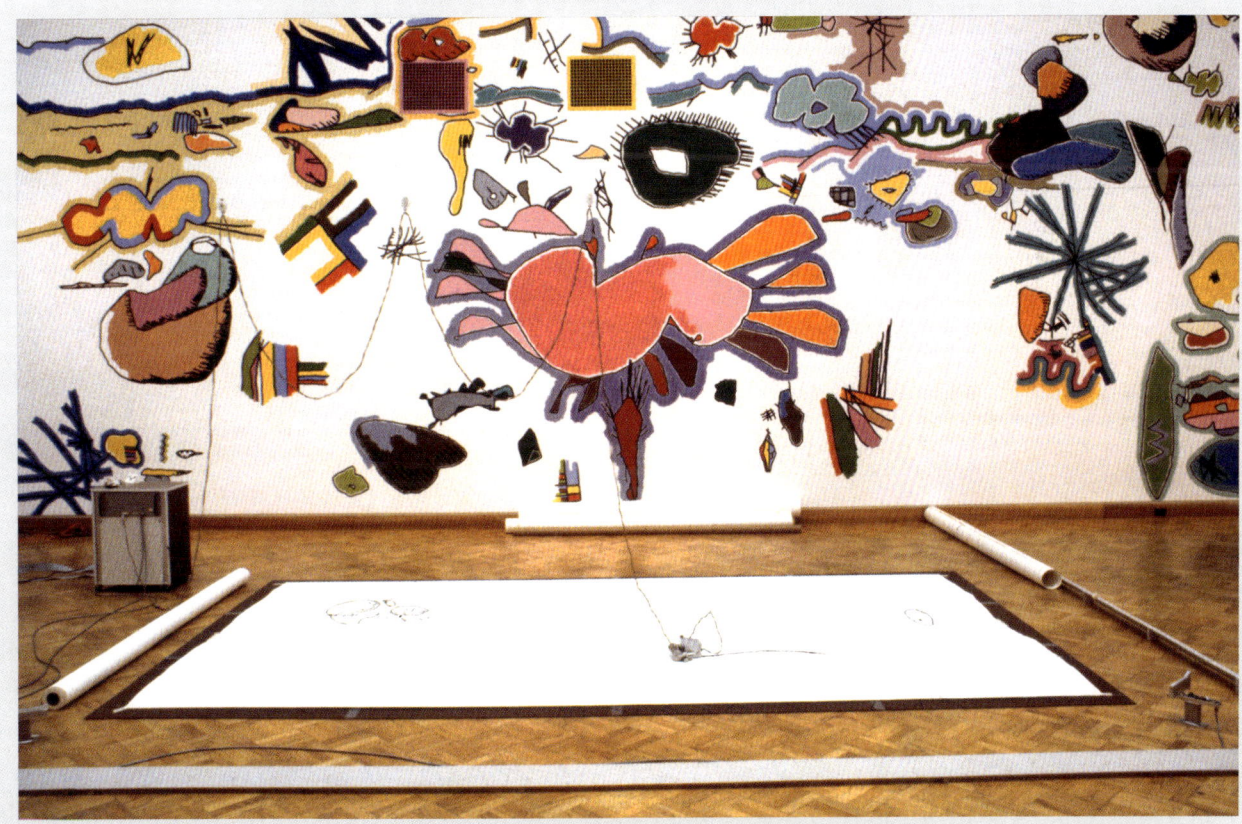

↖ Harold Cohen, *Untitled* 1969
⬈ Becky Cohen, photograph of Harold Cohen with a 'turtle' executing a drawing generated by the AARON software during Cohen's exhibition at San Francisco Museum of Modern Art, 1979

↑ Becky Cohen, photograph of Harold Cohen's exhibition at San Francisco Museum of Modern Art, 1979, with *Untitled* 1979 mural in the background
↪ Harold Cohen, *AARON #1 Drawing* 1979

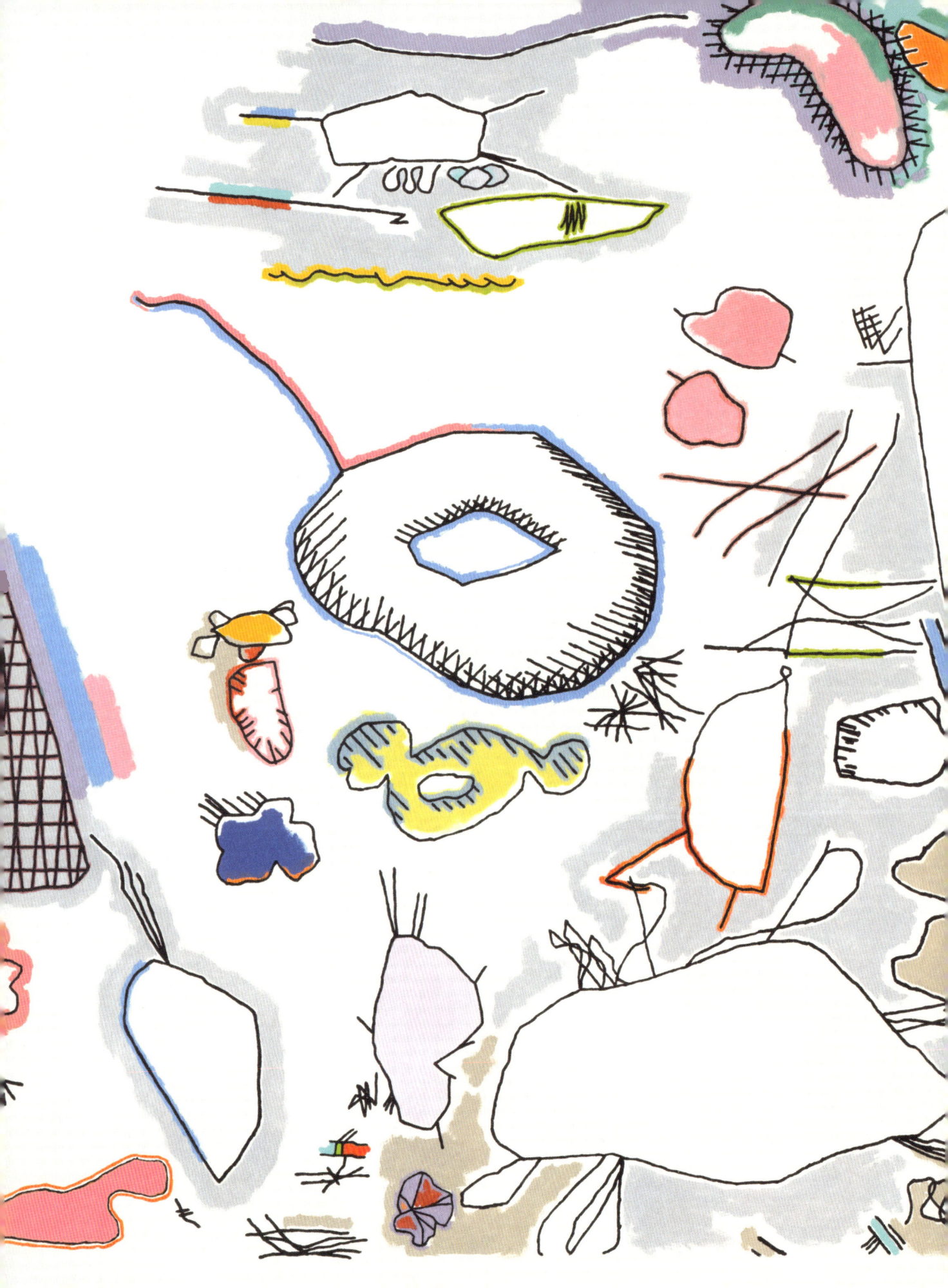

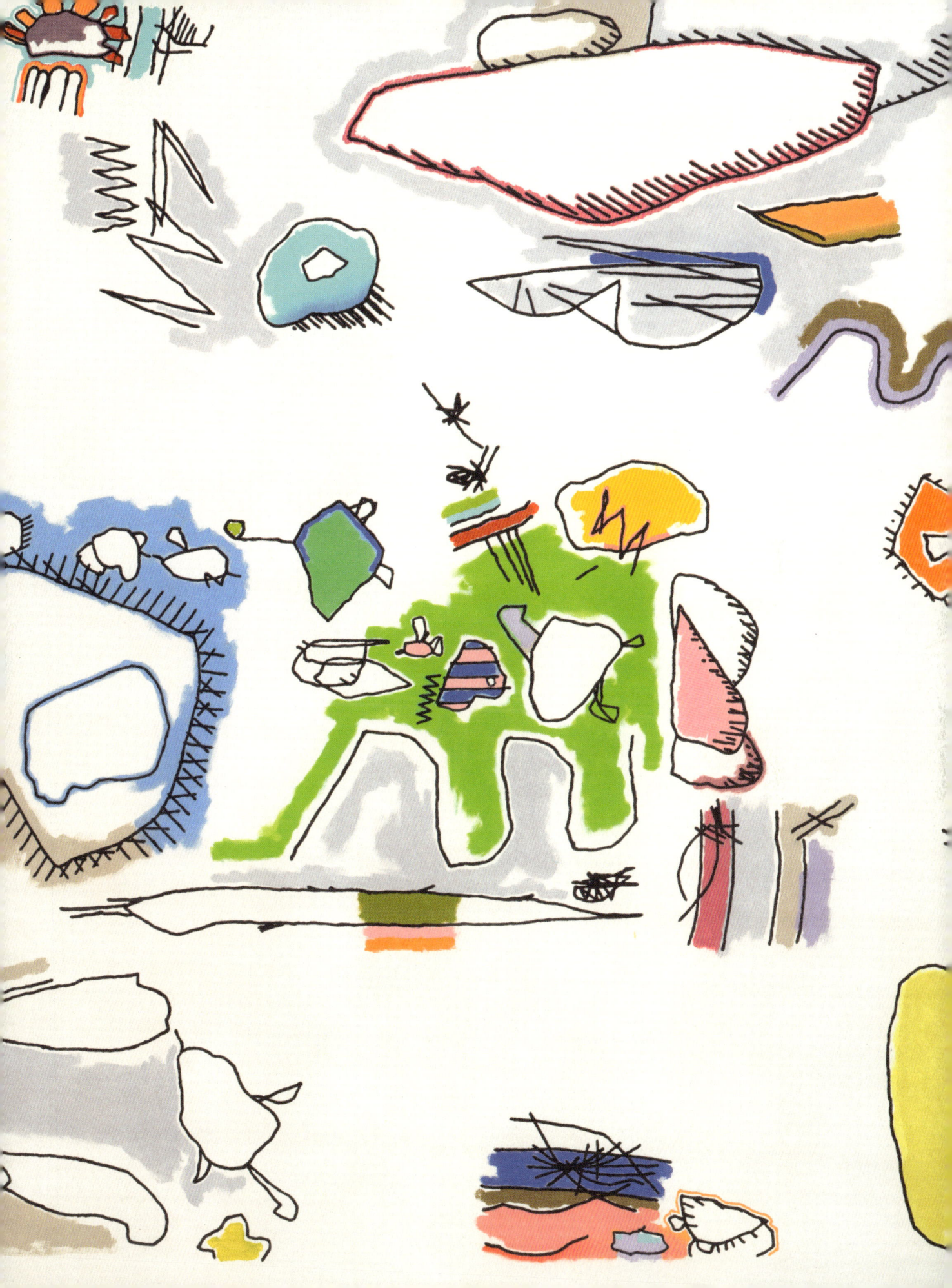

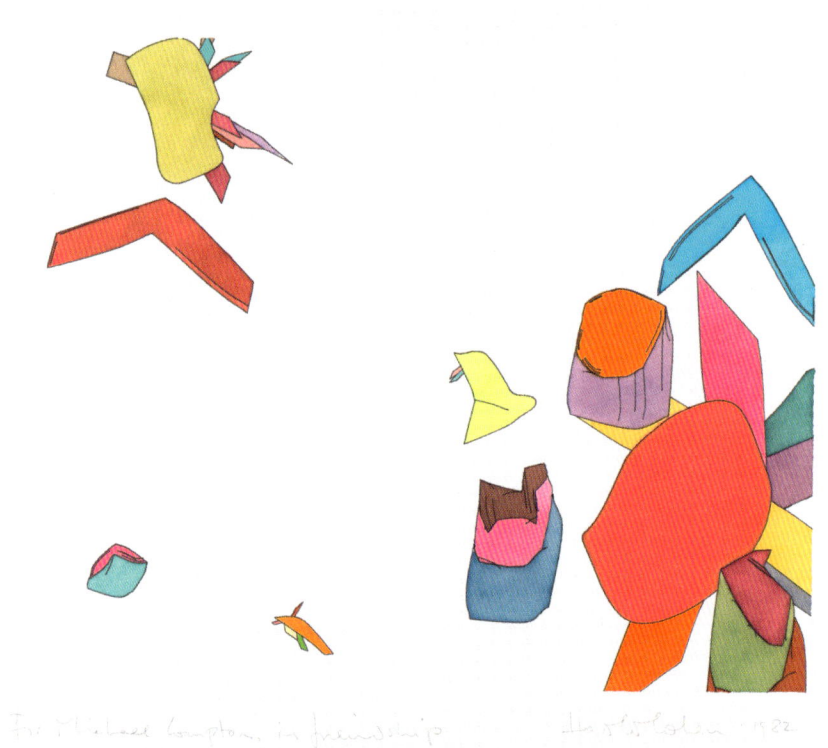

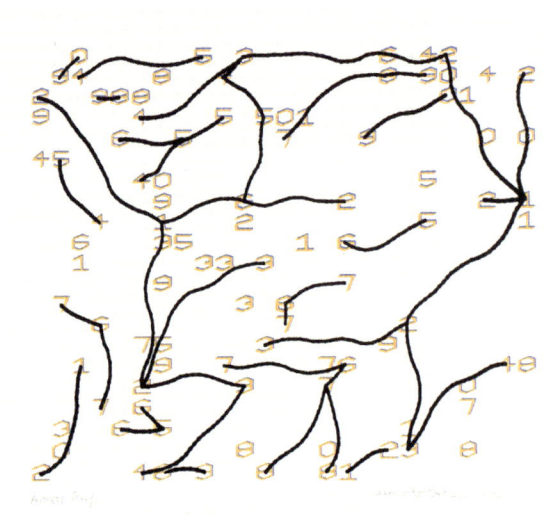

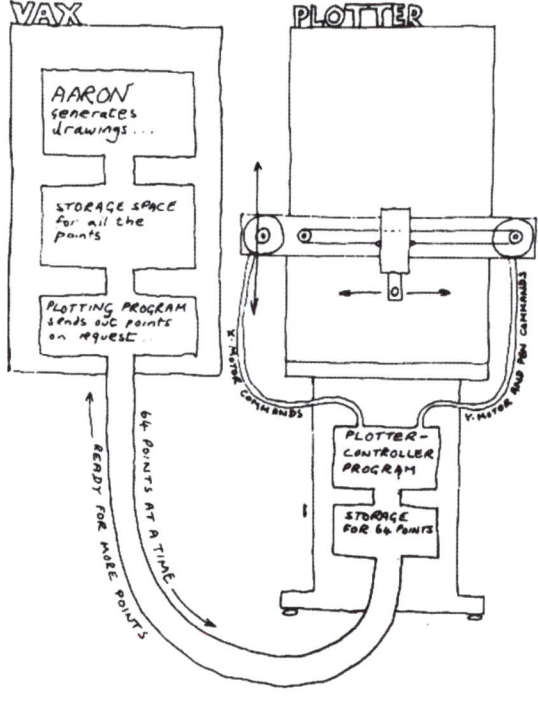

♠ Harold Cohen, *Untitled Computer Drawing* 1982

↑ Harold Cohen, *Untitled* 1971

↗ Diagram of Harold Cohen's computer hardware arrangement
(Digital Equipment Corporation MicroVAX II and a plotter printer)
that runs the computer program AARON

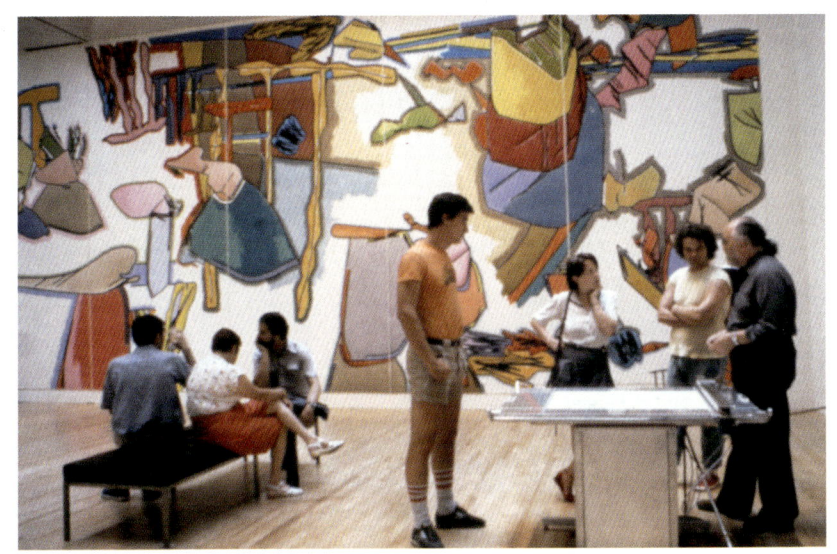

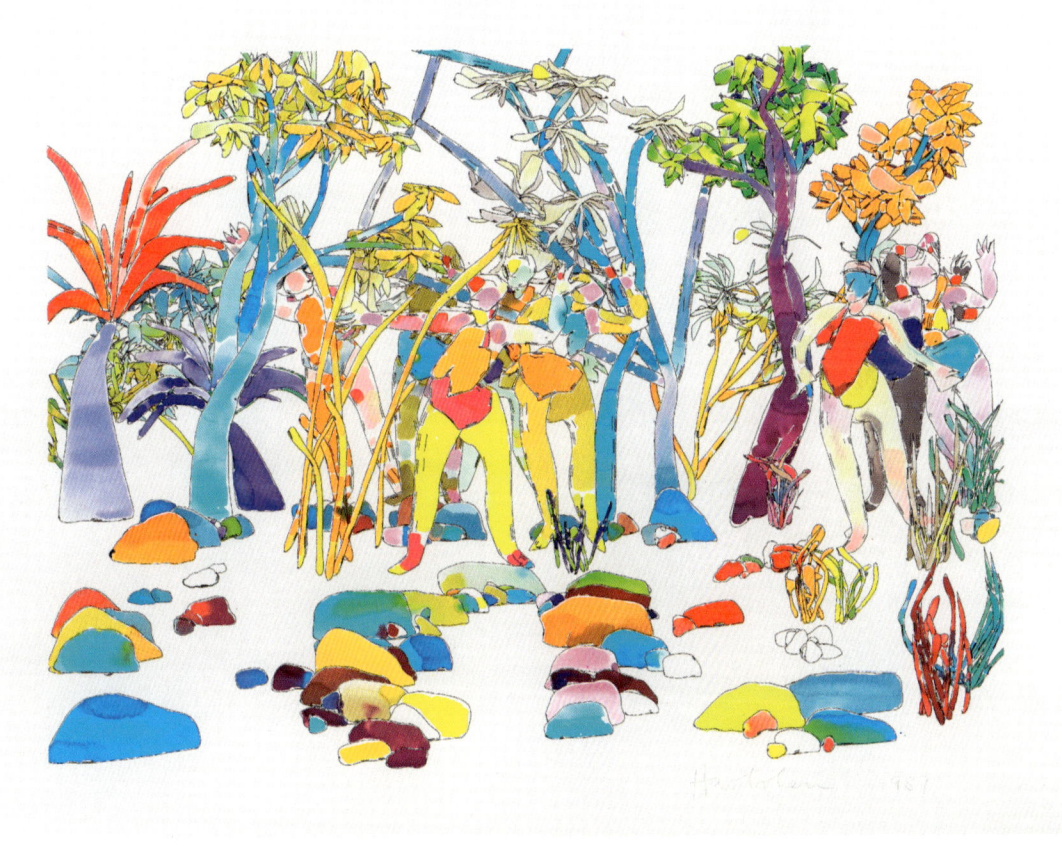

⬆ Becky Cohen, photograph of Harold Cohen at the Tate Gallery, London, 1983, with his *Untitled* 1983 mural in the background
↑ Harold Cohen, *Untitled* 1987

Electronic DIY:
Tinkering
with Tech

Electronic DIY:
Tinkering
with Tech

Electronic DIY

The Patchy History of Artists and Electronics: Typewriter, Telephone, Television, Telecommunications

Sarah Cook

Media 'define what really is'; they are always already beyond aesthetics.
– Friedrich Kittler, quoting Norbert Bolz, in *Gramophone, Film, Typewriter* (1999)[1]

Dear microphone, all things which can be known, all things that have arrived, and that's to say, have gone again (I mean history) we can know in so far as you, in your function and your job, store what has gone.
– Friedrich Kittler, talking to the author's MiniDisc recorder microphone, 2001[2]

What does twenty-first-century art owe to late-twentieth-century artistic experiments with microphones, sensors, audio recorders, telephones, fax machines, televisions, computers, gaming platforms and other technological communication systems?

One answer is a debt, for their uncovering of the potential of these technologies for both modification and (embodied) participation. Telecoms systems cannot be separated from their users, receiving the messages they record, store or broadcast. Media defines what the message is. Today's interest in artists who were using 'mass-media' and early computer systems in the 1970s and the 1980s is in understanding how those technologies were invented, challenged, hacked and tinkered with.[3] While media theorists such as Friedrich Kittler might consider that tinkering futile where all it provided was an aesthetic experience (at Tate, audiences might jokingly call this 'the lights going on and off'), the outcomes of that tinkering might equally, sometimes, have led to those technologies becoming widely adopted by users, and co-opted by corporate initiatives (for better or worse).

Art historian Caroline Seck Langill has warned of looking back to art and technology developments and using them as a yardstick for understanding later works, in part because the art-historical record is so patchy, with great big gaps where the art–technology works should be:

> Scholars of new media art history have cited the inclusion of technologies associated with the sciences, particularly computer science, as one of the factors in the exclusion of new media art from the art historical record. Nevertheless, artists persisted with labour-intensive methods of fabrication associated with electronic media art, knowing there were steep learning curves and with little chance for exhibition of the work once it was finished. Producing work in the 1970s and 1980s, prior to the domestication of digital technologies, they set the bar surprisingly high for artists in subsequent decades who had access to hardware and software bought off the shelf.[4]

This essay will not address why there are gaps in the record, given we know that one definition of new media is that it absorbs all earlier media (and technological obsolescence is a real threat!). However, this reference to off-the-shelf

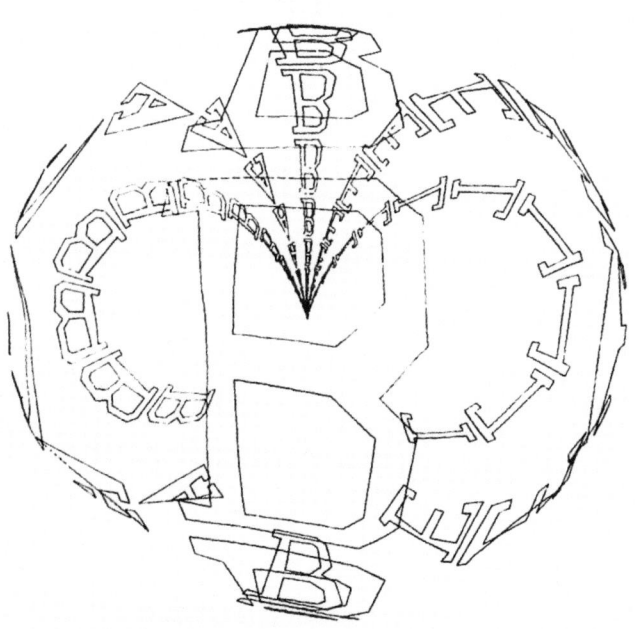

↖ Leslie Mezei, *Babel* 1967

technologies suggests that video and computing technology became more portable, not confined to labs and research centres. This is debateable. Technology's commercial accessibility around the world – what Langill calls 'domestication', but could also be 'democratisation' – has certainly challenged art historians, who (since Vasari published his volumes on *The Lives of the Artists* in the sixteenth century) have long favoured art movements located in particular times and places. In this essay I try not to be such an art historian. I recognise that due to the distributed and network-materialised nature of technology, the history could instead be one of geographically isolated artists finding ways to connect with each other through mass media such as the postal service, telephones and fax machines, leading to the work demonstrating a global telecoms aesthetic.[5] The constraints of the technology of automated writing (typewriters, photocopiers and, later, computers) and their global accessibility (at home, but also through newsrooms, universities and offices) certainly created a new field for art making.

So, in the spirit of Kittler talking to my MiniDisc recorder, which histories have these media telecommunications technologies stored? This is what this essay will try to show.

Electronic tinkering

We call ourselves music workers. We do not purposely use romantic definitions such as 'artists' ... ours is constructivism: we want to manufacture, show a new conception of productivity, of the individual, of society.
– Kraftwerk [6]

In 1975, already a decade after publishing the article 'The Electronic Computer as an Artist' in *Canadian Art Magazine*, and his book *Computer Art*,[7] Toronto-based artist-programmer Leslie Mezei wrote:

The artists, and especially the art students, are willing to learn programming and some mathematics, and to learn to think in an algorithmic, process oriented manner ... The technical computer specialists, on the other hand, have to become aware of the potential contribution of the artists ... Programmer-artists and artist-programmers. Collaboration and multimedia are not impossible, only extremely hard and rarely successful.[8]

If we step out of the university computer science department, where people such as Mezei worked, and consider the DIY side of early electronic art, we can reconsider this earlier separation between artist and programmer. The idea of 'tinkering' (posited by *Electric Dreams*) is indebted to an earlier form of exposition: showing a proof of concept or working model – demonstrating so-called 'contraptions'. To tinker is to mend something without having had any training or gained a professional qualification to do so. Technical institutes and philosophical societies in the UK in the early nineteenth century hosted presentations of useful instruments (such as microscopes): some worked, some didn't. There was little distinction between artists and scientists, or professionals and tinkerers. Just as now

there is a so-called 'demo scene' in software development, so too were demonstrations of robotic and kinetic contraptions (such as in the work of Edward Ihnatowicz, Norman White or Laura Kikauka) a mainstay of the early history of electronic art, where artists had to be self-taught, writing their own programming algorithms to 'run' their works and the texts to theorise them. Likewise, we can listen to Kraftwerk to understand both the history and theory of ~~artists~~-workers creating technologies to manipulate electronic signals (in their case, audio synthesisers, drum machines and sequencers).

Curator Jasia Reichart has characterised the history of computers in art as having two main trajectories, with computers as 'machines for making pictures' and 'tools in the building of responsive sculptures and environments'.[9] She even went so far as to argue that prior to the 1970s it was predominantly 'scientists who made the pictures and the engineer/artists who made the cybernetic sculptures'. While this is a simplified view, it is perhaps not until the invention of video synthesisers (machines that create video signals electronically), by artists Stephen Beck, Nam June Paik and Shuya Abe, and Denise Gallant, among others, that the aesthetics of electronic tinkering and the opportunity to do it live onstage or from a broadcast studio, or open it up to participation, emerges. 'Its possibilities as an artistic medium appear unlimited', wrote the *New York Times* in 1972.[10]

Early pioneers of video art Steina and Woody Vasulka made numerous monitor-based works using a Rutt/Etra scan processor, which manipulates the signal that controls the scanning of the raster, and the resulting creation of an image, in the cathode-ray tube of a television monitor. Users could dial up or down the voltage to the television, creating animations and waveforms of varying height and width to give effects of zooming or flipping the image (as in *Matrix I* 1970, see p.185).[11] The Vasulkas founded The Kitchen in New York as a venue for experimental media artists to gather, watch screenings and install work, hosting the first Women's Video Festival in 1972. In Buffalo they shaped the State University of New York's first media department, and the AKG Art Museum (formerly the Albright-Knox Art Gallery) collection still benefits from the experimental approach to art and technology fostered there.[12] After *Matrix II* 1974 (p.184), 'In 1976, together with computer scientist Jeffrey Schier, Woody built a machine, the Digital Image Articulator, or Imager, which bridged the divide between analogue and digital image-making.'[13] This machine evolved and, a decade later, allowed the multiplication of images into grids with 'a digital pixelation in proportion with the storing capacity or computing memory'. In other words, more memory equalled greater resolution, just as it does today (though at the time the total storage capacity must have been about 16 bits!).[14]

In 1992 the Vasulkas curated an exhibition for Ars Electronica at the invitation of festival director Peter Weibel.[15] *Pioneers of Electronic Arts* included 'early "personal" electronic audio & video instruments used by artists'.[16] The Vasulkas' checklist of technologies of 'video feedback with audio input modulation' was, in their words, 'archaeological', noting that 'the whereabouts of a number of these machines is unknown, and we can only document their existence from ephemeral images on paper,

154

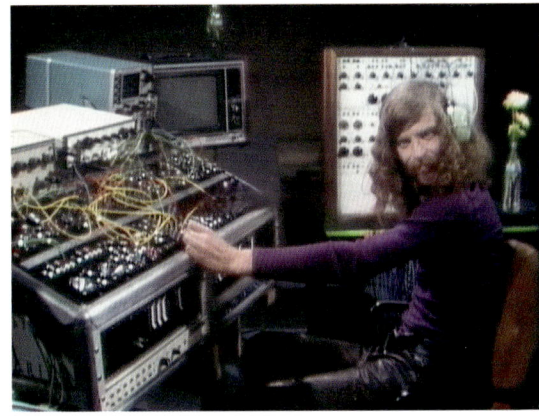
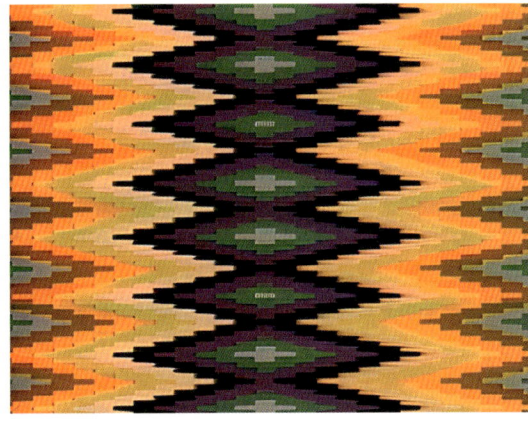
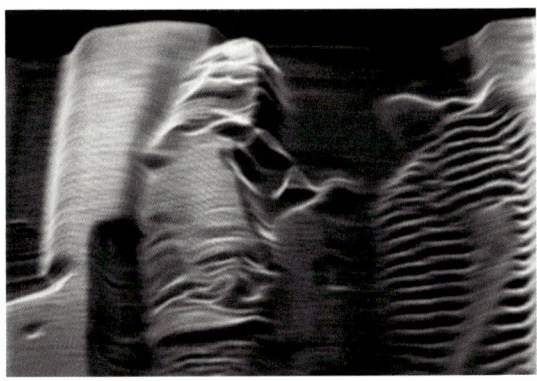
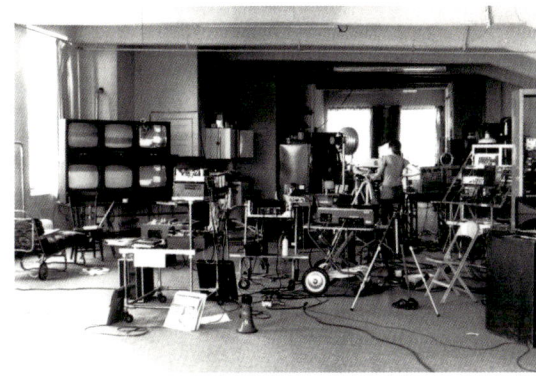
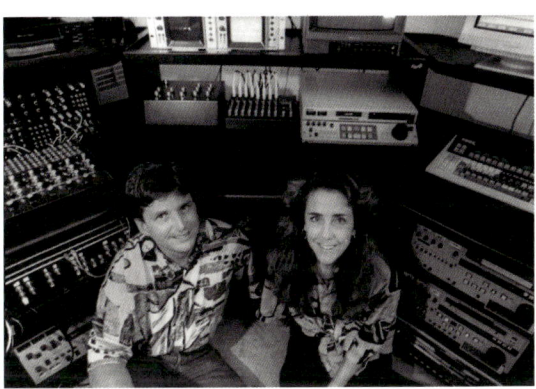
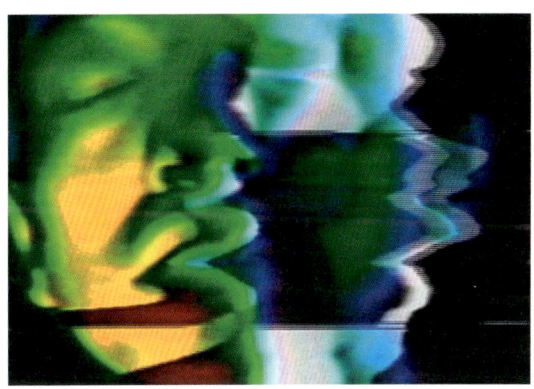

Top: Stephen Beck playing the Beck Direct Video Synthesizer live on KQED-TV for the first performance of *Illuminated Music I*, 19 May 1972
Middle: Woody Vasulka, still from *Reminiscence* 1974
Bottom: Denise Gallant with Kevin Monahan in their studio

Top: Stephen Beck, still from *Video Weavings*, 1973–6
Middle: Steina Vasulka in her and Woody Vasulka's studio, Buffalo, NY, c.1976
Bottom: Denise Gallant, still from a live video editing session for the band Tuxedomoon, 1979

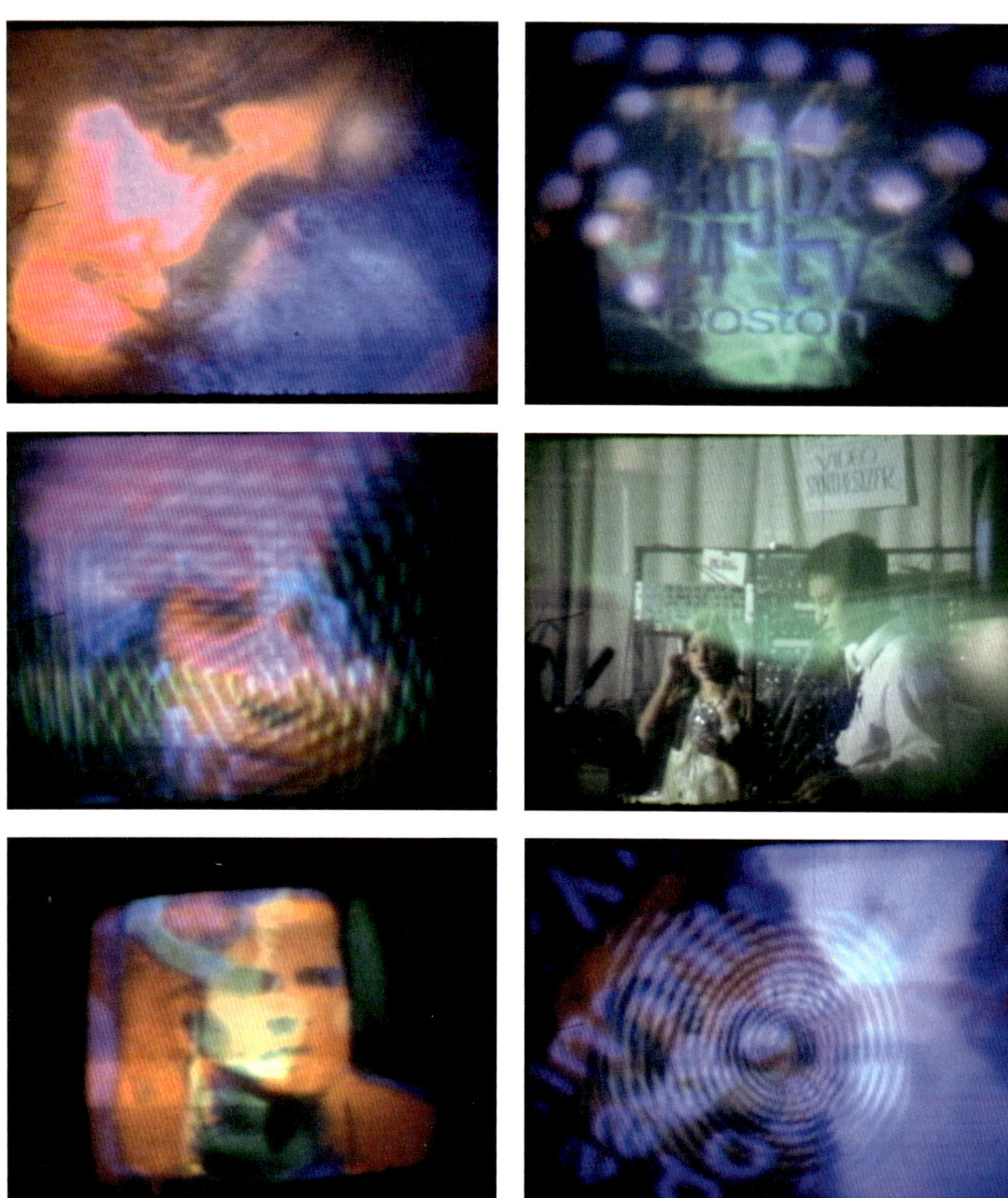

Nam June Paik and Jud Yalkut

Since the 1960s Paik championed the possibilities of telecommunication technologies to distribute art and enable long-distance
live collaborations. Later in that decade he became artist-in-
residence at Boston's WGBH-TV public television network and,
with their funds, worked with engineer Shuya Abe to develop
the Paik-Abe Video Synthesiser, one of the first video-editing
instruments capable of manipulating and mixing several input
channels at once, in real time. In addition to colourisation effects,
the synthesiser enabled other video image distortions that Paik
had already established in his past experiments with TV sets.
Video Commune (Beatles Beginning to End) 1970 (re-edited
1992), the debut broadcast of the synthesiser, took shape as a live
performance lasting several hours, including recorded footage as
well as images captured live in the busy television studio (such as
Paik and Abe in front of the synthesiser). The footage was shot in
collaboration with New York artist and filmmaker Jud Yalkut, and
later turned into a shorter video work. The title comes from Paik's
suggested soundtrack – the Beatles' complete discography. VR

↑ Jud Yalkut, *Video Commune (Beatles Beginning to End)*
1970, re-edited 1992
→ Nam June Paik, *Video-Synthesizer* 1969/92   156

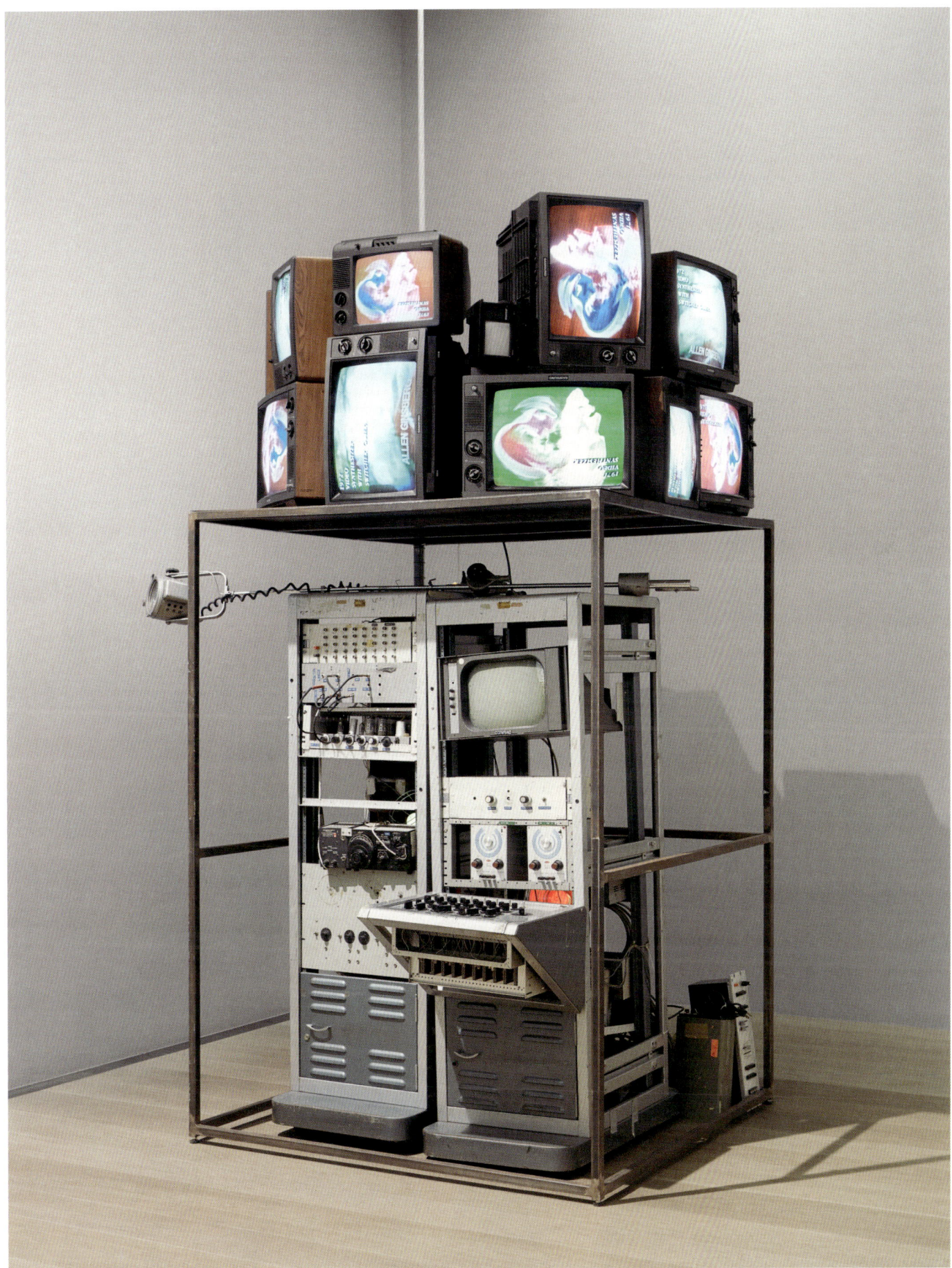

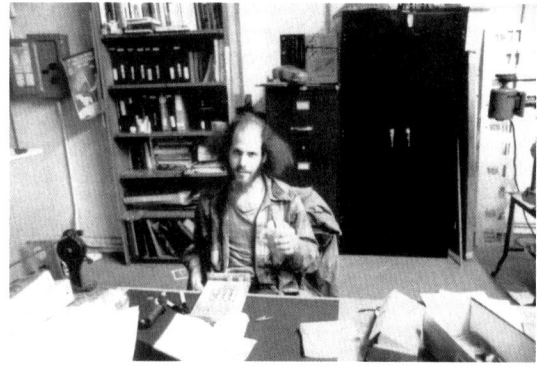 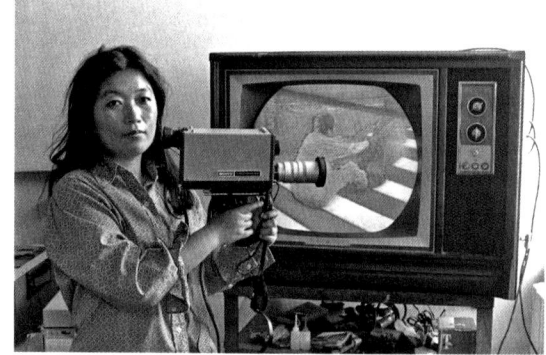

in photographs, and on video tapes.' If in the 1990s it was hard to find the technology artists used in the 1970s, this indicates the speed of change the field was undergoing (and the possible time-lag between creation and museums collecting and preserving the work).

In the US and Canada, a number of video programmes emerged from film departments within museums such as the Whitney Museum of American Art or the Museum of Modern Art (MoMA),[17] many showing the work that resulted from the efforts of television stations to support this experimental media: WNET in New York; WGBH in Boston, which broadcast Paik and Jakult's *Video Commune* (*Beatles Beginning to End* 1970 (p.156); KQED in San Francisco; and earlier in the UK, BBC2 and the ATV television studio at the Royal College of Art. Yet the rise of electronic image manipulation in the mainstream imagination arguably began with the release of early video game systems and the launch of MTV in 1981. This created a wide audience for a new commercial form of culture: the music video.[18] The history of music videos, and the history of video art, is full of rotoscoping (animation drawn, frame by frame, over motion-picture footage), greenscreen performances, vector (mathematically defined) images, and videos made using the Quantel Paintbox. This software allowed users to draw on top of footage, as in the video for the Cars song 'You Might Think', which has the lyrics 'But somewhere, sometimes, when you're curious, I'll be back around', which, when you think about it, could be describing the future of computer art itself.

The only Quantel set-up in Scotland in the 1980s was at the art college in Dundee, the city which was also the site of the production of early home computer the ZX Spectrum – a demonstration of how interlinked these histories are. Earlier, in the 1970s, art students might have used PICASO, a computer plotting and drawing graphics programme developed by John Vince at Middlesex Polytechnic. While it certainly gained public awareness through its use in music videos, Paintbox started out as a competitor to another early art software called EASEL, used by artist Sonia Landy Sheridan. Sheridan had previously made work with photo reproduction and colour layering, when Xerox colour photocopiers were invented by the company 3M (where she was, at one point, artist-in-residence).

Putting aside this brief (and mostly Western/European) account of the development of synths and colourful computer graphics programmes, there is a long, spooling and complicated story of artists experimenting with video technologies.[19] The commonly held view is that, with the invention of portable video recorders like the Sony Portapak, alongside home computing, technology was more readily accessible to artists. Given that he was already famous for, among other things, carrying a tape recorder with him absolutely everywhere he went, and producing TV shows and magazines, it's not a surprise that Andy Warhol was given an Amiga computer in 1985. He promptly used it, live on stage, to draw a portrait of Blondie's lead vocalist Debbie Harry during a performance by the band.

Linking Hollywood production studios, artists' studios and the ground-zero of computing and software development in Palo Alto, California was ACM SIGGRAPH (Association for Computing Machinery, Special Interest Group on Computer Graphics and Interactive Techniques), an annual conference started in 1974, where pioneering artist-programmers or programmer-artists showed their computer-generated and computer-driven works. Exhibitors included, for example, Joan Truckenbrod, Rebecca Allen and Jane Veeder, who had used the computer language Zgrass to make real-time motion graphics using a Datamax UV-1 graphics computer.[20]

The idea that computers 'invaded' the individual artist's studio is still, however, disputed by a number of artists, who know they couldn't have made their work without institutional support or the help of 'scientists', be it in a computer lab in a university, a television studio with monitors and synthesisers, a movie or video game production company, or a corporate think-tank. A number of chapters in the book *White Heat Cold Logic: British Computer Art 1960–1980* point to the importance of particular courses at art schools in the UK for introducing artists to cybernetics, systems thinking and computing technology; see, for example, the founding in 1972 of the Experimental and Electronic Art Department at London's Slade School of Fine Art, which, according to art historian Catherine Mason, 'purchased a Data General Nova 2 minicomputer system ... possibly the first installation of a "high-performance" dedicated computer system in an art school anywhere in the world'.[21]

↑ Jeffrey Schier in the Vasulkas' Buffalo studio
(NY, United States), c.1978
↗ Shigeko Kubota with a Sony Portapak

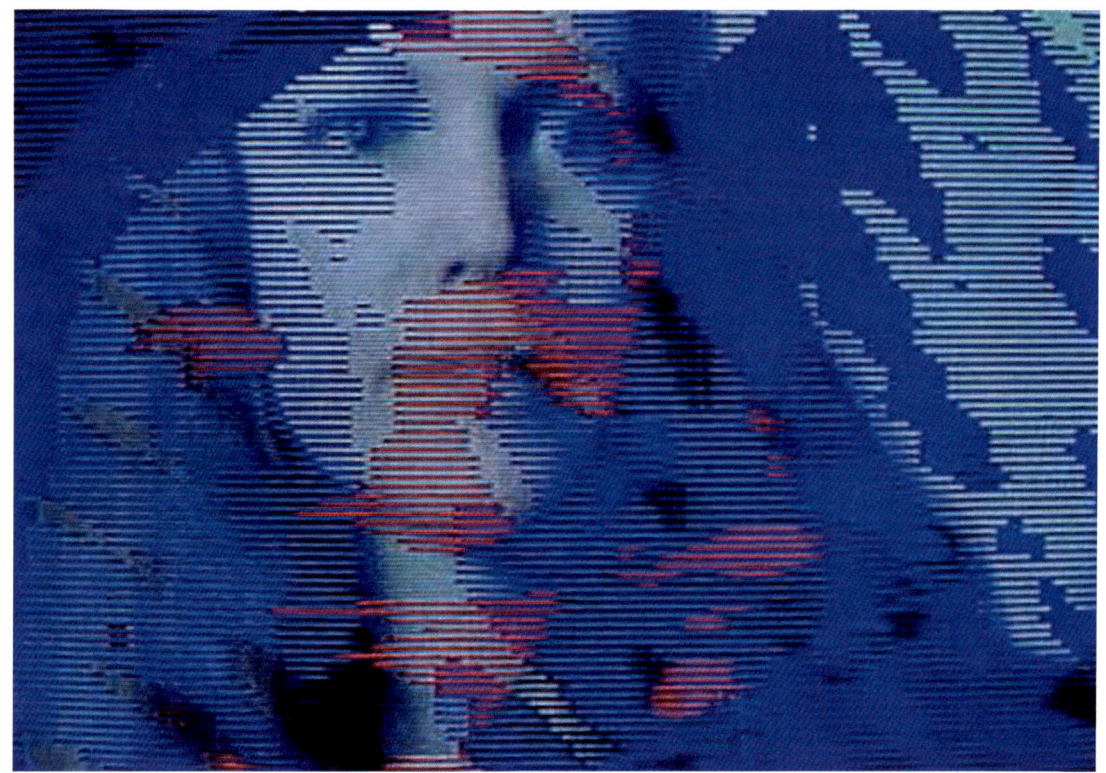

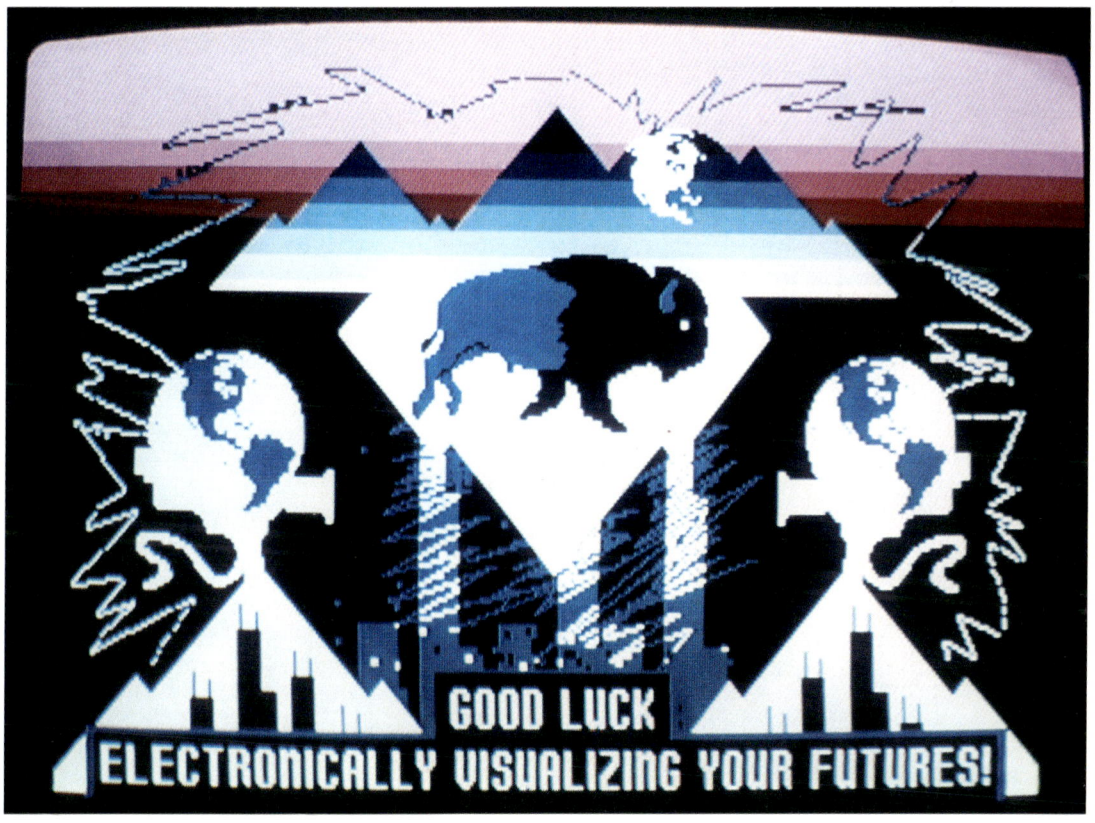

⁂ Joan Truckenbrod, *On Becoming* 1984
↑ Jane Veeder, still from *Montana* 1982

George Barber, of the Scratch video art movement, studied at the Slade and later used Quantel Paintbox to make *1001 Colours Andy Never Thought Of* 1989, reprocessing images from Andy Warhol's Marilyn Monroe screenprints. The facilities of colleges and polytechnics (technical and vocational institutes), as well as the discursive and exhibition activities of societies, clubs or research institutes, are part of this history. For instance, the London-based Computer Arts Society had strong links to the London Film-Makers' Co-op through the efforts of British film-maker Malcolm Le Grice.[22] Around the world, new places for art and technological exchange cropped up, such as community centres to share skills in programming, and art studios with industry-standard technology, like the Banff Centre in Canada, or V2_, Lab for the Unstable Media in Rotterdam, Netherlands. In Europe and North America these organisations, set up to explore the artistic potential of computing, were in all likelihood still outnumbered by the universities, the industry-focused research wings of corporations such as Xerox or Bell Labs, and national initiatives such as the animation wing of the National Film Board of Canada, all of which hosted artists.[23]

These industry collaborations nevertheless allowed artists to experiment with not just computer-generated screen-based graphics and early virtual reality (the Banff Centre is where Lawrence Paul Yuxweluptun created *Inherent Rights, Vision Rights* 1992–3 (p.203), but also networked systems such as slow-scan television and signals sent via satellite, making this a period of global activity. Vera Frenkel's work *String Games: Improvisations for Inter-City Video* 1974, was the first artwork in Canada to use real-time telecommunications technology from the teleconference facilities of the company Bell Canada. Meanwhile, WorldPool, co-founded by artists Judith Doyle, Norman White and others, was a 'means to explore telecommunications technology, including proto-networking, fax transmission, and slow-scan video. Between 1978 and 1984, the aforementioned technologies were used to perform live-to-live TeleXchanges using telenetworking devices borrowed from high-tech businesses'.[24] This included the event Weincouver IV at artist-run centre the Western Front Society in 1983, which saw artists engage in live performance distributed across a worldwide network. Precursors included, in California, Kit Galloway and Sherrie Rabinowitz's Satellite Arts Project and Electronic Cafe Network (and their well-known work *Hole In Space* 1980, and prior to that, Liza Béar and Keith Sonnier's 1977 project that delivered to an audience of 25,000 a two-hour networked performance between New York and San Francisco, broadcast over two days via NASA's CTS Satellite. Earlier still, Argentinian performance artist Marta Minujín was engaging with telecommunications technologies, in relation to the activities of the CAYC/Video Encounters festivals.[25]

Given that the outputs of these communities were shown as much at corporate showcase events and even World Fairs

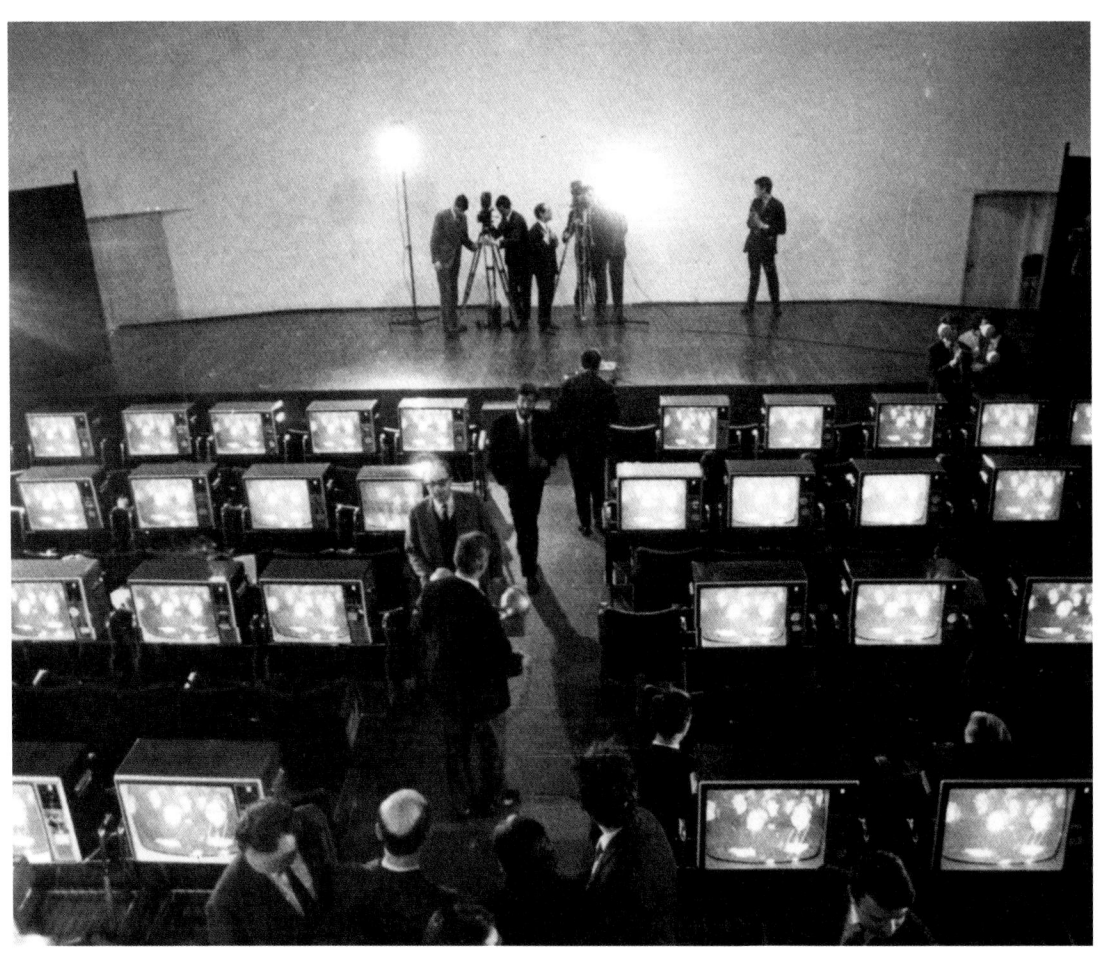

as academic conferences, a reconstituted art history has to consider how the commercial world and the conceptual art world were at odds with one another, especially once artists invited the public to (bodily) participate in the environments they were creating. This clash between practice and theory (DIY/activism and cybernetics) is the subject of a number of important texts detailing the 'systems thinking' pervasive at that time. In 1970 Jack Burnham, curator of the 1972 exhibition *Software*, wrote about society's move from being object-oriented to being systems-oriented. In the catalogue for the show, artist Les Levine wrote about how privacy was dead, and the information environment was controlling us: 'If everybody has computers, then it becomes possible for everybody to talk to everybody else … while companies do have the possibility to control you, if you are hooked in to them you have the possibility to control back.'[26] Many thinkers and artists linked increased participation in the information age to debates about planetary thinking, capitalism, scientific rationality, technological development and technology's links to the military-industrial complex in the wake of the Vietnam War.[27] *The Postmodern Condition*, philosopher Jean-François Lyotard's 1979 report about technology's influence in science and society, let's not forget, was commissioned by an educational body – the Conseil des universités du Québec – in an effort to understand what *living* as information cyborgs might mean for how we come to know the world.

Langill has written:

This tension between the values espoused by artists and the ambitions of industry led to a growing divide between the art world and technology-based art objects. However, there remained pockets of interest; some artists continued to employ new media as a means of production, recognizing a society that was gradually integrating new technologies as critical means of communication.[28]

National government initiatives to foster new electronic telecoms systems for communication between users also offered opportunities for artists, the histories of which are still being revealed. Proto-internet telecoms systems that worked via phone lines – and, later, ISDN and television cable connections (Videotex and teletext) – are crucial steps in the history of participatory text- and image-based electronic art, which eventually leads to net art. The UK had Prestel, Canada had Telidon, which never quite caught on, but France had Minitel, which did, and artists Eduardo Kac, Fred Forest, Vera Molnar, François Morellet and others created work explicitly for it, many at the invitation of artist ORLAN.[29] Minitel was also a key component – used almost like a live journal– in Thierry Chaput and Lyotard's 1985 exhibition at the Centre Pompidou, *Les Immateriaux*.

Industrial collaborations aside, just as with net art of the 1990s, in the 1980s artists like painter Samia Halaby were in their studios programming their own computers, using languages such as BASIC and C. Here is DIY tinkering not in the corporate or cybernetic management sense of a process of optimisation, but, as with the use of other gaming or telecoms platforms that you could access from home, as a process of exploration.

Considered through the lens of software or hardware development, industrial and commercial history is intertwined with art history such that it becomes even more difficult to separate them once video games become a primary driver of new technologies (as, arguably, they still are). A case in point is the work of the groundbreaking artist and human-computer interaction designer Brenda Laurel, who moved to California to work at Atari in 1979. As part of her work at the Interval Research Corporation (a future oriented think-tank founded by Microsoft's Paul Allen), Laurel went to the Banff Centre to build the Placeholder VR system in 1992 with a group of artists including Rachel Strickland, creating interactive installations that allowed users to inhabit avatars of other species, incorporating indigenous belief systems and iconography. In 1996 she founded Purple Moon (bought by Mattel in 1999), the educational game company for girls and women, to address the gender disparity in computer gaming. So not only did artists invent a number of technologies, they also pointed out important aspects of working more inclusively, and more bodily/embodied-ly, with them.

Planetary thinking

Oh, it's beautiful … Ohhh, it's infinite …
Oh, it's fantastic!
– Andy Warhol on releasing one of his silver, helium-filled balloons from the roof of The Factory[30]

In his 2014 interview with electronic video artist Stephen Beck, curator John Hanhardt commented: 'There's a kind of sense that today historians sort of look in the rearview mirror – focus on minimalist and conceptual art and don't often take cognizance of the full complexity of the visual art culture and the media art that you were so integral to.'[31]

The complexity that Hanhardt refers to here isn't just the multimedia convergence, but also the context of social change during this time period (of the 1960s to 1980s) – liberation movements, feminism, anti-war movements, free speech and community groups engaged in activism. Reflecting on this complexity about mass media and the message, Beck, a self-declared 'polymediast', and founding member of (the Chicago branch of) Experiments in Art and Technology (E.A.T.) replies: 'The Race to Space, the landing on the moon, I mean, these were transformative events, and yet to me, I wanted to make something beautiful with that technology to try to offset the destructive nature of it, and I wanted to make something beautiful out of television.'[32]

Artists have wondered whether the confining of technological development to within a corporate and commercial framework meant that society failed to actively redefine art

← Marta Minujín, still from *Simultaneity in Simultaneity*, installation view at Torcuato Di Tella Institute, Buenos Aires, 24 October 1966

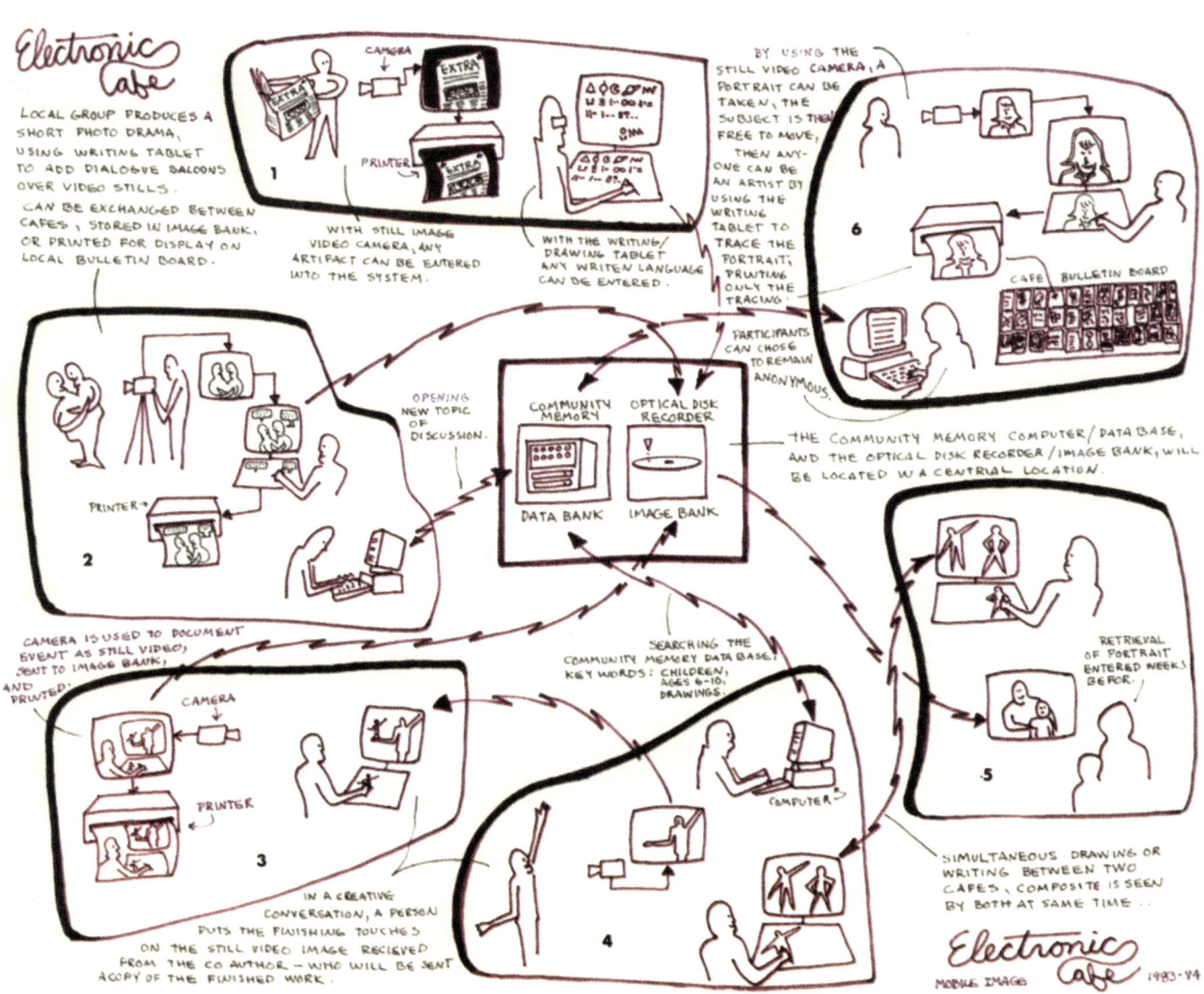

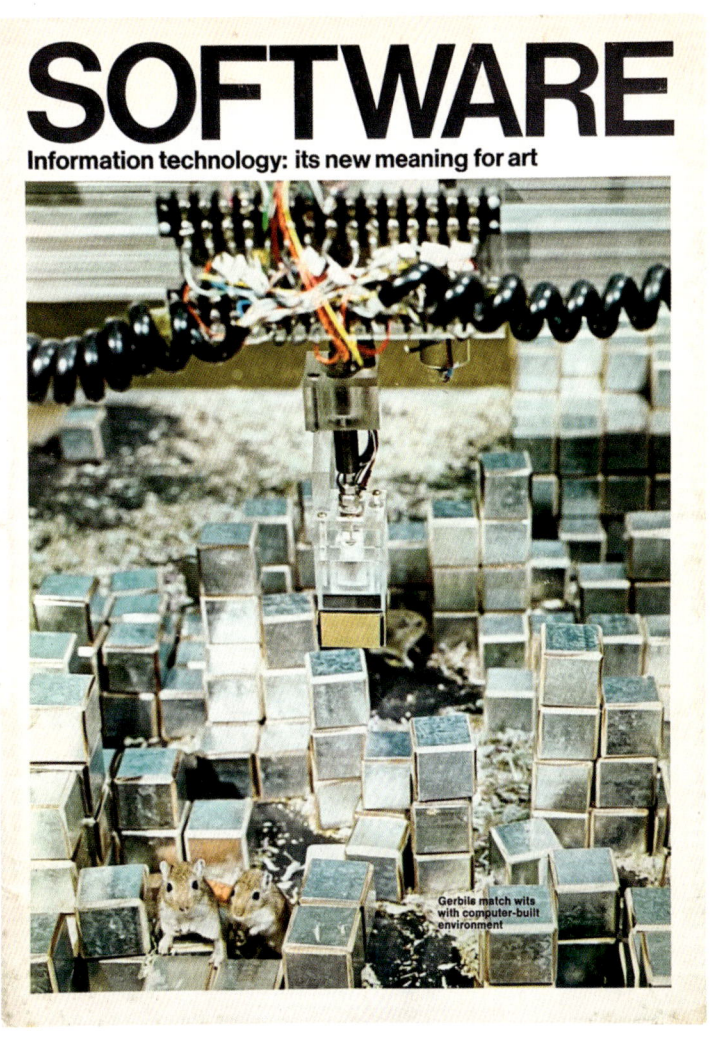

SOFTWARE
Information technology: its new meaning for art

Gerbils match wits
with computer-built
environment

from being an exclusive or privileged activity in the service of private interests or industry, into being a research-driven and more open, participatory creative visual process.[33] Some of the happenin' experimental artists of the 1970s did, in the eyes of some, sell out to Silicon Valley, though arguably it was more that their work got co-opted.[34] Where artists fit, between the military-industrial complex and 'hippie' California planetary thinking, and what future their art might help to build, is exemplified in counter-culture magazine *The Whole Earth Catalog*, and the publishing of the magazine *Radical Software* in the early 1970s. The DIY mandate of these publications – teaching readers not just how to code, but how to think and live as bodies in harmony with the environment in a computerised future, or how to 'bend' technology in order to democratise and demystify it – directly influenced how the internet was first used and built up into a global resource and tool for the good of all.[35] <Sigh>.

As home computing became not just possible, but actually affordable and accessible, plenty of artists continued to work with a DIY ethos, and at what I'm calling the

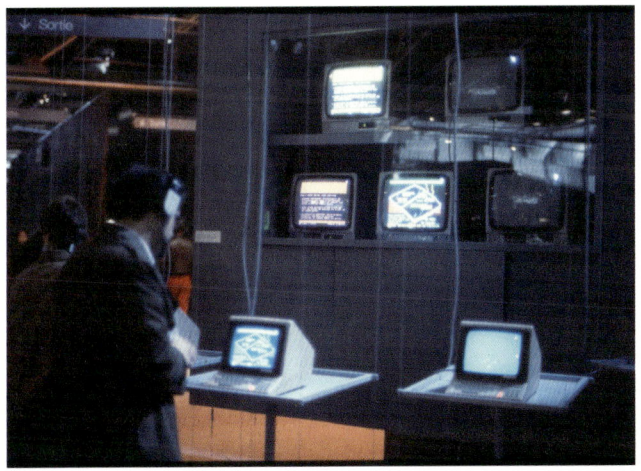

↖ Jaques-Elie Chabert, Jean-Paul Martin, Camille Philibert, Dominique Horviller, *The Lost Object* 1985, installation view at the exhibition *Les Immatériaux*, Centre Georges Pompidou, Paris, 1985

↑ Cover of the exhibition catalogue for *Software: Information technology: its new meaning for art*, Jewish Museum, New York, 1970

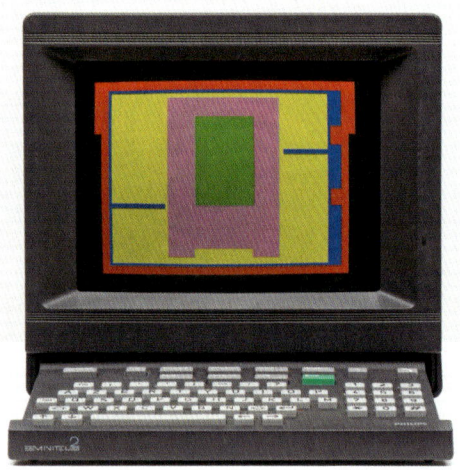

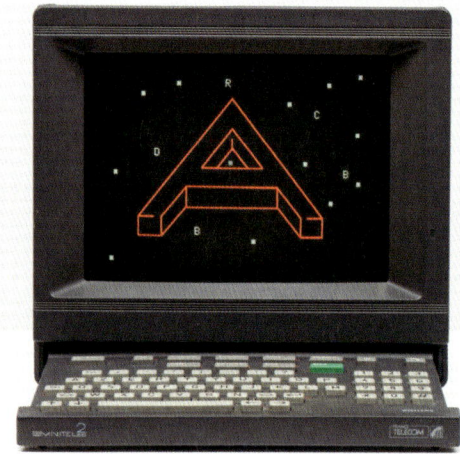

Eduardo Kac

Kac is a multimedia artist with an expansive oeuvre spanning performance, poetry, interactive art, digital art and proto-internet art. In the 1980s he was eager to engage with the discourse around cybernetics in relation to new technologies, and his early works used telecommunication tools such as Xerox, fax machines and slow-scan TV. The Minitel terminal series is an example of his early experiments with animated poetic artworks and is considered an early example of art made specifically for a computer network. The Minitel system, originating in France, allowed users to connect through remote terminals and access information and services through regular phone lines. Kac's works were made for the Brazilian version of this service, the Videotexto network. The series engages with Brazil's rich history of experimentation with concrete poetry, an art form straddling visual art and literature, in which the layout and typography of words shape a poem's meaning. Kac plays with the chromatic and painterly features of the Minitel display, as seemingly abstract geometric forms gradually reveal text. The words hint at Brazil's unstable socio-political context and connect to Kac's previous works exploring the visual and literal language of desire. BP

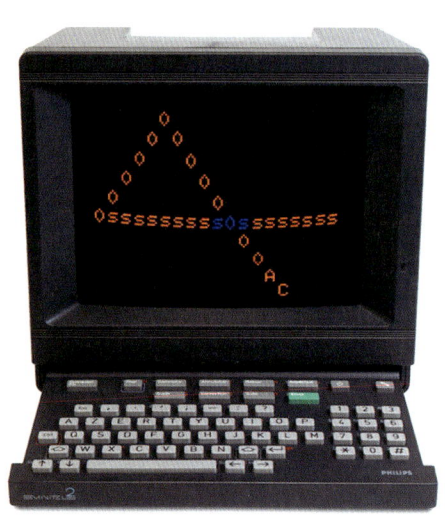

✿ Eduardo Kac, *Horny* 1985/6
↗ Eduardo Kac, *Reabracadabra* 1985
→ Eduardo Kac, *Recaos* 1985–6

embodied or 'corporeal' rather than 'corporate' end of electronic experimentation, in a 1960s spirit of participatory performance. Trying to pull apart these histories now is an aesthetic disintermediation exercise – teasing out the differences between the kind of computer graphics seen on TV shows like *Night Flight* (1981–8) or in movies like *TRON* (1982), and the bodily immersive potential of VR or other interactive installations, of the kind artists such as Brenda Laurel were working on. Sitting somewhere in the middle is a work like *Liquid Views – Narcissus' Digital Reflections* 1992–3 (p.202) by Monika Fleischmann and Wolfgang Strauss. Here the possibility of seeing yourself in the digital environment is actualised, and your bodily actions affect its manifestation. But with that comes the warning that behind that glassy, reflective, slick image must be the truth that the digital environment is also looking back at you.

Futurecasting

We look at the present through a rear-view mirror. We march backwards into the future.
– Marshall McLuhan[36]

In 1985 Kittler warned about this 'convergence media' ending history:

The general digitization of channels and information erases the differences among individual media. Sound and image, voice and text are reduced to surface effects, known to consumers as interface. Sense and the senses turn into eyewash. Their media-produced glamor will survive for an interim as a by-product of strategic programs. Inside the computers themselves everything becomes a number: quantity without image, sound, or voice.[37]

Was Kittler actually describing the rise of AI systems? Is AI art 'eyewash'? We currently find ourselves faced with some of the same challenges artists faced in the 1970s and 1980s – dependent on tools and facilities confined to university labs or corporate R&D programmes (hello, quantum computing). Many artists are also, as in the 1970s, not sure they want to participate in a disembodied techno-capitalism, particularly where military use of those technologies is concerned (hello, AI). Remembering the DIY ethos of these artistic experiments is thus all the more important. Artist Garnet Hertz, in his book *Art + DIY Electronics*, does just this, writing:

DIY practices operate without a commercially motivated endpoint. In other words, finances often force a DIY approach, but financial gain is not usually the goal ... DIY practice rejects, or does not attain, a mass production mode of efficient productivity ... DIY is embodied in and attentive to process, uses authenticity and materiality for political ends, and embraces a fuller and more complex notion of the amateur that rejects management.

Despite hoping to look back to this moment in art history and see an emphasis on a DIY engagement with technologies, the social and political potential of networked

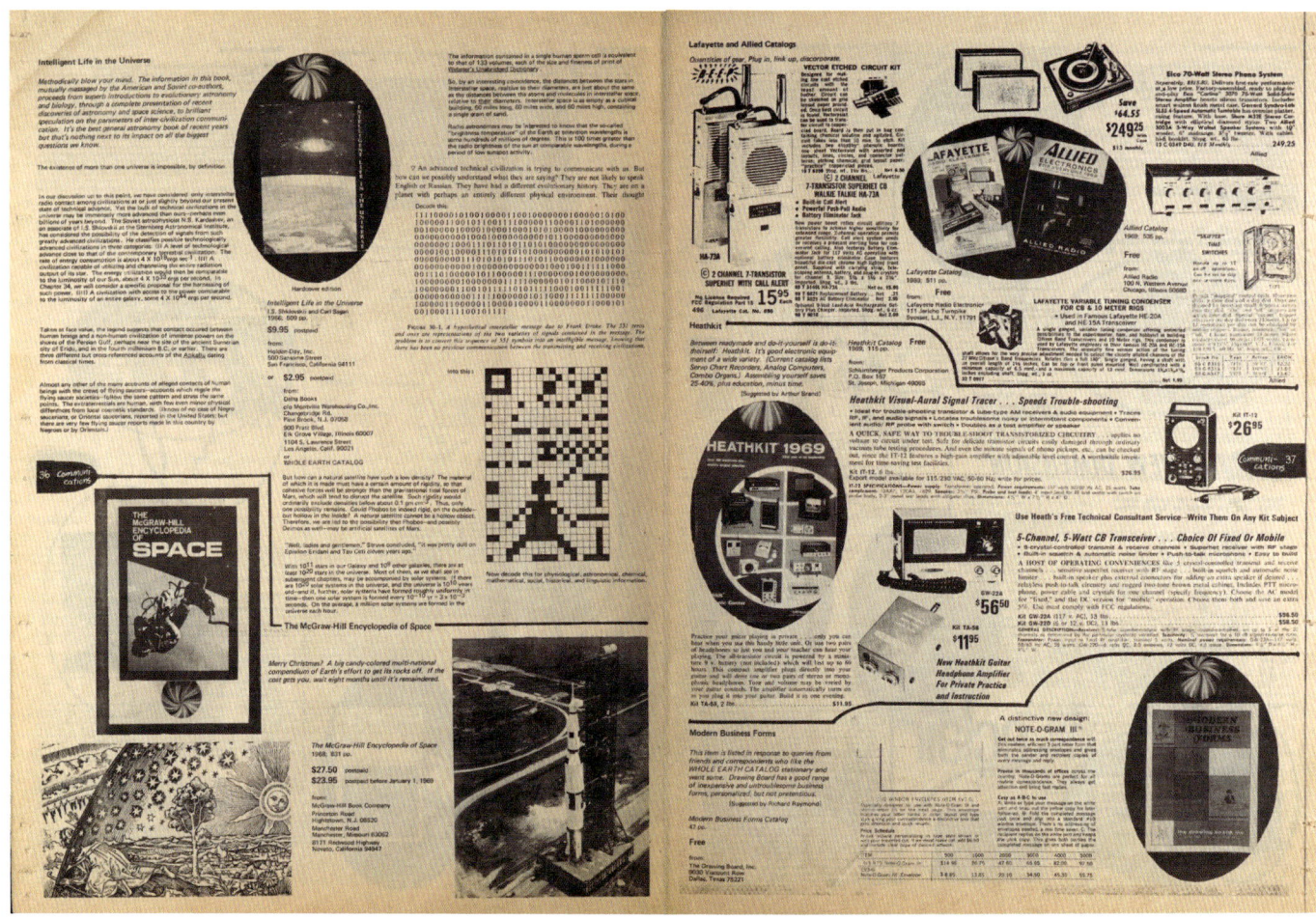

Whole Earth Catalog

The *Whole Earth Catalog* was a countercultural magazine published irregularly by the technologist Stewart Brand from 1968 to 1998 in California. Half research journal, half mail-order catalogue, the publication was initially intended for use by the North American 'back-to-the-land movement' of the 1960s and 1970s, which saw young, politically motivated people move from cities to rural areas, engaging in farming and communal group living. Gathering a diverse range of objects, ideas and resources under the rallying subtitle 'access to tools', the *Catalog* sought to instigate a DIY ethos that bridged technological and ecological practices, brought together to understand the Earth as a 'whole system'. The cover of each edition featured an image of Earth as a full disc seen from space, the first of which images had only been captured in 1967 by NASA.

Catalogue items are grouped into thematic sections, from 'Understanding Whole Systems', which introduces the theoretical background of the *Catalog* through the works of cyberneticist Buckminster Fuller and others, to 'Shelter and Land Use', via tantric art, glass blowing, auto repair, calculators and various examples of early computer tech. The publication functioned as a kind of prototypical search engine for alternative ways of relating to the Earth, its environment and other people populating the planet.

Over time, the *Catalog* generated spin-off publications, such as the *CoEvolution Quarterly* and *Whole Earth Review*. In 1985 Brand would launch the WELL (Whole Earth 'Lectronic Link), one of the first online networked communities. Leaving a complicated legacy, the *Whole Earth Catalog* has been criticised in recent years for its aesthetic and rhetorical relationship to North American pioneerism and its celebration of individualism – trends which became influential among the nascent tech communities and corporations of Silicon Valley. EH & VR

↑ A spread from *Whole Earth Catalog: access to tools*, Fall 1968

electronic systems has sadly only shown us how little agency we have when corporations control the means of production. As curator Val Ravaglia wrote in preparation for launching *Electric Dreams*, there was 'a dialogue, exchange or tension with the more systematic and functionally-minded methods of engineering: both sides were ultimately needed for those experiments to emerge'.[38] We still need the artist-programmers and the programmer-artists to remind us not just that we should DIY, but that we should DIWO (Do It With Others) if we really want to change the corporate technology-dependent world our corporeal bodies live in.

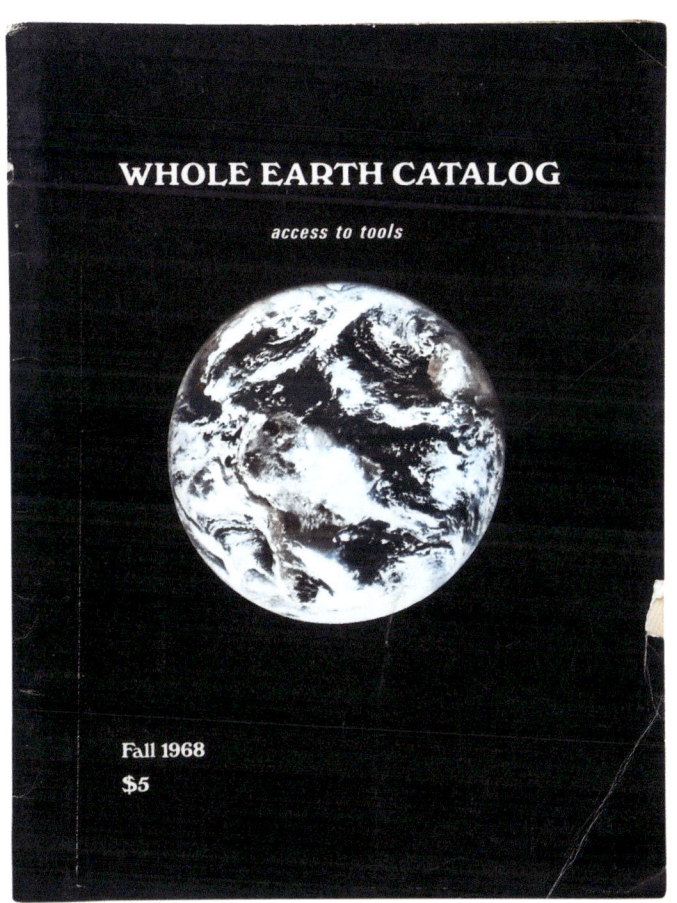

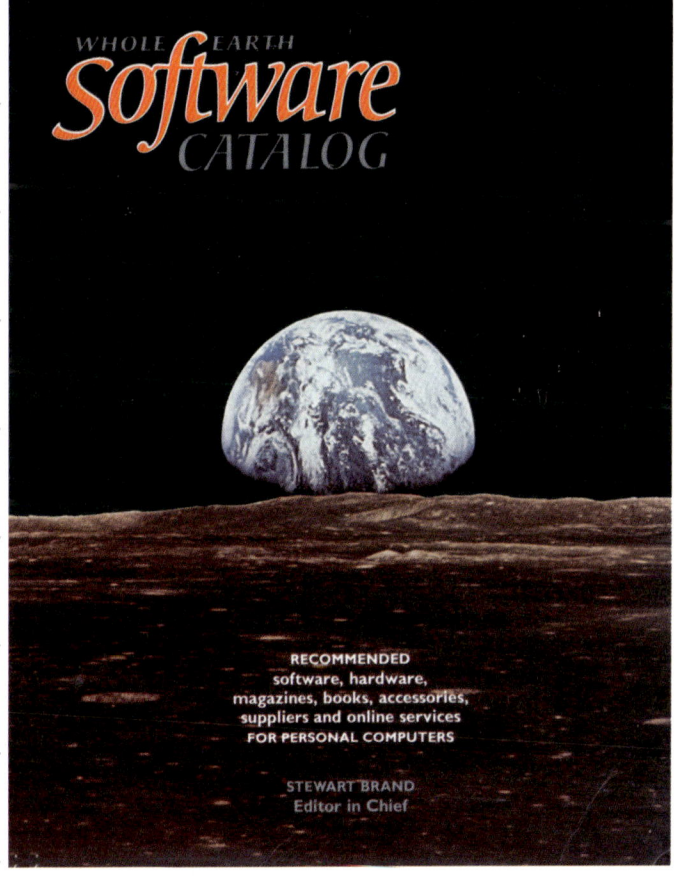

↑ *Whole Earth Catalog: access to tools*, Spring 1969   ↑ *Whole Earth Software Catalog*, June 1984

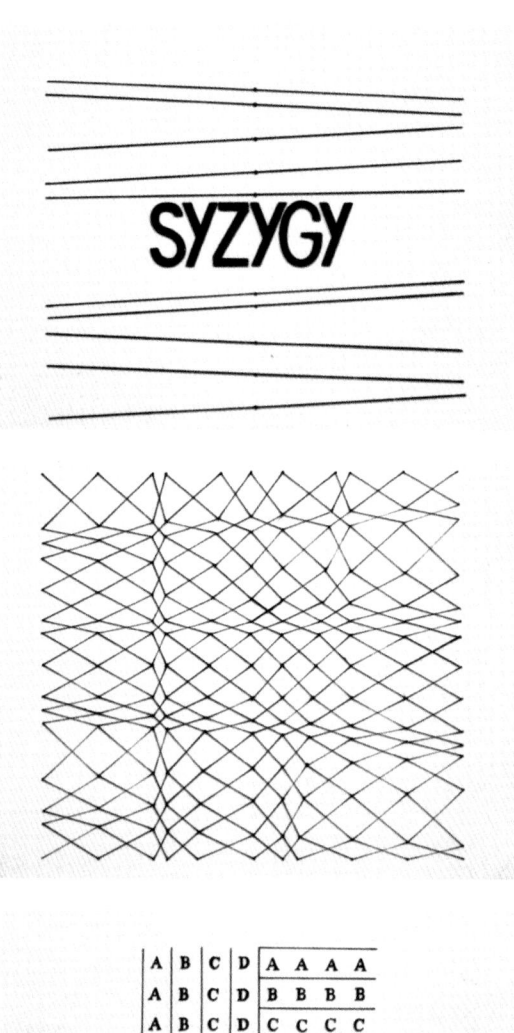

Akbar Padamsee

In 1969 Akbar Padamsee founded the Inter-art Vision Exchange Workshop (VIEW, 1969–71) in Mumbai; it was a short-lived but influential platform for artists to experiment and exchange ideas across disciplines. Padamsee, primarily a painter, made his first short films at VIEW, including *Syzygy* 1972, a collaboration with animator Ram Mohan. The film is an abstract, stop-motion animation created out of nearly 1,000 drawings, in which Padamsee develops sequences of forms from numbers, letters and dots turned into straight, dashed or curved lines. The sequence suggests an order, as if following a code from which the animation is generated, like an idiosyncratic and analogue programming language. Padamsee's inspirations for the film mix his interest in philosophy and astronomy with references to Paul Klee's pedagogical diagrams and possibly to John Cage and Iannis Xenakis. VR

↑ Akbar Padamsee, stills from *Syzygy* 1972

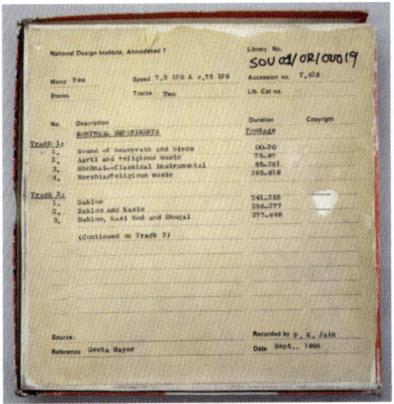

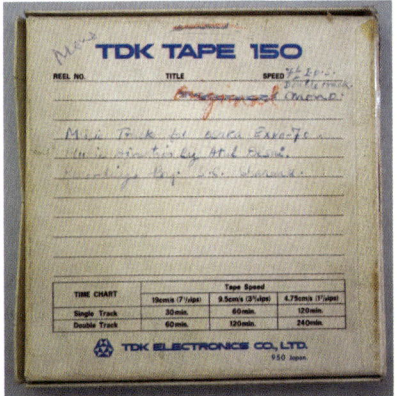

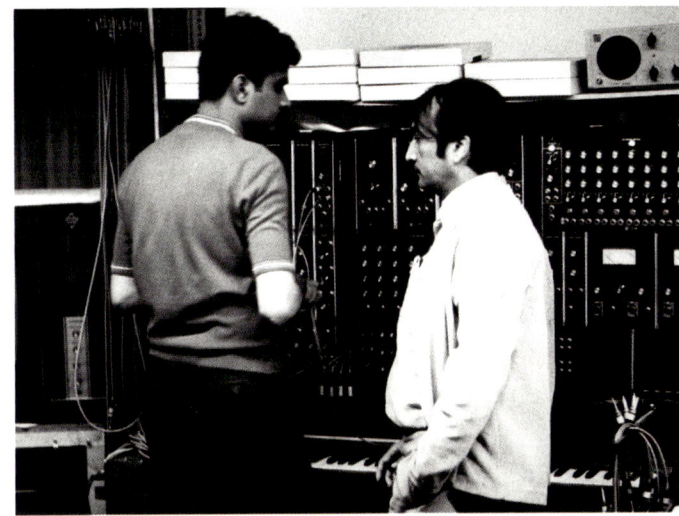

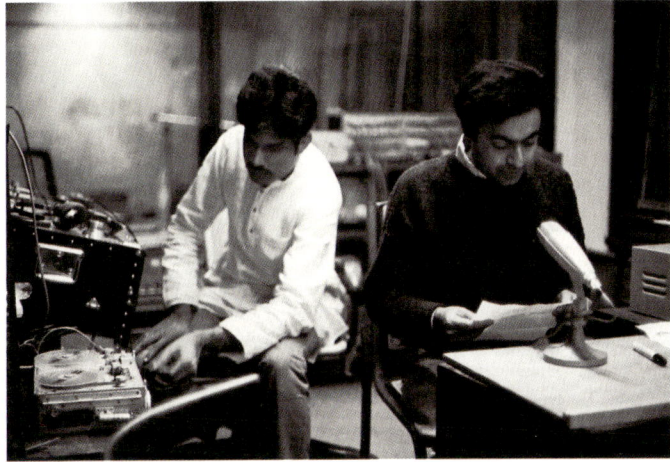

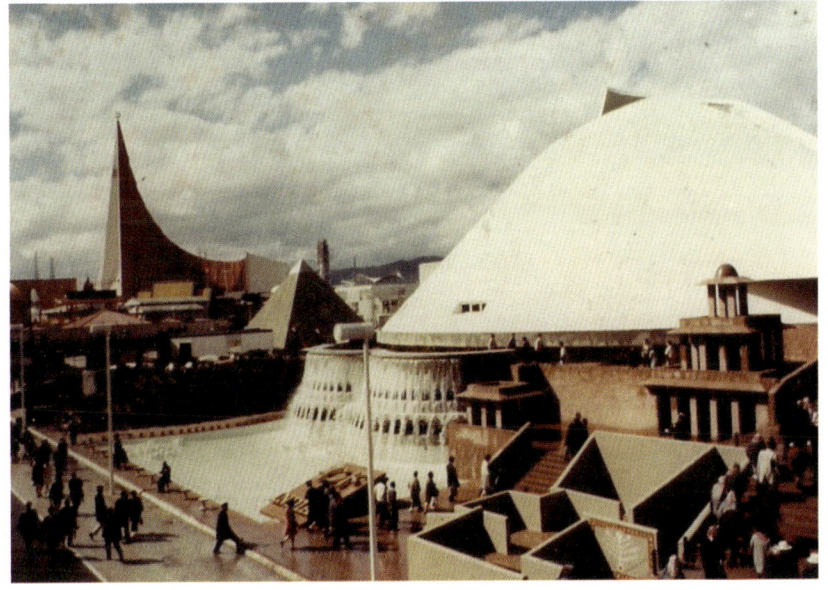

National Institute of Design (NID)

The National Institute of Design was founded in 1961 in Ahmedabad, in the context of a post-war India which was investing significantly in media, design and technology. The institute included India's first electronic music studio, founded in 1969 with the support of the Sarabhai family and composer David Tudor, who helped bring a Moog modular synthesiser to NID. The studio became a hub for pioneering Indian musicians who experimented with the new technology, including Atul Desai, Gita Sarabhai and S.C. Sharma, and produced what are considered the earliest examples of electronic music in India, including the soundtrack for Dashrath Patel's nine-screen projection for the India Pavilion at the Montreal World's Fair in 1967, one of India's first immersive multimedia installations. NID also fostered relationships with international artists, namely Experiments in Arts and Technology (E.A.T.), and took part in both the Osaka Expo in 1970 and the *Utopia Q&A 1981* project of 1971. OW

⤒ Label for the National Institute of Design's
Montreal Experiments tape, 1967

169　⤒ Label for Atul Desai's *Osaka Expo '70* tape, 1967

⤒ I.S. Mathur and Atul Desai working in the NID studio, c.1970
↑ Tape and voiceover work at the NID sound studio, c.1969
↖ India Pavilion at Osaka Expo '70, 1970

Expo '70, the first World Exposition in Asia, took place in Osaka, Japan, between 15 March and 13 September 1970. Against the backdrop of the Cold War, the theme was 'Progress and Harmony for Mankind'. Seventy-seven countries participated, alongside organisations and companies, and a record-breaking sixty-four million people visited the site, designed by architect Kenzō Tange.[1] Technology, central to Japan's post-Second World War economic growth, emerged as a key area of interest. Artists utilising technology were commissioned by governments and corporations to contribute to pavilions, providing an opportunity to work with larger scales and budgets.

The United States Pavilion dedicated a section to 'New Arts', emerging from the Art and Technology programme initiated by curator Maurice Tuchman at Los Angeles County Museum of Art (LACMA): 'a pioneer experiment in which industrial corporations sheltered artists in residence and gave them the opportunity to explore advanced technology'. Works included a 'Strobe light environment' by Boyd Mefferd and 'Cube and concave mirrors with pseudo-scopic images' by Robert Whitman.[2]

The Dutch Pavilion was recognised for its multimedia environment designed by Wim Crouwel, with film footage by director Jan Vrijman. The pavilion included reliefs by Peter Struycken, composed by making decisions through the roll of a die, a precursor to works he later made using a computer as a pioneer of computer art in the Netherlands.[3]

The German Pavilion was a spherical concert hall conceptualised by Karlheinz Stockhausen, composer and pioneer of electronic music. Compositions by Stockhausen were performed daily, including *Expo*, written specifically for the event, in which three performers utilise sounds picked up from short-wave radio receivers.[4] The Indian Pavilion also celebrated electronic music, with an experimental soundtrack by Atul Desai, vocalist, composer and lecturer at Ahmedabad's National Institute of Design (p.169).[5]

Some experiments in art and technology at Expo '70 were less successful than others. Festival Plaza, the Expo's central site, was designed by architect Arata Isozaki as an interactive environment, containing robots, lighting and sound, controlled by a computer. Isozaki saw the plaza as a 'Cybernetic Environment', in which 'humans and machines become unified within space-time to form a dynamic totality'.[6] Contrary to Isozaki's intentions, the programming of traditional music and dance performances in the space meant visitors were positioned as static observers, preventing them from participating freely.[7]

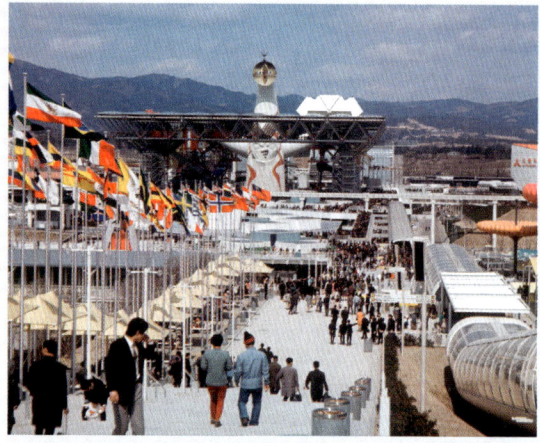

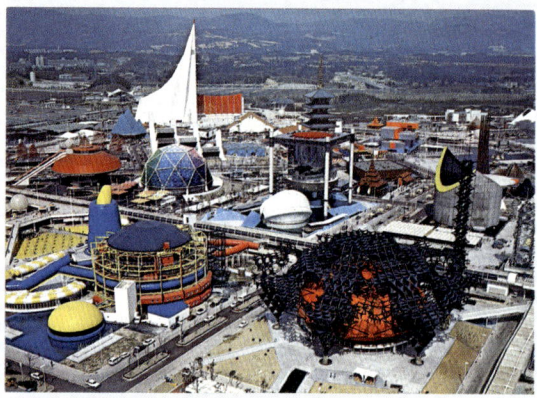

⬆ Osaka Expo '70, the Festival Plaza with Taro Okamoto's *Tower of the Sun* in the background, 1970
↑ Osaka Expo '70, view with Matsui Pavilion and Toshiba-IHI Pavilion in the foreground, 1970

Progress and Harmony for Mankind: Innovation and Commercialisation at Expo '70

Kira Wainstein

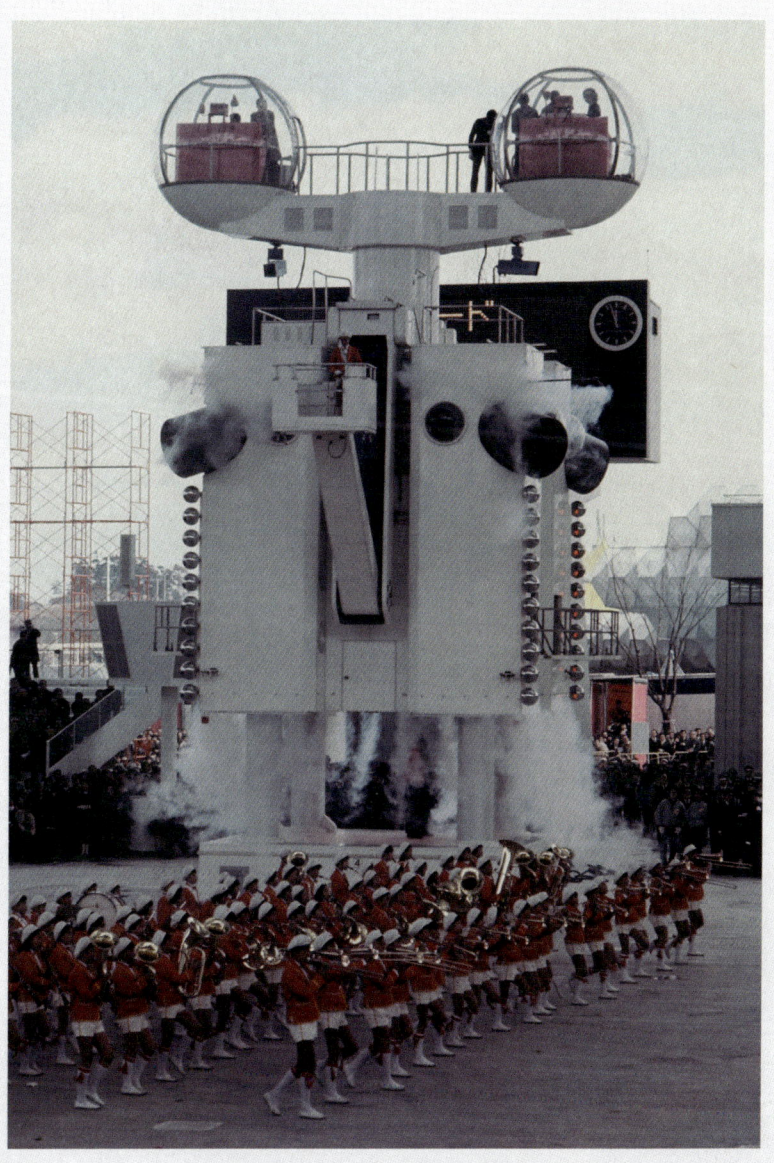

The artist Katsuhiro Yamaguchi designed the pavilion for Japanese corporation Mitsui: an imagining of the future in which motorised platforms transported visitors through projections, strobe lights and sound from 1,726 speakers.[8] Yamaguchi called it 'total theatre', highlighting its intended immersive nature. However, as with Isozaki's Festival Plaza, critics noted the passive experience of visitors, who were 'carried away by a mobile platform operated by technicians sitting in an adjacent control room'.[9]

The corporate presence at Expo '70 prompted criticism among artists. Alongside Mitsui, there were pavilions from major corporations including IBM, Mitsubishi, Sanyo and Hitachi, which presented futuristic consumer products such as mobile telephones and flight simulators. Tjebbe van Tijen, artist and co-founder Research Center Art Technology and Society in Amsterdam, co-wrote a manifesto critiquing Expo '70 for its capitalistic tendencies: 'Don't the World's Fairs force themselves upon us as manifestations of the "freedom" to have to produce things for which there is no need and to have to consume what we were forced to produce?'[10]

The Pepsi Pavilion, designed by US-based collective E.A.T. (Experiments in Art and Technology), complicates this critique. For this participatory environment, Fujiko Nakaya created her first fog sculpture, which covered the exterior of the pavilion, home to the world's largest hemispherical mirror, designed by Elsa Garmire (pp.174–7). Robert Breer's *Float* sculptures moved around outside. The pavilion's coordinating architect, John Pearce, said: 'This is a kind of *anti-Expo* exhibit because we don't show people something we want them to see. Here, each individual is part of the show.'[11] Although the project was viewed as the pinnacle of E.A.T.'s activities, the collective's contract was terminated by Pepsi weeks after opening, with their performance programme cancelled. Whether this was due to budget disagreements or Pepsi's reservations about the anti-Expo nature of the pavilion is unclear.[12]

Criticism of Expo '70 was aimed not only at its commercialisation, but also at its perceived political motives. Many saw Expo '70 as a deliberate distraction from the renewal of the U.S.-Japan Security Treaty, known as Anpo. First signed in 1951, Anpo was met with widespread opposition during its 1960 renewal, and was viewed as a means of allowing America to use Japan as its Cold War base in Asia. This suspicion, coupled with the uncertainty surrounding the Expo site's future, is encapsulated in Genpei Akasegawa's tongue in cheek 1970 text work, *A Redevelopment Proposal for the Expo '70 Site*:

Construct another expo on the former site of Expo '70.
Construct another expo on the former site of Expo '70.
Construct another expo on the former site of Expo '70.
Repeat it every time the Anpo is renewed.[13]

↖ Arata Isozaki, *Robot Deme* performance robot, Osaka Expo '70, 1970

大阪　　人類の進歩と調和

O S A K A　　　　PROGRESS　AND HARMONY　FOR　MANKIND

French and British _national_ industrial exhibitions let to the birth of the
World's Fair. These exhibitions were a festive effect of the " liberté du
travail " which was proclaimed shortly after the French Revolution. After
the guilds were disbanded (1791) the patent was introduced.
1798 The first _national_ industrial exhibition in Paris was a celebration of
  this " freedom of labour ".
   the freedom of labour
   was to be the beginning
   of labour towards freedom
   in order to achieve
   liberation from labour
1851 The motto of the first World's Fair in London was: " the union of the
  human race ". This idea was reflected in the huge glass and steel
  structure (Crystal Palace) which housed the entire exhibition.
1862 This World's Fair once more held in London, (unintentionally) furnished
  a possibility for a meeting of the international proletariat. The idea
  " workers of the world unite " (1848) crystallized when the " international " was founded in 1864.
1867 The idea behind this World's Fair in Paris was to demonstrate world
  unity: " all the countries are here together, enemies live side by side
  in peace ". The building which housed the exhibition of all the participants was supposed to represent the shape of the globe.
1893 This World's Fair in Chicago deliberately opposed the idea of world
  unity as it had been reflected in the large structures of the previous
  Fairs. From now on the participants held their exhibitions in National
  Pavilions.
1967 The motto of the last World's Fair in Montreal was: "terre des hommes ".
1970 The motto of the next World's Fair in Osaka Japan is: " progress and
  harmony for mankind ".
None of the 62 World's Fairs which have been held took place in the Third
World except for those in Lima (1872), Santiago de Chile (1875), Bombay
(1887), Hanoi (1902) and Rio de Janeiro (1922).

The World's Fairs have become Olympian demonstrations of national ideals.
Ideals formed by power monopolies which use their own norms as a standard
to determine the freedom of other people, although these same norms are in-
adequate to allow for freedom within the system where the power monopoly
exists. This has led (in our country) to a consumption society where human
values are no longer of central importance, but where values of life are
imposed upon us, with the inherent aim of increasing profit. In various areas it is becoming clear that this is happening at the expense of human
beings (in the Third World and _also_ here), that it is urgently necessary to
seek alternatives and to oppose further escalation of the situation. It is
important with respect to this process of awakening and becoming aware that
precisely those people who are involved with the formulation of these human
values (e.g. designers, architects, artists, youth leaders, social workers,
city planners, etc.) take a standpoint with respect to this system.

Don't the World's Fairs force themselves upon us as manifestations of the
'freedom' to have to produce things for which there is no need and to have
to consume what we were forced to produce ?

Don't artists, designers, architects, etc. give the World's Fairs a cultural image' and aren't they being (mis)used to present a sham freedom ?

The aim of this publication is to form a basis for a discussion about a
problem that concerns all of us. For this reason everyone is requested to
put down his or her (pro or anti) opinion: designs, signed statements,
essays, cartoons, photographs with caption, etc., etc. and send it to:
Post Box 159 Heerlen Holland (before february '69). Every contribution will
be used without any modification (except those made necessary in translation
for a publication, that will be send again to all contributors all over the
world. So that this World's Fair can form the basis for a combined effort to
find alternatives for the contemporary systems of society and achieve a way
of life in which the human being is of central importance.

↑ Tjebbe van Tijen and Nic Tummers, _Osaka._
Progress and Harmony for Mankind, 1968

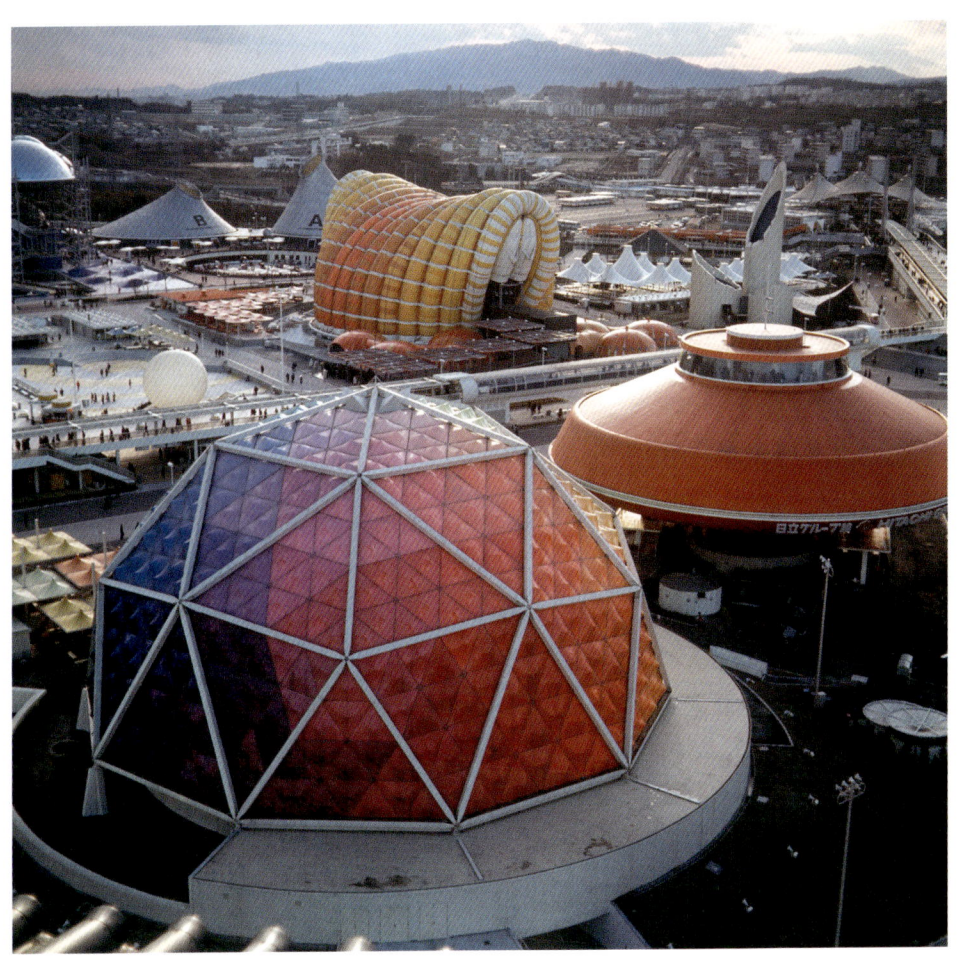

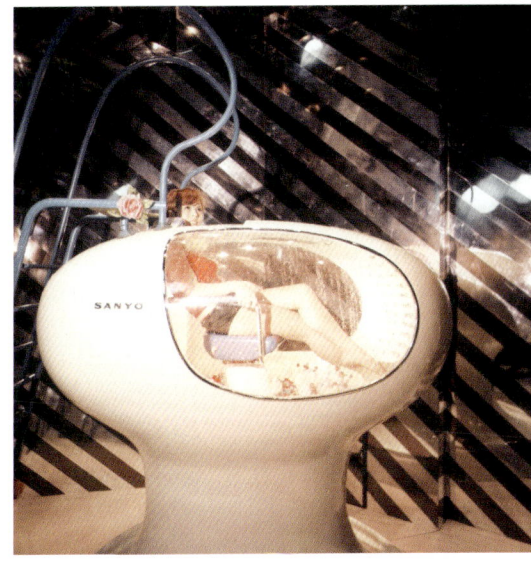

↖ Midoni-Kan (Astrorama), Hitachi Pavilion and Fuji Pavilion
at Osaka Expo '70, 1970
↑ The Ultrasonic Bath on display in the Sanyo Pavilion,
Osaka Expo '70, 1970

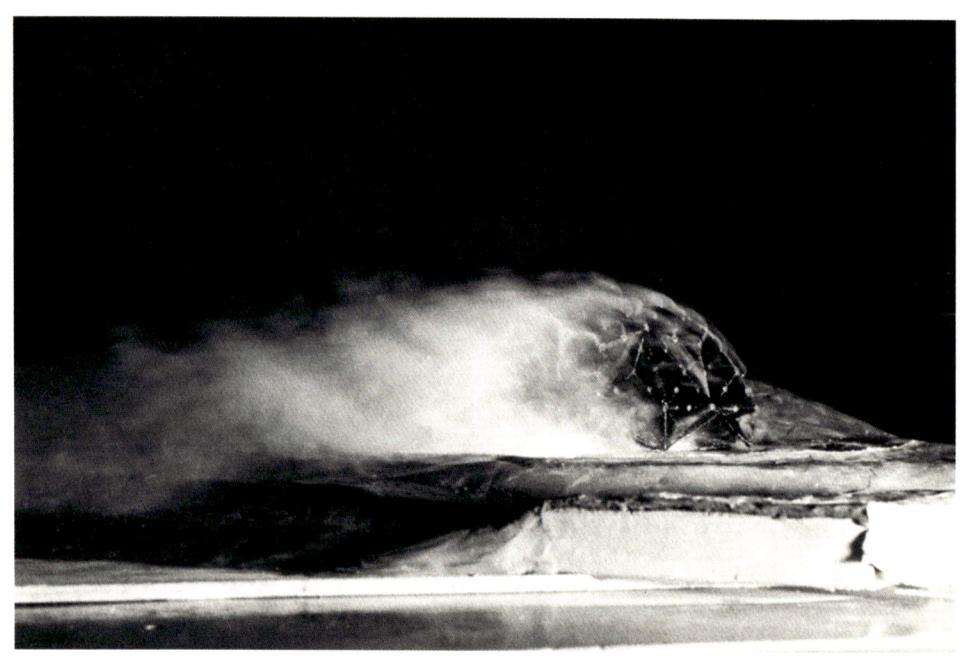

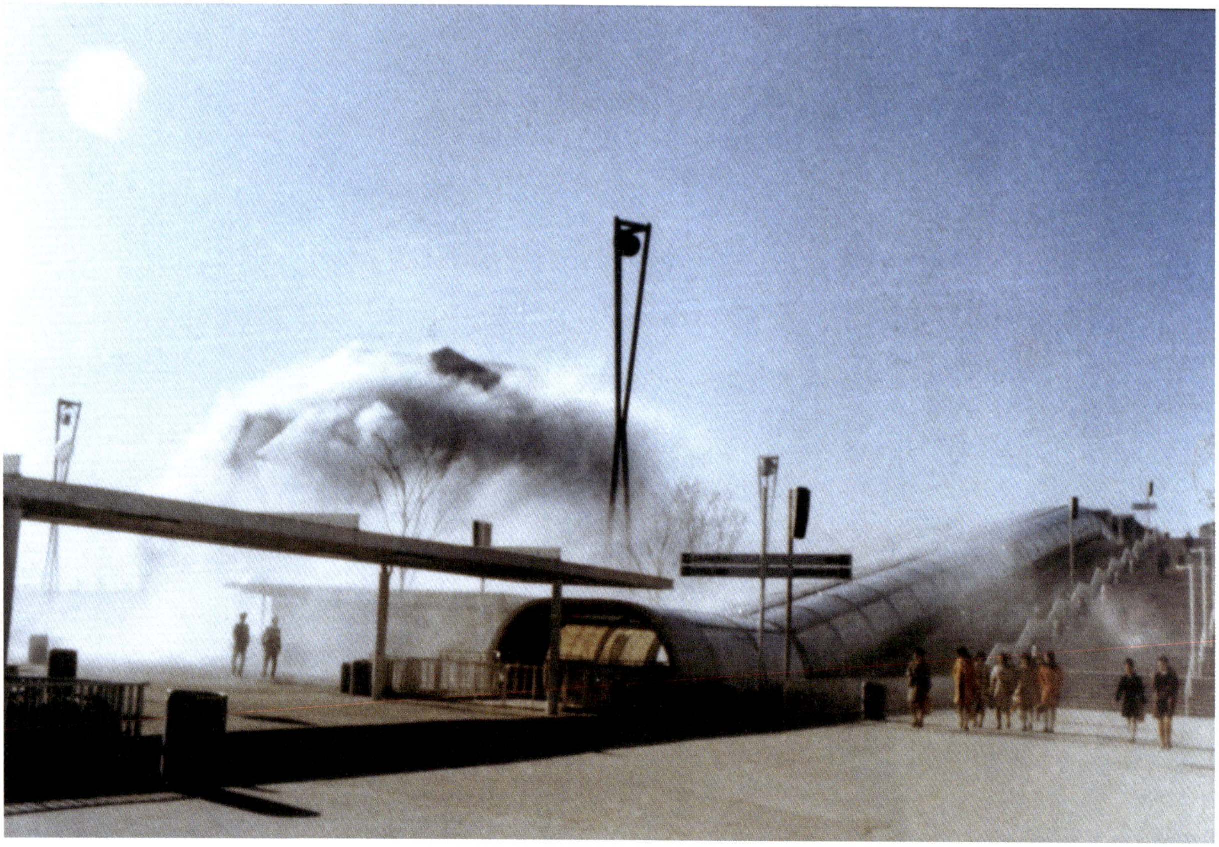

⯯ Fujiko Nakaya, wind tunnel test with 1/200 scale model of Pepsi Pavilion, 1969

↑ Fujiko Nakaya, *Fog Sculpture #47773* 1970, Pepsi Pavilion, Osaka Expo '70

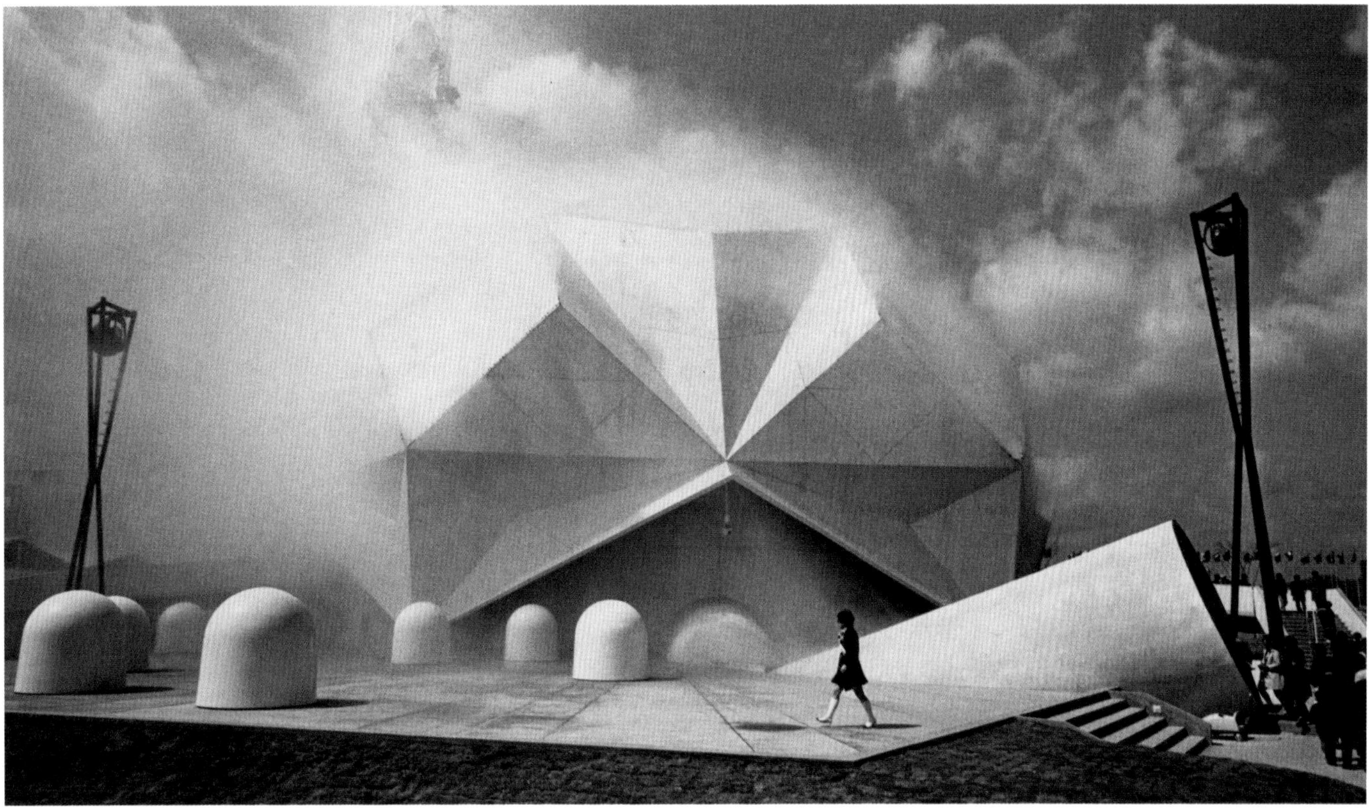

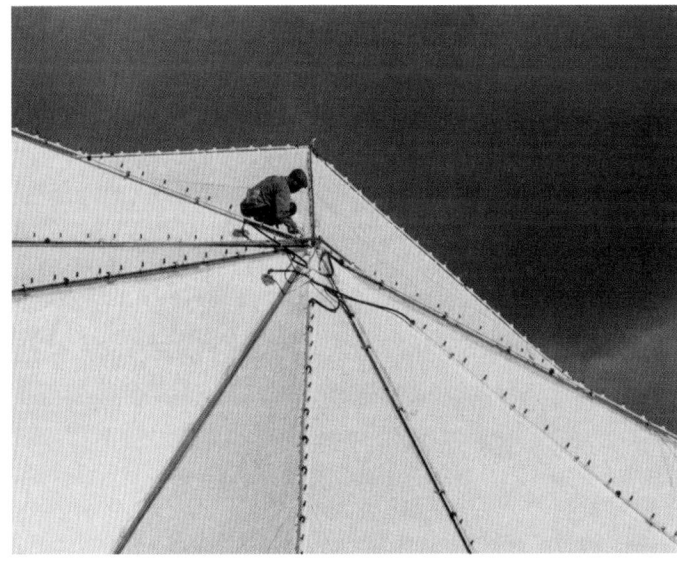

Fujiko Nakaya

Fujiko Nakaya is best known for her fog sculptures, which use water, air currents and the passing of time to create ephemeral structures shaped by their environmental conditions. Working as part of Experiments in Art and Technology (E.A.T.), Nakaya made her first fog sculpture for the Pepsi Pavilion at Expo '70 in Osaka. Nakaya was E.A.T.'s Tokyo representative for the Expo, and eventually founded their Tokyo branch. She is also a prominent video artist and was a central member of the collective Video Hiroba. In 1980 Nakaya also founded SCAN, the first Japanese art gallery to specialise in video. KW

↖ Installation of the nozzles for *Fog Sculpture #47773* on the outer dome of the Pepsi Pavilion, Osaka Expo '70

↑ Fujiko Nakaya walking in front of the Pepsi Pavilion with *Fog Sculpture #47773* 1970, Osaka Expo '70

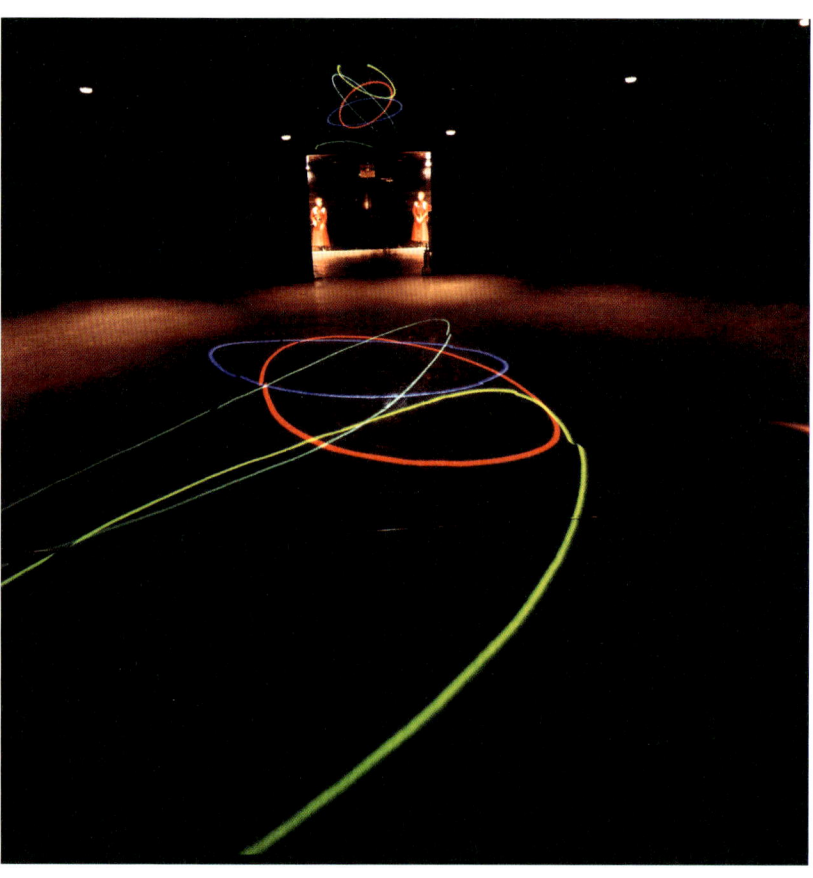

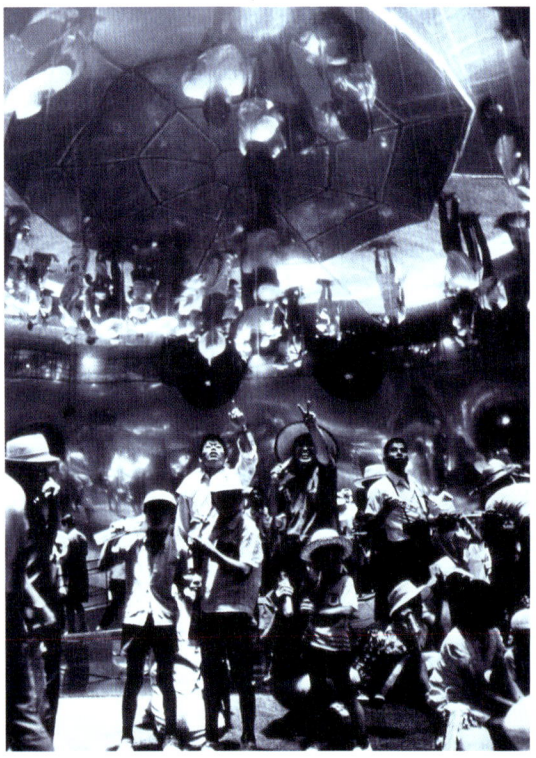

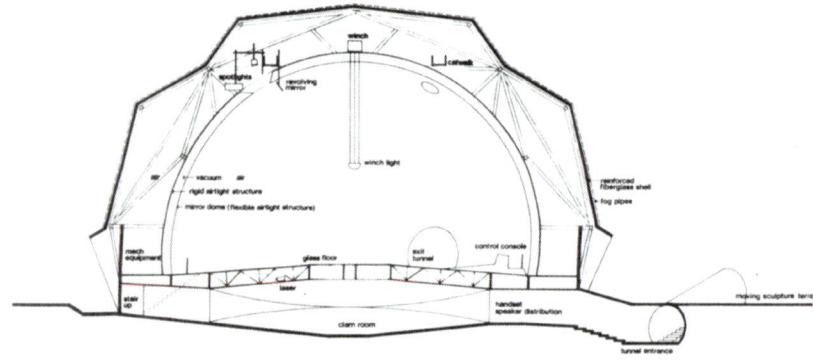

↗ *Laser Deflection System*, Clam Room, Pepsi Pavilion,
Osaka Expo '70
↑ Mirror Dome, Pepsi Pavilion, Osaka Expo '70
→ Elevation diagram of the Pepsi Pavilion, Osaka Expo '70

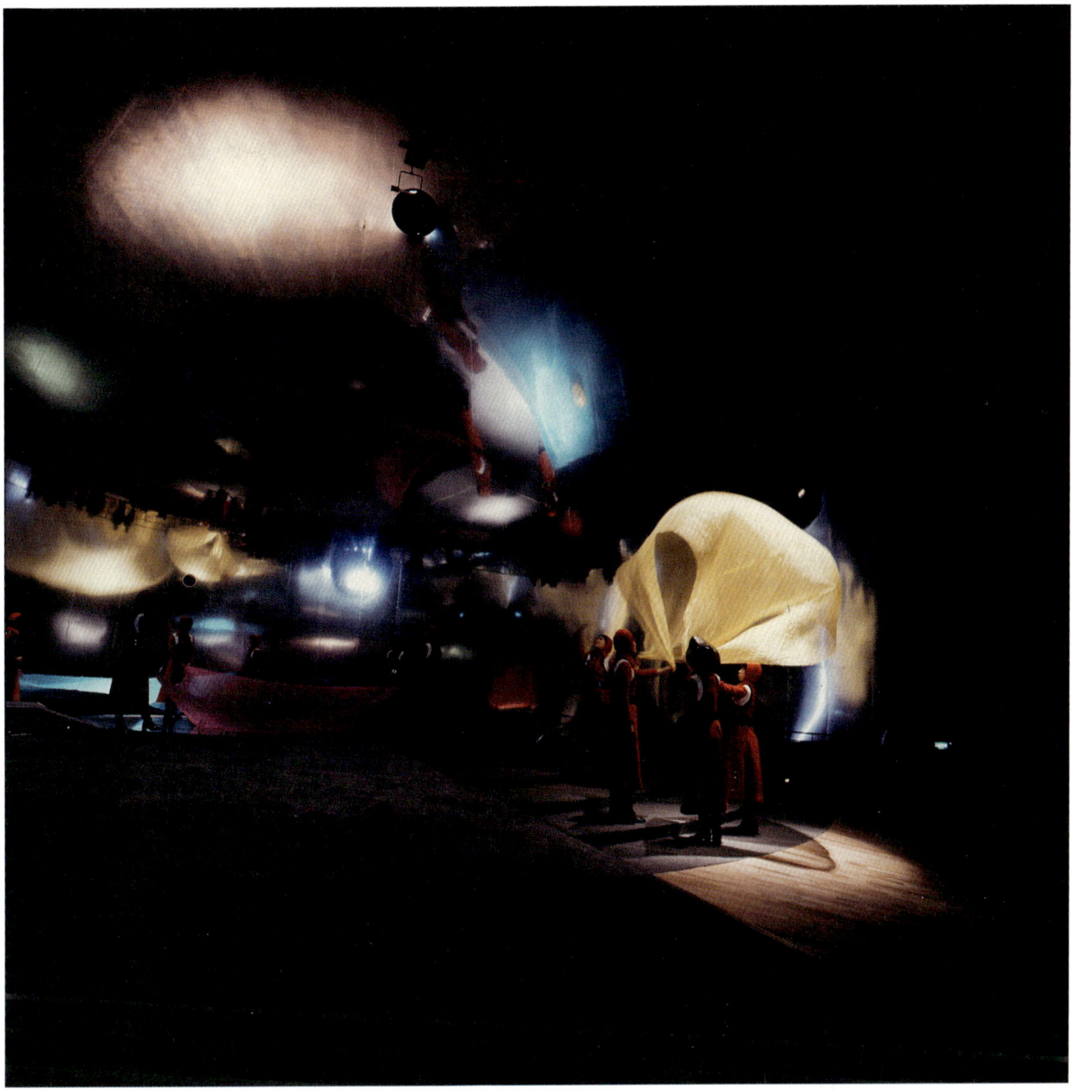

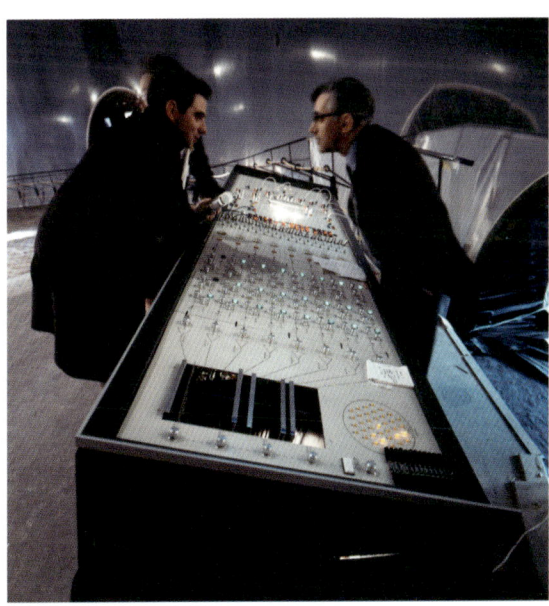

Pepsi Pavilion (interior)

After receiving a small handset – which picked up audio signals emitted from loops embedded in the floor – from a hostess wearing a red uniform, visitors entered the pavilion through a tunnel. On the ground floor was the Clam Room, a darkened space with a concave floor. It featured a *Laser Deflection System*, designed by Lowell Cross and activated with sound by composer David Tudor, which projected colourful moving patterns on the floor. A stairway led up into the Dome Room, with its huge hemispherical mirror reflecting visitors in unexpected ways and places. The entire pavilion was fitted with a programmable sound and light system; Tudor was closely involved with the design of the soundscapes. The Dome Room was conceived as a performance space, to be continuously programmed with events featuring artists, musicians, dancers and poets, as well as scientists and researchers holding talks and demonstrations. VR

↑ Mirror Dome, guides with yellow cloth, Pepsi Pavilion, Osaka Expo '70
↖ David Tudor and Lowell Cross at the console, Pepsi Pavilion, Osaka Expo '70

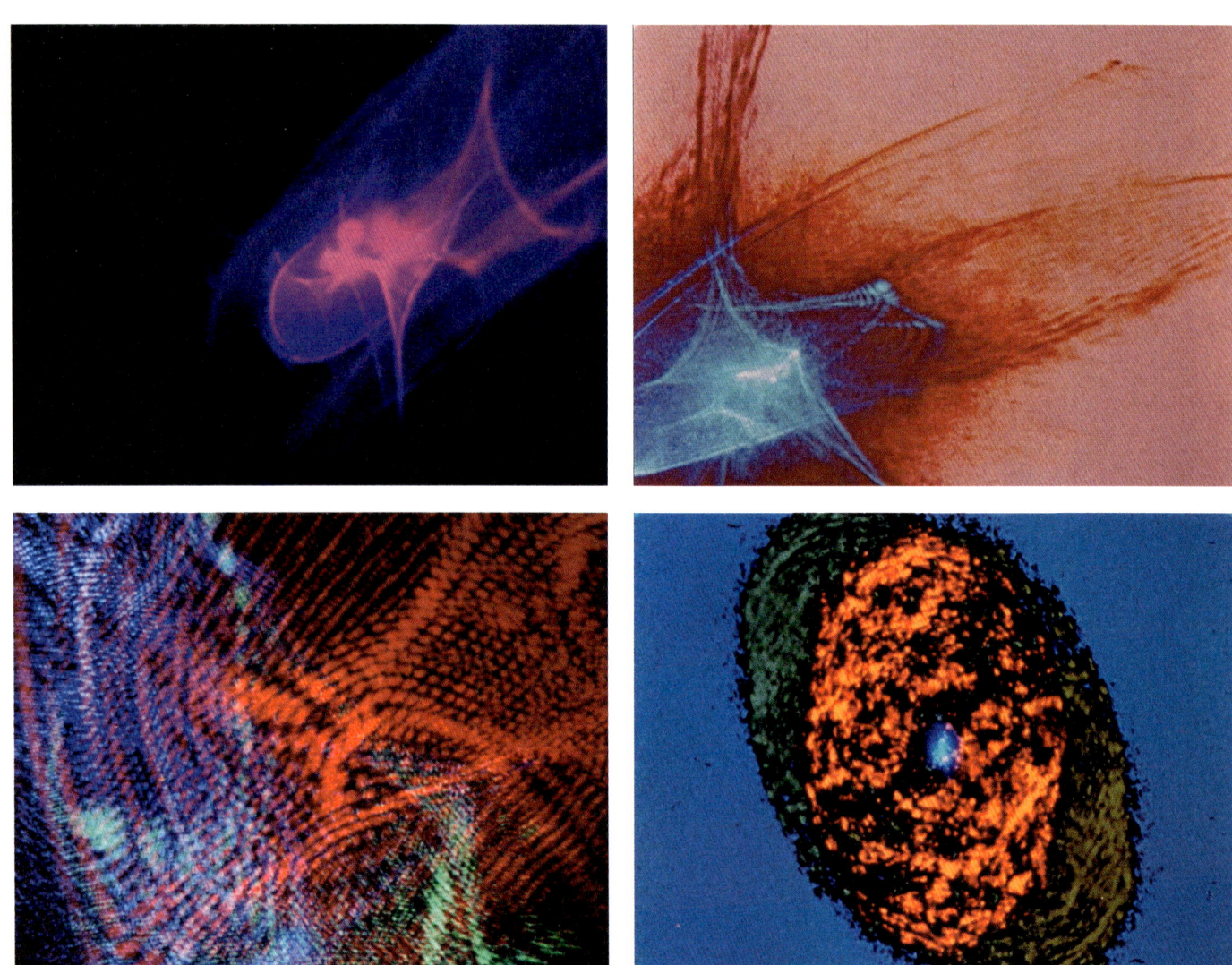

Ivan Dryer and Elsa Garmire

Elsa Garmire is a physicist and engineer known for her pioneering work in laser technology and optics. She partnered with filmmaker Ivan Dryer to create *Laserimage*, which acted as a test for a laser show they were developing for the Griffith Observatory planetarium in Los Angeles. This later became a long-running attraction called *Laserium*. Garmire was a key member of Experiments in Art and Technology (E.A.T.), designing the world's largest hemispherical mirror for the Pepsi Pavilion at Expo '70 in Osaka. She was unimpressed with the laser show produced for the pavilion and, following this, began working on her own laser art. She invented her own techniques for diffracting laser beams, which generate the patterns captured in *Laserimage*. KW

↑ Ivan Dryer and Elsa Garmire, *Laserimage* 1972

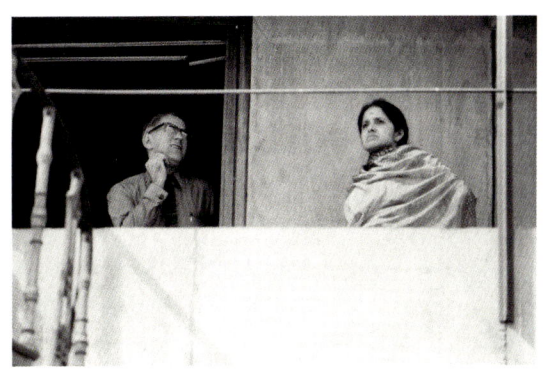

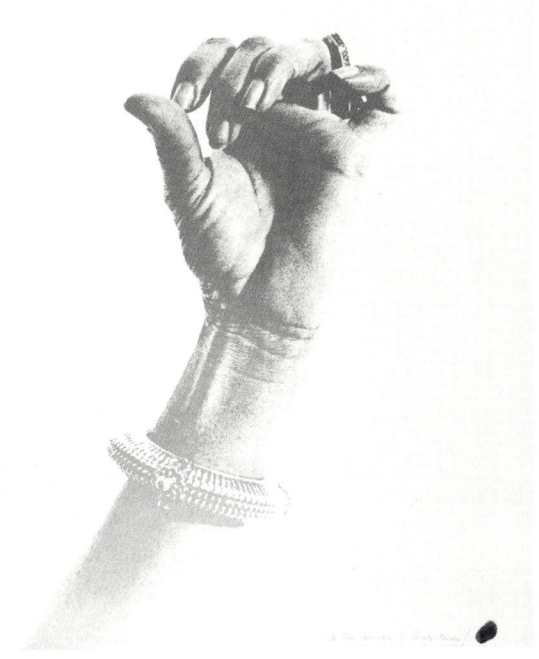

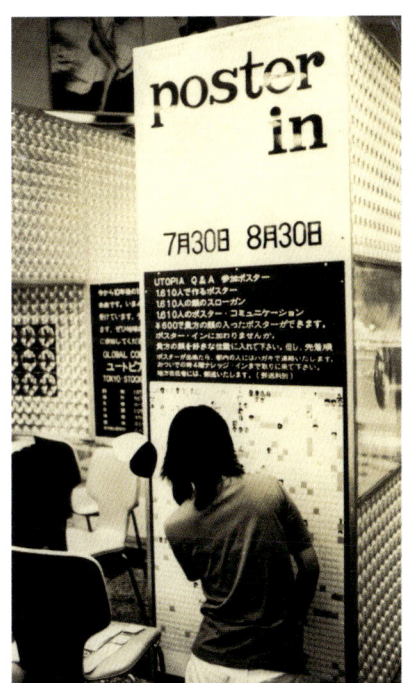

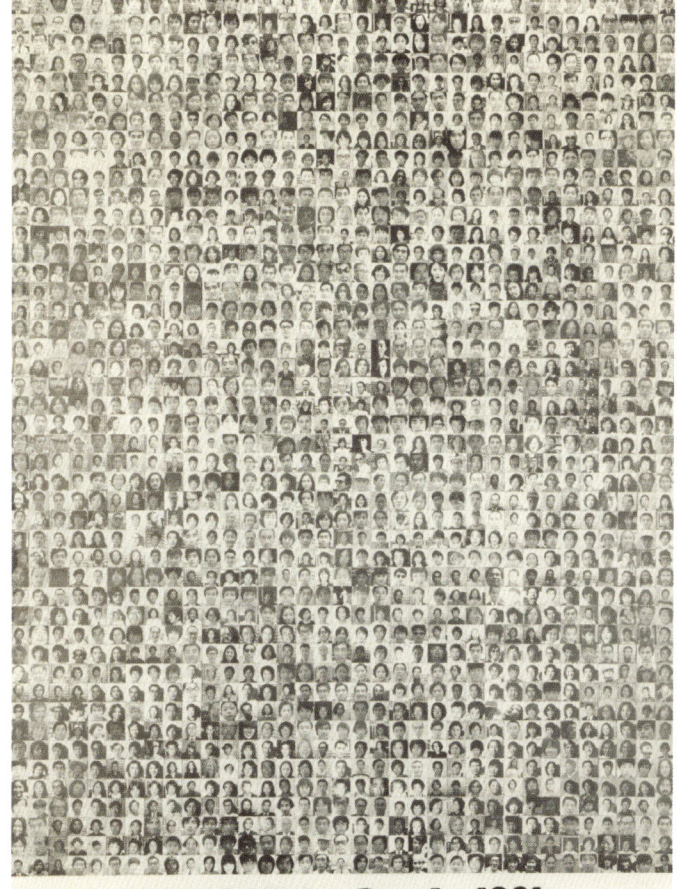

✿ Tom Gormley, Harry Shunk and Janos Kender,
American Artists in India poster, 1970–1
↑ Katsuhiro Yamaguchi, *Poster-in* installation for
Utopia Q&A 1981, Tokyo, 1971

✿ David Tudor and Gita Sarabhai, Ahmedabad, 1969
↑ Katsuhiro Yamaguchi, *Utopia Q&A 1981* poster, 1971

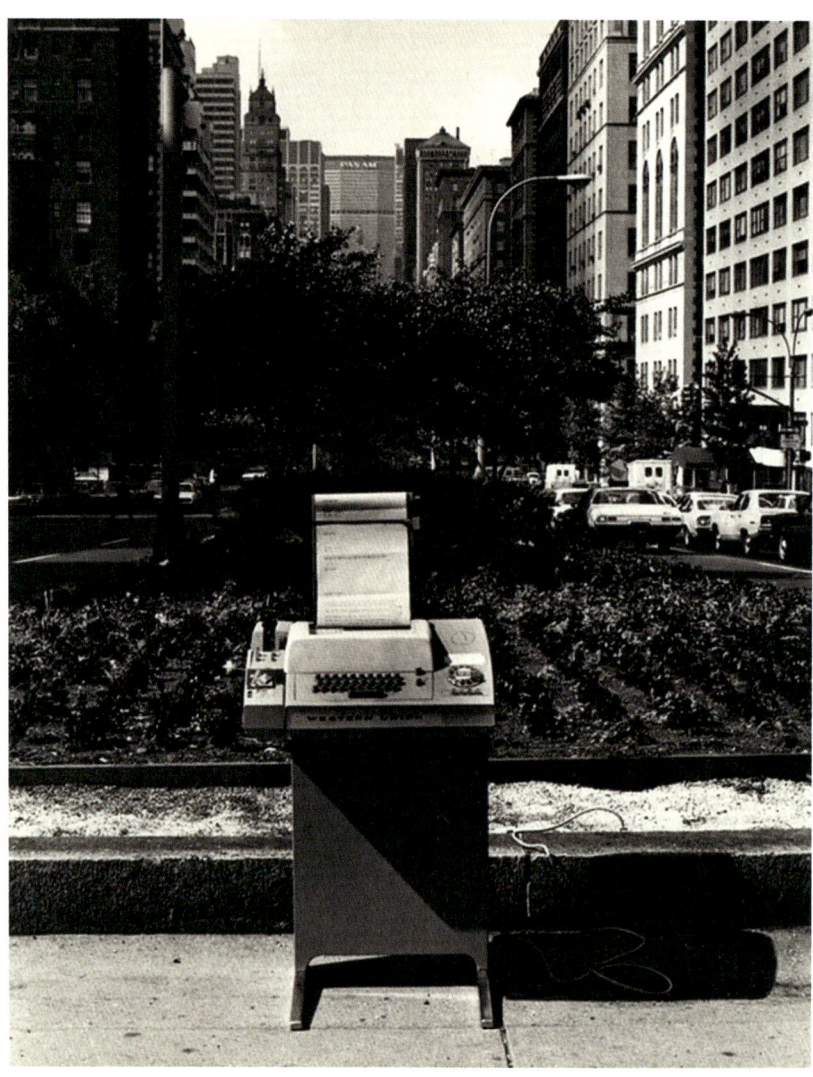

Utopia Q&A 1981

Utopia: Q&A (or *Utopia: Q&A 1981*) was a project organised
by E.A.T. in 1971 on the occasion of the *Utopia and Visions:
1871–1981* exhibition at Moderna Museet, Stockholm. The
work involved the installation of telex machines in four cities:
Stockholm; New York, at the E.A.T. offices at 49 East 68th Street;
in Tokyo, at an exhibition space in the Sony Building; and in
Ahmedabad at the National Institute of Design. The public was
invited to think about society ten years in the future and to send
questions concerning life in the year 1981, which were then
telexed to the other three terminals. Questions and answers were
formulated by various members of the public, including artists
and scientists, and telexed across to the other terminals in a
complex communication chain.

The exchange lasted for a month, during which more than 400
questions were asked and answered. In 1981 E.A.T. followed up on
the project by collecting the *New York Times* for a month to com-
pare the predictions against the reality of that imagined 'future'. BP

↑ E.A.T., *Utopia Q&A 1981*, Telex Machine on Park Avenue
in New York City, 1971
↗ E.A.T. Tokyo, *Utopia Q&A 1981*, Sony Building, Ginza,
Tokyo, 1971 (Fujiko Nakaya pictured in the centre)

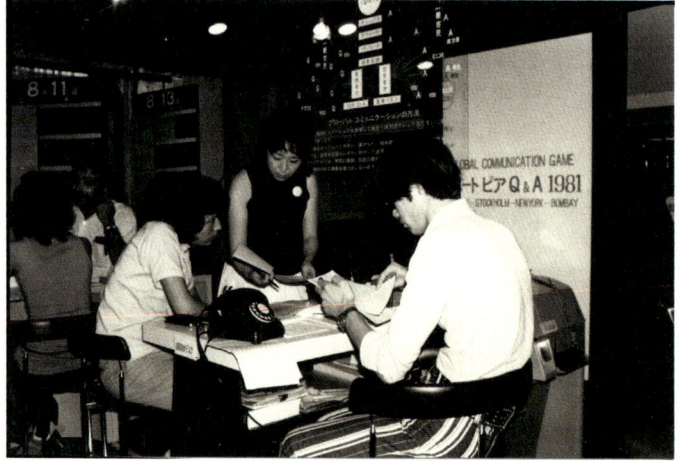

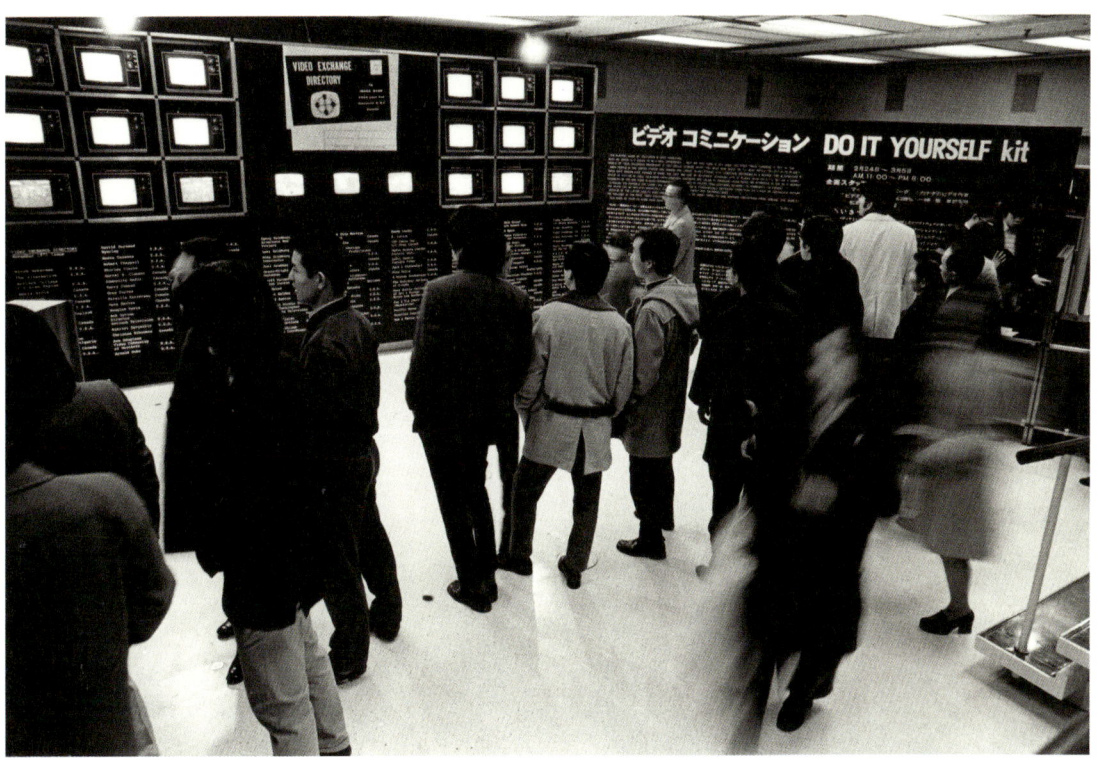

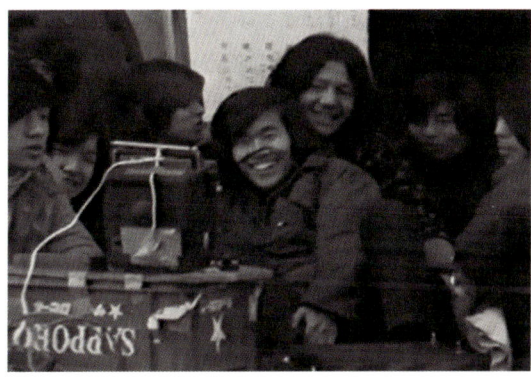

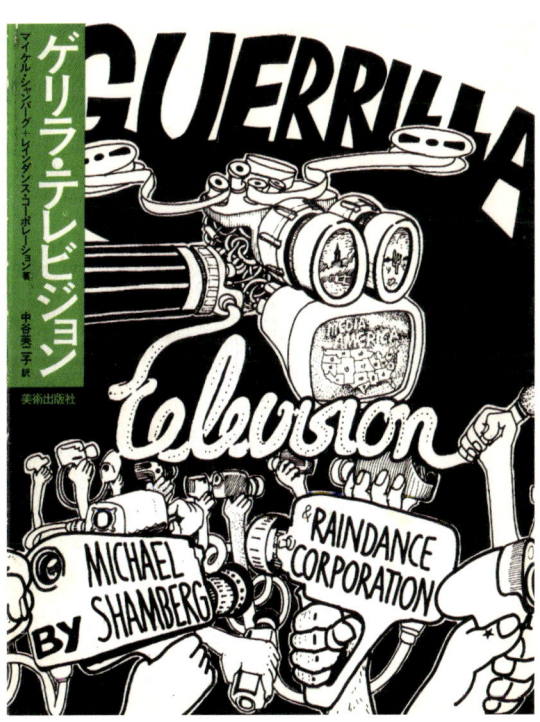

Video Hiroba

Video Hiroba was one of the first experimental video collectives in Japan, founded in Tokyo in 1972 on the occasion of the exhibition *Video Communications: Do-It-Yourself Kit* in the Sony Building. This was organised by Canadian video artist Michael Goldberg as an introduction to the new Sony Portapak video recorder. Led primarily by Fujiko Nakaya and Katsuhiro Yamaguchi, Video Hiroba members used video technology to engage with social movements and strengthen public debate, offering an alternative to mainstream media. For her video *Friends of Minamata Victims – Video Diary* 1972, for instance, Nakaya filmed a sit-in against a company polluting waters with mercury, and played the footage back to offer the protesters a moment of reflection on their action based on immediate feedback. Nakaya was inspired by Paul Ryan's 1973 book *Cybernetics of the Sacred* and in 1974 translated Michael Shamberg's *Guerilla Television* (1971) into Japanese. Shamberg's book criticises television's monopolistic power and invites readers to reclaim the medium by adopting the increasingly portable and affordable video technologies. VR

⚐ *Video Communication: Do It Yourself Kit* exhibition, Sony Building, Ginza, Tokyo, 1972
↑ Cover of the Japanese edition of *Guerrilla Television*, by Michael Shamberg and Raindance Corporation (1972/1974)

↑Fujiko Nakaya, *Friends of Minamata Victims – Video Diary* 1972

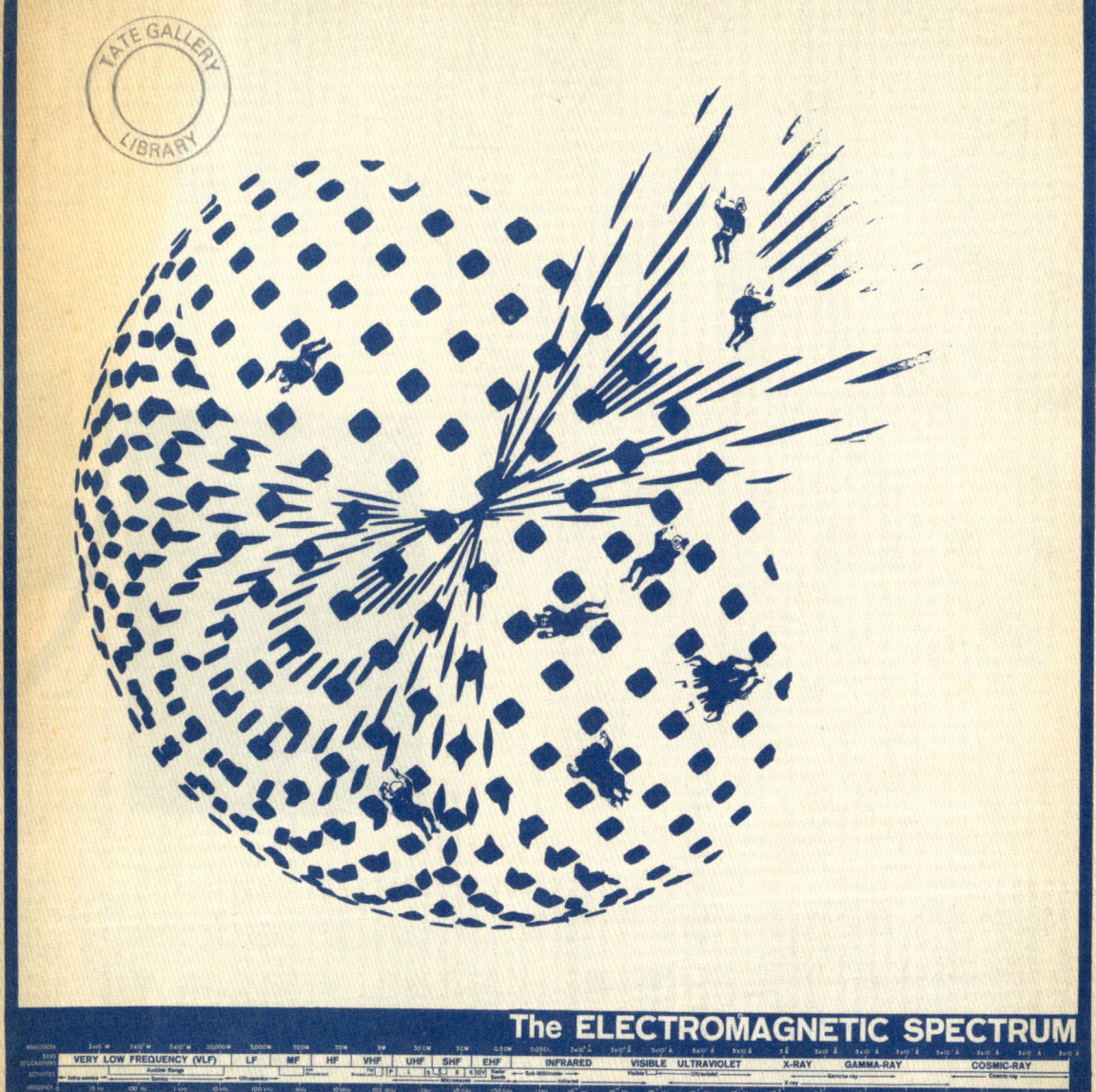

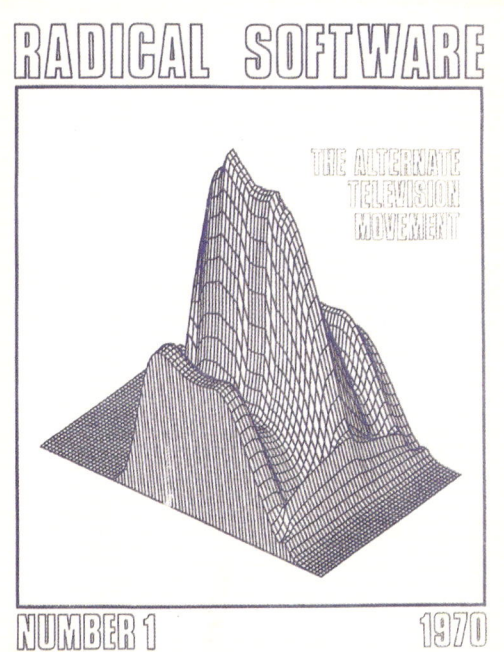

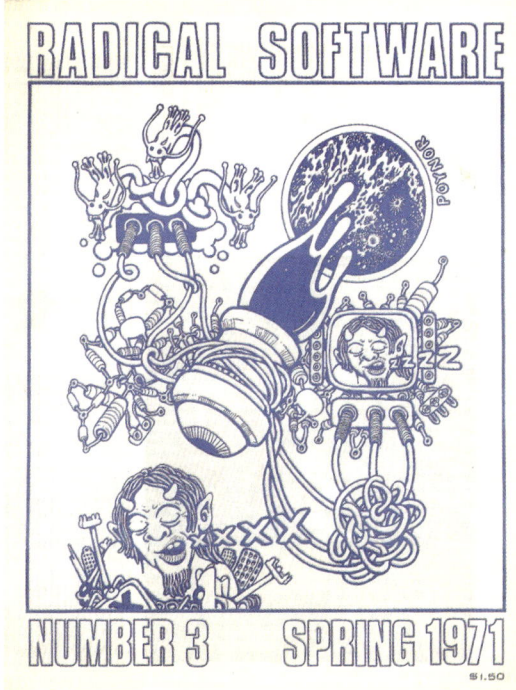

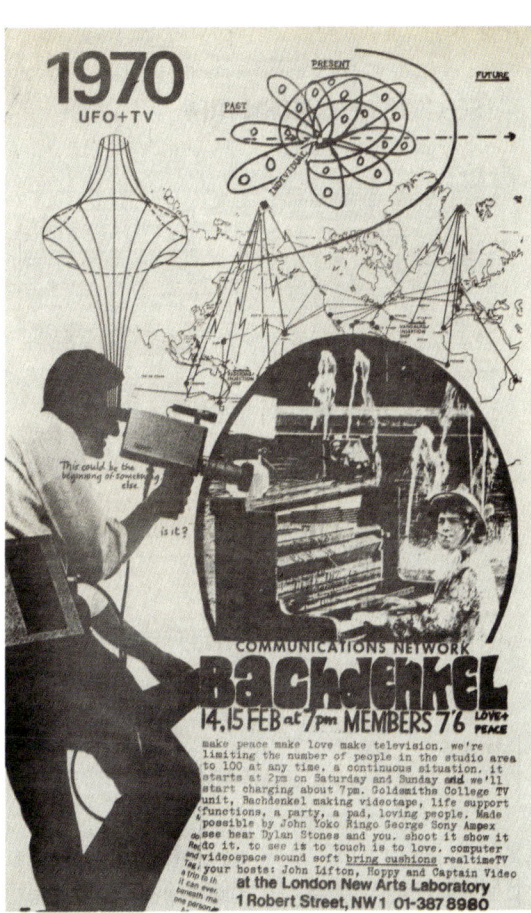

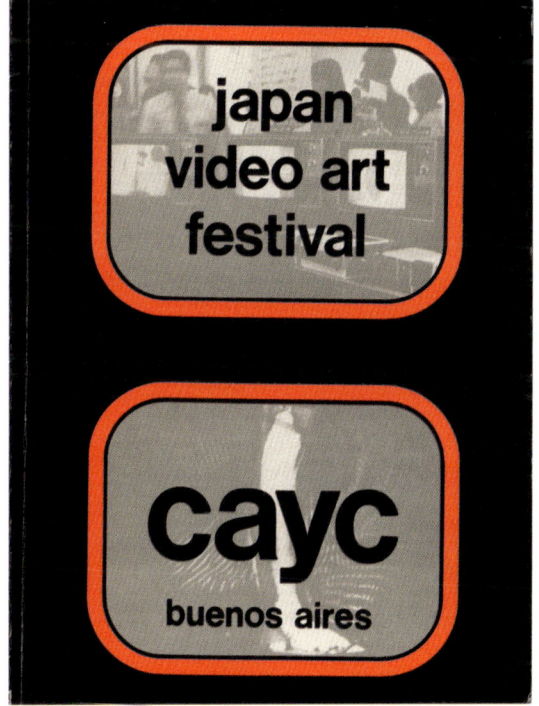

♠ *Radical Software*, vol.1, no.1, 1970
↑ *UFO+TV - Bachdenkel* flyer, New Arts Lab, London, 1970

♠ *Radical Software*, vol.1, no.3, 1970
↑ *Japan Video Art Festival: 33 Artists* exhibition catalogue,
Centro de Arte y Comunicación, Buenos Aires, 1970

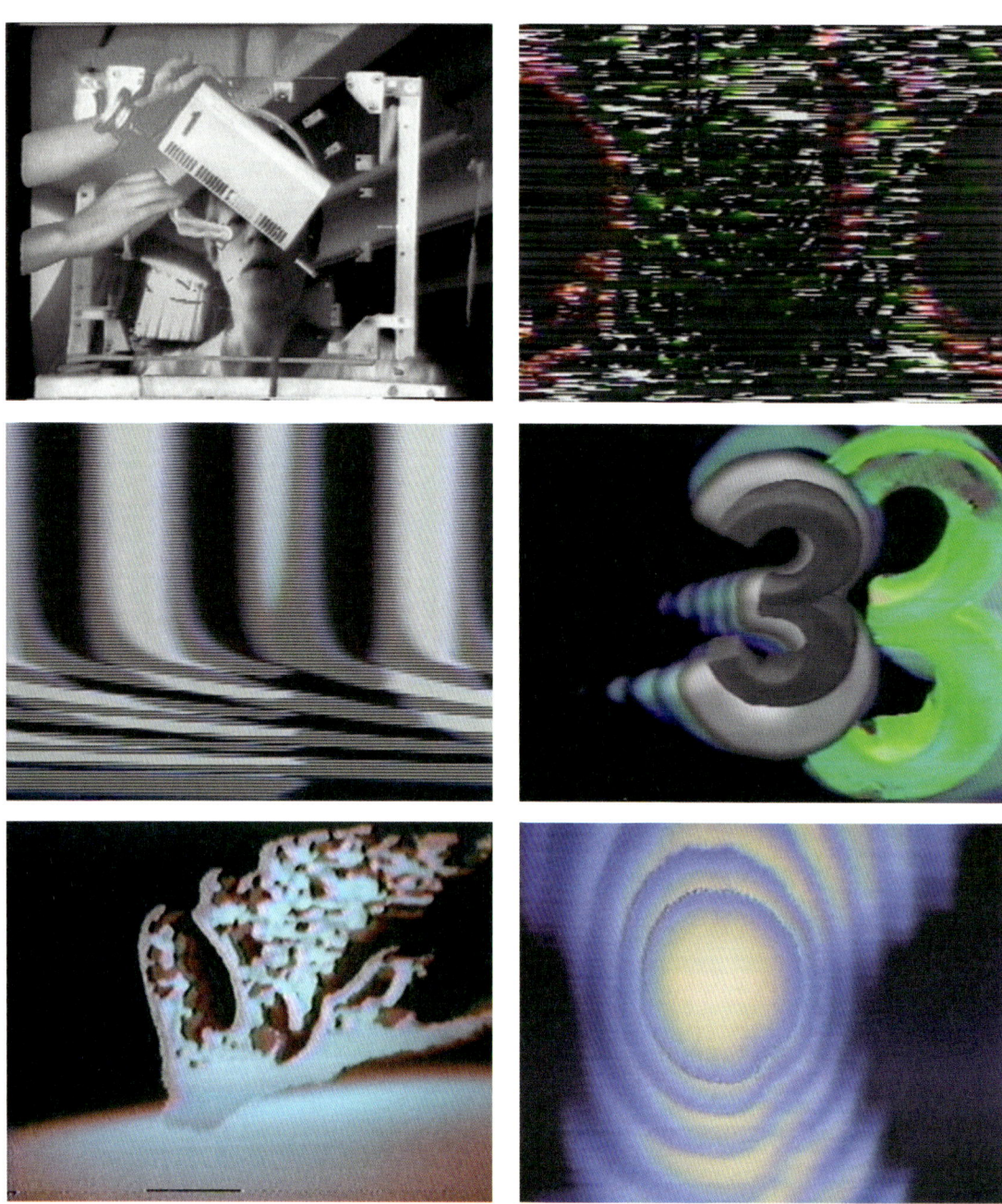

↑ Steina and Woody Vasulka, stills from *Matrix II* 1974

Steina and Woody Vasulka

Steina and Woody Vasulka developed a unique collaborative and multifaceted practice grounded in their respective experiences in music and film. They were highly influential in the development of moving image and sonic arts through their adoption of electronic media and a constant drive to experiment with emerging technical possibilities. Through the use of these technologies, including video synthesis and digital manipulation, their works explore the translation and transmission of signals and the relationship between image and sound. In 1971 they founded The Kitchen, a non-profit space that significantly shaped New York's art, music and performance scenes, and in 1973 they helped develop the Digital Arts Laboratory at Buffalo State University, the first research centre of its kind in an academic institution.

Matrix II 1974 is an installation consisting of a single video input repeated on multiple cathode-ray monitors, arranged in a grid. The work – a montage of various segments created using different image manipulation techniques – shows geometric forms and captured images that can be seen traveling across a matrix of screens. This animated pattern challenges the constraints of each monitor and invites the eye to move back and forth between the individual frame and the composite whole. BP

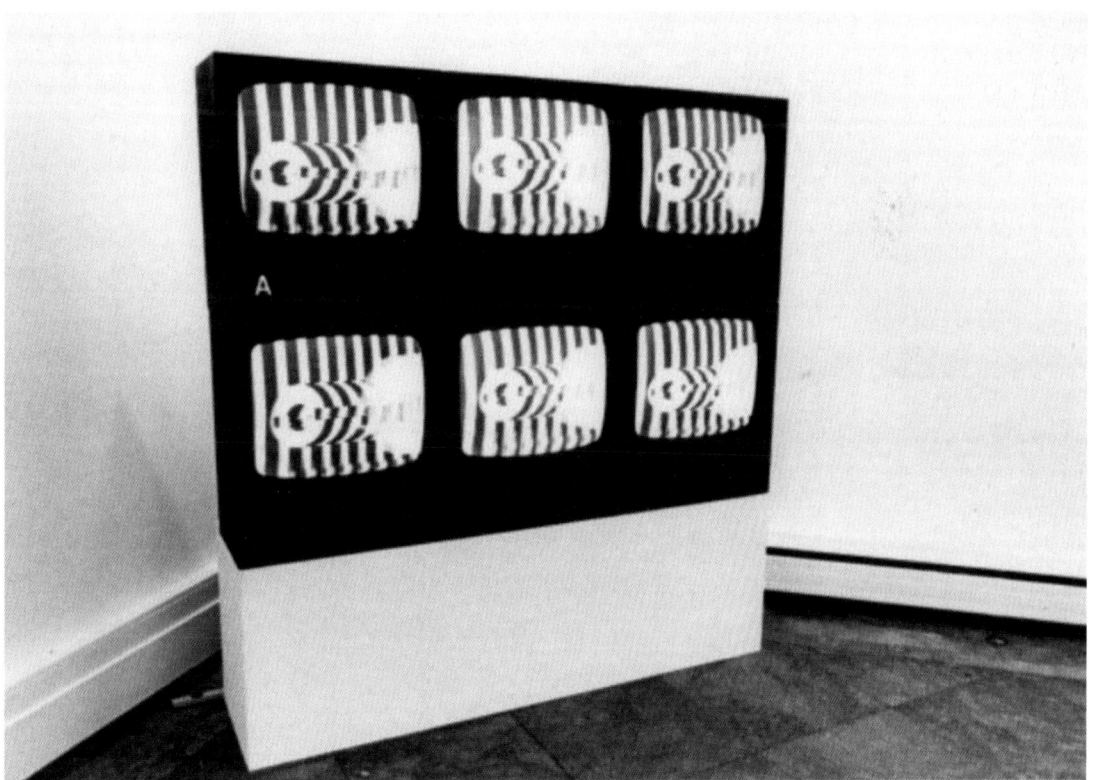

↑ Steina and Woody Vasulka, *Matrix I* 1970

Sonia Landy Sheridan

This selection of works demonstrates Sheridan's experimental reprography techniques, which she taught at the Art Institute of Chicago, where she established the Generative Systems program. *Stan VanDerBeek* c.1970 and *Flowers* 1976 were made using Color-in-Color photocopiers, the first commercially available colour copiers produced by 3M, where Sheridan was artist-in-residence. There, she also created full-scale portraits by scanning sections of the subjects' bodies and collaging them together, sometimes enlarging them to monumental scale. For *Untitled (Process: Electrostatic Thermal)* c.1970 Sheridan exposed the chemically treated surface of a Color-in-Color copy to heat.

Sheridan also worked with Xerox machines, including a Haloid model for *Portrait of Sonia Sheridan* c.1970, and a telecopier (a machine that translates images into audio-frequency tones that can be sent between machines) for *Nathan Lyons* c.1970. To create this work, she recorded the sounds made when an image produced using Color-in-Color was passed through a telecopier. She then played back the sounds through the telecopier, adjusting the volume to create a distorted version of the image. *Sonia through the Time Plane* (1977) was created using a Versatile Quality Copier (again by 3M): covering parts of the paper for the first copy, Sheridan then passed the sheet through the machine again to layer images.

In the 1980s Sheridan created artworks using a black-and-white surveillance camera and a Cromemco Z-2D computer. She manipulated the images using the graphics software EASEL and later Lumena, trailblazing programmes developed by John Dunn, a Generative Systems graduate student. KW

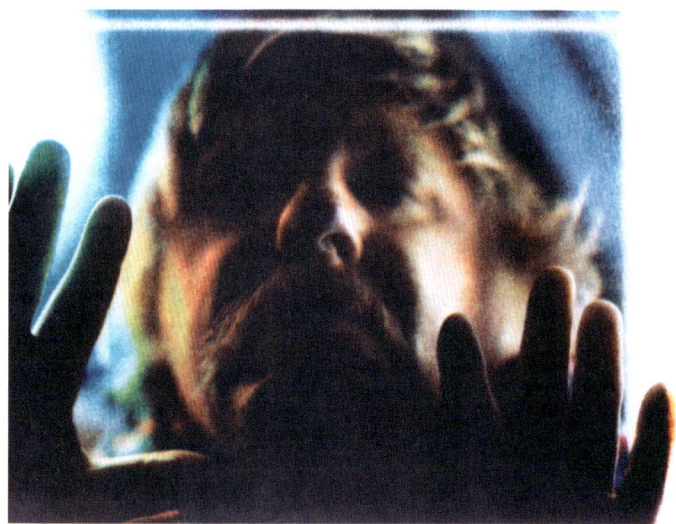

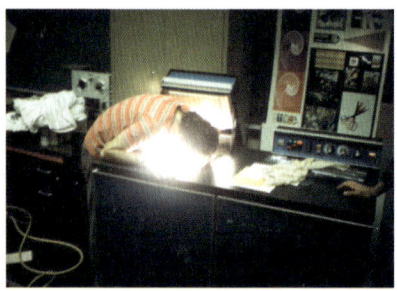

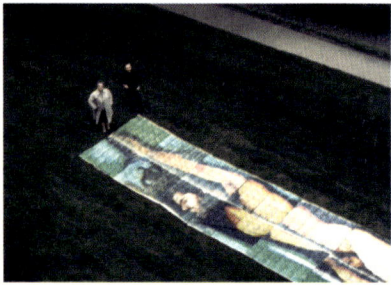

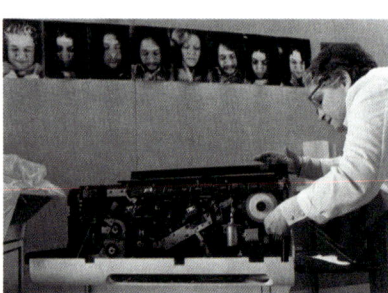

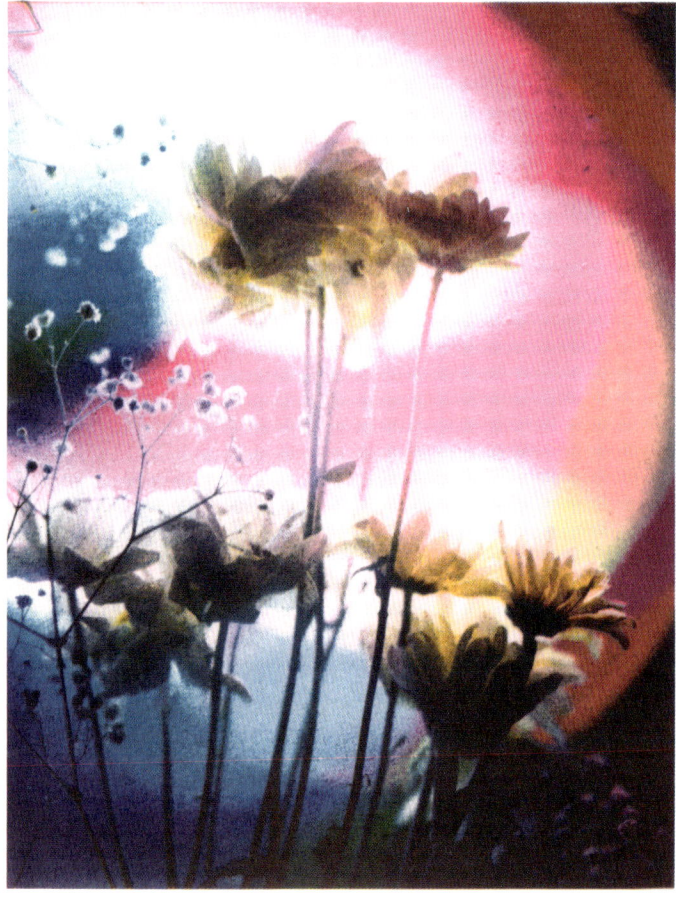

⬥ The Generative Systems classroom, Art Institute of Chicago, 1973
↑ Sonia Landy Sheridan, *Man Scan* with Ric Puls 1974
↑ Sonia Landy Sheridan manipulating a 'VQC' copier in the classroom at the Art Institute of Chicago, 1973

⬥ Sonia Landy Sheridan, *Stan VanDerBeek* c.1970
↑ Sonia Landy Sheridan, *Flowers* 1976

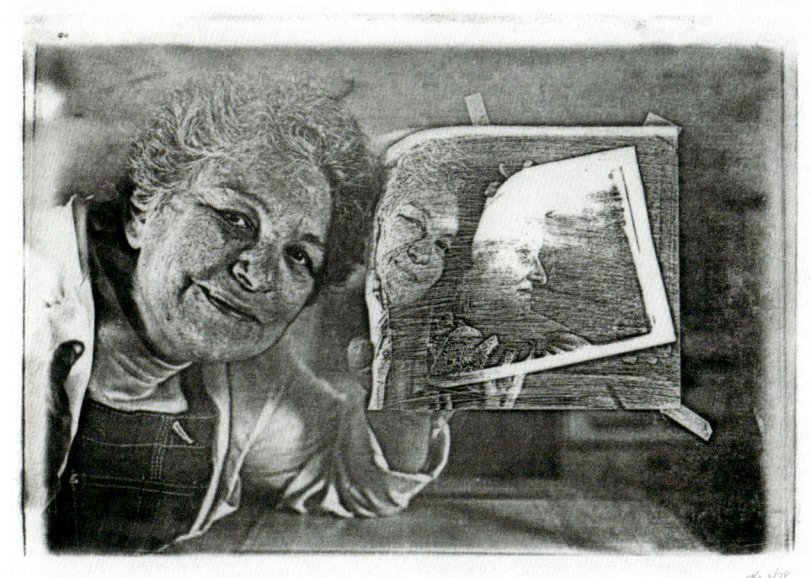

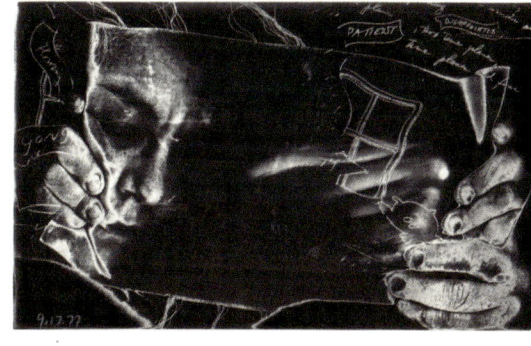

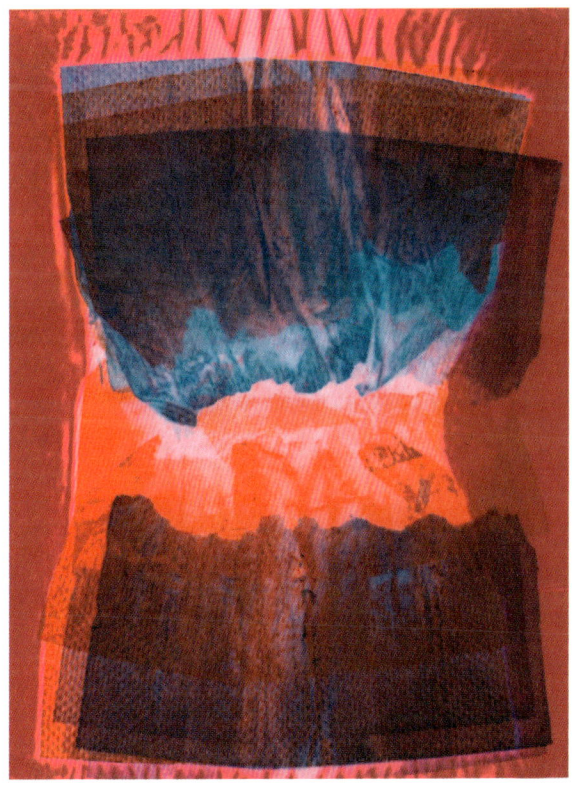

⛊ Sonia Landy Sheridan, *Portrait of Sonia Sheridan* c.1970
↑ Sonia Landy Sheridan, *Untitled (Process: Electrostatic Thermal)* c.1970

⛊ Sonia Landy Sheridan, *Sonia through the Time Plane* 1977
↑ Sonia Landy Sheridan, *Nathan Lyons* c.1970

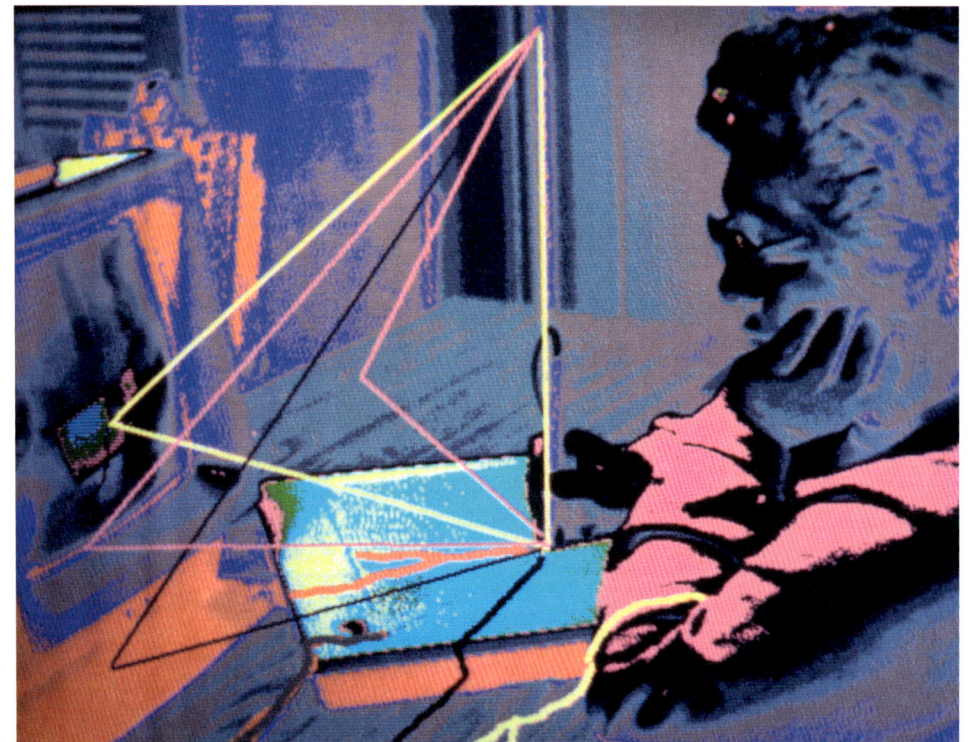

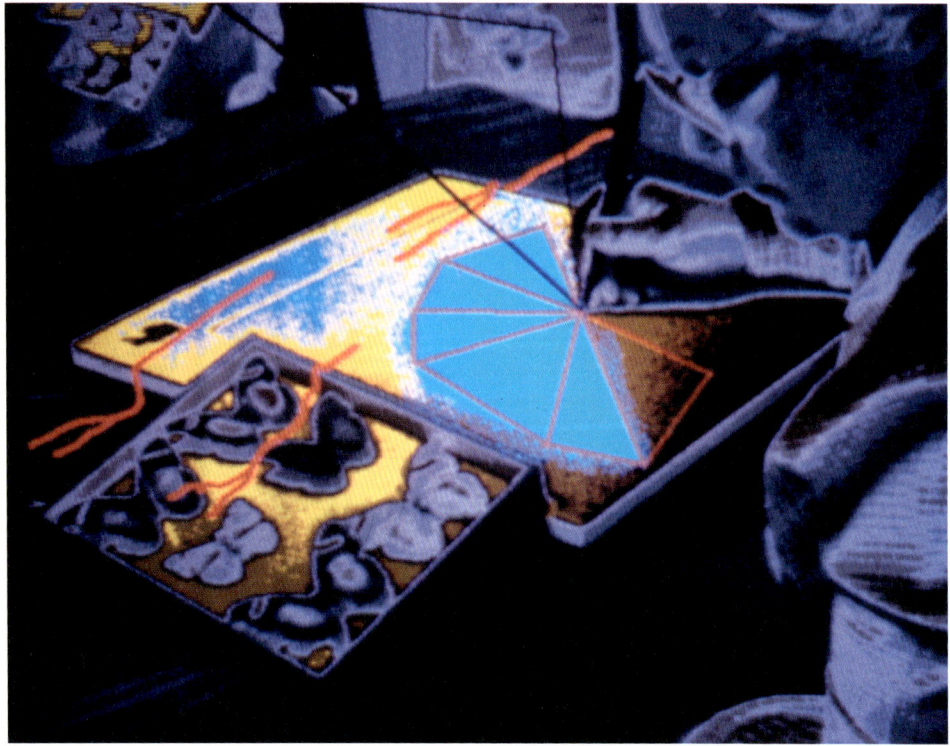

↖, ↑ Sonia Landy Sheridan, *Drawing in Time (Infinite Series)* 1982–3

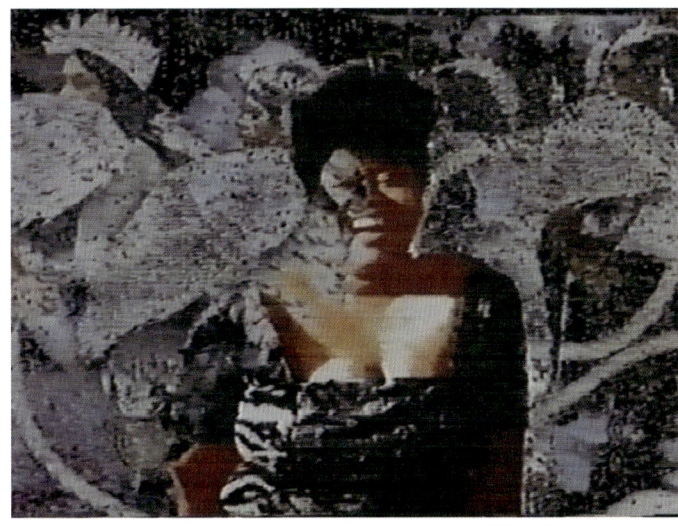

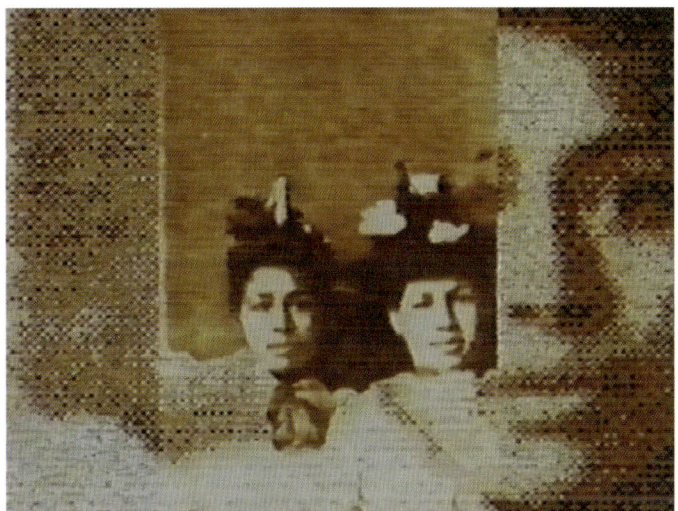

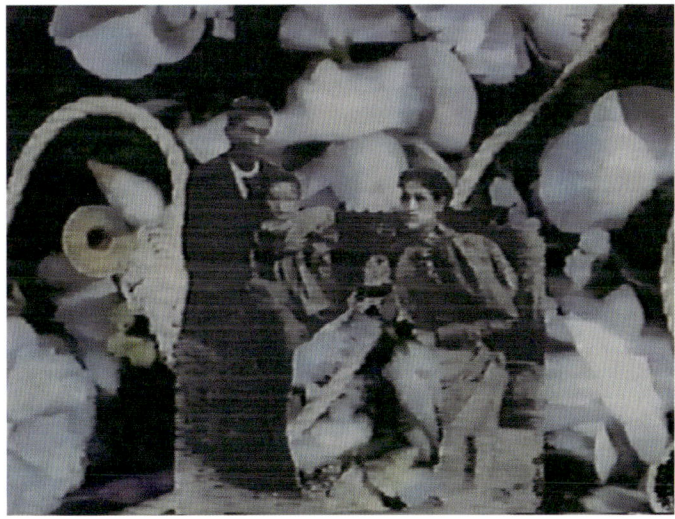

Rita Keegan

Keegan is a multimedia artist working extensively with copy art, collage and digital technologies. Prominently involved with the UK's Black Arts Movement in the 1980s, her practice sits at the intersection of sociohistorical realities, multimedia technologies, archival and collaborative practices. In *Rites of Passage*, Keegan collages photographs of several generations of her family, blending and dissolving them into one another with a digital mixer. These effects create ghostly visuals, echoing her family's 'passages' between continents and generations. This approach to video-making resonates with Keegan's extensive practice of copy art and collaging: she has experimented with the photocopier to manipulate source material in unexpected ways. In the 1980s Keegan co-founded the cooperative print shop Community Copy Art – a key resource for community groups and artists working with scanners, photocopiers and computers as shared resources. BP

↖ Rita Keegan, stills from *Rites of Passage* 1991

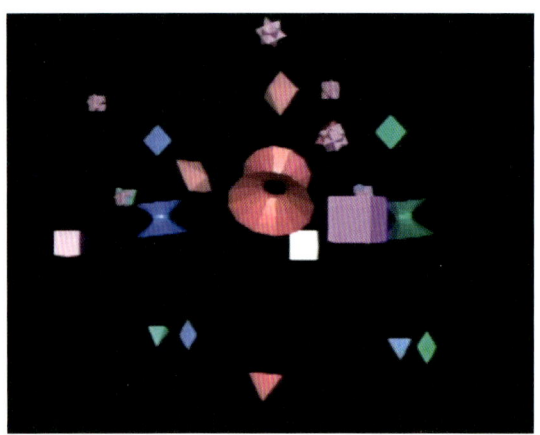

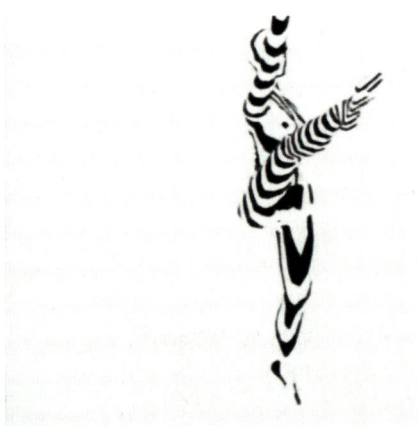

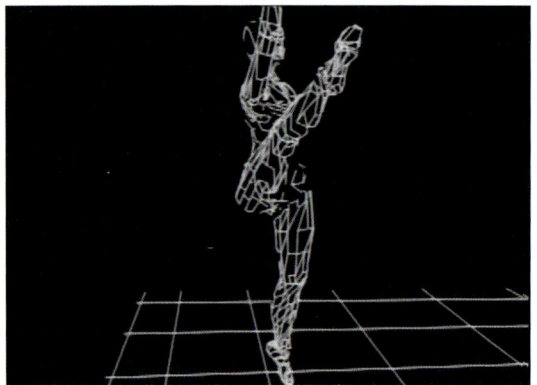

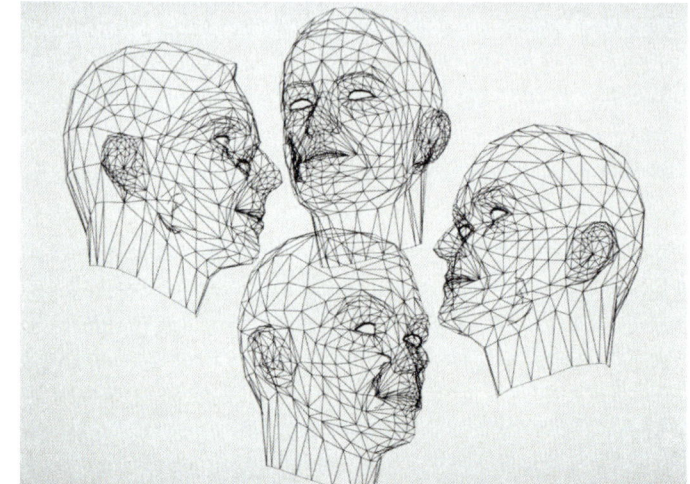

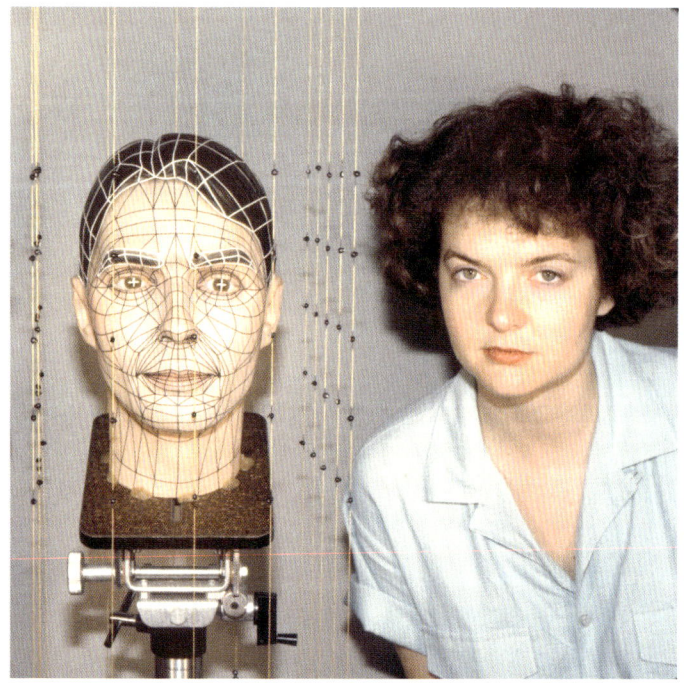

Rebecca Allen

A pioneering female figure in computer art since the mid-1970s, Allen's works include experimental videos, performance, generative art, artificial life systems and virtual and augmented reality (VR/AR) installations that explore gender, identity, simulation and the human experience in the digital age. She was among the first artists to use computers for human motion simulation, eventually leading to present-day motion capture. Her work *Steps* 1982 was inspired by Bauhaus theatre and merged performance with technology to create an illusion of dancing abstract forms. Allen also created the visual material for Kraftwerk's 1986 album *Electric Café,* including the seminal, award-winning music video *Musique Non Stop*. Using facial animation software, Allen brought to life virtual mannequins as technological avatars, simulating the likeness of the band members and creating a new digital aesthetic. OW

↑ Rebecca Allen, stills from *Steps* 1982

✤ Rebecca Allen, *Kraftwerk Wireframe Portrait on Grey* 1984–6
↑ *Rebecca Allen with Kraftwerk Model* 1984

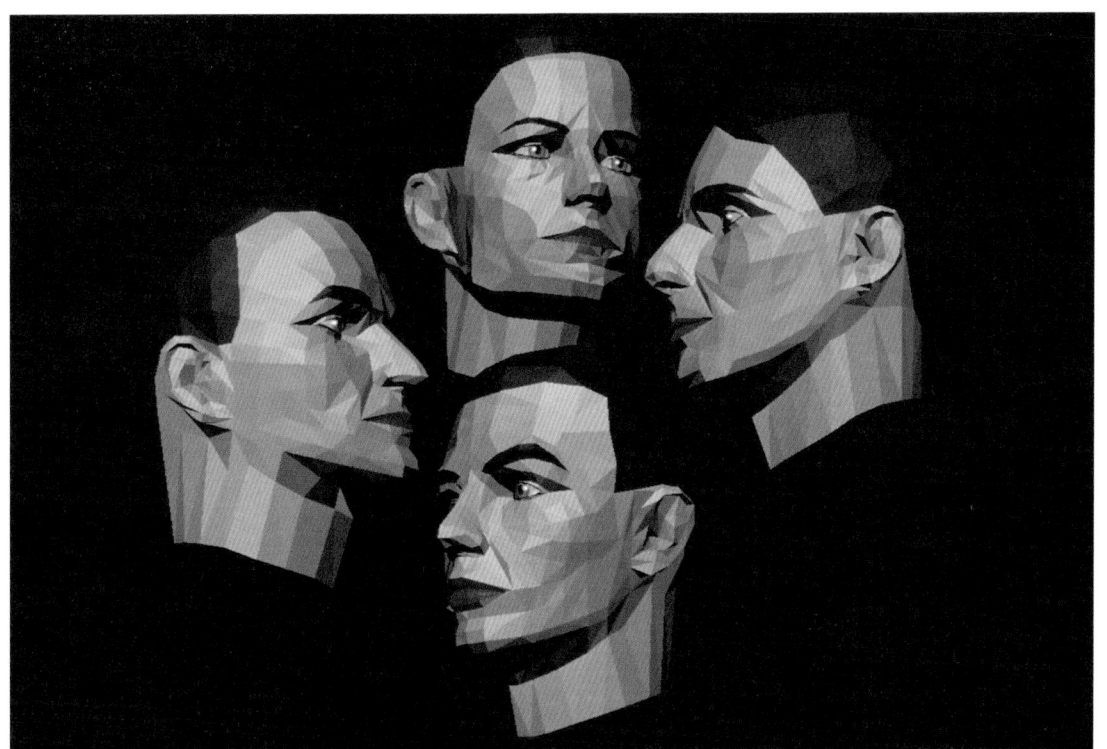

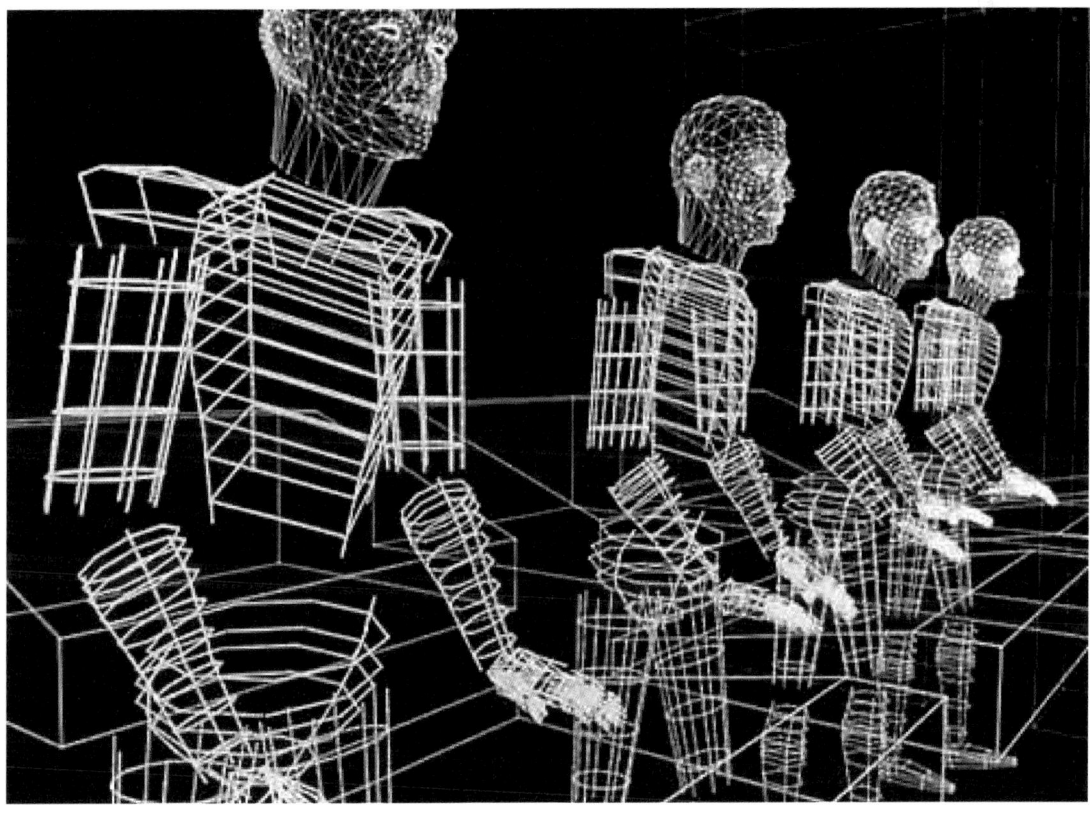

⌃ Rebecca Allen, *Kraftwerk Portrait* 1984–6, album cover for Kraftwerk's *Electric Café*
↑ Rebecca Allen, *Wireframe Kraftwerk Performing*, still from *Musique Non Stop* 1986

Samia Halaby is a multidisciplinary abstract artist and activist from Palestine. Born in Jerusalem in 1936, her family relocated to Jaffa in 1939. Following the *Nakba* in 1948, during which over 750,000 Palestinians were dispossessed of their land, her family fled to nearby Lebanon. A few years later, in 1951, they relocated once more to Cincinnati in the United States. Encouraged by her aunt and her mother, Halaby enrolled in a Bachelor of Science in Design degree at the University of Cincinnati, graduating in 1959. She chose a degree through which she believed she could channel her creativity and also earn a living. This decision would prove fortuitous, as she was trained in draughtsmanship, a skill which taught her perspective and became an enduring interest in her art. She later undertook a Masters degree in painting at Michigan State University, followed by a Master of Fine Arts degree in painting in 1963.

In her early career, Halaby taught at several universities, including the University of Hawaii, Kansas City Art Institute, University of Michigan and Indiana University.[1] In 1972, she became the first full-time female professor at the Yale School of Art. In 1976, she switched to part-time in order to live in New York, where she rented a loft in Tribeca. Her time at Yale ended in 1982, when she parted ways with the school following its decision not to honour her and other women's permanent contracts.

Throughout her teaching years, Halaby continued to develop her artistic practice. In 1966 she received a grant to travel to Egypt, Syria and Turkey to study Islamic art and architecture, and she visited Palestine for the first time since her family's forced displacement.[2] This trip fuelled her interest in geometric abstraction – she was inspired by the Dome of the Rock in Jerusalem and the Great Mosque in Damascus – and had a lasting influence on her work. Indeed, citing her deep admiration for Arabic literature and calligraphy, Halaby described how experimenting with graph paper allowed her to create ambivalent form, rather than attempt to represent ambivalence visually.[3]

She continued this exploration in her series of helix paintings, buying several used books on geometry, written for engineers and technicians.[4] In works such as *Blue and Orange Helix* 1972, Halaby experimented with space on the canvas by creating images with no negative or positive space – no space behind or forward in the painting.[5] Through her use of shading, she created a sense of continuum between volume and surface, a technique inspired by the Islamic architecture she had seen.[6]

Continuing her investigation into abstraction, she began to question the notion of the rectangle as the basic framework for visual language – what she considered 'a window'. Indeed, for Halaby, abstraction is about 'general

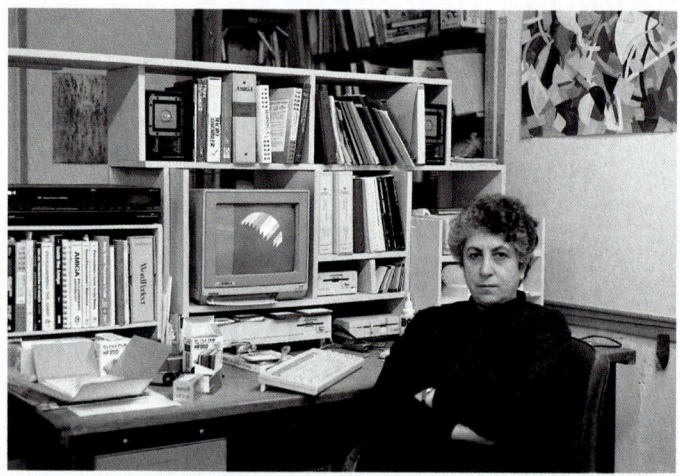

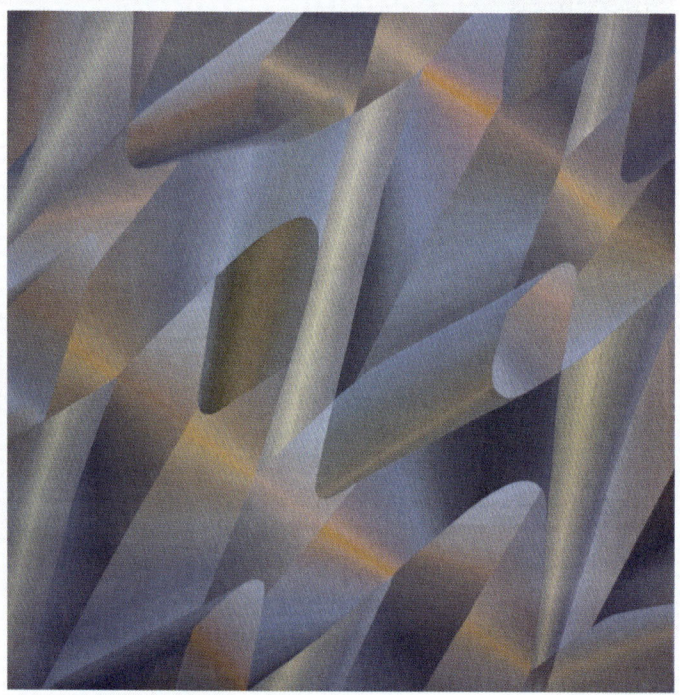

⤢ Samia Halaby working on her Amiga 1000, 1987
↑ Samia Halaby, *Blue and Orange Helix* 1972

principles', not a fixed image of the world.[7] This interest led to her series of kinetic paintings – what she terms 'abstract paintings in motion with sound'.[8]

An exhibition sponsored by IBM in New York in the 1960s on art and cutting-edge technology had a profound impact on Halaby.[9] A few years later, she became interested in the programme Sketchpad, developed by MIT, which allowed the user to draw images in perspective. By the mid-1980s she finally had the opportunity to

Samia Halaby: Kinetic Abstraction

Odessa Warren

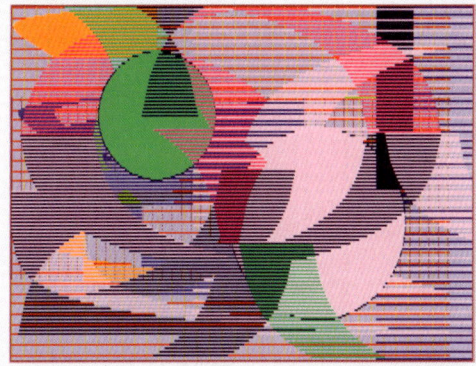

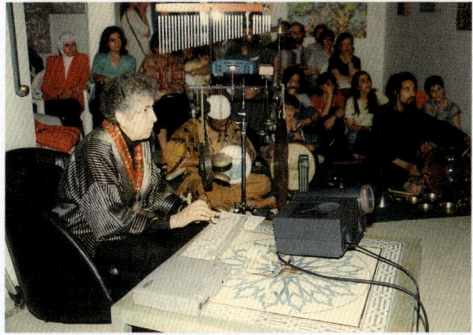

⊼ Samia Halaby, still from *Judith* 1986
↑ Samia Halaby at a Kinetic Painting Group performance,
Mona Atassi Gallery, Syria, 1997

experiment with her sister's Apple II computer, which led her to buy an Amiga, a choice she made based on the computer's ability to display a wide variety of colours.[10] She learnt how to code in BASIC and C languages and began experimenting with computer programming, creating dynamic visual compositions, all the while pursuing her commitment to developing abstract forms.[11]

She first exhibited her kinetic works alongside her still paintings in 1988, in a solo exhibition at Tossan-Tossan Gallery in New York. The show included a live demonstration of a program she wrote called *Spooling Up*, as Halaby brought her Amiga computer along, complete with its table, cathode-ray tube monitor, bulky television and videocassette player.[12]

In the 1990s, inspired by electronic musicians she had seen jamming at a computer conference, Halaby developed the Kinetic Painting Programme with musician Kevin Nathaniel Hylton, and later Hasan Bakr.[13] They went on to perform together at the Lincoln Center and Brooklyn Museum of Art, New York,[14] as well as at Mona Atassi Gallery, Damascus and the Khalil Sakakini Cultural Center, Ramallah.

Often created live and before an audience, shapes fluctuate and evolve visibly in Halaby's kinetic paintings, moving beyond a language of 'static abstraction'.[15] For Halaby, 'It is what the computer could provide that the painting on canvas could not that is significant.'[16]

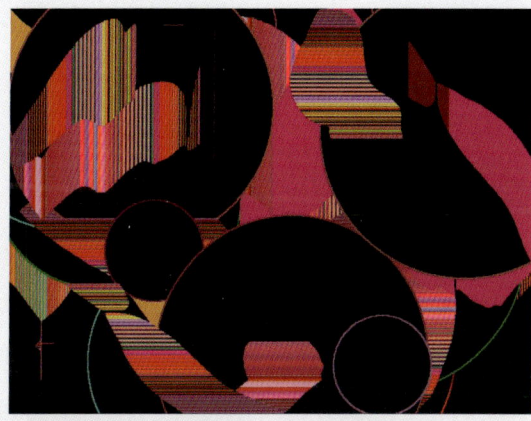

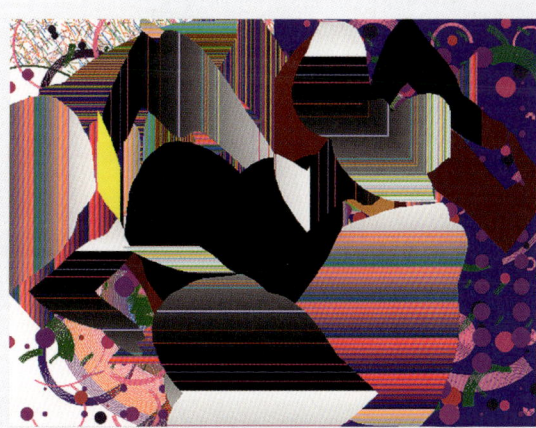

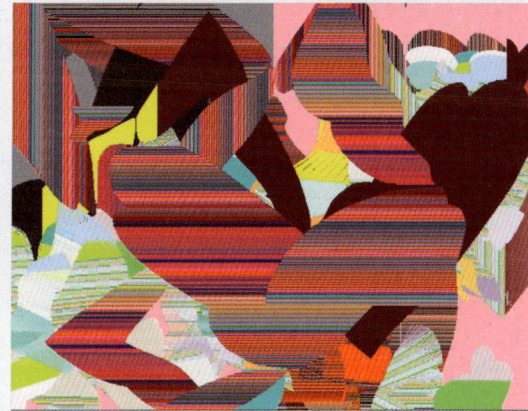

193

↑ Samia Halaby, stills from *Brass Women* 1992

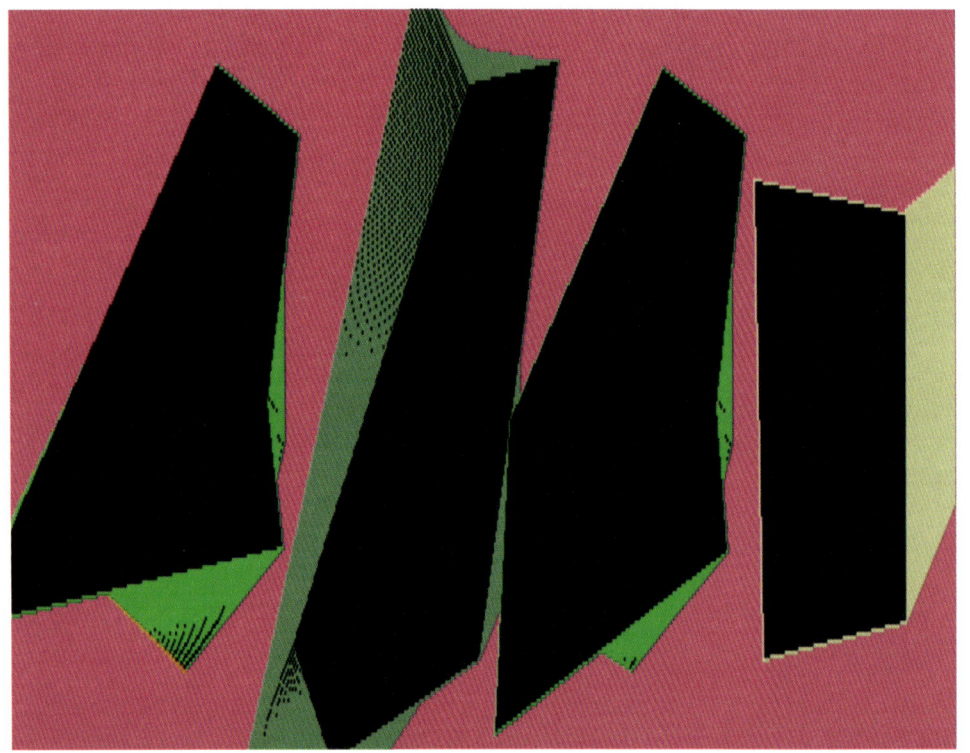

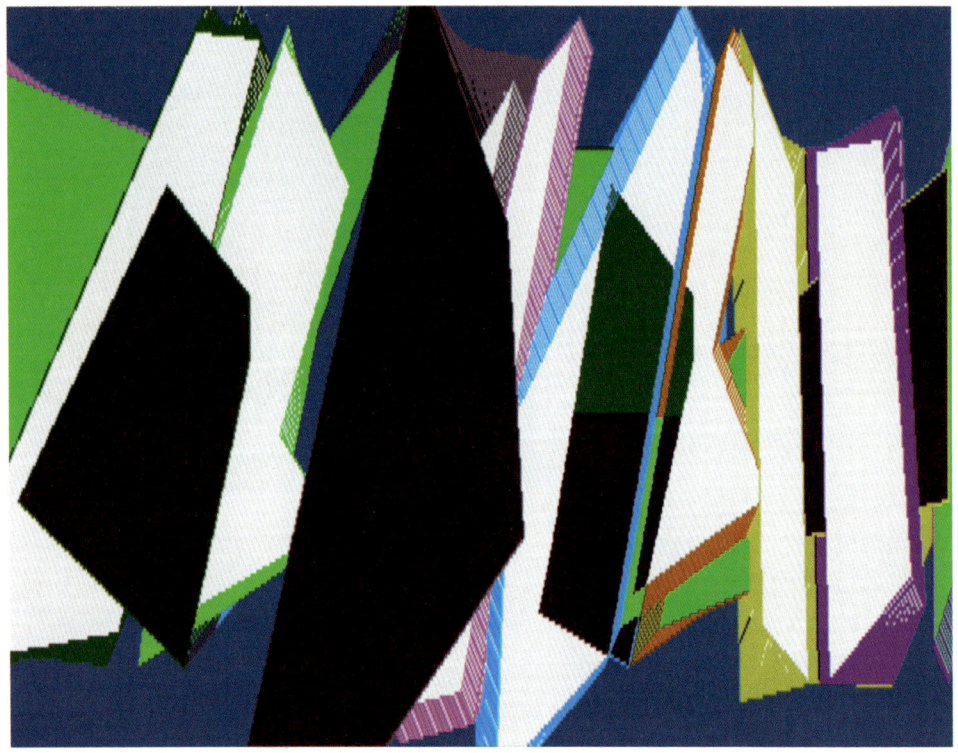

↑ Samia Halaby, stills from *Land* 1988

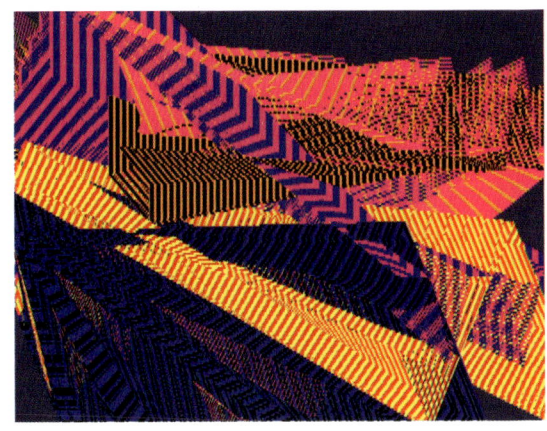
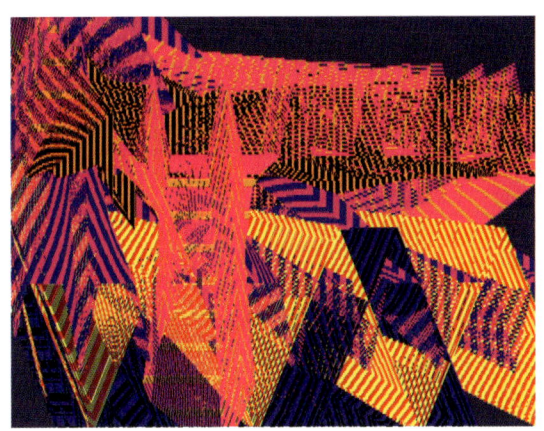

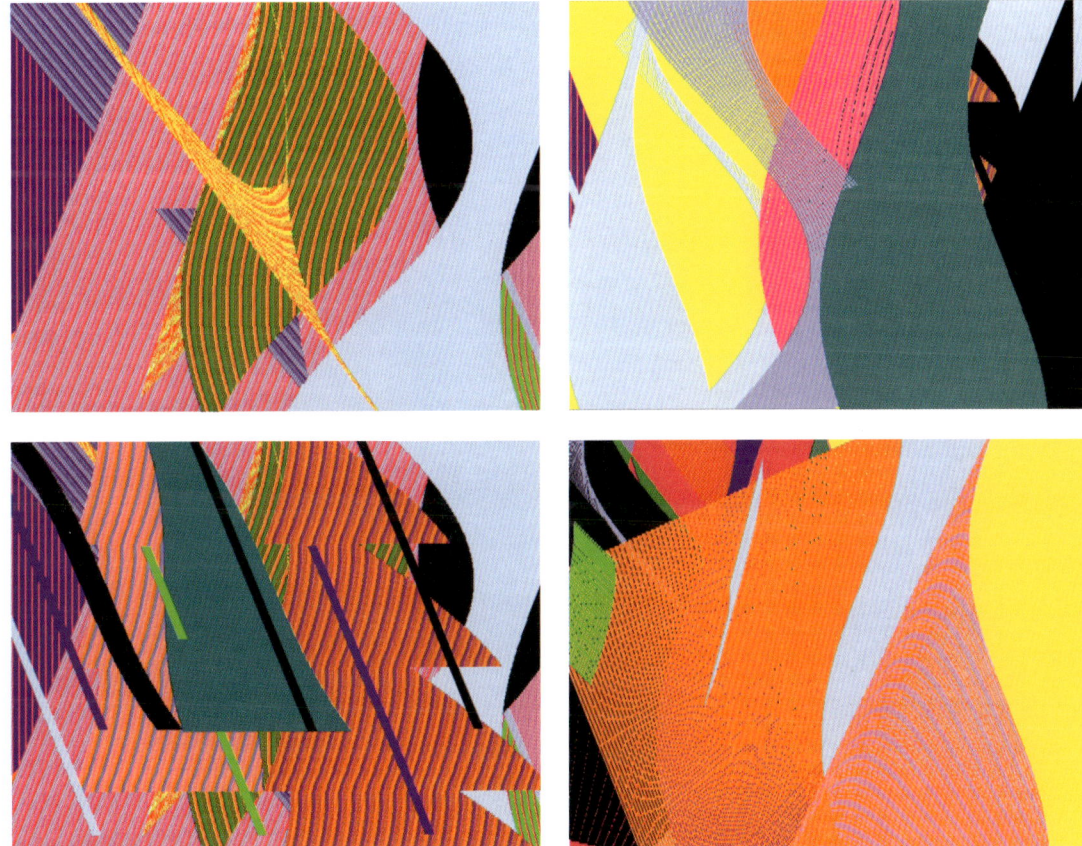

⬆ Samia Halaby, stills from *Fold 2* 1988
↑ Samia Halaby, stills from *Spooling Up* 1988

Combining translucency and materiality, contemplativeness and the dynamics of movement, the pioneering practice of Liliane Lijn has explored light-based art and language for over six decades. Giving form to frequencies and life to vibrations, her work brings to mind Marshall McLuhan's observation in his *Understanding Media* (1964) that 'electric light' is 'pure information' and 'a medium without a message'.[1] In an essay published in 1978, Lijn stated: 'Light becomes the living medium expressing form. The luminous message is more real than its source.'[2]

At the same time, works such as *The Bride* 1988 (p.199) contain powerful messages that speak directly to our contemporary preoccupations. Indeed, from her first moving-light works of the early 1960s, Lijn has been a pathfinder for a technological feminism, creating a now substantial series of works that counter and balance an otherwise often male-dominated narrative with respect to innovative use of industrial materials and processes. Moreover, animating the language of light through making the seemingly intangible visible – and meaningful across the range of the human sensorium – is a defining signature of her oeuvre.

Lijn drew attention to the poetic potential of industrial processes in a series of works made with signs and symbols found on sheets of Letraset that she first came across in London in 1964. She turned these into a unique form of visual poetry in her series of graphic constellations entitled *Electronic Symbols* 1966–9. She used a related approach soon after in a series she entitled *Neurographs* (including *Neurograph: Untitled 1* 1970), which were prompted by her friend, the poet Sinclair Beiles. He showed her a notebook of writings he was developing during psychiatric treatment and asked her if she might consider illustrating this. Lijn readily agreed: 'I thought I could create poignant metaphors for mental disturbance using electronic symbols, relating electrons to neurons. I thought of the brain as an electro-chemical system, a kind of organic machine. I found that using these delicate symbols, code for the control and use of electrical energy, opened up a new imaginative field for me.' She noted that this 'field of visual code' seemed to 'run parallel to poetry'.[3] In her poem series *Six Throws of the Oracular Keys*, written in 1974, she combined visual codes and words together, with each poem composed by the 'random dealing' of a deck of fifty-four oracular cards she invented in 1970.

In 1963 Lijn had an exhibition in Paris showing rotational machines on which lines of language curved and words were fragmented; in her works of this period we see a heightened transition from mechanical to electrical processes. From the mid-1960s she began to make *Linear Light Columns*, based on coils of copper wound around

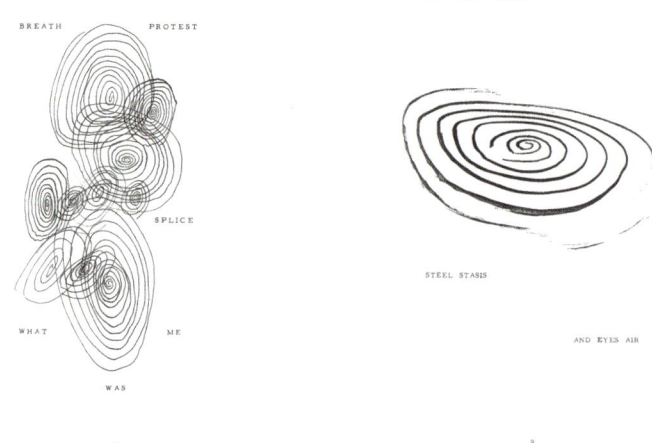

↑ Liliane Lijn, pages from *Six Throws of the Oracular Keys* (1981)

slowly revolving steel cylinders onto which a narrow beam of light is being directed. Lijn has referred to the copper-bound surfaces as a 'reflective skin' for a variegated line of light that 'appears to flow both ways, both upwards and downwards'.[4] The turning of the columns at five rotations an hour is almost imperceptible to the observer, while the dancing line of light is mesmeric and hypnotic.

Lijn probed the physics of light through sustained, artist-led interventions in the production of different versions of this work, having realised early on that by making varying indentations on the surface of the underlying tubes she could alter the way that the light would then fall onto

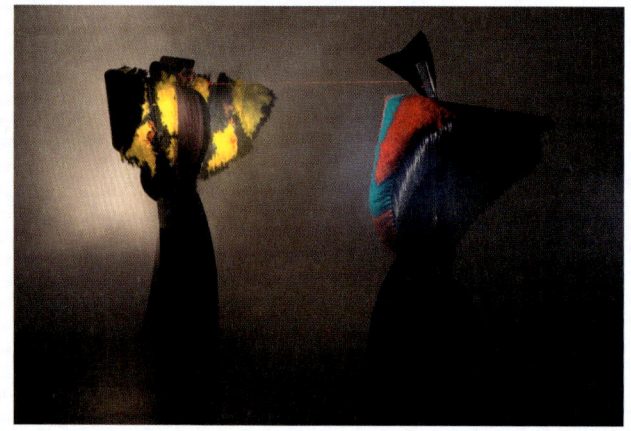

Light as Material and Medium: Liliane Lijn

Bronac Ferran

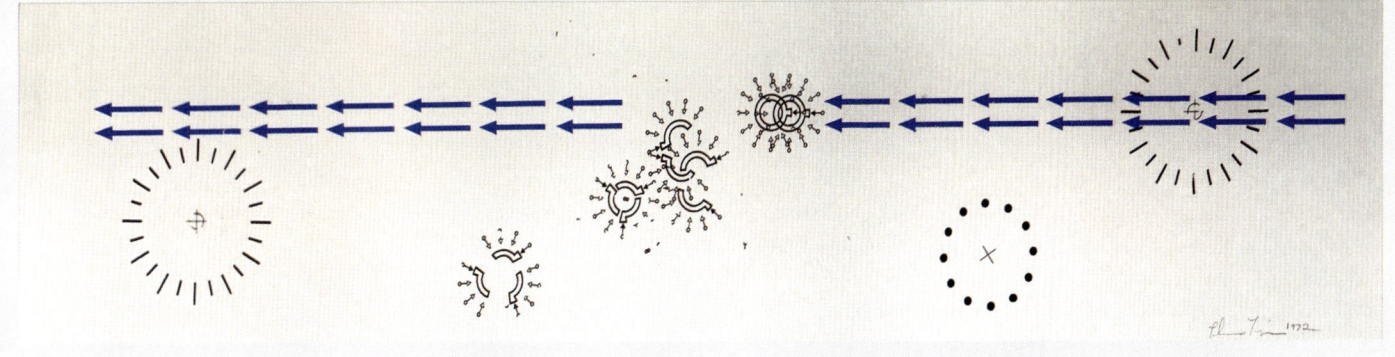

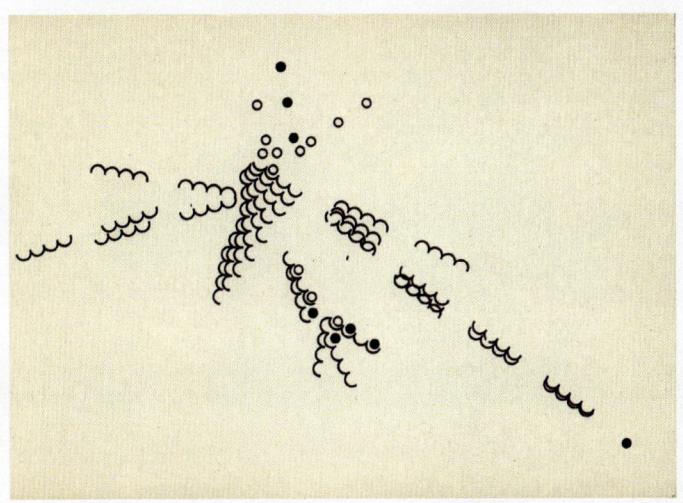

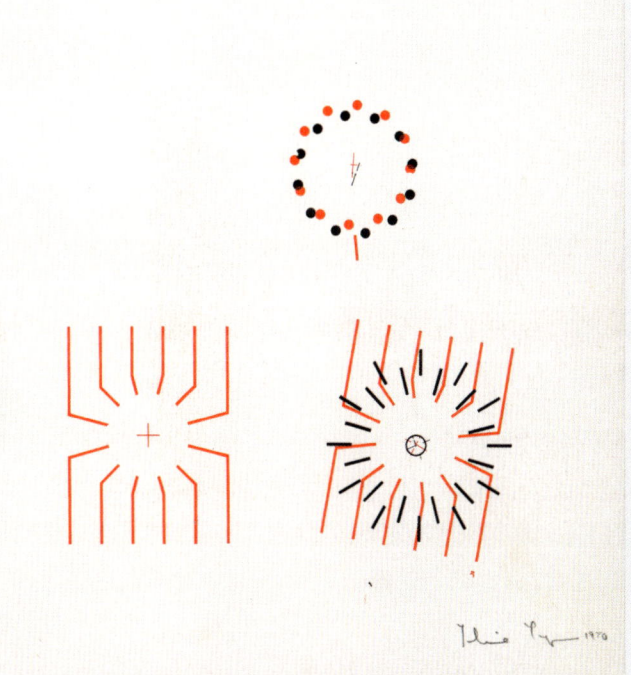

the reflective copper surfaces. This was further extended into *Lines of Power* 1983 (p.198), in which she used narrower, tighter bands of copper coil, secured through a link Lijn made to a major cable manufacturing company and the Post Office in England, giving her access to industrial machinery to wind the lines ever more tightly.[5]

In the 1980s, Lijn also made inroads into construction of a new feminist approach to materiality, manifest in a series of works, including *Conjunction of Opposites*, comprising *The Woman of War* 1986 and *Lady of the Wild Things* 1983, *The Bride* and *The Electric Bride* 1989. All transmit a gestation of energy through a powerful use of contrasts and juxtapositions, of light and sound and quietness and shadows, of extremely hard and extremely soft materials. In *Conjunction of Opposites* and *The Electric Bride*, a soundtrack heightens the dramatic effects, while *The Bride* is a more subdued, bowed, semi-veiled character. There is something of the occult about this shimmering oracular figure, positioned on a glowing bed of mica particles, made out of copper, iron, steel, papier-mâché, blown glass and ostrich feathers, who seems to move as visitors venture closer, although kept in check within a dark metal cage.

Lijn observed of her *Linear Light Column*: 'Narrowing the field of one's sight often allows one to widen one's vision.'[6] This is an apt description of works across her highly prismatic practice, in which poetic effects and technological shifts are fused together in sculpted lines of light and mediumistic messages.

⬧ Liliane Lijn, *Electronic Symbols* 1972
↑ Liliane Lijn, *Neurographs: Untitled I* 1970
← Liliane Lijn, *Conjunction of Opposites: Lady of the Wild Things and Woman of War* 1986

↑ Liliane Lijn, *Electronic Symbols 04* 1966–9

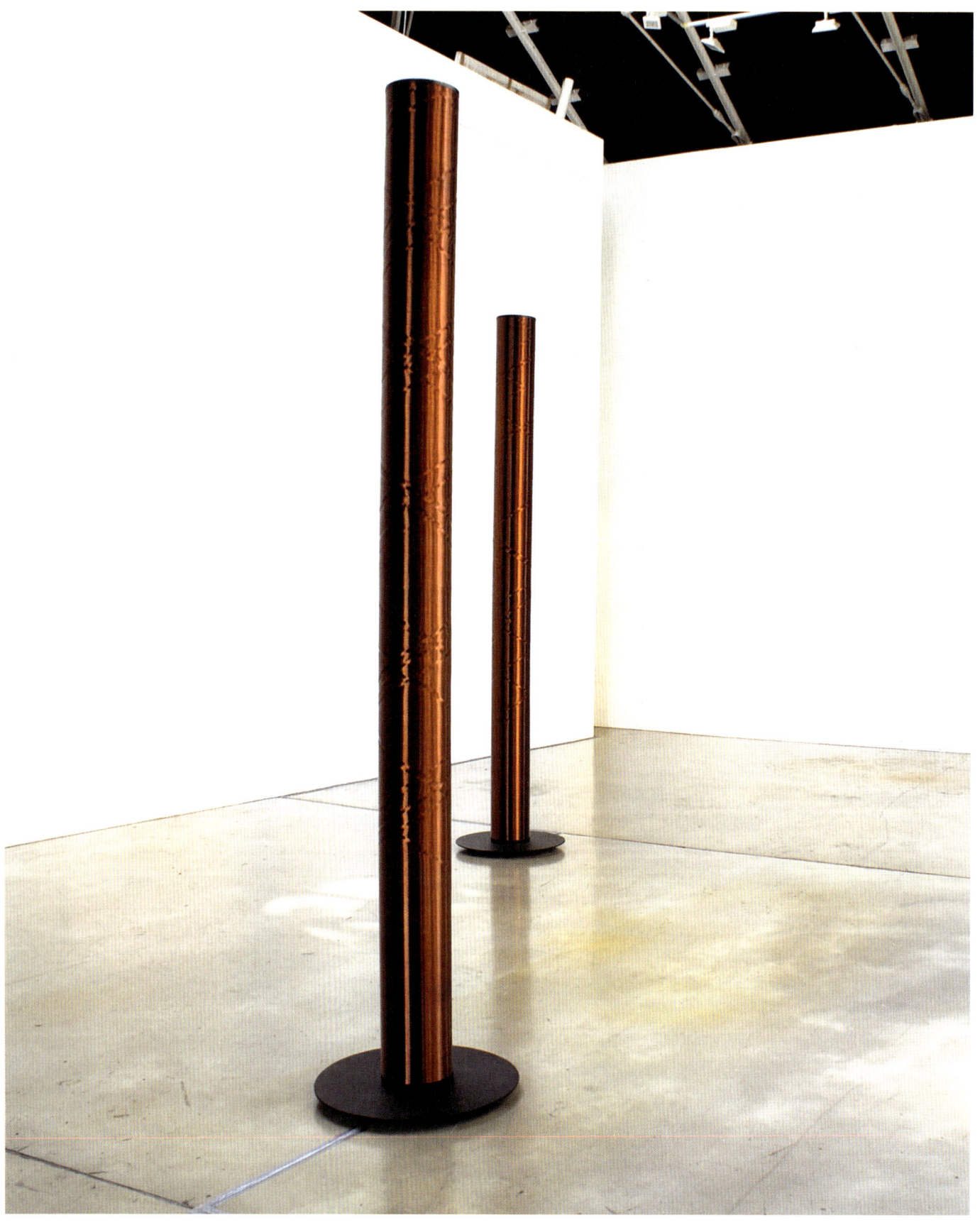

↑ Liliane Lijn, *Lines of Power* 1983

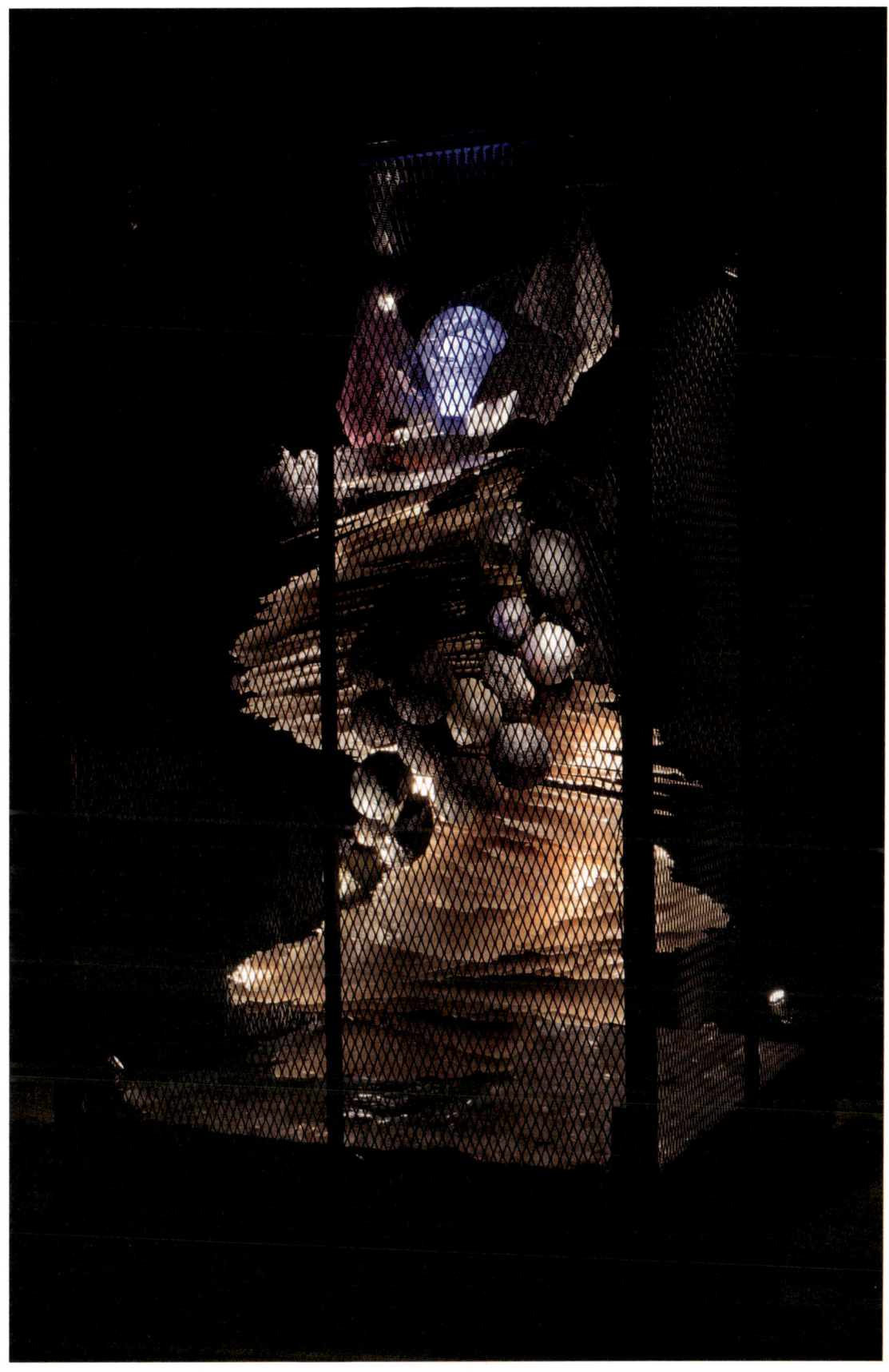

↑ Liliane Lijn, *The Bride* 1988

Tatsuo Miyajima is a Japanese sculptor and installation artist largely known for work that explores notions of time and space through the use of digital light-emitting diode (LED) counters. Born and raised in Tokyo, Japan, Miyajima studied painting at the Tokyo National University of Fine Arts and Music from 1980 to 1986. While waiting to be accepted onto the course, he had a temporary job in a data research company for metereological observation, an experience that piqued his interest in ideas of time and measurement.[1]

Initially, Miyajima experimented with performance, influenced by the Japanese Gutai Art Association of the 1950s and 1960s. Concerned by the transient nature of his performances, Miyajima began working with sculpture to address what he saw as issues of permanence and accessibility in his work.[2] He was also interested in working with materials that were widely available and popular. This led him to his first series of electronic works, developed between late 1984 and 1987, for which he collected and recycled electronic devices from scrapyards and wired them together to create new machines.[3] He later developed these mixed-media constructions into his first installation, entitled It of the Future 1986, which consisted of a room filled with monitors, lights and computers that were triggered by the viewer's movements. At the time, Miyajima was inspired by Jean Tinguely's kinetic objects of the 1950s and 1960s.[4]

Towards the late 1980s, Miyajima began to incorporate LEDs into his work to create customised digital counters. This proved to be an important breakthrough in his practice, and these counting gadgets continue to be fundamental to his work today.[5] The LEDs were initially in red and green – the only colours commercially available at the time. As technology developed, Miyajima quickly incorporated new colours into his work: blue in 1994, followed later by white.[6] His first artwork to use LED digital counters was Sea of Time 1988, which involved 300 connected LED units displayed across the gallery floor.

In 1990 Miyajima began his vast and ongoing series entitled 133651, which involved two-digit LED units that count from one to nine, arranged in geometric formations. The title of the series signals its vastness, the potential of embodying 133,651 works, based on the number of combinations it could engender. For Miyajima, 'The whole is a study of models of the world, of outer space, of time and of human society.'[7] Indeed, the series is an exploration of time and its measurement. For example, the work Lattice B 1990 is a large, wall-based installation – the second in a series of three – consisting of forty LED units arranged in a rectangular configuration that is three and a half metres high and over eight metres wide. Its title refers to the intricate way in which the units are connected, as well as to their physical arrangement on the wall. Each unit displays a digital counter that is individually programmed to move upwards from one to ninety-nine in a unique rhythm, before it restarts again from one. With thirty-five units in red, and five in green, the overall effect is of a flickering and ever-changing display of numbers progressing at different speeds.

In Miyajima's works, the number zero never appears. Instead, a gap or pause is displayed, signalling the space of death before life 'begins again' and the counters restart from one.[8] For the artist, zero is a transitional state and a void. The series 133651 reflects Miyajima's long-standing interest in and exploration of Buddhist philosophy, in particular, its thinking concerning cycles and repetition.[9] Here, numbers represent both individual and collective life cycles. Miyajima's preoccupation with time, space, life and death, the individual and the cosmos, is further explored in the work Mega Death 1999, an installation that fills an entire room. It is a reflection on the massive, unnatural loss of life caused by wars and conflicts in the twentieth century.[10] The viewer is immersed in blue counter gadgets that regularly switch off in unison, plunging the entire space into darkness.

Following Buddhist thought, Miyajima's work is guided by three principles: keep changing; connect with everything; continue forever. Technology, and the use of LEDs in particular, allows him to articulate these philosophical ideas simultaneously through light and movement.[11] For Miyajima, modern technology is not 'an end in itself' but a means of visually representing his ideas and visions.[12] He states: 'It is not about creating a beautiful image or system, it is more about creating an inner spiritual quality in the world. My idea of the future is not a pictorial image but a spiritual concept.'[13]

Tatsuo Miyajima: Light, Movement, Space

Odessa Warren

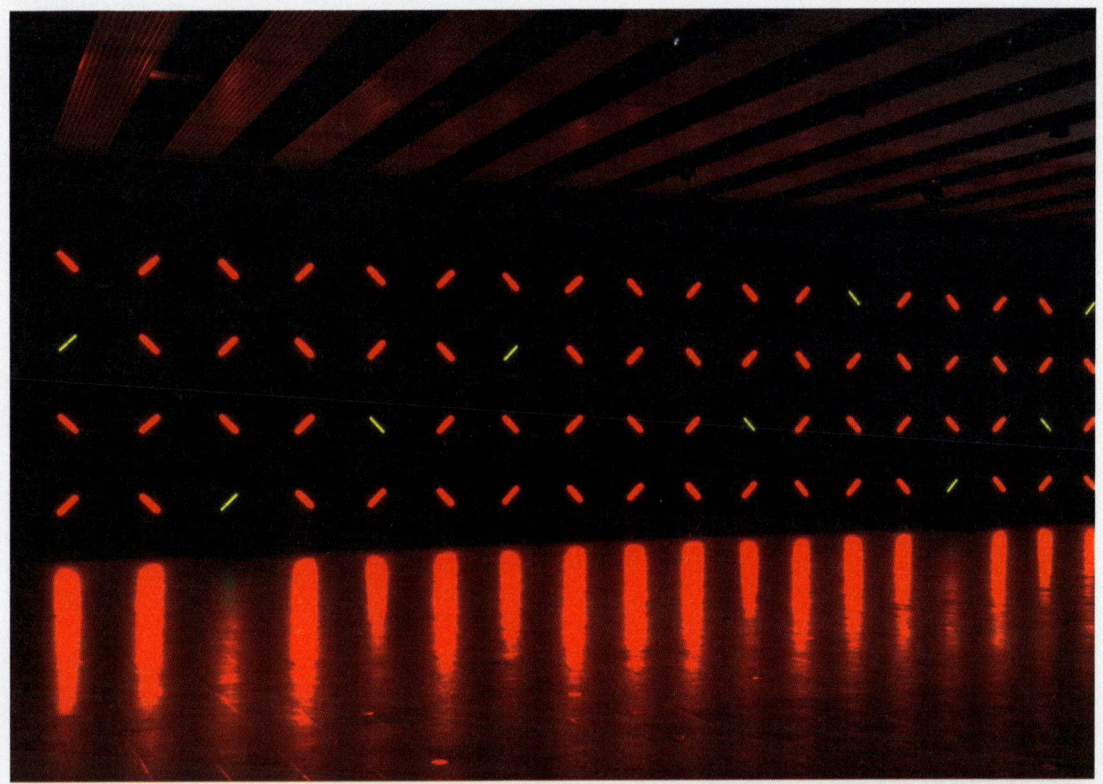

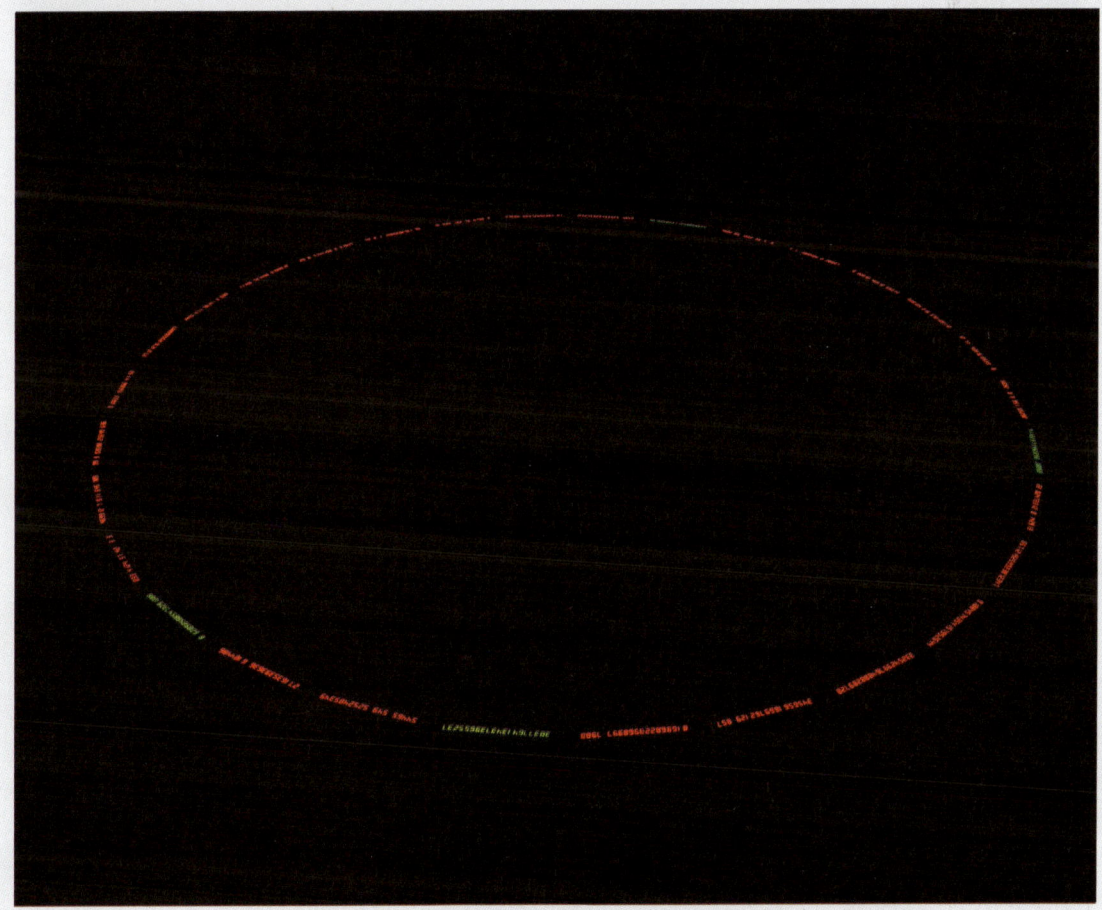

⬆ Tatsuo Miyajima, *Lattice B* 1990
↑ Tatsuo Miyajima, *Opposite Circle* 1991

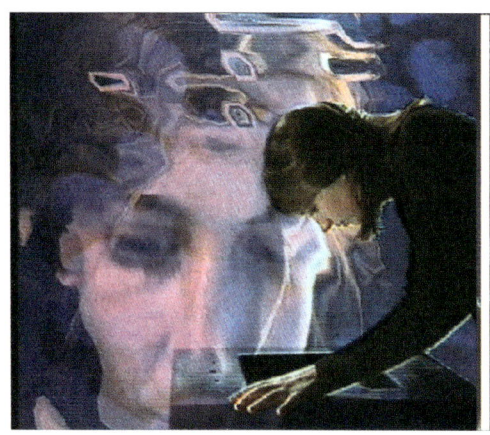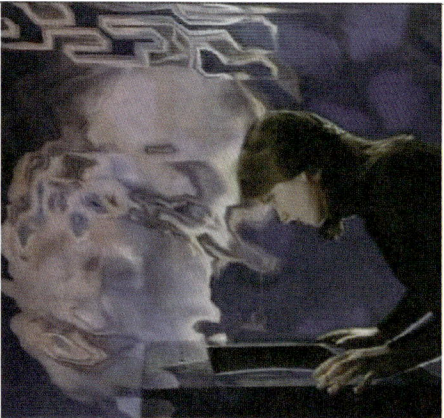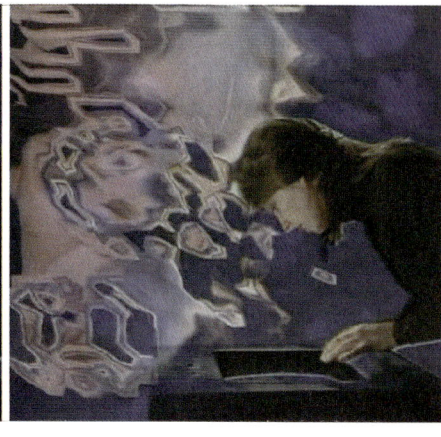

Monika Fleischmann and Wolfgang Strauss, with Christian-A. Bohn

Monika Fleischmann and Wolfgang Strauss are research artists and media scholars, among the very first to create digital artworks featuring immersive virtual and augmented reality. Their work *Home of the Brain* 1989–91 was the first ever to use goggles and a data glove, allowing users to spatially explore philosophical ideas around the rise of digital media technologies. Another of their most notable early works is *Liquid Views – Narcissus' Digital Reflections* 1992, an installation featuring a touch screen simulating a pool of water that reflects the viewer's image, as captured by camera. As visitors interact with the work, they see their distorted reflections in the screen, revealing a mutable second self that blurs in the rippling liquid. The viewer's image is also projected, allowing the audience to watch the person reflected in the water. Although echoing the experience of Narcissus from Greek mythology (Caravaggio's painting *Narcissus* c.1597–9 was a direct inspiration), the work also projects the reflection of the subject outward, engaging both personal and public gazes. The installation merges live video texture, mapping and generative algorithms to experiment with synthetic representation: according to the artists, 'It depicts the encounter of the self with a shadowy virtual doppelganger as a metaphor for the Internet and predicts the emergence of the Second Self as a selfie data body.' OW

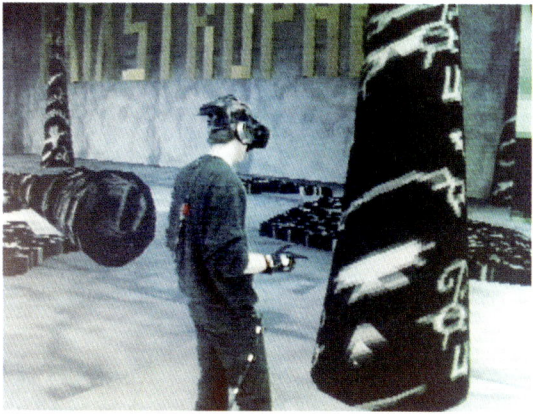

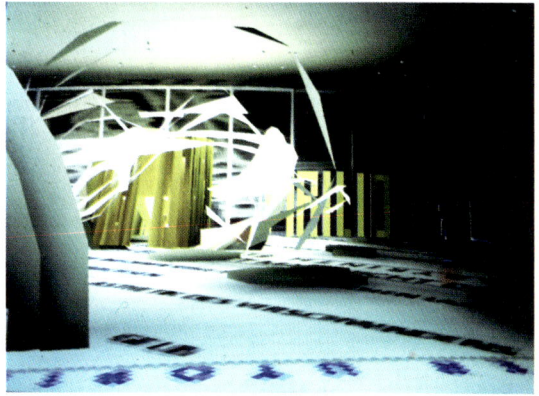

✿ Monika Fleischmann and Wolfgang Strauss with Christian-A. Bohn *Liquid Views – Narcissus' Digital Reflections* 1992

↑ Monika Fleischmann and Wolfgang Strauss, *Home of the Brain* 1989–91

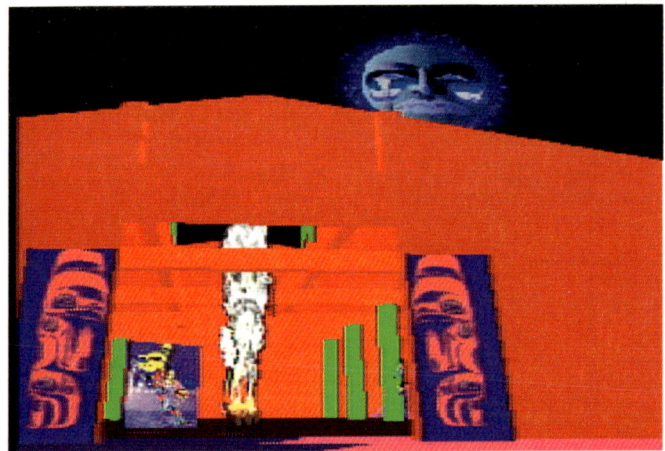

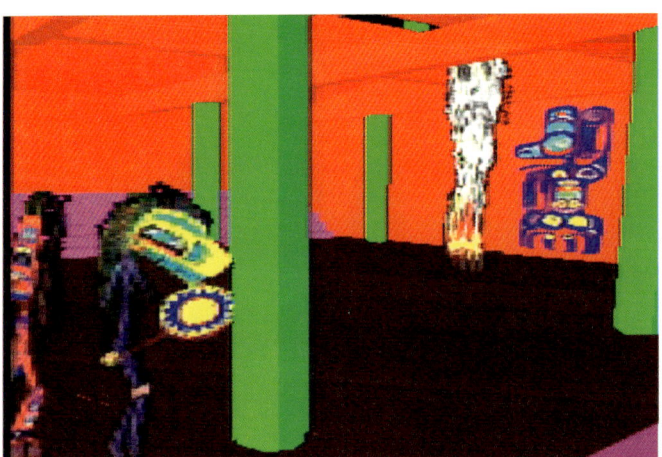

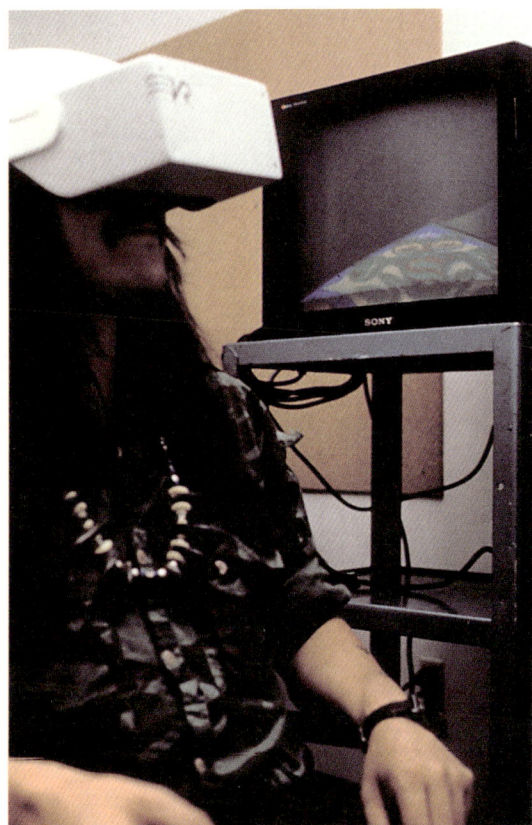

Lawrence Paul Yuxweluptun

The immersive virtual reality (VR) work *Inherent Rights, Vision Rights* 1992–3 simulates the experience of entering a sacred ceremony in a Coast Salish longhouse, a traditional structure used by First Nations peoples from the west coast of Canada. Yuxweluptun populated the longhouse with spirits of Coast Salish folklore, who also prominently feature in his colourful paintings depicting visions of his ancestral mythology, thus establishing a parallel between virtual space and spiritual realm. Yuxweluptun's name means 'man of many masks': besides the oversized animal masks worn by the spirits in his works, the VR helmet he wore to create the work becomes for him another ritual mask. However, the full VR version of the work does not require the use of a helmet or goggles, but rather a cabinet resembling an old stereoscope. Visitors to this world don't get to experience wearing the full mask: a reminder of their status as outsiders. *Inherent Rights, Vision Rights* was produced as part of the landmark Art and Virtual Environments Project (1991–4) of the Banff Centre for Arts and Creativity, one of the first ever workshops dedicated to VR art. VR

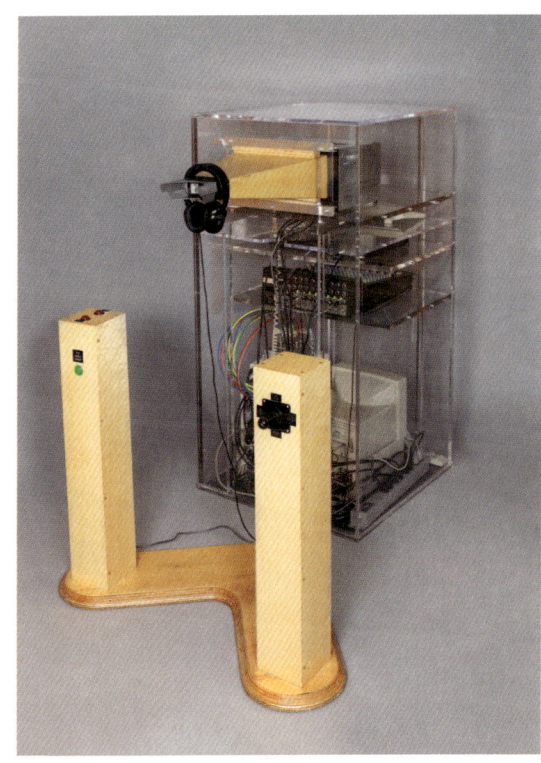

⬈ Lawrence Paul Yuxweluptun at the Banff Centre for New Media, Banff, Canada, c.1991–3
↑ Lawrence Paul Yuxweluptun, cabinet to experience *Inherent Rights, Vision Rights* in VR 1992–3

⬉ Lawrence Paul Yuxweluptun, *Inherent Rights, Vision Rights* 1992–3

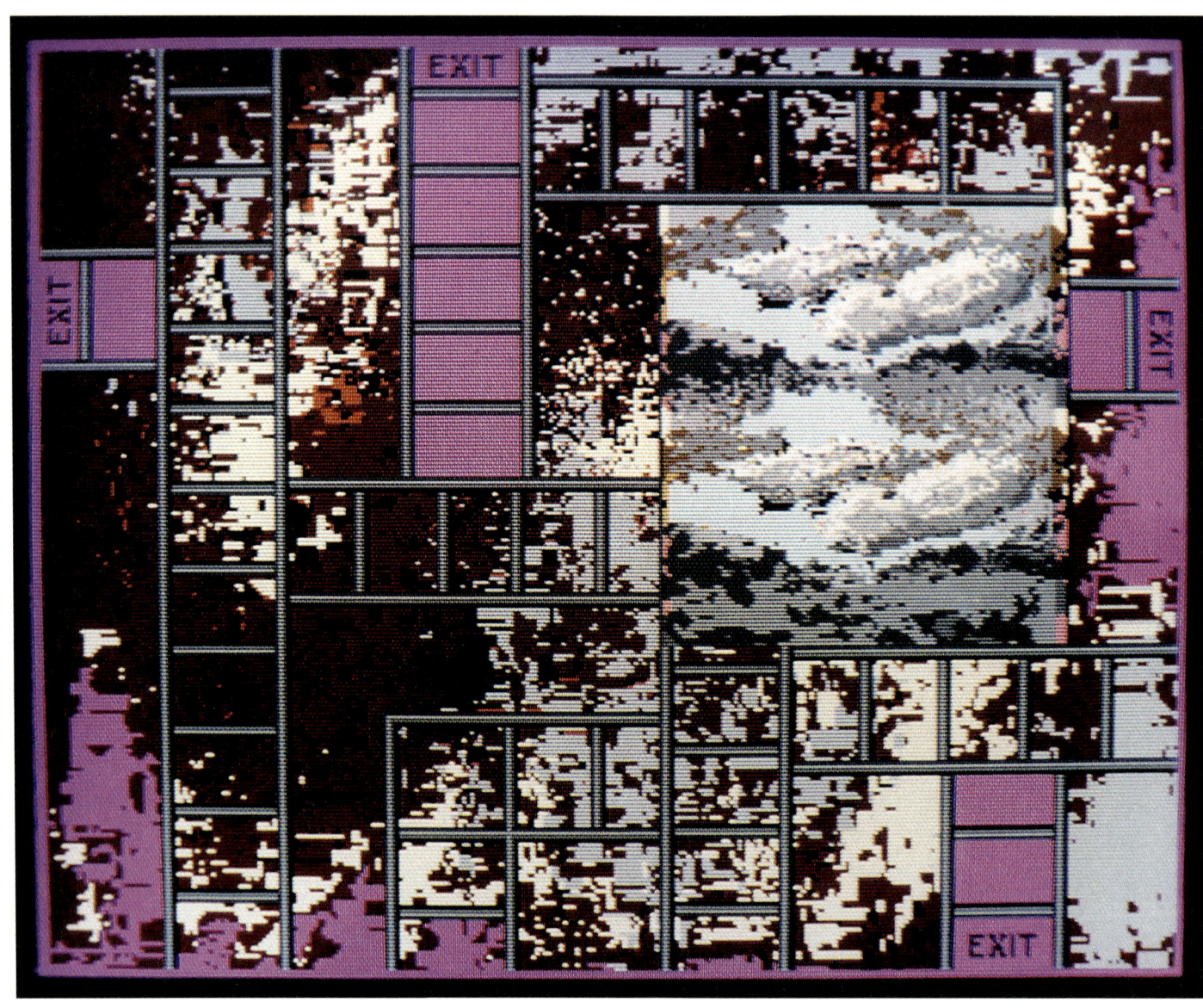

↑ Suzanne Treister, *Fictional Videogame Stills /
Four Exits* 1991–2

Suzanne Treister and Val Ravaglia in Conversation

London, 25 March 2024

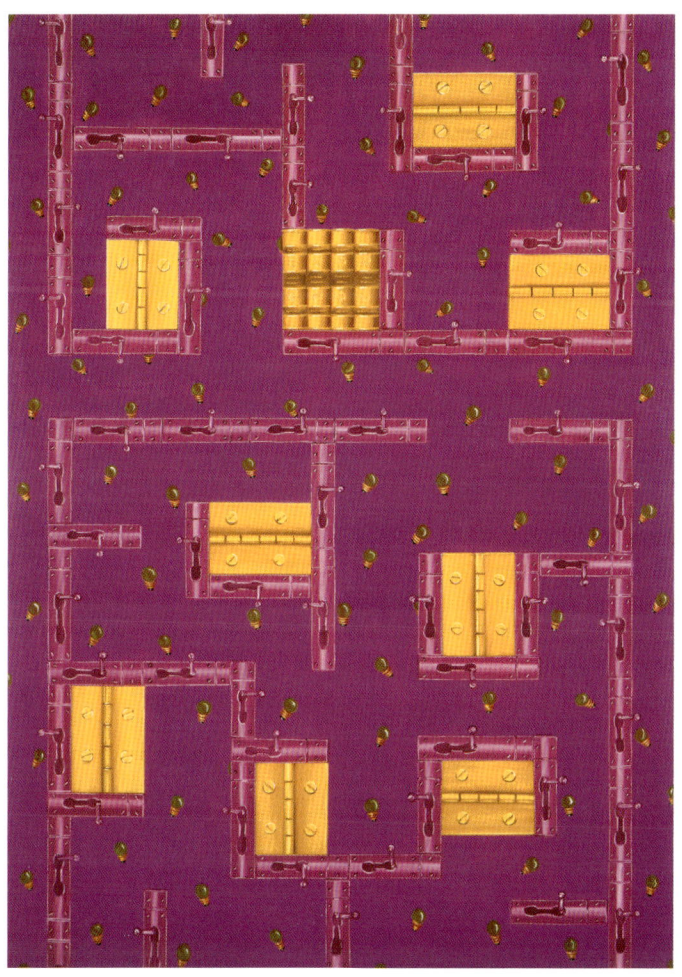

Val Ravaglia: *Let's start by talking about your* Fictional Videogame Stills. *Could you tell me the story of how they came about?*

Val Ravaglia: *Let's start by talking about your* Fictional Videogame Stills. *Could you tell me the story of how they came about?*

Suzanne Treister: From about 1986 onwards I had a boyfriend who used to go to video game arcades in Soho in London in the evenings. I'd go with him and observe, because I wasn't really into playing the games myself. This was the first time I had really seen those kinds of machines and that kind of imagery. So my first exposure to digital imagery was in video games and in a narrative form. The majority of the games had a war-like setting, they were about shooting and destruction. They were predominantly aggressive and militaristic, and this got me thinking about the future of technology as something that I should be concerned about. It was a really critical encounter. Some of my paintings up to that point referenced game structures, so it seemed quite an obvious move for me to start using the language of video games in my paintings, as a way of thinking about new technologies and their future uses. It didn't even seem possible to me at that time that I could *own* a computer. I didn't have any money, and I didn't really know anyone with a computer. That kind of visual imagery seemed to be something that could only be done at a very high end. So I started making paintings about video games instead. I used repeated imagery to form mazes, suggesting game structures and imaginary narratives. For example, one of these paintings was called *Video Game for Primo Levi* 1989 and it was connected with Levi's history of being a concentration camp survivor; one could imagine moving through this maze and trying to escape. Other paintings incorporated scenes from actual video games, which I photographed in the arcade and used as reference. At the time I wasn't aware of anyone else who had made any art about video games.

You have said that reading William Gibson was one of the triggers for you to decide to get a computer and start using it to make your art.

Yes, it was reading *Neuromancer* by William Gibson 1984 that gave me the impetus. By 1991, I had heard that you could get relatively cheap computers, so one Saturday afternoon I bought a Commodore Amiga and started working with this software called Deluxe Paint II to make my first video-game still. Obviously this idea had been brewing with my video-game paintings, but after that I gave up painting more or less overnight. The year before I bought my first computer, I'd met a guy who worked in a digital graphics design company. He told me he had a computer that could paint, and the next day I got a demonstration. It was the first time I'd held a mouse and used a graphics editor with a toolbox. It was a really magical experience. I moved my hand and this bright coloured line flew across the screen, like a big arc. Suddenly I was controlling these amazing, luminous colours on this digital interface. I think I felt a massive paradigm shift at that moment. It was a sense of ecstasy and a sense of panic – almost like a disembodied, transcendent feeling; something quite spiritual. In that first experience I felt the potential embedded in this

↖ Suzanne Treister, *Video Game for Primo Levi* 1989

technology, and a need to make work on computers that would explore not just the aggressive side of video games and their potential militaristic uses, but the multiple possible trajectories and embodiments of new technologies. Because technology is invented by human beings and it can be as complex as human beings are, it just depends who is using it and for what purpose. So that's always been my dream, to somehow navigate technology both critically and holistically.

Were you in any way aware around that time of previous works by older artists that had an interest in electronic technologies, or of early uses of computers in art?
Not really. This was before the World Wide Web, and from around the time I left art school in 1982, I don't remember seeing computer art in any London show I attended. I may have seen works with abstract, computer-generated patterns in books, perhaps, and I might have been aware of someone like Nam June Paik. But there was also a sense that artworks done on computers were more like special effects, they weren't really considered art. I personally wasn't aware of any work being done with computers that was in any way critical. When I first got my computer in 1991, there was a very hostile reaction. The computer was seen as something which was going to kind of ... eat your brain. And I had to explain to people that I wasn't going to make work simply dictated by the machine, but rather that it was going to be about the machine and what the machine could do. People assumed that anything made with a computer was generated by the machine, that it took away individual creativity, and therefore that it was to be dismissed. I think people were as scared then as they are now with AI – scared that the machine would take over. Whereas I thought that as an artist I was responsible for articulating my existence in this world and reflecting on what's happening to it – that I had to take control of this machine before it took control of us.

When you made the Fictional Videogame Stills*, did you have complete scenarios in your head for what the video game was, like what the goals or the characters were?*
They were more like mysterious, suggestive snapshots, really. The text was really important. It would sometimes be in the form of a question. In one, the text said 'Q. There are 10 questions.' That one actually referred to the 10 commandments. I would often tangentially bring in some religious subtext, which was asserting a possible belief system into that digital space, but also questioning it at the same time. Another one was 'You have reached the gates of wisdom', which sounded kind of like a mystical quest. And then there were some that questioned the idea of a virtual paradise. In 1991 I had tried virtual reality games at this place called SegaWorld at the top of the Trocadero, in Piccadilly Circus, where you put on a headset and could move around a virtual environment on a giant chequerboard platform in outer space, where monsters descended from four staircases to try and kill you. I remember going

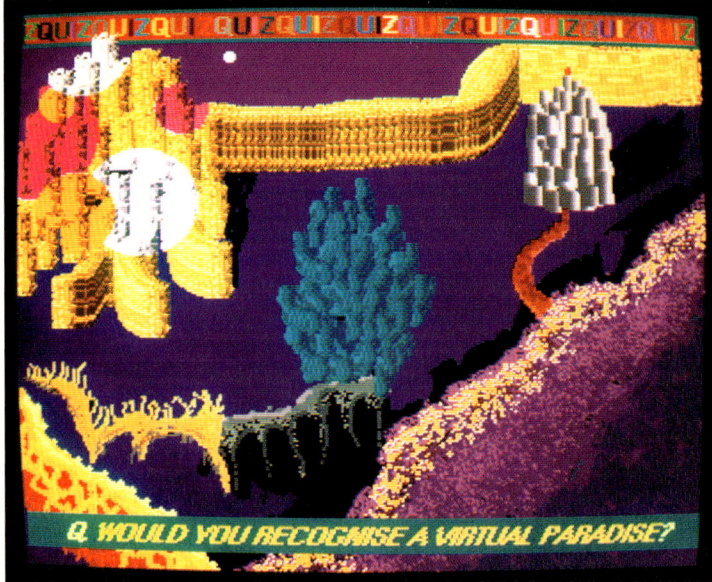

to the edge of this board, looking out onto outer space and trying to jump off. But that's where the interface ended, and the software wouldn't let you leave the platform. So I was interested in the idea of virtual reality from 1991. I did a series of video-game stills called *Would You Recognise a Virtual Paradise?* It was a sequence where the first still is in some strange, imagined digital world, with the title included as text. In the second one a system message comes up saying 'Not enough memory for operation'. My Amiga would often say 'You don't have enough memory', because back then you only got half a megabyte of RAM. Then in the third, another system message pops up, saying 'Presume virtual breakdown'. The fourth said 'Now enter a virtual wilderness', and there's an interference pattern in the original landscape where reality glitches. So it's not as real as you may think it is, because you can see there's the virtual paradise behind bars of interference, and then you've got this strange row of geometric shapes suggesting another reality. So the series starts off with this magical landscape, which gradually gets interfered with.

Do you feel like we are now in a 'virtual wilderness'?
Yes; I imagined it back in 1991 quite clearly. That series was imagining that we would evolve to create a virtual paradise, which I gradually broke down and questioned. I was asking people to challenge this idea of virtual paradise, even though they didn't even know it was possible at the time.

The fifth still in the series says 'Software failure. Please enact repetition of the crime'. What 'crime' exactly?
I think I was possibly imagining people playing that game who may have some guilt on their conscience. I was very interested in psychoanalytic theory at the time and in a kind of 'psychology of the audience' in relation to those technologies, and of the people who were going to go on

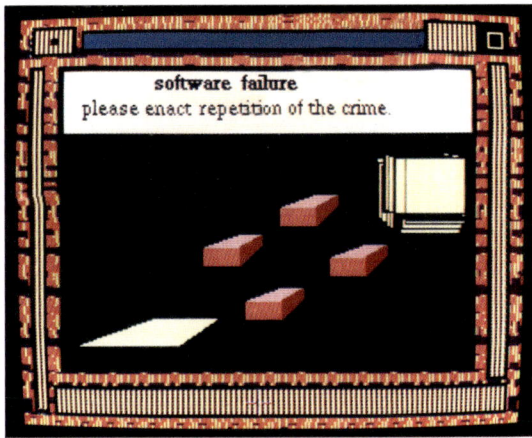
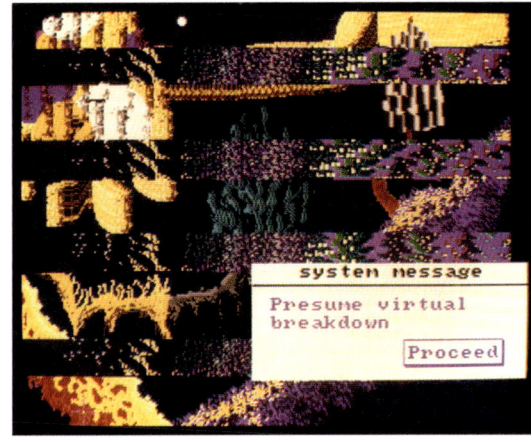
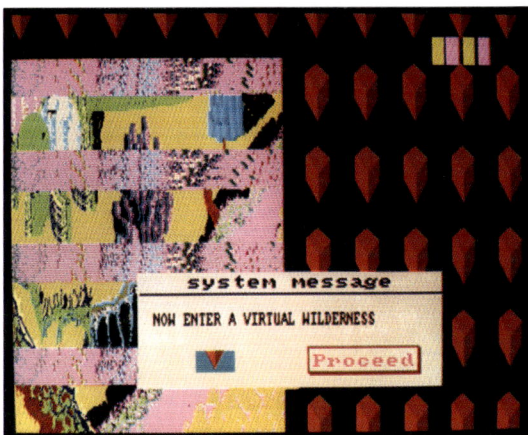
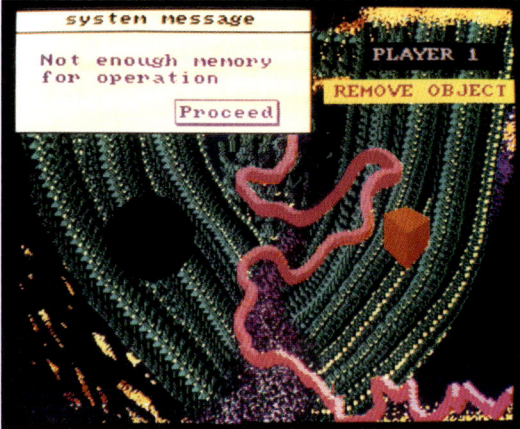
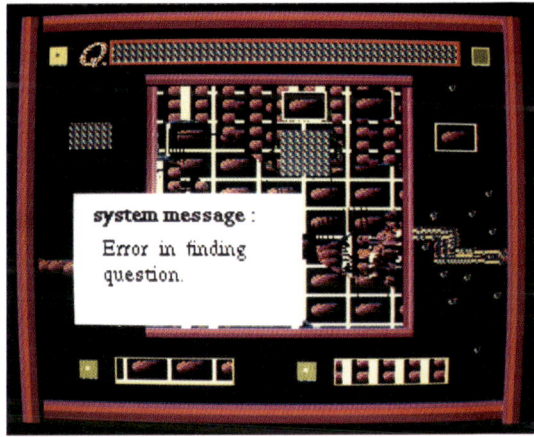
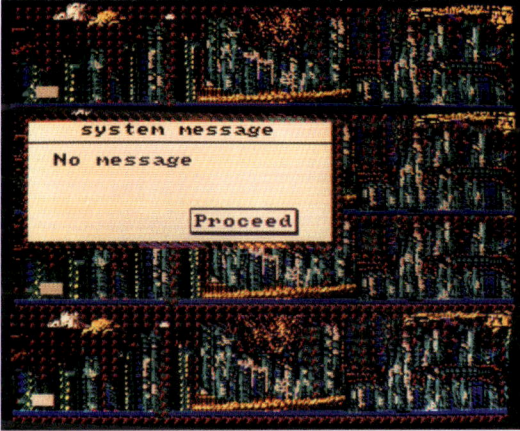

Suzanne Treister, *Fictional Videogame Stills /
Would You Recognise A Virtual Paradise?* 1991–2
Top: *Software failure …*
Middle: *Now Enter A Virtual Wilderness*
Bottom: *Error In Finding Question*

Top: *Presume Virtual Breakdown*
Middle: *Not Enough Memory For Operation*
Bottom: *No Message*

and use them. I wanted to create a kind of ethical questioning, somehow.

I'm particularly struck by the one that says 'Have you been sentenced to a fate worse than death?' Is that because of said crime?

It's more abstract in a sense. I think that's partly because in those games, and in thinking about the potential futures of technology, there was always this feeling that you were under attack – that technology could take control in some way or could be used to control people. A 'fate worse than death' could happen maybe more easily if there were machines involved. We know that in the Holocaust, for example, without the IBM computers used for the census, the Nazis wouldn't have been able to track down so many people. So the idea of digital reporting and the power of data collection were already implicit in those works in a way.

So you were thinking of a state of constant surveillance and fear as a 'fate worse than death'?

I don't think I had a specific idea for it at the time. I think I was abstractly anticipating potentials, and a lot of what I did has proven very prophetic. For example, in 1993–4 I made that series of software packages the *SOFTWARE* series (p.209) that anticipated the whole idea of the app – these different softwares that could digitise different aspects of life. I'm always trying to think the future, to push myself to get beyond what we can imagine, always thinking 'Do we need to worry about this? How do we safeguard?' These things come out in everything I do.

It seems to me that the way that you were engaging with technology at the start had a lot to do with visual storytelling. Were the Fictional Videogame Stills *the first time you used text in your work?*

Yes. My earlier paintings didn't have text, and actually it was a great relief to me to find out that I could just add text instantly in the graphics software. And it would have a different kind of authority to it, because it was on a screen rather than hand-painted. Interestingly, after about six months of making those works on the computer, I wondered what would happen if I went back to painting. There would be no point doing the kind of paintings I had done before, because I had moved on and translated them into digital form. So I found myself doing a series of text paintings with quite weird expressionist fonts that I made up, which combined a kind of techno-spirituality with a rather psychedelic way of painting. That was around 1992.

Was there a moment when you realised that the use of certain technological digital tools allowed you to tell stories differently?

Yes: in 1995, when I created my alter ego Rosalind Brodsky, the time traveller. Firstly I made a series of time travel costumes, which were actually sculptures with various electronic appendages, a group of attaché cases and other works. Then, when I started to make a multimedia

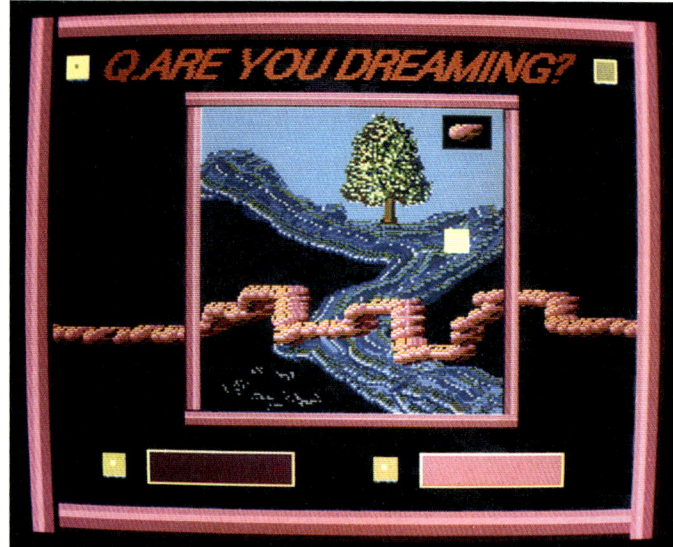

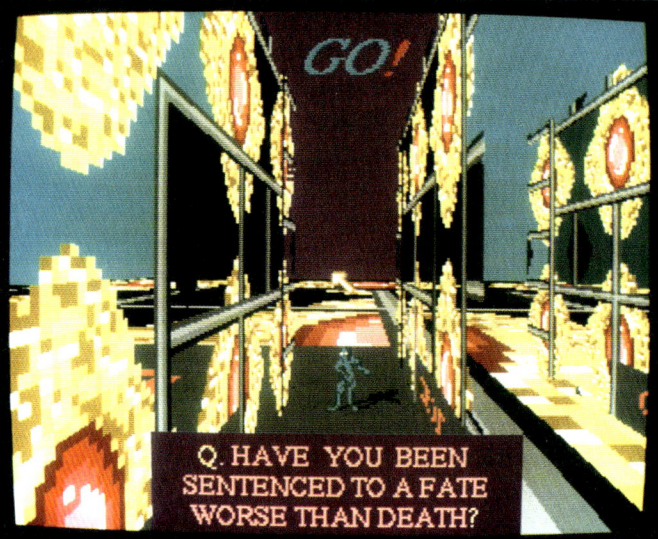

Suzanne Treister, *Fictional Videogame Stills* 1991–2
♠ *Are you dreaming?*
↑ *Fate worse than death?*

CD-ROM about Rosalind Brodsky's time travel-based research, I was able to really create an extended narrative, which was more like an interactive film. The authoring software Director 5 allowed me to include text, images, video, animation, audio and interactivity. It was multi-time-based so people could navigate various different trajectories and directions in a rhizomatic, hypertextual narrative. The internet and these new interactive technologies were allowing artists and writers of the time, such as Mark Amerika, to experiment with non-linearity.

When did you first hear about the internet?
I moved to Australia in 1992, and maybe a year later someone described the concept of email to me. I couldn't envisage that it would catch on – the idea seemed a bit dull to me at first. I think that was due to the fact that computers were used primarily for business and the military. Not many people had a computer to do anything creative with, and the idea of emails seemed like an office thing to me. But then, literally five minutes later, I signed up for an email address. I joined Nettime, which started in 1995, and all these online LISTSERVs, these global discussion lists. I became a huge advocate and I was telling everyone they should get on email, that they could change the world by communicating with people all over the planet at a grassroots level. No one in London listened to me until maybe six years later, when they wanted to buy things on the internet. In 1995 I also made my first web project, which was a precursor of my interactive CD-ROM.

So you were there at a moment when you actually felt like it was possible to use the internet as a grassroots medium.
It *was* possible. It actually was a new counterculture. Me and my friends in Australia were linked up with all these other people in Europe, North and South America, Asia and Eastern Europe and the Balkans, getting information and communicating about what was really happening on the ground all over the world. Of course, it wasn't available everywhere, but when people managed to get access to it, they could communicate what was happening in, say, a village in Bosnia. Instead of reading something in the newspapers, you were getting this information feed instantly, from people who were experiencing a war zone – not through a commentator or a politically filtered system.

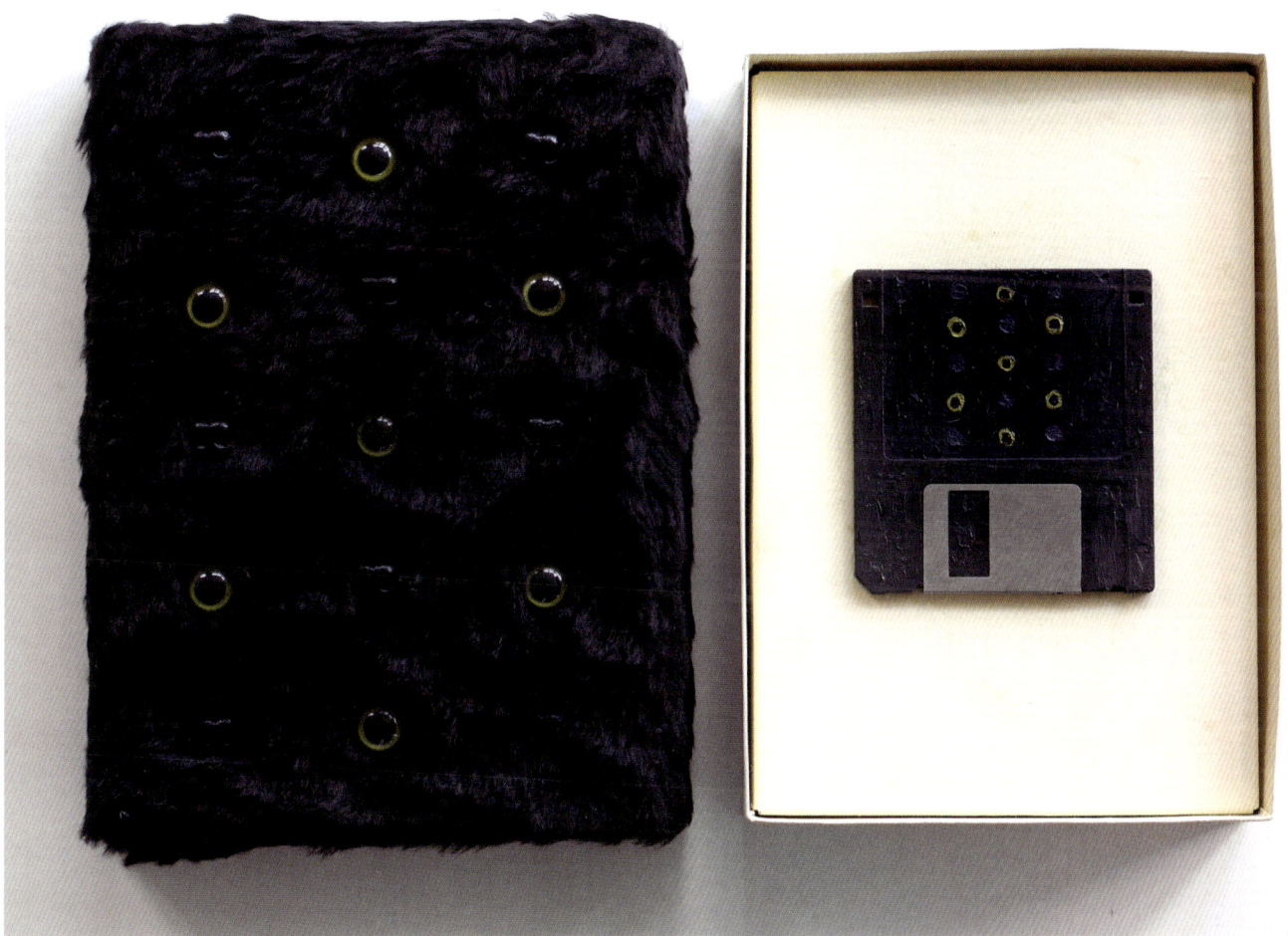

↑ Suzanne Treister, *SOFTWARE / Q. Would you recognise a Virtual Paradise? / Pet Morph (Black)* 1993–4

And that felt like it was going to change everything. At that point there was this idea of a new kind of culture and freedom of exchange, which followed on from various poststructuralist ideas like decentralisation, power to the margins, flattening of hierarchies. It was a huge paradigm shift, and a kind of utopian fantasy that power and control could be more universal, that all those people who had previously been oppressed or marginalised would now be able to speak on a level playing field.

But it was also a very critical environment. There were always conversations on Nettime or other discussion groups monitoring every little step of the way, and people were very aware of potential negative aspects and inequalities that might still be maintained. We were very aware that the internet was historically a military venture, and constantly reminding each other of how privileged we were to have access to it. The people I know from the last thirty years or so of the new media art scene have been part of that questioning from the beginning; we know the history of that 'net politics' period of the 1990s. This separates us from people who only started using new technologies when they wanted to buy something online and didn't know what the internet could have been. Tim Berners-Lee, who invented the World Wide Web in 1989, had more hopeful plans for the future, which he's still working on.

And the fact that it was a technology developed by the military wasn't a deterrent?
Well, just because they developed it didn't mean that they were necessarily going to be able to control it. It was an unusual situation, that suddenly this powerful advanced technology was made generally available to civilians. But then, about five years later governments and corporations started to monopolise it and various American organisations were set up to control domain names and other things. A lot of that is in my *HEXEN 2.0* project (2009–11), a series of works addressing the history of cybernetics and its links with computing, the internet, the military and certain countercultural movements. It became clear to me in 2000 that the internet was no longer a utopian space, and that everything one did could be monitored, controlled and harvested. Since 2000 I've made very little work using technology itself; I've mostly used traditional media, like drawing, to make work about technology. I didn't want to be part of the arms race.

It strikes me that digital warfare emerges in your work as part of the research that you do to look back at the uses of technology, at how the gamification of warfare and the relationship between digital technologies and military research and development (R&D) was something that was present from the get go, first with game theory and then the development of a digital version of those war games that were used by the military for training purposes. It has manifested in literal warfare, with someone in a room piloting a drone to destroy a building on the other side of the planet. In a sense, that was the worst-case scenario you might have envisioned, maybe subconsciously, when you entered the arcade environment and noticed everyone was shooting, right?
Exactly. I couldn't have really anticipated it, but yes. This is also in *HEXEN 2.0*, in the 'History of the Internet' diagram [*From ARPANET to DARWARS via the Internet*]. And in the

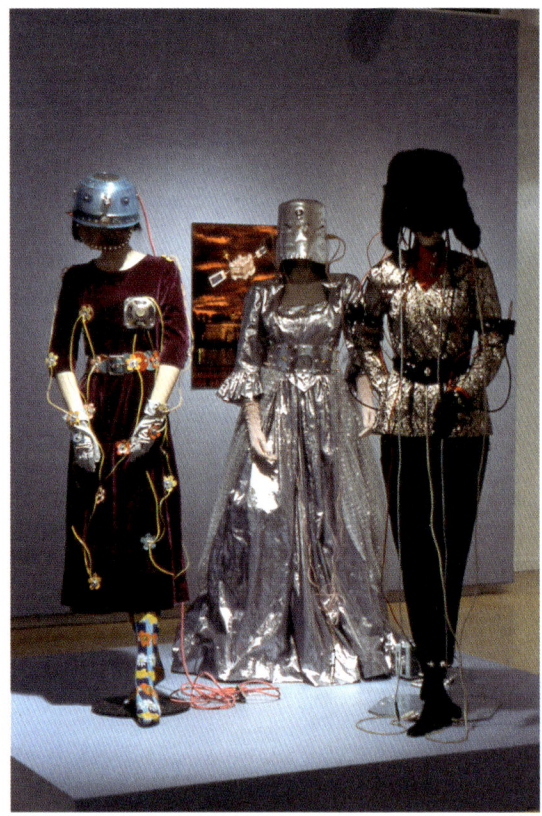

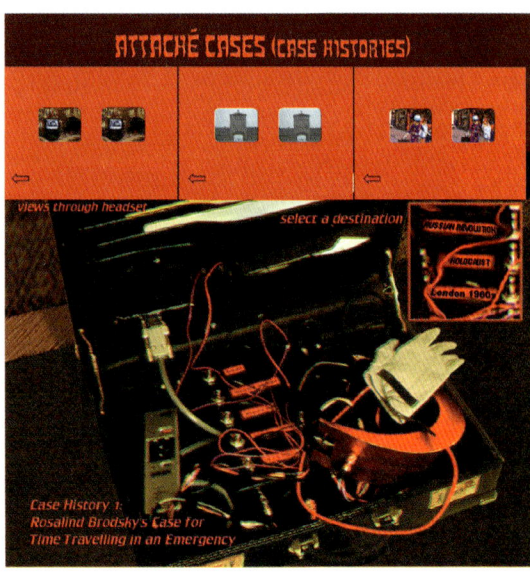

↟ Suzanne Treister, *Rosalind Brodsky's Electronic Time Travelling Costume to go to London in the 1960s; Rosalind Brodsky's Electronic Time Travelling Costume to rescue her Grandparents from the Holocaust; Rosalind Brodsky's Electronic Time Travelling Costume to go to the Russian Revolution* 1995–7. Installation view, 2002 Biennale of Sydney
↑ Suzanne Treister, *Rosalind Brodsky's Attaché Cases / Case History 1. Rosalind Brodsky's Case for getting into Virtual Reality in an Emergency* 1995

210

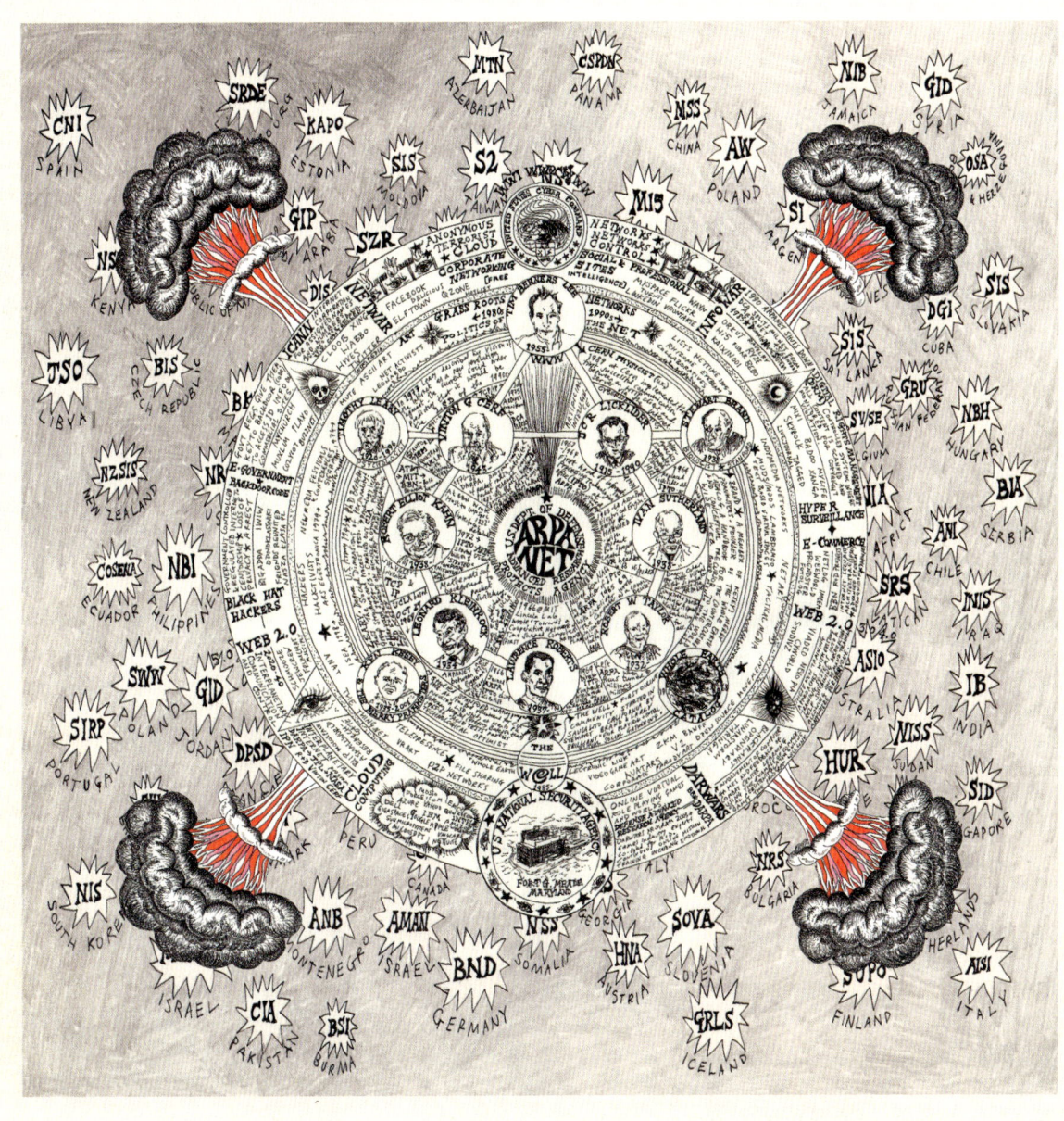

↑ Suzanne Treister, *HEXEN 2.0 / Historical Diagrams /
From ARPANET to DARWARS via the Internet* 2009–11

tarot deck, one of the cards [*Ten of Swords – DARWARS*] has all that stuff that the US military were saying around 2009 about how they wanted to provide online virtual training, 'continuous on-demand training anywhere, anytime for everyone'.

When did you become interested in the history of cybernetics?

I started reading about it in 2009. When I understood what it was really about, I realised it mirrored the way the internet operated as Web 2.0, interactively, as opposed to the read-only first incarnation of the Web. With Web 2.0 there were cybernetic feedback loops that were passing your information up and then feeding things back to you. That was clearly, to me, a cybernetic model. And that really confirmed to me that we needed to start worrying about Web 2.0, because a cybernetic feedback loop is a system of control. I researched cybernetics quite heavily. A useful illustration is Norbert Wiener's anti-aircraft missile prediction system that he developed during the Second World War. Wiener was one of the core participants of the Macy Conferences on cybernetics, which took place in New York from 1946 to 1953. These brought together thirty figures from the hard and soft sciences – from ecology to psychology to computer engineering to anthropology – who gathered in the aftermath of the Second World War to develop a unified theory of the human mind and how to control it. The intention was positive, in the sense that they wanted to try and build a society where fascism could not arise again and there could not be another Holocaust. Those thirty people then moved on in various directions. So, for example, Margaret Mead and some of the others formed the World Federation for Mental Health in 1948, which was supposed to establish some idea of 'normal mental health' across the world. So this idea of cybernetics could apply to all kinds of disciplines. The outcomes of imposed cybernetic systems of control depend on who and what is controlled and by whom, and, for me, in the case of Web 2.0 it raised major alarm bells. I made *HEXEN 2.0* to address these issues.

The word 'cybernetics' comes from the Greek for 'steersmanship'. To me this immediately conjures images of literally being manoeuvered by someone else. On the other hand there are ways of interpreting the whole idea of cybernetics on more neutral ground, as being a study of feedback loops in biological systems. I think it's also useful as a way of rephrasing the idea of interconnectedness in an ecological sense, to drive home the idea that what our species does has ripple effects on the environment that then feed back to us in negative ways. Sadly, only now that these effects manifest in a tangible and catastrophic way do most people finally truly understand what those feedback loops mean on a planetary scale. Do you think that having a better understanding of the origins of cybernetics might help with thinking in ecological terms in a different way? Is there something to recover from the early days of cybernetics?

The Macy Conferences brought together research from so

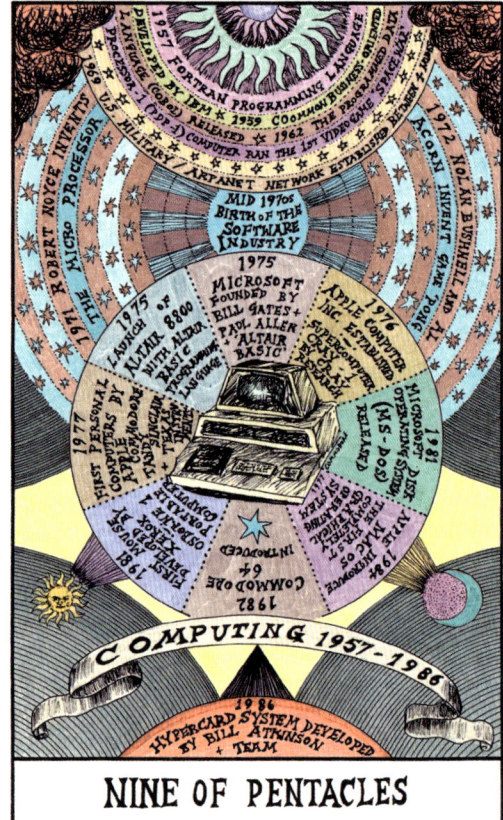

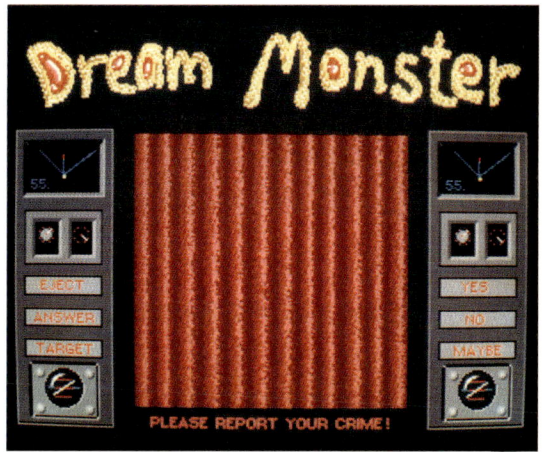

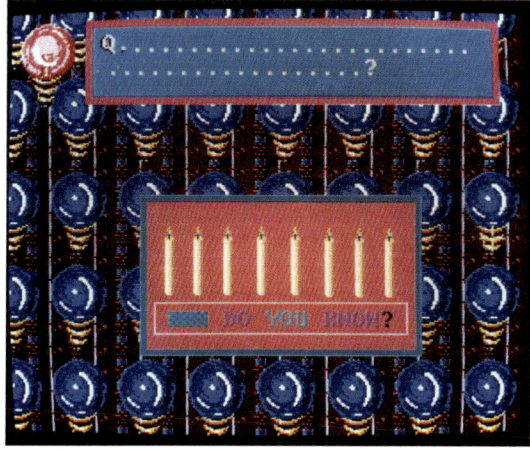

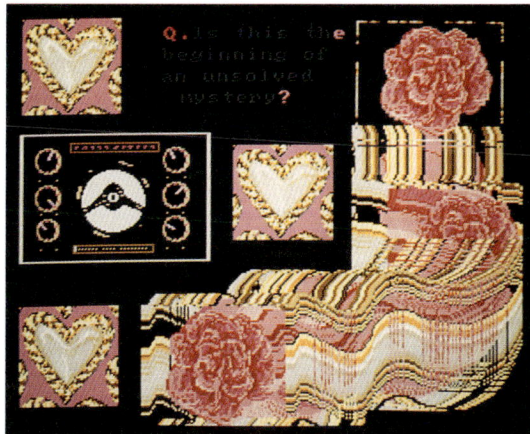

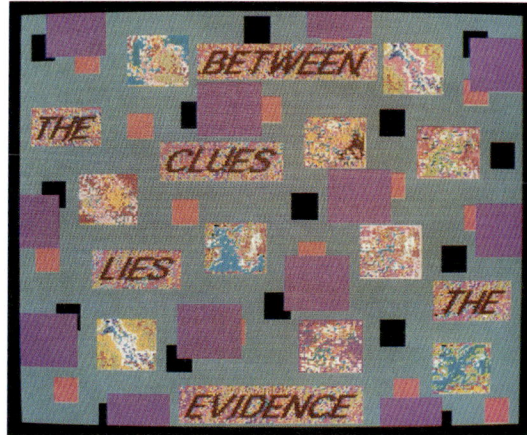

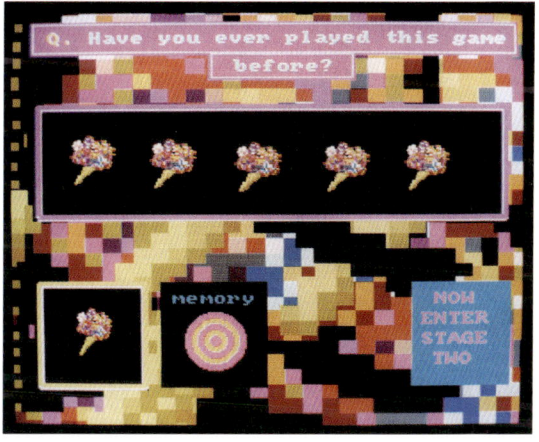

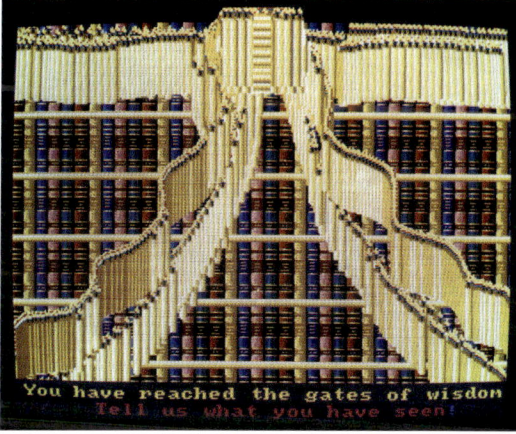

Suzanne Treister, *Fictional Videogame Stills* 1991–2
Top: *Dream Monster*
Middle: *Is This The Beginning Of An Unsolved Mystery?*
Bottom: *Have You Ever Played This Game Before?*

Top: *Do You Know?*
Middle: *Between The Clues Lies The Evidence*
Bottom: *Gates Of Wisdom*

many different disciplines. George Hutchinson, who studied circular causal systems of organisms in relation to their environment, was the only ecologist participant. Gregory Bateson had been developing his theory of schismogenesis in cultural anthropology: a certain human behaviour has repercussions, and the interaction between individuals becomes cumulative; you get a *positive* feedback loop and things escalate out of control, whereas *negative* self-regulating feedback loops, like a central-heating thermostat, produce a self-regulating system. The Macy Conferences wanted to develop society as a self-regulating system. The ecosystem is no longer a self-regulating system controlled by negative feedback. Human intervention has caused positive feedback, sending the system out of control.

Maybe what's particularly helpful from today's ecological perspective is how second-order cybernetics puts the emphasis on the observer in that feedback loop. It's a way of pointing at the observing entity and at how that position is a potentially active one. You're not just observing a closed system: you're part of that ecology, or part of that network or community that you can influence in one way or another. Yes, of course, because we are a crucial part of the ecosystem. Human beings didn't set out to disrupt the equilibrium of the ecosystem in a way that would end in their personal destruction, but we can now see what's happened ecologically as a dangerously positive cybernetic feedback loop that threatens the whole system, which includes us.

Hutchinson saw the ecosystem as a self-regulating system controlled by negative feedback loops, warning that the increase in atmospheric carbon dioxide would lead to a global temperature increase. So using cybernetic modelling to stabilise the ecosystem is an ideal scenario: the re-establishment of negative feedback loops involving ourselves within the total global and universal environment.

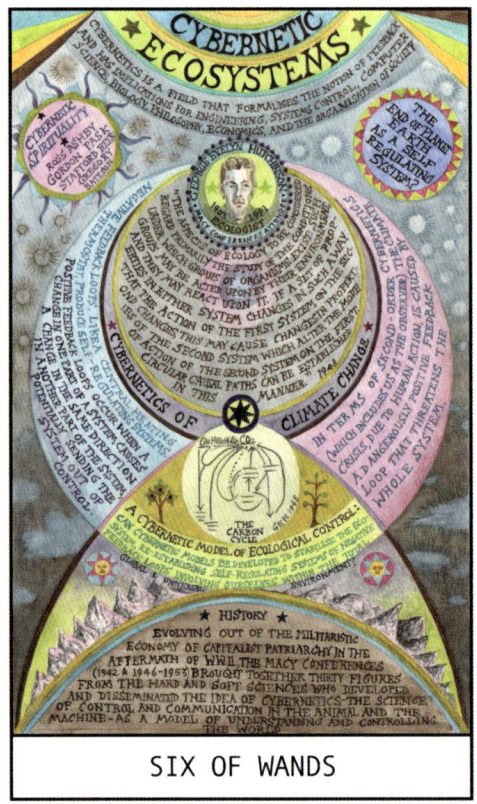

SIX OF WANDS

↑ Suzanne Treister, *HEXEN 5.0 / Tarot / Six of Wands – Cybernetic Ecosystems* 2024

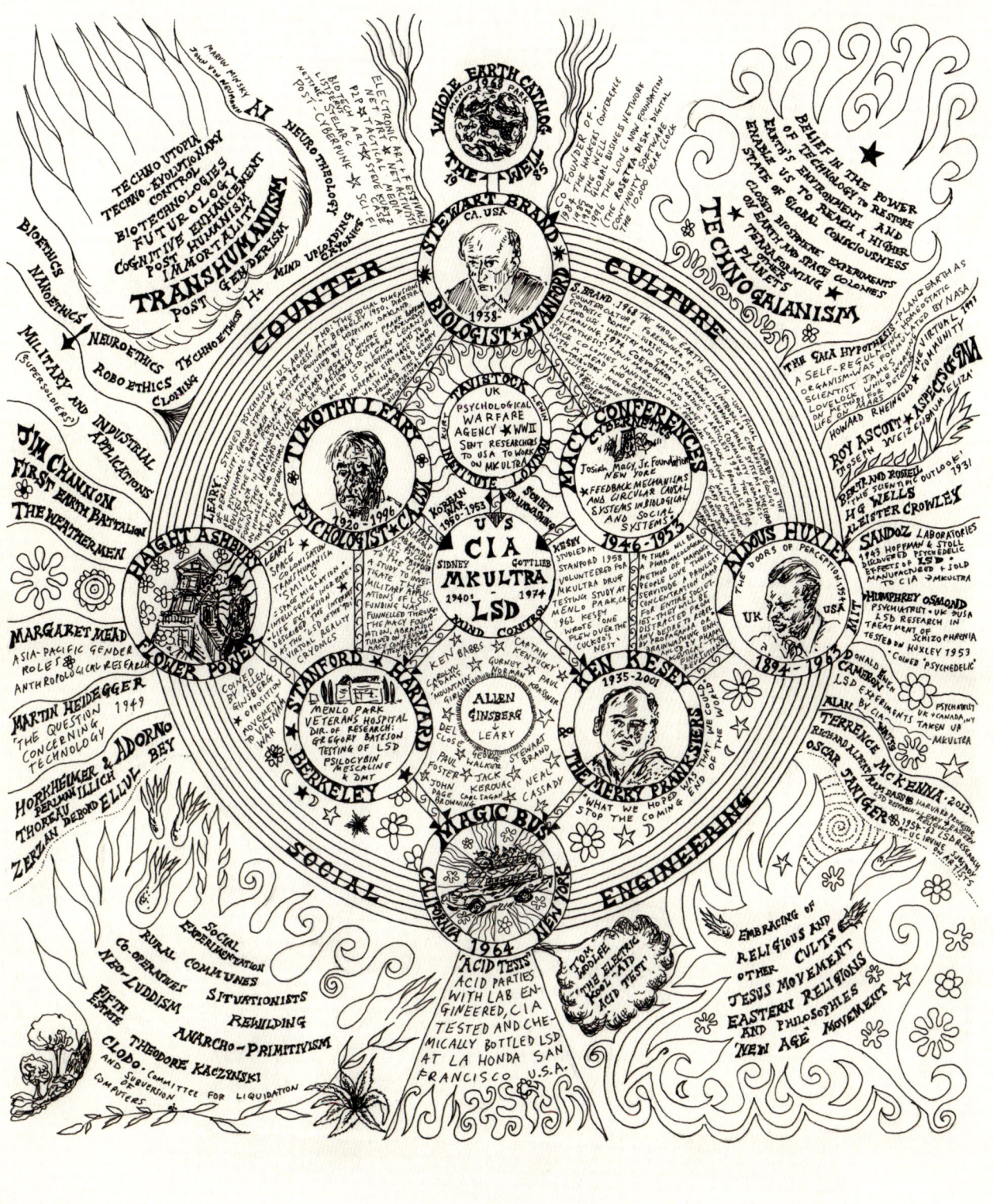

↑ Suzanne Treister, *HEXEN 2.0 / Historical Diagrams / From MKULTRA via the Counterculture to Technogaianism* 2009–11

Notes

Introduction
Val Ravaglia

1   Marshall McLuhan, *Understanding Media: The Extensions of Man*, Berkeley, CA 2013 (1964).
2   Norbert Wiener, *Cybernetics: or, Control and Communication in the Animal and the Machine*, 2nd revised edn, New York 1961.
3   See our p.23
4   François Morellet in *Nove Tendencije 2*, exh. cat., Galerija Suvremene Umjetnosti, Zagreb 1963; quoted in *A Little-Known Story about a Movement, a Magazine, and the Computer's Arrival in Art: New Tendencies and Bit International, 1961–1973*, exh. cat., Neue Galerie Graz am Landesmuseum Joanneum, Graz, and ZKM, Center for Art and Media Karlsruhe, ZKM and The MIT Press, Karlsruhe / Cambridge MA / London 2011, p.28.
5   *Arte Programmata. Arte Cinetica. Opere Moltiplicate. Opera Aperta,* exh. cat., Negozio Olivetti, Milan 1962.
6   Umberto Eco, *The Open Work*, Cambridge, MA 1989 (1964).
7   E.A.T. was founded by artists Robert Rauschenberg and Robert Whitman and engineers Billy Klüver and Fred Waldhauer.

Vera Spencer: Artist Versus Machine
Val Ravaglia

1   Luigi Menabrea, *Sketch of the Analytical Engine invented by Charles Babbage* (1843), translated and annotated by Ada Lovelace, Note A.
2   For a historical perspective on glitch art, see *Glitch: Die Kunst der Störung - The Art of Interference,* exh. cat. Munich 2023. I am indebted to Chris King for his astute interpretation of Spencer's *Artist Versus Machine* as 'early glitch art'.

Electric Worlds
Ming Tiampo

1   Marshall McLuhan, *Understanding Media: The Extensions of Man*, 3rd edn, New York 1964, p.34.
2   Atsuko Tanaka, 'When I make my work', in Ming Tiampo and Kato Mizuho, *Electrifying Art: Atsuko Tanaka, 1954–1968*, exh. cat., Morris and Helen Belkin Art Gallery, Vancouver 2004, p.105.
3   Ming Tiampo, *Gutai: Decentering Modernism*, Chicago 2011.
4   Katō Mizuho, *Tanaka Atsuko to Gutai bijutsu kyōkai* (Atsuko Tanaka and the Gutai Art Association), Osaka 2023; Nakajima Izumi, *Anchi akushon : Nihon sengo kaiga to josei gakka* (Anti-Action: Post-war Japanese art and women artists), Tokyo 2019; Namiko Kunimoto, *The Stakes of Exposure: Anxious Bodies in Postwar Japanese Art*, Minneapolis 2017.
5   Tanaka 2004, p.105.
6   Miyuki Minami, 'The Message of Absence: A Note on Work', in *Tanaka Atsuko: Michi no bi no tankyu, 1954–2000*, exh. cat., Ashiya City Museum of Art & History and Shizuoka Prefectural Museum of Art, Ashiya/Shizuoka 2001, p.158.
7   Sadamasa Motonaga, *A Handbook for Gutai Art*, brochure printed for the *1st Gutai Art Exhibition*, 1955, unpag.
8   Henk Peeters, interviewed by the author, 4 Oct. 2007.
9   For a fuller account of Gutai participation in Nul, see Tiampo 2011 and Atsuo Yamamoto, 'Zero/Gutai/Zero', in *nul=0: The Dutch Nul Group in an International Context*, Rotterdam 2011, pp.76–83.
10   Valerie Hillings, 'Countdown to a new beginning: The Multinational ZERO Network, 1950s–60s', in Hillings (ed.) 2014, p.17.
11   Otto Piene, *Otto Piene: Light Ballet*, exh. cat., Howard Wise, New York 1965, unpag.
12   Ibid.
13   Piene 1961, p.232.
14   For an excellent critical analysis of Piene's *Light Ballets*, see Michelle Y. Kuo, 'Specters', in Otto Piene, João Ribas and Michelle Y. Kuo, *Otto Piene: Lichtballett*, Cambridge, MA 2011, pp.58–77.
15   Isobel Whitelegg, 'Everything Was Connected: Kinetic Art and Internationalism at Signals London, 1964–66', in Jo Applin, Catherine Spencer and Amy Tobin (eds.), *London Art Worlds: Mobile, Contingent, and Ephemeral Networks, 1960–1980*, Philadelphia 2017, pp.21–38.
16   Guy Brett, *Exploding Galaxies: The Art of David Medalla*, London 1995, p.13.
17   Steven Cairns, Fatima Hellberg and Bart van der Heide (eds.), *David Medalla: Parables of Friendship*, Cologne 2022.
18   David Medalla, 'Medalla: New Projects', in Medalla and Keeler (eds.) 1964.
19   A playful erotic joke, *bahag hari* literally translates from the Tagalog as 'the king's loincloth'. The term means rainbow, and is now used to refer to LGBTQ organisations in the Philippines.
20   Brett 1995, p.88.
21   Chanon Kenji Praepipatmongkol, 'David Medalla: Dreams of Sculpture', *Oxford Art Journal*, vol.43, no.3, Dec. 2020, p.355.
22   David Morris, 'Precarious Solidarities: Artists for Democracy in Historical Perspective, Part 1' and 'Part 2', *eflux Journal*, nos.140 and 141, Nov. and Dec. 2023.
23   McLuhan 1964, p.3.

Brion Gysin: Before And After the Dreamachine
Bronac Ferran

1   The Dreamachine's recent transformation into a large-scale immersive experience is described at https://dreamachine.world; further accounts of its ongoing influence include Rick Castro's article 'The Dreamachine, the Execution and the Specter of William Burroughs', *Document*, 25 Aug. 2020, https://www.documentjournal.com/2020/08/the-dreamachine-the-execution-and-the-specter-of-william-s-burroughs/, accessed 16 May 2024.
2   Ian Sommerville was born into a working-class family in northern England in 1940; he won a scholarship to study mathematics at the University of Cambridge and became a computer programmer. He died in 1974 in a car accident, shortly after getting his license, apparently after driving back from sending a telegram to Burroughs, his former lover, wishing him a happy birthday.
3   Burroughs was born in 1914 and was named after his grandfather, William Seward Burroughs I, who held patents for both the world's first calculating machine and the first electric alarm clock in the late nineteenth century. The company the elder Burroughs co-founded was involved in multiple pre-computational, and then computational, innovations of the twentieth century. Yet Burroughs Junior steered clear of any direct role in the business; having shot his common-law wife in the head (allegedly by accident) in 1947, he left the US and became a key figurehead of what came to be known as the 'Beat' or 'Beatnik' generation, fostered by his confessional novel *Junkie* (1953) and *Naked Lunch* (1959). Gysin was born John Clifford Brian Gysin in 1916, in a Canadian military hospital in Buckinghamshire, and spent the first few months of his life living in Streatham, south London. John Grigsby Geiger notes that Gysin, in an autobiographical essay, recounted that his father – who died at the Somme – never saw his son with his eyes open; 'Brion Gysin: his life and times', in José Férez Kuri (ed.), *Brion Gysin: Tuning into the Multimedia Age*, London 2003, p.199.
4   Gysin is cited in Barry Miles, *Ginsberg: A Biography*, New York 1989, p.285.
5   Miles 1989, p.285.
6   Brion Gysin, 'CUT-UPS: a Project for Disastrous Success', in William S. Burroughs and Brion Gysin, *The Third Mind*, New York 1978, p.45.
7   Gysin 1962, pp.31–2.
8   Ian Sommerville, 'Flicker', *Olympia: A Monthly Review from Paris*, no.2, 1962, p.37.
9   Guy Brett, 'Gysin Known and Unknown: The Calligraphic Paintings', in *Brion Gysin: Tuning into the Multimedia Age*, London 2003, p.56, n.8, gives reference as Brion Gysin, October Gallery catalogue, March 1981.
10   *Revue OU Cinquième Saison*, nos.20–1, 1964.
11   Burroughs and Gysin 1978, p.45.
12   Gérard-Georges Lemaire, '23 Stitches Taken by Gérard Georges Lemaire and 2 Points of Order by Brion Gysin', in Burroughs and Gysin 1978, pp.20–1.
13   William S. Burroughs, *The Electronic Revolution*, Bonn 1970, https://www.swissinstitute.net/2001-2006/Images/electronic_revolution.pdf, pp.9, 10, 17 (accessed 2 Sept. 2024).

The City Refracted: Yamaguchi Katsuhiro's Applied Media Theory
Nina Horisaki-Christens

1   While not comprehensive, the most complete compilation of Yamaguchi's writings is Toshino Iguchi (ed.) *Ikiteiru zen'ei: Yamaguchi Katsuhiro hyōron-shū*, Tokyo 2017.
2   Katsuhiro Yamaguchi, 'Katsuhiro Yamaguchi: Experiment on Imaginarium', *ARTiT*, 8 Dec. 2010, https://www.art-it.asia/en/u/admin_ed_feature_e/rijnomatuafxv-1l46bdc/, accessed 5 March 2024.
3   Miwako Tezuka, 'Jikken Kōbō (Experimental Workshop): Avant-Garde Experiments in Japanese Art of the 1950s', PhD thesis, Columbia University, 2005.

No to the Op Art: Visual Research and Programmed Arts of the1960s and 1970s
Darko Fritz

1   See Edward A. Shanken, 'Art in the Information Age: Technology and Conceptual Art', *Leonardo*, vol.35, no.4, 2002, pp.433–8; Christiane Paul (ed.), *A Companion to Digital Art*, Chichester 2016.
2   Darko Fritz, 'Nove tendencije', *Oris*, no.54, 2008, pp.176–91.
3   Ljiljana Kolešnik, 'A Decade of Freedom, Hope and Lost Illusions: Yugoslav Society in the 1960s as a Framework for New Tendencies', *Radovi Instituta za povijest*

umjetnosti, no.34, 2010, pp.221–4, https://www.ipu.hr/content/radovi-ipu/RIPU-34-2010_211-224_Kolesnik.pdf, accessed 20 May 2024.

4   Gruppo N (1959–64) members were Alberto Biasi, Manfredo Massironi, Ennio Chiggio, Toni Costa and Edoardo Landi.

5   François Morellet, untitled, in *Nove tendencije*, exh. cat., Gallery of Contemporary Art, Zagreb 1961.

6   Umberto Eco, *Opera aperta: Forma e indeterminazione nelle poetiche contemporanee*, Milan 1962. Translated by Anna Cancogni as *The Open Work*, Cambridge, MA 1989.

7   François Morellet, 'Pour une peinture expérimentale programmée', in *Groupe de recherche d'art visuel* (pamphlet), Paris 1962, unpag.

8   Ibid.

9   Matko Meštrović, untitled, in *Nove tendencije 2*, exh. cat., Gallery of Contemporary Art, Zagreb 1963. Subsequently published under the title 'Ideologija Novih Tendencija' in the book *Matko Meštrović: Od pojedinačnog općem*, Zagreb 1967, 2005. Translation author's own. Also see, by the same author, the essay 'Scijentifikacija kao uvjet humanizacije' (1963), in *Od pojedinačnog općem*, Zagreb 1967, 2005.

10   Max Kozloff, 'American Painting During the Cold War', *Artforum*, vol.11, no.9, May 1973.

11   Frances Stonor Saunders, 'Modern art was CIA "weapon"', *Independent*, 22 Oct. 1995, https://www.independent.co.uk/news/world/modern-art-was-cia-weapon-1578808.html, acccessed 13 May 2024.

12   For computer visual research in NT, see Darko Fritz, 'Amnesia International', in *I am still Alive*, Zagreb 2000; 'Amnesia International: Early computer art and the Tendencies movement', in *Bitomatik – Art practice in the time of information/media domination*, Novi Sad 2004, pp.23–30; Herbert W. Franke, 'Das Wunder von Zagreb', in Thobias Hoffman and Rasmus Kleine (eds.), *Die Neuen Tendenzen – Eine europäische Künstlerbewegung 1961–1973*, exh. cat., Museum für Konkrete Kunst, Ingoldstadt 2006; Cristoph Klütsch, 'Computer Graphic-Aesthetic Experiments between Two Cultures', *Leonardo*, vol.40, no.5, 2007, pp.421–5; *A Little-Known Story about a Movement, a Magazine, and the Computer's Arrival in Art: New Tendencies and Bit International, 1961–1973*, exh. cat., NeueGalerie Graz am Landesmuseum Joanneum, Graz, and ZKM, Center for Art and Media Karlsruhe, ZKM and The MIT Press, Karlsruhe / Cambridge, MA / London 2011; and Armin Medosch, *New Tendencies: Art at the Threshold of the Information Revolution (1971–1978)*, Cambridge, MA 2016.

13   Matko Meštrović, 'The situation of nt', *Bit International*, no.3, 1968, p.43. Published in Croatian and English (trans. from the Croatian by Vilim Crlenjak).

14   Radoslav Putar, untitled, in *tendencije 4*, exh. cat., Gallery of Contemporary Art, Zagreb 1970, unpag. Published in both Croatian and English translation (six translators are credited for the catalogue as a whole: Sonja Bašić, Nikolina Bićanić, Zeljko Bujas, Vanda Radetić, Josip Rirrig and Viktor Šafranek).

15   Enzo Mari, 'Nouvelle Tendance: Ethique ou Poétique', in *tendencije 4*, 1970.

16   Gordon Hyde, Jonathan Benthall and Gustav Metzger, 'Zagreb Manifesto', *Studio International*, June 1969, p.259, republished in *Bit International*, no.7, 1971, p.4.

17   In association with various IT experts, Metzger calculated and programmed the rhythm and patterns of destruction of five big panels to be placed in an urban environment.

18   Darko Fritz, 'International Networks of Early Digital Arts', in Paul 2016, pp.46–68, and Christoph Klütsch, *The Summer 1968 in London and Zagreb: Starting or End Point for Computer Art? Proceedings of the 5th conference on Creativity & Cognition*, London 2005, pp.109–17.

19   Robert Mallary, 'TRAN 2 - a Computer Graphics Program to Generate Sculpture', *Bit International*, no.7, 1971, pp.118–27.

20   'Constructivism belongs to the past, its content corresponding to the palaeocybernetic age is computer art': Waldemar Cordeiro, 'Analogical and/or Digital Art', in *t-5, Rational and Irrational in Visual Research Today*, symposium reader, Galleries of the City of Zagreb, 2 June 1973, unpag.

21   'A straight line from the midpoint of the left side of the page through the center toward the midpoint of the right side': Sol LeWitt, 'Wall drawing', *tendencije 5*, exh. cat., Gallery of Contemporary Art, Zagreb 1973, unpag.

22   Darko Fritz, 'Notions of the Program in 1960s Art: Concrete, Computer-generated and Conceptual Art', address at the symposium *Art-oriented programming 2*, Amphithéâtre Richelieu, Sorbonne, Paris, 20 Oct. 2007. Published as 'La notion de « programme » dans l'art des années 1960 – art concret, art par ordinateur et art conceptuel', in David-Olivier Lartigaud (ed.), Art++, Orléans 2011, pp.26–39, and Darko Fritz, 'Notions of the Program in 1960s Art – Concrete, Computer-generated and Conceptual Art / Program jako koncepcja w sztuce lat 60. XX w. – sztuka konkretna, komputerowa i konceptualna', in Ryszard W. Kluszczyński (ed.), *The Art+Science Meeting*, Gdansk 2016, online; 'Pojam programa u umjetnosti 1960-ih', in Jadranka Pintarić and Jasna Jakšić (eds.), *Suglasja i razlike: Nove tendencije 60 godina poslije*, Zagreb 2022, pp.88 –103.

23   Radoslav Putar, untitled, in *tendencije 5*, 1973, unpag.

24   Frieder Nake, 'The Separation of Hand and Head', in *t-5, Rational and Irrational in Visual Research Today*, symposium reader, Galleries of the City of Zagreb, 2 June 1973, unpag.

25   In *tendencije 5*, 1973, and audio archive of the symposium *t-5, Rational and Irrational in Visual Research Today*, Zagreb, 2 June 1973.

26   For example, in the general survey *Art since 1900* (Hal Foster and others, 3rd edn, London 2016), NT is not mentioned. There is a tiny reference to GRAV in the significantly recontextualising chapter entitled 'French Conceptualist Painting'.

François Morellet
Val Ravaglia

1   https://www.tate.org.uk/tate-etc/issue-16-summer-2009/65-38-21-4-72

GRAV: Visual Research and the Politics of Participation
Odessa Warren

1   Frank Popper, 'Artistic Groups, Collective Creation and Spectator Participation', in *Groupe de Recherche d'Art Visuel (GRAV): Stratégies de Participation – 1960–1968*, exh. cat., Le Magasin – Centre national d'art contemporain, Grenoble 1998, p.18.

2   Ibid., p.17.

3   Ibid., p.18.

4   Valerie Hillings, '"It is Forbidden Not to Participate": Le Parc and the Groupe de Recherche d'Art Visuel (1960–1968)', in *Julio Le Parc*, New York 2022, p.367.

5   Marion Hohlfeldt, 'Strategies for Participation: The Groupe de recherche d'art visual (GRAV) under the sign of games', in *Groupe de Recherche d'Art Visuel (GRAV): Stratégies de Participation – 1960–1968*, 1998, p.37

6   Popper 1998, p.18.

7   Hohlfeldt 1998, p.37.

8   Umberto Eco, 'L'informale come opera aperta', *Il Verri*, no.3, June 1961, pp.98-127.

9   Ibid., p.37.

10   Ibid., p.38.

11   Hillings 2022, p.370.

12   Hohlfeldt 1998, p.44.

13   Ibid., p.39.

14   Hillings 2022, p.368.

15   Ibid., p.373.

16   Larry Busbea, 'Kineticism-Spectacle-Environment', *October*, no.144, Spring 2013, pp.92–114.

17   Hillings 2022, p.374.

Chromointerferent Environment: A Work in the Making
Carlos Cruz Delgado

1   Carlos Cruz-Diez, 'Laberinto de Descondicionamiento', manuscript, Paris 1965; published in Alfredo Boulton, *Cruz-Diez*, Caracas 1975, p.69.

2   Ibid.

Dialogues with the Machines: Early Computer and Cybernetic Art
Tina Rivers Ryan

1   J. R. Pierce, 'Portrait of the Machine as a Young Artist', *Playboy*, June 1965, p.184. The potential for the computer to become a creative medium was extolled by Allon Schoener, then assistant director of the Jewish Museum, New York, in the pages of *Art in America* the following year. Taking a broader historical view, Schoener justified the turn towards the computer in art as a reflection of the transformation of the means of production in the electronic age; Allon Schoener, '2066 and All That', *Art in America*, March–April 1966, p.40.

2   For more on the shows *Software* and *Information*, and their relation to computer theory (in the form of 'systems aesthetics'), see, for example, Eve Meltzer, 'The Dream of the Information World', *Oxford Art Journal*, vol.29, no.1, 2006, pp.117–35; Luke Skrebowski, 'All Systems Go: Recovering Hans Haacke's Systems Art', *Grey Room*, no.30, Winter 2008, pp.54–83; and Edward A. Shanken, 'The House that Jack Built: Jack Burnham's Concept of "Software" as a Metaphor for Art', in Roy Ascott (ed.), *Reframing Consciousness: Art, Mind and Technology*, Exeter 1991, pp.156–61.

3   Grant D. Taylor, 'The Soulless Usurper: Reception and Criticism of Early Computer Art', in Hannah Higgins and Douglas Kahn (eds.), *Mainframe Experimentalism: Early Computing and the Foundations of the Digital Arts*, Berkeley, CA 2012, p.18. Taylor's own book delves more deeply into the history of

early computer art and its reception; see Grant D. Taylor, *When the Machine Made Art: The Troubled History of Computer Art*, New York 2014.

4   The Howard Wise show followed the very first exhibition of computer art, held in Germany, by only a few weeks. In February 1965, Georg Nees presented his own computer-generated images at the Technische Hochschule Stuttgart; Nees again presented his work, alongside that of Frieder Nake, in November that same year, at Stuttgart's Galerie Wendelin Niedlich.

5   Making reference to the work of both Jonathan Crary and the nineteenth-century invention of the stereoscope, Zabet Patterson has discussed the significance of Julesz's experiments, which proved that 'stereopsis can and does occur in the complete absence of monocular form': 'Perception, for Julesz, was revealed as a process that occurs without our conscious volition. Recognition was displaced onto a secondary plane, removing the question of memory that had been important to the study of contour. Julesz was able to demonstrate that without any training and without our input, vision just happens: it constitutes a "rapid, effortless, and spontaneous process".' Zabet Patterson, *Peripheral Vision: Bell Labs, the S-C 4020, and the Origins of Computer Art*, Cambridge, MA 2015, pp.39, 41.

6   A. Michael Noll, 'Howard Wise Gallery Show of Digital Art and Patterns (1965): A 50th Anniversary Memoir', unpublished manuscript, 21 Aug. 2014, p.2. The designs were produced using an IBM 7094 Digital Computer, which output its data on a General Dynamics SC-4020 Microfilm Plotter.

7   The show also included eight stereographic works, which when viewed with special polarised glasses would make two images merge and appear three-dimensional.

8   A. Michael Noll, 'The Beginnings of Computer Art in the United States: A Memoir', *Leonardo*, vol.27, no.1, 1994, pp.40–41.

9   Howard Wise Gallery, *Computer-Generated Pictures*, press release, Smithsonian American Art Museum, Archives of American Art, Howard Wise Gallery Records, 1965, pp.1–2. The question of who, or what, had 'created' Noll's work ultimately became a bureaucratic one: having filed a patent for his work *Gaussian-Quadratic*, Noll had to go to great lengths to explain that, whereas the work was partially based on randomness and produced with the help of a computer, he, the artist, ultimately had created the computer programme and edited the work (his patent was ultimately granted).

10   A. Michael Noll, 'Computer-Generated Pictures', unpublished, 1965, Harvard University Art Museums Archives, Howard Wise Gallery Records, p.2.

11   This description relies in part on that of Richard Kostelanetz, though by looking at reproductions of the work, it appears his account of which panel is on top of which has them reversed. Richard Kostelanetz, 'Tsaibernetics', in *The Cybernetic Sculpture Environment of Tsai Wen-Ying*, exh. cat., The Center Art and Science Foundation, New York 1997, p.214.

12   The importance of the strobe is underscored by a promotional image for the Wise show that features Tsai standing behind his sculptures, cradling a strobe light in his arms.

13   Cited in Kostelanetz 1997, p.213.

14   Later, as a fellow at Massachusetts Institute of Technology (MIT), Tsai would be visited regularly by Dr Harold Edgerton,

inventor of the strobe, who himself used the device to create artistic photographs of bodies in motion.

15   The technology of Tsai's work was complicated enough to prompt the gallery to explain it on a handout: 'The strobes flash at regular intervals. When the rate of the flashes is the same as the rate of the vibrations of the rods, i.e. 30 per second, the motion of the rods appears fixed, and they appear to be stationary. But they appear to be in the shape of a harmonic curve, and not a straight line as would normally be expected. When the rate of the strobe flashes is altered to slightly slower or greater than the rate of the rods' vibrations (30 per second) then the rods appear to be slowly undulating, like the tentacles of a sea anemone under water. The greater the rate of the strobe flashes deviates from the constant harmonic motion of the rods, the more rapidly the rods appear to be moving and the more excited they seem to become.' Howard Wise Gallery, *Tsai: Cybernetic Sculptures*, 1968, Smithsonian Institution, American Art Museum, Archives of American Art, Howard Wise Gallery Records.

16   Wen-Ying Tsai and Frank T. Turner, 'Report on Collaboration', 1968, Getty Research Institute, Experiments in Art and Technology Archives, Box 24, 94003, 4MSH, folder 16, EAT Exhibitors @ MOMA. Turner's contribution earned the second-place prize, and the work was shown not only at *Some More Beginnings*, but also at its pendant exhibition, *The Machine As Seen at the End of the Mechanical Age*, at MoMA.

17   While such actions appeared to alter the movement of the sculptures, 'in reality your activity does not alter the motion of the rods or plates', the gallery explained. 'These are in a constant and unvarying rate of harmonic motion ... But you are varying the rate of the strobe flashes (one flash lasts about one millionth of a second)' (underline in original). Howard Wise Gallery, *Tsai: Cybernetic Sculptures*, 1968.

18   On this exhibition, see Rainer Usselmann, 'The Dilemma of Media Art: Cybernetic Serendipity at the ICA London', *Leonardo*, vol.36, no.5, 2003, pp.389–96, and Maria Fernandez, 'Detached from HiStory: Jasia Reichardt and Cybernetic Serendipity', *Art Journal*, vol.67, no.3, Fall 2008, pp.6–23.

19   Jasia Reichardt, *The Computer in Art*, London 1971, p.9.

20   In fact, Reichardt claimed that 'cybernetic sculptures such as those by Tsai are the extension or bridge between computer and kinetic art'; Reichardt 1971, p.35.

21   Reichardt 1971, pp.34–5.

22   György Kepes, 'Rhythmic Vitality—The Art of Tsai (1971)', in *The Cybernetic Sculpture Environment of Tsai Wen-Ying*, exh. cat., The Center Art and Science Foundation, New York 1997, p.171.

23   The site is now defunct, but the original URL was www.pathfinder.com/twep/artslink/Tsai

Analivia Cordeiro: The Computer as Choreographer
Kira Wainstein

1   Mariola V. Alvarez, 'Machine Bodies: Performing Abstraction and Brazilian Art', *Arts*, 2020, vol.9, no.1, p.9.

2   Peter Weibel, 'Analivia Cordeiro: From Choreography to Code', in *Analivia Cordeiro: From Body to Code*, exh. cat., ZKM Center for Art and Media, Karlsruhe 2023, p.16.

3   Analivia Cordeiro, 'Brushstrokes', in Analivia Cordeiro (ed.), *Analivia Cordeiro: Human Motion – Impression/Expression*, 2nd edn, São Paulo 2018, p.9.

4   Cordeiro 2018, p.10.

5   Alvarez 2020, pp.6–11.

6   *Analivia Cordeiro: From Body to Code*, 2023, p.166.

7   Analivia Cordeiro, 'Computer Dance', https://www.analivia.com.br/computer-dance-3/, accessed 11 April 2024.

8   *Analivia Cordeiro: From Body to Code*, 2023, p.206.

9   Ibid, p.248.

10   Analivia Cordeiro, 'Nota-Anna: An Expression Visualization System of the Human Body Movements', in *Analivia Cordeiro: From Body to Code*, 2023, p.60.

Meaning Generators:
Harold Cohen and AARON
Val Ravaglia

1   Catherine Mason, 'Infinite Variety: Harold Cohen and Cybernetics in the 1960s', in *Harold Cohen*, exh. cat., Gazelli, London 2024, pp.100-3.

2   Harold Cohen, 'Conversation: Harold Cohen & Becky Cohen. La Jolla, California, March, 1995', in *The Robotic Artist: AARON in Living Color. Harold Cohen at the Computer Museum, 1995*, exh. cat., The Computer Museum, Boston, MA, April-May 1995, p.8.

3   Ibid., p.10.

The Patchy History of Artists
and Electronics
Sarah Cook

Data availability: This chapter is an overview and re-analysis of existing data and therefore all data underlying this study is cited in the references. An extended version of this text is available from the author.

1   Friedrich A. Kittler, *Gramophone, Film, Typewriter*, Stanford, CA 1999, p.3.

2   Friedrich A. Kittler, interview with the author, published posthumously in Sarah Cook (ed.), *Information, Documents of Contemporary Art*, London and Cambridge, MA 2016, p.172.

3   Most quoted as the indispensable tome for this history is Edward A. Shanken, *Art and Electronic Media*, London 2009. There is a telling review of it written by Régine Debatty, to which Shanken has added his comments: https://we-make-money-not-art.com/book_review_art_and_electronic/, accessed 8 May 2024.

4   Caroline Seck Langill, introduction to *Shifting Polarities*, https://www.fondation-langlois.org/html/e/page.php?NumPage=1949, accessed 8 May 2024. Langill's project, *Shifting Polarities: Exemplary Works of Canadian Electronic Media Art Produced Between 1970 and 1991*, drew from the CR+D archives and library at the Daniel Langlois Foundation in order to establish a potential canon of electronic media art. Interviews with the artists can be found at https://www.fondation-langlois.org/html/e/page.php?NumPage=1928, accessed 8 May 2024.

5   Regarding the telecoms aesthetic in art, perhaps this is all the more prevalent with ASCII and the dot matrix printer, or the fax machine. Consider the works in *Electric*

Dreams by Waldemar Cordeiro, or Edward Zajec, and, later, Roy Ascott's *La Plissure du Texte* (1983).

6   Quoted in Uwe Schütte, *Kraftwerk: Future Music from Germany*, London 2020, p.108.

7   Leslie Mezei with Arnold Rockmann, 'The Electronic Computer as an Artist', in *Canadian Art*, vol.21, no.6, 1964, pp.365–7.

8   'Leslie Mezei' (Toronto, July 1975), https://www.atariarchives.org/artist/sec7.php, accessed 8 May 2024.

9   Jasia Reichardt, 'The Computer in Art', talk at *REFRESH! The First International Conference on the Histories of Media Art, Science and Technology*, Banff, 2005, Media Histories Archive, http://95.216.75.113:8080/xmlui/handle/123456789/386, accessed 8 May 202X.

10   Anon (some have guessed this is by Peter Schjeldahl), 'VIEW INTO FUTURE IN COMPUTER ART', *New York Times*, 5 Dec. 1974, https://www.nytimes.com/1972/12/05/archives/view-into-future-in-computer-art-national-endowment-unit-holds.html, accessed 8 May 2024.

11   There is a video showing a demo of the Rutt/Etra on the website of the Daniel Langlois Foundation: https://www.fondation-langlois.org/html/e/page.php?NumPage=456, accessed 8 May 2024. The Vasulkas also had a Putney RCS3 synthesiser from 1970 working with the Alternative Media Center in New York.

12   Along with Paul Sharits, Tony Conrad, Hollis Frampton and others. See Woody Vasulka and Peter Weibel (eds.), *Buffalo Heads: Media Study, Media Practice, Media Pioneers, 1973–1990*, Cambridge, MA 1997.

13   *V_A_S_U_L_K_A*, exh. cat., National Gallery of Iceland, Reykjavik 2014, p.29.

14   Lucinda Furlong, 'Notes Toward a History of Image-Processed Video: Steina and Woody Vasulka;', *Afterimage*, Dec. 1963, pp.12–17, https://monoskop.org/images/1/18/Furlong_Lucinda_1983_Notes_Towards_a_History_of_Image-processed_Video_Steina_and_Woody_Vasulka.pdf, accessed 8 May 2024.

15   The catalogue for the 1992 *Ars Electronica* festival is online at https://webarchive.ars.electronica.art/en/archives/festival_archive/festival_catalogs/festival_catalog.asp%3FiProjectID=8893.html (accessed 8 May 2024) and is an incredibly rich resource.

16   The list of instruments is at https://webarchive.ars.electronica.art/en/archives/festival_archive/festival_catalogs/festival_artikel.asp%3FiProjectID=8858.html, accessed 8 May 2024.

17   See, for example, *Open Circuits: An International Conference on the Future of Television*, held at The Museum of Modern Art on January 23 and 25, 1974. This event led to the expansion of MoMA's film department to take on video as well, as described in this press release: https://www.moma.org/momaorg/shared/pdfs/docs/press_archives/5491/releases/MOMA_1977_0030_29.pdf, accessed 5 June 2024.

18   Steven Shaviro has written about the music video as cultural and artistic form for over twenty years, with articles in mainstream and academic press, such as 'Supa Dupa Fly: Black Women as Cyborgs in Hiphop Videos', *Quarterly Review of Film and Video*, vol.22, no.2, April–June 2005, pp.169–79. See, also, his book *Digital Music Videos*, New Brunswick, NJ 2017.

19   There are too many references to the history of video and digital art to list here, but the more recent scholarship on media art preservation is a good place to start: for example, through the archives of the Time-based Media and Digital Art working group at the Smithsonian, https://www.si.edu/tbma/, accessed 8 May 2024.

20   In 2023 SIGGRAPH held a retrospective of female digital artists including both Truckenbrod and Veeder: see https://history.siggraph.org/artwork/rebecca-allen-copper-frances-giloth-darcy-gerbarg-colette-bangert-joan-r-truckenbrod-barbara-nessim-jane-veeder-retrospective-of-female-digital-art-pioneers/, accessed 9 May 2024.

21   *Leonardo Electronic Almanac*, vol.13, no.4, April 2005, http://www.catherinemason.co.uk/wp-content/uploads/2020/11/RE-SEARCHING-OUR-ORIGINS-Leonardo-Electronic-Almanac-Special-Issue-April-2005-co-edited-with-Paul-Brown.pdf, accessed 9 May 2024. See also Mason's important chapter 'The Routes toward British Computer Arts: The Role of Cultural Institutions in the Pioneering Period' in Charlie Gere et al (eds.), *White Heat and Cold Logic: British Computer Art 1960–1980*, Cambridge, MA 2009. Mason's research points out that cutbacks in arts education also meant artists working in the burgeoning computer graphics industry; this history is also addressed in Andy Darley's chapter 'From Abstraction to Simulation: Notes on the History of Computer Imaging' in Philip Hayward, *Culture, Technology and Creativity in the Late Twentieth Century*, London 1990, pp.39–64.

22   Charlie Gere, in his introduction to Gere and others (eds) 2009: 'In "PICASO at Middlesex Polytechnic" (chapter 26) John Vince describes the genesis of one of the first dedicated graphics programs, PICASO, which he developed at Middlesex Polytechnic in the early 1970s, while, in From "0 to 1: Art Made between the Times of Having and Not Having a Computer" (chapter 27) Brian Reffin Smith writes about using and not using computers in art at various institutions in the period. Jeremy Gardiner's "The Aftermath of Early Computer Art: A Painter's Odyssey" (chapter 28) describes Gardiner's attempts to make art using computers in the context of ebbing support and increasing resistance in the institutions where he was studying, particularly the Royal College of Art, despite the presence of important, pioneering figures such as Patrick Purcell and Brian Reffin Smith.'

23   For more on this history, see Michael Century, *Northern Sparks: Innovation, Technology Policy and the Arts in Canada from Expo 67 to the Internet Age*, Cambridge, MA 2022.

24   Caroline Seck Langill, 'New Media Art and Industry, a Critical Relationship', in Adam Lauder (ed.), *Variable Conditions: Para-computational Arts in Canada, 1965–1995*, Montreal 2023, p.180.

25   The exhibition *Signals: How Video Transformed the World* (MoMA, New York, 2023), curated by Stuart Comer and Michelle Kuo, covers this comprehensively.

26   Les Levine, 'Information Fall-out', in *Software: Information technology: its new meaning for art*, exh. cat., Jewish Museum, New York 1970, https://monoskop.org/images/3/31/Software_Information_Technology_Its_New_Meaning_for_Art_catalogue.pdf, accessed 5 June 2024.

27   See, for example, the work of Stafford Beer, a systems theorist who applied cybernetics to management, and his landmark book *Platform for Change* (1975).

28   Langill 2023.

29   Marie Vicet, 'The French Telematic Magazine *Art Accès* (1984–1987)', *Arts*, vol.11, no.6, 2022, p.112, https://doi.org/10.3390/arts11060112, accessed 9 May 2024.

30   https://www.youtube.com/watch?v=besJaZyPqS8&t=14s, 4 October 1965.

31   John G. Hanhardt (and Gregory Zinman), 'Interview of Artist Stephen (Steve) Beck', Smithsonian American Art Museum, https://americanart.si.edu/research/paik/resources/beck, accessed 5 June 2024.

32   Ibid.

33   This idea was mentioned to me by Catherine Richards, an artist who worked for Canada's National Research Council and was a founding member of the bioapparatus project.

34   For more on this, see Pamela M. Lee, *Think Tank Aesthetics: Midcentury Modernism, the Cold War and the Neoliberal Present*, Cambridge, MA 2020, and her writings about the E.A.T. 9 Evenings: 'Theatre and Engineering' (1966) in her book *Chronophobia: On Time in the Art of the 1960s*, Cambridge, MA 2004.

35   For more on computers and automation, see Ashley Scarlett, 'Excavating the Origins of Network Art in Canada: Leslie Mezei, Peter Milojevic, and Computer Art Journalism of the 1960s and 1970s', in Lauder 2023. The magazine *Computerese* (edited by Bill Perry, from 1981) was published 'online' on Telidon Vista. For the much later debates about the magazine *Make*, inheritor of this tradition, see Garnet Hertz, *Art + DIY Electronics*, Cambridge, MA 2023.

36   Marshall McLuhan and Quentin Fiore, *The Medium is the Massage*, London 1967.

37   Preface to Kittler 1999. There are two different translations of this – the one published in *October* (no.41, 1987) and the one published in the later, full translation of the book.

38   Val Ravaglia, email responding to a query from artist Rebecca Allen, 28 February 2024.

Progress and Harmony for Mankind: Innovation and Commercialisation at Expo '70
Kira Wainstein

1   Midori Yoshimoto, 'Expo '70 and Japanese Art: Dissonant Voices An Introduction and Commentary', *Review of Japanese Culture and Society*, vol.23, 2011, p.1.

2   *United States Pavilion Japan World Exposition Osaka 1970*, guidebook, https://www.state.gov/wp-content/uploads/2019/04/Osaka-Expo-1970-Guidebook.pdf, accessed 11 April 2024

3   Sheila D. Muller, *Dutch Art: An Encyclopedia*, New York 1997, p.368.

4   Sean Williams, 'Osaka Expo '70: The Promise and Reality of a Spherical Sound Stage', paper presented at *InSONIC2015: Aesthetics of Spatial Audio in Sound, Music and Sound Art*, Karlsruhe, Germany, 27–28 November 2015.

5   Matt Williams, '1– 6 March 2020, Ahmedabad, Gujarat, India', in Paul Purgas (ed.), *Subcontinental Synthesis: Electronic Music at the National Institute of Design, India 1969–1972*, London 2024, p.95.

6   Yuriko Furuhata, 'Multimedia Environments and Security Operations: Expo

'70 as a Laboratory of Governance', *Grey Room*, no.54, 2014, p.65.

7   Haryū Ichirō and Ignacio Adriasola, 'Expo '70 as the Ruins of Culture (1970)', *Review of Japanese Culture and Society*, vol.23, 2011, pp.48–9.

8   Machiko Kusahara, 'A Turning Point in Japanese Avant-garde Art, 1964–1970', in Andreas Broeckmann and Gunalan Nadarajan (eds.), *Place Studies in Art, Media, Science and Technology: Historical Investigations on the Sites and the Migration of Knowledge*, Weimar 2008, p.139.

9   Furuhata 2014, p.64.

10   Tjebbe van Tijen and Nic Tummers, *Progress and Harmony for Mankind*, self-published 1969.

11   Hiroko Ikegami, '"World Without Boundaries?": E.A.T. and the Pepsi Pavilion at Expo '70, Osaka', *Review of Japanese Culture and Society*, vol.23, 2011, p.174.

12   Ikegami 2011, p.182. Carl Tomkins, 'Outside Art', *Pavilion*, New York 1972, p.162.

13   Akasegawa Genpei and Reiko Tomii, 'A Redevelopment Proposal for the Expo '70 Site (1970)', *Review of Japanese Culture and Society*, vol.23, Dec. 2011, pp.148–9. Translated into English by Reiko Tomii.

Samia Halaby: Kinetic Abstraction
Odessa Warren

1   Nathalie Handal, 'Crossing the Submarine: A Life in Color and Strokes', in *In Conversation with Samia Halaby*, exh. cat., Ayyam Gallery, Dubai 2008, p.5.

2   Ibid.

3   Maymanah Farhat, *Samia Halaby: Five Decades of Painting and Innovation*, London 2014, p.54.

4   Ibid., p.57.

5   Handal 2008, p.20.

6   Farhat 2014, p.59.

7   Handal 2008, p.28.

8   Elliot Josephine Leila Reichert (ed.), *Samia Halaby: Centers of Energy*, Munich 2024, p.30.

9   Samia Halaby, 'My History with Digital Art', in Elliot Josephine Leila Reichert (ed.), *Samia Halaby: Centres of Energy*, Munich 2024, p.135.

10   Ibid., p.136.

11   Reichert (ed.) 2024, p.19.

12   Halaby 2024, p.144.

13   Ibid., p.146.

14   Farhat 2014, p.17.

15   Halaby 2024, p.140.

16   Ibid., p.138.

Light as Material and Medium: Liliane Lijn
Bronac Ferran

1   Marshall McLuhan, *Understanding Media: The Extensions of Man*, New York 1964, p.8.

2   Liliane Lijn, 'The Code of Form', *Upstart Magazine*, no.2, 1978.

3   Liliane Lijn, 'Poetry Language Code Industry', in Bronac Ferran (ed.), *Visualise: Making Art in Context*, Cambridge 2013, pp.36-45 (40).

4   Lijn 1978.

5   Both organisations were testing the potential of copper wires for use in tele-communication networks, a development eventually superseded by high-speed fiber-optic systems.

6   Lijn 1978.

Tatsuo Miyajima: Light, Movement, Space
Odessa Warren

1   Michael Auping, 'Theatre of Time', in *Counter Pieces*, exh. cat., Galerie der Stadt Stutttgart 1991, p.28.

2   Ibid., p.29.

3   Ibid.

4   Ibid.

5   Rachel Kent, 'Tatsuo Miyajima: Connect with Everything', Museum of Contemporary Art Australia (MCA), 3 November 2016, https://www.mca.com.au/stories-and-ideas/tatsuo-miyajima-connect-everything-curatorial-essay, accessed 5 June 2024.

6   Ibid.

7   'Tatsuo Miyajima in conversation with Bernhard Bürgi', in *Tatsuo Miyajima*, exh. cat., Berliner Kunsthaller Zürich and Oktagon Verlag, München & Stuttgart 1993, p.27.

8   Kent 2016.

9   Auping 1991, p.20.

10   Kent 2016.

11   Ibid.

12   'Tatsuo Miyajima in conversation with Bernhard Bürgi', 1993, p.27.

13   Auping 1991, p.42.

Works are listed alphabetically by artist, and chronologically within each artist section. Measurements of works are given in centimetres, height before width and depth. All information was correct at the time of going to press.

REBECCA ALLEN (b.1953)
Steps 1982
Video, shown digitally; colour, sound
2 min, 30 sec
Courtesy of the artist

Musique Non Stop 1986
Video, shown digitally; colour, sound
4 min, 10 sec
Courtesy of the artist

MARINA APOLLONIO (b.1940)
Circular Dynamics 6S+S II 1968–1970
Dinamica Circolare 6S+S II
Silkscreen on lacquered wood, motor
102 diam.
Tate. Presented by the artist 2024

MANUEL BARBADILLO (1929–2003)
Untitled (Cuadro Numero) (c.1968–72)
Impact print on fanfold paper
36.2 × 36.2
The Anne and Michael Spalter Digital Art Collection

ALBERTO BIASI (b.1937)
Light Prisms. Spectral Kinetic Mesh 1966
Light Prisms. Cinereticolo spettrale
Mobile crystal prisms; acrylic blocks, electric engines, wooden case
100 × 100 × 40
ZKM | Center for Art and Media Karlsruhe

VLADIMIR BONAČIĆ (1938–1999)
GF.E 16 – NS 1969
Custom-made hardware (Galois field generator); aluminium, analogue and digital electronics, 256 glow lamps
36 × 36 × 12
Dunja Donassy-Bonačić, bcd-Cybernetic Art Team – on permanent loan to ZKM | Karlsruhe

GF.E 16 – S 1969–79
Custom-made hardware (Galois field generator); aluminium, analogue and digital electronics, 256 glow lamps
36 × 36 × 12
Dunja Donassy-Bonačić, bcd-Cybernetic Art Team – on permanent loan to ZKM | Karlsruhe

PLN 6 1969
Gelatin silver print
22.5 × 18.1
Dunja Donassy-Bonačić, bcd-Cybernetic Art Team

Random 63 1969
Aluminium, electronics, 63 glow switch starters, 63 lightbulbs
76 × 76 × 6.5
Dunja Donassy-Bonačić, bcd-Cybernetic Art Team – on permanent loan to ZKM | Karlsruhe

RS. PLNS. 0374. 1024. 0064 1969
Gelatin silver print
22.7 × 17
Dunja Donassy-Bonačić, bcd-Cybernetic Art Team

DAVIDE BORIANI (b.1936)
Magnetic Surface 1965
Superficie Magnetica

Aluminium, iron filings, polyurethane foam, magnets, motor, sensor
80 × 87 × 26
Private collection

MARTHA BOTO (1925–2004)
Helicoidal Chromokinetics 1968
Chromocinétique helicoïdal
Plywood, polished stainless steel, plexiglass, light bulbs, plastic, motor
202 × 80 × 44
Musée d'Art Moderne de Paris

POL BURY (1922–2005)
3069 White Dots on an Oval Background 1966
3069 Points blancs sur un fond oval
Wood, nylon and motor
67.3 × 120.6 × 25.4
Tate. Purchased 1967

HAROLD COHEN (1928–2016)
AARON #1 Drawing 1979
Acrylic paint on canvas
471.3 × 281.5
Tate. Purchased 2015

Untitled Computer Drawing 1982
Ink and textile dye on paper
57.5 × 76.5
Tate. Presented by Michael Compton 1986

ANALIVIA CORDEIRO (b.1954)
0°⟶45° Version I 1974
0°⟵⟶45° Versão I
Video shown digitally; black and white, sound
3 min, 23 sec
Courtesy of the artist

0°⟵⟶45° Version III 1974/1989
0°⟵⟶45° Versão III
Video shown digitally; colour, sound
1 min, 59 sec
Courtesy of the artist

0°⟵⟶45° Version V 1974/2024
0°⟵⟶45° Versão V
Video shown digitally; black and white, sound
2 min, 1 sec
TokenAngels Collection

WALDEMAR CORDEIRO (1925–1973)
*People Ampli*2* 1972
*Gente Ampli*2*
Computer output on paper
134.5 × 72.5
The Museum of Modern Art, New York. Latin American and Caribbean Fund, 2016

CARLOS CRUZ-DIEZ (1923–2019)
Chromointerferent Environment 1974–2009
Environnement Chromointerférent
Software, projections
Dimensions variable
Courtesy of Atelier Cruz-Diez

CHARLES CSURI (1922–2022)
Sine Curve Man 1967
Screenprint on acrylic
92 × 94
The Anne and Michael Spalter Digital Art Collection

DADAMAINO (1930–2004)
Volume of Displaced Modules 1960
Volume moduli sfasati
Plastic, paint and wood
69 × 49
Tate. Presented by Tate Members 2011

LUCIA DI LUCIANO (b.1933)
Discontinuous Structural Articulation 1964
Articolazione strutturale discontinua
Household emulsion paint on hardboard
75 × 75 × 30
Tate. Presented by Archivio Lucia di Luciano e Giovanni Pizzo and 10 A.M. Art Gallery, Milan 2023

MONIKA FLEISCHMANN (b.1950)
WOLFGANG STRAUSS (b.1951)
Collaborator: **CHRISTIAN-A. BOHN**, computer scientist (b.1963)
Liquid Views – Narcissus Digital Reflections 1992
Interactive installation; touch screen, computer: PC, operating system: Windows XP; individual software, loudspeaker, camera, projection screen
Dimensions variable
ZKM | Center for Art and Media Karlsruhe

HERBERT W. FRANKE (1927–2002)
Untitled from the DRAKULA Series 1971
Plotter drawing on paper
21 × 29.2
The Anne and Michael Spalter Digital Art Collection

ELSA GARMIRE (b.1939)
IVAN DRYER (1939-2017)
Laserimage 1972
Film, 16mm, shown digitally; colour, sound
10 min
Courtesy of David Dryer

BRION GYSIN (1916–1986)
Dreamachine no.9 1961
Perforated metal, electronic motor and lamp
height 118.5 × diameter 30
Musée d'Art Moderne de Paris

Am I That? c.1961
Photograph, scratched 35mm slide transferred to digital image file, projected
Original: 3.5 × 2.3
Courtesy of Musée d'Art Moderne de Paris

Am I That I Am? c.1961
Photograph, scratched 35mm slide transferred to digital image file, projected
Original: 3.5 × 2.3
Courtesy of Musée d'Art Moderne de Paris

That I Am Am I c.1961
Photograph, scratched 35mm slide transferred to digital image file, projected
Original: 3.5 × 2.3
Courtesy of Musée d'Art Moderne de Paris

Self-Portrait c.1961
Autoportrait
Photograph, two superimposed 35mm slides transferred to digital image file, projected
Original: 3.5 × 2.3
Courtesy of Musée d'Art Moderne de Paris

Self-Portrait c.1961
Autoportrait
Photograph, two superimposed 35mm slides transferred to digital image file, projected
Original: 3.5 × 2.3
Courtesy of Musée d'Art Moderne de Paris

Self-Portrait c.1961
Autoportrait
Photograph, two superimposed 35mm slides transferred to digital image file, projected
Original: 3.5 × 2.3
Courtesy of Musée d'Art Moderne de Paris

Self-Portrait c.1961
Autoportrait
Photograph, scratched 35mm slide
transferred to digital image file, projected
Original: 3.5 × 2.3
Courtesy of Musée d'Art Moderne de Paris

Self-Portrait c.1961
Autoportrait
Photograph, two superimposed 35mm slides
transferred to digital image file, projected
Original: 3.5 × 2.3
Courtesy of Musée d'Art Moderne de Paris

Self-Portrait c.1961
Autoportrait
Photograph, scratched 35mm slide
transferred to digital image file, projected
Original: 3.5 × 2.3
Courtesy of Musée d'Art Moderne de Paris

Self-Portrait c.1961
Autoportrait
Photograph, four identical superimposed
35mm slides transferred to digital image file,
projected
Original: 3.5 × 2.3
Courtesy of Musée d'Art Moderne de Paris

Ian Ian c.1961
Photograph, scratched 35mm slide
transferred to digital image file, projected
Original: 3.5 × 2.3
Courtesy of Musée d'Art Moderne de Paris

No Writers Don't Own Words c.1961
Photograph, 35mm slide with ink markings
transferred to digital image file, projected
Original: 3.5 × 2.3
Courtesy of Musée d'Art Moderne de Paris

Self-Portrait c.1961–4
Autoportrait
Photograph, superimposed 35mm slide and
painted and scratched film transferred to
digital image file, projected
Original: 3.5 × 2.3
Courtesy of Musée d'Art Moderne de Paris

W. S. Burroughs in front of the Beat Hotel
c.1961–4
W. S. Burroughs devant le Beat Hôtel
Photograph, scratched 35mm slide
transferred to digital image file, projected
Original: 3.5 × 2.3
Courtesy of Musée d'Art Moderne de Paris

Brian Sings Ono c.1961–80
Photograph, scratched 35mm slide
transferred to digital image file, projected
Original: 3.5 × 2.3
Courtesy of Musée d'Art Moderne de Paris

Electronic Revolution 1971
Lithograph
32 × 23
Musée d'Art Moderne de Paris

Electronic Revolution 1971
Lithograph
32 × 23
Musée d'Art Moderne de Paris

Untitled c.1973
Photograph, scratched 35mm slide
transferred to digital image file, projected
Original, 3.5 × 2.3
Courtesy of Musée d'Art Moderne de Paris

Untitled c.1973
Photograph, scratched 35mm slide with ink
markings transferred to digital image file,
projected
Original: 3.5 × 2.3
Courtesy of Musée d'Art Moderne de Paris

Untitled c.1973
Photograph, scratched 35mm slide
transferred to digital image file, projected
Original: 3.5 × 2.3
Courtesy of Musée d'Art Moderne de Paris

Untitled c.1973
Photograph, two superimposed scratched
35mm slides transferred to digital image file,
projected
Original: 3.5 × 2.3
Courtesy of Musée d'Art Moderne de Paris

Untitled c.1973–9
Photograph, scratched 35mm slide
transferred to digital image file, projected
Original: 3.5 × 2.3
Courtesy of Musée d'Art Moderne de Paris

Untitled c.1973–9
Photograph, scratched 35mm slide with ink
markings transferred to digital image file,
projected
Original: 3.5 × 2.3
Courtesy of Musée d'Art Moderne de Paris

Painting c.1973–9
Peinture
Photograph, scratched 35mm slide with ink
markings transferred to digital image file,
projected
Original: 3.5 × 2.3
Courtesy of Musée d'Art Moderne de Paris

Untitled c.1976
Photograph, scratched film on 35mm slide
transferred to digital image file, projected
Original: 3.5 × 2.3
Courtesy of Musée d'Art Moderne de Paris

The color of a tree 1976–9
Photograph, 35mm slide with ink markings
transferred to digital image file, projected
Original: 3.5 × 2.3
Courtesy of Musée d'Art Moderne de Paris

Art is the Tail of a Comma c.1977
Photograph, scratched 35mm slide with ink
markings transferred to digital image file,
projected
Original: 3.5 × 2.3
Courtesy of Musée d'Art Moderne de Paris

Art is the Tail of a Comma c.1977
Photograph, 35mm slide with ink markings
transferred to digital image file, projected
Original: 3.5 × 2.3
Courtesy of Musée d'Art Moderne de Paris

Weapon Tear Alarm c.1978
Arme Larme Alarme
Photograph, scratched film on 35mm slide
transferred to digital image file, projected
Original: 3.5 × 2.3
Courtesy of Musée d'Art Moderne de Paris

Self-Portrait c.1980
Autoportrait
Photograph, three identical superimposed
35mm slides transferred to digital image file,
projected
Original: 3.5 × 2.3
Courtesy of Musée d'Art Moderne de Paris

Brion Gysin c.1981
Photograph, scratched film on 35mm slide
transferred to digital image file, projected
Original: 3.5 × 2.3
Courtesy of Musée d'Art Moderne de Paris

Light Structure c.1982
Structure Lumière
Photograph, electric light print on 35mm slide
transferred to digital image file, projected
Original: 3.5 × 2.3
Courtesy of Musée d'Art Moderne de Paris

SAMIA HALABY (b.1936)
Land 1988
Kinetic painting coded on an Amiga
computer; video shown digitally; colour,
sound
1 min, 15 sec
Tate. Purchased with funds provided by the
Middle East and North African Acquisitions
Committee 2023

Spooling Up 1988
Kinetic painting coded on an Amiga
computer; video shown digitally; colour,
sound
4 min, 16 sec
Tate. Purchased with funds provided by the
Middle East and North African Acquisitions
Committee 2023

Fold 2 1988
Kinetic painting coded on an Amiga
computer; video shown digitally; colour
45 sec
Tate. Purchased with funds provided by the
Middle East and North African Acquisitions
Committee 2023

DESMOND PAUL HENRY (1921–2004)
Untitled 1962
Ballpoint ben plotter drawing and black
duplicator ink on ultra-smooth white card
stock
38.1 × 27.9
The Anne and Michael Spalter Digital Art
Collection

HERVÉ HUITRIC (b.1945)
MONIQUE NAHAS (b.1940)
No.3 (from the Handmade Pixel Series) 1971
Computer-generated print and gouache on
paper
20.3 × 21
The Anne and Michael Spalter Digital Art
Collection

EDWARD IHNATOWICZ (1926–88)
SAM (Sound Activated Mobile) 1968
Aluminium, fibreglass, electrical components
174 × 41 × 46.5; without the plinth: 61 × 41x
46.5
Richard Ihnatowicz

EDUARDO KAC (b.1962)
Horny 1985–6
Tesão
Minitel
24.5 × 25 × 24.5
Lent by the Tate Americas Foundation,
courtesy of the Latin American Acquisitions
Committee 2018

Reabracadabra 1985
Minitel
24.5 × 25 × 24.5
Lent by the Tate Americas Foundation,
courtesy of the Latin American Acquisitions
Committee 2018

Recaos 1985–6
Minitel
24.5 × 25 × 24.5
Collection of Catherine Petitgas, London

HIROSHI KAWANO (1925–2012)
3 of 7 d2 // Design 1–4 1964
3 No 7 d2/ / dezain 1–4
Gouache on paper after computer-generated
design
34.4 × 25.2
ZKM | Center for Art and Media Karlsruhe

KD 29- Artificial Mondrian 1969
Gouache on paper after computer-generated
design
71.4 × 50
ZKM | Center for Art and Media Karlsruhe

RITA KEEGAN (b.1949)
Blue III 1988
White cartridge paper, sugar paper and toner ink
46.4 × 31
Courtesy of the artist

Rites of Passage 1991
Video, shown digitally; colour, sound
8 min, 57 sec
Courtesy of the artist

BEN LAPOSKY (1914–2000)
Electronic Abstraction 4 1952
Gelatin silver print on paper
24.1 × 19
The Anne and Michael Spalter Digital Art
Collection

Electronic Abstraction 27 1952
Gelatin silver print on paper
24.1 × 19
The Anne and Michael Spalter Digital Art
Collection

RUTH LEAVITT (b.1944)
Computer Milled Sculpture 1971
Aluminium
14.6 × 14.6, 36.2 × 28.6 framed
The Anne and Michael Spalter Digital Art
Collection

JULIO LE PARC (b.1928)
Continual Light on Ceiling 1966/1996
Continuel Lumière au Plafond
Painted wood, steel, nylon and spotlights
220 × 220 × 150
Atelier Le Parc

Four Double Mirrors 1966–2016
Quatre doubles miroirs
Wood, plastic
38 × 24 × 1 each
Atelier Le Parc

LILIANE LIJN (b.1939)
Electronic Symbols 01 1966–9
Letraset letters and electronic symbols and
card
10.5 × 10.5
Collection of the artist and Sylvia Kouvali,
London/Piraeus

Electronic Symbols 04 1966–9
Letraset letters and electronic symbols and card
10.5 × 10.5
Collection of the artist and Sylvia Kouvali,
London/Piraeus

Prism Flares 1967
Polymer lenses on acrylic and acrylic
prisms in metal frame, lights and detachable

programmed digital switching controller
50 × 109 × 12.5
Collection of the artist and Sylvia Kouvali,
London/Piraeus

Neurographs: Untitled I 1970
Letrafilm and Letraset electronic symbols
on card
23.1 × 20.4
Collection of the artist and Sylvia Kouvali,
London/Piraeus

Electronic Symbols 1972
Letrafilm and Letraset electronic symbols
on card
52.2 × 11.2
Collection of the artist and Sylvia Kouvali,
London/Piraeus

The Bride 1988
Steel mesh cage, blown glass, epoxy bonded
mica, ostrich feathers, lacquered papier-
mâché balls, crocheted stainless steel and
enamelled copper, forged iron
244 × 155.5 × 155.5
Collection of the artist and Sylvia Kouvali,
London/Piraeus

Lines of Power 1983
Steel, copper wire and motors
2 columns 300 × 23 diam.; base 60 diam.
(each)
Collection of the artist and Sylvia Kouvali,
London/Piraeus

HEINZ MACK (b.1931)
Light Dynamo 1963
Aluminium, glass, wood and motor
57.8 × 57.1 × 22
Tate. Purchased 1964

Tele-Mack 1968
16mm film, shown as digital video; colour,
sound
45min, 40 sec
Courtesy of Atelier Mack and SWR Media
Services GmbH

ROBERT MALLARY (1917–97)
Quad III 1969
Plywood, metal and resin on plywood base
213 × 35 × 33.6
Tate. Purchased with funds provided by the
Tate Americas Foundation 2019

MARY MARTIN (1907–69)
Permutation of Six 1966
Ink, paint and papers on paper
46 × 46
Tate. Purchased with funds provided by
Catherine Petitgas 2015

ALMIR MAVIGNIER (1925–2018)
*Structure grey/pink/orange/white/yellow
on red* 1964
Struktur grau/rosa/orange/weiß/gelb auf rot
Oil paint on canvas
140 × 100 (155.5 × 114.2 × 8.5 with acrylic
box frame)
Atelier Almir Mavignier and 10 A.M. ART
Gallery Milan

DAVID MEDALLA (1942–2020)
Sand Machine Bahag – Hari Trance #1
1963–2015
Wood, brass, sand, bamboo, acrylic sheet,
glass beads and other materials
68.5 × 60 × 60
Tate. Purchased with funds provided by the
Asia-Pacific Acquisitions Committee 2019

TATSUO MIYAJIMA (b.1957)
Lattice B 1990
40 light emitting diode units and 10
transformers
Displayed: 308 × 872 × 3.5
Tate. Presented by Janet Wolfson de Botton
1998

Opposite Circle 1991
30 light emitting diodes units, 3 transformers
and aluminium panel
Displayed: 3.5 × 322 × 322
Tate. Presented by Janet Wolfson de Botton
1996

MANFRED MOHR (b.1938)
P-026 Logical Inversion 1970
P-026 Inversion Logique
Benson plotter drawing on paper
22.9 × 22.9
The Anne and Michael Spalter Digital Art
Collection

VERA MOLNAR (1924–2023)
Transformations 1-21 1976
Átalakulás 1-21
21 digital prints on paper, each 55 × 30
Display dimensions variable
Tate. Purchased with funds provided by the
Russia and Eastern Europe Acquisitions
Committee 2020

FRANÇOIS MORELLET (1926–2016)
2 Warps and Wefts of Short Lines 0° 90°
1955–6
2 Trames de Tirets 0°-90°
Oil paint on canvas
Support: 100 × 100; frame: 110.5 × 110.6 × 6.7
Tate. Purchased 1974

*Random distribution of 222,048 squares
using the π number decimals, 50% odd digit
blue, 50% even digit red* 1963, remade 2024
*Répartition aléatoire de 222,048 carrés
suivant les chiffres pairs et impairs d'un
annuaire de téléphone, 50% bleu, 50% rouge*
Wallpaper (exhibition copy)
Dimensions variable
Courtesy of the François Morellet Estate

FRIEDER NAKE (b.1938)
Matrix Multiplication Series 29 1967
Matrizenmultiplikation Serie 29
Plotter print on paper
47.6 × 47.6
The Anne and Michael Spalter Digital Art
Collection

GEORG NEES (1926–2016)
Hall (Corridor) 1966, printed 1970
Flur (Korridor)
From the *Computergrafik Computerplastik*
(*Computer Graphics Computer Sculpture*)
portfolio
Offset lithograph on paper
30.5 × 30.5
The Anne and Michael Spalter Digital Art
Collection

KIYOJI OTSUJI (1923–2001)
*Tanaka Atsuko, Electric Dress, 2nd Gutai
Exhibition* 1956, printed 2012
*Tanaka Atsuko, Denki-fuku, Dai-2kai Gutai
Bijutsu-ten*
Photograph, gelatin silver print on paper
20.7 × 31.5
Tate. Purchased with funds provided by the
Asia-Pacific Acquisitions Committee 2019

Tanaka Atsuko, Stage Clothes, Gutai Exhibition on the Stage 1957, printed 2012
Tanaka Atsuko, Butai-fuku, Butai o shiyo suru Gutai Bijutsu-ten
Photograph, gelatin silver print on paper
20.7 × 31.5
Tate. Purchased with funds provided by the Asia-Pacific Acquisitions Committee 2019

KIYOJI OTSUJI
KATSUHIRO YAMAGUCHI (1928–2018)
Composition for APN 1953-4, printed 2002
'APN' no tame no kōsei
Photograph, gelatin silver print on paper
16.5 × 16.4
Tate. Purchased 2012

Composition for APN 1953-4, printed 2002
'APN' no tame no kōsei
Photograph, gelatin silver print on paper
21 × 15
Tate. Purchased 2012

Composition for APN 1953-4, printed 2002
'APN' no tame no kōsei
Photograph, gelatin silver print on paper
17 × 11.4
Tate. Purchased 2012

Composition for APN 1953-4, printed 2002
'APN' no tame no kōsei
Photograph, gelatin silver print on paper
14.5 × 12.5
Tate. Purchased 2012

Composition for APN 1953-4, printed 2002
'APN' no tame no kōsei
Photograph, gelatin silver print on paper
16.5 × 12.3
Tate. Purchased 2012

AKBAR PADAMSEE (1928–2020)
SYZYGY 1972
Video shown digitally; black and white
16 min, 33 sec
Courtesy of Future East Film/Akbar Padamsee Studio

NAM JUNE PAIK (1932–2006)
JUD YALKUT (1938–2013)
Video Commune (Beatles Beginning to End) 1970, re-edited 1992
16mm film shown digitally; colour, sound
8 min, 32 sec
Tate. Licence purchased with funds provided by the Tate Americas Foundation 2020

IVAN PICELJ (1924–2011)
New Tendencies 2 1963
Nove tendencije 2
Screenprint on paper
Support: 70.5 × 50.2; Mount: 84.2, 59.7, 0.7; Frame 111.6 × 63.8 × 3.5
Tate. Presented by Anja Picelj-Kosak 2016

Tendencies 4 1969
Tendencije 4
Screenprint on paper
Support: 97 × 49.5; Frame 111.6 × 63.8 × 3.5
Tate. Presented by Anja Picelj-Kosak 2016

OTTO PIENE (1928–2014)
Light Room (Jena), exhibited 2007
Lichtraum (Jena)
Rubber, metal, foamboard, wood, electric motor, control unit and light
Dimensions variable
Tate. Purchased with Art Fund support and with funds provided by Tate Members, Tate Patrons and Tate International Council 2022

PAOLO SCHEGGI (b.1940–71)
Inter-ena-cubo 1970
Enamel paint on aluminium
51 × 51 × 13
Tate. Presented by Franca and Cosima Scheggi 2022

LILLIAN F. SCHWARTZ (b.1927)
Enigma 1972
Film, 16mm, shown digitally; colour, sound
4 min 20 sec
Courtesy the Collections of The Henry Ford. Gift of the Lillian F. Schwartz & Laurens R. Schwartz Collection

SONIA LANDY SHERIDAN (1925–2021)
Natasha Lyons c.1970
Impression on paper
22 × 28
The Daniel Langlois Foundation Collection of the Cinémathèque Québécoise. Sonia Landy Sheridan fonds

Portrait of Sonia Sheridan c.1970
Impression on paper
22 × 28
The Daniel Langlois Foundation Collection of the Cinémathèque Québécoise. Sonia Landy Sheridan fonds

Untitled (Process: Electrostatic Thermal) c.1970
Photocopy on paper
22 × 28
The Daniel Langlois Foundation Collection of the Cinémathèque Québécoise. Sonia Landy Sheridan fonds

Stan VanDerBeek c.1970
Photocopy on paper
22 × 28
The Daniel Langlois Foundation Collection of the Cinémathèque Québécoise. Sonia Landy Sheridan fonds

Flowers 1976
Photocopy on paper
22 × 28
The Daniel Langlois Foundation Collection of the Cinémathèque Québécoise. Sonia Landy Sheridan fonds

Sonia Through the Time Plane 1977
Photocopy on paper
22 × 28
The Daniel Langlois Foundation Collection of the Cinémathèque Québécoise. Sonia Landy Sheridan fonds

JESÚS RAFAEL SOTO (1923–2005)
Cardinal 1965
Cardenal
Wood on chipboard, metal rods and nylon threads
156.2 × 106 × 25.4
Tate. Purchased 1965

VERA SPENCER (1926–2021)
Artist versus Machine c.1954
Gouache on card, paper and cotton on paper
35.5 × 129.5
Tate. Presented by Tate Members 2018

ALEKSANDAR SRNEC (1924–2010)
Luminoplastic 1965-7
Luminoplastika
Metal, motor, projector
Dimensions variable
Museum of Contemporary Art, Zagreb

TAKIS (1925–2019)
Télélumière No.4 1963-4
Iron machine parts, light bulbs, wood, brass, steel, electromagnet, string and paint
Overall display dimensions variable
Tate. Purchased with assistance from Tate International Council, Tate Members, Tate Patrons and with Art Fund support 2019

Electro-Magnetic Music 1966
Électromagnétique Musical
Wood, paint, magnet, electromagnet, spark plugs, amplifier, metal wire and needle
125 × 43 × 5.5
Tate. Purchased with assistance from Tate International Council, Tate Members, Tate Patrons and with Art Fund support 2019

ATSUKO TANAKA (1932–2005)
Drawing after 'Electric Dress' 1956
Denki-fuku no tame no sobyō
Crayon, oil-based ink, water-based ink on paper
109 × 77
21st Century Museum of Contemporary Art, Kanazawa

Drawing after 'Electric Dress' 1956
Denki-fuku no tame no sobyō
Ink, crayon and watercolour on paper
109 × 77
21st Century Museum of Contemporary Art, Kanazawa

Work 1957
Sakuhin
Permanent marker and poster colour on paper
109.8 × 79.3
Ashiya City Museum of Art & History

JEAN TINGUELY (1925–1991)
Metamechanical Sculpture with Tripod 1954
Méta-mécanique à trépied
Steel, cardboard, plastic and electric motor
236 × 81.5 × 91.5
Tate. Purchased 1984

SUZANNE TREISTER (b.1958)
Fictional Videogame Stills/Would You Recognise A Virtual Paradise? series, 1991–2:
Would You Recognise A Virtual Paradise?
Would You Recognise A Virtual Paradise? Not Enough Memory
Would You Recognise A Virtual Paradise? Presume Virtual Breakdown
Would You Recognise A Virtual Paradise? Virtual Wilderness
Would You Recognise A Virtual Paradise? Software Failure …
Would You Recognise A Virtual Paradise? Error Finding Question
Would You Recognise A Virtual Paradise? No Message – Proceed
Original photographs: 50.8 × 40.6
Courtesy the artist, Annely Juda Fine Art, London and P.P.O.W. Gallery, New York

A selection of Fictional Videogame Stills 1991–2:
All Exits Are Closed
Are You Dreaming?
Between The Clues
Disappearing Trick
Do You Know?
Dream Monster.
Either It Explains All
Examine The Evidence
Extinguish Targets
Fate Worse Than Death

Four Exits
Gates Of Wisdom
Have you ever played this game before?
Incidents Reported
Is This The Beginning?
Look No Further
Mutant Territories – Grand Prix
No Quiz
Voyage Of Discovery
What Is Implied?
What Would You Say?
Where Are You Now?
You Have Lost Control – Change Identity
Photographs of original designs displayed on
Amiga 1000 computer screen, digitised and
presented as video
Original photographs: 50.8 × 40.6
Courtesy the artist, Annely Juda Fine Art,
London and P.P.O.W. Gallery, New York

WEN-YING TSAI (1928–2013)
Cybernetic Sculpture: Square Tops 1969
Aluminium, steel, concrete, electric motor,
audio-control unit and strobe light
111.8 × 71.1 × 55.9
Tate. Lent by the Tate Americas Foundation,
courtesy of Lee & Betsy Turner in recognition
of their friendship with the artist 2022

Umbrella 1971
Metal, concrete, wood and motor
265.4 × 180.3 × 180.3
Tate. Purchased 1972

GÜNTHER UECKER (b.1930)
White Field 1964
Weisses Feld
Painted nails on canvas and board
87 × 87 × 7.6
Tate. Purchased 1964

GRAZIA VARISCO (b.1937)
Variable Light Scheme R. VOD. LAB 1964
Schema Luminoso Variabile R. VOD. LAB
Black wooden box, blue acrylic, electric
motor 3/2rpm, neon lamp
91 × 91 × 12.5
Archivio Varisco

STEINA VASULKA (b.1940)
WOODY VASULKA (1937–2019)
Matrix II 1974
Video installation, 1-12 monitors (displayed as
12-monitor version), colour, sound
Duration variable
Tate. Purchased jointly by Pamela and
Richard Kramlich, Tate, London, Museum of
Modern Art, New York, and San Francisco
Museum of Modern Art, presented by Tate
Patrons 2021

MOHSEN VAZIRI MOGHADDAM
(1924–2018)
Untitled (Geometric Relief Series) 1968,
remade 2015
Aluminium, wood and paint
Composed of 4 pieces each 100 × 100 × 15
Tate. Presented by Fondazione Mohsen Vaziri
Moghaddam 2024

MIGUEL ÁNGEL VIDAL (1928–2009)
Untitled 1969
Screenprint on paper
36.3 × 36.3
Tate. Presented by the estate of Miguel Angel
Vidal and Ungallery, Buenos Aires 2020

Untitled 1970
Screenprint on paper
28 × 47.4

Tate. Presented by the estate of Miguel Angel
Vidal and Ungallery, Buenos Aires 2020

NANDA VIGO (1936–2020)
Chronotope 1960–5
Cronotopo
Aluminium, glass, neon, tubes, electrical
components
100 × 100 × 10
Archivio Eredi Nanda Vigo

Chronotope 1960–5
Cronotopo
Aluminium, glass, neon tubes, electrical
components
60 × 60 × 20; base: 111 × 60 × 20
Archivio Eredi Nanda Vigo

Chronotope 1963
Cronotopo
Aluminium, glass, neon tubes, electrical
components
100 × 100 × 5.5
Archivio Eredi Nanda Vigo

Chronotope 1966
Cronotopo
Aluminium, glass
140 × 50 × 50
Archivio Eredi Nanda Vigo

Diaphragm 1960–5
Diaframma
Aluminium, glass, neon tubes, electrical
components
100 × 100 × 25
Archivio Eredi Nanda Vigo

STEPHEN WILLATS (b.1943)
Visual Automatic No.5 1965
Plywood, wood, plastic, metal, light bulbs,
electrical components and motor
76.5 × 133 × 24.5
Tate. Purchased from funds provided by the
Knapping Fund 2004

KATSUHIRO YAMAGUCHI (1928–2018)
Barnacle 1966, restored 2017
Fujitsubo
Acrylic, light
84.5 × 84.5 × 21
Annely Juda Fine Art, London

Vitrine: Deep into the Night 1954
Vitorīnu: Yoru no shinkō
Watercolour on paper, oil on wood,
corrugated glass, acrylic, plywood
65.5 × 56.5 × 9
Museum of Contemporary Art Tokyo

Trial Object in Acrylic Plastic 1960s
Akuriru jushi no shisaku obuje
Acrylic sheet
90 × 90 × 25
Tate. Purchased with funds provided by the
Asia-Pacific Acquisitions Committee 2015

Mesh Sculpture 1961
Kanaami chōkoku
Painted wire mesh
46 × 34 × 27
Tate. Purchased with funds provided by the
Asia-Pacific Acquisitions Committee 2015

*Environmental installation for Jikken Kōbō's
concert 'Musique Concrète/Electronic Music
Audition'* 1956, remade 2024
*Myūjikku konkurēto / denshi ongaku ôdishon'
no tame no kankyô insutarêshon*
String, wood, hardware

Dimensions variable
Courtesy of the estate of the artist

Image Modulator 1969
Eizō henchō-ki
Reconstruction; colour cathode-ray tube
monitor, acrylic plastic, wood
Dimensions variable
Courtesy of the estate of the artist

KATSUHIRO YAMAGUCHI
HIROYOSHI SUZUKI (1931–2006)
Adventure of the Eyes of Mr W.S., a Test-Pilot
1953/86
Shiken hikōka W.S.-shi no Me no Bōken
Slideshow, projected from DVD
4 min, 55 sec
Courtesy of Yokota Tokyo Gallery

LAWRENCE PAUL YUXWELUPTUN (b.1957)
Inherent Rights, Vision Rights 1992–3
Video documentation of original VR
experience; colour, sound
Courtesy of Lawrence Yuxweluptun and
Vtape

EDWARD ZAJEC (1938–2018)
RAM 2 V.3
Plotter print using india ink on paper
22.1 × 30.4
The Anne and Michael Spalter Digital Art
Collection

Supporting material (selection)

SINCLAIR BEILES (1930–2000)
WILLIAM S. BURROUGHS (1914–97)
GREGORY CORSO (1930–2001)
BRION GYSIN (1916–86)
Minutes to Go 1960
Book, print on paper
Tate Archive

Bit International 7: Dialogue with the Machine, 1971
Magazine, print on paper
Tate Library

Black Chip, issue 86:1, Spring 1986
Magazine, print on paper
Peter Harrington, London

RICHARD BRAUTIGAN (1935–84)
All Watched Over By Machines Of Loving Grace 1967
Print on paper
Peter Harrington, London

WILLIAM S. BURROUGHS
BRION GYSIN
The Exterminator 1960
Book, print on paper
Tate Archive

WILLIAM S. BURROUGHS
BRION GYSIN
Electronic Revolution 1970–1
Book, print on paper
Tate Archive

WILLIAM S. BURROUGHS
BRION GYSIN
The Third Mind 1979
Book, print on paper
Peter Harrington, London

CEAC (CENTRO DE ESTUDIOS DE ARTE Y COMMUNICACIÓN)
Arte y Cibernética 1969
Poster, print on paper
Tate Archive

HAROLD COHEN (1928–2016)
Drawing Machine ('Turtle') 1980
Steel, copper, plastic
The Harold Cohen Trust and Gazelli Gallery

Copy Art Newsletter, Sep. Oct. Nov. 1986 1986
Print on paper
Tate Library

Cybernetic Serendipity (Late Night Lineup) 1968
Video
7 min, 16 sec
Courtesy of the BBC

Cybernetic Serendipity Music 1968
Vinyl record
Tate Archive

ATUL DESAI (1934–2013)
Music Track for Osaka Expo 70 tape 1970
Audio track
2 min 50 sec
Courtesy of the National Institude of Design, Ahmedabad

EXPERIMENTS IN ART AND TECHNOLOGY (E.A.T.)
Selected documents from the E.A.T. Papers
Tate Archive

EDWARD IHNATOWICZ (1926–88)
Cybernetic Art of Edward Ihnatowicz
Film, transferred to video, colour and sound
4min, 3 sec
Courtesy of Richard Ihnatowicz

LILIANE LIJN (b.1939)
Crossing Map 1983
Book, print on paper
Tate Library

GUSTAV METZGER (1926–2017)
Maquette for Five Screens with Computer 1969
Ink and glue on paper
Tate Archive

BRUNO MUNARI (1907–98)
Xerografia: Documentazione sull'uso creativo delle macchine Rank Xerox 1970
Book, print on paper
Tate Archive

NEW ARTS LAB
UFO+TV – Bachdenkel flier 1970
Photocopy on paper
Tate Archive

Olympia: A Monthly Review from Paris, No.2 1962
Magazine, print on paper
Bronac Ferran

Radical Software Volume I, N.1 1970
Magazine, print on paper
Private Collection

Radical Software Volume I, N.2 1970
Magazine, print on paper
Tate Library

Radical Software Volume I, N.3 1971
Magazine, print on paper
Private Collection

Radical Software Volume I, N.4 1971
Magazine, print on paper
Private Collection

Radical Software Volume II, N.5 1973
Magazine, print on paper
Peter Harrington, London

ERIC SAARINEN (b.1942)
The Great Big Mirror Dome 1970
Film transferred to digital video; colour, sound
18 min
Courtesy of the artist and Getty Research Institute

NICOLAS SCHÖFFER (1912–92)
La Ville Cibernetique 1969
Book, print on paper
Tate Archive

MICHAEL SHAMBERG (b.1945), RAINDANCE CORPORATION
Guerrilla Television 1971 – Japanese edition, 1974, trans. Fujiko Nakaya and Nobuhiro Kawanaka
Book, print on paper
Private Collection

SONIA LANDY SHERIDAN (1925–2021)
A selection of digitised slides of artworks created using computer graphic software EASEL
Sonia Landy Sheridan fonds, Daniel Langlois Foundation Archives at the Cinémathèque Québécoise, Montreal, Canada

FRANCISZKA THEMERSON (1907–88)
Poster for *Cybernetic Serendipity* 1968
Screenprint on paper
Gregor Muir

JEAN TINGUELY (1925–1991)
Drawing executed by Meta-matic no.13 c.1982
Felt-tip pen on paper
Tate Archive

NIC TUMMERS (1928–2020)
TJEBBE VAN TIJEN (b.1944)
Osaka. Progress and Harmony for Mankind. 1968
Poster, print on paper
Private Collection

Whole Earth Catalog – access to tools, Spring 1969
Magazine, print on paper
Peter Harrington, London

Credits

The publishers have made every effort to trace the copyright holders of the works illustrated in this book and apologise for any omissions or errors that may inadvertently have been made.

Front cover © Samia A. Halaby
Back cover © ALBERTO BIASI, by SIAE/DACS 2024 / ZKM | Center for Art and Media Karlsruhe
2 © Estate of Carlos Cruz-Diez. All rights reserved 2024 / Atelier Cruz-Diez Paris / Bridgeman Images
10 © Liliane Lijn. All Rights Reserved, DACS 2024 / Courtesy Studio Liliane Lijn. Photo: Tomek Sierek
11 © Estate of Richard Brautigan / The Communications Company, San Francisco, 1967 / Photograph Peter Harrington Rare Books
12 © Suzanne Treister. Courtesy the artist, Annely Juda Fine Art, London and P.P.O.W. Gallery, New York
13 © André Morain
14 Getty Research Institute, Los Angeles (2014.R.20) Gift of the Roy Lichtenstein Foundation in Memory of Harry Shunk and Janos Kender. Photograph: Shunk-Kender © J. Paul Getty Trust.
15, 16 Courtesy Museum of Contemporary Art, Zagreb
17 *Black Chip* no.86:1, Spring 1986. Photograph Peter Harrington Rare Books
18–19 © Vera Spencer. Photo: Tate. Artist versus Machine, c.1954. Gouache on card, paper and cotton on paper. 35.5 x 129.5 cm. Tate.
20 © Estate of Gustav Metzger. All Rights Reserved, DACS 2024 Photo: Tate. Tate Archive
21 © Estate of Gustav Metzger. Photo: Tate. *Recreation of First Public Demonstration of Auto-Destructive Art*, 1960, remade 2004, 2015, Gustav Metzger
23 © Tetsuo Otsuji. © Kanayama Akira and Tanaka Atsuko Association. Photo: Tate
24 top left © Kanayama Akira and Tanaka Atsuko Association. Photo: Moderna Museet.
24 top right © Tetsuo Otsuji. © Kanayama Akira and Tanaka Atsuko Association. Photo: Tate
24 bottom © Kanayama Akira and Tanaka Atsuko Association. Photo: The 21st Century Museum of Contemporary Art, Kanazawa
25 top left © Kanayama Akira and Tanaka Atsuko Association. Courtesy: © Kanayama Akira and Tanaka Atsuko Association
25 top right © Kanayama Akira and Tanaka Atsuko Association. Collection of the Mudima Foundation, Roma. Photo: Moderna Museet
26 © Kanayama Akira and Tanaka Atsuko Association. Photo: Ashiya City Museum of Art & History, Ashiya City, Japan
27 © Kanayama Akira and Tanaka Atsuko Association. Photo: The 21st Century Museum of Contemporary Art, Kanazawa
28 © Kanayama Akira and Tanaka Atsuko Association. Osaka Museum of Art, Nakanoshima.
29 © Estate of Suburo Murakami. © Estate of Michio Yoshihara. © Estate of Jiro Yoshihara. © Estate of Tsuroko Yamazaki. © Estate of Sadamassa Motonaga. © Kanayama Akira and Tanaka Atsuko Association. © Estate of Shozo Shimamoto. Photo: © Philip Mechanicus/Maria Austria Institute Amsterdam
30 top left © Henk Peeters, c/o Pictoright. DACS 2024
30 top right Heinz Mack © DACS 2024. ZERO Foundation, Düsseldorf
30 centre right Otto Piene © DACS 2024. Photo: Paul Brandenburg
30 bottom right Otto Piene © DACS 2024. EIN FEST FUR DAS LICHT, 9th Night Exhibition, at the artist's studio, Gladbacherstrasse 60, Dusseldorf, Germany 1960. Photo: Manfred Tischer © The estate of Manfred Tischer
31 Otto Piene © DACS 2024. Photo: Museum of Art Pudong
32–3 Otto Piene © DACS 2024. Photo: Museum of Art Pudong
34 © Estate of David Medalla. Photo: Tate. *Cloud Canyons No.3: An Ensemble of Bubble Machines (Auto Creative Sculptures)*, 1961, remade 2004, metal,

perspex, 2 compressors, 2 timers, water and soap, dimensions variable
35 top © Estate of David Medalla. Photo: Tate
35 bottom © Estate of David Medalla. Photo: Tate. © Clay Perry, England & Co Gallery, London
36–7 © Estate of David Medalla. Photo: Tate. © Clay Perry, England & Co Gallery, London. Photo: Tate. Tate Archive
38 © The estate of Jean Tinguely. Photo: Tate
39 Jean Tinguely © ADAGP, Paris and DACS, London 2024. © Centre Pompidou, MNAM-CCI, Dist. GrandPalaisRmn / Philippe Migeat. Jean Tinguely, Meta-matic n°1 1959, felt-tip pen, paper, 96 x 85 x 44
40 Jean Tinguely © ADAGP, Paris and DACS, London 2024. Associated Press / Alamy Stock Photo
41 Heinz Mack © DACS 2024. ZERO Foundation, Düsseldorf
42 top Heinz Mack © DACS 2024. Photo@ Edwin Braun
42 bottom Heinz Mack © DACS 2024. Photo: Tate
43 Heinz Mack © DACS 2024. Photo: Edwin Braun
44 Günther Uecker. All rights reserved. DACS 2024. Photo: Tate
45 top Pol Bury © ADAGP, Paris and DACS, London 2024. © Centre Pompidou, MNAM-CCI Bibliothèque Kandinsky, Dist. GrandPalaisRmn / Jean-Claude Planchet. Pol Bury, CLICHÉ 1957, wood, 117 x 65.5 x 162.5
45 bottom Pol Bury © ADAGP, Paris and DACS, London 2024. Photo: Tate
46 top © Estate of Paul Brandenburg. Photo: Paul Brandeburg / Atelier Heinz-Mack
46 bottom Photo by Reiner Ruthenbeck. © Stiftung Kunstfords, Estate Reiner Ruthenbeck
47 Heinz Mack Estate, ZERO Foundation, Düsseldorf
48–9 © Nanda Vigo Heirs
50 Otto Piene © DACS 2024. © Aldo Tambellini Art Foundation. Courtesy ZKM Center for Art and Media Karlsruhe
51 © Archivio Dadamaino. Photo: Tate
52 top © Estate of Mary Martin. Photo: Tate
52 centre © Estate of Mary Martin. Photo: Tate. Mary Martin, *Perspex Group on Orange (B)* 1969, perspex on wood, 60.7 x 60.9 x 233. Tate
52 bottom © Estate of Mary Martin. Photo: Tate. Mary Martin, *Inversions* 1966, aluminium, oil paint and wood, 182.9 x 731.5 x 27.9. Tate
53 © Stephen Willats. Photo: Tate
54–5 © Takis. Photo: Tate
56 Takis © ADAGP, Paris and DACS 2024. Photo: Tate. Tate Archive
57 top Photo © Clay Perry, England & Co Gallery, London. © Lilianne Lijn. All Rights Reserved, DACS 2024. Takis © ADAGP, Paris and DACS 2024. © "THE WORLD OF LYGIA CLARK" CULTURAL ASSOCIATION. © Estate of Sergio de Camargo. Jesús Rafael Soto © ADAGP, Paris and DACS, London 2024. Courtesy © "THE WORLD OF LYGIA CLARK" CULTURAL ASSOCIATION
57 bottom © Clay Perry, England & Co Gallery, London
58 Jesús Rafael Soto © ADAGP, Paris and DACS, London 2024. Photo: Tate
59 top © Clay Perry, England & Co Gallery, London
59 bottom © Lilianne Lijn. All Rights Reserved, DACS 2024. Courtesy Studio Liliane Lijn. Photo: Richard Wilding
60 top © 1970, William Burroughs and Brion Gysin, used by permission of The Wylie Agency (UK) Limited. © Charles Gatewood / TopFoto
61–2 © Brion Gysin, used by permission of The Wylie Agency (UK) Limited. © Paris Musées, Musée d'Art modern. Dist. GrandPalaisRmn / image ville de Paris
63 top Brion Gysin, used by permission of The Wylie Agency (UK) Limited. © Paris Musées, Musée d'Art modern. Dist. GrandPalaisRmn / image ville de Paris
63 bottom left Brion Gysin, used by permission of The Wylie Agency (UK) Limited. Courtesy The Wylie Agency (UK) Limited
63 bottom right Brion Gysin, used by permission of The Wylie Agency (UK) Limited. Los Angeles County Museum of Art (LACMA), Los Angeles (CA), USA. Digital image Museum Associates/LACMA/Art Resource NY/Scala, Florence

64–5 Brion Gysin, used by permission of The Wylie Agency (UK) Limited. © Paris Musées, musée d'Art modern, Dist. GrandPalaisRmn / image ville de Paris
66 © Estate of Katsuhiro Yamaguchi. Courtesy YOKOTA TOKYO
67 top © Estate of Katsuhiro Yamaguchi. Courtesy YOKOTA TOKYO. Courtesy Electronic Arts Intermix (EAI), New York
67 bottom © Estate of Katsuhiro Yamaguchi. Courtesy YOKOTA TOKYO
68 © Estate of Katsuhiro Yamaguchi. Courtesy YOKOTA TOKYO. ©Tetsuo OTSUJI. Photo: Tate
69 © Estate of Katsuhiro Yamaguchi. Courtesy YOKOTA TOKYO. Museum of Contemporary Art Tokyo
70 top L'eve Future from "Experimental Ballet Theater" performed at the Haiyuza Theater, Tokyo, 1955. Photographed by Kiyoji Otsuji. ©Tetsuo OTSUJI; Courtesy Musashino Art University Museum & Library
70 centre left © Estate of Katsuhiro Yamaguchi. Courtesy YOKOTA TOKYO. ©Tetsuo OTSUJI
70 centre right © Estate of Katsuhiro Yamaguchi. Courtesy YOKOTA TOKYO
70 bottom © Estate of Katsuhiro Yamaguchi. Courtesy YOKOTA TOKYO
71 top © Estate of Katsuhiro Yamaguchi. Photo: Tate
71 bottom © Estate of Katsuhiro Yamaguchi. Courtesy YOKOTA TOKYO. Photo courtesy Annely Juda Fine Art, London
73 Courtesy Museum of Contemporary Art, Zagreb
74 © Estate of Paul Talman. Julio Le Parc © ADAGP, Paris and DACS, London 2024 © Courtesy Museum of Contemporary Art, Zagreb
75 © Ivan Picelj Estate. Photo: Tate
76 top © Estate of Gianni Colombo. Courtesy Museum of Contemporary Art, Zagreb
76 bottom © Estate of Joël Stein. Courtesy Museum of Contemporary Art, Zagreb
77 top Courtesy Museum of Contemporary Art, Zagreb
77 bottom © Estate of Rudolf Kämmer. Courtesy Museum of Contemporary Art, Zagreb
78 Courtesy: 10 A.M. ART Gallery, Milan and Delmar Mavignier, Hamburg. Photo by Mattia Mognetti
79 top © Ivan Picelj Estate. Photo: Tate. Ivan Picelj, *Suasum*, 1965, metal, wood and paint, 70 × 70 × 5.7. Tate
79 bottom © Ivan Picelj Estate. Photo: Tate
80 Courtesy Museum of Contemporary Art, Zagreb
81 top © Petar Milojević. Courtesy Museum of Contemporary Art, Zagreb
81 bottom Courtesy Museum of Contemporary Art, Zagreb
82 Jesús Rafael Soto © ADAGP, Paris and DACS, London 2024. Courtesy Museum of Contemporary Art, Zagreb
83 © Art Research Center. Courtesy Museum of Contemporary Art, Zagreb
84–5 Julio Le Parc © ADAGP, Paris and DACS, London 2024. Courtesy Atelier Le Parc
86 Martha Boto © ADAPG, Paris and London and DACS, London 2024. © Centre Pompidou, MNAM-CCI Bibliothèque Kandinsky, Dist. GrandPalaisRmn / Jean-Claude Planchet
87 © Family Srnec. Courtesy Museum of Contemporary Art, Zagreb
88 © Davide Boriani. Photo: Private collection, Italy
89 Thomas Libis Milano and Courtesy Archivio Varisco
90 Alberto Biasi © ADAGP, Paris and DACS, London 2024. Courtesy ZKM Center for Art and Media Karlsruhe
91 © Marina Apolollonio. Courtesy the artist.
92 top Courtesy 10 A.M. ART Gallery, Milan and Archivio Lucia Di Luciano & Giovanni Pizzo, Rome. Photo by Mattia Mognetti
92 bottom Courtesy Archivio Lucia di Luciano & Giovanni Pizzo, Rome
93 © Associazione Paolo Scheggi. Photo: Tate
94–5 Fondazione Mohsen Vaziri Moghaddam
96 top © Estate Morellet. Photo: Tate
96 bottom © Estate Morellet. Photo: SPA, Lisboa 2024
97 © Estate Morellet
98–9 © Atelier Le Parc
100–1 © Estate of Carlos Cruz-Diez. All rights

reserved 2024 / Bridgeman Images. Courtesy Galleria Continua. Art Basel Unlimited Fair
102 top © Estate of Carlos Cruz-Diez. All rights reserved 2024 / Bridgeman Images
102 bottom © Estate of Carlos Cruz-Diez. All rights reserved 2024 / Bridgeman Images. Caracas Museum of Contemporary Art (MACC), Venezuela 1974
103 top © Estate of Carlos Cruz-Diez. All rights reserved 2024 / Bridgeman Images. Ostwell Museum, Germany 2009
103 centre © Estate of Carlos Cruz-Diez. All rights reserved 2024 / Bridgeman Images. Hester + Hardaway Photographers. Buffalo Bayou Park Cistern, Houston, United States.
103 bottom © Estate of Carlos Cruz-Diez. All rights reserved 2024 / Bridgeman Images. *Light Gallery*, Hayward Gallery, London 2013
105 © Estate of William Fetter. Photo: © Boeing Images
106 © A. Michael Noll. © Victoria and Albert Museum, London
107 left © A. Michael Noll
107 right © Mondrian/Holtzman Trust. Photo © NPL – DeA Picture Library / © Mondrian/ Holtzman Trust / Bridgeman Images
108 © 2024 Tsai Art and Science Foundation / Artists Rights Society (ARS), New York / DACS London, 2024
109 © 2024 Tsai Art and Science Foundation / Artists Rights Society (ARS), New York / DACS London, 2024. Photo: © Estate of Nishan Bichajian. Massachusetts Institute of Technology
110–11 © 2024 Tsai Art and Science Foundation / Artists Rights Society (ARS), New York / DACS London, 2024. Photo: Tate
112 © 2024 Tsai Art and Science Foundation / Artists Rights Society (ARS), New York / DACS London, 2024. Photo: © Estate of Nishan Bichajian. Massachusetts Institute of Technology
113 © 2024 Tsai Art and Science Foundation / Artists Rights Society (ARS), New York / DACS London, 2024
114 © Estate of Franciszka Themerson. Photo: Tate. Tate Archive
115 top © Cybernetic Serendipty, 1968 © Estate of Edward Ihnatowicz
115 bottom left © Estate of Franciszka Themerson and Stefan Themerson. © Donald K. Robbins. © Charles Csuri
115 bottom right © Cybernetic Serendipty, 1968 © Estate of Peter Zinovieff
116 top © Estate of Gordon Pask. Courtesy ZKM Center for Art and Media Karlsruhe. Photo © Jasia Reichardt
116 bottom © Estate of Gordon Pask. Courtesy ZKM Center for Art and Media Karlsruhe. Photo: TJ McLeish
117 top Nicolas Schöffer © ADAPG, Paris and DACS, London 2024 – Photo: Jacques L'Hoir/ adapg images
117 bottom Nicolas Schöffer © ADAPG, Paris and DACS, London 2024
118 © Estate of Edward Ihnatowicz. Photo: © Science & Society Picture Library, London
119 © Estate of Edward Ihnatowicz
120 left © Estate of Hiroshi Kawano. Courtesy ZKM Center for Art and Media Karlsruhe. Hiroshi Kawano, *Design 6 Data A* 1965, painting after computer-generated design; computer: OKITAC 5090A, programming language: OKISIP; gouache on graph paper, 164 x 30
120 right, 121 © Estate of Hiroshi Kawano. Courtesy ZKM Center for Art and Media Karlsruhe
122 © D. P. Henry Archive. Desmond Henry. www.desmondhenry.com. Anne and Michael Spalter Digital Collection. Photography © Jillian Freyer
123 top © Estate of Ben Laposky. Anne and Michael Spalter Digital Collection. Photography: Jillian Freyer
123 bottom © Estate of Vladimir Bonačić. Courtesy Museum of Contemporary Art, Zagreb
124 top left © Estate of Ivan Picelj. Photo: Tate
124 top right © Estate of Ivan Picelj. Courtesy Museum of Contemporary Art, Zagreb
124 bottom © Estate of Vladimir Bonačić, © Estate of Ivan Picelj
125 © Estate of Vladimir Bonačić, Courtesy ZKM Center for Art and Media Karlsruhe
126–7 © Estate of Vera Molnar. Photo: Tate
128 © Frieder Nake. Anne and Michael Spalter Digital Collection. Photography: Jillian Freyer
129 top © Estate of Herbert W. Franke. Anne and Michael Spalter Digital Collection. Photography: Jillian Freyer
129 bottom © Georg Nees. Anne and Michael Spalter Digital Collection. Photography: Jillian Freyer
130 top © Manfred Mohr. Anne and Michael Spalter Digital Collection. Photography: Jillian Freyer
130 bottom © Tomislav Mikulić. Anne and Michael Spalter Digital Collection. Photography: Jillian Freyer
131 © Charles Csuri. Anne and Michael Spalter Digital Collection. Photography: Jillian Freyer
132 top © Edward Zajec. Anne and Michael Spalter Digital Collection. Photography: Jillian Freyer
132 bottom Manuel Barbadillo © DACS 2024. Anne and Michael Spalter Digital Collection. Photography: Jillian Freyer
133 © Estate of Miguel Ángel Vidal. Photo: Tate
134 top © Roth Estate. Photo: Tate
134 bottom left © Roth Estate. © Computer Technique Group (CTG). Photo: Tate
134 bottom right © Roth Estate
135 top © Roth Estate. © Estate of Gustav Metzger. All Rights Reserved, DACS 2024
135 centre © Estate of Gustav Metzger. All Rights Reserved, DACS 2024
135 bottom © Estate of Gustav Metzger. All Rights Reserved, DACS 2024. Generali Foundation Collection-Permanent Loan to the Museum der Moderne Salzburg, © Generali Foundation, Photo: Werner Kaligofsky
136–7 © Lilian F. Schwartz. From the Collections of The Henry Ford. © The Henry Ford
137 top left © Estate of Robert Mallary. Photo: Tate
138 top right, bottom © Estate of Robert Mallary. Courtesy The Mayor Gallery, London. Private collection
139 © Ruth Leavitt. Anne and Michael Spalter Digital Collection. Photography: Jillian Freyer
140 © Hervé Huitric and Monique Nahas. Anne and Michael Spalter Digital Collection. Photography: Jillian Freyer
141 left © Estate of Waldemar Corderio. Digital Image, The Museum of Modern Art, New York/ Scala, Florence
141 right © Estate of Waldemar Cordeiro. Photo courtesy Ana Cordeiro
142–3 © Ana Cordeiro. Photo courtesy Ana Cordeiro
144 © Ana Cordeiro. Photo courtesy Ana Cordeiro
145 top © Ana Corderio. 'The Programming Choreographer', Computer Graphics and Art 2, no.1, 1977, pp.27–31. Photo courtesy Ana Cordeiro
145 bottom © Ana Cordeiro. Photo courtesy Ana Cordeiro
146 © Harold Cohen Trust. Courtesy Gazelli Art House. © Becky Cohen. Photo: © Becky Cohen. Private collection
147 © Harold Cohen Trust. Courtesy Gazelli Art House. Photo: © Becky Cohen
148–9 © Harold Cohen Trust. Courtesy Gazelli Art House. Photo: Tate
150 top, bottom left © Harold Cohen Trust. Courtesy Gazelli Art House. Photo: Tate
150 bottom right © Harold Cohen Trust. Courtesy Gazelli Art House
151 top © Harold Cohen Trust. Courtesy Gazelli Art House. Photo: © Becky Cohen
151 bottom © Harold Cohen Trust. Courtesy Gazelli Art House
153 © Estate of Leslie Mezei
155 top © Steve Beck. www.stevebeck.tv
155 centre left © Woody Vasulka. Reminiscence, 1974 1/2" Open Reel Video, b&w, sound, 4.52 min. Courtesy Steina Vasulka and BERG Contemporary
155 centre right Courtesy Steina Vasulka and BERG Contemporary. The Daniel Langlois Foundation Collection of the Cinémathèque Québécoise. Steina and Woody Vasulka Fonds. Steina in the Vsaulkas' studio, Buffalo, NY, United States, cira 1976. B&W photographic print, 20 x 26
155 bottom © Denise Gallant
156 © Estate of Nam June Paik. Photo: Tate
157 © Estate of Nam June Paik. Kunsthalle Bremen – Tobias Hübel – ARTOTHEK. Nam June Paik, Video-Synthesizer, 1969/92, original synthesizer in two frames, partially disassembled, 12 monitors of different sizes, 2 video disc players, 305 x 155 x 150
158 left The Daniel Langlois Foundation Collection of the Cinémathèque Québécoise
158 right Photo by Tom Haar © Estate of Shigeko Kubota. Estate of Shigeko Kubota archive, Tom Haar. Portrait of Shigeko Kubota with Portapak
159 top Courtesy the Artist. Artist Represented by RCM Galerie, Paris
159 bottom © Jane Veeder
160 © Marta Minujin Archive
162 Kit Galloway and Sherrie Rabinowitz Archives
163 top Shunk-Kender © J. Paul Getty Trust. The Jewish Museum, New York, USA. Photo The Jewish Museum/Art Resource/Scala, Florence. Cover of exhibition catalogue *Software: Information Technology: Its New Meaning for Art* (16 Sept. – 8 Nov. 1970)
163 bottom © Jaques-Elie Chabert. © Jean-Paul Martin. © Camille Philibert. © Dominique Horviller. Paris, Centre Pompidou-MNAM/CCI-Bibliothèque Kandinsky, Dist. GrandPalaisRMN/ Jean-Claude Planchet
164 © Eduardo Kac. Courtesy England & Co. Gallery. Photo: Tate
166–7 Courtesy Stewart Brand
168 Courtesy Future East Film / Akbar Padamsee Studio
169 top left Photography courtesy Paul Pargas
169 right top The state51 Conspiracy
169 right bottom Archives, National Institute of Design, Ahmedabad
170 top akg-images / picture-alliance / dpa
170 bottom Osaka Expo 70
171 The Asahi Shimbun Collection / Getty images
172 © Tjebbe van Tijen and Nic Tummers. Photo: Tate
173 top akg-images / picture-alliance / dpa
173 bottom The Asahi Shimbun Collection / Getty Images
174 top © Fujiko Nakaya. Photo: Tatsuro Murota
174 bottom © photo: Fujiko Nakaya
175 Getty Research Institute, Los Angeles (2014.R.20) Gift of the Roy Lichtenstein Foundation in Memory of Harry Shunk and Janos Kender. Photograph: Shunk-Kender © J. Paul Getty Trust
176 top Getty Research Institute, Los Angeles (2014.R.20) Gift of the Roy Lichtenstein Foundation in Memory of Harry Shunk and Janos Kender. Photograph: Shunk-Kender © J. Paul Getty Trust
176 bottom Klüver/Martin Archive
177 Getty Research Institute, Los Angeles (2014.R.20) Gift of the Roy Lichtenstein Foundation in Memory of Harry Shunk and Janos Kender. Photograph: Shunk-Kender © J. Paul Getty Trust
178 © Ivan Dryer and Elsa Garmine
179 top left © Estate of Tom Gormley. Shunk-Kender © J. Paul Getty Trust. Photo: Moderna Museet
179 top right Archives, National Institute of Design, Ahmedabad
179 bottom left © Estate of Katsuhiro Yamaguchi. Courtesy YOKOTA TOKYO. © Courtesy: Experiments in Art and Technology Tokyo. Photo: Shoji Fukazawa
179 bottom right © Estate of Katsuhiro Yamaguchi. Courtesy YOKOTA TOKYO. Photo: Moderna Museet
180 top © Klüver/Martin Archive
180 bottom Courtesy: Experiments in Art and Technology Tokyo. Photo: Shoji Fukazawa
181 top Photo by Michael Goldberg
181 centre right © Photo: Fujiko Nakaya
181 bottom © Ant Design. Courtesy Fujiko Nakaya
182 © RADICAL SOFTWARE
183 top © RADICAL SOFTWARE
183 bottom left © John 'Hoppy' Hopkins Archive. Photo: Tate. Tate Archive
183 bottom right © Roth Estate. Photo: Tate. Tate Archive
184 Courtesy Steina Vasulka and BERG Contemporary. Photo: Tate
185 Courtesy Steina Vasulka and BERG Contemporary
186–8 Cinémathèque Québécoise / Fondation Daniel Langlois. Sonia Sheridan Landy Fonds
189 © Rita Keegan
190 top right and left © Rebecca Allen. Courtesy the artist
190 bottom © Rebecca Allen. Courtesy the artist. Photo: Linda Law
191 © Rebecca Allen. Courtesy the artist
192 top © Samia A. Halaby
192 bottom Courtesy the artist and Sfeir-Semler Gallery, Beirut/Hamburg
193 top Courtesy the artist and Sfeir-Semler Gallery, Beirut/Hamburg
193 centre © Samia A. Halaby
193 bottom Courtesy the artist and Sfeir-Semler Gallery, Beirut/Hamburg
194–5 Courtesy the artist and Sfeir-Semler Gallery, Beirut/Hamburg
196 top © Liliane Lijn. All Rights Reserved, DACS 2024 / Courtesy Studio Liliane Lijn and Sylvia Kouvali, London/Piraeus
196 bottom © Liliane Lijn. All Rights Reserved, DACS 2024 / Courtesy Studio Liliane Lijn
197 © Liliane Lijn. All Rights Reserved, DACS 2024 / Courtesy Studio Liliane Lijn
198 © Liliane Lijn. All Rights Reserved, DACS 2024 / Courtesy Studio Liliane Lijn. Photo: Michael Petry
199 © Liliane Lijn. All Rights Reserved, DACS 2024 / Courtesy Studio Liliane Lijn. Photo: Tomek Sierek
201 top © Tatsuo Miyajima; Courtesy the artist and Hayward Gallery. *Lattice B*, 1990. 40 light emitting diode units, 10 transformers. 872 x 308. Installed in *Big Time*, Hayward Gallery, 1997
201 bottom © Tatsuo Miyajima; Courtesy the Artist. Photography by Hirouki Yazumi. *Opposite Circle,* 1991. 30 light emitting diode (LED) units, 3 transformers and aluminium panel. Dimensions displayed: 3.5 x 322 x 322. Installed at Luhring Augustine Gallery, New York
202 top © Monika Fleischmann and Wolfgang Strauss. © Christian-A. Bohn. Courtesy ZKM Center for Art and Media Karlsruhe
202 bottom © Monika Fleischmann and Wolfgang Strauss. Courtesy ZKM Center for Art and Media Karlsruhe
203 top left © Lawrence Paul Yuxweluptun. Courtesy the Museum of Anthropology, University of British Columbia
203 top right Lawrence Paul Yuxweluptun. Courtesy Banff Centre for Arts and Creativity
203 bottom © Lawrence Paul Yuxweluptun. Courtesy the Museum of Anthropology, University of British Columbia. Photo by Kyla Bailey
205–15 © Suzanne Treister. Courtesy the artist, Annely Juda Fine Art, London and P.P.O.W. Gallery, New York

Supporting Tate

Tate relies on a large number of supporters – individuals, foundations, companies and public sector sources – to enable it to deliver its programme of activities, both on and off its gallery sites. This support is essential in order for Tate to acquire works of art for the Collection, run education, outreach and exhibition programmes, care for the Collection in storage and enable art to be displayed, both digitally and physically, inside and outside Tate. Please contact us at:

Development Office
Tate
Millbank
London SW1P 4RG

Tel: +44 (0)20 7887 4900
Fax: +44 (0)20 7887 8098

Tate Americas Foundation
520 West 27 Street Unit 404
New York, NY 10001
USA

Tel: 001 212 643 2818
Fax: 001 212 643 1001

Donations, no matter the size, are gratefully received, either to support particular areas of interest, or to contribute to general activity costs.

Legacies

A legacy to Tate may take the form of a residual share of an estate, a specific cash sum, or an item of property such as a work of art. Legacies to Tate are free of inheritance tax and help to secure a strong future for the Collection and galleries. For further information please contact the Development Office.

Offers in lieu of tax

Inheritance Tax can be satisfied by transferring to the Government a work of art of outstanding importance. In this case the amount of tax is reduced. It can be made a condition of the offer that the work of art is allocated to Tate. Please contact us for details.

Tate Members

Tate Members enjoy unlimited free admission throughout the year to all exhibitions at Tate, as well as a number of other benefits such as exclusive use of our Members' Rooms and a free annual subscription to *Tate Etc*. Whilst enjoying the exclusive privileges of membership, members also help secure Tate's position at the very heart of British and modern art. Members support actively contributes towards new purchases of important art, ensuring that Tate's collection continues to be relevant and comprehensive, as well as funding projects in London, Liverpool and St Ives that increase access and understanding for everyone.

Tate Patrons

Tate Patrons share a passion for art and are committed to supporting Tate on an annual basis. The Patrons help enable the acquisition of works across Tate's broad collecting remit and support the staging of major exhibitions in the galleries. They also give their support to vital conservation, learning and research projects. The scheme provides a forum for Patrons to share their interest in art and meet curators, artists and one another in an enjoyable environment through a regular programme of events. These events take place both at Tate and beyond and encompass curator-led exhibition tours, visits to artists' studios and private collections, art trips both in the UK and abroad, and access to art fairs. The scheme welcomes supporters from outside the UK, giving the programme a truly international scope.

Corporate Membership

Corporate Membership at Tate offers companies opportunities for corporate entertaining and the chance for a wide variety of employee benefits. These include special private views, special access to paying exhibitions, out-of-hours visits and tours, invitations to VIP events and talks at members' offices.

Corporate Investment

Tate has developed a range of imaginative partnerships with the corporate sector, ranging from international interpretation and exhibition programmes to local outreach and staff development programmes. We are particularly known for high-profile business to business marketing initiatives and employee benefit packages. Please contact the Corporate Partnerships team for further details.

Charity Details

The Tate Gallery is an exempt charity; the Museums & Galleries Act 1992 added the Tate Gallery to the list of exempt charities defined in the 1960 Charities Act. Tate Foundation is a registered charity (number 1085314).

Tate Americas Foundation

Tate Americas Foundation is an independent charity based in New York that supports the work of Tate in the United Kingdom. It receives full tax exempt status from the IRS under section 501(c)(3) allowing United States taxpayers to receive tax deductions on gifts towards annual membership programmes, exhibitions, scholarship and capital projects. For more information please contact the Tate Americas Foundation office.

This information is correct as of the beginning of June 2024

Tate Trustees

Dame Jayne-Anne Gadhia, DBE
Katrin Henkel
Anya Hindmarch, CBE
Kwame Kwei-Armah, OBE
Michael Lynton
Rosalind Nashashibi
Danny Rimer, OBE
Roland Rudd (Chair)
Howard Shore
Lord Ed Vaizey

Tate Foundation Trustees and Honorary Members

Dr Maria Balshaw, CBE*
Abigail Baratta
Joseph P Baratta II*
Victoria Barnsley, OBE
Mrs Debby Brice
The Lord Browne of Madingley, FRS, FREng
Susan Burns
Christina Chandris
Melanie Clore
Sir Howard Davies
Dame Vivien Duffield, DBE
George Economou
Edward Eisler*
Maryam Eisler
Mala Goankar*
Sasan Ghandehari
Noam Gottesman
Jonathan Grad*
Anthony Gutman (Chair)*
Oliver Haarmann
Peter Kellner
Catherine Lagrange
Ronald McAulay
The Hon Mrs Rita McAulay
Scott Mead*
Mandy Moross
Elisabeth Murdoch
Marilyn Ofer
Simon Palley*
Franck Petitgas
Sir John Ritblat
Lady Ritblat
Emmanuel Roman*
The Rt Hon Sir Timothy Sainsbury
Sir Anthony Salz*
Howard Shore*
Peter Simon
Jon Snow
Lord Stevenson of Coddenham, CBE*
Mercedes Stoutzker
John Studzinski, CBE
Lance Uggla*
Sir David Verey, CBE
Anita Zabludowicz, OBE
*Executive Trustee

Tate Members Council

Sean Burns
Lorraine Candy
Nicole Crentsil
Roger Hiorns
Aynsley Jardin
Nick Smith
Emma Thompson
Matteo Vallone
Steve Wills
Stephen Witherford (Chair)

Tate Americas Foundation Trustees

Dr Maria Balshaw, CBE
Abigail Baratta*
Paul Britton (Chair)
Estrellita Brodsky (Emeritus)
Tiqui Atencio Demirdjian (Emeritus)
Wendy Fisher
Glenn Fuhrman
Heloisa Genish*
Kevin McNamara
Bob Rennie (President)
Jay Rivlin
Erica Roberts*
Charlotte Santo Domingo
Kim Shirley
Jay Smith
John Studzinski, CBE (Emeritus)
Amanda Waldron
George Wells*
*Ex-officio

Tate Modern Donors to the Founding Capital Campaign

29th May 1961 Charitable Trust
Alan Cristea Gallery
AMP
The Annenberg Foundation
Arts Council England
The Asprey Family Charitable Foundation
Lord and Lady Attenborough
The Baring Foundation
Ron Beller and Jennifer Moses
Alex and Angela Bernstein
David and Janice Blackburn
Mr and Mrs Anthony Bloom
BNP Paribas
Mr and Mrs Pontus Bonnier
Lauren and Mark Booth
Mr and Mrs John Botts
Frances and John Bowes
Ivor Braka

Mr and Mrs James Brice
The British Land Company plc
Donald L Bryant Jr Family
Melva Bucksbaum
Cazenove & Co
CGU plc
Clifford Chance
The Clore Duffield Foundation
Edwin C Cohen
The John S Cohen Foundation
Ronald and Sharon Cohen
Sadie Coles
Carole and Neville Conrad
Giles and Sonia Coode-Adams
Douglas Cramer
Thomas Dane
Michel and Hélène David-Weill
Julia W Dayton
Gilbert de Botton
Pauline Denyer-Smith and Paul Smith
Sir Harry and Lady Djanogly
The Drapers' Company
Energis Communications
English Heritage
English Partnerships
The Eranda Foundation
Esmée Fairbairn Charitable Trust
Donald and Doris Fisher
Richard B and Jeanne Donovan Fisher
The Fishmongers' Company
Freshfields Bruckhaus Deringer
Friends of the Tate Gallery
Bob and Kate Gavron
Giancarlo Giammetti
Alan Gibbs
Mr and Mrs Edward Gilhuly
GKR
GLG Partners
Helyn and Ralph Goldenberg
Goldman Sachs
The Horace W Goldsmith Foundation
The Worshipful Company of Goldsmiths
Lydia and Manfred Gorvy
Noam and Geraldine Gottesman
Pehr and Christina Gyllenhammar
Mimi and Peter Haas
The Worshipful Company of Haberdashers
Hanover Acceptances Limited
The Headley Trust
Mr and Mrs André Hoffmann
Anthony and Evelyn Jacobs
Jay Jopling
Mr and Mrs Karpidas
Howard and Lynda Karshan
Peter and Maria Kellner
Madeleine Kleinwort
Brian and Lesley Knox
Pamela and C Richard Kramlich
Mr and Mrs Henry R Kravis
Irene and Hyman Kreitman
The Kresge Foundation
Catherine and Pierre Lagrange
The Lauder Foundation
    – Leonard and Evelyn Lauder Fund
Lazard Brothers & Co., Limited
Leathersellers' Company Charitable Fund
Edward and Agnès Lee
Lehman Brothers
Lex Service Plc
Ruth and Stuart Lipton
Anders and Ulla Ljungh
The Frank Lloyd Family Trusts
London & Cambridge Properties Limited
London Electricity plc, EDF Group
Mr and Mrs George Loudon
Mayer, Brown, Rowe & Maw
Viviane and James Mayor
Ronald and Rita McAulay
The Mercers' Company
The Meyer Foundation

The Millennium Commission
Anthony and Deirdre Montagu
The Monument Trust
Mori Building, Ltd
Mr and Mrs M D Moross
Guy and Marion Naggar
Peter and Eileen Norton,
    The Peter Norton Family Foundation
Maja Oeri and Hans Bodenmann
Sir Peter and Lady Osborne
William A Palmer
Mr Frederik Paulsen
Pearson plc
The Pet Shop Boys
The Nyda and Oliver Prenn Foundation
Prudential plc
Railtrack plc
The Rayne Foundation
Reuters
Sir John and Lady Ritblat
Rolls-Royce plc
Barrie and Emmanuel Roman
Lord and Lady Rothschild
The Dr Mortimer and Theresa Sackler
    Foundation
J Sainsbury plc
Ruth and Stephan Schmidheiny
Schroders
Mr and Mrs Charles Schwab
David and Sophie Shalit
Belle Shenkman Estate
William Sieghart
Peter Simon
Mr and Mrs Sven Skarendahl
London Borough of Southwark
The Foundation for Sports and the Arts
Mr and Mrs Nicholas Stanley
The Starr Foundation
The Jack Steinberg Charitable Trust
Charlotte Stevenson
Hugh and Catherine Stevenson
John J Studzinski, CBE
David and Linda Supino
The Government of Switzerland
Carter and Mary Thacher
Insinger Townsley
UBS
UBS Warburg
David and Emma Verey
Dinah Verey
The Vintners' Company
Clodagh and Leslie Waddington
Robert and Felicity Waley-Cohen
Wasserstein, Perella & Co., Inc.
Gordon D Watson
The Weston Family
Mr and Mrs Stephen Wilberding
Michael S Wilson
Poju and Anita Zabludowicz
and those who wish to remain anonymous

Donors to The Tate Modern Project
Artist Rooms Foundation
Joseph and Abigail Baratta
Blavatnik Family Foundation
Lauren and Mark Booth
The Deborah Loeb Brice Foundation
The Lord Browne of Madingley, FRS, FREng
John and Michael Chandris,
    and Christina Chandris
James Chanos
Pierre Chen
Paul Cooke
The Roger De Haan Charitable Trust
Ago Demirdjian and Tiqui Atencio Demirdjian
Department for Digital, Culture, Media and Sport
George Economou
Stefan Edlis and Gael Neeson
English Partnerships
Mrs Donald B. Fisher

Jeanne Donovan Fisher
Mala Gaonkar
Yassmin and Sasan Ghandehari
Thomas Gibson in memory of Anthea Gibson
Lydia and Manfred Gorvy
The Granville-Grossman Bequest
The Hayden Family Foundation
Peter and Maria Kellner
Madeleine Kleinwort
Catherine Lagrange
Pierre Lagrange
London Development Agency
LUMA Foundation
Allison and Howard W. Lutnick
Donald B. Marron
Scott and Suling Mead
Sami and Hala Mnaymneh
Anthony and Deirdre Montagu
Mori Building Co Ltd
Elisabeth Murdoch
Eyal Ofer Family Foundation
Maureen Paley
Simon and Midge Palley
Stephen and Yana Peel
Daniel and Elizabeth Peltz
Catherine Petitgas
Franck Petitgas
The Roman Family
The Dr Mortimer and Theresa Sackler
    Foundation
The Sackler Trust
Lily Safra
Stephan Schmidheiny Family / Daros Collection
Helen and Charles Schwab
London Borough of Southwark
John J Studzinski, CBE
Tate Americas Foundation
Tate Members
Julie-Anne Uggla
Lance Uggla
Nina and Graham Williams
Manuela and Iwan Wirth
The Wolfson Foundation
and those who wish to remain anonymous

Tate Modern Benefactors and Major Donors
10 A.M. Art
Abakanowicz Arts and Culture Charitable
    Foundation
Nassib Abou-Khalil
Alireza Abrishamchi
acb Galéria
The Estate of Albert Adams
Aicon Gallery
Shane Akeroyd
AKO Foundation
Ola Al Dajani and Hisham El-Khazindar
The Estate of Edward Allington
Annenberg Foundation
The Estate of Denise Antenen
Art Fund
Art Mentor Foundation Lucerne
Artangel
Arts and Humanities Research Council
Arts Council England
Asymmetry Art Foundation
Celia and Edward Atkin, CBE
Bishoy Azmy and Mary Habib
Fayez Barakat and Hwasun Lee Barakat,
    Barakat Contemporary
Abigail and Joseph Baratta
Rosa Barba
Barbro Osher Pro Suecia Foundation
Perihan Bassatne
Corrine Bellow Charity
Péter Bencze and Réka Lőrincz
Allison Berg
Mr. Timm Bergold
Executors of Julia Berlin
David Bermant Foundation

Anna Boghiguian
The Charlotte Bonham-Carter Charitable Trust
Sophie Bowness
Bowness Family Foundation
Ivor Braka
The Estate of Emmy Bridgwater
The Britton Family Foundation
The Daniel & Estrellita Brodsky Family
  Foundation
The Rory and Elizabeth Brooks Foundation
The John Browne Charitable Trust
Beatrice Bulgari | In Between Art Film
The Estate of Ruth J Bullock
The Estate of Andrew Burt
John Bute
The Estate of Reg Butler
Andrew Cameron, AM and Cathy Cameron
The Estate of Lady Caro (Sheila Girling)
E. Rhodes and Leona B. Carpenter Foundation
Mrs Kavita Chellaram
Pierre Chen
Earls of Clarendon
The Clore Duffield Foundation
Denise Coates Foundation
Mr and Mrs Oliver Colman
The Cosman Keller Art and Music Trust
Executors of Chris Nolan Crozier
Dimitris Daskalopoulos
The Estate of Professor Martyn Davis
François-Xavier and Natasha de Mallmann
Rachel Deakin
Tiqui Atencio Demirdjian and Ago Demirdjian
Department for Culture, Media and Sport
Harry A Dickinson
Maryam Diener
Joe and Marie Donnelly
Lonti Ebers
Efie Gallery
Maryam and Edward Eisler
Embassy of Sweden, London
Embassy of the Kingdom of the Netherlands
Endeavor
Everybody Needs Art and László Vágó
Warren, Amanda and Jeremy Felson, and Lucy Sun
Margaret and Richard Finch
Jeanne D Fisher
Wendy Fisher and The Kirsh Foundation
Fluxus Art Projects
Eric and Louise Franck
Helen Frankenthaler Foundation
Freelands Foundation
The Estate of Lucian Freud
Josef W. Froehlich
The Fuhrman Family Foundation
Larry Gagosian
Mala Gaonkar
Bill & Melinda Gates Foundation
General Atlantic Foundation
Raghida Ghandour Al Rahim
The Hon HMT Gibson's Charity Trust
Lorraine Gill
Louise Giovanelli / White Cube
Gladstone Gallery
Janice Goble
Amy Gold and Brett Gorvy
Golden Bottle Trust
Nicholas and Judith Goodison's Charitable
  Settlement
Goodman Gallery
Lydia & Manfred Gorvy
Nicholas Leonidas Goulandris
The Granville-Grossman Bequest
Grosvenor Gallery
Wang Guangyi
Guaranty Trust Bank Plc
Agnes Gund
Anthony & Sandra Gutman
Hakuta Family
Paul Hamlyn Foundation
Yasser Hashem

Taimur Hassan
Hauser & Wirth
Tudor Havriliuc
The Drue Heinz Charitable Trust
The Barbara Hepworth Estate
The Estate of Susan Hiller
Lubaina Himid, CBE
Damien Hirst
The Robert H. N. Ho Family Foundation
David Hockney
Stanley and Valery Jacqueline Honeyman
The Estate of Jill Hood & the Mortimer Family
Alexandra Howell
Huo Family Foundation
Lalla Hurst & Family
Mr Phillip Hylander and Ms Ellie Harrison-Read
Institut Français du Royaume-Uni
Saodat Ismailova
Japanese Friends of Tate
Pamela J. Joyner and Alfred J. Giuffrida
Mohamed and Huda Kanoo
Ivan Katzen
Judi Kaufman and Arthur Rubin
Chris Keesee
Mike Kelley Foundation for the Arts
Peter and Maria Kellner
Charles Kim
Tina Kim Gallery
Jack Kirkland in honour of Yasufumi Nakamori
Korean Foundation for International Cultural
  Exchange
Josef Koudelka
Lachaise Foundation
The Lagrange Family
Edward Lee
Miyoung Lee and Neil Simpkins
The Leverhulme Trust
Ruben Levi
Lévy Gorvy
James Lindon in honour of Khalid bin Sultan
  Al-Qasimi
Loewe
Andrew and Amanda Love
Lillian and Jon Lovelace
LUMA Foundation
Michael Lynton
The Mactaggart Third Fund
The Estate of Sir Edwin Manton
The Manton Foundation
Agnes Martin Foundation
The Walter and Shirley Massey Fund
Theo Matoff
Lord McAlpine of West Green
The Mead Family Foundation
Paul Mellon Centre for Studies in British Art
Mellon Foundation
MEM Gallery
Joel Meyerowitz
The Estate of Catherine Ann Meyrick
Milani Gallery
Gregory R Miller
Phil Mohr
Henry Moore Foundation
Simon Mordant, AO and Catriona Mordant, AM
Mottahedan Family
National Heritage Memorial Fund
The National Lottery Heritage Fund
Mark and Louise Nelson
New Carlsberg Foundation
Simon Nixon and Family
Open Hand
Oranges & Sardines Foundation
OUTSET Germany_Switzerland
The Pace Gallery
Gretel Packer, AM
Maureen Paley
Irene Panagopoulos
Véronique Parke
Yana and Stephen Peel
Catherine Petitgas

Estate of Rosemary Ann Phelps
The Stanley Picker Trust
Estate of Murray Ashley Pickering
Pilgrim Trust
Polish Cultural Institute in London
Professor Richard Portes, CBE, FBA
David W. Posnett, OBE
Mr Gilberto and Mrs Daniela Pozzi
PPOW Gallery
Ramzy Rasamny in memory of Maya Rasamny
Bob Rennie
RocioSantaCruz Gallery
The Roman Family Collection
The Estate of William George Roper
The Estate of Peter Rose
The Estate of Eugene and Penelope Rosenberg
Rossi Rossi
Rothschild Foundation
Roland Rudd
The Estate of Simon Sainsbury
Gillian and Simon Salama-Caro
Jean and Melanie Salata
The Estate of Martin T Salmon
Sammlung Hoffmann Gbr
Tarana and Tarun Sawhney
Susan Sawyers
Clare Scherrer
Jake and Hélène Marie Shafran
Jack Shainman
Jack Shear
Kimberly R and Jon A Shirley
Sikkema Jenkins & Co.
The Estate of David Smith
Jay Smith and Laura Rapp
Sang Mo Son and Kyung Soon Lee
Norah and Norman Stone Collection
  (Tate Americas Foundation)
Mercedes and Ian Stoutzker
John J. Studzinski, CBE
Hiroshi Sugimoto
Maria and Malek Sukkar
Family and Executors of the Estate
  of Maud Sulter
Tamares Real Estate Holdings, Inc. in
  collaboration with the Zabludowicz Collection
Faisal Tamer and Sara Alireza
Lorraine Tarabay
Tate 1897 Circle
Tate Africa Acquisitions Committee
Tate Americas Foundation
Tate Asia Pacific Acquisitions Committee
Tate Central and Eastern Europe Plus
  Acquisitions Committee
Tate European Collection Circle
Tate International Council
Tate Latin American Acquisitions Committee
Tate Members
Tate Middle East North Africa Acquisitions
  Committee
Tate North American Acquisitions Committee
Tate Patrons
Tate Photography Acquisitions Committee
Tate South Asia Acquisitions Committee
Teiger Foundation
Terra Foundation for American Art
The Nicholas Themans Trust
The Estate of Milly Thompson
Tiwani Contemporary
The Turner Family
Luc Tuymans
The Tymure Collection
UK Research & Innovation
V-A-C Foundation
Axel Vervoordt Gallery
Paulo A W Vieira
Mercedes Vilardell
The Estate of Derek von Bethmann-Hollweg
Marie-Louise von Motesiczky Charitable Trust
The Estate of Manfred von Rosenberg-Lipinksy
Wagner Foundation

Amanda and John E Waldron
Dr Anne Walmsley
George Wells
Westminster City Council
Ali and Michael-Hue Williams
The Michael G. and C. Jane Wilson 2007 Trust
The Lord Leonard and Lady Estelle Wolfson
    Foundation
Terry Wu
Mr Hasnaine Yavarhoussen
Qiao Zhibing, in honour of Gregor Muir
and those who wish to remain anonymous

Platinum Patrons
Eric Abraham
Walid Abu-Suud
Mr Shane Akeroyd
Celia and Edward Atkin, CBE
Mr Bishoy Azmy and Mrs Mary Habib
The Hon Ms A Bagri
Lars Bane
Alex Beard
Beecroft Charitable Trust
Francesca Bellini Joseph (Co-Chair)
    and Allan Hennings
Natalia Bondarenko
John Booth
Rory and Elizabeth Brooks
The John Browne Charitable Trust
Karen Cawthorn Argenio
Chargeurs Philanthropies
XiaoMeng Cheng
Lord and Lady Davies of Abersoch
Ms Miel de Botton
Pascale Decaux
Sophie Diedrichs
Sima Ganwani Ved
Alexander Green
David Herro
Kristin Hjellegjerde
Mr Yan Huo
Mr Phillip Hylander (Co-Chair)
    and Ms Ellie Harrison-Read
Natascha Jakobs-Linssen
Elli Jason Foster
Maya Junger
Maria and Peter Kellner
Ms Matilda Liu
Mr M J Margulies
Svetlana Marich
Scott and Suling Mead
Mary Moore
Batia and Idan Ofer
Simon and Midge Palley
Dr Fiona Pathiraja and Søren Fryland Møller
Jan-Christoph Peters
Mr Gilberto and Mrs Daniela Pozzi
Frances Reynolds
Sybil Robson Orr
Bianca Roden
Jake and Hélène Marie Shafran
Andrée Shore
Amar Singh
Grey Skipwith
Maria and Malek Sukkar
Michael and Jane Wilson, CBE
Lady Wolfson of Marylebone
Chizuko Yashiro
Mr Mingfang Yu
Jessica Zirinis
and those who wish to remain anonymous

Gold Patrons
Marc Anani-Isaac
Ms Mila Askarova
Angela Choon
Beth and Michele Colocci
David Corbell
Harry G David
Émilie De Pauw

Valentina Drouin
Edwin Fox Foundation
Hugh Gibson
Amanda Gowing
Olga Grishina
Eykyn Maclean
Asta Paulauskaite
Mathew Prichard
Valerie Rademacher
Almine Ruiz-Picasso
Tatiana Salomon
Hahnah Seminara
Lord Snowdown
Jennifer N C Stahl
Kimberly Stallvik
Matthew Steinmetz
Brunhild Stelter
Yuko Takano
Manuela and Iwan Wirth
and those who wish to remain anonymous

Silver Patrons
Cameron Amiri
The Anson Charitable Trust
Toby and Kate Anstruther
Hannah Armstrong
James Arnell
Aspect Charitable Trust
Charles Banner, QC
Peter Barham
Mrs Jane Barker
Oliver Barker
Victoria Barnsley, OBE
Jim Bartos
Ms Anne Berthoud
Madeleine Bessborough
David Blood and Beth Bisso
Harry and Fabiana Bond
Caroline Boseley
Elena Bowes
Viscountess Bridgeman
Basia Briggs
Laura Brimson
Laura and William Burlington
Michael Burrell
Mrs Marlene Burston
Mrs Aisha Cahn
Timothy and Elizabeth Capon
Countess Castle Stewart
Liza Cawthorn
Roger Cazalet
Lord and Lady Charles Cecil
Sandrine Chelmy
David Cheng
Dr Peter Chocian
Miss FangChing Chou
John F Clappier
Frank Cohen
Mrs Jane Collins
Terrence Collis
Mr and Mrs Oliver Colman
Giles and Sonia Coode-Adams
Pilar Corrias
Tommaso Corvi-Mora
Mr and Mrs Bertrand Coste
Kathleen Crook and James Penturn
Averil Curci
Sir Howard Davies
Giles de la Mare
Mr Damon and The Hon Mrs de Laszlo
Anne Chantal Defay Sheridan
Pier-Luigi del Renzio
Mr Robert Devereux
Lord and Lady Egremont
Jake Elsley
John Erle-Drax
Paul Ettlinger
Stuart and Margaret Evans
Ernest Fasanya
Mrs Margy Fenwick

The Sylvie Fleming Collection
Mr and Mrs Laurent Ganem
Mala Gaonkar
Mr Mark Glatman
Ms Emily Goldner and Mr Michael Humphries
Kate Gordon
Dimitri Goulandris
Martyn Gregory
Richard and Odile Grogan
Professor John Gruzelier
Jill Hackel Zarzycki
Mark Harris
Michael and Morven Heller
Soo Hitchin
Muriel Hoffner
James Holland-Hibbert
Lady Hollick, OBE
Holtermann Fine Art
Jeff Horne
Ben Houston
Tina Hughes
Mr Haydn John
Mike Jones
Jay Jopling
Mrs Brenda Josephs
Tracey Josephs
Niki Kalamida
Andrew Kalman
Mr David Kaskel
Dr Martin Kenig
Mr and Mrs Simon Keswick
Neha Khosla
Mrs Mae Khouri
Gerald Kidd
David Killick
Mr and Mrs James Kirkman
Jennifer Klein
Brian and Lesley Knox
David P Korn
Kowitz Trust
Sergey Kozlov
Mr and Mrs Herbert Kretzmer
Silvana Lagos
Judith Lamb
Simon Lee
Norman Leinster
Sharron Lewis
Sophia and Mark Lewisohn
Linwan Li
Yimeng Lin
Mr Gilbert Lloyd
Mrs Elizabeth Louis
Alison Loyd
Kate MacGarry
Nadia Mahmud
Audrey Mandela
Marlborough Fine Art
Marsh Christian Trust
Daniele Mattogno
Mazzoleni Art
Professor Rob Melville
Shahid Miah
Victoria Miro
Mrs William Morrison
Ms Deborah Norton
Reine and Boris Okuliar
Julian Opie
Pilar Ordovás
Leslie Osterling
Gulsah Ozturk
Desmond Page
Maureen Paley
Sir Michael Palin
Mrs Kathrine Palmer
Anthea Peers
Alexander V Petalas
Frederique Pierre-Pierre
Mary Pollock
Professor Richard Portes, CBE, FBA
Susan Prevezer, QC

Mr and Mrs Ryan Prince
Chelsea Purvis
Ivetta Rabinovich
Irith Rappaport
Frankie Rossi
Mr David V Rouch
Mr Charles Roxburgh
Mr Alex Sainsbury and Ms Elinor Jansz
Cherrill and Ian Scheer
Mrs Cara Schulze
Melissa Sesana
The Hon Richard Sharp
Sadie Sherman
James Shoreland
Neville Shulman, CBE
Oliwia Siem
Louise Spence
Linda Streit
Mr James Swartz
Elaine Thomas
Marita Thurnauer
Ian Tollett
Karen Townshend
Mr Philippos Tsangrides
Celine Valligny
Ewan Venters
Gisela von Sanden
Andreas Vourecas-Petalas
Audrey Wallrock
Linda Waterhouse
Offer Waterman
Miss Cheyenne Westphal
Professor Sarah Whatmore
Mr Douglas Woolf
Adam Wurr
Phoebe and Arthur Yates
Clara Zevi
and those who wish to remain anonymous

Young Patrons
Khaled Abu-Suud
Omar Abu-Suud
Tarek Abu-Suud
Nadine Adams
Estelle Akeroyd Hunt
Elsa Akesson
Tasneem Aliewi
HRH Princess Alia Al-Senussi
Fiona Amitai
Aishwarya Anam
Mihai Anca
Aurore E Ankarcrona Hennessey
Gulru Arvas (Co-Chair, Young Patrons
    Ambassador Group)
Miss Olivia Aubry
Isabel Bardawil
Katrina Beechey
Penny Johanna Beer
Eleni Beveratou
Dr Maya Beyhan
Jennifer Brown
Oliver Cain
Sarah Cannon
Federika Chaimowicz
Matthew Charlton
Ariel Chen
Claudia Cheng
Joyce Chin
Nowk Choe
Bianca Chu (Co-Chair, Young Patrons
    Ambassador Group)
Gretchen Cline
Charlotte Cobb
Thamara Corm
Stephanie Courmont
Huguette Craggs
Douglas Cuadrado
Helena Czernecka
Giuliana D'Amieo
Henry Danowski

Countess Charlotte de la Rochefoucauld
Alexandre de Royere
Sophie Dickson
Eleanor Dilloway
Indira Dyussebayeva
Christina Eberli
Lara Eckes-Chantré
Lena Economides
Alexandra Economou
Jennifer Ellis
Phoebe Emerson
Zhiyi Fang
Kate Fensterstock
Faridah Folawiyo
Thomas Forwood
Jane and Richard Found
Sylvain Fresia
Brian Fu
Mr Andreas Gegner
Stefano Giulietti
Pierre-Antoine Godefroy
Javier Godino de Frutos
Elissa Goldstone
Frederick Gordts
Mr Taymour Grahne
Beth Greenacre
Andrea Grigsby
Richard Grindy
Ari Helgason
Patrick Hennessey
Max Edouard Friedrich Hetzler
Elise Huff
Lola Hylander
Molly Ingleby
Phoebus Istavrioglu
Marley Jellie
Faye Jiang
Daniel Jones
Peter Jones
Jasmine Kailey
Miss Meruyert Kaliyeva
Melih Kaplan
Zoe Karafylakis Sperling
Joe Kennedy
Ms Chloe Kinsman
Daria Kocherova
Daria Kravchenko
Natalia Kritsali
Lamb Gallery
Giulia Lecchini
Megan Leckie
John Lellouche
Marianna Lemos
Alexander Lewis
Samuel Lewis
Ines Leynaud
Jonathan Lim
Alexandra Lindsay
Phoebe Liu
Joanna Lowe
Mr J Lueddeckens
Alica Maclean
Giulia Magnani
Ms Sonia Mak
Mr Jean-David Malat
Mary McNicholas
Stefan Miesner
Amanda Millwood
Mr Fernando Moncho Lobo
Ottavia Morfino
Laura Moses
Tilak Nathwani
Jingxiu Niu
Muchun Niu
Ikenna Obiekwe
Nnamdi Obiekwe
Hilla Olsson
Rory B O'Sullivan
Cuppy Otedola
Periklis Panagopoulos

Pietro Pantalani
Divya Pathak
Alonso Peña Alfaro
Samantha Pickett
Christopher Pullen
Miss Yasmine Rahimzadeh
Nikki Ramirez
Sasha Reviakin
Dr Konrad Rotthege
Alexander Santema
Sinclair Schäfer
Sneha Shah
Wei Shi
Ms Marie-Anya Shriro
Joshua Silver
Louise Simpson
Mandeep Singh
Stephanie Stevens
Jana Suhani Soin
Ilgin Surel
Molly Susman
Yaroslav Syzonov
Evangeline Tawil
Ryan Taylor
Lorna Tiller
Omer Tiroche Contemporary Art
Mr Giancarlo Trinca
Ms Navann Ty
Valentina Vangelista
Selina Ved
Nicholas Walker
Luning Wang
Thomas Williams
Benedict Winkler
Wen Xiao
HRH Princess Eugenie of York
Duo Zhang
Tiffany Zhang
Rui Zhuang
Alexandra Zirinis
and those who wish to remain anonymous

International Council Members
Staffan Ahrenberg, Editions Cahiers d'Art
Mr Geoff Ainsworth, AM
John Auerbach and Edward Tang
Anne H Bass Foundation
Mrs Anita Belgiorno-Nettis, AM
Nicolas Berggruen
Jo and Tom Bloxham
Pontus Bonnier
Paloma Botín O'Shea
Mr William Bowness, AO
Ivor Braka
The Deborah Loeb Brice Foundation
Rory and Elizabeth Brooks
Andrew Cameron, AM
Christina Chandris
Pierre Chen, Yageo Foundation, Taiwan
Mr Euisun Chung and Mrs Geesun Chung
Mr Dimitris Daskalopoulos
Ms Miel de Botton
Suzanne Deal Booth
Tiqui Atencio Demirdjian and Ago Demirdjian
Robert and Renée Drake
Mrs Olga Dreesmann
Füsun and Faruk Eczacıbaşı
Désiré Feuerle and Sara Puig
HRH Princess Firyal of Jordan
Mrs Wendy Fisher
Kathrine Fredriksen
Fuhrman Family Foundation
Hideaki Fukutake, Chairman of Fukutake
    Foundation
The Gaudio Family Foundation
Candida and Zak Gertler
Mrs Yassmin Ghandehari
Lydia and Manfred Gorvy
Bianca and Noam Gottesman
Laurence Graff, OBE

Mimi and Peter Haas Fund
Mrs Susan Hayden
Ms Ydessa Hendeles
Ms Katrin Henkel
Marlene Hess and James D. Zirin
Ms Maja Hoffmann
Sangita Jindal
Dakis and Lietta Joannou
Ms Monica Kalpakian
Richard and Pamela Kramlich
Andreas Kurtz (Vice Chair) and Ulrike Kurtz
Ms Catherine Lagrange
Mr Pierre Lagrange
Judy and Leonard Lauder
Agnès and Edward Lee
Seo Hyun Lee
Jacqueline and Marc Leland
Christian Levett
Ms Joyce Liu
Andrew J Love
Anthony Medich
David Meitus and Angela Westwater
Naomi Milgrom, AC
Audrey and David Mirvish, Toronto
Professor Cav. Simon Mordant, AO (Vice Chair)
    and Catriona Mordant, AM
Mrs Yoshiko Mori
Gael Neeson
Dr Mark Nelson
Hélène Nguyen-Ban
Mr and Mrs Takeo Obayashi
Mr and Mrs Eyal Ofer
Andrea and José Olympio Pereira
Hideyuki Osawa
Ms Gretel Packer, AM
Midge and Simon Palley
Irene Panagopoulos
Véronique Parke
Yana and Stephen Peel
Catherine Petitgas
Sydney Picasso
Ana Pinho
Lekha Poddar
Miss Dee Poon
Smita Prabhakar
Ms Miuccia Prada and Mr Patrizio Bertelli
Laura Rapp and Jay Smith
Patrizia Sandretto Re Rebaudengo and Agostino
    Re Rebaudengo
Frances Reynolds
Paulina Rider Wilhelmsen
Michael Ringier
Sybil Robson Orr and Matthew Orr
Ms Hanneli M Rupert
E. Melisa Sabanci Tapan
Rajeeb and Nadia Samdani
Alejandro Santo Domingo
Tarana and Tarun Sawhney
Czaee Shah
Dasha Shenkman, OBE
Dr Gene Sherman, AM
Jon and Kimberly Shirley
Poonam Bhagat Shroff
Uli and Rita Sigg
John J Studzinski, CBE
Maria and Malek Sukkar
Mr Christen Sveaas
Lorraine Tarabay
Richard and Maggie Tsai
Mrs Ninetta Vafeia
Paulo A W Vieira (Chair)
Mercedes Vilardell
Robert and Felicity Waley-Cohen
Diana Widmaier Picasso
Christen and Derek Wilson
Mrs Sylvie Winckler
The Hon Dame Janet Wolfson de Botton, DBE
Terry Wu
Yang Yang
Poju Zabludowicz and Anita Zabludowicz, OBE

and those who wish to remain anonymous

Africa Acquisitions Committee
Aki Abiola
Kathy Ackerman Robins
Kola Aina
John Basnage de Beauval
The Beachum Charitable Fund
Mrs Kavita Chellaram
Harry G David
Lana de Beer David
Mrs Wendy Fisher
Samallie Kiyingi
Alexander Klimt
Caro Macdonald
Dale Mathias
Valentina Mintah & Kwame Mintah
Wissam and Hiba Nesr Art Foundation
Charlotte L. Newman
Alain F Nkontchou
Emile Stipp
Josef Vascovitz and Lisa Goodman
Jorge Fernández Vidal
Mercedes Vilardell (Chair)
Mr Hasnaine Yavarhoussen

and those who wish to remain anonymous

Asia-Pacific Acquisitions Committee
Shane Akeroyd
Jim Amberson
Director of Arario Museum
Arndt Foundation, Matthias Arndt
Mrs Victoria Bruhn
Lito and Kim Camacho
Mrs Marisa Chearavanont
Adrian Cheng
Jonathan Cheung
Lawrence Chu
Yan Du
Mrs Yassmin Ghandehari
Nathaniel P Gunawan
Esther Heer-Zacek
Philippa Hornby
Shareen Khattar Harrison (Co-Chair)
Ms Ellie Lai
Alan Lau (Co-Chair)
Woon Kyung Lee
Alexander Lewis
Ms Dina Liu
Alan and Yenn Lo
Ms Kai-Yin Lo
Yoonwhe Leo Moon & Young Ran Yun
Lynn Ou
Francis and Eleanor Shen
Kazunari Shirai
Raksha Sriram
Arif Suherman
Mr Patrick Sun
Timothy Roy Tan
Dr Andreas Teoh
Rudy Tseng
Janice S Y Wang
Margaret M Wang
Yang Bin
Jenny Yeh
Dayea Yeon
Fernando Zobel de Ayala

and those who wish to remain anonymous

**Central and Eastern Europe
Plus Acquisitions Committee**
Stella Beniaminova
Attila and Emese Brezóczki
Francise Hsin-Wen Chang
Artur Dela
Gabriela Gantenbein
Jan Hammer
Patrick Hessel
Kasia Kulczyk
Peter Kulloi (Co-Chair)

Vita Liberte
Danica and Eduard Maták
Luba Michailova
Christl Novakovic
Florin Pogonaru
The Pudil Family Foundation
András Réti
Ivana & Martin Ridler
Valeria Rodnyansky
Robert Runták
Ovidiu Şandor
Simon Sicko
Ms Kory Sorenson
The Terziev Family
Attila G. Vizi
Tomasz Wardyński, CBE
Mr Jānis Zuzāns

and those who wish to remain anonymous

European Collection Circle
Mandy Cawthorn Argenio
Lonti Ebers
Trustees of the Gaudio Family Foundation (UK)
    Limited
Edward Lee (Chair)
Monica Reitan
Danny Rimer, OBE
Stichting Hartwig Foundation

and those who wish to remain anonymous

Latin American Acquisitions Committee
Monica and Robert Aguirre
María Amalia León
Giselle Araoz and Mirko Stiglich
Juan Ball
Celia Birbragher
Estrellita Brodsky
Teresa AL Bulgheroni
Simone Coscarelli Parma
HSH the Prince Pierre d'Arenberg
Tiqui Atencio Demirdjian
Isabela Mosconi Katchuian Galvao
Heloisa Genish (Co-Chair)
Jonathan Grad
Barbara Hemmerle Gollust
Julian Iragorri
Marjorie and Michael Levine
José Luis Lorenzo
Denise and Felipe Nahas Mattar
Susan McDonald
Gabriela Mendoza
Alexandra Mollof
Veronica Nutting
Mario Pacheco
Silvia Paz-Illobre
Jorge and Darlene Pérez
Thibault Poutrel
Erica Roberts (Co-Chair)
Alin Ryan Lobo
Lilly Scarpetta
Maria Fernanda Vilela

and those who wish to remain anonymous

**Middle East North Africa
Acquisitions Committee**
Nassib Abou-Khalil
Walid Abu-Suud
H.E. Huda Alkhamis-Kanoo, Founder of the Abu
    Dhabi Music & Arts Foundation
Nora Hamza AlKholi
HRH Princess Alia Al-Senussi
Abdelmonem Bin Eisa Alserkal
Marwan T Assaf
Bishoy Azmy
Perihan Bassatne
Mrs Elisabeth Bauchet-Bouhlal
Maryam Eisler
Ola Al Dajani and Hisham El-Khazindar
Shirley Elghanian
Dr Farhad Farjam

Hossein and Dalia Fateh
Raghida Ghandour Al Rahim
Mareva Grabowski
Mary Habib
Yasser Hashem
Fady Jameel
Rasheed Kamel
Mr Elie Khouri
Maha Kutay
Hashem Montasser
Dina Nasser-Khadivi
Mr Moshe Peterburg
Maria (Co-Chair) and Malek Sukkar
Faisal Tamer (Co-Chair)
Mr Zahid and Ms Binladin
Roxane Zand
and those who wish to remain anonymous

North American Acquisitions Committee
Abigail Baratta (Co-Chair)
Dr. Eraka Bath
Allison Berg
Dr. Tyson Boudreaux
Alla Broeksmit
Lewis Cheng
Dillon Cohen
Michael Corman and Kevin Fink
Laura Fisch
Lisa Garrison
Joshua Greenberg
Jennifer Hawks Djawadi
Craig Hollingworth
Peter Kahng
Patricia Kaneb
Christian Keesee
Charles Kim
Ekaterina Klim
Marc J. Lee & Armando Abounce
Margarette Lee
Miyoung Lee
Marjorie and Michael Levine
James Lindon
Matt McClure
Samantha McManus
Gregory R Miller
Sami Mnaymneh
Shabin and Nadir Mohamed
Yana Peel
Alexander V. Petalas
Holly Peterson
Laura Rapp and Jay Smith
Stephanie Robinson
Leo Rogath
Susan Sawyers
Ralph Segreti and Richard Follows
Francis and Eleanor Shen
Kimberly and Jon Shirley
Ann Tang Chiu
Charlotte Wagner
George Wells (Co-Chair)
Christen Wilson and Derek Wilson
Debi Wisch
Mary Zlot
and those who wish to remain anonymous

Photography Acquisitions Committee
Ryan Allen
Nicholas Barker
Cynthia Lewis Beck
Pierre Brahm
Elizabeth (Co-Chair) and Rory Brooks
Lisa and Mark Caputo
XiaoMeng 'Cherry' Cheng
Michael A Chesser
Beth and Michele Colocci
Lucy and Andrew Darwin
David Fitzsimons
Natascha Jakobs-Linssen
Elizabeth and William Kahane
Jack Kirkland (Co-Chair)

Nathalie Lambert-Besseddik and Cyril Besseddik
Suling Mead
Nicholas Stanley
Maria and Malek Sukkar
Tia Tanna
Francois Trausch, in memory of Caroline Trausch
Juan Carlos Verme
Michael and Jane Wilson, CBE
Chizuko Yashiro
and those who wish to remain anonymous

South Asia Acquisitions Committee
Dr Arani and Mrs Shumita Bose
Surabhi K Chaudhary, Unnati Foundation
Krishna Choudhary
Akshay Chudasama
Jai Danani
Taimur Hassan
Blanca Hirani
Dr Amin Jaffer
Neha and Sumedh Jaiswal
Sonam Kapoor Ahuja
Deepanjana Klein
Simran Kotak and Vir Kotak
Ms Aarti Lohia
Hiroo and Haresh Motwani
Moklasur Rahman Pinto
Lekha Poddar (Co-Chair)
Alka and Amit Ruia
Saffronart Foundation
Isheta Salgaocar
Nadia Samdani, MBE
Rajeeb Samdani (Co-Chair)
Mrs Tarana Sawhney
Sally Eugenia Schwartz
Damian Vesey
Manuela and Iwan Wirth
and those who wish to remain anonymous

The 1897 Circle
Lynn Allan
Maureen Bampton
Anne Berthoud
Marilyn Bild
James Birch
David and Deborah Botten
Geoff Bradbury
Charles Brett
Eloise and Francis Charlton
Paul Cumming-Benson
Alex Davids
Sally Davies
Jonathan Davis
Sean Dissington
Ronnie Duncan
Joan Edlis
Vikki-Louise Fabian
Ian Fletcher
Mr and Mrs R.N. and M.C. Fry
Richard S. Hamilton
L.A. Hynes
John Iddon
John Janssen
Dr Martin Kenig
Vanessa Koster-Goodliffe
Isa Levy
Tony Miller
David and Sonya Newell-Smith
Miss Susan Novell and Mr Graham Smith
Martin Owen
Ruth Rattenbury
Simon Reynolds
Dianne Roberts
Dr Claudia Rosnowski
Ann M Smith
Alan Sprince
Deborah Stern
Jennifer Toynbee-Holmes
Audrey Wallrock
Rosie Watts

Professor Brian Whitton
Kay and Dyson Wilkes
Simon Casimir Wilson
Andrew Woodd
Mr. and Mrs. Zilberberg
and those who wish to remain anonymous

Tate Modern Corporate Partners
Bank of America
Bloomberg LP
Bloomberg Philanthropies
CHANEL
Deutsche Bank
Genesis
General Atlantic Foundation
G . F Smith
GUCCI
Hyundai Motor
La Caixa Foundation
Lockton
LVMH Moët Hennessy Louis Vuitton
PJT Partners
Sotheby's
Swatch
UNIQLO
Van Cleef & Arpels

Tate Modern Corporate Members
Aspen Insurance Group
Bentley Systems UK Ltd
Beringea
BIG / Bjarke Ingels Group
Chartered Management Institute (CMI)
Clifford Chance LLP
CRA International (UK) Limited
Dalkia
Dentsu UK Limited
DLA Piper UK LLP
FGS Global
Foster + Partners
Freshfields Service Company
FRP Advisory
Hayfin Capital Management LLP
Heidrick & Struggles
HKA Global Ltd
Howden M&A
Imperial Health Charity
JATO Dynamics Ltd
Linklaters LLP
MatthewsDaniel
McDermott Will & Emery UK LLP
Morgan Stanley UK Limited
Pentagram Designs
Portland Communications
PVH Europe B.V.
Ropes & Gray International LLP
Siegel+Gale
STATE STREET BANK AND TRUST
  – London Branch
T. Rowe Price
The Up Group
WIRED
Worldpay UK Ltd
and those who wish to remain anonymous

First published 2024 by order of the Tate Trustees by
Tate Publishing, a division of Tate Enterprises Ltd,
Millbank, London SW1P 4RG

www.tate.org.uk/publishing

on the occasion of the exhibition
Electric Dreams: Art and Technology Before the Internet

Presented in the Eyal Ofer Galleries

in partnership with

GUCCI

Tate Modern, London
28 November 2024 – 1 June 2025

Supported by

ANTHROP\C

With additional support from The Electric Dreams Exhibition Supporters Circle:
The David Bermant Foundation
Marcin and Izabela Wiszniewski

Tate Americas Foundation, Tate International Council, Tate Patrons

Research supported by Hyundai Tate Research Centre: Transnational
In partnership with Hyundai Motor

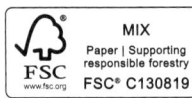 **HYUNDAI**

© Tate Enterprises Ltd 2024
'Chromointerferent Environment: A Work in the Making' © Atelier Cruz-Diez 2024

All rights reserved. No part of this book may be reprinted or reproduced or utilised
in any form or by any electronic, mechanical or other means, now known or hereafter
invented, including photocopying and recording, or in any information storage or
retrieval system, without permission in writing from the publishers or a licence from
the Copyright Licensing Agency Ltd, www.cla.co.uk.

A catalogue record for this book is available from the British Library

ISBN 978-1-84976-923-5 (hbk)
ISBN 978-1-84976-924-2 (pbk)

Senior Editor: Nicola Bion
Production: Bill Jones
Picture Research: Emma O'Neill
Design: Johanne Lian Olsen

Printed and bound in Italy by Industria Grafica SIZ
Colour reproduction by DL Imaging, London

Measurements of artworks are given in centimetres,
height before width and depth

Front cover: Samia Halaby, still from *Fold 2* 1988 (detail, see p.199)
Back cover: Alberto Biasi, *Light Prisms. Spectral Kinetic Mesh* 1966 (detail, see p.90)
Frontispiece: Carlos Cruz-Diez, *Chromointerferent Environment* 1974/2009,
installation view, *Luminous Reality*, Phillips, London, 2018

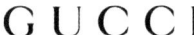

MIX
Paper | Supporting
responsible forestry
FSC® C130819